Journal of Semitic Studies Supplement 22

VOICES OF EXILES:
A STUDY OF AL-ṬAYYIB ṢĀLIḤ AND HIS WORK

by

Ami Elad-Bouskila

Published by Oxford University Press
on behalf of the University of Manchester
2007

OXFORD JOURNALS
OXFORD UNIVERSITY PRESS

Great Clarendon Street, Oxford OX2 6DP

Oxford University Press is a department of the University of Oxford.
It furthers the University's objective of excellence in research, scholarship, and education by publishing worldwide in

Oxford New York

Athens Auckland Bangkok Bogotá Buenos Aires Cape Town
Chennai Dar es Salaam Delhi Florence Hong Kong Istanbul Karachi
Kolkata Kuala Lumpur Madrid Melbourne Mexico City Mumbai Nairobi
Paris São Paulo Shanghai Singapore Taipei Tokyo Toronto Warsaw

with associated companies in Berlin Ibadan

Published in the United Kingdom
by Oxford University Press, Oxford

First published 2007

A catalogue for this book is available from the British Library

Library of Congress Cataloguing in Publication Data
(Data available)

ISSN 0022-4480
ISBN 0-19-921512-X
ISBN 978-0-19-921512-6

Subscription information for the *Journal of Semitic Studies* is available at the journal website:
jss.oupjournals.org

Printed in Great Britain by Bell & Bain Ltd, Glasgow

For Osnat

CONTENTS

PREFACE vii

ACKNOWLEDGMENTS viii

CHAPTER ONE
The Author's World: The Case of al-Ṭayyib Ṣāliḥ 1
Some Notes on his World 1
The Author and Modern Sudanese Literature 7
Possible Sources of Impact 11
Translations and the Critical Reception of his Works 16
Comparison of Textual Versions 20

CHAPTER TWO
Poetic Elements in al-Ṭayyib Ṣāliḥ's Works 25
Titles 25
Dedications 38
Expositions 40
Endings 50
Dialogues and Monologues 58
Place, Space and Time 66

CHAPTER THREE
Status of the Characters in al-Ṭayyib Ṣāliḥ's Works 75
Importance of the Characters 75
Dawmat Wad Ḥāmid 80
Two Later Short Stories 90
'Urs al-Zayn 93
Mawsim al-Hijra ilā al-Shamāl 100
Bandar Shāh: Ḍaw al-Bayt 123
Bandar Shāh: Maryūd 129

CHAPTER FOUR

Development of the Characters in al-Ṭayyib Ṣāliḥ's Writing 133

How to Define the Characters 133

Defining the Character 134

Fiction and Reality in the Figure of the Narrator 142

CHAPTER FIVE

The Migration to the North/West: On East/South and West/North in the Works of al-Ṭayyib Ṣāliḥ 155

Between East/South and West/North in Modern Arabic Literatures 155

East/South and West/North in the Works of al-Ṭayyib Ṣāliḥ 165

Women, Sex and Violence 166

Politics, Nation and Nationality 174

Culture, Education and Art 176

Science and Technology 179

EPILOGUE

An Attempt at Evaluating al-Ṭayyib Ṣāliḥ's Writing 183

APPENDICES 191

A. Places and Dates of Publication of al-Ṭayyib Ṣāliḥ's Works 191

B. A Short Summary of his Works 197

C. Translations of his Works into Other Languages 202

D. Dissertations, Theses and Diplomas about his Works 206

E. Reviews, Introductions and Articles by al-Ṭayyib Ṣāliḥ 208

F. Films and Plays Based on his Works 209

G. Interviews Conducted with al-Ṭayyib Ṣāliḥ 209

H. The Path and its Stations: An Interview with al-Ṭayyib Ṣāliḥ in London, 22 August, 2000 213

NOTES 233

BIBLIOGRAPHY 287

INDEX 327

PREFACE

In 1980 I was asked by the Department of Arabic Language and Literature at the Hebrew University of Jerusalem to write (in Hebrew) a seminar paper for my M.A degree. The subject of this paper was 'Three Novels between East and West: *'Uṣfūr min al-Sharq*, by Tawfīq al-Ḥakīm, *al-Ḥayy al-Lātīnī*, by Suhayl Idrīs and *Mawsim al-Hijra ilā al-Shamāl* by al-Ṭayyib Ṣāliḥ'. The novel *Mawsim al-Hijra ilā al-Shamāl* (Season of Migration to the North, 1966) by the Sudanese author al-Ṭayyib Ṣāliḥ (b.1929) impressed me deeply and my M.A. thesis was the turning point in my attitude towards modern Arabic literatures in general, and particularly towards al-Ṭayyib Ṣāliḥ's literary works. I continued my study of al-Ṭayyib Ṣāliḥ's works with my Master's thesis entitled *The World of al-Ṭayyib Ṣāliḥ* (1981, in Hebrew). Since then I have not stopped teaching al-Ṭayyib Ṣāliḥ's literary works, first at the Department of Arabic Language and Literature at the Hebrew University of Jerusalem and later at the Beit Berl College Department of Arabic Language and Literature, where I teach them to this day.

In addition to those in Hebrew, I have published a number of articles in Arabic, Hebrew, English and French (see Appendices and Bibliography). Sections of two chapters of the present study appeared as: 'Al-Ṭayyib Ṣāliḥ: The Author and his Works', in Ami Elad-Bouskila and Ahmed Al-Shahi (eds), *Al-Ṭayyib Ṣāliḥ: Seventy Candles, Edebiyât,* 10 (1999), pp. 7–34. Chapter Four is based on two articles: 'Taṭawwur al-Shakhṣiyya fī A'māl al-Ṭayyib Ṣāliḥ', *al-Karmil*, 10 (1989), pp. 7–26, and 'Shaping the Cast of Characters: The Case of al-Ṭayyib Ṣāliḥ', *Journal of Arabic Literature*, XXIX: 2 (1998), pp. 59–84. Some of the Appendices were published under the title 'Appendices: Writing by and on al-Ṭayyib Ṣāliḥ', in Ami Elad-Bouskila and Ahmed Al-Shahi (eds), *Al-Ṭayyib Ṣāliḥ: Seventy Candles, Edebiyât,* 10 (1999), pp. 129–51.

Even today, after twenty years of reading and writing about the works of al-Ṭayyib Ṣāliḥ, I still wonder why I am so attracted to his world. I am quite certain that even this study will not give me the full answer.

Ami Elad-Bouskila
Beit Berl College, Israel
February 2003

ACKNOWLEDGEMENTS

I first wish to thank those who supported this research: Beit Berl College and its generous financial contribution that allowed me to prepare the manuscript for publication, with special thanks to the Rector, Dr Aharon Seidenberg. I would also like to express my gratitude to St Antony's College, Oxford University, which gave me the opportunity to conduct research there during the 1996–8 academic years as Senior Associate Member and Israeli Junior Research Fellow. I wish to thank especially the Middle East Centre of St. Antony's College and its current director Dr Eugene Rogan, and former director Dr Derek Hopwood, as well as my colleagues at the centre, Dr M.M. Badawi, Dr Ahmed Al-Shahi, and Professor Avi Shlaim. Dr Yossi Amitay, former director of the Israeli Academic Centre in Cairo, has provided a great deal of help. Thanks also to colleagues who read the entire manuscript and offered their suggestions, Professors: Irene Eber, Moshe Piamenta, Jacob M. Landau and Shmuel Moreh, of the Hebrew University of Jerusalem. Some of my colleagues gave me much useful information and I therefore wish to express my thanks to the Sudanese writer and critic Muḥammad Khalaf Allāh of London, Dr Aḥmad Muḥammad el-Badawi of Manchester, Dr Ḥaydar Ibrāhīm 'Alī, director of the Sudanese Studies Centre in Cairo, Professor Barbara Michalak-Pikulska, director of the Institute of Oriental Philology at the Jagiellonian University in Kraków, Professor Syrine Hout of the American University of Beirut, Dr Zahia Smail Salhi of University of Leeds, Dr Daniela Merolla of the University of Leiden, Professor Joseph Zeidan of Ohio State University, Professor Heather Sharkey of Trinity College, Hartford, Connecticut, Professor Nobuyoshi Fukuhara of Osaka University and Mr Doron B. Cohen of Jerusalem. My appreciation goes to my research assistants at various stages of the writing: Ms Sharon Shitrit-Sasson, Ms Shani Payes, Ms Shīrīn Nāṣir, Ms Ofrah Ayalon and Ms Ḥanīn Ḥājj Yaḥyā. I also wish to thank my students from both the Arabic and Comparative Literature Departments at Beit Berl College, and the Department of Arabic, Language and Literature at the Hebrew University of Jerusalem. I would like to acknowledge with gratitude the help I have received during the research years of this project from the librarians Mr Mu'īn Ḥājj Yaḥyā, Ms Dian Mizrachi, Ms Michal Belachsen, Ms Hanna Dar and Ms Vered Rubin of Beit Berl College, Ms Shoshana Adelstein, Ms Esti Shapira, Ms Michal Tzadok, Ms Yael Eitan and Mr Uri Palit of the Hebrew University of Jerusalem, and Mr Haim Gal of Tel Aviv University. The skillful English editing by Mr Anthony Berris, Ms Margalit Rodgers and Ms Gila Svirsky is deeply appreciated. I am also grateful to have had exceptional collaboration with al-Ṭayyib Ṣāliḥ and his wife Julia, and the tremendous contribution of my wife Osnat. Finally I wish to thank the editors of the *Journal of Semitic Studies* for accepting to publish my work in the Supplement series and in particular Dr Philip Sadgrove and Ms Bronwen Campbell for their cordial attitude all along and the beautiful work with the final shape of the book.

CHAPTER ONE

The Author's World: The Case of al-Ṭayyib Ṣāliḥ

Fiction as reality is part and parcel of the author's world. While it is very difficult to follow the sources of the fictional part in the author's literature, it is less difficult to follow some biographical elements through his literary and non-literary writing. Therefore, it is small wonder that some literary critics insist on the importance of the text alone, as everything beyond its confines bears no significance or relevance to the text's study. Although I, too, am among those who argue that the text is of primary importance, I still maintain that an author's cultural, political, social and economic background is significant and in many ways assists in elucidating his or her works.

Why is an author's biography important? To gain a more profound and broader understanding of works of fiction we ought to familiarize ourselves with the writer's cultural and biographical background. The poetic world alone does not suffice in allowing the reader a deeper familiarity with the writer's literary world: the mimetic world reflects only one aspect of the text. Therefore, acquaintance with the writer's poetic, mimetic and real world assists the reader as well as the literary critic in understanding additional matters of which they might otherwise remain unaware.

Some Notes on his World

The above is especially applicable to a better reading of al-Ṭayyib Ṣāliḥ's works. Therefore extensive use will be made of those parts of the recently published portions of his autobiography, and also of the numerous interviews conducted with him.[1] The fact that al-Ṭayyib Ṣāliḥ delivered in these interviews few particulars about his family (and these carefully controlled and selected) made our quest a difficult one. Nonetheless, from the details he provided in the various interviews, we have brief glimpses of his real and fictional worlds. Thus we learn that al-Ṭayyib Ṣāliḥ was born in 1929 in al-Dabba village in northern Sudan[2] to middle-class parents, Muḥammad and 'Ā'isha, as were his two siblings, 'Alawiyya and Bashīr.[3] His father, a man of Sufist leanings, named him al-Ṭayyib after a venerated local sheikh who was buried in the village, and also out of a desire that his son be blessed. Al-Ṭayyib Ṣāliḥ went to the village primary school, to junior high school in Port Sudan, and completed his secondary studies at the Wādī Sīdnā high school north of Omdurman, from which he graduated *cum laude*. He moved to Khartoum where he enrolled in the Faculty of Natural Sciences, but he did not persevere with his studies for various reasons, among them his strong literary inclinations. Al-Ṭayyib Ṣāliḥ began teaching, but here, too, he did not last long and his urge to travel led him to England where he took a degree in international relations at the University of London. He settled there, married a Scottish woman and they have three daughters. He was director of the BBC's Arabic drama department, then served a stint as Director General of the Ministry of Information in Qatar and also worked for a short period in the Sudan. He did not return to the Sudan to work, for, in his own words, he did not wish to settle there permanently. The nature of his work would have required him to assume a political position, which is something he has always avoided.[4] Al-Ṭayyib Ṣāliḥ worked for UNESCO in Paris and was later employed as that organization's representative in Qatar and Jordan.

Two central facts in al-Ṭayyib Ṣāliḥ's life, in fact two principal axes around which his writing revolves, are first, that he was born in a village – in which he lived for part of his childhood – and second, his prolonged residence in England. It may be assumed that someone born in a remote village, like the subject of these pages, is bound to give expression to this in his work. In the works of village-born Arab authors, even after the majority left the village for the city, their villages, distant in time and place, appear time and again. Some obvious examples are the Egyptian authors 'Abd al-Raḥmān al-Sharqāwī (1920–87), 'Abd al-Ḥakīm Qāsim (1935–90) and Muḥammad Yūsuf al-Qa'īd (b.1944), and the Sudanese author Ibrāhīm Isḥāq Ibrāhīm (b.1946). To the above can be added a long list of authors, particularly from the Arab Mashriq.[5]

As will be obvious in some of the chapters in this study, the village is employed as the central stage in the majority of al-Ṭayyib Ṣāliḥ's works, either fully ('Nakhla 'alā al-Jadwal', 'Ḥafnat Tamr', 'Dawmat Wad Ḥāmid', '*Urs al-Zayn, Bandar Shāh: Ḍaw al-Bayt, Maryūd*), or partially ('Risāla ilā Aylīn', *Mawsim al-Hijra ilā al-Shamāl*, 'al-Rajul al-Qubruṣī').[6] Despite the fact that al-Ṭayyib Ṣāliḥ left his village, at first temporarily for high school, and later when he was twenty-four and left for London, the village remained etched in his heart, his thoughts and his emotions as a central part of his very existence.[7] It is therefore hardly surprising that some of the characters, events and customs in the author's works are villagers, and that they all are given such full expression in these works.[8] Al-Ṭayyib Ṣāliḥ never dissociated himself from his village even when he went to live in England; his move was neither planned nor due to economic reasons, nor because he wanted to acquire an education; according to him, it was mere chance that brought him to England.[9] Over the years he made a point of visiting the village at varying times, even though he never went back there to settle.[10] Despite the distance in time and place, the author invariably describes the village from the inside as someone for whom the real village is etched in his heart, adding further layers, some realistic and semi-realistic, and some fictional. The distance has not harmed his relationship with his village and its inhabitants. On the contrary, it enables him to present the village as a kind of 'Paradise Lost' to which he only returns as a visitor or tourist, not as a native villager.[11] Thus separated from his village, even at the beginning of his stay in England, he seems to have moved closer to it. Lonely in a foreign land, and in order to maintain contact with it, he wrote stories about the village. In his own words:

> When I reached London in February 1953, I found myself suffering during one of the coldest winters England had ever known. The cold seared me and when I recall it my teeth still chatter. I began blaming myself severely asking: 'how did I land myself in the first place in this country and what misfortune has driven me here?' It was then, when burdened by longing for my family, my country and my clan, that I wrote a short story entitled 'Nakhla 'alā al-Jadwal' [A Date Palm by the Stream]. That was in 1953 and it was published later in the anthology of stories, *Dawmat Wad Ḥāmid*. A simple story written very simply. Now when I reread it, I realise how much I was influenced by an all-embracing longing for my homeland. The story was an expression of longing for its environment and an attempt to evoke it.[12]

Beyond his descriptions of life in the village, its customs and traditions, al-Ṭayyib Ṣāliḥ's characters are the most enthralling and important aspects of his work. Indeed, the author's success in shaping his characters is precisely that of village characters, as characters of his first home rather than as characters of his adopted home in the West. Evidence of this can be found in riveting descriptions of al-Ṭayyib Ṣāliḥ's village characters, including that of the narrator. It seems that the author has made no real effort to go deeply into the Eastern characters that are not an organic part of the Sudanese village, like Muṣṭafā Sa'īd (*Mawsim al-Hijra ilā al-Shamāl),* who is Sudanese but an outsider in the village, and describe them convincingly and credibly, and this is certainly true in the case of the Western characters. They always remain foreign, alienated and distant, not only from us, the readers, but first and foremost from al-Ṭayyib Ṣāliḥ himself. Possibly the only instance in which al-Ṭayyib Ṣāliḥ describes, forcefully and importantly, 'Eastern' characters who are not from his village is that of Rabāb and her parents in the story 'Yawm Mubārak 'alā Shāṭi' Umm Bāb' (A Blessed Day on the Umm Bab Shore).[13] Because the story was written in Qatar, and the action takes place in that region, the author was able to shape the local characters credibly and with the insight of one who lived in the region (1974–81) and is familiar with it. Here, too, we can see the relationship between real life and fiction and when the point in question is his native home, the author describes his simple characters extremely well.

The second axis of al-Ṭayyib Ṣāliḥ's life is London. He came to England when he was twenty-four. Thereafter he never lived permanently in the Sudan. Without a doubt, leaving for England at a relatively young age, like his work in Paris and Qatar, continued to be expressed in one way or another in his works. Indeed, the encounter of al-Ṭayyib Ṣāliḥ the real author, the Sudanese intellectual, with the West, has provided much material for his works. In contrast to other Arab writers who left for the West and later returned to the Middle East or Africa to settle there (see Chapter Five), al-Ṭayyib Ṣāliḥ has only returned to his homeland for visits. Some of these Arab writers are from the Mashriq, such as the Egyptian authors Ṭāhā Ḥusayn (1889–1973) in his novel *Adīb* (Man of Letters, 1935), Tawfīq al-Ḥakīm (1898–1987) in his novel *'Uṣfūr Min al-Sharq* (A Bird from the East, 1938), or Yaḥyā Ḥaqqī (1905–92) in the novel *Qindīl Umm Hāshim* (The Lamp of Umm Hashem, 1944), the Syrian author Shakīb al-Jābirī (b.1912) in the novel *Qaws Quzaḥ* (The Rainbow, 1946), and Lebanese author Suhayl Idrīs (b.1924) in his novel *al-Ḥayy al-Lātīnī* (The Latin Quarter, 1954). From the Arab Maghrib we might mention the Moroccan author Muḥammad Zifzāf (1945–2001) and his novel *al-Mar'a wa'l-Warda* (The Woman and the Rose, 1972), and Algerian author Sa'dī Ibrāhīm and his novel *al-Marfūḍūn* (The Rejected, 1981).[14]

That these writers returned to the Middle East or North Africa while al-Ṭayyib Ṣāliḥ remained abroad not only distinguishes him from them, but also raises a question that the majority of literary critics have ignored: is al-Ṭayyib Ṣāliḥ in fact a Sudanese Arab author? This raises a related question of how we determine a writer's nationality. Is it according to his own wishes and definition, or is it according to other parameters connected to the language in which he writes?[15] Thus, for example, is an author like Moroccan writer al-Ṭāhir Ibn Jallūn (b.1944) who was born in Morocco, but is permanently domiciled in France, a Moroccan? In contrast to al-Ṭayyib Ṣāliḥ, al-Ṭāhir Ibn Jallūn not only lives in Europe, but also writes in French. Moreover, his prestige is due to his works in the French language, not in Arabic.[16] In regard to language, a parallel case may be made for other modern Arab writers like, for example, Palestinian writers who were born in British Mandate Palestine, but who reside abroad, such as Jabrā Ibrāhīm Jabrā (1920–94). Is he a Palestinian writer as he is usually presented, or perhaps he should be viewed as an Iraqi author as some writers and literary critics claim?[17] This phenomenon is also true of some Palestinian writers who live outside their own country and who write mainly in Arabic, but also in English (Jabrā Ibrāhīm Jabrā) and French (Afnān al-Qāsim), in addition to those Palestinian writers who live in Israel and write some of their works in Hebrew (Anṭōn Shammās, Na'īm 'Araidī, 'Aṭāllāh Manṣūr).[18] This circle of comparison can be widened to include the *Mahjar* poets and authors, and first and foremost Jubrān Khalīl Jubrān (1883–1931) who was born in Lebanon and lived in the United States, some of whose works were written in Arabic and others in English.[19]

To return to al-Ṭayyib Ṣāliḥ, one should consider it quite extraordinary that this writer who has lived outside the Sudan for most of his life (forty-six years at the time of writing), and yet continues writing in Arabic for either cultural or political reasons.[20] Therefore, I would rather consider al-Ṭayyib Ṣāliḥ a post-*Mahjarī* writer as is the case with other Arab authors who have either chosen or been forced by Arab authorities to leave their countries mostly for the West, but not for America. This was the case with the Mahjar authors who went to Europe, where they continue to write in Arabic, such as the Syrian poet Adūnis (b.1930) and the Syrian short-story writer Zakariyyā Tāmir (b.1931), the Lebanese author Ḥanān al-Shaykh (b.1945) and the Sudanese author Ṭāriq al-Ṭayyib (b.1959). Others went to the Arab states, as is the case with the writer of Saudi extraction 'Abd al-Raḥmān Munīf (1933–2004), who prefers to live in Syria, or the Sudanese writer and critic Ibrāhīm Mukhtār 'Ajūba (b.1946), who prefers to live in Saudia Arabia. In addition to these authors' output we should note the activity of literary periodicals such as *al-Nāqid*, *al-Kātiba* and *Mawāqif* that were published in exile, i.e., outside the Arab world and especially in Europe.[21] However, al-Ṭayyib Ṣāliḥ did not publish any literary works prior to 1953 ('Nakhla 'alā al-Jadwal' – A Date Palm by the Stream), before moving to England in February of that year. Eventually the distance and separation from his homeland gave him the initial impetus to write, and writing may have compensated him for the loss of his home.[22] In any event, al-Ṭayyib Ṣāliḥ has written most of his works in England, France and Greece where Europe is a marginal framework, in contrast to the Sudanese village in which he lived for but a brief part of his life. Therefore, two extraordinary works are worthy of note in this context. The first is 'al-Rajul al-Qubruṣī' (The Cypriot Man, 1973) where the action takes place in Cyprus, thus maintaining the relationship between the autobiographical elements and reality, as we shall see later. The second is the author's most recent work, 'Yawm Mubārak 'alā Shāṭi' Umm Bāb' (A Blessed Day on the Umm Bab Shore, 1993), with the action taking place in the Umm Bab area, not far from al-Doha in Qatar. As we already know, al-Ṭayyib Ṣāliḥ spent two relatively long periods in Qatar, first as Director General of that country's Ministry of Information, and later as the UNESCO representative there.

Al-Ṭayyib Ṣāliḥ's command of English was good even before he reached England and after residing there his expertise developed sufficiently for him to be able to write in English.[23] Yet he did not do so. Despite his command of English and his familiarity with English culture and literature, he apparently made a conscious choice to write in Arabic.[24] He is also less interested in writing about himself and far more interested in preserving the memory of his childhood and youth in the remote northern Sudanese village where he was born. The majority of his works, characters and subjects, and the use of the Sudanese village as a framework, is evidence of this. To this must be added his vast knowledge of and erudition about the hidden treasures of classical Arabic literature, which he loves passionately. This is particularly true of its poetry, and first and foremost with respect to two classical Arabic poets, Abū Nuwās (747/762–813/815) and Abū al-Ṭayyib al-Mutanabbī (919–55).[25] Al-Ṭayyib Ṣāliḥ's love of classical Arabic literature and his knowledge of modern Western literatures, particularly English literature, are evident in his works, as we shall see later.

We should bear in mind that his life in the Sudan as well as in England, in addition to his acquaintance with historical and literary sources and his knowledge of Arabic and English, were reflected not only in his literary works but also in his journalistic writing. Al-Ṭayyib Ṣāliḥ considers his journalistic writing, especially in the periodical *al-Majalla*, not a 'waste of time' or an obstacle to his contribution in the field of 'pure literature', but rather as a unique literary genre.[26] Furthermore, al-Ṭayyib Ṣāliḥ is very proud of this genre and his answer to my question during an interview is very clear:

> Ami Elad-Bouskila: I'd like to ask you if there are any differences between your journalistic and fictional writing? Please.
>
> Al-Ṭayyib Ṣāliḥ: Yes, of course. Although I brought to what you call journalistic writing some of the fictional techniques, I was not actually writing journalism as such. I was writing, I think, what is known in this country as literary journalism. I would take a topic or a poet or a writer or a philosopher or a historian, and go a little deeper into the subject than is usually done in journalism. And some of the products I feel rather proud of.[27]

The Author and Modern Sudanese Literature

Al-Ṭayyib Ṣāliḥ did not appear out of nowhere on the firmament of modern Arabic literatures, for modern Sudanese literature existed for years before his arrival on the scene.[28] A brief review of modern Sudanese literature might help us define al-Ṭayyib Ṣāliḥ's place in this, as well as in modern Arabic literatures.[29] Sudanese literature is different from other modern Arabic literatures in many ways. It is influenced by three specific conditions: first, because of the Sudan's geographic location, numerous elements of popular local fiction have penetrated its literature, as have non-Arabic words,[30] second, due to the Sudan's demography, its religious population includes Muslims, Christians and animists.[31] Thus modern Sudanese literature abounds with non-Muslim motifs, the majority of which are Christian. Third, due to the Sudan's proximity to Egypt, Egyptian literature has influenced the development of modern Sudanese literature and the latter has similarly had an impact on Egyptian writers.

Except for al-Ṭayyib Ṣāliḥ, neither modern Sudanese prose nor poetry succeeded, as discussed later, in having an impact on other Arab literatures. Three main reasons may be cited for modern Sudanese authors' failure to influence the cultural centres of the Arab world: the first is the Sudan's political and economic marginality relative to other Arab countries; the second is linked to the Sudan's relatively underdeveloped press, printing and publishing houses; the third reason is the Sudanese dialect with its combination of non-Arabic and Arabic words that makes the reading of Sudanese texts difficult for readers from other Arab states. No doubt one of the knottiest problems facing Sudanese authors, past and present, is the use of the literary language, especially in protracted dialogues in the local dialect.[32] This problem, which has troubled all Arab authors since the beginning of the twentieth century, has been particularly acute in the Sudan not only because of the composition of the population, but also because of the influence of African languages. Initially, sporadic attempts were made to write dialogues in literary Arabic based on the desire to reach a wider audience but, ironically, some of the authors who wrote fictional dialogues in the popular Sudanese dialect (al-Ṭayyib Ṣāliḥ, Ibrāhīm Isḥāq Ibrāhīm) were precisely those who reached larger audiences both in Arab countries and beyond.

Modern Sudanese literature is still in its initial stages. It has neither been sufficiently studied nor is it well known. Up to the early 1930s, poetry was the most prominent literary genre, and it was only from that period onward that we witness the appearance of fiction in the Sudan.[33] Some scholars of literature tend to link the emergence of literary genres in the Sudan, particularly the short story and poetry, with the Sudanese literary journals of the 1930s, such as *al-Nahḍa* (The Awakening, 1931–2) under the editorship of Muḥammad ‘Abbās Abū Rīsh (1908–35) and *al-Fajr* (The Dawn, 1934–7) under the leadership of ‘Arafāt Muḥammad ‘Abd Allāh (1897–1936).[34] This process in the development of Sudanese fiction, which is considered to be its first stage, continued until the end of World War II. At the time, Sudanese literature, like others in the Arab world, was characterized by romantic writing and was influenced by Egyptian authors like Muṣṭafā Luṭfī al-Manfalūṭī (1876–1924), as well as by translations from Western literatures, especially French and English romantic fiction.[35] Mu‘āwiya Muḥammad Nūr (1909–41) and ‘Uthmān ‘Alī Nūr (b.1925) are the prominent authors of this trend. Not many writers were productive in that period, and of these ‘Arafāt Muḥammad ‘Abd Allāh is a good example.[36] The second period of Sudanese literature began towards the end of World War II and continued until Sudan was granted independence on January 1, 1956 or, as some scholars indicated, at the beginning of the 1960s. The most notable change that occurred in this period was the transition from mainly romantic works to works of realism. Sudanese literature here is similar to the development of most other modern Arabic literatures. Outstanding romantic works in the second stage are characterized by *Mawt Dunyā* (Death of a World, 1946) by Muḥammad Aḥmad Maḥjūb (1910–76). However, realistic writing, and especially social realism, gained a foothold among Sudanese writers, for example, in *Mudhakkirāt Aghbash* (Memories of A Simple Man, 1950) by ‘Abd Allāh Rajab (b.1915) and of Malikat al-Dār Muḥammad ‘Abd Allāh (1922–69) in her short stories and novel particularly these which were published during the 1940s and 1950s. The subjects of fiction were the problems of poverty, city and village, women’s status, government and the citizen, and the like, and were similar to earlier topics, but were now dealt with differently and by means of a different technique. Discernible influences on Sudanese authors are Egyptian, Lebanese and Russian realistic writers. In this stage the role played by journals and periodicals was crucial since they reached a wider audience and encouraged educated readers to be open to new ideas, which were connected to their increased awareness of nationalism. The appearance in 1945 of *Kurdufān*, Sudan’s first provincial paper, and *al-Ra’y al-‘Āmm* (Public Opinion) are important. In addition to the role of the press, radio, a new medium, was established in 1940 in Omdurman.[37] The third stage in the development of modern Sudanese literature begins after the country attained independence and continues to this day. The development of the press, in addition to radio (1940) and television (1963), encouraged Sudanese awareness of the changes through political, social and cultural ideas on the one hand, while on the other the coups of 1958–64, 1969–85, 1989–present, cancelled out most cultural achievements in the Sudan and even led to a decline in these periods.[38]

In the development of modern Sudanese prose and poetry, the last forty years are of the greatest interest. Sudanese literature developed as rapidly as other Arabic literatures in those four decades, with significant changes occurring in the 1960s. Independence may have provided a major impetus. In addition, the Sudan was increasingly influenced by the Arab world, particularly Egypt. This influence was not limited to political, economic and social spheres alone; cultural influences also played a role. Sudanese writers were receptive to the literatures of the Arab world and drew on them. Egyptian writers like Ṭāhā Ḥusayn, Maḥmūd Taymūr (1894–1973), Najīb Maḥfūẓ (b.1911), Yūsuf Idrīs (1927–91), and ʻAbd al-Raḥmān al-Sharqāwī, exerted a significant influence. Lebanese authors, particularly Suhayl Idrīs and Laylā Baʻlabakkī (b.1936), were no less important. In addition to the great influence of writers from Latin America such as Gabriel García Márquez and Jorge Amado, and from Europe such as Albert Camus and Franz Kafka.

Magazines appeared in the Sudan in the 1960s and played an extremely significant role in the dissemination of modern Sudanese poetry and prose. These also included studies by Sudanese scholars on Sudanese literatures and language. Important Sudanese magazines from this period are *al-Ḥayāt* (Life) from the end of the 1950s, *al-Qiṣṣa* (The Story, 1960–1) and *al-Kharṭūm* that began publication in 1965.[39] Similar to modern Arabic literatures generally, from the 1960s onward Sudanese fiction supplanted poetry. The changing emphasis from poetry to prose was accelerated by the success achieved and the respect gained in the Arab world and outside it by Arab writers – particularly the award of the Nobel Prize for Literature to Najīb Maḥfūẓ and the prestigious *Prix Goncourt* to Moroccan author al-Tāhir Ibn Jallūn in 1987 and the Lebanese writer Amīn al-Maʻlūf (b.1949) in 1993. The fictional works of Sudanese writers employed for the most part a realistic style, extensive use of the stream of consciousness, and subjects that were drawn largely from Sudanese experience. During this period, the most prominent short-story authors are al-Ṭayyib Ṣāliḥ, al-Ṭayyib Zarrūq (b.1935), ʻAlī al-Makk (1937–92), ʻĪsā al-Ḥilū (b.1940) and Buthayna Khaḍir Makkī (b.1948).[40] Writers of novels are authors al-Ṭayyib Ṣāliḥ and his *Mawsim al-Hijra ilā al-Shamāl* (Season of Migration to the North, 1966), Abū Bakr Khālid (1934–76) with his *al-Nabʻ al-Murr* (The Bitter Spring, 1967), and Ibrāhīm Isḥāq Ibrāhīm who wrote *Ḥadath fī al-Qarya* (An Event in the Village, 1969).[41] Despite the more limited poetic output, mention should also be made of the poet of Sudanese extraction, Muḥammad Miftāḥ al-Faytūrī (b.1930), and the Sudanese poets Muḥammad al-Mahdī al-Majdhūb (1919–82) and Ṣalāḥ Aḥmad Ibrāhīm (1933–93).[42]

Within the context of modern Sudanese literature the African element cannot be overlooked, although this is not always mentioned when discussing Arabic literature and culture.[43] We should remember that just as the Sudan is an Arab Muslim country, with Christian and animistic elements, it is also an African country. African elements have a place in the literary language and in the choice of subject matter.[44] In two anthologies of selected African short stories, edited by the literary scholar C.L. Innes and the noted Nigerian author Chinua Achebe (b.1930), the stories are arranged according to four geographical areas, one of which is North Africa, and it is there, in both anthologies, that the editors locate the Sudanese story.[45] The African element, sometimes no less than the Arabic one, is so important to some Sudanese writers that the word *Ifrīqiyā* (Africa) is included in the titles of some of their works. The most prominent exponent of this is Muḥammad Miftāḥ al-Faytūrī, four of whose books have the word 'Africa' in their titles: *Aghānī Ifrīqiyā* (Songs of Africa, 1956), *'Āshiq min Ifrīqiyā* (A Lover from Africa, 1964), *Aḥzān Ifrīqiyā* (Sorrows of Africa, 1966), and *Udhkurīnī Yā Ifrīqiyā* (Remember Me, Africa, 1970).[46] Concerning content, contact with the white man is often expressed as the local African's blackness in contrast with the English, French, Portuguese and Arabic-speaking colonial societies, not only in al-Ṭayyib Ṣāliḥ's works ('Risāla ilā Aylīn', 'Khuṭwa li'l-Amām', 'al-Ikhtibār', *Mawsim al-Hijra ilā al-Shamāl*), but also in quite a few African works as well.[47]

African writers, like other writers known as 'Third World authors', often write about their cultural encounters with their past or present occupiers. Thus, a new and important channel of writing is opened in which participate, first and foremost, the intelligentsia of the occupied nation that comes into contact and maintains a dialogue with the people controlling it. This contact between occupier and occupied frequently exists under the impression of the independence attained by the people of the occupied country. That is to say, the cultural occupation by colonialism and imperialism continues, sometimes in the guise of culture, expressed in the language of writing, reading and speaking.[48] Accordingly, we find the people of the occupied country moving, this time out of choice, towards the classical and canonical cultural centers of Europe, and it is irrelevant whether the name is Paris, London, or any other location.

Possible Sources of Impact

Writers are also readers and, consciously or not, they internalize and express the stimulus or influences they have received as readers in their writing. It is the same with al-Ṭayyib Ṣāliḥ.[49] World literature has had an impact on modern Arabic literatures, and indeed, most literary genres found in the Arab world today were borrowed from modern Western literatures, especially the novel and the short story. We need only consider the impact existentialists like Camus, Sartre and Kafka had on Arab authors in the Arab Mashriq (Maḥfūẓ, Ghānim, Ba'labakkī, Suhayl Idrīs) from the 1950s up to the present, and in the Arab Maghrib (Barrāda, Zifzāf, al-Misnāwī). Clearly, the existential and philosophical significance in these writers' works is due to their exposure to Western writers.[50] Thus it is impossible, for example, to understand the works of Najīb Maḥfūẓ from the 1960s without understanding the philosophy and literary values of Western existentialist intellectuals.[51] Maḥfūẓ was one of the pioneers who accepted both literary and intellectual influences in the late 1960s and the beginning of the 1970s, especially from Latin American literature and from the Colombian author Gabriel García Márquez (b.1928) and his novel *One Hundred Years of Solitude*. His *Malḥamat al-Ḥarāfīsh* (The Harafish, 1977) was a product of the Latin American literary impact.[52] By the same token we may note the influence of the *nouveau roman* on modern Arabic literatures. Thus, particularly in the 1960s, one of the most notable examples is the influence of this school on Muḥammad Yūsuf al-Qa'īd in his novels of the 1970s, especially *Yaḥduth fī Miṣr al-Ān* (It's Happening in Egypt Now, 1977).[53] Al-Ṭayyib Ṣāliḥ, who uses elements of fantastic realism in some of his works, is aware of the South American writers' influence on modern Arabic literature. However in his own case he rejects it and notes the differences,[54] as he also draws on the local, traditional, oral African culture that was part and parcel of everyday life prior to European colonialism in Africa.[55]

Resorting to classical Arabic literature can be seen in the novels *Bandar Shāh: Ḍaw al-Bayt* and *Bandar Shāh: Maryūd*, where he uses verses by an anonymous Sudanese poet, by Muḥammad Miftāḥ al-Faytūrī, and verses by the classical Arabic poet Abū Nuwās, in addition to two paragraphs of *Kalīla wa-Dimna*. In contrast to some other contemporary Arabic writers, al-Ṭayyib Ṣāliḥ does not merely use quotations from the texts of modern writers; he also uses classical expressions and proverbs from the Koran.[56] His great love of classical Arabic literature has led him to the religious literary type, known as *al-Faraj ba'd al-Shidda* (Relief after Distress) found in 'Nakhla 'alā al-Jadwal', and even more so in 'Dawmat Wad Ḥāmid'.[57] Sufi elements and figures appear in 'Dawmat Wad Ḥāmid' and 'Yawm Mubārak 'alā

Shāṭi' Umm Bāb', where he also mentions figures from Arabic and/or Muslim history, such as 'Antara b. Shaddād, and some Sufi figures like al-Shahrazūrī, Ibn al-Fāriḍ, and Rābi'a al-'Adawiyya.[58]

Classical Arabic and Eastern literatures also appear in texts like *Alf Layla wa-Layla* and *Kalīla wa-Dimna.* These literatures are a frequent topic in interviews conducted with al-Ṭayyib Ṣāliḥ who greatly admires prominent poets and writers such as al-Mutanabbī, Abū Nuwās, Abū Tammām, Imru' al-Qays, al-Nābigha al-Dhubyānī and al-Jāḥiẓ.[59] But above all he reveres the two classical Arabic poets al-Mutanabbī and Abū Nuwās. He says:

> The genius of Abū Nuwās is in the fact that he is an artist. I personally consider him to be an artist par excellence of Arabic literature. He is certainly not the greatest poet when compared to al-Mutanabbī, but he is an artist in the contemporary meaning of the word. He used the term 'vain thoughts' in its contemporary sense i.e., 'illusion'...[60]

Al-Ṭayyib Ṣāliḥ values the Arabic past, both from the literary and cultural standpoints. In his words:

> The past, with regard to all of us and with all its flaws, had clear characteristics and this is the sad thing about it. I have met Sudanese communists whose thinking is, of course, based upon the rejection of this past, but when truly facing oneself, one finds that one owns nothing but this past. For if we look at our present, and intend to compare present contributions of the Arab nation with high cultural standards – claimed from us as a large plot on the face of our planet – we find that they are very small achievements indeed. Accordingly, the past is the only truth that exists for us till now. Henceforth, in my opinion, is our longing for this past, and what seems to be a condition of adherence to it, is nothing but an outpouring of our concern. Thus, when we compare ourselves today with what had been achieved by our ancestors yesterday, we find ourselves dwarfs in aspiration and deed, despite all the great achievements that have taken place in definite locations and in certain situations.[61]

Aside from the past, so necessary to present existence, and yet so much superior to what is now, al-Ṭayyib Ṣāliḥ furthermore draws a comparison between himself and other writers.

> I wish to say that these friends [Tawfīq al-Ḥakīm and Suhayl Idrīs] have, in fact, not influenced me, except in an unconscious way [...] but I do not want to reject totally any form of influence [...], for a writer does not read another seeking to copy him; however, these readings are in a way accumulating points of departure for the writer. Yet, I cannot define by whom I have been influenced. I might have been influence by some Western writers, and had I been able, I would have said in all sincerity that my artistic path is similar, to a great extent, to that of Shakespeare or Conrad. Consequently, in Arabic literature, I cannot deny the high status enjoyed by a writer like Najīb Maḥfūẓ [...] There are also many authors whom I respect, like Yūsuf Idrīs, Maḥmūd al-Mas'adī, who discusses problems in Arabic culture most profoundly, 'Abd al-Salām al-'Ujaylī and 'Abd al-Raḥmān Munīf. There are many voices and illustrious authors, each abiding by his own system.[62]

Despite his respect for modern Arabic authors, al-Ṭayyib Ṣāliḥ feels that he has not been overly influenced by them, although some of their works may have made an impact at various stages of his life. In interviews that were conducted with him he has mentioned Egyptian authors such as Tawfīq al-Ḥakīm, Najīb Maḥfūẓ, Yaḥyā Ḥaqqī, Yūsuf Idrīs and Ibrāhīm 'Abd al-Qādir al-Māzinī (1890–1943), the Syrian authors 'Abd al-Salām al-'Ujaylī (b.1918), Zakariyyā Tāmir and Ghāda al-Sammān (b.1942), the Palestinian-Lebanese author Tawfīq Ṣā'igh (1923–71), and the Tunisian author Maḥmūd al-Mas'adī (1911–81). To these Arab authors he adds modern Sudanese writers such as 'Alī al-Makk in addition to modern Sudanese poets and critics who published their works especially in the 1950s and/or the 1960s, like Aḥmad al-Ṭayyib (b.1921) and Jamāl Muḥammad Aḥmad (b.1915), Muḥammad Miftāḥ al-Faytūrī, 'Uthmān Abū Bakr, Ṣalāh Aḥmad Ibrāhīm, Muḥammad al-Makkī Ibrāhīm (b.1939), and Muḥammad 'Abd al-Ḥayy (1944–89).[63]

Western, particularly English authors, have had a greater influence on al-Ṭayyib Ṣāliḥ, as he has often stated in interviews. These are primarily William Shakespeare, Jonathan Swift, Joseph Conrad, William Faulkner, Samuel Beckett, W.B. Yeats, Johann Wolfgang von Goethe, Thomas Mann, D.H. Lawrence, E.M. Forster, Ford Madox Ford, Charles Dickens, Eugène Ionesco, and T.S. Eliot.[64] Among other non-Arab writers, although al-Ṭayyib Ṣāliḥ does not mention them by name, whose influence is apparent in some of his works, especially in *Mawsim al-Hijra ilā al-Shamāl*, are Albert Camus, despite al-Ṭayyib Ṣāliḥ's reservations,[65] and to a lesser degree Stendhal, pseudonym of Henri Marie Beyle, Jorge Amado, and Emily Brontë, as has been noted by some literary critics.[66] Camus' relationship, similarity, closeness and, to a certain extent, influence on al-Ṭayyib Ṣāliḥ is important. These are not related to the latter's writing technique but rather to his assimilation of Camus' existentialist ideas, at least with respect to the novel *Mawsim al-Hijra ilā al-Shamāl* and more regarding the figure of Muṣṭafā Sa'īd than that of the narrator.[67] We shall deal with similar relationships between Camus' *The Outsider,* Conrad's *Heart of Darkness* and Shakespeare's *Othello* later (see Chapter Four).

To conclude this issue of influence(s) on al-Ṭayyib Ṣāliḥ by Western writers the following table summarizes points in common, similarities, and possible influences of Western works on *Mawsim al-Hijra ilā al-Shamāl.*

A Table of Comparison Between *Mawsim al-Hijra ilā al-Shamāl*, *Othello*, *Heart of Darkness*, *The Outsider*, *The Red and the Black*, and *Wuthering Heights*

Subject of comparison	*Mawsim al-Hijra ilā al-Shamāl*	*Othello*	*Heart of Darkness*	*The Outsider*	*The Red and the Black*	*Wuthering Heights*
The characters	Muṣṭafā, the Narrator, Maḥjūb, Ḥusna, Wad al-Rayyis, Bint Majdhūb, the Grandfather	Othello, Iago, Desdemona, Cassio	Kurtz, Marlow	Meursault, the Arab	Julien Sorel, Madame de Rênal, Mathilde	The Narrator, Heathcliff, Catherine
Writing technique	◆ Breaking the unity of time and place ◆ Stream of consciousness ◆ Monologues ◆ Dialogues ◆ Archetypical characters ◆ Use of historical events ---	◆ Non-observance of unity and place --- ◆ Monologues ◆ Play dialogues ◆ Archetypical characters ◆ Use of historical events ---	◆ Breaking the unity of time and place --- ◆ Monologues ◆ Dialogues ◆ Mixed characters ◆ Use of historical events ---	◆ No unity of time and place ◆ Stream of consciousness ◆ Monologues ◆ Dialogues --- ◆ Use of historical events ---	◆ Unity of place not maintained --- ◆ Monologues ◆ Dialogues --- ◆ Use of historical events ◆ Chronological story	◆ Unity of time and place maintained --- ◆ Monologues ◆ Dialogues ◆ Archetypical characters --- ◆ Chronological story
Themes	◆ East and West ◆ Past and future ◆ City and village ◆ Imperialism and localism ◆ Foreignness ◆ Life and death ◆ Violence ◆ Sex ◆ Culture ◆ Education ◆ Racism (anti-black) ◆ Jealousy ◆ The sun --- --- ◆ The victim – Mustafā ◆ Religion ◆ Alienation	◆ East and West ◆ Past and future ◆ City ◆ Colonialism ◆ Foreignness ◆ Life and death ◆ Violence ◆ Sex ◆ Culture --- ◆ Racism (anti-black) ◆ Jealousy --- --- --- --- --- ◆ Alienation	◆ East and West ◆ Past and future ◆ City and village ◆ Imperialism ◆ Foreignness ◆ Life and death ◆ Violence ◆ Sex ◆ Culture --- ◆ Racism ◆ Madness --- --- --- --- --- ◆ Alienation	◆ East and West ◆ Past and future ◆ City and village ◆ Colonialism ◆ Foreignness ◆ Life and death ◆ Violence --- ◆ Culture ◆ Education ◆ Racism --- ◆ The sun --- --- --- --- ◆ Alienation	--- ◆ Past and future ◆ City and village --- ◆ Foreignness ◆ Life and death --- ◆ Sex --- ◆ Education --- --- --- ◆ Class struggle ◆ Ambition --- ◆ Religion ◆ Alienation	--- ◆ Past and future ◆ City and village --- ◆ Foreignness ◆ Life and death ◆ Violence ◆ Sex ◆ Culture ◆ Education --- ◆ Jealousy --- ◆ Classes ◆ Ambition ◆ The victim – Heathcliff --- ◆ Alienation

Translations and the Critical Reception of his Works

Three main motives stimulate one society to learn about another through translated literary works: curiosity, politics and artistic qualities. The translation of various sciences into Arabic, together with Western literature, had a decisive influence on the development and growth of Arab society. In the golden ages of Arabic culture, especially in the tenth century, translations were mainly from Greek, Latin and Persian works. In the nineteenth and twentieth centuries, translations of Western literary works have been intensively pursued, which also included new genres previously unknown to Arab readers. Accordingly, the quantity of Western works translated into Arabic is far greater than of works translated into Western languages from Arabic.[68]

Al-Ṭayyib Ṣāliḥ's fiction has been translated into numerous languages, among them English, French, German, Polish, Russian and Hebrew.[69] This is one of the few cases, perhaps the only one in modern Arabic literatures, where almost all the works of an Arabic writer are rendered into foreign languages. Of his five books, four novels[70] were translated into English, as were most of his short stories.[71] The accessibility of al-Ṭayyib Ṣāliḥ's works in English, and significantly the translation of the novel *Mawsim al-Hijra ilā al-Shamāl*,[72] has clearly been a major factor in the acceptance of his works in the Western world and the enhancement of his reputation as a modern Arabic author.[73]

He is a unique case, for he is an Arabic author who first established his reputation in the West, mainly in England and Scotland, and only later in the Arab world, thus proving the inherent connection between translation, literary criticism and acceptance of the translated text. Indeed, the numerous translations of al-Ṭayyib Ṣāliḥ's works also had a decisive influence on literary criticism of his works in the Arab world. Al-Ṭayyib Ṣāliḥ published the majority of his works in the 1960s, yet Arab critics paid little attention to them and when they did, they did not view him as an author of stature, except for the Egyptian critic Rajā' al-Naqqāsh.[74] A study of works published by al-Ṭayyib Ṣāliḥ in the 1960s shows that apart from the two novels, *Mawsim al-Hijra ilā al-Shamāl* (1966) and *'Urs al-Zayn* (1964–6), only his collection of stories, *Dawmat Wad Ḥāmid* (1967), was published. By the end of the 1960s, some of his works, novels and short stories, aside from various new editions, had also appeared in magazines in the Arab world and outside it.[75] The turning point in his recognition as a major literary figure came, therefore, when his works were published in Egypt and when the Egyptian edition of *Mawsim al-Hijra ilā al-Shamāl* was published by the large Egyptian publishing house *Dār al-Hilāl* in 1969.[76] It was similarly important that his first two novels and some of his short stories were published in English in 1968 and 1969.[77] Hence, the publication of the majority of al-Ṭayyib Ṣāliḥ's works in Arabic, together with the translations of others in the latter 1960s, was the catalyst in enhancing al-Ṭayyib Ṣāliḥ's reputation as one of the most prominent modern Arabic writers.[78]

The importance of al-Ṭayyib Ṣāliḥ's acceptance, and more precisely the acceptance of his works into the canon of modern Arabic literatures, that began in the mid-1970s and which continues to this day, is important in understanding his special status among readers and literary critics. Most likely it was because he is an author from an Arab country whose literature is marginal at best, together with other facts mentioned above, such as the problem of the dialogues written in popular Sudanese dialect and the fact that he lives in London and not in the Arab world, that only little interest was shown in his works at the end of the 1960s. Together with these factors, two others were obstacles during that period. First, some of his works, particularly *Mawsim al-Hijra ilā al-Shamāl*, were published in the Lebanese magazine, *Ḥiwār*.[79] In the 1960s, this magazine was involved in what was known as 'the *Ḥiwār* scandal'. Rajā' al-Naqqāsh, who was one of the Arab literary critics who early on praised al-Ṭayyib Ṣāliḥ's works and the novel *Mawsim al-Hijra ilā al-Shamāl*, concluded his enthusiastic review of the book with the words:

> One lamentable observation remains, and that is that this great novel was only published in an earlier issue of the Beirut *Ḥiwār* magazine. The magazine's pages were later a platform for free nationalist ideas as the magazine represented the World Organization for Freedom of Culture, financed and directed by American Intelligence. I have no doubt that al-Ṭayyib Ṣāliḥ has no connection with the World Organization for Freedom of Culture for as every letter of his novel testifies, Arab genius throbs with true nationalism that is neither sick nor perverse. If it is a sad fact that this novel was published only in *Ḥiwār*, I hope that an Arab publishing house in Cairo or Beirut will shortly publish the complete version for Arab readers everywhere, so that they may grasp with their intellect and emotions the rise of a new genius in the firmament of the Arabic novel...[80]

It should also be mentioned that al-Ṭayyib Ṣāliḥ's relationship with *Ḥiwār*'s editor, the Palestinian Lebanese poet and critic Tawfiq Ṣāyigh, was close and warm. Al-Ṭayyib Ṣāliḥ viewed him not only as a talented and important poet, but also as an excellent literary critic.[81] Secondly the slow acceptance of al-Ṭayyib Ṣāliḥ's works in the Arab world may also have occurred for political reasons. The 1960s was the period of Nasserism, and al-Ṭayyib Ṣāliḥ's first two books were published close to the Six-Day War of 1967. During that period, al-Ṭayyib Ṣāliḥ presumably made neither political statements nor voiced views on this subject. When one considers the trauma which the Arab world experienced at the time, it is quite possible that the proximity of the publication of his works, and *Mawsim al-Hijra ilā al-Shamāl* in particular, to the Six-Day War, caused the suppression of the book's publication in the late 1960s.

However, starting with the mid-1970s, al-Ṭayyib Ṣāliḥ burst into the consciousness of readers and literary critics both inside and outside the Arab world.[82] Three main reasons may have brought about this turning point; the first was the changing political circumstances in the Arab world (especially in Egypt) and the waning of the *Ḥiwār* scandal. The second is linked to the translation of his works into additional Western languages and the praise by Western literary critics. The third reason was the appearance of two further novels, *Bandar Shāh: Ḍaw al-Bayt* (1971) and *Bandar Shāh: Maryūd* (1976–7),[83] and reprints of his earlier books in Lebanon, Egypt, Tunisia and Israel.[84] Telling evidence is that al-Ṭayyib Ṣāliḥ and his works were not only accepted, but enthusiastically received by readers and literary critics in the Arab world, as were the numerous articles, books, interviews and doctoral dissertations in Arabic, Hebrew, and in Other languages (see Appendices and Bibliography).[85] For the past twenty-odd years al-Ṭayyib Ṣāliḥ has thus been received into the highly regarded canon of modern Arabic literatures, and he is one of the best known, loved and admired authors in the Arab world and beyond it. Like their Western counterparts, Arab critics consider the novel *Mawsim al-Hijra ilā al-Shamāl* a turning point in modern Arabic literatures.[86] Calling the novel a work of *'abqariyya* (genius) – a word not commonly used in the Arab world of letters – some even called this work not by the word *riwāya* (novel), but *malḥama* (epos).[87] The Palestinian poet, author and translator Jabrā Ibrāhīm Jabrā expressed his feelings about *Mawsim al-Hijra ilā al-Shamāl* as follows:

> It [*Mawsim al-Hijra ilā al-Shamāl*] is quite possibly the most brilliant novel I have read in Arabic. It may be said that al-Ṭayyib Ṣāliḥ has achieved in one fell swoop the depth, structure and fervour that no other writer in our Arabic literature, in my opinion, has achieved before. *Mawsim al-Hijra ilā al-Shamāl* forges a link between the problems of character, time, imagination and reality, cohesively and flowingly, in a way that we have unsuccessfully sought for a long time, and which has recently been fulfilled by al-Ṭayyib Ṣāliḥ, and what a lyrical fulfillment it is.[88]

Indeed, this is one of the rare cases when an author has succeeded in expressing himself deeply, intelligently, sensitively, simply, cleverly and impressively. Clearly, not all al-Ṭayyib's works equal this one. Others are good and even excellent, but in this novel, replete with autobiographical elements, the author has risen to unprecedented heights regarding both the poetics of writing and content. His intense, flowing and fiery writing stimulates the reader's curiosity, and forces him to continue turning the pages.

How does al-Ṭayyib Ṣāliḥ consider his novel? Although he is aware that his reputation rests, first and foremost, on this novel and its many translations, he nonetheless prefers the novel *'Urs al-Zayn*. Al-Ṭayyib Ṣāliḥ, moreover, considers the novel *Bandar Shāh* to be of greater importance than *Mawsim al-Hijra ilā al-Shamāl.* In his words:

> So you find me saying that my most important work to date, despite its flaws, is *Bandar Shāh*. This is the most important work as far as I am concerned, despite the fact that it has not been completed, because I have published two parts of the novel, *Maryūd* and *Ḍaw al-Bayt*, and I hope to complete this work. I am convinced that this will take a very long time [...] so therefore I feel that *Bandar Shāh* is the best text I have written, and that the best work as far as I am concerned is the last chapter of *Ḍaw al-Bayt.*[89]

But to return to *Mawsim al-Hijra ilā al-Shamāl.* Among the subjects dealt with in the text, sex is most important and central to the novel. True, there are many other important subjects, but readers and literary critics alike have found it appropriate to devote much space to the way in which al-Ṭayyib Ṣāliḥ writes about women and sex. The importance of sex in the text is beyond all doubt, and we need not inquire further whether al-Ṭayyib Ṣāliḥ (as he says of himself) was influenced by Freud at the time, or whether psychological and/or psychoanalytical analysis is related to this.[90] Although literary critics ascribed great significance to this subject, they touched on it hesitantly, which is perhaps indicative of the problem this subject raised. Al-Ṭayyib Ṣāliḥ was, of course, conscious of the great sensitivity of Muslim Arab society towards the subject of sex: therefore, when he gave the manuscript to his friend, the translator Denys Johnson-Davies, for translation into English, he suggested restoring passages he had written but which he had deleted from the original, being concerned that these would prevent the book's publication in Arabic. According to the translator, he refused to do so, and with the author's agreement these passages were also removed from the translation.[91] Regrettably, because of the way the subject of 'sex' and 'immoral expression' were dealt with in *Mawsim al-Hijra ilā al-Shamāl*, it was forbidden to distribute this novel in Kuwait in 1966 (as it was forbidden to distribute the Egyptian edition of 1969), and thirty years later, for the same reasons, the rector of Cairo University asked Professor Sayyid al-Baḥrāwī to stop teaching the novel. Eventually, for political reasons, at the end of 1996, the Sudanese authorities ordered the cessation of teaching the novel at Sudanese universities. Needless to say, al-Ṭayyib Ṣāliḥ and many of his colleagues in the Arab world roundly criticized this step.[92]

Comparison of Textual Versions

Authors who make changes in a text both prior to its publication and after, are nothing out of the ordinary in world literature, although it occurs infrequently in modern Arabic literatures. There are at least two factors that make a writer change part or parts of his original text, the first possible one of which is the existence of diglossia and/or multiglossia in Arabic.[93] Briefly stated, two languages exist in Arabic, literary and spoken Arabic. Literary Arabic is common to all Arabs wherever they may be, as this is the language of the Koran. It has many and varied strata, but it is essentially one language. Arabic dialects separate countries, cities, villages, neighbourhoods and quarters in the Arab states, and when an Arab author has to address the problem of dialogues, he must first decide which of the two languages he should use. The most notable example of this is the Egyptian author Maḥmūd Taymūr who published hundreds of stories and plays during his career. Over a period of almost forty years (1920–59) he decided to change almost half of his stories for artistic and aesthetic reasons and, in addition, for reasons of his own, he changed everything related to the use of dialogues and moved from writing in spoken Egyptian Arabic to literary Arabic. The principal cause of his change of attitude towards the language of dialogue is connected with the author and thinker Ṭāhā Ḥusayn. Ḥusayn, who was a member of the Egyptian Language Academy, rejected outright the use of spoken Egyptian Arabic in literary writing, and viewed its use as a mistake, arguing that the Egyptian dialect, like any other Arabic dialect, is not a language and therefore should not be used for literary purposes. Taymūr, who also became a member of the Egyptian Language Academy (1949), changed the language of his dialogues under the influence of Ṭāhā Ḥusayn.[94] The second possible factor that causes a writer, Arab or non-Arab, to change part of a published text is connected to the art of storytelling. Authors, like everyone else, change in the course of life and these changes may be expressed either in the poetics of writing or in the thematic field.

There are five instances in which al-Ṭayyib Ṣāliḥ made changes and/or amendments to his works, the first of which is connected to 'Muqaddimāt' (Preludes, 1966) that are part of the *Dawmat Wad Ḥāmid* collection of short stories (pp. 83–93). The 'Muqaddimāt' includes five short short stories and that is how they appear in the Egyptian magazine *al-Hilāl*.[95] Interestingly, they first appeared in the Beirut magazine *Ḥiwār*, where other works by al-Ṭayyib Ṣāliḥ had also appeared, and at their first publication there were six, not five, stories.[96] Two possible assumptions might explain this: the first is that this is simply a technical error; when 'Muqaddimat' was printed in the *Dawmat Wad Ḥāmid* collection, one was inadvertently left out and *al-Hilāl* simply followed suit in its own edition. The second assumption is that the short short story 'al-Shay' al-Ākhar' (The Other Thing), which appeared in *Ḥiwār*,[97] was not omitted as the result of a technical error, but intentionally by the author. If this is true, the reason could be connected to the poetics of al-Ṭayyib Ṣāliḥ's writing, because this story is characterized by three components that set it apart from the other short short stories in 'Muqaddimāt'. From the thematic standpoint, the subject of this story is not the encounter between East and West. The story's plot is set in Khartoum; and all five short short stories in 'Muqaddimāt' open with different forms of the same verb, *kāna*, to be, while the opening of 'al-Shay' al-Ākhar' does not begin this way!

The second instance of amending a text or the location of parts of it concerns the novel *'Urs al-Zayn* (The Wedding of Zein, 1964–6). Three years before the novel appeared in book form, several portions appeared in *Ḥiwār*.[98] The editor notes that these are 'the first two chapters of *'Urs al-Zayn*, a short novel, which will appear together with another of the author's short novels next year'.[99] The two chapters mentioned are not the first two chapters of the novel, which appears as a book in various editions (see Appendix A and Bibliography), but appear in the edition we are using on pages 73–90. It is clear, then, that the author could have opened the novel in the same way as the two chapters that appear in the magazine. It should be remembered that in this book, the *imām* and the groups that make up the village population have a special significance in the text. However, the way the novel begins in book form is more convincing and credible. At times the chronological order of the final text may be abandoned in its serialized form, but we should note that the novel appeared in its complete form in the Sudanese magazine *al-Kharṭūm* just as it appears in various book length editions of the book.[100]

The third instance is the novel *Mawsim al-Hijra ilā al-Shamāl*. As mentioned above, when al-Ṭayyib Ṣāliḥ gave the manuscript for translation into English to Denys Johnson-Davies he omitted certain sexually explicit passages, suggesting to the translator that they be included in the translation. The reason may be that despite the fact that al-Ṭayyib Ṣāliḥ was living in London at the time, he knew full well that this subject was controversial and sensitive, and that some of his readers, even in the second half of the 1960s, would not accept direct, blunt and even coarse descriptions. And indeed, some literary critics expressed their concern with the way al-Ṭayyib Ṣāliḥ dealt with this sensitive subject. Moreover the current Sudanese regime prohibited teaching the novel, not because it feared offending religious sensitivities, as was the cases with Najīb Maḥfūẓ, the Syrian Ḥaydar Ḥaydar (b.1936) and Salman Rushdie (b.1947), but because of the sexual explicitness that in their opinion harmed the moral standards of Arab and/or Muslim society. It is probably true that the current regime was settling accounts with al-Ṭayyib Ṣāliḥ, who had criticized it harshly, and now used his sexual explicitness as a pretext for prohibiting the teaching of his works. To my knowledge, the charge of the perverted use of sex has been used in at least one other famous case, that of the Lebanese author Laylā Baʿlabakkī. After she published her collection of stories *Safīnat Ḥanān ilā al-Qamar* (Spaceship of Tenderness to the Moon, 1963), she was accused of harming her society's moral standards.[101] As a result, Baʿlabakkī stopped publishing her literary works and moved into journalism.[102] To return to *Mawsim al-Hijra ilā al-Shamāl,* the translator decided that it was inappropriate to include passages in the English translation that did not exist in the original Arabic text, and so with the author's consent the offending passages were removed from both the original and the translation.

The fourth instance of changing a text or parts of it is 'al-Rajul al-Qubruṣī' (The Cypriot Man, 1973).[103] This story was published in January 1976 in the Qatari magazine *al-Dōḥa*, together with the editor's comment: 'This short story was written in Beirut in the summer of 1972 and was first published in *al-Thaqāfa al-ʿArabiyya*, 2 (1973). The author rewrote its first paragraphs and as a result, it is possible that it [the story] is not completely identical with the text published in the above-mentioned magazine [*al-Thaqāfa al-ʿArabiyya*]'.[104] A further comment by the same editor appears at the end of the story: 'al-Ṭāhir Wad al-Rawwāsī, one of the characters who appears in the author's novels, appears in the novels *ʿUrs al-Zayn* and *Ḍaw al-Bayt*, and is one of the principal characters in the novel *Maryud*, soon to be completed by the author'.[105] The last six lines in the first version (*al-Thaqāfa al-ʿArabiyya*) were omitted from the text of the second version (*al-Dōḥa*).[106]

And so we find two editorial comments, one on the changes at the beginning of the text and the second on the character al-Ṭāhir Wad al-Rawwāsī, about whom the editor, as someone familiar with the author's works, sought to enlighten his readers.

In any event, beyond the amendments made to the first paragraphs of the text, made for artistic considerations, the story is preceded by four lines taken from a poem by Muḥammad Miftāḥ al-Faytūrī. These lines contain motifs of death, life, and government, all of which appear in the works of al-Ṭayyib Ṣāliḥ. It is also worth noting that the author quotes an excerpt from one of al-Faytūrī's poems in his novel *Bandar Shāh: Ḍaw al-Bayt.*[107]

The fifth instance is that of the novel *Bandar Shāh: Maryūd* (1976–7).[108] In this case there were no changes of the text itself, but in the chapter order. In all the published editions of the novel in book form, there is a set chapter order. The first chapter (pp. 11–23) deals with Muḥaymīd, the second (pp. 25–32) with Sa'īd 'Ashā al-Bāyitāt al-Qawī, the third (pp. 33–66) with al-Ṭāhir Wad al-Rawwās, and the fourth and last chapter (pp. 67–88) with Maryūd. In contrast, the novel, two chapters of which were published in *al-Hilāl*, is published in a different order. The editor states categorically that 'The great Arab artist and author al-Ṭayyib Ṣāliḥ has completed his new novel, *Maryūd*, which will soon be published in book form. *Al-Hilāl* is pleased to publish the first chapter of this superb novel here'.[109] The first chapter deals with Bilāl and it appears as part of the third chapter of *Maryūd* (pp. 46–55). The second chapter in *al-Hilāl* deals with al-Ṭāhir Wad al-Rawwās, while in *Maryūd* he appears only partly in the third chapter (pp. 33–45). In other words, the first and second chapters in *al-Hilāl* reverse the order of the third chapter of the book. With regard to the book's publication in four parts in *al-Dōḥa*, here, too, there is an order different from that found in the *al-Hilāl* and the novel as it appears in the book *Maryūd*. The first part is about Muḥaymīd, as he appears in the book, but it is different from the order in *al-Hilāl*. The second part deals with Sa'īd 'Ashā al-Bāyitāt al-Qawī and al-Ṭāhir Wad al-Rawwās (pp. 25–34), that is to say all of the book's second chapter and half of the third (pp. 35–45). The third part deals with Bilāl, and this, too, is different from the order in *Maryūd*, where he appears in the second half of the third chapter (pp. 46–66). The fourth part deals with Maryūd, exactly as it is in the book *Maryūd*. To summarize, the author made changes after completing *Maryūd*, and decided that in the book itself he would change both the chapter order and their apportionment. It is difficult to see any reasons other than aesthetic that compelled him to make these changes in accordance with his conception and understanding. One other small but important change is the addition of interpretations of words and expressions in the Sudanese dialect in *al-Dōḥa*, which was not done in *Maryūd* in the *Dār al-'Awda* editions but was in the Tunisian editions of the novel.[110]

This chapter has attempted to draw a portrait of the world, including the literary one, of al-Ṭayyib Ṣāliḥ, to assist the scholar of literature and the reader in gaining a better understanding of the author's texts. The details of his spiritual and personal life help us to discern aspects in his works that might otherwise escape attention. Al-Ṭayyib Ṣāliḥ's personal life, as I suggest, is of prime importance in the understanding of his works. It is very true that his way of life – like the fact that he is, in a certain sense, a post-*Mahjarī* writer is amply reflected in his works and finds a different guise, not only because of the fiction, but because every shift of the writer's 'piece of life' to creation, in the present case to literature, is subject to change, adaptation and emptying in a manner suited to the world to which they are removed. Therefore, the 'location' of his writings becomes more and more 'globalized' through the various translations of his literary works. As we shall see later (especially in Chapters Two and Five) his local and globalized writing connected with what I prefer to call complementary opposites.

CHAPTER TWO

Poetic Elements in al-Ṭayyib Ṣāliḥ's Works

In the first chapter we saw that al-Ṭayyib Ṣāliḥ's worldview is influenced by four principal sources: modern Western literatures, particularly English literature; modern Arabic literatures, particularly Egyptian literature; classical Arabic literature and African literature, especially its folk literature. In this chapter I shall attempt to analyze al-Ṭayyib Ṣāliḥ's poetical worldview. It can be assumed that an author's poetical worldview is not constant and varies according to circumstances, not only in his artistic life but also in his personal life. Whereas writing, technique and style may not vary drastically from work to work, they can characterize each work at various levels and in varied parameters. Nonetheless, despite this assertion al-Ṭayyib Ṣāliḥ's works may be considered as a single, long, multi-faceted text, with different facets gaining expression in various works as will be shown. It can be furthermore assumed that there is no distinction between the author's fictional texts and the author himself.[1] In this chapter we shall examine the following parameters: the titles of the works, dedications and introductions, expositions of the texts, endings of the texts, dialogues and monologues, and place, space and time.

Titles[2]

The title selected by the author for his text is of paramount importance. This is the first contact between the text, the author and the reader, and to a certain degree, determining the title of the work delineates the author's position. The significance of a title exists today, the beginning of the twenty-first century, just as it has existed for hundreds of years in poetry and prose in both Western and Eastern literatures. Clearly, authors who chose the name of a man or woman for their book sought to focus maximal interest on the hero or heroine whose name the work bears. Works of this kind are to be found in various periods in canonical Western literatures.[3] For example, *Don Quixote* (1605–16), by the Spanish author Miguel de Cervantes (1547–1616), serves as a means to discuss and criticize the unrealistic literature of the knights' or the rulers' way of life; regarding *Père Goriot* (1835) by the French author Honoré de Balzac (1799–1850) some critics indicate that the real hero is Paris; other examples are *Tess of the D'Urbervilles, A Pure Woman* (1891) by the English author Thomas Hardy (1839–1928) and *Ulysses* (1922) by the Irish author James Joyce (1882–1941).[4] This literary usage is also known from the beginnings of modern Arabic literatures and an outstanding example of it may be seen in the following works by

Egyptian authors: *Zaynab, Manāẓir wa-Akhlāq Rīfiyya* (Zaynab, Rural Scenes and Manners, 1914) by Muḥammad Ḥusayn Haykal (1888–1964), and *Rāma wa al-Tinnīn* (Rama and the Dragon, 1979) by Edwār al-Kharrāt (b.1926). The Palestinian author Jabrā Ibrāhīm Jabrā in the novel *al-Baḥth 'an Walīd Mas'ūd* (The Search for Walid Mas`oud, 1978); Syrian author Ḥannā Mīna in the novel *Ma'asāt Dīmitrīyū* (The Tragedy of Dimitriou, 1985), Iraqi author Dhū al-Nūn Ayyūb (1908–88) in the novel *al-Duktūr Ibrāhīm* (Doctor Ibrahim, 1939), and the Sudanese author al-Ṭayyib Ṣāliḥ in the novels *Bandar Shāh: Ḍaw al-Bayt* (1971) and *Bandar Shāh: Maryūd* (1976–7).[5]

The titles of works may focus on elements other than the character of the hero or heroine. It can, for example, be related to the confines of a place such as a train, a ship or the sea. Titles are sometimes attributed to well defined places like a house, as in the case of a collection of short stories by Najīb Maḥfūẓ, *Bayt Sayyi' al-Sum'a* (The House of Ill-Repute, 1965). The place is sometimes even smaller and becomes a room as, for example, in the novel *Qadar al-Ghuraf al-Muqbiḍa* (The Fate of the Oppressive Rooms, 1982) by the Egyptian author 'Abd al-Ḥakīm Qāsim. The place can be a city as, for example, in the collection of stories *Madīnat al-Mawt al-Jamīl* (The City of Beautiful Death, 1985) by the Egyptian author Sa'īd al-Kafrāwī (b.1939). The title is sometimes associated with a part of the city or one of its neighbourhoods as in Maḥfūẓ's novel *Al-Qāhira al-Jadīda* (New Cairo, 1946). The plot can unfold in a village as in the case of the Egyptian author Maḥmūd Ṭāhir Lāshīn's (1894–1954) story 'Ḥadīth al-Qarya' (Talk of the Village, 1928). The village locale is sometimes limited to an estate as in the novel by Egyptian author Muḥammad Yūsuf al-Qa'īd in his novel *Akhbār 'Izbat al-Manīsī* (News From al-Manisi Estate, 1971).[6]

As in world literature, titles in modern Arabic literatures can focus on the element of time as, for example, in the novel *Ṭuyūr Aylūl* (September Birds, 1962) by the Lebanese author Emily Naṣrallāh (b.1931). Titles are sometimes related to a specific day as, in the novel *Yawm Qutila al-Za'īm* (The Day the Leader was Killed, 1985) by Maḥfūẓ. Titles may reduce the period of time to a time of day as in the collection of stories by the Egyptian author Yūsuf Abū Rayya (b.1955), *al-Ḍuḥā al-'Ālī* (In the Late Morning, 1985). We sometimes find a combination of two periods of time as in the story 'Layla Shatawiyya' (A Wintery Night, 1984) by 'Abd al-Ḥakīm Qāsim, and also the seasons in general as in the story *Kull Tilka al-Fuṣūl* (All Those Seasons, 1987) by Sa'īd al-Kafrāwī.[7]

Thus the title of a work is used as a kind of declaration of intent by the author. A title is sometimes chosen as the result of the author adopting a stand vis-à-vis the text on the one hand, and the reader, on the other. Accordingly, this might be a reader whom the author is addressing as he writes. It is clear that the choice of a title for the text is indicative of the way in which the author seeks to create a dialogue with the reader and attract his or her attention. Therefore, the choice of giving the text the name of one its heroes is quite commonplace and the choice of a name like 'Zaynab', 'Ibrāhīm', etc., is far from unique. The moment the writer chooses an uncommon title he succeeds in capturing the reader's attention (the same applies to literary criticism) and in creating a close, immediate dialogue. Thus, for example, when Najīb Maḥfūẓ chose the title 'Za'balāwī' for one of his best-known stories, he immediately aroused the reader's curiosity. Za'balāwī is not a common name and it is doubtful if it exists in Egyptian reality, yet the author has already achieved a double objective: on the one hand, he has enmeshed the reader in his net, while on the other, he has imbued the text with an atmosphere of ambiguity and mystery that is appropriate to the content of the story.[8] A title of this kind can employ a word or term unfamiliar to at least some of the readers, as in the case of Moroccan author Muṣṭafā al-Misnāwī (b.1953), in his 'al-Ūṭūrūṭ' (The Autoroute, The Road, 1977)[9]. Some Arab readers in Mashriq will possibly not understand the title as this word has been borrowed from French. But the word itself arouses curiosity by virtue of its choice as a title that is dependent on a non-Arabic word. Had an Arabic word been chosen, it would not have achieved the desired effect.

Let me move on to the titles chosen for his works by al-Ṭayyib Ṣāliḥ and examine them one by one. We shall begin with the collection of stories *Dawmat Wad Ḥāmid, Sab' Qiṣaṣ* (1967).[10] Numerous collections have titles taken from one of the stories they contain and this is true in the present case. Why was this particular literary work chosen? Because the author himself, and quite a few of his readers, translators and literary critics consider it the jewel in the crown of his short stories.[11]

'Nakhla 'alā al-Jadwal' (A Date Palm by the Stream)[12] dates from 1953 and was first published in 1960. It is the opening story of the collection. It was not by chance that the author opened this collection with this particular one. The first reason might be chronological as the stories in the collection appear in order of their writing. The second reason could be related to the author's worldview as the story's title embodies his clear position on the centrality of the two elements of the title, the palm tree and the stream. These two components are central elements in Sudanese village life. The author seeks to give expression to his feelings and emotions during the period in which he wrote the story, when he was in a foreign country, England, and suffered from loneliness and homesickness for his village. The story was therefore a bridge between him and his homeland.[13] It could have been entitled 'Maḥjūb' after its central character, but in so doing the author would have been missing the mark, for the story, like so many of al-Ṭayyib Ṣāliḥ's works, was written more about nature, the village and its inhabitants, and less about Maḥjūb. The palm tree and the stream, one of the tributaries of the Nile, are not only parts of nature but also the villagers' source of life. The palm tree, like other kinds of palm trees of the same family, appears in al-Ṭayyib Ṣāliḥ's works as they do in other Arabic works, and are often used in the titles of additional modern Arabic texts.[14] The tree, as we shall see in other works by al-Ṭayyib Ṣāliḥ, is not merely a symbol but rather part and parcel of the village scene. The author's perception is based on the principle that people, trees, birds and animals are part of nature and live together in harmony. In so doing in 'Nakhla 'alā al-Jadwal' as in other stories ('Ḥafnat Tamr', 'Dawmat Wad Ḥāmid'), al-Ṭayyib Ṣāliḥ has personified trees and animals.[15]

'Ḥafnat Tamr' (A Handful of Dates)[16], was written in 1957 and first published in 1967. It is the second story written and published by al-Ṭayyib Ṣāliḥ, and like its predecessor it was written in England. The author could have named the story after one of the two central characters, the narrator's grandfather or Mas'ūd, or even often the narrator himself. He chose, however, to maintain the same line of thought that characterized his choice of title for the first story. In other words, the representation of the village world remains and the date, the fruit of the palm tree, is employed as a central axis for the story itself. It is the grandfather who gives the narrator, his grandson, a handful of dates which he eats, but in the wake of the injustice done to Mas'ūd during the date harvest, he forces himself to vomit the dates he has eaten.

'Risāla ilā Aylīn' (A Letter to Aileen)[17], the third story, was written in 1960 and first published in 1967. Here we see a different kind of title, which does not continue the principle of the two previous stories. The change in the title conforms to the changes of content and characters. Although this story takes place both in the village and in England, one of the central characters, Aileen, is Scottish. In other words, subject, characters and content have changed and therefore the choice of the text's title has changed too. The story's title testifies to the beginning of a new direction of writing by the author; for it is no longer only the small Sudanese village with which he seeks to maintain contact through his writing and visits that concerns him, but also the West. The title indicates, as does the entire story, his first step in coping with Western culture, the beginnings of the relationship between the Eastern hero and the Western woman. It should be noted that the choice of genre – correspondence – exists in classical Arabic literature in the literary genre known as *al-Rasā'il* (Correspondence Literature), as it is also present in modern Arabic literatures.[18]

'Dawmat Wad Ḥāmid' (The Doum Tree of Wad Hamid)[19] the fourth and best known story dates from 1960 and was first published in 1961. We have already mentioned that al-Ṭayyib Ṣāliḥ, his readers, translators and literary critics view this story as the author's best short text. The title reflects the continuity with the titles of the first two stories, 'Nakhla 'alā al-Jadwal' and 'Ḥafnat Tamr'. With regard to the doum palm, which is different from the date palm, *nakhla*, it typifies both the Sudan and Egypt. In this respect it is more distinctive and typical than the date palm or the date that characterize numerous Middle Eastern and North African countries. The title of the story is comprised of two parts: the first is the name of the tree, *dawma*, which is employed as the plot's central motif and embodies a great deal of symbolism with regard to the villagers' struggle against progress, in addition to the fact that it was considered to be immutable, sacred and rooted.[20] The tree is essentially an altar symbol, not only of the villagers' struggle against progress and a site of miracle and legend, but also a symbol of continuity. Moreover, from an etymological standpoint, the name *dawma* is derived from *d.w.m.*, which in Arabic means continuity, and the same root occurs in *al-Dā'im*, which is one of the ninety-nine names of Allah. The second part of the story's title is *Wad Ḥāmid*, the righteous man after whom the village is named.[21] Both parts of the title are connected to mystery, legend and the village inhabitants, and together they characterize the content of this etiological story. In addition, because the real author considers all his texts as a whole text, his latest short novel *Bandar Shāh: Maryūd*, mentions that the village of Wad Ḥāmid was named after the al-Ḥawāmida tribe whose members were the rulers and noblemen of Wad Ḥāmid.[22]

'Idhā Jā'at' (If She Comes)[23] was written in 1961 and first published in 1967. It is the title of the fifth story in which al-Ṭayyib Ṣāliḥ deviates totally from his previous stories in both the story's content and its title. Neither the content nor the scene of the plot are connected to the village. The subject, tourism, is completely different as it belongs to the modern world. There is no mention of the Sudanese village and the plot's three characters are city dwellers. The title refers to Bahā', one of the three central characters, who hopes that despite the office being closed, the beautiful Swedish woman he is expecting will arrive on time.

In some respects, 'Hākadhā Yā Sādatī' (That's The Way It Is, Gentlemen)[24], which dates from 1961 and was published in 1962, continues the line of perception of 'Risāla ilā Aylīn' and 'Idhā Jā'at'. This is another step along the author's long road of his East-West encounters. The title is decisive and declarative while at the same time it addresses the reader in a style uncommon in modern Arabic literatures.[25] The kind of address to the reader in this text is the same as at the beginning of the novel *Mawsim al-Hijra ilā al-Shamāl.*[26] Possibly this title reflects an English language influence. In the course of the events related in this story, the narrator uses the word *sayyidatī* (Madam) on one occasion, when he addresses the woman (p. 70), but on two occasions he addresses his implied readers: once when he seeks to include the readers, *yā sādatī* (O, Gentlemen), because he has managed to resist the hostess's temptations despite the fact that he was about to succumb to them (p. 73), and the second time when he uses the title of the story 'Hākadhā Yā Sādatī'. At the end of the story, he again chooses to address his readers and make us part of his marriage (p. 82). But it is also possible that we find here the influence of classical Arabic on al-Ṭayyib Ṣāliḥ's world, with this kind of title the real author has chosen to address us not as readers but as listeners. In other words the real author, who has been influenced by *The Arabian Nights*, used the technique of the listener and the teller. Therefore, what matters is the telling of the story as *al-ḥakawātī* (the popular storyteller) and not as *al-rāwī* (narrator).

'Muqaddimāt' (Preludes)[27], was written in 1962 and published in 1966. It is the last in al-Ṭayyib Ṣāliḥ's only collection of stories. This is not one story but rather a cluster of very short tales and each has its own subject. The author probably preferred to group them under the title 'Preludes' not only for convenience, but also because each one is autonomous, has its own right of existence and certainly bears the same defined characteristics borne by all these very short stories from the standpoint of content, subject, exposition, ending and formation of characters. This unique formula is an aggregate despite the fact that the formula's components function autonomously in the stories. Accordingly, the author decided to unify them under one title, yet it does not explain the title itself, for the author does not provide any reason for calling them 'Preludes' and we have no explanation for his choice. It seems unlikely that the author chose this title to draw for the reader, and perhaps even for himself, brief sketches or formulae of possibilities of encounters between East and West. A more convincing explanation is that they are introductions to the following texts, or to the long and important one, *Mawsim al-Hijra ilā al-Shamāl.*

'Al-Rajul al-Qubruṣī' (The Cypriot Man)[28], from 1972 and published in 1973 is grouped with the two stories that are not included in al-Ṭayyib Ṣāliḥ's only collection. This work deals partly with the characters and the village of Wad Ḥāmid, while the second one deals with the Qatari village of Umm Bāb.[29] In this text, al-Ṭayyib Ṣāliḥ chose the appellation of a person and not a defined name, a style uncommon in modern Arabic literatures.[30] Thus, as we shall see later, the author continues with similar titles and defined names of people that constitute the principal character and the key of the plot. Who the Cypriot Man really is is unknown; we do not know his name or other important details about him, but only that this is what the narrator calls him because he met him in Cyprus. Perhaps we can conclude from the story's ending that he is the Angel of Death, who on this occasion is satisfied with the narrator's father, but next time it will be the narrator's turn to die. Possibly the author's father died during the same period (see later) which exerted some influence on the writing of the story and the forbidding atmosphere permeating it.

'Yawm Mubārak 'alā Shāṭi' Umm Bāb' (A Blessed Day on the Umm Bab Shore, 1993)[31] is the last story the author has published so far. The story's title is the longest of any of al-Ṭayyib Ṣāliḥ's works and it relates to one day in the life of a couple who have a daughter, and who spend a day on the shore in the Umm Bab area. The story is different from others by al-Ṭayyib Ṣāliḥ in that the location is not Wad Ḥāmid and the characters are not the village characters familiar to us from his previous works.[32] Yet the Sufi atmosphere and the high degree of ambiguity in the text characterize it, just as they do other stories. The word *mubārak* could be understood literally to mean 'blessed', but we may certainly view it as a word with Sufi or religious connotations. The name Umm Bāb, which is not far from Doha in Qatar, distinguishes the scene of the plot from the Sudan, and thus al-Ṭayyib Ṣāliḥ takes a step further than the one he has taken in the previous story, the main part of which does not take place in Wad Ḥāmid. Perhaps the author is thus evoking places where he lived while outside the Sudan, like Qatar, for example, a country in which he spent seven years (1974–81) and which is one of the Arab countries that is closest to his heart.[33]

The novel *'Urs al-Zayn* (The Wedding of al-Zein)[34], was written in 1960–2, and was first published in 1966. It is the first long text written by the author. Its name is brief and to the point. What could be more 'natural' than the wedding of a man called al-Zayn, i.e., 'the good' or 'the handsome'? As al-Zayn is not particularly good-looking, the 'good' meaning of his name is more appropriate and in contrast to al-Shayn, it hints at a pandect of positive and good meanings.[35] Apparently the choice of title suggests al-Ṭayyib Ṣāliḥ's condition at the time he wrote this work. He gave a short, concise and clear title to a work that deals with simple people and at the same time with extremely complex events. Al-Zayn's wedding is the axis around which the entire novel revolves; he is the hero and his wedding is the climax of the book. This knowledge opens the novel, becomes exciting village news and reaches its culmination at the end of the book. Although marriage is not an uncommon event, one that occurs frequently in modern Arabic literatures, a title that includes the word *'urs* (wedding, marriage) is extremely rare.[36] Clearly, the author could have chosen the title 'The Wedding of Ni'ma', but despite the importance of this character he did not do so, placing instead al-Zayn at the centre of the novel, because his life is a chain of miracles and extraordinary events linking him to the character of al-Ḥanīn, the man of miracles.

Mawsim al-Hijra ilā al-Shamāl (Season of Migration to the North),[37] was written in 1962–6, and first published in 1966. It is al-Ṭayyib Ṣāliḥ's second novel and has the most complicated, complex and charged title of all his works. If the novel *'Urs al-Zayn* is a continuation of the author's short stories, like 'Nakhla 'alā al-Jadwal', 'Ḥafnat Tamr' and 'Dawmat Wad Ḥāmid', then in *Mawsim al-Hijra ilā al-Shamāl* we see, on the one hand, a continuation of some of the above-mentioned stories, while on the other, it continues stories like 'Risāla ilā Aylīn', 'Idhā Jā'at', 'Hākadhā Yā Sādatī', and particularly 'Muqaddimāt'. *Mawsim al-Hijra ilā al-Shamāl* has two central motifs: the Sudanese village and the relationship between Eastern and Western cultures, the title expressing this duality. My perception is that al-Ṭayyib Ṣāliḥ, especially in his novels, makes extensive use of complementary opposites and binary oppositions by means of three words: *mawsim, hijra* and *shamāl.*[38] It is possible to show how the author's life is reflected and expressed by these terms that include the clash between West/North and East/South, as we shall see later (Chapter Five). The word *mawsim* has two meanings: the first, a season and the second a festival or holiday.[39] The first meaning indicates a field that delimits us to the natural world, that is a season, a circumscribed time. It is not defined as in the word *faṣl* (season), for then it would be completely clear that the subject was the four seasons of the year, but rather a constant or recurring period of time, a season that recurs each year, or a temporary phenomenon that has permanency or a permanent phenomenon that has varying temporariness. This might be a season related to animals or birds, the world of animals. A further meaning is related to Man in the context of the sowing seasons or any other activity connected to agriculture. Certainly, most of Sudanese society is rural-agricultural and temporariness, permanency and particularly periodicity are what characterize the word *mawsim* in Arabic. The second meaning is related to the religious aspect of the word. That is to say it indicates a festival, a celebration, albeit one which is not necessarily of a religious character, but which is related to a celebration, and there are those who suggest interpreting the word in this way.[40] Moreover, the word *mawsim* may be also interpreted as a season in the political context, namely the fate of imperialism – an extremely important subject in the novel – a temporary phenomenon that will pass. Imperialism is compared to a bacterium that attacked the European conqueror and was transmitted to the conquered Arabs, but it is a seasonal bacterium.[41] Another meaning of the word *mawsim* is related to the character of Ḥusna, an important character who is viewed by some as a symbol of the modern Arab woman who rebels against accepted norms, disobeying the dictates of tradition and customs accepted in her community. In short, this is not a total and sweeping migration, symbolizing a continuing situation, but rather a temporary, seasonal one.[42] Indeed, the first part of the title relates to its second part, that is the migration, in the sense of a phenomenon that also characterizes educated Sudanese when they emigrate from their country. People migrate as do animals, regularly and periodically.

With regard to the word *hijra* (migration), here, too, there are two meanings, the religious and the secular one.[43] In its religious sense, the intention is, of course, to *hijra*, the word that signifies for the Muslim the Prophet Muḥammad's reluctant migration from Mecca, where he and his disciples were persecuted by some of that city's inhabitants. The year of the *hijra* has been determined as 622, the first year of the Muslim Era. The attendant connection to this is both positive and negative. The negative aspect is related to the fact that the Prophet and his disciples were forced to leave Mecca, while the positive side of the coin is that they were accepted by part of the citizenry of Medina, the city to which they migrated and which offered them sanctuary. The non-religious meaning of the word deals with migration or wandering in two spheres, such as the movement of natural phenomena from one place to another, in this case sand dunes, a motif and symbol in Arab society, while another movement or migration is that of birds. The second sphere concerns human beings, in this case Muslim-Arab society, such as the migration of Sudanese. Here, too, the subject under discussion is the African-Arab society in which nomadism is not extraordinary, for part of Arab society, like its African counterpart, lives a nomadic life. Nomadic inhabitants are part of the social fabric that characterizes Sudanese society as it finds expression in this novel and particularly in *'Urs al-Zayn.*

During numerous periods, inhabitants of the Sudan emigrated and in the present case from northern Sudan, the birthplace of the author. In the forties, for example, as a result of economic hardship, many northern Sudanese emigrated northwards (to Egypt) and southward (to Khartoum and the Jazira).[44] Yet they maintained contact with the region and their families during vacations and festival times. It should be remembered that the Bedouin, like Gypsies, maintained a reverse migration, that is they came to the area in which al-Ṭayyib Ṣāliḥ lived for a specific period, and some remained and mingled with the local inhabitants. Furthermore, during earlier periods, the Sudanese people's love of science and learning caused them to migrate to famous cities in cultural centres outside the Sudan, like Fez, Baghdad, Tunis and Cairo.[45] In any event, nomadism or migration is perceived as temporary, and not as permanent state. The importance is in the place from which the migration was begun, for the destination is temporary, provisional and just another way-station on the migrational journey. Therefore, this migration is both on the collective and individual level. In addition, this migration (*hijra*) is possible from one internal situation to another. The issue of internal migration as a temporary event arises in the case of the narrator and in some respects in the case of Muṣṭafā Sa'īd as well.

The word *shamāl* in Arabic signifies a northerly direction. Thus, if the migration is to the north, the migrants do not come from the north but from another direction, and in the present case, from the south. The entire title, 'Season of Migration to the North', simultaneously expresses the two elements that dialectically support an ambivalent equation in which permanency and temporariness are used as two varying and constant factors. Nature's migration is from north to south in the cold season when the birds arrive from cold countries seeking refuge in warmer climates. But here the author reverses the significance of this movement and perhaps this is indicative of his view of natural phenomena. Instead of from north to south, the migration is in the opposite direction, like the flow of the Nile in the narrator's village. Perhaps this is the author's response to the migration of Sudanese from south to north. The northerners, in this case the English, like various other European peoples in the modern era, had, since the end of the eighteenth century, begun to reach the south (the East) to conquer parts of the Arab and/or the African world. Their stay in the south, like that of birds, was temporary and at the end of a constant periodicity they returned to their home countries. The symbolism of the title is clear, i.e., from the end of the first half of the twentieth century, educated Sudanese who migrated from south to north were not permanent migrants, but left for Western, Northern society and always returned from it after acquiring their education. This is the case with Muṣṭafā Sa'īd who lived in Europe for thirty years, or in the case of the narrator who spent seven years in England. The difference between the emigration of Muṣṭafā Sa'īd and that of the narrator is not solely one of a period of time, seven years as opposed to thirty years, or the way that each of them did return to the Sudan,[46] but it is related to place. Whereas the narrator only emigrated to England and returned to the Sudan, Muṣṭafā

Sa'īd emigrated to Cairo, England, Paris, Copenhagen, Delhi and Bangkok. Furthermore, Muṣṭafā Sa'īd left for Cairo when he was twelve years old and for England at fifteen, while the narrator went to England when he was older, only after completing his high school studies.

The problem is that the real author emigrated from the south to the north in 1953, only returning for visits, not permanent residency, and so the title is testimony more to the fictional characters rather than the real ones. Both the emigration and the north are nothing but way-stations on the heroes' journey, but with clear contrasts: East and West, North and South, women and men, life and death, desert and water are not so much an outward voyage like the one they undertook in real life, but a prolonged inward spiritual journey, into themselves. In this journey they seek their own belonging on the personal and collective level, and face up to two cultures with all the alienation and foreignness this entails.[47] This is a journey that contains elements of apprenticeship, and some autobiographical features in addition to the typical elements of the *Bildungsroman*, or as Plato put it, *anagnorisis*.[48] The north is a transit station through which the educated Sudanese has to pass in a personal ceremony of maturation just as he does in the collective ceremony. The northward migration is not merely from the Sudan to England. In fact, Muṣṭafā Sa'īd's whole life is one big migration in which there are numerous stops on the way north: from Khartoum to Cairo, Cairo to London and then a southward migration from London to Khartoum, from Khartoum to the narrator's village and from the village to the river. The narrator, too, passes through a number of way-stations on his migration from his village to England, from England to his village, from his village to Khartoum, from Khartoum to his village, from himself to Muṣṭafā and from Muṣṭafā to himself until he reaches his village and the land of the living. People are compared to birds that undertake the journey in a temporary yet permanent way.

And yet the title of the novel does not relate only to people, because it relates first and foremost to birds. The novel contains a specific reference to this when the narrator is struggling with the river and the decision between south and north, and it is, in fact, a deliberation between life and death: 'In a state between life and death I saw formations of sand grouse heading northwards. Were we in winter or summer? Was it a casual flight or a migration?'[49] On the subject of the river, the importance of the Nile in relation to the title of the novel and the entire text is also significant. The Nile flows from south to north and despite the fact that it changes its course because of natural obstacles, it reaches the north in the end. Why? Because the sea lies to the north and rivers flow to the sea. This natural flow of the Nile has symbolic implications. Educated Arabs, in our case educated Sudanese, indicating Muṣṭafā Sa'īd, go northwards, first to Cairo and then to London, to become educated. During that period (and today), the culture of the north, or the West, is the central culture where science, technology, industry and education are concerned. In other words, the northward migration, even though it be temporary, is towards Western culture that symbolizes progress, particularly scientific progress. At the same time it is a symbol of the foreign conqueror.[50] One might go even further and say that the author gave the novel its title as a provocation, not of the Arab, but rather the Western, and the English reader in particular. Hence although the text is presented in the form of a novel, which is, of course, a Western literary genre, its content is totally different from what the English reader might expect.[51]

Bandar Shāh: Ḍaw al-Bayt was written in 1967–70 and first published in 1971. It is a novel built upon two books of which this is the first. In addition to its subtitle, which we shall discuss later, the novel has two titles. These titles also have a meaning expressed in the names of two important characters in this book, i.e. Bandar Shāh and Ḍaw al-Bayt. The order of the titles is also interesting: first, *Bandar Shāh,* the common title of both books. First comes *Bandar Shāh*, the name by which 'Īsā Wad Ḍaw al-Bayt, (one of the central characters), is known. Therefore, the author chose to put the son's name before that of the father, which runs contrary to natural, biological and chronological order. *Ḍaw al-Bayt* (a major character) means 'light of the house' and this is the name, not the original one that the villagers gave to the stranger whom the waves carried to their village. This name has positive connotations in Sudanese society, meaning a respected man with positive attributes. It was possibly unavoidable that this name also bears a folkloristic Sufi meaning because the figure is characterized by an aura of legend, ambiguity and mystery. Another interpretation emerges when the two names are combined. They then mean 'light of the house', as well as 'lighthouse' which is connected to his background: first, he came from the sea and disappeared into the sea, and secondly Ḍaw al-Bayt's extraordinary character almost served the villagers as a lighthouse. The words *Bandar Shāh* are not derived from Arabic but from Persian;[52] *Bandar* means 'harbour' or 'trading town', and *Shāh* means 'sovereign'.[53] Al-Ṭayyib Ṣāliḥ explains the significance of the title thus:

> I chose the name Bandar Shāh since our problem is one of searching for a city (that is, al-Bandar) and the second point is the invention of a form suitable for governing ourselves, which is the sovereign (*shāh*).[54]

The novel is about these two matters and the assumption in *Bandar Shāh* is that 'both past and future are constantly plotting against the present, or the grandfather and the grandson are constantly plotting against the father'.[55] Indeed, these connections are perhaps proof of the relations between the city and the village, on the one hand, and the relations between past and future on the other, both in terms of complementary opposites and quite often as binary oppositions. The last part of these remarks is directed towards the novel's subtitle, 'A story of the father who is the victim of his own father and son'. In this subtitle, al-Ṭayyib Ṣāliḥ intends to point out the relationship between the grandfather, Bandar Shāh, and his grandson, Maryūd. This may be viewed as suggesting another type of novel the author has chosen, the Period Novel.[56] The author is consistent in this regard, as the relationship between Bandar Shāh and Maryūd, like that between the narrator (Muḥaymīd) and his grandfather, does not exist solely in this novel. The special relationship, with which we shall deal in Chapter Three, exists in al-Ṭayyib Ṣāliḥ's earlier works, particularly 'Ḥafnat Tamr' and *Mawsim al-Hijra ilā al-Shamāl*. It is difficult to determine whether these relationships exist in modern Arab society, and in our case, in Sudanese village society. However, this is an unusual relationship, for the common one is between father and son or mother and son. Clearly, a relationship also exists between the narrator's father and the narrator, or between the mother and the narrator, but they are described in a minor key. Moreover, at the centre stands the special relationship between the narrator and his grandfather in several of al-Ṭayyib Ṣāliḥ's works. In the novel *Bandar Shāh: Ḍaw al-Bayt*, the author delineates an extraordinary relationship between Bandar Shāh, the grandfather, who has eleven children, and the grandson. This relationship is more than merely symbolic; for example, the Biblical story of Joseph and his brothers and his father preferring him, but there the relationship is between father and son and not grandfather and son.[57] The relationship between Bandar Shāh and his grandson Maryūd exists on two levels: the legendary and the realistic; though both become coalexe when the eleven children murder the grandfather and his grandson and are imprisoned for the crime. We may also note that the first word of the subtitle, *uḥdūtha*, is in both singular and plural use in modern Arab literatures, although not commonly used thus.[58] The symbolic level indicates the main issue: in a traditional Arabic way the real author relates the generational struggle by employing a modern Western technique. The present is the real victim between past and future since it has lost the connection with the past and the future and only rarely can play the role of go-between.[59]

Bandar Shāh: Maryūd[60] (The Beloved) was written in 1976 and first published in 1976–7. It is the second of the three or possibly five planned parts of the novel *Bandar Shāh: Ḍaw al-Bayt.* Hence the title *Bandar Shāh* remains constant; in the first part it was *Ḍaw al-Bayt,* Bandar Shāh's father, while in the second part it is *Maryūd.* The name *Maryūd* is used exclusively in the Sudan. Al-Ṭayyib Ṣāliḥ himself interprets the name: '*al-Rīd* in the Sudan means 'love' and *Maryūd* is the loved one'. The name *Maryūd* appeared in the first book, *Bandar Shāh: Ḍaw al-Bayt.* The choice of this name, meaning not simply 'liked' but 'beloved', testifies to the author's decision of placing the stage at the disposal of this special character. He is prefered over his uncles and his father and reveals that the grandfather skips the generation of children, preferring the generation of grandchildren. Or in the author's words, 'And Maryūd is the continuation of lasting characters in a long, uninterrupted line'.[61] The author clearly prefers the past and the future at the expense of the present and thus, from his point of view, there is a direct continuation of the first book of *Bandar Shāh*'s subtitle. We may assume that the author is expressing his personal feelings and worldview: the present is always the less important time in relation to past and future.[62] Moreover, the title reveals not only a preference for the future and the hopes it embodies but it also indicates the importance of love as the author views it in various contexts. Love can be mundane as the love between Maryūd and Maryam and Bilāl and Ḥawwā', or indicative of the Sufi context of which we find traces in earlier works ('Nakhla 'alā al-Jadwal', *'Urs al-Zayn, Bandar Shāh: Ḍaw al-Bayt*) and the author's last work, 'Yawm Mubārak 'alā Shāṭi' Umm Bāb'.

Dedications[63]

In modern Arabic literatures – those that were influenced by modern Western literatures – we find the authors' dedications to relatives in part of the texts. Some Arab writers also employ the verse of a poem or a proverb at either the head of the text or at the head of certain chapters.[64] In three of the five books al-Ṭayyib Ṣāliḥ has published to date, he has included dedications. The first book, *Dawmat Wad Ḥāmid: Sab' Qiṣaṣ* (1967), is dedicated to Fatḥ al-Raḥmān al-Bashīr, his good friend from their student days and from the period in which they studied at the same institution.[65]

The fourth book, *Bandar Shāh: Ḍaw al-Bayt* is dedicated to his parents Muḥammad and 'Ā'isha and his two siblings, 'Alawiyya and Bashīr,[66] thus supplying the names of the author's parents and those of his sister and brother who, at the time of writing, were still alive. A further interesting fact is that while al-Ṭayyib Ṣāliḥ puts the name of his father before that of his mother, he places his brother's name after that of his sister. In this novel, regarding the use of another text as a motto or motifs of other writers, al-Ṭayyib Ṣāliḥ uses the texts of three writers: 'an anonymous Sudanese poet', Abū Nuwās and al-Faytūrī. Therefore, we may conclude firstly that the three writers are Eastern, not Western, secondly, all three are poets, and thirdly, one of them is a classical poet, one is a modern poet and we know nothing of the third. Who are these poets and why did the author quote their texts? It is well known, both from interviews and his narrative texts, that the author has expressed his love of, and familiarity with, Arabic poetry. It is therefore hardly surprising that beyond inserting verses in his works, his writing itself is characterised by lyrical language.[67] Regarding the anonymous and unknown Sudanese poet, the content of his verses, and in particular his use of the word *bandar* (city), justify the inclusion of the quotation. The second writer is Abū Nuwās, a classical poet who enjoyed wide fame both in the Abbassid period, when he was active, and later, in the twentieth century. Abū Nuwās's verses are connected to the novel itself as they relate to the subjects of imagination and reality, knowledge and ignorance and their limits. The third poet whose verses al-Ṭayyib Ṣāliḥ chose to quote is Muḥammad Miftāḥ al-Faytūrī and who was born and lives in Egypt. Probably al-Ṭayyib Ṣāliḥ chose a quotation from his works because al-Faytūrī writes copiously about Africa and gives his collections of poems titles that are linked to that continent.[68] Al-Ṭayyib Ṣāliḥ apparently selected these verses because of their subject matter like longing, loss, love, slavery and rule, subjects that appear in the novel *Bandar Shāh: Ḍaw al-Bayt*.

In the novel *Bandar Shāh: Maryūd*, the following dedication appears: 'My father, Muḥammad Ṣāliḥ Aḥmad was rich in his poverty and strong in his weakness, lived as a lover and a beloved, and died satisfied and wanted'. (p. 5). As in the previous dedication in *Bandar Shāh: Ḍaw al-Bayt*, the author dedicated the novel to his father, *inter alia*, because he had died after the publication of the first book of *Bandar Shāh* and before the publication of the second. Therefore, this is a beautiful dedication in the form of a poetic verse and the integration of contrasts in it: poverty and wealth, weakness and strength, lover and loved one, satisfied and accepted. His father is the only person to whom the author has dedicated more than one book, both the collective and personal father does not enjoy special status in al-Ṭayyib Ṣāliḥ's works, neither in comparison to the mother and certainly not to the grandfather. This is true of the two *Bandar Shāh* books in which the father plays a minor role, not to mention the interpretation given to the father by the author himself as someone who symbolizes the present, and is therefore a victim of plots laid by the grandfather and grandson. In addition to the dedication in this book, there are verses of a poem, (p. 7) again by the classical Arab poet Abū Nuwās,[69] which are directly related to the content of the novel. The verses deal with thoughts, the falsehood of what eyes see, and the meanings and expressions in imagination and reality. Indeed, the novel has a philosophical stratum and the author has chosen a motto with philosophical significance taken from Abū Nuwās. For exactly the same reason he chose a quotation from *Kalīla wa-Dimna*. This philosophical stratum is linked to the fact that the legend quoted is partly understood and partly ambiguous, partly clear and partly obscure, partly known and partly unknown. Abū Nuwās analyzes the legend precisely.[70] For the first time in any of his texts, al-Ṭayyib Ṣāliḥ adds two pages (pp. 9–10), taken from the book *Kalīla wa-Dimna*, from the chapter of Barzawayh the Physician.[71] Moreover, al-Ṭayyib Ṣāliḥ uses a text as a motif that is not taken from poetry, but rather from prose. The author's unique integration of prose texts into his own here and elsewhere illustrates his preference for classical prose over Arabic or Western prose. Al-Ṭayyib Ṣāliḥ may be compared to the Palestinian author Emīl Ḥabībī, who also demonstrated his clear preference for classical Arabic literature over the modern in interviews and in various parts of his works.[72]

But al-Ṭayyib Ṣāliḥ's selection from *Kalīla wa-Dimna* needs explaining. It seems that the answer is to be found in the fable quoted in this book and no less in its moral lesson.[73] Al-Ṭayyib Ṣāliḥ uses the fable and its moral lesson to indicate the subjects of time, place and fate, but mainly the principal points of his perspective on man's insignificance and the lack of value in human life. Occupied with the vanities of this world a person does not know what fate has in store. In short, freedom of choice in the life of man may exist, but this freedom is circumscribed. Indeed, the objectives that man sets himself in this world are unimportant and often unworthy. They are of absolutely no significance in the next world. While in the process of writing, the author realizes that during the time allotted to man in this world, there is something else – the presence of both the Koran and the *Ḥadīth.*[74]

Expositions[75]

The authorial awareness of important literary components has not bypassed texts in modern Arabic literatures. This awareness became heightened in Western literature at the end of the nineteenth and the beginning of the twentieth centuries. Some notable writers who gave it significant poetical expression were James Joyce, Virginia Woolf, and William Faulkner, and later, Latin-American authors like Jorge Borges, Gabriel García Márques and the Cuban-born Italian author Italo Calvino. These writers, particularly Joyce, Borges and Calvino, emphasized the relationship between the designated or casual reader and the real author. One of the central literary components of this relationship occurs in the opening section of some of their works. In modern Arabic literatures a similar style appeared during the second half of the twentieth century, particularly from the end of the sixties onward. Arab authors influenced by Western writers dwelt on the importance of the relationship between reader and author. This relationship was accorded great importance in expositions as this was the initial contact, apart from the title, between reader and author. An Arab writer who has employed this means, usually cleverly but not always judiciously, is Muḥammad Yūsuf al-Qa'īd in his novel *Yaḥduth fī Miṣr al-Ān* (It's Happening in Egypt Now).[76] In this novel, the exposition is connected with the reader and the author, as follows:

> From the moment your eyes fall on the beginning of this line and until you reach the concluding words at the bottom of the last page, a relationship would be established between us that will be conducted around a novel we will create together about what is happening in Egypt today. I do not know what your reading rate is, but undoubtedly in the time it will take you to read this novel a great deal will happen in the other Egypt – Egypt of the rīf and the fellahin. To put it all on paper will take volumes, and to relate it – millions of mouths and tongues. I said that we would create a novel. There is no novel without a beginning. But on the blank pages reserved for an introduction or preface, in the words of the innovators among contemporary story-tellers, I shall begin my novel without further ado.[77]

Apart from this attempt at cleverness and irony, al-Qa'īd seemingly tries to create an unusual textual exposition, and to a great extent he succeeds in doing so. On the one hand, there is clearly a double-play here: the real author writes of the reader's cooperation in writing the novel, while on the other, there is no relationship between reader and author because the novel has already been written, and therefore both parties are aware that this is a game with obvious rules. Al-Qa'īd has other writing techniques to his credit, like the use of subtitles or author's footnotes. And he deftly adopts writing techniques from theoretical and scientific writing for the benefit of writing fiction. He is not the only Arab author using such techniques; for example, the Egyptian author Muḥammad Mustajāb (b.1938) employs them intelligently and cleverly in his book *Min al-Tarīkh al-Sirrī li Nu'mān 'Abd al-Ḥāfiẓ* (From the Secret History of Nu'aman Abd al-Hafez, 1982), as do the Moroccan authors Muḥammad Barrāda (b.1938) in his novel *La'bat al-Nisyān* (The Forgetting Game, 1987), and Muṣṭafā al-Misnāwī in his story 'al-Ūṭūrūṭ', who put the subtitle to good use.[78]

The majority of al-Ṭayyib Ṣāliḥ's works were published in the 1960s and 1970s when he was well aware of the importance of literary and poetical elements like expositions. He therefore devoted much thought to this, particularly since he is an author who meticulously plans both the subjects of his writing and the use of his varied writing techniques. Let us consider the exposition of the first story, 'Nakhla 'alā al-Jadwal' (A Date Palm by the Stream) which he begins with the words '*Yiftaḥ Allāh!*' (p. 7) or 'May Allah open a way to success', which symbolizes the entire text. Maḥjūb, who has become impoverished, decides not to sell the date palm and puts himself at the mercy of God, and in the end he meets with success. Therefore, the principal motif of the story is trust in God (*Tawakkul*),[79] a religious and Sufi element, which opens and concludes the text. The narrator stresses beyond doubt that the word *fatḥ* or *fātiḥa* (the name of the first *Sūra*) means here *al-faraj* (relief), in the sense of *al-Faraj ba'd al-Shidda* (Relief after distress) as we can find in 'Dawmat Wad Ḥāmid'.[80] Regarding the writing technique, this exposition also reveals that the first is related to the three ellipsis points following the opening words, *Yiftaḥ Allāh*, are significant and this is furthermore the concluding sentence of the story. Concerning the first, we know that Arab printers use two points for various needs, including the three ellipsis points, to indicate a comma and the like. However, the author of this story uses three points to conclude the first line, to mark an open ending of the opening sentence, which means he suggests an opening or gap that the reader himself will fill as his imagination sees fit. With regard to the opening sentence as the concluding one, a well-known literary device in poetry is using a word or sentence that opens the poem for its conclusion. This principle is also prevalent in works of fiction. Thus, for example, in Najīb Maḥfūẓ's short story, 'Za'balāwī' (1961), the opening sentence of the story is the one that concludes it: 'I was finally convinced that I had to find Sheikh Za'balawi' compared with 'I was totally convinced that I had to find Sheikh Za'balawi, yes, I had to find Za'balawi'.[81] Clearly the principle guiding the authors in both instances is that the sentence that opens the story is one for opening a circle and the concluding sentence closes it.[82] But there are two important differences between the same words in the exposition and in the ending, aside from this common formula: first while in the opening sentence there are three ellipsis points indicating open options, the ending has no ellipsis points but a full stop, which stresses the closed circle of this story. The second difference is that the first sentence is spoken by Ḥusayn the merchant trying to press Maḥjūb into selling him the date palm, whereas the ending of the story is by Maḥjūb who concludes his experience in trust and hope. Therefore, what has happened from the exposition until the end is not just a question of trust in God and 'relief after distress': it is also a journey by the hero/anti-hero of the story, and this is exactly what happened to the narrator of *Mawsim al-Hijra ilā al-Shamāl* in terms of *anagnorisis* and the *Bildungsroman*, as we shall discuss later.

The short story 'Ḥafnat Tamr' opens as follows: 'I must have been very young at the time' (p. 19), which is an excellent example of the remembrance technique. The narrator describes an extremely significant experience he had in his childhood and the opening of the story is used as an exposition through which the author clarifies his position towards the specific event that occurred in his village. The extraordinary event, in which the narrator is compelled to vomit the handful of dates given to him by his grandfather, is employed as a metaphoric adoption by the author vis-à-vis the event itself. An exposition of this kind presents an aperture to the reader through which he is able to glimpse the author's childhood world. Thus we have a successful attempt in lending reliability to the child-narrator's experience. [83] Nevertheless, while in 'Nakhla 'alā al-Jadwal' the author prefers to open the story at a crucial moment and then, by using the flashback technique, to tell Maḥjūb's story, in 'Ḥafnat Tamr', he prefers to open the story with a very pastoral description of rural life in a remote village. But apparently this ideal situation is shattered and suddenly the idyll is transformed from harmony to confrontation, from innocence to the cruel facts of life. In short, the promising exposition of the story was a literary device or an introduction to the 'real' story as told by the narrator.

In the story 'Risalā ilā Aylīn', the narrator opens with the words 'My dear Aileen'. This is probably a direct translation from the English, but in fact the letter to Aileen is used as the framework of the story. The author chose to open the story with these words to create clear observation points around the relationship between the addressor – the narrator, and the addressee – Aileen. Aileen however, is only an interim addressee or a kind of mediator between narrator and reader. In this equation the relationship between fiction and reality are delineated: on the one hand, Aileen links the narrator and the reader, while on the other, she mediates between the narrator and the author. Even at the beginning of the story the author employs Aileen as a passive, secondary character, an addressee, whose nature is made known to us solely through the narrator, something that might damage the credibility of the text. The narrator seems to hold a dialogue with her, but in fact he delivers a long monologue, similar to 'Dawmat Wad Ḥāmid' where the dialogue appears to resemble the one mentioned above, but is actually a long monologue directed at a passive addressee.

'Dawmat Wad Ḥāmid' opens with an exposition about life in the village and its inhabitants. They are the centre of the story whereas the others are the young listener or any other addressee: 'Were you to come to our village as a tourist, it is likely, my son, that you would not stay long' (p. 33). In the continued sentence the narrator broadens the exposition, providing reasons why he would not stay long. Obviously the opening sentence is of great importance and should be analyzed as follows: the first word is 'were…', introducing a void conditional sentence or, it may be assumed that you would not come to our village, and if you were to come, then you would do so only as a tourist. Then the author uses the phrase 'it is most likely' (*aghlab al-ẓann*), which means that it may be assumed with a great degree of probability that you would not stay long.[84] The expression *yā bunayya* which means 'oh, my son' should be regarded as adjacent and sympathetic. In this story, as we shall see later, this kind of close relationship between the old narrator and the young listener was established by using the expression *yā bunayya* exactly as in 'Ḥafnat Tamr', when the grandfather, on the one hand, and Mas'ūd, on the other, also called the narrator *yā bunayya* (pp. 21–2, 24). This kind of appeal stresses the special and warm relations with the addressee who in our case is the child. In addition, the use of this expression proves the differences between the old teller and the young listener. Indeed, here the author opens the story with two words as he did in 'Nakhla 'alā al-Jadwal', when he also used 'Yiftaḥ Allāh', which served him as a leitmotif for shedding light on rural life in a remote village in the Sudan, and the question of trust in God. Al-Ṭayyib Ṣāliḥ opened the story with two leitmotif words which allows the real author to send the reader messages and hints concerning the encounters between Western and Eastern (Northern and Southern) cultures on both the individual and collective levels. The negation *lan* (no) is used, but this is not a regular negative word, it is 'would not' referring to the future. The use of the negative *lan* expresses total negation, 'no', 'definitely not'. It is therefore clear that the interrogative and negative words used by the author were chosen with great care. Their sole objective is to show that the young listener, the addressee, does not belong to the village and his visit, if it takes place at all, is nothing but a figment of the author's imagination when the listener-character is used as previously in early classical Arabic and Eastern texts, like *The Arabian Nights*.[85] In the exposition, the author chooses to present a two-part equation, one part are the city characters that come to the village and are unable to live in it. This part includes the implied, passive listener, or the addressee. The other part consists of the villagers, including the old narrator, who are not only able to live the hard village life, but are also able to enjoy it.

'The World Office of Tourism Arts' opens the story 'Idhā Jā'at' (p. 53) and thus the author continues his one-sentence expositions as he did in the previous stories, 'Naklah 'alā al-Jadwal' and 'Risāla ilā Aylīn'. The words appear to be a title, or more precisely a subtitle, which could be the framework of the story, or perhaps the dimension of place. The entire story takes place in the office bearing this name. Amīn, one of the three central protagonists, feels uncomfortable both with the length of the name and with the name itself, which he considers hackneyed. And indeed, the bombastic name his colleagues have chosen is used as a focus of irony by the author who seeks to place this occupation in a mocking light, mocking as well the arrogance of some of the company's owners, or alternatively, the younger generation intent on making easy money as quickly as possible. The exposition is further testimony to the author's views than to those of the fictitious characters who participate in the plot.

In the opening sentence of the story 'Hākadhā Yā Sādatī', the author raises the dilemma faced by the narrator: 'This girl did not smile at me because I am a foreigner? Or because she has a big nose, a wide mouth and blue eyes?' (p. 69). Two characters face one another as strangers at the exposition of the story, but at the story's end enter a marital relationship. The narrator's sense of foreignness opens the story with question marks that remain unanswered throughout the text. The cultural differences between the man and woman support the plot and are employed as the axis around which the relationship between the narrator, the young woman and their hosts, revolves: he faces the other, the different, those who symbolize and behave according to norms and codes that are different from his own.

The 'Muqaddimāt' all open uniformly with a verb, 'to be'. In the first short story, 'Ughniyat Ḥubb', he uses the first person, *kuntu*, 'I was' or 'I liked to' or 'I used to' (p. 84). 'Khuṭwa li'l-Amām', opens with *kānat*, 'she was'. In the third one, 'Laka ḥattā al-Mamāt', the opening is once again *kānat*, 'she was' (p. 82). The fourth begins with *kānā*, the dual form of 'to be' (p. 90), while the last story, 'Sūzān wa 'Alī', employs 'to be' in the third person. However, in the story 'Al-Shay' al-Ākhar' (The Other Thing),[86] which is not included in the collection *Dawmat Wad Ḥāmid*, the author does not begin with the verb *kāna,* 'to be', which appears only in the second sentence. Perhaps this is the reason it was removed from the 'Muqaddimāt'; because it does not open in the constant format of the other stories in the collection.

'Al-Rajul al-Qubruṣī' has a slightly different exposition than those mentioned so far.[87] For the first time the story opens with a description of time and place. The place is Nicosia in Cyprus; the time is the month of July, and here the author compares Khartoum with Damascus; the streets are in English style, and this surprises the narrator who expected to find a city with Hellenistic characteristics. By the end of the exposition we become acquainted not only with time and place, but also with an additional principal character, that of the Cypriot Man in the story's title, about whom the readers do not know a great deal. The exposition resembles a play in which the playwright determines the location, the time, the sets and the characters.

In 'Yawm Mubārak 'alā Shāṭi' Umm Bāb', al-Ṭayyib Ṣāliḥ elected to open the text with a dialogue.[88] At this stage of the exposition we only learn that one of the speakers is someone named Rabāb; and apart from that we have no idea who the second speaker is. What characterizes the two protagonists? What is the level of their relationship? It is only later in the story that we realize that the dialogue is between a father, whose name is not given, and his nine year-old daughter, Rabāb. We might say by reversing the order of questioner and answerer, the author has put the cart before the horse. We should expect the daughter to ask the questions and the father to answer them, but we realize that the opposite is true: the father asks the questions and the nine-year old girl answers them. Yet, there is no inconsistency in this story, because the author imbues the nine-year-old girl with mythical, observational and legendary dimensions, one of these being the status he accords her in the text. This status is completely different from that usually reserved for a girl her age, and from what a reader might expect to find in Arab society.

In the novel *'Urs al-Zayn* the author opens the text with the announcement of al-Zayn's wedding. The announcement is made by Ḥalīma the milk seller to Āmina, who had come for her milk as usual before sunrise.[89] Indeed, what could be more 'natural' than to spread the news through this character, and in a conversation between women? The novel's exposition tells of the extraordinary event in an entire chapter,[90] and is an attempt to use cinematic or television drama techniques in which the camera pans over characters, events and places, while the reader, through the exposition, becomes aware of the microcosm created by the author.[91] The author transmits the news of al-Zayn's coming wedding through various people in the village, beginning with Āmina the milk-seller and ending with the headmaster of the village school. Generally, we expect that news of a villager's wedding would not cause such uproar and that it would not be the subject of gossip.[92] Why this simple and existential event becomes a stormy subject is only clear in the course of the novel and not at its beginning. Obviously, al-Zayn, a strange and not particularly good-looking man, is about to marry the most beautiful girl in the village. These details emerge later and this is the path often taken by al-Ṭayyib Ṣāliḥ; he prefers to open the text with the climax and then move on, explaining the opening declaration as he goes on. In this exposition he presents al-Zayn's peculiarities from the moment of his birth. The fact that his birth was out of the ordinary imbues him not only with an indefinable aura, but also with a certain saintliness.[93] The novel opens with the surprising news on the first page (p. 5), then moves on to several events connected with other characters in the village, and after a long break of twenty-three pages the author continues the exposition (pp. 29, 32). In the second part of the exposition, the author stresses the headmaster's reaction to the news of the wedding of Zayn and Ni'ma (pp. 5–6) and sixty pages later (pp. 65–6) he comes back to the headmaster. Then, once again he returns after twenty-six pages (p. 92) to complete the exposition. This technique of an interrupted exposition further supports the exceptional and successful camera use as an artistic device.

Among al-Ṭayyib Ṣāliḥ's works *Mawsim al-Hijra ilā al-Shamāl* has the most impressive exposition.[94] The narrator speaks in the first person and in the exposition the real author presents a series of contrasts that only become clear to the reader in the course of the novel. At the same time, he makes a statement about the West and its culture. The first line of the exposition reads, 'It was, gentlemen, after a long absence – seven years to be exact, during which I was studying in Europe.' (p. 5). What do we learn from this first sentence? There are four central points: first, the narrator addresses the reader in the first sentence to create closeness and a relationship with him; that is the real author establishes a dialogue with the reader through the narrator-witness. Yet, this address also demonstrates a certain distance as it were, for he uses the word 'gentlemen' and not, for example, 'dear reader'. The form of address probably hints at an ironic use of the word 'gentlemen', as it contains a certain measure of politeness. This address using the word 'gentlemen' occurs again in the opening of the fourth chapter (p. 65) when the narrator seeks direct contact with the reader in order to convince him of the truth of his words. But as I mentioned earlier, the novel is full of contradictions, as well as being a good example of al-Ṭayyib Ṣāliḥ's writing style that combines classical literatures (especially Arabic) and modern literatures (especially Western). Therefore, another interpretation is possible. According to this, the word 'gentlemen' may indicate in classical Arabic literatures either a direct call to the reader, *sādatī* (gentlemen), or as it was in the past and still exists in Arabic oral and popular literature, when the teller or the *ḥakawātī*, addresses his audience in a very direct way, saying 'gentlemen'.[95] The second point is that the narrator has been away from his village for seven long years. The third is that he was in Europe pursuing his studies. And the fourth point is that the subject is returning, not leaving. In the original Arabic text the author uses the word *'udtu* which means 'I have returned'. Possibly, this kind of opening is the ending of one or more chapters in the narrator's previous life, and he simply tells us his story in the present tense. In addition, it is not a 'normal' opening but rather an exposition, which deals with a continuity. Nor is it a regular returning, but rather a return from there to here, from outside to inside, from the other and otherness to the homeland and the family. In short, this is the final return of the narrator, as in the case of Muṣṭafā Sa'īd, because the migration is over. Now it is time to find (once more) balance and stability. This literary device is well known in modern world literature as well as in classical Arabic and Eastern literary works such as *Alf Layla wa-Layla* (The Arabian Nights).[96]

The opening sentence, however, tells us almost nothing. We do not know who the speaker is, his marital status, his occupation, what exactly he studied in Europe and what else he did there. More is concealed than apparent in the first sentence. Only after the opening sentence are there further expositional sentences that slowly reveal additional details about the narrator and his perception. The second sentence suggests the narrator's dual evaluation of the West: 'I learnt much and much passed me by – but that's another story' (p. 5). In other words, his praise of study for he had 'learnt much', is immediately followed by the 'but', the reservation – just as I learnt much, much passed me by. Although we might expect the author to place the narrator at center stage to relate what had passed him by, but in a kind of game with the reader and with a kind of irony, he describes it without reasons and asserts, 'that's another story'. On the narrator's attitude towards the East and the West we can learn not only from 'what' but also from 'how':

> They rejoiced at having me back and made a great fuss, and it was not long before I felt as though a great piece of ice were melting inside of me, as though I were some frozen substance on which the sun had shone – that life warmth of the tribe which I had lost for a time in a land 'whose fishes die of the cold'. (p. 5)[97].

Therefore, the pair of contrasts, East and West, stands against heat and cold, and beyond all the assertions stands the author's irony to express the narrator's attitude towards the other culture. The author could have used many and varied phrases to express the terrible cold prevailing in the country mentioned (which only later is revealed as England), but he chose to do so through ironic illustration – not only do people freeze there, animals do as well. These lines can be linked to the first steps al-Ṭayyib Ṣāliḥ took in England:

> I reached London in the winter of 1953, and on my arrival the cold seared me. The weather took me by surprise, having come from a hot region, to a very cold one [...]. When London cold seared me, I said to myself: 'how did I ever land myself into this trouble?!' My early days in London were grim as I had left my family, my beloved ones, spacious houses, and my social ties to find myself in a small room where cold was unbearable, in a foreign land among strangers.[98]

Europe's two most prominent characteristics, the cold and being away from home, are expressed not only in the author's semi-autobiography but also in the present novel's fictional text, in which the narrator gives them ironic and critical expression. In the concluding part of the exposition, before the narrator connects himself and his soul to his tribe, he says, '...something rather like fog rose between them and me the first instant I saw them. But the fog cleared and I awoke, on the second day of my arrival.' (p. 5). In this last sentence the narrator's decision regarding his affiliation is clear-cut and henceforth he develops and improves it.

With regard to the novel *Bandar Shāh: Ḍaw al-Bayt*, the text opens with a relatively long piece describing Maḥjūb. This is followed by an exposition that deals with Maḥjūb's aging band of friends and the narrator who has returned to the village after a long absence.[99] Indeed, the author opens the novel with a detailed description of Maḥjūb, which repeatedly gives prominence to the changes that have taken place in him. We must remember that in all the previous novels, Maḥjūb was described as a young *fallāḥ* and the village leader (*'Urs al-Zayn, Mawsim al-Hijra ilā al-Shamāl*), or sometimes as a relatively old *fallāḥ* ('Nakhlah 'alā al-Jadwal'). The author's objective is to detail the changes in the village of Wad Ḥāmid through those undergone by its leaders, in this instance Maḥjūb and his fellow villagers. Thus throughout the novel he unwinds a thread, and a kind of prophecy is fulfilled: we see how Maḥjūb and his fellows lose the positions of power they had held for many years to the village's young men.[100] In other words, the changes undergone by Maḥjūb describe those of the entire village. Maḥjūb, as in other instances presented by al-Ṭayyib Ṣāliḥ (the doum palm, for example), is a collective symbol rather than an individual one. By means of this description, the author achieves two results: one is the long period of time of the narrator's absence from the village, as noted by Maḥjūb: 'You've been a long time away from the village'. (p. 9). The other is linked to the narrator, for he is Maḥjūb's age and so Maḥjūb's growing old is also the aging of the narrator. The narrator left his village initially because his work was in Khartoum (*Mawsim al-Hijra ilā al-Shamāl*). His absences were not long ones, but as time went on they became longer and reached their climax in *Bandar Shāh: Ḍaw al-Bayt*. That is why the author opens the novel as a kind of continuation of other texts, particularly *'Urs al-Zayn* and *Mawsim al-Hijra ilā al-Shamāl;* he continues to tell the story of Wad Ḥāmid village, its inhabitants – especially his contemporaries – and relates his own life story for the greater part indirectly.

The exposition of the novel *Bandar Shāh: Maryūd* describes the narrator who is in Wad Hāmid village. The exposition is not long,[101] and it begins with the narrator's description of dawn, paralleling the one in the first book, *Bandar Shāh: Ḍaw al-Bayt*. The main difference is in the character: the first book opens with the character of Maḥjūb and the narrator is, as it were, secondary, while the exposition of the present novel focuses on the narrator. Here we have a direct exposition, for this is a description of the narrator's life, while on the other hand the exposition is presented within a religious, mystical and obscure atmosphere, which, incidentally, characterizes the entire novel. The exposition is significantly different from those found in *'Urs al-Zayn* and *Mawsim al-Hijra ilā Shamāl* where it is direct, clear and a leitmotif of the entire novel. Nonetheless, before *Bandar Shāh: Maryūd* appeared in book form, parts of it were published in the *al-Hilāl* periodical and the novel itself was published in serial form in the Qatari periodical *al-Dōḥa*.[102] In the case of *al-Dōḥa*, the chapter order is identical to that of the book, while in *al-Hilāl* the chapter order is different, with the first chapter about Bilāl, one of the novel's principal characters. In this periodical, the author does not open with the character of Muḥaymīd and this is an interesting fact because the character of Bilāl is veiled in the mystery and ambiguity that characterizes the novel itself.

Endings

Expositions of a literary work as described earlier are important as they are the first contact between reader and author, both of whom are characters acting outside the fictional world and both react to this world with all its advantages and disadvantages. For this reason endings of literary works are similarly important.[103] The ending of a text is the final connection between reader, text and author. It is the taste left in the reader's mouth, or more precisely, his imagination. The body of the text is, to be sure, also important, but if it is uninteresting its ending is of no significance as most readers will not bother to read it. Clearly, some authors plan the components of the text's structure meticulously; they devote much attention to the title, the exposition, the building of characters and the ending. The ending does not necessarily have to be dramatic, though it may be. But even if the ending is not dramatic, it contains either a direct continuation of the course of the plot or a coherent relationship with the text, its beginning and continuation. An author's work is successful if it contains three traditionally accepted parts: beginning, middle and end.

Al-Ṭayyib Ṣāliḥ, an author who diligently plans the structure of his texts, is meticulous in the endings in a way that is not always dramatic but planned, and in which they have a rationale of their own. As we have seen he has texts with varying expositions, likewise the endings of his texts, and on this point – as with other poetical points – he makes no distinction between short and long narratives. The ending of his first story, 'Nakhla 'alā al-Jadwal' describes in the concluding paragraph Maḥjūb's return home after receiving the money his son had sent from Egypt. Nature, too, is happy about Maḥjūb's good fortune and it seems to him that the leaves of the palm tree quiver, praising him with the words, 'May Allah open a way. May Allah open a way' (p. 18). The narrator described Maḥjūb's life from cradle to adulthood, his meteoric economic rise and his sudden decline. Therefore, on the brink of the abyss, namely, the sale of Maḥjūb's date palm, his life flashes before him like frames of a film and then, in the midst of his distress, he finds solace and salvation from the Almighty, and with man's help.

In the second story, 'Ḥafnat Tamr', the ending is more dramatic and poignant. The narrator, who sees his neighbour Mas'ūd's wretched state and the high price he has to pay for being a much-married man, cannot stand the sight and flees the scene. He puts his finger into his throat and spews up Mas'ūd's dates that his grandfather had given him to eat. It is clear that al-Ṭayyib Ṣāliḥ, faithful to the use of symbols, makes intentional use of symbolism here. The child-narrator is unable to witness the exploitation of Mas'ūd, especially by his own grandfather, the one who gave Mas'ūd's dates to his grandson. The latter is not prepared to be a party, even passively, to the festival of shame and due to his great sensitivity to the lack of justice, and also because of his human sensibilities, wants no part of the fruit and so vomits it. Thus he extricates himself from participation in an event forced upon him: the exploitation of Mas'ūd.

In the story 'Risāla ilā Aylīn', we find a significant difference between the narrator's situation at the beginning of the story and at its end. At the beginning, the narrator sends a letter to his wife Aileen, while at the end, after having told her what had been happening to him in his village, he imagines her parting words to him that she hopes he will find his family as he left them. However, the narrator at the end of the letter is cleverer and more realistic; it is obvious to him that not only has he changed, yet also the people of his village and especially the members of his own family. On the face of it, the relationship between him and his family has not changed, but both the narrator and his family realize that their relationship will never be as it once was because of his numerous absences from the village. In the last sentence the narrator reconciles himself to the fact that two factors, more than anything else, reveal the chasm between him and his family – time and uprooting; time as a factor in his distancing himself from them, and uprooting as someone who seemingly bears the stigma of the foreigner on his forehead.

In 'Dawmat Wad Ḥāmid', the old interior narrator addresses the young listener saying, 'Tomorrow, without doubt, you will be leaving us. When you arrive at your destination, think well of us and judge us not too harshly'. (p. 52) The old narrator who throughout the story is sure of his unassailable position regarding modernization, considers how to transmit the message about the changes that will surely come. The point of the story is in its ending. The old narrator's words on the need to accept change, but that the people causing the change must accept that it cannot be forced upon others, express the author's philosophy more than anything else. He gets this message across in an extremely clever way through an old, rather than a young, narrator. The old and interior narrator addresses his young listener, who is an exterior narrator or addressee, and asks him to carry the message onwards. To the same degree it is probable that the message of the old narrator is directed at you, the reader, so that you will see, understand, and if necessary, even judge – but leniently. It is a kind of wink at the reader who will empathize with the old man and his story. It should be noted here that al-Ṭayyib Ṣāliḥ places great importance on the reader in his dialogue with the text.[104] In addition, on the face of it this story ends with the triumph of tradition over progress or the triumph of the villagers in their struggle with the government. But since we consider al-Ṭayyib Ṣāliḥ's writings as one text (see Chapter Four), by doing so we find in *Mawsim al-Hijra ilā al-Shamāl* (pp. 66–7) another ending to 'Dawmat Wad Ḥāmid', namely that the water pump and steamer had become part and parcel of the village.

In contrast, the ending of the story 'Idhā Jā'at' is not dramatic. Once the three partners decide to close the office, a dramatic step might well be expected in the wake of the event. But in contrast to the level of expectation (the reader's, perhaps), the story has a rather banal ending, a kind of anti-climax. It ends with a description of Bahā' who is not disappointed by the closing of the office; he thinks about and imagines the Swedish blonde with great satisfaction, provided she comes. Indeed, he has not learned a thing. In contrast to Amīn and Sanā' who learned that establishing a business is no simple matter, he remains as he was, continuing to dream foolish dreams and perpetuating the stereotype of the spoiled, shallow, educated man whose every thought is devoted to one blonde or another.

The title of 'Hākadhā Yā Sādatī' reflects the narrator's words and the end of the text. The narrator in this story maintains continuous eye contact with the implied reader and his dialogue with the addressee is constant, whereas the rest of the participants in the plot are simply extras with whom the author does as he wishes. We, the readers, are employed as witnesses to the narrator's life and we, non-fictional characters, play an integral part in the fictional plot. We are the story's principal addressees; the narrator addresses us at the end of the story with the important information that he has married the young woman and he hopes the Englishwoman will forgive him; in fact he is not sure with which of the two he is living. As readers we are passive listeners who are unable to participate in the fiction.

In 'Muqaddimāt', all the stories except one ('Khuṭwa li'l-Amām') end either with death or with the ending of a relationship between a couple. The man is from the East, the woman is Western, and their relationship cannot endure for various reasons. Unlike the expositions, in these stories with their clearly defined formula, no set ending in these short stories occurs.

In 'al-Rajul al-Qubruṣī', the relationship ends between the narrator and the Cypriot Man and the narrator weeps at his father's grave at the end of the story. Here the author's voice is heard because his father indeed passed away in the year 1973. The Cypriot Man explains to him that this time he has taken his father, but next time he will take the narrator. Despite the fact that the narrator does not explain who the Cypriot Man is and what their relationship might be, we gather that the Cypriot Man is the Angel of Death who meticulously plans how next to come to the narrator. The narrator weeps as he explains to himself that the Cypriot Man has taken his father and now no one will protect him from death when the time comes. Therefore, only in the story's last lines does the narrator undergo a kind of epiphany when he realizes for the first time how close he was to death, and he, like the reader, understands now exactly who the Cypriot Man is.

The story 'Yawm Mubārak 'alā Shāṭi' Umm Bāb' has a symbolic ending with Sufi characteristics. It ends with the father hearing his daughter's call and his swimming back to shore to the mother and daughter. The three leave the beach, get into the car and only when they start up do they see the camel turn its back to the sea and rejoin its herd. The story, which is not always entirely clear, as noted by Egyptian critic al-Ṭāhir Aḥmad Makkī,[105] is replete with insinuations and Sufi expressions as well as obscure characters. It has an unconventional exposition and strange relationships between the father, mother and daughter. It has an extraordinary ending in which the author's message, beyond its ambiguity, obscurity and its Sufism, is about the relationship between man and animals and the place of modernization in religion and mysticism, or alternatively, the status of Sufism in times of modernization.

At the end of the novel *'Urs al-Zayn,* al-Zayn, on the eve of his wedding, goes to visit al-Ḥanīn's grave. Maḥjūb and his fellows find him lamenting al-Ḥanīn's passing and drag him off to his wedding. Al-Zayn joins the celebrants, he has drawn energy from the experience and adds even more joy to the celebration. We thus find that whereas the exposition of the novel focused on the news of al-Zayn's wedding, the novel ends with the wedding ceremony itself. As in other works, al-Ṭayyib Ṣāliḥ uses the ending of this work to conclude what he began. We have here a kind of closing of a circle. Whereas at the beginning of the novel we read the news of al-Zayn's wedding but did not understand the reactions to it, between the novel's beginning and end we have become more familiar with the character of al-Zayn as an extraordinary man and we, the readers, stand in the shoes of the fictional characters from the beginning of the novel who were unable to digest the news of al-Zayn's wedding. The novel's ending is closer to those accepted in the nineteenth century rather than those of the twentieth, because it contains more symbols of a 'happy ending' than a tragic one: the wedding, reconciliation between the camps in the village, and al-Zayn's realization that life surmounts death.

In *Mawsim al-Hijra ilā al-Shamāl* the author has chosen catharsis, but in fact he does not use a 'happy ending' or a closed ending; on the contrary, he uses an open one. The ending seems clear; the narrator, struggling against the destructive forces of the river, deliberates between life and death and, as Muṣṭafā had done, chooses life.[106] Here there is more than a mere suggestion of 'To be, or not to be?' from Shakespeare's *Hamlet.* In contrast to his trenchant and parodied attitude towards Shakespeare's *Othello,* in which al-Ṭayyib Ṣāliḥ sees the author's lack of understanding of Othello, he transmits, through the narrator, not only his personal struggle, but also the collective one, that of the Sudan. He explains his decision to choose life thus:

> All my life I had not chosen, not decided. Now I am making a decision. I choose life. I shall live because there are a few people I want to stay with for the longest possible time and because I have duties to discharge. It is not my concern whether or not life has meaning. If I am unable to forgive, then I shall try to forget. I shall live by force and

> cunning. I moved my feet and arms, violently and with difficulty, until the upper part of my body was above water. Like a comic actor shouting on a stage, I screamed with all my remaining strength, 'Help! Help!'[107]

Indeed, had the author decided to end the novel without the last sentence, the ending and the message would have been perfectly clear, namely that the narrator had extricated himself, once and for all, from his internal struggles and especially from his relationship with Muṣṭafā Sa'īd, in life and in death. However, the last sentence is difficult to explain. Clearly the author has decided not to make things easy for the reader.[108] He seeks to emphasize that the narrator has overcome the destructive forces of Muṣṭafā Sa'īd and concluded that life is better than death. On the other hand, the conclusion might also stress the author's desire for reconciliation with those around him. There is here a wish to bring his world, the village, the Sudan and Sudanese intellectuals back into the order preceding chaos, that is to say before the appearance of Muṣṭafā Sa'īd. Some might view this as the completion of the narrator's individuation process.[109] Yet it may also be that through the last sentence, the author seeks to convey an unequivocal message to the reader: yes, in this battle the narrator has vanquished his foe, life has overcome death, but this has been only one battle of a long series that forms a single, great war in which it is still too early to decide who is victorious. In other words, the author has intentionally chosen to end the novel with a sentence indicating that the narrator has not rid himself of Muṣṭafā. The words 'Help! Help!' at the end of the novel, are Muṣṭafā-like; there is something satanic, Faustian or Draculaean in them. Although good was victorious, its victory is only temporary and evil continues to await its chance. There is perhaps also a suggestion of the author's position of seeing the duality of all phenomena. Similar to the American author Herman Melville (1819–91), al-Ṭayyib Ṣāliḥ views the narrator's reality and to a lesser extent that of Muṣṭafā Sa'īd, as human reality in its double-faced form. In addition, when the narrator compares himself to a comic actor he may hint at the author's philosophy that life is but a huge stage on which we perform. Moreover, it should be remembered that the narrator struggling against the river is in fact performing solo on stage. The audience is on the riverbank, in the village, not in the realistic world but in the fictional one. The description expresses al-Ṭayyib Ṣāliḥ's world view about the theatre. We can find here statements of the way in which Irish author and playwright Samuel Beckett (1906–89) views the actor-audience relationship, as he described it to director Peter Brook:

> Imagine very high cliffs, the cliffs of Dover for example. Below a stormy sea and a drowning man shouting 'Help! Help!' On the cliff top there are people looking down, completely frozen, expressionless, watching the drowning man crying for help. Even if they wanted to save him they couldn't, because the cliffs are very high and the stormy sea separates them from the drowning man. The drowning man is the actor and the people watching from the cliff are the audience, and that is how what happens on the stage should be viewed.[110]

A slightly different interpretation of the above quotation brings us back to the world of the text and links the writer with the reader. Members of the theatre audience have no possibility of offering help and the author does not address them, but you, the reader, as he does in the last sentence of 'Dawmat Wad Ḥāmid'. Therefore, the author seeks the reader's help and it is to him that he reaches out after holding a dialogue with him, beginning with the opening sentence. The author says, I will help you, reader, and you help me to decipher the text and the difficult situation in which we find ourselves. In so doing the author is hinting at another world he presents as an alternative to the hollow, decayed and hopeless world of Muṣṭafā Sa'īd. We can therefore sum up by saying that some of the literary critics who found difficulty in explaining this strange and theatrical ending were right, because the author, in other texts ('Nakhla 'alā al-Jadwal', 'Ḥafnat Tamr', *'Urs al-Zayn*), all with clear endings that close the circle opened at the text's beginning, has here an ending that is completely different. It is possible that the ending is not only Muṣṭafā-like but that it also has the same point of departure as the sentence 'The horror! The horror!' spoken by Kurtz in *Heart of Darkness* (1902) by Joseph Conrad (1857–1924).[111] In any event, possibly the last sentence does not come from the same place or places as the previous ones, but from one of the dark corners within the narrator, which the river waters were unable to cleanse at the very end. This being the case, then why provide a pretext for that same spirit at the ending (or perhaps because of it)?[112] In contrast with *'Urs al-Zayn* where the novel had a happy ending, here the ending is more characteristic of the modern novel; it has an open ending concerning the future of both the narrator and the Sudan.

Bandar Shāh: Ḍaw al-Bayt is the first of three, or possibly five, planned books, two of which have been published.[113] Therefore, the ending should not be a closed one as the author had planned a continuation. But this is not the case here as the ending of the book concludes the text and presents it as autonomous and independent. The first book opens with the character of Maḥjūb and the changes occurring in the village, and the novel ends with the character of Ḥasab al-Rasūl lamenting the disappearance of Ḍaw al-Bayt. Why? Because it was Ḥasab al-Rasūl who found Ḍaw al-Bayt in the river and it was he whom Ḍaw al-Bayt saved from drowning, while Ḍaw al-Bayt disappeared. There is, in Ḥasab ar-Rasūl's words at the end of the novel, a characterization of not only Ḍaw al-Bayt but also of the entire novel:

> Hasab ar-Rasoul's eyes fill with tears as he says, 'God have mercy on Dou al-Beit. He paid with his life for the porridge he ate with us the first day. He passed away like a dream, as though he had never been – were it not for his son Isa who was born three months after his death. We look at his face but we do not see Dou al-Beit; we look at his eyes and we see the exact replica of Dou al-Beit'.[114]

At the end of the novel the author's message is perfectly clear: Ḍaw al-Bayt, in life and death, is symbolic of the entire text. Therefore, he seems to say that Ḍaw al-Bayt is characterized not only by legend and mystery but also by reality, and the entire novel, dear reader, is replete with legend and mystery together with a grain of reality. Thus ends the first book of *Bandar Shāh*, but it is not the end, for the life and death of Ḍaw al-Bayt and his son 'Īsā continue into the second book.

Indeed, in the second book, *Bandar Shāh: Maryūd*, the author continues to discuss the life and death of Ḍaw al-Bayt and 'Īsā, who is known as Bandar Shāh; above all he describes the character of Maryūd. The second book ends with a dramatic scene in which Maryam, Maḥjūb's sister, lies on her deathbed. She is the beloved of Muḥayamīd but married to another, and with Maryūd, who is Muḥayamīd and the narrator, she holds an incisive dialogue about his life, her life and both their lives. She berates him for his weakness and helplessness, for choosing his grandfather and his grandfather choosing him, though in the final accounting his father is greater than both. Maryūd's response to Maryam's accusations is: 'I said yes. I said yes. I said yes. But the way back was harder because I had forgotten'.[115] This is a confession by the narrator who totally agrees with Maryam and expresses his acceptance of the way of life he has chosen, from which there is no going back. Perhaps he hints at his childhood to which there is no return. On the face of it, the words appear vague but they are actually very clear if we assume that other texts can shed light on this one. In fact, the narrator, Muḥayamīd/Maryūd, wanted to be a farmer but according to his grandfather he became an intellectual. Maryūd also wanted to marry Maryam, but the grandfather said 'no' and the narrator was forced to accept his decision. On her deathbed Maryam reminds him that he did not stand up for himself and disobeyed his grandfather. Maḥjūb and al-Ṭāhir Wad Rawwāsī testify to Maryam's words in the first book, *Bandar Shāh*: *Ḍaw al-Bayt*; there the narrator's and his grandson's mistake and the father's rectitude appear. Moreover, the narrator himself says in the same place: 'A man must say "no" right from the start.'[116] The ending remains open and it is closer to the ending of *Mawsim al-Hijra ilā al-Shamāl*, which concludes with the narrator's questions and wonder, rather than that of *'Urs al-Zayn*. This open ending is connected to the search for the meaning of life or for the self determination of his community, the African and the Sudanese, on both the collective and personal level at a time of rapid change.[117]

Dialogues and Monologues

Dialogue and monologue in modern Arabic literatures occur more frequently since the 1960s.[118] One school of thought that supported increased use of these writing techniques was the one which advocated the 'stream of consciousness' linked in one form or another to the definition of existentialism as a philosophical and literary term. Since the early 1920s, employing dialogue and monologue has raised the characteristic question of the old *vs.* the new regarding language use mainly in dialogue, but also of monologue and description in novels, plays and poetry in modern Arabic literatures.[119] As a writer who is well aware of Western literary techniques, particularly in English literature, al-Ṭayyib Ṣāliḥ makes extensive use of varied writing techniques, especially dialogue and monologue together with stream of consciousness, as we shall see later. Clearly, because of its genre he uses these more in his novels than in the short stories. Still, he makes varied use of both dialogue and monologue either regarding the poetics of his writing, or because he must deal with the problem of literary Arabic and the Sudanese Arabic dialect.[120] Thus, in some of his short stories al-Ṭayyib Ṣāliḥ uses dialogue and monologue sparingly ('Nakhla 'alā al-Jadwal', 'Ḥafnat Tamr', 'Risāla ilā Aylīn', 'Ughniyat Ḥubb') and in others more frequently ('Idhā Jā'at', 'Hākadhā Yā Sādatī', 'Laka ḥattā al-Mamāt', 'al-Shay' al-Ākhar', 'al-Rajul al-Qubruṣī', 'Yawm Mubārak 'alā Shāṭi' Umm Bāb'). In contrast to other short stories and novels, al-Ṭayyib Ṣāliḥ's use of dialogue in 'Dawmat Wad Ḥāmid' has special features, because dialogue in the accepted sense of the term does not take place. It takes place only prima facie between the old narrator and his young listener. We are familiar with this technique from *The Arabian Nights*, where there is a narrator and a listener. The writer holds, as it were, a dialogue between the two principal characters – but only as it were. In fact, it is a monologue spoken by the narrator and heard by the young listener. It should be noted that the young listener does not participate in the apparent dialogue, because in fact there is no dialogue except at the end of the story. Indeed, al-Ṭayyib Ṣāliḥ employs the old narrator as an interior narrator who relates the story of Wad Ḥāmid village to his young listener, who is his addressee. However, the young listener who is the interior addressee is used as an exterior narrator for exterior addressees who do not exist in fiction, or simply, the readers. The real dialogues take place at the end of the story when the young listener asks the old narrator two questions linked to the heart of the story. The questions are short but the answers long because they are the central message that the author seeks to convey to the exterior addressee in the real world, far more than to the interior addressee who is a participant in the text's fictional world. The dialogues are as follows:

> 'And when,' I asked, 'will they set up the water-pump, and put through the agricultural scheme and the stopping-place for the steamer?'
>
> He lowered his head and paused before answering me, 'When people go to sleep and don't see the doum tree in their dreams.'
>
> 'And when will that be?' I said.
>
> 'I mentioned to you that my son is in the town studying at school,' he replied. 'It wasn't I who put him there; he ran away and went there on his own, and it is my hope that he will stay where he is and not return. When my son's son passes out of school and the number of young men with souls foreign to our own increases, then perhaps the water-pump will be set up and the agricultural scheme put into being – maybe then the steamer will stop at our village – under the doum tree of Wad Hamid.'
>
> 'And do you think,' I said to him, 'that the doum tree will one day be cut down?' He looked at me for a long time while as though wishing to project, through his tired, misty eyes, something he was incapable of doing by word.
>
> 'There will not be the least necessity for cutting down the doum tree. There is not the slightest reason for the tomb to be removed. What all these people have overlooked is that there's plenty of room for all these things; the doum tree, the tomb, the water-pump, and the steamer's stopping-place.'
>
> When he had been silent for a time he gave me a look which I didn't know how to describe, though it stirred within me a feeling of sadness, sadness for some obscure thing which I was unable to describe. Then he said: 'Tomorrow, without doubt, you will be leaving us. When you arrive at your destination, think well of us and judge us not too harshly.'[121]

Common to the corpus of stories in which the author uses dialogue, to a greater or lesser extent, and the novel *Mawsim al-Hijra ilā al-Shamāl*, in this novel he uses classical Arabic, whereas in others the dialogues are in the popular Sudanese dialect. However, the popular Sudanese dialect does not occur directly, but in a literarized form. Accordingly, dialogues in the novel have a popular, local Sudanese scent, particularly those between rural characters.[122] Nearly all are between the narrator and Muṣṭafā Sa'īd, but some are also between minor characters. Through the dialogues in *Mawsim al-Hijra ilā al-Shamāl*, the author succeeds in conveying information about the situation of the characters and locales, showing dramatically and with increasing tension the reciprocal relations between the characters. A notable example is the dialogue between Muṣṭafā Sa'īd and the narrator, which is also an introduction to Muṣṭafā's own story and which tears the veil from his face and enables the reader – and the narrator – to enter his unknown world. To quote Muṣṭafā:

> 'I shall say things to you I've said to no one before. I found no reason for doing so until now. I have decided to do so lest your imagination run away with you – since you have studied poetry.' He laughed so as to soften the edge of scorn that was evident in his voice. 'I was afraid you'd go and talk to the others, that you'd tell them I wasn't the man I claimed, which would – would cause a certain amount of embarrassment to them and to me. I thus have one request to make of you – that you promise me on your honour, that you swear to me, you won't divulge to a soul anything of what I'm going to tell you tonight.'
>
> He gave me a searching look and I said to him: 'That depends on what you say to me. How can I promise when I know nothing about you?'
>
> 'I swear to you,' he said, 'that nothing of what I shall tell you will affect my presence in this village. I'm a man in full possession of my faculties, peaceful, and wanting only good for this village and its people.'[123]

In the other novels, al-Ṭayyib Ṣāliḥ presents the dialogues that take place mainly between the leading characters in the popular Sudanese dialect, because the Sudan is not a central country in the Arab world and its literature, too, does not occupy a central place. The fact that quite a few Sudanese writers have preferred to write dialogues in Sudanese dialect has not helped them to break out of the circle of their Sudanese readers and they, like al-Ṭayyib Ṣāliḥ, had to interpret some of the words and phrases used in popular Sudanese dialect.[124] It should be remembered that al-

Ṭayyib Ṣāliḥ wrote most of his works at a time when Pan-Arabism held sway and this exerted a great influence on Arab intellectuals.

In al-Ṭayyib Ṣāliḥ's first novel, *'Urs al-Zayn,* he made extensive use of dialogues, all of them in the popular dialect of Northern Sudan.[125] Whereas in the novel *Mawsim al-Hijra ilā al-Shamāl* he was partially justified in using literary Arabic because of the characters, the plot and the locale, in *'Urs al-Zayn,* the entire novel, the characters, the plot and the locale are in the Sudanese village. Therefore, it was out of the question to have the dialogues in anything but the local dialect if the author wanted to lend credibility to the speakers, their words, and in fact to the entire text.[126] But al-Ṭayyib Ṣāliḥ distinguishes between speakers. A good example of this is the second dialogue on the first page of the novel. It is held between the Headmaster and al-Ṭarīfī, a young pupil who is late for school:

> 'Yā walad ya ḥumār, eih akhkharak?'
> Wa-lama'a al-makr fī 'aynay al-Ṭarīfī.
> 'Yā fandī simi't il-khabar?'
> 'Khabar betā' eih yā walad ya bahīm?'
> Wa-lam yuza'zi' ghaḍab al-Nāẓir min ribātat ja'sh al-ṣabī, faqāla wahuwa yaktumu ḍahkatahu:
> 'Il-Zein māsh ya'qdū loh ba'd bākir'.'[127]

And in English:

> 'You ass of a boy, what's made you so late?'
> A look of cunning flashed momentarily in Tureifi's eyes.
> 'Sir, have you heard the news?'
> 'News about what, you animal of a boy?'
> The Headmaster's anger, however, did not shake the boy's composure. Checking his laughter, he said: 'They're marrying off al-Zayn the day after tomorrow'.

Not surprisingly, the author, who wanted to show this headmaster in a negative light, preferred to do so not just through his features but also by his manner of speech which was totally different from those of the villagers. By so doing he successfully introduces him as a ridiculous character. Therefore we find that the headmaster did discuss the issue of the wedding of Zayn with al-Shaykh 'Alī:

(Yā ragul dī sana gharība giddan wallā anā ghaltān?)
Lam yakun al-nāẓir yasta'milu 'ibārat
(zōl), ay (shakhṣ) ka-baqiyyati ahl al-balad, bal
Kāna yaqūlu (ragul) fī bidāyati jumla [...]
Waqāla al-nāẓir:
(Lākīn il-mu'giza il-kubrā mawdū' zawāg il-Zein)
Hādhihi kānat 'ādatuhu, yazujj al-kalimāt al-fuṣḥā fī ḥadīthihi.[128]

And in English:

My dear fellow, this is a most strange year – or am I wrong? The headmaster did not use the expression 'chap' or 'man' like the other villagers, but would begin his sentences by using the phrase 'my dear fellow' [...] 'But the biggest miracle of all', said the headmaster, 'is the business of Zein's betrothal' (he had the habit of interspersing his speech with words in the classical language).

In the first book of *Bandar Shāh: Ḍaw al-Bayt*, the author continues the extensive use of dialogues which are all in various spoken Sudanese dialects, while the narrator's descriptions and remarks are in literary Arabic.[129] Thus, for example, the following dialogue between Maryūd and the grandfather provides an authentic picture of both the characters and the author's opinions:

'Bandar Shāh yiqūl inno ishtarā al-'igil minnak.'
Fa-qāla jaddī:
'Bandar Shāh yishtarī wallā mā yishtarī huwwa ḥurr. Lākin anā mā bi't.'
Fa-qāla Maryūd ḍāhikan:
'Idhā kān Bandar Shāh ishtarā minnak lā budd innak bi't.'
Fa-qāla jaddī:
'Gaddak 'araḍ itnāshar wa-anā tāleb saba'tāshar.'
Lam yaqul Maryūd shay'an wa-lākinnahu akhraja min jaybhi rizmata junayhāt maddahā li jaddī, fa-'akhadhahā dūna an ya'uddahā wa-lākinnahu abqāhā burhatan fī rāḥati yadihi ka'annahā yazinuhā thumma qāla:
Il-'igl marbūṭ fī al-murāḥ, imshi khudhhu'
Fa-qāla Maryūd ḍāhikan wa-huwa yata'ahhab li'l-khurūj:
Il-'igl anā suqthu ma'a shurūq al-shams Laḥmuh dilwaqti fawq il-nār
wi-yimkin yakūnū akalūh kamān.'[130]

And in English:

'Bandarshah says he's bought the calf from you.'

'Bandarshah's free to buy or not to buy,' said my grandfather. 'I, though, have not sold.'

'If Bandarshah has bought from you,' said Meryoud, laughing, 'then you must have sold.'

'Your grandfather offered twelve,' [pounds] said my grandfather, 'and I'm asking seventeen.'

Saying nothing, Meryoud took from his pocket a roll of pound notes, which he handed to my grandfather, who took them without counting them, though he kept them for an instant in the palm of his hand as though weighing them, then said, 'The calf's tied up in the pen – go and take it.'

'I drove the calf off at daybreak,' said Meryoud, laughing, as he made to leave. 'Its meat is now cooking over the fire, maybe they've even eaten it.'

In the second book of *Bandar Shāh: Maryūd*, dialogue is frequently employed. As in the first book, they are in the dialect of northern Sudan while the connecting pieces and the author's remarks are in literary Arabic. As in the previous novels, al-Ṭayyib Ṣāliḥ's objective in this novel is to accord a dimension of credibility and authenticity to the leading, secondary and peripheral village characters. A dialogue of this kind is between al-Ṭāhir Wad al-Rawwās and the narrator and it typifies the thought processes of the old villager. From the dialogue we learn of the woman's characteristics:

Faj'atan ṣarakha: 'Bint il-kalb, al-layla waq'at ma'āy!'

Qultu lahu: 'Kayf 'irift innahā unthā?'

Qāla: 'Ḥattā fī al-ḥūt, il-mara mara, wi'l-rāgil rāgil.'[131]

And the translation:

Suddenly he exclaimed, 'The bitch – tonight I shall get her.'

'How do you know it's a she?' I said to him.

'Even in fishes a woman's a woman and a man's a man', he said.

Regarding monologues, the technique used conveys the hero's internal world, opinions and ideas. In Western literature, the monologue, like dialogue, conveys the character's interior world; it illuminates his consciousness by means of the stream of consciousness technique. Eminent European authors (James Joyce, Virginia Woolf, Marcel Proust) and American writers (William Faulkner), have employed this technique. In modern Arabic literatures, similar use has been made of the stream of consciousness technique since the late 1950s, particularly in the sixties as well as today. Some Arab authors use it intensively. Among the latter are Najīb Maḥfūẓ, Laylā Ba'labakkī, and Palestinian author Ghassān Kanafānī (1936–72), to whom we can add from the 1970s onward, authors like Moroccan author Muḥammad Barrāda, Syrian author Salīm Barakāt (b.1951), 'Abd al-Raḥmān Munīf, Jordanian author Ibrāhīm Naṣrallāh (b.1954) and Algerian author al-Ṭāhir Waṭṭār (b.1936).[132]

The term 'monologue' includes within its accepted meaning the 'interior monologue'. While the monologue is usually directed towards another or others, the interior monologue is a delicate tool that enables characters to express their own hidden feelings. Al-Ṭayyib Ṣāliḥ makes excellent use of both types of monologue, providing further proof of how he has internalized modern Western writing techniques that call for extremely sensitive powers of attention and discernment. He uses both types of monologue extensively to convey truths and messages to the reader with the optimal involvement of both author and implied author. Among his writings is an entire corpus of works in which al-Ṭayyib Ṣāliḥ uses only the monologue ('Risāla ilā Aylīn', 'Dawmat Wad Ḥāmid') and a second corpus in which he employs only the interior monologue ('Nakhla 'alā al-Jadwal', 'Ḥafnat Tamr', 'Idhā Jā'at'). In the latter, the author makes extensive use of the interior monologue by the three main characters, placing the interior monologue in parentheses, as for example when he supplies Amīn's thoughts about Bahā': ('Who does he think he is?').[133] However, the use of parentheses in modern Arabic literatures in not a common feature.[134] In the third corpus that comprises the majority of al-Ṭayyib Ṣāliḥ's works ('Hākadhā Yā Sādatī', 'Ughniyat Ḥubb', *'Urs al-Zayn, Mawsim al-Hijra ilā al-Shamāl, Bandar Shāh: Ḍaw al-Bayt, Bandar Shāh: Maryūd*), both forms of monologue are employed with great emphasis placed on the interior monologue. Thus, for example, the author uses the interior monologue form when the narrator is speaking, while the monologue is employed when Muṣṭafā is the speaker. An example of one of Muṣṭafā's monologues is the story he relates to the narrator, thereby revealing his past.[135] With regard to the narrator, there are numerous examples of interior monologues and it is they that are used by the implied author as a literary tool with which he brings the reader into his interior world. Such a case can be found in the following interior monologue of the narrator:

> Was it likely that what had happened to Mustafa Sa`eed could have happened to me? He had said that he was a lie, so was I also a lie? I am from here – is not this reality enough? I too had lived with them. But I had lived with them superficially, neither loving nor hating them. I used to treasure within me the image of this little village, seeing it wherever I went with the eye of my imagination.[136]

Al-Ṭayyib Ṣāliḥ's monologues are in literary Arabic except for *'Urs al-Zayn* where they occur in the vernacular of northern Sudan. In this novel the extensive monologues occur as interior monologues in parentheses, especially not exclusively by the central characters, like al-Zayn and Maḥjūb. An example is the scene in which Maḥjūb reflects on the miracle that had happened to Sayf al-Dīn, while we, the readers (but not the characters around him) become privy to his reflections:

> Seif ad-Din has decided to go on the pilgrimage. By God, do you credit it, friend? Do you or don't you believe it? A miracle, friend, without the shadow of a doubt.[137]

The novel also contains ordinary monologues as when al-Zayn, on the eve of his wedding, laments the death of Ḥanīn: 'For a while they stood watching him in bewilderment, then al-Zayn said in a broken voice choked with tears: "If he hadn't died our revered father Haneen would have attended the wedding."'[138] In both *Bandar Shāh: Ḍaw al-Bayt* and *Bandar Shāh: Maryūd,* in contrast to the monologues in Sudanese vernacular are also some in literary Arabic. The logic of the use of dialogues in Sudanese vernacular is clear and has already been explained. But now we must ask why the author uses monologues in literary Arabic in these two books. One might have expected him to be consistent by using the same language both in dialogue and monologue, as he did in *'Urs al-Zayn,* since credibility and authenticity are his guiding lights. Generally, al-Ṭayyib Ṣāliḥ maintains a correlation between writing style, language and the language of monologue and dialogue not only in the events that take place, but also by the various characters. Possibly the novel *Mawsim al-Hijra ilā al-Shamāl* is in this respect most successful. Some literary critics rightly noted that with this novel the author broke one of the traditional narrative conventions of modern Arabic literatures. The writing style is adapted to the interior and exterior events of the book; the writing style differs where plot is concerned; and simple and convincing language is used; while the story of Muṣṭafā Sa'īd is written in rhetorical, perhaps overly rhetorical, language.[139] In any event, his writing style in this work is simple, clear and fluent. The author uses literary Arabic, albeit greatly simplifying it, while 'literarizing' words from everyday language. The dialogues between the various characters are held in literary language in a not particularly high register. However, the speech and style are so close to everyday language that they lend authenticity, realism and credibility to the dialogues. Thus al-Ṭayyib Ṣāliḥ upholds one of the principles of the realistic story, i.e., that of adapting the language to the speaker. We must remember that the majority of the dialogues in this novel are between villagers and therefore the author has made a great effort to have his characters speak simple literary Arabic. To illustrate this, here follow three examples written in different registers:

In the first example, an everyday Arabic word is inserted into a descriptive section: *'Wa-stayqaẓtu thānī yawm wuṣūlī'* ('I awoke on the second day of my arrival').[140]

In the second example we can see a simplification of the dialogue in literary language: *'Wa-qālat Bint Majdhūb wa-hiya ḍāḥika: khifnā an ta'ūda ilaynā bi Naṣrāniyya ghalfā'* ('Bint Majzoub laughed, "We were afraid," she said, "you'd bring back with you an uncircumcised infidel for a wife"').[141] In the third example we find Sudanese vernacular terms like: *'marīsa'*, a type of beer.[142]

In the novel *'Urs al-Zayn,* al-Ṭayyib Ṣāliḥ employs a language and dialogues for the text. The dialogues in this book are all in northern Sudanese dialect and this is what sets this novel apart from the other novels, especially *Mawsim al-Hijra ilā al-Shamāl.* The difference is obvious: events, plot, characters and locale dictate the above-mentioned usage. The locale is Sudanese and the plot and events take place in the closed society of a Sudanese village. There are, however, two exceptions: the *imām* and the Headmaster. The *imām* usually speaks fluent literary Arabic while the Headmaster scribbles words in the literary style. The author has a clear reason for characterizing them in this way; by this, as well as other artistic means, he taunts them. In addition, in the story 'Nakhla 'alā al-Jadwal' the author stresses his dislike of Ḥusayn the merchant, not only through speech that is very close to literary, but also by suggesting that he is different, even foreign. Accordingly, he uses the literary word *rajul* (man) or *rāgil/ragil* (man or person) widely used in Egyptian and Sudanese dialects, as opposed to *zōl* (man or person) of the dialect of northern Sudan.[143]

Place, Space and Time

In all al-Ṭayyib Ṣāliḥ's works, without distinction between the various literary genres, place, space and time play a very important role. Place and space are of great significance whether the place is realistic because it exists in reality or not, or whether the place or space has historical or religious significance whether they existed or not, and there are also instances in which the place and space exist only in the mind of the author. Clearly, in all the cases mentioned these functions are used as a framework for the plot. In modern Western literature similarly, authors like William Faulkner have their plot take place in a Mississippi township in the southern part of the United States, where the reader wonders whether the town indeed exists, or whether its name is fictional or not. Another case in point is the imaginary and legendary town of Macondo used by Gabriel García Márquez in the plots of his works (see Chapter Four). In modern Arabic literatures there are places of legendary, historical and spiritual significance, like Ṭība, for example, that is a source of inspiration for Najīb Maḥfūẓ in his novel *Kifāḥ Ṭība* (Thebes at War 1939), or by 'Abd al-Raḥmān Munīf in his novel *al-Ashjār wa-Ightiyāl Marzūq* (The Trees and the Assassination of Marzuk, 1973).[144] The village is a realistic place and it is generally the village in which the real author spent his childhood. We must therefore remember that the majority of Arab societies are basically rural.[145] There are authors who reduce the plot locale to a train, like Egyptian author and playwright Muḥammad Taymūr (1892–1921), or to a hotel, like Maḥfūẓ, or to a ship, like Jabrā Ibrāhīm Jabrā.[146] There are texts in which the central plot shifts between two places remote from one another, one in an Arab country and the other in Europe, and this enables the author to move between the poles, for example Cairo and Paris in *'Uṣfūr Min al-Sharq*, by the Egyptian author Tawfīq al-Ḥakīm, or Beirut and Paris in the novel *al-Ḥayy al-Lātīnī* by the Lebanese author Suhayl Idrīs, or Cairo and London in the novel *Qindīl Umm Hāshim* by the Egyptian author Yaḥyā Ḥaqqī.[147]

Al-Ṭayyib Ṣāliḥ chose to locate the majority of his works and their plots in a village in northern Sudan.[148] This is the village of Wad Ḥāmid whose full name appears in 'Dawmat Wad Ḥāmid', *Bandar Shāh: Ḍaw al-Bayt* and *Bandar Shāh: Maryūd*, or which is a setting for other works that do not mention its full name, like 'Nakhla 'alā Jadwal', 'Ḥafnat Tamr', *'Urs al-Zayn* and *Mawsim al-Hijra ilā al-Shamāl*. In some works the central plot unfolds in the village, while sub-plots take place in a city (Cairo, Khartoum, London or Nicosia) as in *Mawsim al-Hijra ilā al-Shamāl* and 'al-Rajul al-Qubruṣī'. Sometimes the entire plot takes place outside the Sudan, as in 'Hākadhā Yā Sādatī' and 'Yawm Mubārak 'alā Shāṭi' Umm Bāb'. Wad Ḥāmid village, whether mentioned by name or not, is nearly always the permanent setting for al-Ṭayyib Ṣāliḥ's works and it indeed exists in northern Sudan. The author uses it in both the realistic and mythical, legendary dimension because of the broad canvas it affords him. He was born and spent his childhood there, and to him the village is a mould of place and space into which he can cast content, meanings and fictitious plots as his mood dictates. The author's move from the village, despite the fact that he visits it from time to time, has distanced him from the realistic elements, for he writes about them from outside, not from within, but it enables him as well – because of the distancing in place and space – to employ it more easily, even though he sometimes idealizes the place and its people.

Time has numerous and important functions in a literary work. In most cases we find that in the term 'time' we are able to pinpoint three different levels: the first is the time of the plot, or when the events related take place in their chronological order (i.e. *fabula*), or according to the author's order (i.e. *sjuzet*); the second is the use made by the author in the narrative continuity of the text; and the third is the time of modernization. Therefore, the author may perceive the present in relation to time past, and express the view that the present is a better time than the past, or in contrast, he may perceive the present as a cursed time when compared to the past.

Al-Ṭayyib Ṣāliḥ uses the three levels of time extensively. He does not employ one writing style when dealing with time, but changes it from work to work. The subject of his writing is far from the author not only in terms of place and space, but also in terms of time. Moreover, as we view all the author's works as a single large text, we shall see the play on time in certain works in relationship to others.

The most intelligent use of the three levels of time are employed by the author in *Mawsim al-Hijra ilā al-Shamāl*. He does not use a single defined time nor does he maintain a chronological order, and he exploits time in various ways in accordance with the development of the plot. He makes deliberate use of dates and numbers with total awareness of their hidden significance, as for example, his use of the number seven in this and other works. The narrator has been away from his village for seven years, the same number of years that Muṣṭafā spent in jail, and apparently this is no mere coincidence.[149] The narrator returns to his village from Khartoum where he works, for the first time after a seven-month absence.[150] Seven is the number of dead (killed, murdered, suicides and disappearances) in this novel – four in Europe and three in the Sudan. In al-Ṭayyib Ṣāliḥ's short story 'Yawm Mubārak 'alā Shāṭi' Umm Bāb' (1993), Rabāb, the main character, was born after seven months of her mother's pregnancy which is unusual, exactly as Rabāb is an unusual person. Indeed, the element of uniqueness in the meaning of time is part and parcel of her unique character. The number seven is of great importance in the three monotheist religions and also in the ancient Orient, particularly in Babylon.[151] Seven is not only of great importance in the Sudan and especially in popular Sudanese literature,[152] but also in modern Arabic literatures where its use is quite common. We find examples of this in the titles of novels like *Ayyām al-Insān al-Sab'a* (The Seven Days of Man, 1969) by Egyptian authors such as 'Abd al-Ḥakīm Qāsim, and *Fī al-Usbū' Sab'at Ayyām* (Seven Days in the Week, 1975) by Muḥammad Yūsuf al-Qa'īd,[153] or *Qindīl Umm Hāshim* by Yaḥyā Ḥaqqī. In the latter novel Ismā'īl, the novel's central character, returns from Europe after an absence of seven years: 'Seven years have gone by and the ship has come home', and in another place Ni'ma (a marginal character) comes to Sheikh Dardīrī and fulfills her vow after seven years.[154] In the novel *al-Marfūḍūn* (The Rejected, 1981) by Algerian author Sa'dī Ibrāhīm, Aḥmad, the novel's central character, leaves his village in Algeria when he is fifteen and goes to France to work. After seven years, he returns to the village to marry one of the village girls.[155] Most of the central characters in the novels mentioned above underwent some experiences on their journey, as did Sindbad in his seven journeys. The number seven in Ṣāliḥ's writing is not the only important number since he also uses other numbers which have great importance in the three monotheist religions, especially the number four. In the story 'The Doum Tree of Wad Hamid', the villagers visited the tomb of Wad Ḥāmid every week on Wednesday at four o'clock in the afternoon; this is also the exact time the government wants as 'The official replied that the time fixed for the steamer to stop by their village would be four o'clock on Wednesday afternoon' (p. 42). The old man was very impressed by the lofty doum tree: 'Wherever you happen to be in the village you can see it; in fact, you can even see it from four villages away' (p. 38), or when the old man tells the young listener about another attempt by the new government to cut down the doum tree: 'So things went on till four years ago when a new government came to power' (p. 48). In *'Urs al-Zayn*, when Umm al-Zayn sees her son injured: 'She gave a scream which was heard by Hajj Ibrahim, Ni'ma's father, four houses away…' (p. 43). In *Mawsim al-Hijra ilā al-Shamāl*, the narrator decides to discuss with Ḥusna the offer of Wad al-Rayyis to marry her, and 'At approximately four o'clock in the afternoon I went to Mustafa Sa'eed's house' (p. 91). When Maḥjūb and the narrator discuss how many changes had taken place in their village, Maḥjūb indicates that they would become real when people like him would become ministers, adding laughingly: 'Wa-hādhā ṭab'an min rābi' [Fourth] al-mustaḥīlāt' (p. 103) which means: 'and naturally that is an out-and-out impossibility'.[156]

In the novel *Mawsim al-Hijra ilā al-Shamāl* the author works on three levels of time: The time related by the narrator, which is the time when he returns from England after an absence of seven years, telling us exactly how long he spent in

Europe, without telling us when he was there. With the help of the events related in the novel we are able to estimate that he went to England not earlier than 1941 and returned to the Sudan not earlier than 1948. This calculation is based on the fact that the narrator met Muṣṭafā Sa'īd when he was twenty-five and Muṣṭafā was fifty, or perhaps a little older, and we know that Muṣṭafā was born in 1898, so they could not have met earlier than 1948. As the narrator was then twenty-five, we can assume that he was born around 1923, the year in which Muṣṭafā was sent to jail for seven years.[157]

The time of Muṣṭafā Sa'īd is defined in accordance with the various stages of his studies and his growing up in Khartoum, Cairo and Oxford. These milestones enable us to estimate the year in which Muṣṭafā's activities are related. The problem is that there is a discrepancy between the dates provided. He was born in 1898 (clearly, al-Ṭayyib Ṣāliḥ chose this date deliberately because of its political significance in Sudanese history),[158] for his exit visa was stamped in 1916 in Cairo and renewed in London in 1926.[159] But there are facts in the body of the text that do not fall into line with this date and thus we find that he reached Cairo when he was twelve years old, hence the year was 1910.[160] He arrived in London when he was fifteen, i.e., in 1913, and here again is a discrepancy in the dates.[161] A general, albeit solid, historical date is Muṣṭafā's arrival in London when: 'London was emerging from the war and the oppressive atmosphere of the Victorian era'.[162] Apparently mention of this date, in addition to the fact that at his trial in London the date 1922–3 occurs and that he first met Jean Morris when he was twenty-five,[163] proves that the second series of dates is correct, while the first series is inexact. In any event, Muṣṭafā was sentenced to seven years in prison and was therefore in London until 1930. Another precise date, 1928, also appears without coinciding with other dates. A Sudanese Minister claims that Muṣṭafā was one of his lecturers in 1928,[164] which is impossible if Muṣṭafā was in prison between 1923 and 1930 I suggest two possibilities: either the author sought to characterize the Sudanese minister as untrustworthy or he was lax in his choice of the date. The way the combined time of the narrator and of Muṣṭafā are joined defies separation. Muṣṭafā's time and the time related to the villagers intermingle, making it difficult for the reader to follow the course of the plot. This is possibly a deliberate ploy by the author, who seeks to emphasize the relationship between them again and again, and his unwillingness (or inability) to separate them.

Time in *Mawsim al-Hijra ilā al-Shamāl* is perceived by the villagers in two ways. The first is the time of the new era as the root of all the troubles and catastrophes that befall the village. These catastrophes are part of the tragedy that the village experienced following the murder of Ḥusna, Muṣṭafā Sa'īd's wife, and the suicide of Wad al-Rayyis's wife. After these deaths the villagers use terms like 'modern women', 'modern plagues', 'modern times have brought things like this upon us' and 'you have become a modern lover'.[165] Indeed, time past indicates the good times before the village catastrophies of the present, with the onset of modernization, as well as a result of Western culture and its influence. Villagers in the Sudan felt threatend by the city in the narrow sense and by Western culture in the wider one[166].

A second significance of time for the villagers is the way it is related to special events and the mystical and legendary implications connected with it. These are related to night and darkness, dawn and dusk and winter and summer when events occur, significant not only for the creation of legends and mystery in the present, but also in the future.[167] In some of these events we can discern a sense of unreality that overcomes the narrator; in *Mawsim al-Hijra ilā al-Shamāl,* he leaves Muṣṭafā Sa'īd's house and feels that he is lost in place, space and time, and the village, that symbol of stability, is hanging between heaven and earth. But the feeling passes after he walks among the village houses.[168] Time, as employed by the author has symbolic significance. The time related to Muṣṭafā Sa'īd, whether in London or the Sudanese village, is the night, in direct contrast to the narrator's grandfather whose time is at dawn. The narrator is in the middle, and while he is conscious of the significance of the night, he also sees positive things in it, just as he understands that not only positive events occur during the day, but also negative ones that are related to the sun.[169]

In his works, al-Ṭayyib Ṣāliḥ makes extensive use of descriptions of the time of events and their unfolding – not in chronological order – which is particularly prominent in the novels rather than the short stories. In so doing the author uses various times in different ways for different aims, to persuade the reader of his (Ṣāliḥ's) willingness to shed light on characters and events as well. Therefore, as noted earlier, there are in his literary works a variety of uses of dawn, morning, noon, afternoon, evening and night. Nevertheless, it is true that the author does have a favoured time and that is *al-ḍuḥā,* meaning forenoon or more precisely early forenoon, the time of one of the five daily prayers. Morever, as already indicated, al-Ṭayyib Ṣāliḥ is influenced by and makes use of the Koran, and we should bear in mind that the word *al-ḍuḥā* is mentioned in the Koran several times.[170] *Al-ḍuḥā* occurs in many of his literary works concerning various important and unimportant events and can be divided into four categories: the first as the time connected to legendary events such as the case of the doum tree in 'Dawmat Wad Ḥāmid', or the legendary connection between Maryūd and the narrator's grandson to the past and the future in *Bandar Shāh: Ḍaw al-Bayt,* or the connection between the narrator and Maryam in terms of the legendary world in *Bandar Shāh: Maryūd.* The second category is used by the villagers as a unit of time in several cases, such as in 'Dawmat Wad Ḥāmid' or in *'Urs al-Zayn.* The third category is used by the author to indicate important village events, such as the news of the wedding of Zayn in *'Urs al-Zayn,* or some events connected with Ḍaw al-Bayt, Bandar Shāh and Maryūd, characters in *Bandar Shāh: Ḍaw al-Bayt,* or with the narrator and his old friends in *Bandar Shāh: Maryūd.* The fourth category belongs to the religious sphere, which in turn is connected to legendary events as in *Bandar Shāh: Ḍaw al-Bayt,* when the *imām* reads the chapter of *al-Ḍuḥā*, as well as several other cases in this chapter.[171] The short story in which times are mixed in a flashback and events are not in chronological order is 'Nakhla 'alā al-Jadwal'. In this story the opposite occurs; he first places us in the specific situation in which Maḥjūb finds himself and then moves us along, through Maḥjūb's memories, to different periods of time in his past. Through Maḥjūb's reflections, thoughts and deliberations the author takes the reader through the course of Maḥjūb's life. The time of the plot and the interior time of Maḥjūb's reflections converge with the news of the receipt of Ḥasan's letter.[172]

The novel *Bandar Shāh: Maryūd* exemplifies the author's use of the dimension of time. On the one hand, there are references to historical and political events that are related to the Sudan's distant past, like the Arab invasion in the seventh century, or references to the kingdom of Sennar that existed between 505–1820. There is also mention of the more recent past like, for example, the late Christian period in the nineteenth century or the activities of Muḥammad Aḥmad al-Mahdī between 1881 and 1885 and his successor, 'Abd Allāh al-Ta'īshī, who was active between 1885 and 1898.[173] On the other hand, these events are intermingled with legends related to the mystical figure of 'Īsā, known as Bandar Shāh.[174] Different versions of the wonderful figure of Bandar Shāh, his life and death, are combined with legends; in these combined versions the author exploits his historical and political knowledge of the Sudan to fabricate reality and imagination within narrative fiction. Echoes of this approach are present in al-Ṭayyib Ṣāliḥ's semi-autobiographical work in which he says, *inter alia*:

> We thereupon find that Maḥjūb 'Abd al-Ḥafīẓ, al-Ṭāhir Wad Rawwāsī and others, are ordinary farmers, but yet by the novel *Bandar Shāh* I have turned them into myth... into

> legend... and the legend as I understand it means giving reality broader dimensions in time, as Homer did. He took the Greeks and turned them into symbols that interacted with a legendary world [...] The author looks at what is called reality, but when we think about it more deeply, reality from a philosophical standpoint does not exist. There is no reality; there is a dream, as Shakespeare said, if you regard it from a historical point of view. It is not stable.[175]

The present chapter, and indeed, all al-Ṭayyib Ṣāliḥ's works, might be concluded with these words. For the author has tried, in most cases successfully, to weave into fictional texts material taken from the Sudanese past and present history together with fictional material. This wonderful admixture also includes materials from classical Arabic literature and Western philosophies and literatures with which he is very familiar. This is not a superficial familiarity, but rather a profound knowledge and internalization of both cultures successfully expressed, especially in the poetics of his writing. Thus he makes highly intelligent use of the character as listener, basically taken from *The Arabian Nights*, together with the 'Theory of Narrative Gaps' taken from Western literature. In 'Dawmat Wad Ḥāmid', he also makes delightful use of modern interpretations of the same religious literature, *al-Faraj ba'd al-Shidda* (Relief after distress), that originated in the eighth century. The use of numerous elements of the poetics of writing in the works of al-Ṭayyib Ṣāliḥ, which include various literary devices, is done naturally and flowingly, varying from text to text. Nonetheless, al-Ṭayyib Ṣāliḥ's poetics and the characteristics of his literary writing are not cut from the same cloth. He does not rest on his laurels, but leaves the unique contours of his works that are made of both local and borrowed materials. Place, explicitly Wad Ḥāmid village, and time, especially past and future, remain constant, with the author changing them according to his needs deriving from his perception that the entire congeries of his works is one big text. The most prominent element of all is al-Ṭayyib Ṣāliḥ's use of characters. I suggest that characters and characterization are the keystone of his texts. To this topic the following two chapters will be devoted.

CHAPTER THREE

Status of the Characters in al-Ṭayyib Ṣāliḥ's Works

Importance of the Characters

In Chapter Two we examined fiction and reality in the works of al-Ṭayyib Ṣāliḥ and discussed the fine line between the real world in which the author lives and works and the fictional one created by the writer or real author. Obviously, one of the expressions of living between these two worlds is manifested in the construction of the characters. There is no disputing the fact that characters filling a role in an artistic work have, in one form or another, a connection with the author's real life. Furthermore, we shall see that in works of an autobiographical nature, either partly or wholly, one character has greater importance since it embodies autobiographical characteristics of the author. I do not wish to claim that in a fictional work a total similarity or identity exists between the author and the leading character or one of the central characters, but obviously the author gives one or more characters the nature, qualities or characteristics that indicate an autobiographical relationship with his own life in everyday reality.

As we know, since the 1950s some literary critics and even several authors of novels have spoken with some certainty of the death of the character in literature. Here a totally converse conception is presented (and this is why two chapters are devoted to the subject of characters) that will focus on the importance of the characters. Shaping characters is an integral part of the fabric of fashioning the text, and the character itself is used as a means of achieving the author's literary objectives. But a distinction must be drawn between three main types of character: central or leading, secondary, and marginal characters. This does not mean that only the central character or characters have a special status that leads to a presentational role at the individual or collective level, and likewise, secondary characters and sometimes even marginal characters have a defined and important role. The point is that the characters are not simply a reflection of reality, or *mimesis* in Auerbach's definition. He claims that 'imitation of reality is imitation of the sensory experience of life on earth – among the most essential characteristics of which would seem to be its possessing a history, its changing and developing'.[1] This has no bearing on the extent to which these characters are 'rounded' or 'flat', according to Forster's definition,[2] whereby each character has at least one function it is supposed to fill in the text. The character's persuasiveness, or lack of it, depends on the way it fills its role, and not on its centrality or marginality. It is therefore clear that in a complete text authors do not usually create only a central character or characters, and nothing else. On the contrary, no matter how developed and convincing the central character is, it must still fill the role given to it by the author. Few are the writers who do not use their characters – and their degree of centrality is of no importance – to convey their credo or messages from various spheres of life that they seek to express through the fictional text they have built. Constructing a character is only one of the author's main objectives, that is to say, when shaping a fictional text the authors employ various devices to fill various functions in the structuring of the text. In the present case, shaping the character, either central or secondary, is not an end in itself but rather a means. We believe that building characters at different functional and central levels is connected to persuasion and credibility with regard to the reader, and in accordance with the author's level of understanding. Thus, for example, if the central character in a novel is an anti-hero, it means that by constructing this type of character, the author has sought to convince the reader of the existence of a character of this type in reality or in the fictional life. The manner in which the author seeks to delineate his protagonists may be attained in a number of ways. This may be summed up as follows:[3]

Outward appearance – The ways in which the author describes his characters' outward appearance are many and varied. A character which is ugly or beautiful, dressed in tatters or finery, who is short and stocky or tall, will clearly attract or repel the reader – all according to the author's concealed and sometimes overt intentions; the author almost exclusively determines the character's credibility and the way in which the reader identifies (or does not identify) with it. The empathy or lack of it that the author seeks to impart to it directly affects the way in which it is shaped and built.

Habits and manners – The author employs the character's habits and manners as a single, but important, means of characterizing it. Clearly the character's habits and manners at the individual or collective level are merely a function of its role in the community in which it lives; its social status, the manners deriving from this status, its relationship with the surrounding society, its everyday behaviour, are all perceived as mainly external social characteristics which bear witness to the character's inner world.

The character's speech – The character's speech has an important function in shaping the ideas that the author seeks to convey to the reader. The way in which the character speaks and the linguistic register used will, of course, position it in a specific social class. Common, coarse speech in contrast to refined, literary speech can, each according to its definition, remove the character to another social class.

Thus a writer like William Faulkner (1897–1962) who wrote about the southern states of America, will 'naturally' have his characters use southern speech – imparting to his work and its characters a high degree of credibility.[4] In modern Arabic literatures, the register of speech has special significance. Dialogues held in a literary Arabic, or alternatively, in everyday spoken Arabic, will impart credibility (or the lack of it) to the character speaking the words. In the case of an Egyptian text, the use of the Egyptian dialect presents no difficulties for non-Egyptian Arab readers, but in cases of less central dialects in the Arab world – the Sudanese dialect, for example – their use limits the number of readers and forces the writer or publisher to use footnotes to clarify the meaning of words and sentences for readers not au courant with its intricacies.[5]

Life story and its relationship with the environment – The protagonist's or central character's place of birth and life story can, at least in the eyes of the reader, characterize him. One of the main questions in this context is how does the author present the life story to the reader? Here writing techniques are generally divided into two categories. The first draws the character using direct reporting on its life and origins, while the second usually provides the reader with the protagonist's life story, or that of the central characters, indirectly, and not through the character itself. The character's relationship with its 'natural' environment is depicted to locate and characterize him against his social background and the human landscape in which he grew up. When a character(s), comes from the lower class, for example, he is liable to be shackled throughout his life as portrayed throughout the text. In Western literature, Sorel in the novel *The Red and the Black* (1830) by Stendhal (1783–1842), was born a carpenter's son and as a result of his social status he was persecuted by the people of his first environment, aspiring throughout the novel to move up the social scale, which was, of course, in direct contradiction of the iron-clad rules of French society of the time.[6] In modern Arabic literatures there are a number of cases of members of the lower classes who attempt to move into the upper classes, especially in the wake of nationalist aspirations of the 1950s and 1960s. A notable example of a man's origins that pursued him throughout his progress up the Egyptian social ladder is Yūsuf 'Abd al-Ḥamīd al-Suwayfī in the novel by Fatḥī Ghānim, *al-Rajul Alladhī Faqada Ẓillahu.*[7]

Accordingly, characters in literary works generally and the novel in particular have a major role. We reiterate that the three categories of characters (central, secondary, and marginal) have a significant function in modern Arabic literatures; even in the initial period of the development of modern Arabic literatures especially the novel, novella, and the short story. Arab writers assigned great importance to the shaping of characters and the functions they perform. No doubt this was due to the tremendous influence of modern Western literatures on Arabic literatures, beginning at the end of the 19th century and continuing well into the seventh decade of the 20th. Therefore, no single characterization technique exists in modern Arabic literatures, but rather a wide variety is employed. For instance, the techniques employed in his works by Najīb Maḥfūẓ are many and varied. Indirect characterization is used in his short story 'Za'balāwī', and in the majority of his works from the 1960s onwards.[8] This writing technique is combined with an allegorical style in some of his works of the late 1950s, as seen in the novel *Awlād Ḥāratinā* (*Children of Gebelawi*, 1959).[9] In the 1970s, and with even greater force in the 1980s and 1990s, writing techniques became diversified, and not a few Arab writers devote much thought in their texts to characterization, especially of the central characters. In most cases writers paid much attention to shaping the protagonists' various dimensions and allowed them to fill important functions in the construction of the text. These modern and post-modern attempts were made by Egyptian authors like Ṣabrī Mūsā (b.1932) in his novel *Fasād al-Amkina* (The Corruption of Places, 1973), or by writers from the Arab Mashriq and Maghrib, like Syrian authors Khalīl al-Nu'aymī (b.1941) in his novel *Tafrīgh al-Kā'in* (Emptying of Existence, 1995) and the Canadian-domiciled Egyptian author, Sa'd al-Khādim in his book *Thulāthiyyat 'Ūlayis* (The Ulysses Trilogy, 1988).[10]

Al-Ṭayyib Ṣāliḥ places his characters at the centre of his works, weaving the story's plot around them.[11] This author is a fine example of a writer who constructs narrative texts in which the characters play a major role, and thus he maintains a tradition of Arabic and world writing that places at its centre a character or characters who function as an axis around which the entire text revolves. In modern Arabic literatures, however, there are also fictional texts in which atmosphere is far more important than the characters. Such texts are primarily works of atmosphere rather than of character, and one such work that clearly illustrates this is the story 'al-Bashar al Thalātha' (The Three Men, 1984), by the Egyptian author Muḥammad al-Makhzanjī (b.1954).[12] Al-Ṭayyib Ṣāliḥ's construction of a wide range of central, secondary and marginal characters at the centre of his works has earned him high praise from critics, who have singled out the way he shapes his characters and integrates them into the events that take place in the work.[13] The convincing manner in which the characters are constructed results from the author's use of realistic figures he knew in life in his own village as well as other villages in the Sudan. The majority of al-Ṭayyib Ṣāliḥ's characters therefore have biographical characteristics of people he knew in the past, and in this regard his novels and short stories are alike. Al-Ṭayyib Ṣāliḥ said the following on this point in the interview he gave to the Sudanese critic and journalist Ṭalḥat Jibrīl, in the context of the novel *Bandar Shāh: Ḍaw al-Bayt* (1971) and *Maryūd* (1976–7):

> I relied on the special features of the environment of northern Sudan, for no other reason than that I know them well. I represented them by ordinary people, farmers living in that environment, turning them into legendary figures. Thereupon, we find that Maḥjūb, ʻAbd al-Hafīẓ, al-Ṭāhir Wad al-Rawwāsī, and others are ordinary farmers, yet in the novel *Bandar Shāh* I have turned them into myth... into legend... and legend as I understand it means giving reality broader dimensions in time, as Homer did.[14]

The main characteristics of al-Ṭayyib Ṣāliḥ's works can be summarized under five categories:

- Al-Ṭayyib Ṣāliḥ's novels and short stories teem with characters, consisting of the three above-mentioned groups: central, secondary, and marginal.
- A large number of the characters in his works are developed by relying on his acquaintance with them. Therefore, both the text's central character and most other characters are based on people who lived in reality and possess biographical characteristics. The charcteristics are not those of the author.
- The majority of the characters represent and symbolize certain classes, mainly classes in Sudanese society, particularly in the village society of northern Sudan, far more than they constitute individual and autonomous characters. In short, a large number of characters have the function of archetypal characters.
- In many cases, the characters' names are charged with meaning, symbols and allusions. Thus, for example, in the novel *ʻUrs al-Zayn*, there are names like al-Zayn (the good or the handsome), al-Ḥanīn (the merciful), and Niʻma (the graceful), or in the novel *Mawsim al-Hijra ilā al-Shamāl*, names like Muṣṭafā (the chosen), Saʻīd (the happy), and Ḥusna (the good), and in the novel *Bandar Shāh: Ḍaw al-Bayt*, a name like Ḍaw al-Bayt (light of the house), and in the novel *Bandar Shāh: Maryūd*, the character of Maryūd (the beloved).
- A large number of the characters in al-Ṭayyib Ṣāliḥ's works reappear in the author's various works. Their centrality and status, and the developments they undergo, symbolize more than anything the changes that have taken place in Sudanese society since the 1950s. In Chapter Four I shall discuss their development and the way in which al-Ṭayyib Ṣāliḥ shapes and plays with them.

A discussion and analysis of the central characters in al-Ṭayyib Ṣāliḥ's works, stories and novels alike, according to the chronological appearance and/or genre of the works, provides a picture of the character's importance in the author's texts. Furthermore, it demonstrates indirectly the main points of our hypothesis with regard to the character's centrality in modern literatures, not only in Arabic.

Dawmat Wad Ḥāmid

Dawmat Wad Ḥāmid contains seven short stories according to the chronological order of their writing:

- 'Nakhla 'alā al-Jadwal' – In this short story the author's concept of the importance of the characters finds full expression. The major character is Maḥjūb, the secondary character is Ḥusayn the merchant, and the marginal ones are Ḥasan and Khadīja, Maḥjūb's children, his cousin Ismā'īl, Ramaḍān, Sitt al-Banāt and her son. Maḥjūb is the central protagonist in this story,[15] a man of about fifty-five, a successful farmer in the past but who is currently in dire financial straits. The only course open to him to extricate himself from his problems is to sell the date palm from which he makes his living and which is his pride and joy. He places his trust in God and is saved by the money his son, Ḥasan, sends him from Egypt. Maḥjūb is thus the central character who fills a number of functions that the author seeks to convey. They are: Maḥjūb symbolizes the Sudanese farmer whose recklessness, combined with the modernization that is overtaking his country, deprives him of his higher economic status. He also symbolizes the social, economic, and political exploitation current in the Sudan in general and the Sudanese village in particular. In this story, as occurs in additional works, Maḥjūb lives in a time of change. Ḥusayn the merchant is an extremely important secondary character: he is a wealthy merchant who seeks to exploit Maḥjūb's financial situation in order to buy from him the date palm that is his source of income. Ḥusayn is the axis around which the author weaves the story of the ravages of the times and the economic, social, and political corruption in the Sudan. Moreover, in contrast to Maḥjūb, who gains both the author's affection and criticism of his recklessness, Ḥusayn is the object of the author's ridicule and criticism. Yet al-Ṭayyib Ṣāliḥ does not express his negative attitude towards Ḥusayn directly. The devices used by the author are irony and ridicule directed at him, as for example, in the scene in which he pleads with Maḥjūb to sell him the date palm: 'The donkey of Husein the merchant shifted restlessly. Its owner hadn't dismounted for he didn't want to show Sheikh Mahjoub his eagerness to buy the date palm…' (p. 7). In another place the author mocks Ḥusayn's excellent financial circumstances and his dress (aside from criticizing him), which stand in stark contrast to Maḥjūb's harsh economic conditions:

> Husein the merchant, with his flowing white robes, and his black `aba he had bought on a visit to Khartoum, and his turban made of top quality crêpe, and his red shoes, the best that the craftsmen of Fasher had ever turned out, with his plump, gleaming white donkey and the red-painted saddle with the dark brown pelt hanging down so low it almost touched the ground, was a living picture of haughty arrogance. (p. 8).

The way in which al-Ṭayyib Ṣāliḥ indirectly depicts Ḥusayn the merchant in a negative light, through his dress, is greatly reminiscent of the short story 'Za'balāwī' by Najīb Maḥfūẓ, mentioned above. In 'Za'balāwī', the real author expresses his negative opinion on the economic, social, and especially the moral status of Sheikh Qamar, one of the characters encountered by the narrator in his search for a cure for his sickness. We can hear the author's voice criticizing the *nouveaux riches* of the Egypt of post-July 1952 revolution, as he describes the sheikh:

> On asking to see him I was ushered into a room just as a beautiful woman with a most exciting perfume was leaving it. The man received me with a smile and motioned me towards a fine leather-upholstered chair. My feet were conscious of the costly lushness of the carpet despite the thick soles of my shoes. The man wore a lounge suit and was smoking a cigar; his manner of sitting was that of someone well satisfied both with himself and his worldly possessions. The look of warm welcome he gave me left no doubt in my mind that he thought me a prospective client and I felt acutely embarrased at encroaching upon his valuable time.[16]

Al-Ṭayyib Ṣāliḥ similarly exploits the confrontation between Ḥusayn the merchant and Maḥjūb the farmer, to convey his positive attitude towards Maḥjūb, in contrast to the negative attitude he has towards Ḥusayn. Apart from the economic and human spheres, he also deals with religion. While Maḥjūb's trust in God wins the reader's support, exactly the opposite occurs with Ḥusayn, who says insolently to Maḥjūb: 'Man, what are you standing there like an idiot without saying anything? Just say the word and let's get going'. (p. 16). And later, when Maḥjūb decides to place his trust in God and send Ḥusayn on his way, Ḥusayn's response is scathing:

'...saying in a voice as cold as a whiplash: "May Allah open a way. May Allah open a way – tomorrow you'll come looking for a loan"'. (p. 17).

The roles of the rest of the marginal characters in the story highlight the two central characters, Maḥjūb and Ḥusayn. They are not important and are there solely as scenery with the task of filling voids and gaps in the story. They function to vary, expand, and cast light both upon the central characters and the plot itself.

- In the second story, 'Ḥafnat Tamr', instead of a single central character, there are three: the grandson, the grandfather, and Mas'ūd, and three marginal characters: Ḥusayn the merchant and another two merchants who are strangers. The first two, the narrator and the grandfather, appear in a series of texts in which they fill various roles, and the relationship between them is reinforced in *Mawsim al-Hijra ilā al-Shamāl* (1966) and *Bandar Shāh: Ḍaw al-Bayt* (1971), and later becomes even more complex in the novel *Bandar Shāh: Maryūd* (1976–7). The grandson is the narrator who describes the events taking place in his village and although his viewpoint is that of a boy, it is also an adult's, employed as memory and remembering. The fact that the author presents this character in two periods of life lends credibility to the text. Child narrators are used widely in world literature as well as in modern Arabic literatures. 'Abd al-Raḥmān al-Sharqāwī, in his novel *al-Arḍ*,[17] also employs a child narrator who relates events that took place in his village twenty years earlier. The failure of the child in al-Sharqāwī's novel is the inadequate and unconvincing way in which the author shapes the narrator's character from both the literary and logical point of view, when the boy states facts and makes judgments that could not possibly be provided by a child with only a primary school education.[18]

In our case, the entire story of the relationship between grandson and grandfather is related solely by the narrator. It is therefore difficult to assess the credibility of the boy's story, as we are not privy to the details of their relationship from the grandfather's perspective. Thus, for example, when the grandson tells that he was his grandfather's favorite grandchild, we can find nothing to support his claim from the grandfather. The grandson's world, as we shall see in others of al-Ṭayyib Ṣāliḥ's works, is limited during his childhood to three central spheres: the mosque, the river, and the field. Among the three the mosque holds primary status, and as the child says: 'Yes, I used to love the mosque, and I loved the river too'. (p. 19). It is interesting to note that the narrator's favouring the mosque changes in others of the author's texts, as we shall see later.

The author also employs the child in another way: he turns him into the voice of conscience. The child is sensitive to social and economic injustice and when he hears that his grandfather has, over a period of many years, gradually acquired Mas'ūd's land and that he intends to acquire all his land, he views this with apprehension. In contrast with his feelings of shame and anger that border on hate towards his grandfather, he identifices with Mas'ūd, their goodhearted neighbour. This reaches a climax in the scene in which Mas'ūd's crop is divided. Here is the young narrator's reaction: 'For some unknown reason, I experienced a sharp sensation of pain in my chest. I ran off into the distance [...] I felt at that moment that I hated him [grandfather]'. (p. 25).

The grandfather is described solely by the grandson, and in this way the author uses a series of texts in which the grandfather appears as an important character with symbolic attributes. The grandfather's importance varies from work to work. We do not know much about him or what he does, but we do know that he is not a native villager but came to the village forty years earlier, prior to the event related in the story.[19] He is revealed as a tough, practical man who shows Mas'ūd no mercy; on the contrary, he despises Mas'ūd for being forced to sell his land in order to pay for his numerous marriages. Where the grandfather is concerned land has supreme value, so anyone who sells his or his family's land is, in his view, beyond the pale. In other works, however, the grandfather symbolizes the grass-roots farmer and his attitude towards land is utterly convincing and is consistent in all al-Ṭayyib Ṣāliḥ's works. What is perhaps surprising is that the grandfather is not a local man, and this provides an opening for weaving threads leading to other characters in al-Ṭayyib Ṣāliḥ's later works.

Mas'ūd, the grandfather's neighbour, is a man of means inherited from his father, but with the passage of time he has become impoverished due to his many marriages. Maḥjūb, in the story 'Nakhla 'alā al-Jadwal', becomes, on the other hand, impoverished due to the depredations of nature and everything entailed in progress. Mas'ūd still has land, while Maḥjūb only has his date palm. Both are central characters and the author, by means of riveting descriptions, wants the reader to identify with their wretched financial plight and to sympathize with them. Still, the narrator identifies more with Mas'ūd than with his grandfather. The narrator conveys to the reader Mas'ūd's manifold emotions and his sensitivity, similar to those of Maḥjūb. As conveyed by the narrator in our story: 'I heard him make a noise in his throat like the rasping of a lamb being slaughtered' (p. 25), he describes the scene in which his neighbour Mas'ūd's crop is being sold to his creditors. Mas'ūd means 'happy', but paradoxically his situation is anything but that. It reminds us of Muṣṭafā's surname (*Mawsim al-Hijra ilā al-Shamāl*) which in Chapter Two is Sa'īd, or ‘happy’, and which in his case, too, is decidedly not the quality that would characterize him.

Additional characters that play secondary roles in this story are Ḥusayn the merchant and the two strangers. Their roles are negative and they are mentioned only in one context: collecting Mas‘ūd’s debt. As in ‘Nakhla ‘alā al-Jadwal’, in this story, too, the author depicts merchants and moneylenders in the most negative light. The fact that the two other merchants are nameless strangers further emphasizes the reader’s inability to identify with them, and their role in the author’s socio-economic message is transparent.

- In the third story, ‘Risāla ilā Aylīn’, the author employs two major characters, the narrator and Aileen, and also marginal characters who are members of the narrator’s family whose names we do not know. This is the first text in which a Western character participates in the plot, and thus Aileen is the first in a series of Western women who will continue to appear in the author’s later works. Aileen, a young Scotswoman from Aberdeen, is fully aware of the difficulties and differences existing between her and the Eastern narrator. Nevertheless they marry after knowing one another for a year, and he returns to his village for a visit. The character of Aileen is portrayed positively, which is quite uncommon in modern Arabic literatures, especially in the fiction defined as East-West (see Chapter Five). Her great sensitivity and high level of awareness make her a model female character who views the ‘other’ in a human, not demonic, way. In contrast, the character of the narrator is far more complex; he has no name and this positions him as the prototype Easterner who has left his homeland for the West. The narrator, too, is well aware of the differences between him and Aileen regarding religion, origin, and colour. He tries to convince her and himself that a relationship of this kind cannot possibly lead to marriage, but after an eight-month acquaintance they indeed marry. As in others of al-Ṭayyib Ṣāliḥ’s works, the narrator is employed more as a prototype rather than as an independent character who expresses his own self. Thus he symbolizes the generation of educated Sudanese who leave their country for the West, where he feels himself a stranger. He says in the story: ‘What made you fall in love with me? I’m a strange lost wretch. In my heart I carry all the cares of my generation’. (p. 27). As we saw with Muṣṭafā Sa‘īd (*Mawsim al-Hijra ilā al-Shamāl*), the narrator’s problem is that he is a stranger not only in Europe, but also to a certain extent in his own country, the Sudan. After a year in Europe he returns to his village for a thirty-day vacation, and there the narrator character appears who has the autobiographical characteristics of the author, al-Ṭayyib Ṣāliḥ himself. Indeed, in the author's autobiography there are references to the connection between his visits, the people and village:

> ...even when I came from London to Khartoum I would fly directly to my [home] region, and sometimes within 24 hours of my departure to London, I'd be still on the sand hill [in my vision] with my old friends and contemporaries, as if nothing had happened, leaving them after my vacation was over and returning to London.[20]

The narrator's absences, like those of the author, distance him from his family despite his frequent visits to his village. He is fully aware of the changes taking place not only in himself, but also in the villagers; he knows that this time his absence has been longer than usual, and here we witness the first seeds of the tragedy, because 'They [the young women] look on me as a date palm on the bank of a river uprooted by the current and swept away far from where it grew up'. (p. 30). The feeling of distance and foreignness that surrounds him in the village is hard for him this time and he is conscious of the breach between himself and them:

> Then, all of a sudden, an idea which horrified him filled the whole of his mind. These people were his people. A huge tribe of which he was a member. But in spite of this, they were strangers to him, and he was a stranger among them. A few years back he had been a living cell in the closely knit body of the tribe. When he used to go away he left a void which stayed unfilled till he returned. When he used to come home, his father would greet him without embarrassment, and his mother would laugh her usual laugh, and the rest of his family would treat him unaffectedly as long as he was there with them. But this time his father had hugged him tight and his mother had shed tears and the rest of the family had given him an exaggerated welcome. It was this exaggeration which upset him. It was as though the warmth of their natural feeling for him had cooled and that they felt compelled to show more than they felt. (p. 31)[21]

- The story 'Dawmat Wad Ḥāmid' is in the opinion of many literary critics and readers, and the author himself, the most famous, successful, and most translated of all al-Ṭayyib Ṣāliḥ's stories. The two major characters are the old villager, the interior narrator, the young city man and the exterior narrator. They are accompanied by characters of secondary importance like the preacher and the holy man Wad Ḥāmid, and also by marginal characters like the minor government official with the big hat, seers from among the villages, and government officials. The interior narrator is an old man whose name we do not know and to whom the exterior narrator listens. This narrator can possibly be identified with the character of the grandfather who, as mentioned earlier, appears in others of al-Ṭayyib Ṣāliḥ's works. In his wisdom the old man understands that there is no possibility of sealing the village off from modernization, and he supports a compromise:

> What all these people [the government officials] have overlooked is that there's plenty of room for all these things: the doum tree, the tomb, the water-pump, and the steamer's stopping-place. (p. 52).

The compromise, according to the old narrator, is also joined to a gradual movement towards modernization and he suggests that there be no coercion or hasty acceptance of it by the villagers. Thus, for example, his son ran away to the city to study, but only when his son's son completes his studies will there be room enough for everyone. Compromise as understood by the old man, like the entire story, is conveyed ironically, and thus the sting is drawn from the difficult and painful problem facing not only this specific Sudanese village, but also the entire Arab world.[22]

In this story the interior narrator's credibility seems problematic. It is puzzling that the author has chosen the character of an old man to convey messages of compromise and acceptance of the new, for it is generally the older generation that expresses opposition to innovation. Possibly, however, the author chose an old, wise, and experienced man to prove that there is no escaping acceptance of the new, underscoring as well the astuteness of compromise. This character knows everything that happens in the village and the city; between the authorities and the citizens; and he seems to accomplish all this without being an educated man who is nonetheless au courant with the complexities of what is currently happening in the Sudan. In other words, the old narrator's credibility is unconvincing. It is safer to assume that the words were attributed to him by the author, and furthermore, although the old narrator holds a dialogue, as it were, with his young listener, he is in fact the only speaker and through him we see the events unfolding in the story. The exterior narrator's role is that of listener as it exists in modern world literatures and classical literatures, like in *Alf Layla wa-Layla*, for example.

In contrast to the description of the old narrator's life, the details the author provides about the young listener are minimal. He comes from the city and hears the old man's story. He plays a double role of listener, but interior listener, while at the same time he functions as an exterior narrator. He is employed as the connecting link between the old man and his story and the reader and the outside world. Broadly speaking there is a division between the old narrator's world, which symbolizes the world of the villagers, and that of the young listener representing the world of the educated, the urbanites, those who are alien to the village. In the course of the old man's story, the young listener interrupts only twice with two questions at the end of the story. But these two questions are extremely important and constitute the essence of the conflict between the old and new in this story. The young listener's role is that of a stranger: he came to the village for only a short time; he listens to the old narrator's story, asks two questions, and then we listen to the message of the old narrator: 'Tomorrow, without doubt, you will be leaving us. When you arrive at your destination, think well of us and judge us not too harshly'. (p. 52).

The secondary characters in the story are mainly government officials who are portrayed in a negative light. They are described by the old narrator as people whose only interest is their personal benefit. Their representatives in the village are both unaware of, and are insensitive to the difficulties bound up in the changes that progress entails. The narrator moveover does not differentiate between the representatives of the pre-independence Sudanese governments, and those who have come after independence. The author criticizes them and in numerous instances employs irony and ridicule, just as he does with the villagers.[23] One of the techniques used to ridicule the government representatives is to describe their outward appearance, as for example, in the case of the new official: 'We awoke one day to find an official with an enormous hat and a small head' (p. 48). Al-Ṭayyib Ṣāliḥ embraces here the tradition of other Arab writers who use unflattering descriptions to ridicule disliked characters, especially religious leaders. There is the character of the preacher, a government appointee, who is also depicted negatively and is poles apart from the popular cleric. But clerical characters in al-Ṭayyib Ṣāliḥ's works are also often negative, as tends to be the case generally in modern Arabic literatures.[24]

Wad Ḥāmid is a secondary, but nonetheless important character. A righteous man after whom the tree, the village and the story are named, he is the antithesis of the character of the preacher and of other official clerics. Together with the mythic elements that surround this character, the author takes pains to provide a realistic background of his existence. In the majority of his works, al-Ṭayyib Ṣāliḥ describes the characters of saints and holy men at length, such as Sheikh Wad Dulayib in his first story, 'Nakhla 'alā al-Jadwal', as well as in his later works, particularly *'Urs al-Zayn*, and the two *Bandar Shāh* books. Wad Ḥāmid's appearance in the story is more than a literary device: he is an integral part of the village fabric that al-Ṭayyib Ṣāliḥ seeks to convey. The doum tree that bears his name, like the village and the tomb, are employed as milestones in the village tradition, and therefore it is an integral part of the human and legendary landscape.

- 'Idhā Jā'at' contains three major characters: Sanā', Bahā' and Amīn, and in addition, the character of the plumber's apprentice. The story differs from previous ones on two counts: one, it is the first story in which there are three central and more or less equally dominant characters; two, as in 'Nakhla 'alā al-Jadwal', the narrator does not appear in the text. Sanā' is a young woman with a tawdry outward appearance that is somewhat misleading both to strangers and her partners in the travel agency. The author heaps ridicule on her superficial, hollow world, but gives her credit for being the first to want to close down after only a month the tourist agency she had opened with Bahā' and Amīn. Still, she has another side, her strong personality that allows her to choose either to study at the university or to leave the job.[25] Amīn is an educated and well-to-do young man whose world is narrow and limited, though he despises Sanā's commonness. Bahā' is an educated young man with aspirations in two directions, business and women, and he fails in both. More than Amīn, Bahā' represents a young man who seeks to impress women and whose whole world revolves around them. His world, like that of his two partners is empty, and the author ridicules him and his world of women.

The three central characters' lack of psychological depth and plausibility are the exception that proves the rule in al-Ṭayyib Ṣāliḥ's works. There is not even one village character in this text, and with this story the author begins a series of works in which the modern world holds sway. Apparently these characters are part of the array of characters employed as a preliminary sketch by the author with the objective of improving and developing them and then integrating them into the character of the educated Arab, as will be shown later.

- 'Hākadhā Yā Sādatī' is one of the stories in which the narrator predominates, aside from two secondary Western characters, the woman and the young girl, and a collection of marginal English men and women. As in the previous story, the author does not employ village characters. The plot is located in England and the narrator is an Eastern man (unstated in the story) who has come to the West. Generally speaking, the narrator resembles the narrator in 'Risāla ilā Aylīn', and his interests – women and sex – remind us, as we find in the majority of the 'Muqaddimāt' (Preludes), of the model of Muṣṭafā Sa'īd (*Mawsim al-Hijra ilā al-Shamāl*).

Foreignness is the most prominent element of the narrator's emotions. He draws a line between 'them', his British hosts, and 'me', and this alienation does not disappear as a result of his relationships with Western women. It is, however, somewhat dulled when he marries the English girl and she bears him two daughters. It is difficult to ignore the similarity between the real author, i.e., al-Ṭayyib Ṣāliḥ and this central character, just as occurs in several of the author's other works. As early as the narrator's first encounter with the girl, we find an expression of his acute sense of alienation: 'Is it because I'm a foreigner?' (p. 69).

British women are represented in this story by the woman and the young girl. The English woman has no name, she is forty, and married. These particulars do not change the fact that as far as the narrator is concerned, she is the story's most powerful sex object. On the one hand, she reminds us of the English women in *Mawsim al-Hijra ilā al-Shamāl* because of the sexuality she radiates and the struggle between her and the narrator, while on the other, she is revealed as a compassionate woman who comes to his aid when all the other Britishers attack him. She even confesses: 'Perhaps it was me who encouraged him'. (p. 82).

The young British girl, whose name is not given, opens and closes the story. Her outward appearance is unflattering, but she has a nice voice. The initial contact between her and him does not work well and causes his outburst against his hosts, but in the end she marries him. This girl provides a second model or second possibility of a Western woman, a British woman.

The story's marginal characters are all British and the narrator sees them as distinguished by their hypocrisy, their xenophobia, and by excessively praising their beautiful country. They are portrayed in a negative light, the narrator does not manage to form a real relationship with them and they arouse in him feelings of anger and hatred. As in some of al-Ṭayyib Ṣāliḥ's other works, the narrator's alienation in this story is only one part of the equation; the other is the English people's attitude towards him.

- The 'Muqaddimāt' consist of five short short stories. Regarding the characters, there is a set formula for the order of their appearance except for one story ('al-Ikhtibār') in which there are three central characters and one secondary character. Two major figures are at the centre of the stories. The two central characters in the 'Muqaddimāt' stories have several things in common: they are always young and are the Eastern man and the Western woman. The man has come to Europe in search of higher education and he is therefore better educated than the woman ('Khuṭwa li'l-Amām', 'Laka ḥattā al-Mamāt', 'al-Ikhtibār'). He is portrayed as sensitive, introverted and human ('Ughniyat Ḥubb', 'Laka ḥattā al-Mamāt', 'al-Ikhtibār'). The character of the man bears autobiographical characteristics reminiscent of the author ('Khuṭwa li'l-'Amām', 'Laka ḥattā al-Mamāt').

In the context of the 'Muqaddimāt', two facts should be noted. When published in the Lebanese journal *Ḥiwār,* the 'Muqaddimāt' included five stories, while in the Egyptian *al-Hilāl,* the story 'al-Shay' al-Ākhar' does not appear.[26] Concerning the characters, we should note that the 'al-Shay' al-Ākhar' story deviates slightly from the usual formula we find in the 'Muqaddimāt' stories, in that there are two central characters, the narrator and the sensitive Eastern protagonist, and in the background there are only echoes of the protagonist's relationship with a Western woman. We know nothing of what happened in the past directly, and as for the elements that we mentioned above, they do not exist in this story. Moreover, in contrast to the other 'Muqaddimāt' stories where the plot is set in England, here it is set in Khartoum.

The second noteworthy fact concerns the characters. These texts are sketches that al-Ṭayyib Ṣāliḥ used in his later works, particularly in the novel *Mawsim al-Hijra ilā al-Shamāl* and in the stories appears the formula contained in some of the author's short stories. Together with the characters, the events, the place, the writing technique and the subjects exist in one form or another in the author's other short stories, and especially in the novel *Mawsim al-Hijra ilā al-Shamāl.* In his short stories between 1953–62 and the novel *'Urs al-Zayn* written between 1962–4, al-Ṭayyib Ṣāliḥ developed characters with a defined objective in mind: to prepare figures in these texts for the important task of constructing central, secondary, and marginal characters for *Mawsim al-Hijra ilā al-Shamāl.*

Two Later Short Stories

Al-Ṭayyib Ṣāliḥ's two later works, published in journals and not in the collection *Dawmat Wad Ḥāmid,* are 'al-Rajul al-Qubruṣī' and 'Yawm Mubārak 'alā Shāṭi' Umm Bāb'.

- The short story 'al-Rajul al-Qubruṣī' contains two major characters: the narrator, Muḥaymīd, and the Cypriot Man. There are also secondary and marginal characters with whom we are familiar from al-Ṭayyib Ṣāliḥ's earlier works, like al-Ṭāhir Wad al-Rawwāsī, Maryam, Fāṭima bint Jabr al-Dār, 'Abd al-Ḥafīẓ, and the narrator's father. These characters function to delineate the narrator who returns to his village having suffered bereavement, where he recalls scenes linked to characters belonging to his past.

The narrator appears here for the first time as a tourist, which is certainly unusual in al-Ṭayyib Ṣāliḥ's texts. The plot shifts on two axes of time and two axes of place: in the present, the narrator comes to Cyprus to meet his childhood friend al-Ṭāhir Wad al-Rawwāsī, while in the past that is also linked to another place, he comes to the village of Wad Ḥāmid. Because of the story's obscurity, it is difficult to discuss the nature of the two central characters, but of the two it is easier to define the character of the narrator, as we have already encountered him in the author's other works. Like the author, the narrator is married, and has daughters whom he has left in Beirut, which is one of al-Ṭayyib Ṣāliḥ's favoured cities, as he himself indicates.[27] The narrator, who is distressed by the Cypriot Man's words and actions, turns to the past, to the characters and events in his village, in order to grasp at something firm and save himself, even if temporarily, from the Cypriot Man and his words. He tells the Cypriot Man that he has come to Cyprus to meet his old friend al-Ṭāhir Wad al-Rawwāsī, as, on the one hand, the latter refused to visit him in London, while on the other, the narrator failed to meet him in Beirut. The Cypriot Man tries to offer the narrator a young woman but the latter, as in other works, refuses because this was not the reason for his visit to Cyprus. In this story, as in others (*Mawsim al-Hijra ilā al-Shamāl, Bandar Shāh: Maryūd*), the narrator faces death but is saved. The Cypriot Man tells him that he has evaded death this time because he preferred to take the soul of his father (another true autobiographical fact, for the author's father died between the publication of the first and second volumes of *Bandar Shāh*). Obviously, the narrator is aware that death is an inseparable part of life and that now he is closer to death than ever. Possibly the author wants to convey through the narrator feelings of growing old and also that life is fleeting and that a human being has but his allotted time to live.

The story's other major character is the Cypriot Man. This is what the narrator calls him, we know neither his name nor his origins, for he is proud of the fact that people do not know where he comes from. In his opinion it is unimportant. He is an elderly man of seventy-five, so he says, who has made a lot of money, retired to the good life, and now all his activities are centered around women. Presumably he lost a leg in one of the wars, and yet the narrator is not at all sure of this. But the fictional sphere is the interesting one here; the way in which he relates to the narrator and the subject of death is important. Possibly he belongs to imaginary spheres, the obscure, the unclear, a minion of the Angel of Death or even the Angel of Death himself. He does not take leave of the narrator the way two strangers would, whose meeting was unplanned. He leaves with the words 'au revoir' and furthermore, he meets the narrator later, at his father's grave in Wad Ḥāmid. The narrator tells us that in deciding whether to take his soul or that of his father, he took the one that belonged to the better of the two men, his father. The Cypriot Man goads the narrator not only on the subject of women but also on the subject of death. The game of death he plays with him is slightly reminiscent of the game of death in *The Seventh Seal*, Swedish director Ingmar Bergman's famous film.[28] In any event, the Cypriot Man is connected with death and the narrator, who writes an elegy on the death of his father, thus serves the author's objective.

- 'Yawm Mubārak 'alā Shāṭi' Umm Bāb' is al-Ṭayyib Ṣāliḥ's most recently published story and is, therefore, not included in the collection *Dawmat Wad Ḥāmid*. It has three major characters: the daughter, Rabāb, and her parents, about whom we know very little. A prominent fact is that the characters, and indeed the entire plot, are surrounded by an air of obscurity and mystery.[29]

This is one of al-Ṭayyib Ṣāliḥ's texts in which a female character is at the centre of the story, or by another definition, the female voice is the most dominant presence. Although Rabāb is only nine years old, she is an extraordinary child and with her the author continues the list of extraordinary girls that appear in his works: Ni'ma (*'Urs al-Zayn*), Ḥusna (*Mawsim al-Hijra ilā al-Shamāl*), Fāṭima (*Bandar Shāh: Ḍaw al-Bayt*), and Maryam and Ḥawwā' (*Bandar Shāh: Maryūd*). But Rabāb is special, not only as the story's central and most important character, but also as a Wunderkind with supernatural powers. Her knowledge, talents, power, leadership, and her great love of religion and Muslim mysticism place her above her peers, and even above her parents. Rabāb is employed as the central axis around which the story's reconditeness revolves. The entire text is shadowy and mystic, in which the child is her parents' teacher in a kind of reverse world. Rabāb is an extremely good swimmer and feels that she is part and parcel of the water. She, like Ḍaw al-Bayt, might be the energy which al-Ṭayyib Ṣāliḥ mentioned very often, and that Ḍaw al-Bayt symbolized when he made his appearance from the water, after Muṣṭafā Sa'īd disappeared.

The character of the father is central, but he too is obscure, and we do not know his name, his life story, or his origins; he and his wife are employed to reveal the character of Rabāb. We know that he married Umm Rabāb when he was fifty, and this is the only identifying detail, for we do not know where he lives and what his occupation is. He has no other relatives and like the author, he is well versed in classical Arabic literature. As in others of al-Ṭayyib Ṣāliḥ's works, he is no stranger to love of the sea or the Nile, and familiarity with death and the game played with it (*Mawsim al-Hijra ilā al-Shamāl, Bandar Shāh: Maryūd*).

The mother has a minor role in this story. She married her husband when she was forty. In contrast to her husband who has no relatives, she has a mother, an older brother, and a sister. But we are not told whether or not she has a father, but we are given to understand that she has no father and that the narrator has neither parent. She is happy with her husband and daughter, yet it seems she is outside her daughter's world, a world in which, however, her husband has a place. This character, in short, is overshadowed by her daughter and to a lesser degree by her husband.

'Urs al-Zayn

The characters in the novel *'Urs al-Zayn* have a status, role, and function quite different from those of others in al-Ṭayyib Ṣāliḥ's works, particularly in his novels. There are three main differences between *'Urs al-Zayn* and other texts, a major one (especially the novel *Mawsim al-Hijra ilā al-Shamāl*) being that it does not contain any active Western characters. Thus the place of *'Urs al-Zayn* is with the author's other village works that preceded it, such as 'Nakhla 'alā al-Jadwal', 'Ḥafnat Tamr', and 'Dawmat Wad Ḥāmid'. A second difference is the absence of the narrator, whom we have encountered in earlier stories like 'Ḥafnat Tamr' and the later novels. The third difference is that there is only one major character (al-Zayn) in this novel and not several, but there are some important secondary characters, like Ni'ma and Maḥjūb. The novel contains a large number of marginal characters, such as the *'umda* (village headman) and the *imām*, and the role played by some of these is to highlight certain facets of the character of al-Zayn, while the status of others is different and their role in the novel is not obvious.[30]

The Major Character

The character of al-Zayn is the axis around which the entire plot and the function of the majority of the other characters revolves and who are inextricably linked to al-Zayn.[31] The name itself is quite common in the Sudan and is an abbreviation of 'Zayn al-Dīn' (the beauty of religion). Al-Zayn can be a personal noun of 'the good' or 'the handsome', but as he is neither good looking nor splendid, in addition to his love of life and his fellow men, the 'good' meaning is more appropriate here. Al-Ṭayyib Ṣāliḥ lavishly praises his qualities, saying:

> al-Zayn is a character who is all heart and love. He gives without demanding… he is a generous giver and the village comes together around him. He is the factor around which

> all the opposing forces in the village are brought together in 'Urs al-Zayn, with no effort on his part, but simply because he is full of a love that embraces the entire village.[32]

People like al-Zayn can in fact be found throughout the Arab world and not only in numerous villages in north-western Sudan, where the novel's action takes place. More than that, it seems that such an extraordinary, different, and charming character may exist in any rural society. This character, from the day of his birth to the day he dies, experiences various events that place him at the centre of the society in which he functions. To some extent al-Zayn symbolizes 'the village idiot', or fills the role of court jester, something for which parallels occur in modern Arabic literatures as well as in world literature.[33]

Al-Zayn is a complex character and his power is not always revealed to the reader. However, if we examine the character in accordance with two circles, this figure will become clearer. The first circle consists of al-Zayn's childhood, his youth, and his family. In the second circle I will discuss the entire gamut of his relationships with the village and its inhabitants.

The first circle: his childhood, youth and family – Al-Zayn's childhood is notable for two elements that set him apart from other village children. First, he was different from the others, and in the author's words:

> At first, as is well known, children meet life with screams With Zein however, it is recounted – and the authorities for this are his mother and the women who attended his birth – that no sooner did he come into this world than he burst out laughing. And so it was throughout his life. (p. 11).

The second element is connected with the myths and mystery that surrounded his birth. With his mother's help, the author recounts events linked with al-Zayn's birth that had implications for his life. Thus, for example, the author gives the following reasons for al-Zayn having only two teeth:

> His mother, though, says that his mouth was once filled with pearly white teeth, but that when he was six she took him one day to visit some relatives of hers; at sunset, passing by a deserted ruin rumoured to be haunted, Zein had suddenly become nailed to the ground and had begun shivering as with a fever. Then he let out a scream. After that he took to his bed for several days, and on recovering from his illness it was found that all his teeth had fallen out – except for one in his upper jaw and one in the lower. (ibid.)

It should be noted here that both Muṣṭafā (*Mawsim al-Hijra ilā al-Shamāl*) and al-Zayn are connected, albeit in different ways, to their mothers, for neither has a father, and to this the author assigns considerable importance. Apart from other characteristics, it is a justification for their being different from the society that surrounds them and this difference enables them to rebel against social norms[34]

Aside from this, the author does not provide many particulars about al-Zayn's family, childhood, and education, and this leaves his character somehow opaque. Although one might have expected that a novel's major protagonist should be painted in detail, it must be assumed that the author intentionally omitted details about his family.

The second circle: his relationships with the village and its inhabitants – Al-Zayn's relationships with the villagers do not belong to a single category, but move in different and contradictory circles and worlds connected with him.[35] There are four categories: his relationships with men; with 'the strange people'; with the village women; and with Ni'ma.

His relationships with the village men – Al-Zayn has good relationships with the villagers in general and with his peers in particular. Maḥjūb is his best friend. His relationships with mature and old men are derived from his exploits. He has a gang of eight young men with whom he spends much of his time and to whom he recounts his adventures. The village is divided into camps and groups,[36] and al-Zayn may be said to be a camp unto himself, even though he spends most of his time with Maḥjūb's gang. In contrast to Maḥjūb, the village *imām* is the man with whom he does not have a good relationship, and the author describes the *imām*'s as a man who symbolizes official religion, who lacks the qualities that characterize al-Ḥanīn and al-Zayn: sanctity, blessings, mysticism, and a love of life.[37]

His relationships with 'the strange people' (*shawādhdh*) – Every society, including rural society, has a person or persons who are abnormal, who are different and who are frequently ridiculed by the rest of the villagers, especially children. In al-Zayn's village there is a number of strange people and his attitude towards them is not one of ridicule, and it is with them that he joins up. This group consists of four characters: al-Ḥanīn, Deaf 'Ashmāna, Mūsā the Lame, and Bakhīt the Cripple; al-Zayn treats them with great love, and none more than al-Ḥanīn. Against the background of al-Zayn's womanizing this relationship is interesting, for he is known as one brimming with joie de vivre, who enjoys the pleasures of life. This, however, is only one side of al-Zayn; the other is his relationship with al-Ḥanīn, whom he views as the supreme spiritual and religious authority. These relationships, when added to his mother's stories about al-Zayn, endow him with an aura of holiness, strangeness, mystery and Sufism.[38]

His relationships with the village women – Al-Zayn's relationships with the village women became legendary. He had three great loves that drew special attention in the village: his love for 'Izza, the *'umda*'s daughter, for Ḥalīma the Bedouin girl, and for 'Alawiyya, his friend Maḥjūb's daughter. But al-Zayn's loves were always one-sided; the girls' parents exploited him for hard work and then married their daughters to others. Al-Zayn's loves, the villagers noted, were always with girls at the height of their flowering and beauty. The village women therefore saw him as a kind of talisman who was endowed with the scent of love and they hoped he would bring good luck and blessings to their daughters. But while the women viewed him as the emissary of blessings, the author ridicules him:

> And then would begin another romance and from each romance Zein would emerge unscathed and, to all appearances, unchanged: his laugh unaltered, his tomfoolery in no wise lessened, and his legs were never weary of bearing his body to the outlying parts of the village. (p. 23).

Al-Zayn's relationship with Ni'ma – Al-Zayn's relationship with Ni'ma, and above all their wedding, is the plot's central axis. The news of al-Zayn's wedding is employed both as the novel's exposition and ending. The news that creates an uproar in the village constitutes an attraction and new opening points for the many and varied parts of the book. At first we do not know whom al-Zayn is marrying, and even whether the news is credible, but the picture slowly becomes clear and the reader is made aware of the amazing fact that not only is this wedding about to take place, it has been preordained.

Al-Zayn's relationship with Ni'ma is different from those he had with other girls, including his three big romances. Their relationship is mysterious, allusive, whispered, and it is difficult for the reader – at least at first – to accept that any kind of relationship exists between the two. The relationship takes place in seven stages: first, information is conveyed to us, the readers, about the relationship through the involvement of the author who emphasizes the ending of al-Zayn's romances and his standing among the village women thus:

> Yet with all this, there was one girl in the district about whom Zein did not speak and with whom he never played the fool. She was a girl who would observe him from afar with beautiful, sullen eyes and whenever he saw her approaching he would fall silent and leave off his raillery and buffoonery. If he spotted her from far off he would flee from her presence, leaving the road to her. (p. 24).

In the second stage the author brings Ni'ma and al-Zayn together, giving Ni'ma center stage:

> And all the while there was a young girl in the community, of sweet dignified countenance and flashing eyes, who watched Zein at his horse-play and raillery. One day, finding him amidst a group of women, joking with them in his usual way, she rebuked him with the words, 'Why don't you give up this nonsensical chatter and go off and get on with your work?' And she glared at the women with her beautiful eyes. Zein stopped laughing and lowered his head in shame. He then slunk out from among the women and went his way. (p. 28).

In the above, we are made aware of the relationship between Ni'ma and al-Zayn and furthermore, as Ni'ma had numerous suitors, their families could not understand how Ni'ma was about to marry 'this boorish dolt of a man'. (p. 31).

In the third stage, the author intervenes and conveys Ni'ma's thoughts about marrying al-Zayn, since she sees the marriage as the hand of fate:

> He could, again, be Zein, and when Zein came to Ni'ma's mind, she experienced a sensation of warmth in her heart, of the kind a mother feels for her children. Intermingled with it was another feeling: of pity. She would see Zein as being an orphan in need of being cared for. In any case he was her cousin, and there was nothing unusual in the fact that she should feel concern for him. (p. 39).

In the fourth stage, when the completely hysterical villagers gather round al-Zayn, who has been wounded in an affray, the extraordinary character of Ni'ma stands out:

> Ni'ma stood looking on from afar, silent, her eyes fixed on Zein's face, the sullenness in them having been replaced by a great tenderness. (p. 43).

In the fifth stage al-Ḥanīn, the pious, mystical, righteous man of the village, prophesies on more than one occasion that al-Zayn will indeed marry Ni'ma: 'Tomorrow he'll be marrying the best girl in the village'. (pp. 48–9, 67).

In the sixth stage al-Zayn tells his friends that it was Ni'ma who had come to his house and asked him to marry her. This is, of course, a deviation from accepted village norms here, and it is evident that this is not the first time that al-Ṭayyib Ṣāliḥ turns the exception into the rule. He does so, for example, in the novel *Mawsim al-Hijra ilā al-Shamāl* when Ḥusna, Muṣṭafā Sa'īd's widow, refuses to marry Wad al-Rayyis because she wants to marry the narrator. The narrator's stunned mother berates him thus:

> 'Why did you leave your work and come?' my mother said to me.
> 'The two boys.' I said to her.
> She looked at me searchingly for a while and said: 'The boys or the boys' mother? What was there between you and her? She came to your father and her very words to him were: "Tell him to marry me!" What an impudent hussy! That's modern women for you! That was bad enough, but the terrible thing she did later was even worse.'[39]

In the seventh and final stage, Ḥājj Ibrāhīm announces al-Zayn's marriage to Ni'ma, and the villagers and many guests from outside the village attend the celebration. The marriage, which comes in the wake of the rumors of it actually taking place, finally dashes the hopes of Ni'ma's many suitors. The author has to provide good reasons for this strange marriage and in so doing he cleverly uses the technique of mixing reality and fantasy, while immersing reality in mystery to such a degree that there is no one clear and authoritative version. As we shall see later, he does the same thing in *Bandar Shāh*. In the present case he gives five different versions in which truth and reality are intermingled, these versions are supplied by the fictitious characters in the novel (Ḥalīma the milk seller, al-Ṭarīfī, 'Abd al-Ṣamad, and al-Zayn), including the author, who intervenes and states that it was indeed Ni`ma who initiated the marriage.[40]

Secondary Characters

Al-Ṭayyib Ṣāliḥ fills the novel with a number of secondary and marginal characters who appear in other works (see Chapter Four), the most important being Ni'ma and al-Ḥanīn. The character of Ni'ma, I suggest, is more archetypal than individual and it embodies a greater degree of idealization than realism. Possibly, therefore, al-Ṭayyib

Ṣāliḥ emphatically delineates her strangeness by portraying her as an extraordinary young woman in order to justify the way in which she exists in the text. In fact, whenever the author describes her she is revealed as a young girl who is different from her peers and who is unique. These extraordinary qualities are apparent at her birth and by receiving an education, which is completely uncharacteristic of Sudanese village girls of the time. Ni'ma grew up in a family in which all her siblings were boys. As a young woman of extraordinary strength of character she was ardently pursued by many whom she turned down and vehemently asserted her desire to marry only al-Zayn, the other extraordinary figure in her village:

> When she was sixteen, her mother began talking about the young men who would make suitable husbands: the rich, the educated, the handsome, and those whose mother and father would be suitable as 'in-laws'. But Ni'ma would shrug her shoulders and say nothing. And when Amna had come to talk to Saadiyya about Ni'ma marrying Ahmed and Saadiyya had said to her, 'The decision lies with the girl's father', she had known in her heart of hearts that it lay with no one but Ni'ma herself. She had had to be informed, at which she had shrugged her shoulders and said, 'I'm not ready to marry yet', and it was senseless to argue with her – especially as Saadiyya was not keen on becoming related to Amna's family.
>
> Not long after that another suitor made his appearance: Idris. Many girls in the village would have been only too happy to be his wife, for he was an educated man, worked as a teacher at an Intermediate School, was of a gentle disposition and well respected locally. Though he was not from one of the well-connected and prominent families in the village, his father had nevertheless made a place for himself through his diligence and good neighbourliness. It was a good, comfortably-off family. Hajj Ibrahim, Ni'ma's father, her mother Saadiyya, and her three brothers, were for accepting Idris. Ni'ma, however, was of another opinion. 'He's not for me,' she said with shrug of her shoulders [...] 'He could, again, be Zein.' [41]

Aside from Ni'ma, the other important secondary character is al-Ḥanīn who is symbolic of the Sufi adherent to whom the villagers ascribe miraculous deeds. This Sufi character, who wanders from place to place, exists in village societies throughout the Arab world, including the Sudan:

> Sheikh al-Ḥanīn is a very common character in Sudanese society to this day for the Sufi men in it – especially in the more remote villages and among the desert dwellers – meet

> preordained death face to face, and it [the society] still believes in their wondrous deeds and their miracles still hold sway over the intelligence of many of them.[42]

As pointed out, al-Ḥanīn is counted among the group of uncommon figures known as *shawādhdh,* and he is the most prominent of them all. Yet he is different from the others in that he is thought of as a saint, together with some other strange characteristics, or as the villagers see it:

> No one knew where he went, though people related strange stories concerning him, one swearing that he had seen him in Merowi at a particular time, while another swore he'd caught sight of him in Karma at that very same time, though a distance of six days' journey separates the two places. People stated that Haneen would meet up with a group of those itinerant holy men who wander about devoting themselves to the service of God. Haneen seldom talked to any of the villagers, and if asked where he went for six months of the year would make no reply. No one knew what he ate or drank, for he carried no provisions on his long journeys. (p. 25).

The relationship between al-Ḥanīn and al-Zayn is unique. They are linked by bonds of love and in their extremely close relationship they refer to one another as *al-Mabrūk* (the blessed one). Their relationship appears to be ordained by fate. Another common facet of their relationship is their identical attitude towards the village *imām.* The author places al- Ḥanīn in direct confrontation with the *imām*, thus bringing to the reader's attention his clear preference for the *Ṣūfī* al-Ḥanīn over the *imām*, who represents the government and official religion. Thus al-Ṭayyib Ṣāliḥ continues the tradition laid down by earlier Arab writers who stipulated a confrontation between members of the *Ṣūfī* sect, and the religious establishment. Also their affection for *Ṣūfī* sheikhs is in this case obvious, although the criticism levelled at them remains unchanged. A notable example of this approach is the Egyptian author Ṭāhā Ḥusayn.[43]

Mawsim al-Hijra ilā al-Shamāl

The novel *Mawsim al-Hijra ilā al-Shamāl* abounds with major, secondary and marginal characters. Al-Ṭayyib Ṣāliḥ chose characters representative of various levels of Sudanese and English society, with some of these decidedly more archetypal than individual. But as a rule the author succeeded in enlivening and animating them. Regarding the Sudanese characters, the leading ones, Muṣṭafā Sa'īd and the narrator, respectively symbolize different generations of educated local figures. In the Sudanese village, Maḥjūb is symbolic of the young villagers, while Ḥājj Aḥmad represents the old traditional Sudanese; Bint Majdhūb – the old woman of the village – is fully conversant with the village's comings and goings. The author's Western characters represent different classes in English society, such as the four leading women figures who had relationships with Muṣṭafā Sa'īd and met with death. Balance is a salient element in positioning and shaping the characters, in particular the English ones; thus, for example, the author's dislike of Jean Morris is counterbalanced by a positive description of the Robinson couple. A similar principle is employed regarding the Eastern characters. Thus, for example, the author's deep affection for the grandfather, Ḥājj Aḥmad, is opposed to his dislike of Wad al-Rayyis, and is expressed both explicitly and implicitly.

The Major Characters

The author weaves the main and secondary plots around two major characters in this novel. The leading characters, the narrator and Muṣṭafā Sa'īd, can be viewed from two different perspectives: according to the first, the narrator is seen as containing two diametrically opposed, yet at times parallel, forces. One, demonic and dark, represents Muṣṭafā Sa'īd. He is the first Eastern character in the novel to encounter Europe and symbolizes the 'first alternative'. This encounter was based on an unhealthy and superficial relationship between both parties and ultimately led to killing and death. The other force is the narrator who symbolizes the 'second alternative', i.e., the second-generation educated class of Sudanese who left for the West and returned home. Their encounter with the West, which did not end in death, showed them both the negative and positive sides of English society.[44] Another way is to view the narrator and Muṣṭafā as two separate characters whose paths cross; they bear similar identification marks that are at times even identical. It is, however, precisely against the background of their similar intersecting traits that the great difference between them is underscored, as we shall see later.

The narrator – I share the author's opinion and that of most literary critics who believe that Muṣṭafā Sa'īd and not the narrator is the major character.[45] Nonetheless, the narrator is the most important character in the novel, more complex and less unidimensional, and his development serves as the primary axis in the development of the main plot. The first prominent fact relating to him is that we do not know his name. The author followed in the footsteps of earlier Arab writers who preferred not to name their heroes (*al-Ḥayy al-Lātīnī*). We should bear in mind that in this novel the narrator is the same as the one who appeared in both earlier novels and later works. In earlier works ('Ḥafnat Tamr', 'Risāla ilā Aylīn') the author preferred not to name the narrator, but in later works, such as *Bandar Shāh: Ḍaw al-Bayt* and *Maryūd*, he has a name for reasons we shall discuss later in this chapter. The narrator is a villager who went West, acquired an education, wrote a doctoral dissertation on literature, returned to live in his village, married a local woman and worked in the city. The narrator's life revolves around three main circles: the personal one – his life, education and work; the social one – his relationship with the village and its inhabitants; and the inner one – his relationship with Muṣṭafā Sa'īd.

The personal circle – his life, education and work – The author provides limited information, at least at the beginning, about the narrator and his personal life. The narrator serves the author by relating what is happening to him and Muṣṭafā Sa'īd. Clearly the first person narrative is subjective for the purpose of establishing the reader's identification with the narrator. By doing so, there may be a possible influence of other writers on al-Ṭayyib Ṣāliḥ, for example Camus in *The Outsider* (see Chapter One) or Conrad in *Heart of Darkness* (see Chapter Four). The narrator appears at the point of his return and not at his point of departure, when he returns to his village after a seven-year absence during which he studied in Europe[46]. His ambivalent attitude towards Western culture is expressed as early as the exposition: 'I learnt much and much passed me by – but that's another story'. (p. 5). In comparison with his cold attitude towards chilly Europe, his attitude towards his family is very warm. The villagers are overwhelmed by the fact that he acquired an education and was awarded a doctorate. But studying literature does not contribute much to the village, and it is Muṣṭafā Sa'īd, and not the author, who voices this sentiment: 'The man [Muṣṭafā] laughed unashamedly and said: "We have no need of poetry here. It would have been better if you'd studied agriculture, engineering or medicine."' (p. 13). The narrator, too, considers the subject and thinks to himself: 'True, I studied poetry, but that means nothing. I could equally well have studied engineering, agriculture, or medicine; they are all means to earning a living'. (p. 50). Obviously, acquiring an education is of extreme importance, as al-Ṭayyib Ṣāliḥ, however, says in an interview with Talḥat Jibrīl:

> Despite my literary bent I enrolled in the faculty of science – as I have mentioned earlier – because at the time our Sudanese society was in need of people who would take upon themselves to solve the country's problems, problems related to growth, development and building. People could understand why you would become a physician, engineer,

veterinarian, agriculturist or scientist, but a writer – that was incomprehensible; even the Fakiyy [= *Faqīh*], the village school-master, despite his importance, had no defined social status, after all, he was not like an agriculturist.[47]

The narrator's expertise is literature: '...and [he] had returned to teach pre-Islamic literature in secondary schools before being promoted to an Inspector of Primary Education'. (p. 61).[48] Indeed, he is aware that he is becoming an official: '"Civil servants like me can't change anything," I said to him...' (p. 123). The villagers, in contrast to the narrator, see the advantages and disadvantages of officialdom. On the one hand they appreciate official work, as Maḥjūb tells him: 'You have become a senior civil servant...' (p. 61), while on the other, education, as we will see later, is a barrier between the narrator and the villagers.

The social circle – the narrator's attitude to the village and its inhabitants – In contrast to his ambivalent attitude to the Western world, the narrator expresses his profound regard for the village and its inhabitants. It is clear to him that his place is in the village, even at distressful times when he is confronted with Maḥjūb and Wad al-Rayyis, he thinks positively about his place in the village. Not only did his seven-year absence from the village not detract from his love for the villagers, but on the contrary, it was intensified: 'The important thing is that I returned with a great yearning for my people in that small village at the bend of the Nile. For seven years I had longed for them, had dreamed of them...' (p. 5). The narrator is, however, aware that his prolonged absence has affected their relationship: '...something rather like fog rose up between them and me the first instant I saw them'. (p. 5). This barrier disappears when the narrator returns from Khartoum, after a seven-month absence: 'This time no fog stood between me and them' (p. 67). I might point out that the narrator in 'Risāla ilā Aylīn' undergoes a reverse process; in the beginning his frequent visits to the village do not create a barrier between him and his family, nor do they alienate him from them, but later, when his visits become increasingly infrequent, a wall rises between them.[49]

The narrator reacquaints himself with the village through his numerous wanderings in its physical surroundings, for he understands that his ties with the village are the source of the stability, roots and continuity of his life. Despite his long separation from the village he is aware that his years in the West have not distorted his soul, as it did Muṣṭafā Sa'īd's. He strives, therefore, to find an inner equilibrium in his relationship with the village, the city of Khartoum and England. It is quite obvious that his attitude is extremely complex:

> I am from here – Is this not reality enough? I too had lived with them [the English]. But I had lived with them superficially, neither loving nor hating them. I used to treasure within me the image of this little village, seeing it wherever I went with the eye of my imagination. Sometimes during the summer months in London, after a downpour of rain, I would breathe in the smell of it, and at odd fleeting moments before sunset I would see it. At the latter end of the night the foreign voices would reach my ears as though they were those of my people out here. I must be one of those birds that exist only in one region of the world [...] I would imagine the faces over there as being brown or black so that they would look like the faces of people I knew. Over there is like here, neither better nor worse. But I am from here, just as the date palm standing in the courtyard of our house has grown in our house and not in anyone else's. The fact that they came to our land, I know not why [...] Sooner or later they will leave our country, just as many people throughout history left many countries. (pp. 52–3).

The inner circle – the narrator's attitude toward Muṣṭafā – The relationship between Muṣṭafā Sa'īd, in both his life and death, and the narrator is complex, intricate and interesting. It is no wonder, therefore, that al-Ṭayyib Ṣāliḥ himself, who testifies that at that time he was influenced by Freud, is like many other literary critics, aware of the psychological aspects which exist in this context[50]. The relationship between the narrator and Muṣṭafā Sa'īd is symbiotic. The narrator is another, different, alternative, which the author has created in the image of the young educated Sudanese who encounters English society. In complete antithesis to Muṣṭafā, he was not fashioned as a monstrous legendary character, but he is mostly in a state of confrontation with Muṣṭafā Sa'īd throughout the novel. It is a confrontation between two worlds, between two different *Weltanschauungen*, that at times intersect and even run parallel to one another. Muṣṭafā Sa'īd's life and death are part of the narrator's life, whether he wants them to be or not. Only at the end of the novel does he reach the conclusion that he wants to part ways with Muṣṭafā, but even then a question lingers in light of the last sentence that contains something 'Muṣṭafā-like'. Therefore, in some ways their personalities may be considered as complementary opposites rather than binary oppositions.

The narrator is attracted to Muṣṭafā Sa'īd from the outset; he finds excuses by declaring that this character, so alien to him, makes him wonder: 'I do not know what exactly aroused my curiosity but I remembered that the day of my arrival he was silent'. (pp. 6–7). 'I do not know what it was that brought Mustafa to mind but suddenly I remembered him…' (p. 10). 'I was silent for a while as numerous questions crowded into my head: Where was he from? Why had he settled in this village? What was he about?' (p. 13). 'I feared that the man [Muṣṭafā] would slip away before I had found out anything about him – my curiosity reached such a pitch…' (p. 14). But Muṣṭafā Sa'īd does not run away; on the contrary, he relates his life story to him. The narrator as the author's mediator, tries to create for the reader a mysterious atmosphere which surrounds Muṣṭafā Sa'īd. The problem is that only the narrator, not the villagers, is aware of this air of mystery. Few realize that Muṣṭafā has other sides, of which the narrator, Ḥusna, and to a certain extent Maḥjūb, are unaware. The rest of the villagers have no part in the narrator's act. They are simply not part of the drama that takes place between the narrator and Muṣṭafā Sa'īd. This confrontation, of which they are unaware, leads the narrator to a sense of unreality and illusion: 'All of a sudden there came to me the ghastly, nightmarish feeling that we – the men grouped together in that room – were not a reality but merely some illusion'. (p. 18). This horrendous feeling of unreality and uncertainty in terms of existence and reality leads to a confrontation between the narrator and Muṣṭafā, and is climaxed by a shout. But no one hears him, not even his close friend Maḥjūb. This is the turning point at which Muṣṭafā decides to relate his story to the narrator. From the moment Muṣṭafā enters the narrator's world and reveals his secret to him, the latter's world changes. Latent forces begin to emerge, similar to those that emerged in the Western characters who came in contact with Muṣṭafā Sa'īd, including his wife Ḥusna. The narrator's dark sides become apparent and he will never be the same person he was prior to meeting Muṣṭafā and hearing his life story. Not by accident did the author choose the night as the appropriate time to tell the story to the narrator. The exterior world corresponded to the interior one:

> As for me […] and with darkness all around us outside as though satanic forces were combining to strangle the lamplight. Occasionally the disturbing thought occurs to me that Mustafa Sa'eed never happened, that he was in fact a lie, a phantom, a dream or a nightmare that had come to the people of that village one suffocatingly dark night, and when they opened their eyes to the sunlight he was nowhere to be seen. (p. 50).

The narrator listens to Muṣṭafā's story throughout the night and, symbolically, only at dawn's approach does he leave Muṣṭafā's home. For the narrator these elements of darkness and blackness disappear since he prefers to see the optimistic side of life. The effect of Muṣṭafā's life story on the narrator was so great that even the village, the epitome of stability, traditional background and continuity, seems to him thereafter suspended between heaven and earth. But the sense of instability and unreality fade away and:

> Suddenly I felt my spirits being reinvigorated as sometimes happens after a long period of depression: my brain cleared and *the black thoughts stirred up by the story of Mustafa Sa'eed were dispersed.* Now the village was not suspended between sky and earth but was stable: the houses were houses, the trees trees, and the sky was clear and far away. (p. 52, my emphasis, A.E-B.)

As mentioned earlier, Muṣṭafā Sa'īd's character has had a greater impact on the narrator after he relates his life story to him, as if the germ has been passed on to him and the narrator realizes that though Muṣṭafā has died he will not be able to escape him:

> Mustafa Sa'eed died two years ago, but I still continue to meet up with him from time to time. I lived for twenty-five years without having heard of him or seen him; then, all of a sudden, I find him in a place where the likes of him are not usually encountered. *Thus Mustafa Sa'eed has, against my will, become a part of my world, a thought in my brain, a phantom that does not want to take itself off.* (pp. 53–4, my emphasis, A.E-B.).

The narrator's crisis stems from his awareness that despite Muṣṭafā's death he will remain part of his being.[51] Moreover, he was chosen by Muṣṭafā to continue the struggle of the new Arab intellectual and his confrontation with modernization, as exemplified by Western culture. Therefore, it would seem that Muṣṭafā handed on the torch to the narrator. But the problem is that Muṣṭafā did not, or maybe more precisely could not, bequeath to the narrator the new dress, the new weapon or the new keys for the challenges of the encounter with the new world. This can be seen, for example, when he is travelling by train from Khartoum and meets a retired civil servant who had studied with Muṣṭafā (pp. 67–8). A month later the narrator is staying in Khartoum, and Muṣṭafā's figure once more rises like a spectre in the narrator's conversations with a group of people, which includes, *inter alia*, a Sudanese lecturer named Manṣūr, who had studied with the narrator in England (pp. 58–60). These meetings with Muṣṭafā, or more precisely, with Muṣṭafā Sa'īd's spirit or heritage, cause the narrator to look into his inner self. He embarks on a vicious circle: on the one hand, he meets Muṣṭafā's spirit outside his village, as well as inside it. On the other, the narrator understands clearly that if he wants to cease meeting Muṣṭafā's ghost, *he has to cope not only with Muṣṭafā Sa'īd but first and foremost with himself.* The problem is that the narrator has been appointed as the legal guardian of Muṣṭafā's wife and children and was given the key to his room in the village. Now the narrator's ambivalence towards Muṣṭafā Sa'īd is transferred to Muṣṭafā's widow, Ḥusna. He is aware that he is physically attracted to her and is in fact in love with her, but at the same time he is afraid of her. He tries to avoid Ḥusna and stays away from the village, spending as much time in Khartoum as he can. But when Ḥusna murders Wad al-Rayyis and takes her own life, he is forced to return to cope with death, his heritage and the inevitable inner confrontation. Therefore, when his good friend Maḥjūb calls Ḥusna 'mad', the narrator turns against him in anger and nearly kills him: 'The world has turned suddenly upside down. Love? Love does not do this. This is hatred. I feel hatred and seek revenge; *my adversary is within and I needs must confront him'*. (p. 135, my emphasis, A.E-B.)

The narrator is aware of having reached a stage in his life when he must take decisions and choose a way of life. He regards the dead Muṣṭafā as a rival and an object of revenge. He is afraid that he is Muṣṭafā's disciple. The narrator is horrified by the very thought that Muṣṭafā surpasses him, since, after all, he was the one who chose his end. He realizes that he can no longer avoid confronting his own self. He goes to Muṣṭafā's room to 'meet him', but actually in order to meet himself:

> The light exploded on my eyes and out of the darkness there emerged a frowning face with pursed lips that I knew but could not place. I moved towards it with hate in my heart. It was my adversary Mustafa Sa'eed. The face grew a neck, the neck two shoulders and a chest, then a trunk and two legs, and I found myself standing face to face with myself. *This is not Mustafa Sa'eed – it's a picture of me frowning at my face from a mirror.* (p. 136, my emphasis, A.E-B.).

This passage constitutes a climax among others, when the narrator contends with Muṣṭafā and with himself. The author applies an interesting psychological technique, having the narrator's character split into two and then reunited. The reflection of his face first as Muṣṭafā's, and later as his own are masterful. Playing with and shifting between his own reflection to that of Muṣṭafā, and then back to his own face is deliberate, skillful and arouses curiosity. He intends to set fire to the room that was Muṣṭafā's miniature English world in the heart of the Sudan. Ultimately he decides against it however, and instead sets out on his final confrontation with Muṣṭafā and himself in a different way. He leaves at dawn, at the same hour he had left Muṣṭafā's home after the latter told him his life story. The author could not have chosen a better means than the river since water, which means life, flows in the river, and thus the river serves not only as a place of purification (as in the narrator's case), but also as the place of death, as in Muṣṭafā Sa'īd's case, or as a place of impurity, as at times, in the works of William Faulkner[52].

The narrator struggles with himself and the 'Muṣṭafā' within him. When he is halfway between North and South, a flock of sand grouse fly over on their migration north. They are a symbolic illustration of the struggle between North and South and life and death. Midway is a symbolic illustration of the narrator's situation, since he has attained an inner equilibrium, in direct contradiction to Muṣṭafā Sa'īd. The narrator has symbolically entered the river at a moment of equilibrium, unlike Muṣṭafā who went into it during the floods, but not during the dry period; Muṣṭafā moreover went into it during the night, when disasters take place; whereas the narrator enters the river at dawn, when day breaks and the sun rises, and good things happen; not tragically, like Muṣṭafā, but dramatically; not as an act of hopelessness or despair as Muṣṭafā did, but as an act of hope and struggle.[53] Although at that moment the narrator feels that he is surrendering to the river's destructive forces, it is at this crucial moment that he pulls himself together and returns to his senses. The narrator decides to go on living and for the first time in his life to truly make his own decisions, not letting himself be drawn along by life's forces. His reasons:

> Then my mind cleared and my relationship to the river was determined. Though floating on the water, I was not part of it. I thought that if I died at that moment, I would have died as I was born – without any volition of mine. All my life I had not chosen, had not decided. Now I am making a decision. I choose life. I shall live because there are a few people I want to stay with for the longest possible time and because I have duties to discharge. It is not my concern whether or not life has meaning. If I am unable to forgive, then I shall try to forget. I shall live by force and cunning. (pp. 170–1).

The end is clear. The narrator goes into the river to swim and after a cruel and enthralling struggle decides to remain alive. He is purified, as it were, reborn; presumably he can return to a situation in which his world is no longer plagued by dark and black forces like those of Muṣṭafā. But is this really the case? It seems that this question would not have arisen if not for the strange, cynical, demonic and theatrical finale, which raises doubt and suspicions that perhaps matters are not really as smooth and crystal-clear as they are described. Indeed, in the following sentence the narrator's alleged victory is challenged: 'Like a comic actor shouting on a stage, I screamed with all my remaining strength, "Help! Help!"' (p. 171).

The narrator struggles to live and the solution he chooses, therefore, is totally different from that of Muṣṭafā Sa'īd. The narrator, upon completing his process of individuation, overcomes all obstacles and embarks on a new life. He realizes that his roots are in the Sudan particularly in his village; they are deep and have enabled him to surmount his problems which derived, at least partially, from the confrontation between Eastern and Western cultures[54]. Al-Ṭayyib Ṣāliḥ's words about the narrator illuminate the essence of his character:

> This character is of extreme importance and symbolizes our ability, as Arabs, to create a moral life and cope with it despite obstacles and difficult situations.[55]

Muṣṭafā Sa'īd – Whether the author chose this name intentionally or not, there is an inescapable irony in its meaning. Muṣṭafā means 'the chosen' (it is worth noting that this was one of the names of the Prophet Muḥammad), and Sa'īd means 'happy'.[56] But even if the first name was not intended to have ironic connotations, the last name definitely is the antithesis of Muṣṭafā Sa'īd. According to the Aristotelian poetic tradition, the author apparently intends to portray this character as a tragic hero. But this tragic hero is characterized by conceit and complacency, which are part of the concept of hubris. The tragic hero regards himself as the one chosen by the gods to fulfill an act of bravery, but his flaws cause him to err and fail in his role, this being revealed to him during his travails. Neither does this type of hero regard himself as someone who is dependent on fate; its archetype is *King Oedipus* (430 B.C.) by Sophocles (496–405 B.C.).[57]

Muṣṭafā Sa'īd is different because he was chosen to symbolize the tragic hero in relation to his flaws, and the mistakes he makes during his lifetime are mainly in England. He differs from the Aristotelian model, because he is aware that he is only a tool in the hands of fate. His attempt to return to the remote Sudanese village and begin his life anew is largely a failed catharsis. The majority of readers, like the literary critics, regard Muṣṭafā Sa'īd as the leading and most important character in the novel. Even if Muṣṭafā serves as the plot's axis he is actually a symbol rather than a character, as we often find in al-Ṭayyib Ṣāliḥ's works. As a character he is entirely cerebral, devoid of heart, in short, an antithesis to al-Zayn (*'Urs al-Zayn*). Al-Zayn represents harmony, while Muṣṭafā symbolizes various disharmonies and struggles. To use Freudian terms, by whose theory al-Ṭayyib Ṣāliḥ was influenced in the sixties, we can say that while al-Zayn symbolizes love (eros), Muṣṭafā Sa'īd stands for death (thanatos). But al-Zayn and Muṣṭafā Sa'īd perhaps share – in a very surprising way – a legendary mythical figure connected to the Muslim heritage. This is *al-Nabiyy al-Khaḍir*. Each is regarded by his community as an unusual and outsider person, but from different points of view. Al-Zayn does not belong to one party or camp in his village. He belongs to himself. This is also the case with Muṣṭafā Sa'īd who was rootless and belongs to none but himself. Nonetheless, their uniqueness contradicts the differences between them.[58] Muṣṭafā was regarded by his teachers and colleagues in Khartoum as a miracle (*mu'jiza*). *Mu'jizāt* (miracles) are connected with prophets and apostles while *karāmāt* (miracles) are connected with holy men and/or saints.[59] Muṣṭafā represents first and foremost the first educated Sudanese who encounters Western culture, an encounter that revolves around women and sex and is the negative and base aspect of this type of relationship. Muṣṭafā is an example of how not to behave and what not to do. He may possibly have no alternative, since he, like other tragic heroes in world and classical literature, is predestined to be a symbol of the failure of the cultural encounter. His is also a personal failure; he has no chance against the inevitability of fate, as this is depicted by the author. From another perspective he also symbolizes the Arab/Moslem/African, who dons fictitious robes and sets out on a vengeful journey to the North/West. He seeks revenge because of the imperialistic British conquest of the Sudan. Muṣṭafā Sa'īd, therefore, comes to England as conqueror and avenger of his own culture by vanquishing Western women.[60]

Muṣṭafā Sa'īd was born in Khartoum on August 16, 1898, which was an important and symbolic date in the Sudan's political history (several weeks before the occupation of the Sudan by Kitchener), several months after his father's death. His mother, Fāṭima 'Abd al-Ṣādiq, is said to have been a slave from the south who was forced to bear the burden of parenthood. She, like Muṣṭafā, is revealed as a strange woman, devoid of emotions. Muṣṭafā, who is raised as an orphan,[61] feels no sorrow but is happy to be free, growing up in a different way than his peers:

> Yet I had felt from childhood that I – that I was different – I mean that I was not like other children of my age: I wasn't affected by anything, I didn't cry when hit, wasn't glad if the teacher praised me in class, didn't suffer from the things the rest did. I was like something rounded, made of rubber; you throw it in the water and it doesn't get wet, you throw it on the ground and it bounces back. (p. 24).

Muṣṭafā's scholastic excellence enables him to leave Khartoum and move to Cairo, his first stop in a long journey.[62] It is difficult not to be shocked by his totally emotionless parting from his mother, as he is, after all, her only son:

> Then she disappeared for a while and brought back her purse, which she placed in my hand. 'Had your father lived', she said to me, 'he would not have chosen for you differently from what you have chosen for yourself. Do as you wish, depart or stay, it's up to you, it's your life and you're free to do with it as you will. In this purse is some money which will come in useful'. That was our farewell; no tears, no kisses, no fuss. *Two human beings had walked a part of the road together, then each had gone his way.* (p. 27, my emphasis, A.E-B.)

In Cairo, Muṣṭafā is adopted by the Robinsons, a childless couple who lavish love on him. He stays in Cairo for three years, graduates with honours and decides to move on to his next stop, London. For Muṣṭafā London is nothing more than 'Another mountain, larger than Cairo'. (p. 30). The purpose of his journey to London is to acquire education, but it turns out that destiny provides him with another axis in life, which revolves around women and revenge. Muṣṭafā forms unique relationships with four English women, three of whom commit suicide, and the fourth he kills. For the murder of his wife, Jean Morris, the court sentences him to seven years imprisonment. On his release he continues his wanderings in Europe, but ultimately decides to leave Europe and return to Khartoum, the city of his birth, where he engages in commerce. He cannot find peace of mind and therefore moves on to the third station in his life, the narrator's village. The village is Muṣṭafā's final attempt to rehabilitate himself and try to build a life based on solid ground. He thus explains his motives for moving to the village:

> All my life I've longed to settle down in this part of the country, for some unknown reason. I took the boat not knowing where I was bound for. When it put in at this village, I liked the look of it. Something inside me told me that this was the place. And so, as you [the narrator] see, that's how it was. I was not disappointed either in the village or its people. (p. 14).

Eventually the author chose to solve Muṣṭafā's problems by bringing him back to the village, to use a Conradian term (see Chapter Four), from the 'heart of darkness', from the height of Western culture and its allure. There, the implication is, he would be able to try and rehabilitate himself and build a proper and healthy life, which might be achieved in the most basic of places for the Sudanese, the village. This device is similar to that used by earlier Arab writers who wrote novels on the subject of East and West (*'Uṣfūr min al-Sharq*, *Qindīl Umm Hāshim*, *al-Ḥayy al-Lātīnī*) and who brought their protagonists back to the East, to the source, in order to rehabilitate themselves in their natural environment (see Chapter Five).[63]

Muṣṭafā indeed settles in the village, buys a plot of land, marries Ḥusna, and they have two children. He adjusts to village life, helps the inhabitants and although they regard him as a stranger, they praise his assistance in village development. In the village Muṣṭafā seemingly finds the stability and traditional roots which he sought. But the crux of the matter is that he understands he cannot escape his fate, not only in England, but also in the Sudan. An awareness arises and he confesses his failure to rehabilitate his life and build it anew. As a result Muṣṭafā disappears in the waters of the Nile.[64] The questions: Did Muṣṭafā die? And if not, where is he? Is it possible that he returned to live in the North? Did he commit suicide or did he drown? The questions are of vital importance, but it is difficult, perhaps impossible, to answer them since the author's intention is to leave them ambiguous and unresolved. In other words, the author's intent is to blur and obscure not only the particulars pertaining to Muṣṭafā's life, but perhaps even mainly, his disappearance. On the one hand, we have allusions which testify to the fact that Muṣṭafā chose to die, but on the other, one must not forget that he did not find the courage to end his own life together with Jean Morris. His hope that the court would 'come to his rescue' did not materialize.

The time and place that relate to Muṣṭafā's disappearance are characteristic of the mystery that enshrouds his character. The event took place on a warm July night when the Nile was at high tide, during one of the floods which occur periodically every few decades. Over time these floods have become legends passed down from father to son. The backdrop is perfect. On the night of the Nile's high tide Muṣṭafā does not return home. The village loses several of its inhabitants, but Muṣṭafā's body is not among those washed up by the river. His end is obscure, yet one other reason may be suggested, i.e., Muṣṭafā blended with the river after purifying himself in it[65] in order to depart in a different way, perhaps as did Ḍaw al-Bayt (to be discussed below).

The opinions and assumptions relating to Muṣṭafā's disappearance in the river can be summarized as follows:

The villagers – Muṣṭafā Sa'īd died in the river and his body is now in the belly of the crocodile, with which the waters teem in this area (p. 50). In another place, Maḥjūb says with finality:

> After his death there were rumours that they [the Omda and the merchants] had planned to kill him – mere talk. He died from drowning – tens of men were drowned that year. (p. 105).

Ḥusna – Muṣṭafā's wife states categorically that Muṣṭafā had a part in his own death, or at least that he knew he would die:

> 'It was as though he felt his end drawing near,' said Hosna. 'A week before the day – the day before his death – he arranged his affairs. He tidied up odds and ends and paid his debts. The day before he died he called me to him and told me what he owned and gave me numerous directions about the boys. He also gave me the letter sealed with wax and said to me, "Give it to him if anything happens". He told me that if anything happened you were to be the boys' guardian. "Consult him in everything you do", he said to me. I cried and said to him, "God willing, nothing bad will happen". "It's just in case", he said, "for one never knows in this world"'. (p. 95).

Clearly, this passage can confirm that Muṣṭafā planned his death, or alternatively, knew that his end was near. One may find further proof in Ḥusna's words when she says to the narrator that Muṣṭafā had told her he was a good swimmer.

Muṣṭafā – As mentioned earlier, Muṣṭafā was aware that his fate was sealed. He finds support for this in his encounter with Jean Morris and in their relationship. When he appoints the narrator as his children's' guardian, he says to him:

> I do not know which of the two courses would be the more selfish, to stay on or to depart. In any event I have no choice, and perhaps you will realize what I mean if you cast your mind back to what I said to you that night. (p. 70).

Muṣṭafā feels in his heart that his fate is sealed and he cannot escape it, as he says to the narrator:

> It's futile to deceive oneself. That distant call still rings in my ears. I thought that my life and marriage here would silence it. But perhaps I was created thus, or my fate was thus – whatever may be the meaning of that I don't know. Rationally I know what is right: my attempt at living in this village with these happy people. But mysterious things in my soul and in my blood impel me towards faraway parts that loom up before me and cannot be ignored. (pp. 70–1).

The narrator – The narrator wonders and asks himself time and again what has really happened to Muṣṭafā Sa'īd, and does not reach a conclusion. He reacts in four ways: his first reaction to Muṣṭafā's drowning: 'Mustafa Sa'eed was, as far as I knew, an excellent swimmer' (p. 49). Muṣṭafā Sa'īd had confirmed this to Ḥusna (p. 95). Yet the narrator ponders whether Muṣṭafā committed suicide or perhaps drowned:

> If Mustafa Sa'eed had chosen his end, then he had undertaken the most melodramatic act in the story of his life. If the other possibility was the right one, then Nature had bestowed upon him the very end which he would have wanted for himself. (p. 71).

When he meets the retired official the narrator reflects again: 'that he had been drowned, had perhaps committed suicide…' (p. 56). Here the narrator is inclined to accept the version which holds that Muṣṭafā died and did not take his own life. In the fourth instance, when the narrator argues with several friends and criticizes Manṣūr, a fellow student from the time he studied in England, he refers to Muṣṭafā's death as beyond question: 'On his death Mustafa Sa'eed left…' (p. 59).

We have seen that the narrator deliberated long and hard regarding the question of Muṣṭafā's death or disappearance, and the real author very cleverly used this ambiguity and legend as part and parcel of his literary perception.[66] This question, whether Muṣṭafā drowned or possibly committed suicide, preoccupies the narrator for a good reason. After all, he, the narrator, ultimately achieved serenity – he met with death, which he sought and from which he ran away. This is one facet of Muṣṭafā Sa'īd's end. The narrator's fate is intertwined with Muṣṭafā in a Gordian knot. They have been linked from the beginning of the novel, but this becomes crystal-clear to the narrator after Muṣṭafā chooses him (the narrator) as the witness who will listen to his life story. The relationship between the two characters exists not only because of their similarity, but mainly as result of their dissimilarity.[67] The similarities and dissimilarities between them can be summarized thus:

Muṣṭafā Sa'īd	**The Narrator**
The narrator denies any similarity between them	To a great extent – the image of the real author
Grew up in the city (Khartoum)	Grew up in a village (on the northern Nile)
Lived in England for thirty years	Lived in England for seven years
Wrote his Ph.D. in political science	Wrote his Ph.D. on poetry
Returns troubled to his village and lives as a farmer	Returns to his village but lives as a government official in Khartoum
Meets Jean Morris at the age of 25	Meets Muṣṭafā at the age of 25
The river – the place of his probable death	The river – the place where he is reborn
Women and sex as his life's axis	Women and sex are not his life's axis
Married a Sudanese woman but before that – an Englishwoman	Married a Sudanese woman
Encounter with the West – death of Western women	Encounter with the West – superficial
Regards the West negatively	Regards the West positively and negatively
Continuity – married and has two children	Continuity – married and has a daughter
Symbolizes the present but particularly the past	Symbolizes the present but particularly the future
Negative and tragic hero	Positive and non-tragic non-hero
Self-destruction	Self-construction

Muṣṭafā Sa'īd's demonic, surrealistic, legendary, absurd and bizarre figure, which is detached and tragic, captivated not only readers and critics but also the author himself:

> I soon felt that his character [Muṣṭafā Sa'īd] was growing and trying to gain control, so I attempted to encircle it with secondary characters. However, I believe that my attempt failed. I believe that – as a writer – despite the success of this novel, among the things in which I feel I failed is the fact that I did not gain control and did not restrain this character in relation to its role which is clear from the very course of the story. But perhaps this is not the novel's main problem.[68]

In another place al-Ṭayyib Ṣāliḥ emphasizes the fact that Muṣṭafā Sa'īd with his Faustian characteristics, is not realistic, since it is not possible for one person to have so many characteristics and counter-characteristics.[69] Muṣṭafā Sa'īd boasts of his conquests of cities (Cairo, London) and women, but it seems that these conquests do not lessen his attendant feelings of foreignness and alienation, both in Europe and in Cairo. The problem is that his tragedy derives not only from these feelings experienced in both West and East, but that he also succumbs to them in the village. Despite his efforts to integrate into the village and despite the fact that the villagers greatly appreciated him, he is regarded by them, during his stay in the village, as a stranger. Thus the narrator's father describes him:

> My father said that Mustafa was not a local man but a stranger who had come here five years ago, had bought himself a farm, built a house and married Mahmoud's daughter – a man who kept himself to himself and about whom not much was known. (p. 6).

Even the narrator's grandfather, who praises Muṣṭafā's behaviour, complains that Maḥmūd married off his daughter to Muṣṭafā: 'That tribe doesn't mind to whom they marry their daughters'. (p. 10). In other words, Muṣṭafā Sa'īd is different, foreign and alien wherever he goes. Indeed, Muṣṭafā is a victim of the environment, any environment, because of his struggle, and he is therefore essentially different from the narrator, who is naturally at home in his environment, country, his homeland and his village. Moreover, the author built the character with a plethora of characteristics which are related to his mind and therefore he must bring a foreign character, someone from the outside, to the village. To a certain extent this victim's foreign character arrives at the village with some features of an imperialist.[70]

Whereas Muṣṭafā's foreignness in Europe can be regarded as natural, his failure to put down roots in his own country, in Khartoum, the city of his birth, or his attempt to return to the remote Sudanese village is not.[71] Displacement and lack of roots are curiously combined. In London Muṣṭafā had a room which contained the Eastern world, while in the far-off Sudanese village he had a room which contained the Western world. The displacement, foreignness, alienation and restlessness are what ultimately cause the author to conceal him in the river, rather than to declare that Muṣṭafā died:

> It may well be that his [Muṣṭafā's] disappearance is structured because he was the product of a different kind of generation. His disappearance is a type of energy, which doubtless exists, because I believe that, like in physics, energy never disappears. It has to exist in another form that will change.[72]

Even twenty years later, al-Ṭayyib Ṣāliḥ remains consistent in relation to Muṣṭafā Sa'īd's disappearance and his connection to Ḍaw al-Bayt:

> You can, therefore, see that Muṣṭafā Sa'īd was carried on the waves. People ask: where did he go? It is unimportant. Years before or after, only God knows, Ḍaw al-Bayt emerges from the sea, and it is as if energy itself appears in a different form and a different time. This is what is important. What is important is that the energy reappeared. Muṣṭafā Sa'īd too is shrouded in ambiguous elements, like Ḍaw al-Bayt, but when Muṣṭafā Sa'īd arrives in the village, he acquires a name, status and a history. The villagers did not know this, but Muṣṭafā Sa'īd related his life story to the narrator. In other words, he determined it in both time and place, but Ḍaw al-Bayt was fixed neither in time nor place.[73]

Muṣṭafā Sa'īd's foreignness and more so that he is a victim in both Sudanese and English society is a leitmotif throughout the novel. Thus the author expresses the psychological, philosophical and literary influences of Western culture on him. The stranger, as society's victim, appears in numerous works in world literature and particularly in works by European writers like Shakespeare (*Othello*, 1604), Stendhal (*The Red and the Black*, 1830), Emily Brontë (*Wuthering Heights*, 1846), Josef Conrad (*Heart of Darkness*, 1902) and Albert Camus (*The Outsider*, 1957), and American writers such as William Faulkner (*The Sound and the Fury*, 1929).[74] Arab and Western critics who have discussed the similarity between these works and *Mawsim al-Hijra ilā al-Shamāl,* and Muṣṭafā Sa'īd in particular, dealt with the thematic basis of both the collective aspect of the encounter between Eastern and Western cultures, and the subject of Muṣṭafā Sa'īd's tragic disappearance.[75]

Despite the considerable number of similarities between Muṣṭafā Sa'īd and several of these novels' protagonists, we may note three major characters who served, in one way or another, as inspiration for al-Ṭayyib Ṣāliḥ: Othello of Shakespeare's *Othello*, Kurtz of Conrad's short novel *Heart of Darkness,* and Heathcliff of Brontë's *Wuthering Heights* (see Chapters One and Four). But in *Mawsim al-Hijra ilā al-Shamāl* al-Ṭayyib Ṣāliḥ relates directly only to the character of Othello. The author's choice may possibly derive from the fact that Othello, like Muṣṭafā Sa'īd, is both an African and an Arab. Therefore, when Isabella Seymour asks him: 'What race are you?' 'Are you African or Asian?' (p. 42), he answers: 'I'm like Othello – Arab-African'. On one occasion in the novel, Othello appears as truth, as opposed to Muṣṭafā who is a lie, and once as a lie, since Muṣṭafā is the real Othello. The explanation for this may possibly be that Othello, despite the difference of colour, nationality and age, was in love with Desdemona, whereas Muṣṭafā Sa'īd's relationships with English women were not based on love. The author negates the possibility of real love (at least at the stage described here) between the two cultures represented by the heroes. The relationship cannot end as a romantic one: here are two societies in confrontation with one another. The situation is, therefore, also more difficult on the personal level (although this was not the case with the real author) and does not allow for a love relationship. Moreover, the relationship between Muṣṭafā and the English women is more on the symbolic collective level, in contrast to Othello and Desdemona whose involvement was emotional and personal. Furthermore, Othello destroyed his happiness with his own hands by killing Desdemona because he was jealous, while Muṣṭafā, though not a happy man, kills Jean Morris, not because he is jealous; he has other motives, such as the desire to control her and continue being the hunter, and not the victim, or perhaps also because of his desire to contend with the white culture, the imperialistic Christian Crusader. When Muṣṭafā claims that he is not Othello, but a lie, he means this on the collective level, since he himself symbolizes the world that killed Jean Morris because she was the symbol of another, Western, Crusader, Christian world. The conclusion then could be that both Muṣṭafā Sa'īd and Othello are a lie, fakes and forgeries, each on a different level.[76] Al-Ṭayyib Ṣāliḥ addresses this point when he says:

> He [Muṣṭafā] connected himself to Othello. And in many aspects of the novel he compares himself with Othello. And from time to time he says that Othello is the true... and he is a false Othello. But at the end of the novel he says that Othello is the fake and he is the true one. Shakespeare described Othello as a character totally accepted by European society as it was at the time. Venice was the acme of European culture at that time. He was a military commander who wed Desdemona; the struggle between Othello and Desdemona was not an emotional one. He was the one who created this struggle. Personally I have always felt that Othello's weak point was, despite all that he had undergone, the fact that it was not possible that he could accept all this so easily and turn the struggle into one involving only Desdemona, and I believe that some of the critics allude to this... Perhaps it would have been better if we said, before we discussed Shakespeare, that Muṣṭafā Sa'īd's character should have been the real Othello [...] He said I am not Othello. Othello was false, and that is my point of view on the matter.[77]

It may be that what al-Ṭayyib Ṣāliḥ does not state explicitly in the text, but in my opinion emerges in the novel, is the author's sharp criticism of Othello's character, and indirectly of Shakespeare, for presenting an implausible and unfamiliar character. Therefore, al-Ṭayyib Ṣāliḥ's attitude towards Othello and the playwright tends at times toward parody and even sarcasm. The author frequently uses florid and ornate language in all matters pertaining to Muṣṭafā Sa'īd's life story; and parody within parody; or criticism within criticism. The problem is that Muṣṭafā Sa'īd, like Othello, is not a tragic hero. He is not because he chooses to disappear in the river, and in contrast to his earlier life, is now the master of his fate. Othello, like other Shakespearean heroes (Romeo, Juliet, Brutus, Anthony, Cleopatra), commits suicide and also controls his fate.

Al-Ṭayyib Ṣāliḥ has said in interviews that Muṣṭafā Sa'īd's character is a combination of different characters, and cannot exist in reality. He regards him as a composite of violent, satanic and angelic elements, an image of Don Juan who is simultaneously a good husband and a criminal who destroys his female victims, and yet has the image of a genius who processes, builds and contributes to life. He sees in Muṣṭafa an imaginary character in whom political, spiritual and cultural aspects are connected with human problems This character was created from dreams, hypotheses and probabilities, made up entirely of the cerebral, fraud, as well as a complex psychological struggle. He symbolizes a world diametrically opposed to the harmonious world as portrayed in other al-Ṭayyib Ṣāliḥ texts, particularly in *'Urs al-Zayn.*

Secondary and Marginal Characters

As we have seen, al-Ṭayyib Ṣāliḥ populates his novels with numerous secondary and marginal characters. He maintains a balanced system, between Eastern (Ḥusna, Maḥjūb, Ḥājj Aḥmad) and Western characters (Jean Morris, Ann Hammond, Isabella Seymour, Sheila Greenwood, the Robinsons); young people (Maḥjūb, Ḥusna, Ann Hammond) and the elderly (Ḥājj Aḥmad, Wad al-Rayyis, Bint Majdhūb); men (Maḥjūb, Wad al-Rayyis, Mr Robinson); women (Ḥusna, Bint Majdhūb, Jean Morris); the evil (Jean Morris) and the good (Mr Robinson). The entire spectrum of these secondary and marginal rural characters might be found in Sudanese and Arab villages, if not in any village in the world. They have been discussed in previous chapters and need not be mentioned further. I want to discuss briefly three important secondary Eastern characters: Maḥjūb, Ḥājj Aḥmad and Ḥusna.

- **Maḥjūb** – More than any other figure, Maḥjūb symbolizes the young Sudanese, and as we shall see in Chapter Four, he appears in others of Ṣāliḥ's texts. Maḥjūb, the narrator's good friend, grew up with him but developed differently. He remained in the village and served as a member of several committees. Maḥjūb thinks that the narrator was more successful than he, whereas the narrator is convinced that Maḥjūb is the one who was truly successful:

> We would occasionally chat about our childhood in the village and he would say to me, 'But look where you are now and where I am. You've become a senior civil servant and I'm a farmer in this god-forsaken village.' 'It's you who've succeeded, not I' I would say to him with genuine admiration, 'because you influence actual life in the country. We civil servants, though, are of no consequence. People like you are the legal heirs of authority; you are the sinews of life, you're the salt of the earth.' 'If we're the salt of the earth,' Mahjoub would say with a laugh, 'then the earth is without flavour.' (pp. 101–2).

Maḥjūb adheres moderately to village tradition. His attitude to progress is ambivalent: on the one hand, he finds progress useful to the villagers and their wellbeing, but on the other he believes that it has not led to significant changes in the village. He also has an ambivalent attitude toward education: the narrator's education is valuable, he concedes, but he is satisfied with being literate and knowing basic arithmetic. Regarding politics, Maḥjūb is involved in social and political activities on several village committees and in various parties, but he attacks the Khartoum politicians.

- **Ḥājj Aḥmad** – Ḥājj Aḥmad is the narrator's grandfather. This figure appears in several other texts, as we shall see later. More than any other character in the novel, the grandfather symbolizes the old village Sudanese, rooted in tradition, who holds on to his land and is a source of simplicity and stability. He is ninety years old, and still vigorous.[78] He observes the rules of tradition and religion, and thus differs from the other group of old people, such as Wad al-Rayyis and Bint Majdhūb. Ḥājj Aḥmad is a focal point of the narrator's admiration, but to an even greater extent for the admiration of Muṣṭafā Sa'īd, the man with no roots. Since simplicity is the secret of life, and Ḥājj Aḥmad is its symbol, the grandfather knows the secret of life. Therefore, the young villager Maḥjūb, like other young villagers, cannot understand Muṣṭafā Sa'īd's admiration for him, which contrasts with their own view of him as a garrulous old man. Muṣṭafā Sa'īd says to Maḥjūb:

> 'You know, Mahjoub, Hajj Ahmed is a unique person'. 'Hajj Ahmed's an old windbag', I would reply and he would get really annoyed. 'No, don't say that', he'd say to me. 'Hajj Ahmed is a part of history.' (pp. 105–6).

The grandfather stands as firm as the Rock of Gibraltar against time and its vicissitudes. The only time we, like the narrator, see him in a state of crisis is when Ḥusna murders Wad al-Rayyis and later commits suicide. He is shocked to find his grandfather crying like any man would, but this is the exception that proves the rule. The grandfather is perceived by the narrator as part of nature and the physical environment of the Sudanese village. He, more than anyone else, serves as an example of the differences between East and West, not only in relation to the different attitudes of the two cultures towards life, but also towards death.

- **Ḥusna** – She is symbolic of the young village woman, whom the author hopes to see in the Sudan and who embarks on a new path after years of British occupation.[79] She may represent a not entirely convincing and credible character, but partly a product of the author's wishful thinking. Ḥusna is more likely a model of an extraordinary young village woman that al-Ṭayyib Ṣāliḥ develops more convincingly in his later novels, as we shall see in Chapter Four. In any case, from the day of her marriage to Muṣṭafā Sa'īd, Ḥusna changed drastically. Similar to the Western women who maintained relationships with Muṣṭafā and like the narrator, she, too, is infected by his germ. Latent forces were released after her marriage to Muṣṭafā.[80] It is difficult to know what her overall and essential relationship with Muṣṭafā was, but perhaps it is indicated in her answer to the narrator's question of whether she loved Muṣṭafā Sa'īd:

> 'He was the father of my children.' If I am right in my belief, the voice was not sad, in fact it contained a caressing tenderness. I let the silence whisper to her, hoping she would say something further. Yes, here it was: 'He was a generous husband and a generous father. He never let us want for anything in his whole life.' (p. 93).

In other words she does not say that she loved him and this is perhaps disappointing from a Western perspective. Yet it is in keeping with Sudanese village norms; it is not a matter of love but of fulfilling obligations, as is customary in traditional Eastern society. The fact that Ḥusna does not want to marry after Muṣṭafā's disappearance, having changed after her marriage, may reinforce this view. The extent of her transformation can be heard in Maḥjūb's words:

> It's true, though, that Mahmoud's daughter [Ḥusna] changed after her marriage to Mustafa Sa'eed. All women change after marriage, but she in particular underwent an indescribable change. It was as though she was another person. Even we who were her contemporaries and used to play with her in the village look at her today and see her as something new – like a city woman, if you know what I mean. (p. 104).

When Wad al-Rayyis courts her, she urges family members and the narrator to convey her rejection of him, but from the moment she understands that Wad al-Rayyis is determined to marry her, she warns them and says: 'If they force me to marry, I'll kill him and kill myself.' (p. 99). Her defiance of tradition and village norms brings down on her the wrath of the entire village and is further evidence of the change.[81] The narrator is the only one who understands this because he, too, knew part of Muṣṭafā Sa'īd's world. Therefore, they are both isolated from the other villagers and when she is forced to marry Wad al-Rayyis and he wishes to consummate the marriage, she keeps her promise, murders him and takes her own life. Ḥusna's deed shocks the village, and its inhabitants blame the horrendous crime on the plagues of the modern era. Wad al-Rayyis' murder can be compared with that of Jean Morris despite the differences between the two, since the common denominator is Muṣṭafā Sa'īd.[82] In both cases the germ of violence is triumphant. The missing part in the equation is the narrator: he, too, was infected by Muṣṭafā Sa'īd and he is the only one in the village who opposed Wad al-Rayyis' and Ḥusna's marriage. Moreover, Ḥusna had asked him to marry her. The question is why did the narrator, who loved her and was attracted to her, not marry her? Events could have taken their natural course, as he was appointed by Muṣṭafā himself as the childrens' guardian; the fact that he was already married would not have run contrary to Muslim religious law. Possibly, the answer to this question is within the person of the narrator: he refused to continue his relationship with Muṣṭafā Sa'īd, especially not after he died. To complete his personal identity, he wanted to totally sever his ties with everything related to Muṣṭafā Sa'īd. The villagers paid a terrible price for the murder because the village after the event was no longer the same. But why did Wad al-Rayyis desire so passionately to marry Ḥusna when other marriageable village women who were not divorced were available? After all, a divorced woman in the Arab/Moslem village has a low status. The answer, I suggest, is in Wad al-Rayyis' love not only of women but of foreign women. Ḥusna was married to a foreigner and thus she too became foreign and alien, someone who bore the label of being different. Through her, Wad al-Rayyis sought to taste the foreign women about whom he had heard so much.

Bandar Shāh: Ḍaw al-Bayt

Unlike earlier novels, in *Bandar Shāh: Ḍaw al-Bayt* there are three major characters: the narrator, Ḍaw al-Bayt and Bandar Shāh, as well as many secondary and marginal characters. We have met numerous secondary and marginal characters in earlier novels, and in *'Urs al-Zayn* in particular, but these will be discussed in the following chapter. In this novel the number of characters is reduced from four to three (p. 73) to two and to one character (p. 101) and that is of Ḍaw al-Bayt.[83]

Central Characters

- **The Narrator** – As to the major characters, only the narrator is familiar, having appeared in the short stories ('Nakhla 'alā al-Jadwal', 'Risāla ilā Aylīn', and some of the 'Muqaddimāt') and in *Mawsim al-Hijra ila al-Shamāl.* I shall also deal with the narrator's character in *Bandar Shāh: Ḍaw al-Bayt* in the following chapter, but let me state briefly here that the subject is a fifty or sixty year-old man (p. 46) who comes back to his village after a prolonged absence and tries, not always successfully, to renew his acquaintance with the villagers who are his peer group. He returns to the village, Wad Ḥāmid, not only in order to be buried there, but to try and reconstruct the simple life of his past: 'I want to return to the past, to the days when people were people and Time was Time'. (p. 85).

The 'telltale' facts, or specifically, the autobiographical details common to the narrator and the real author, al-Ṭayyib Ṣāliḥ, can be summarized as follows: the plot takes place in the small village of Wad Ḥāmid, located in the Marawī region of northern Sudan. Like the author, the narrator acquired an academic education, and despite his strong desire to engage in agriculture he is employed as an official. Due to the many years he spent abroad, outside the village, he now evinces a strong desire to overcome the sense of estrangement. Characters and events which appear in some of the author's stories and novels are also mentioned in this novel.

- **Ḍaw al-Bayt** – The character of Ḍaw al-Bayt, the founder of the family line that is at the heart of the novel, is the source of all the legends and mysteries shrouding the ancestral line. He is, however, not only the source of legends but also of reality, this being the key to understanding the duality and dualism which attends it. The river is the first station, but also the last, in Ḍaw al-Bayt's life. We know nothing of his past, just as we do not know whether he really drowned in the river, or perhaps was saved and moved to another place. Here there is a similarity between this story and that of Muṣṭafā Sa'īd in the novel *Mawsim al-Hijra ilā al-Shamāl.* True, Muṣṭafā did not emerge from the river, although he did come by way of it since he came to the village from Khartoum by boat. As to Muṣṭafa's disappearance, we know that he disappeared in the river, and no one knew what had happened to him. But the difference between the novels is in the manner of the two men's disappearance; Muṣṭafā possibly committed suicide, which is not the case with Ḍaw al-Bayt. Al-Ṭayyib Ṣāliḥ was asked about this while he was writing the novel *Bandar Shāh* and he answered:

> It may well be that the meaning of his [Muṣṭafā Sa'īd's] disappearance is that it is mandatory that another kind of generation should emerge. His disappearance is a kind of energy. It is a burst of energy which undoubtedly exists, since I believe that as in physics, energy does not disperse, no matter what happens [but] must exist in another form that will change. Something of this kind may appear during my search in my last novel. I do not know how, but something may appear.[84]

We mentioned earlier the fact that even after a lapse of twenty years, al-Ṭayyib Ṣāliḥ consistently maintained this view, returning to it in the context of Ḍaw al-Bayt as continuity and renewal of energy.[85] Ḍaw al-Bayt's first appearance occurs when he emerges from the river and thus initiates the mysterious stories and legends associated with him. He finds it difficult to answer the villagers' questions in his faulty Arabic. His past was seemingly erased and he cannot reconstruct it. In any event, the villagers circumcise him and give him the name Ḍaw al-Bayt, i.e., 'light of the house'.[86] He is given a plot of land, works it, and prospers. He slowly integrates into village life, but when he wishes to marry, the villagers are disconcerted because he is, after all, a stranger and they know nothing about him. Here again, is an obvious similarity to the villagers' reaction to Muṣṭafā Sa'īd's marriage to one of the village girls. Ultimately, as in the case of Muṣṭafā Sa'īd, the villagers marry him to Fāṭima. He succeeds in business and becomes wealthy. But five years pass and he returns to the river. This happens when he tries to save Ḥasab al-Rasūl, the first villager to see Ḍaw al-Bayt emerge from the river, and he drowns. The villagers describe his mysterious disappearance thus:

> We waited day after day between despair and expectancy, saying to ourselves that maybe there was still hope. But Dau al-Beit had disappeared without trace; he had gone whence he had come, from water to water, from darkness to darkness, with Hasab ar-Rasoul weeping and saying, 'It can't be, it can't be.' (p. 133).

Once again, as in the case of Muṣṭafā Sa'īd, no one saw him drown. As to Ḍaw al-Bayt, despite all the legends and mysteries which enveloped him, there is also a realistic part; he left behind a widow, Fāṭima, who three months later gives birth to his son who is named 'Īsā, and is known as Bandar Shāh. Here, as in the case of Muṣṭafā Sa'īd who left a widow and two children, Ḍaw al-Bayt also leaves a widow and a child.

- **Bandar Shāh ('Īsā)** – Bandar Shāh is one of two names after which the novel is named and Bandar Shāh is one of the major characters in the novel. His past, his relationship with his grandson Maryūd, and their death, serve as an axis for the entire text. His real name is 'Īsā, but the villagers call him Bandar Shāh. Through Ḥamad Wad Ḥalīma's story (p. 34) the author explains the event when 'Īsā was nicknamed Bandar Shāh. These two words are borrowed from the Persian, and mean: *Bandar*: city (region, commerce, port); *Shāh*: king or ruler.[87] In an interview, al-Ṭayyib Ṣāliḥ explains and interprets the name Bandar Shāh:

> I chose the name Bandar Shāh since our problem is one of searching for a city (that is al-Bandar) and the second point is the invention of a form suitable for governing ourselves, which is the sovereign (Shāh)[88].

Be that as it may, the name Bandar Shāh indicates remote areas, different from the Sudan. This is stated when Ḍaw al-Bayt is asked about his name and he answers: 'I certainly had a name'. 'Bahloul. Bahdour. Shah. Khan. Mirza. Mirhan – I don't know' (p. 106), and here the name *Shāh* has several possibilities. But only Persian and not Sudanese names are stated. This is confirmed when Ḍaw al-Bayt is asked where he came from and he answers: 'Caucas, Ahwaz. Khorassan, Azerbaijan, Isphahan, Samarkand, Tashkent. I don't know. From some faraway place. I was tired, hungry and ill'. (p. 107). From both of Bandar Shāh's replies it can be seen that he did not come from an Arab country since his Arabic was faulty, and certainly not from an Islamic environment, as he would have been circumcised. These details of his past, like the obscurity that characterizes his name and origin, add mystery to Ḍaw al-Bayt's character, and hence to his son's. We learn that Bandar Shāh's real name was 'Isā but we do not know who gave him this name. One may assume that al-Ṭayyib Ṣāliḥ, in his customary way, did not choose the name by chance. It may be that Jesus, together with the implications of his birth, were in the author's mind, considering the Christian (Coptic and Ethiopian) influences on the Sudan, and on northern Sudan in particular.[89]

We do not know much about Bandar Shāh's childhood and youth. A large part of the story takes place when he already has eleven children and one grandchild named Maryūd. His financial situation is solid and he lives in a luxurious home. Bandar Shāh's attitude towards his children is strict and so is his attitude towards Maryūd's father. He favours his grandson Maryūd over his eleven sons, an unusual occurrence in rural society, although several of al-Ṭayyib Ṣāliḥ's texts ('Ḥafnat Tamr', *Mawsim al-Hijra ilā al-Shamāl*) also contain relationships based on preference, like very special relationships between grandfather and grandson, where the person of the father is nearly absent. This relationship, based on preference which Bandar Shāh shows towards his grandson Maryūd, is explained in the novel's sub-title, 'A story of the father who is the victim of his own father and son' (p. 3), and is reinforced in al-Ṭayyib Ṣāliḥ's words: 'The past and the future continually conspire against the present, or the grandfather and grandson continually conspire against the father'.[90] In this scheme of chronological reversal, Bandar Shāh is the one who brings change and transformation to the village, while his grandson Maryūd follows him. In any event, Bandar Shāh lives with his eleven sons and grandson Maryūd. He appoints his grandson to manage his affairs, both his business affairs and those as ruler over his father and uncles. He furthermore appoints Maryūd his sole heir. Maryūd rules over them and one day his eleven brothers (one cannot ignore the Biblical association with Joseph and his eleven brothers) rise against him and Bandar Shāh and murder them.

The narrator does not directly describe Maryūd and Bandar Shāh's murders. He hears rumours, stories and legends and tries to reconstruct the events. The trouble is that in the case of Bandar Shāh, we are again confronted with a problem of legend and reality, as in the context of Muḥaymīd. It is hard to know precisely how they were killed. There are rumours that the sons strangled or stabbed them, while others claim they were beaten to death (p. 75). The villagers are shocked by the murders, regarding them as an ominous sign for their village. In contrast with Wad al-Rayyis' murder by Ḥusna who later committed suicide (*Mawsim al-Hijra ilā al-Shamāl*), the villagers in this case conceal the murder from the authorities. But in *Bandar Shāh* the villagers' solidarity is weak, and the murder is brought to the attention of the authorities who arrive and incarcerate the murderers. The reason for the murder, as presented by the villagers, is identical to the murder of Wad al-Rayyis: 'It was an accursed time'. (p. 74). Still, the reaction is stronger here and various events take place in the village, leading to the pervasive feeling that the village is cursed. The villagers believe that a rift has taken place in their lives; there is a feeling of unreality, like after the murder of Wad al-Rayyis, or in the case of the narrator in *Mawsim al-Hijra ilā al-Shamāl*, who hears Muṣṭafā Sa'īd's story.[91] The villagers' traumatic reaction apparently stems from Bandar Shāh, and even more from Ḍaw al-Bayt. But whereas the reaction to Ḍaw al-Bayt's disappearance was one of sadness and grief, here, in the case of murder, it is one of anxiety, fear and danger to the bedrock of society. The villagers admired Bandar Shāh and his father because they attributed supernatural powers to them. The aura of mystery and legend also derives from the astonishing similarity between Bandar Shāh and his grandson Maryūd, who were depicted by the villagers as kings in their mysterious and wondrous palace. To reiterate, the murder that takes place here, like the murder in *Mawsim al-Hijra ilā al-Shamāl*, ultimately was committed by the relative of the two strangers: Ḍaw al-Bayt and Muṣṭafā Sa'īd. According to Sa'īd 'Ashā al-Bāyitat's interpretation of Bandar Shāh's murder, he was killed because of his hubris, because he regarded himself as king and heir of this world (p. 65).

Secondary and Marginal Characters

In this, as in al-Ṭayyib Ṣāliḥ's other novels, there are many secondary and marginal characters. We will mention only the prominent ones and begin with the most important secondary character, Maryūd, who can, in some respects, be regarded as a central character. Who was Maryūd? As his name suggests he was liked and beloved.[92] He is beloved by his grandfather and liked by the villagers. Maryūd is Bandar Shāh's grandson, the great-grandson of Ḍaw al-Bayt, a fact of great importance regarding Maryūd's status in the novel's plot. The aura of mystery and legend that surrounds his grandfather and great-grandfather veils Maryūd as well, but not his father and brothers. The narrator is deeply impressed by his courage and because he is an extraordinary person even at the age of fifteen. The relationship between Maryūd and his grandfather is exceptional. Their similarity begins with their external appearance, their way of sitting, posture and gait, and in the author's words: 'And when you stood between them, it was as though you were standing between two mirrors placed opposite each other, each reflecting the same image in an endless extension'. (p. 21). The villagers are clearly impressed by this similarity and attribute it to the hand of God, while the narrator regards it as an act of fate. He believes that Bandar Shāh formed Maryūd in his own image, since he wanted the latter to be his continuation on earth. The author does not conceal his basic perception of life in this context and says:

> The assumption in *Bandar Shāh* is that the past and the future continually conspire against the present, or the grandfather and grandson continually conspire against the father. Maryūd is an extension of continuing characters who follow a long, unbroken line.[93]

But in the end, Maryūd's uncles kill him and his grandfather Bandar Shāh, and thus put an end to the legend.

- **Maḥjūb** – This character appears in the short story 'Nakhla 'alā al-Jadwal' as an adult, but in the novels *'Urs al-Zayn* and *Mawsim al-Hijra ilā al-Shamāl* he is the village leader, a young and energetic man who symbolizes the young Sudanese farmer (see Chapter Four). In this novel Maḥjūb is an old man of seventy. He still is one of the mainstays of the band or gang, as it is called by the villagers. A problem arises when the young people of the village, led by al-Ṭarīfī, convince the villagers to dismiss Maḥjūb and his band from the key positions they hold. Moreover, even Maḥjūb's sons vote against him, further proof of the changes that have occurred in the Sudanese village together with the rift in tradition, customs and social codes.
- **The grandfather** – The narrator's grandfather played an important and central role in the story 'Ḥafnat Tamr' and the novel *Mawsim al-Hijra ilā al-Shamāl*, while here he has only a marginal one. He does not appear directly, but is employed by the narrator as one with whom he settles past, and not future, accounts. Two parallel relationships are developed: that of the narrator and his grandfather, which receives minor treatment, and the other between Maryūd and his grandfather, which is central to the plot[94].
- **The *imām*** – In al-Ṭayyib Ṣāliḥ's earlier works, the *imām* is not depicted sympathetically by the author, narrator, or the villagers. But in this novel the *imām* holds an important position and he is neither the object of the narrator's wrath nor his ridicule. He is perceived by the villagers as a reliable person. The *imām*, like the other villagers, is shocked by the murder of Bandar Shāh and Maryūd, and upbraids them: 'The Imam refused to pray with the people and said they were all cursed. Neither prayer nor preaching would help them, and then he traveled to Mecca to die there'. (p. 75). We may compare this with his words in the story 'Dawmat Wad Ḥāmid', when he chides the villagers after he becomes ill: 'These are people who have no need of me or of any other preacher'.[95] Common to both *imāms* is that they leave their village never to return.

Bandar Shāh: Maryūd

Maryūd is the second part of the novel *Bandar Shāh*. Against the background of that novel we must examine the various characters: major, secondary and marginal, who take part in both works. In this novel there is one leading character, the narrator, and he is attended by numerous secondary and marginal characters, the most important of them being the grandfather, Maryam, Bandar Shāh and Bilāl.

The Major Character

- **The narrator** – The character of the narrator is the dominant figure in the novel. Here we will discuss him only briefly, as we shall devote a large part of Chapter Four to him. Two main periods exist in the narrator's story: the first is his life in the present, and the second, his life in the past, both connected to his relationship with his grandfather and Maryam. The narrator, Muḥaymīd, returns to his village Wad Ḥāmid in order to record its history. He himself understands that at present the essence of life is in Wad Ḥāmid, and not outside it. The second level of the story records the narrator's life in the past. His childhood is depicted as a wonderful period for which he longs and to which he knows he will never return. His relationship with his grandfather in the past and present may prove that the narrator is Muḥaymīd, and Maryūd.[96] This relationship has come a long way. The narrator shifts from feelings of love and admiration for his grandfather as it was in the past, to feelings of resentment and hate in the present, for two reasons. First because the grandfather forced him to leave in order to study, despite the fact that he had wanted to be a farmer, and the second is that his grandfather did not allow him to marry Maryam. Muḥaymīd's relationship with Maryam, which was only briefly mentioned in *Bandar Shāh: Ḍaw al-Bayt,* is extensively described in this novel. Her death shocks him deeply and leads him to an accounting with himself and his grandfather.

Secondary Characters

The majority of the secondary and marginal characters are familiar to us from earlier works, and *Bandar Shāh: Ḍaw al-Bayt,* in particular. The character of the grandfather in this novel is limited to a passive one and his role is limited to his relationship with his grandson. I have indicated above the similarity between the two relationships: Bandar Shāh and Maryūd, and the grandfather and the narrator: both prefer their grandson to their sons. Both leave their entire property to their grandsons (Maryūd and Muḥaymīd). The grandfather bears a physical resemblance to Muḥaymīd, as does Bandar Shāh to Maryūd. The grandfather, like Bandar Shāh, symbolizes the past. But there are also differences between these two relationships: no hatred exists between the grandfather and Muḥaymīd, while in the relationship between Bandar Shāh and Maryūd it is overlooked. Bandar Shāh is murdered, while the grandfather simply dies under unknown circumstances.

- **Maryam** – The character of Maryam appears in several of al-Ṭayyib Ṣāliḥ's works of fiction (see Chapter Four). As in earlier texts, she is depicted in this novel not directly, but through the narrator. It emerges that she is Maḥjūb's sister, the youngest of four sisters. She is the model of the extraordinary young village woman, as found in others of al-Ṭayyib Ṣāliḥ's works. The love story of Maryam and Muḥaymīd is not related chronologically, but is dispersed throughout the novel. It begins when they were children, told first through the eyes of Muḥaymīd the child, the adult and finally the old man. Maryam marries Bakrī and bears his children. She dies at approximately fifty years of age, deeply shocking the narrator.[97]

- **Bandar Shāh** – The character of Bandar Shāh belongs to other characters like Bilāl, Sheik Naṣrallāh Wad Ḥabīb and others, who take part in the secondary and not in the main plot. Bandar Shāh fills the gaps and voids that existed in the first part of *Bandar Shāh: Ḍaw al-Bayt*, particularly regarding the origins of Bandar Shāh and Ḍaw al-Bayt. Who is Bandar Shāh? As in a legend or mystery tale, there are several versions; in this case – four, and a fifth by Ibrāhīm Wad Ṭāhā, who is known as a reliable informant, conversant with Wad Ḥāmid's history.[98]

- **Bilāl** – The character of Bilāl is described in the secondary plot, though he is strongly connected to the main one. Bilāl is none other than the father of al-Ṭāhir Wad al-Rawwāsī, one of the narrator's close friends. Like Bandar Shāh, whose real name was 'Īsā, Bilāl is a sobriquet for a man named Ḥasan. The name Bilāl was given to him because of his beautiful voice. Here emerges the Muslim Arab past, as Bilāl was not just the first muezzin of Islam; he was born in slavery and his mother was African.[99] Bilāl is bizarre and is surrounded by legend. His character can shed light on certain aspects of Bandar Shāh and Ḍaw al-Bayt. His origin is obscure. According to Ibrāhīm Wad Ṭāhā, the village informant, Bilāl is not one of king Bandar Shāh's slaves, but 'Īsā's twelfth son, the son of Ḍaw al-Bayt. Although the son of a beautiful black woman, whom 'Īsā loved and preferred to his other servant women, Ḍaw al-Bayt denies him his name and lineage. After Bandar Shāh's death his brothers are ashamed of his becoming an ordinary black slave, while on the other hand, they do not regard him as a free man nor do they want to share their inheritance with him.

Bilāl did not grow up with the villagers and it is small wonder that the village children do not remember him as a child, but as a young person between the ages of fifteen and twenty (as mentioned in relation to Maryūd and Muḥaymīd). The narrator describes in detail the relationships between Bilāl and Sheik Naṣrallāh Wad Ḥabīb. Bilāl serves him in ritual ceremonies and the Sheik appoints him the village *muw'adhdhin* – as the Prophet Muḥammad did with Bilāl. Our Bilāl ceases to be the village *muw'adhdhin* when the Sheik dies. Precisely one year after Sheik Naṣrallāh Wad Ḥabīb's death, Bilāl, too, dies, adding a mysterious touch.

Al-Ṭayyib Ṣāliḥ devotes a great deal of space to these characters. He is not satisfied with constructing one or a number of central characters, but carefully shapes secondary and marginal figures as well. Some of these characters are partially convincing, and some, as the author testifies,[100] were modelled on real characters, yet others are rather archetypal and less individualized, particularly when compared to the central character in the novel *Mawsim al-Hijra ilā al-Shamāl* (more in the case of Muṣṭafā Sa'īd and less in the case of the narrator). Legendary, mysterious and ambiguous elements characterize some of the leading and secondary characters in the novels. The fine line between realistic and mythical characters apparently appeal to the author. However, the blurring of the boundaries between legend and fiction and reality adds depth, variety and interest to the texts. The return of numerous characters, who take part in more than one work, functioning on stage in accordance with the author's wishes, is an interesting phenomenon. It confirms my earlier assumption, namely that all of al-Ṭayyib Ṣāliḥ texts, with the exception of his most recent short story 'Yawm Mubārak 'alā Shāṭi' Umm Bāb', are one large text, for the characters he has shaped are part of this fabric, just as the subjects, time, place and plot are an inseparable part of that larger text.[101] The following chapter is devoted to this topic.

CHAPTER FOUR

Development of the Characters in al-Ṭayyib Ṣāliḥ's Writing[1]

How to Define the Characters

In Chapter Three we tried to indicate the importance of the character not only in al-Ṭayyib Ṣāliḥ's writing, but in fiction writing in general and the novel in particular. What warrants emphasis, however is the important role played by the character in the work of al-Ṭayyib Ṣāliḥ. The real author insists on giving his characters a status and presence and it is this which marks his writing, providing a better understanding of manners, customs and way of life, especially in the Sudanese village.

The role of the character is of prime importance in modern literature, as well as in classical Arabic writings and classical Western literatures, especially classical Greek literature. Several literary 'prophets' of the twentieth century who predicted the death of the character in literature, like the death of God or the end of humanism, have been proven wrong. Indeed, the opposite can be claimed: on the threshold of the twenty-first century and the beginning of the third millennium, I can state without hesitation that some of the most successful novels have assigned key roles to characters in building the story.[2] This is true of prominent Western or Latin American writers such as Umberto Eco (b.1932), Italo Calvino (1923–85), or Gabriel García Márquez, as well as contemporary Arabic writers such as Salīm Barakāt, Muḥammad Barrāda, Ibrāhīm Naṣrallāh, Rashīd al-Ḍa'īf (b.1945) and Ilyās Khūrī (b.1948).[3]

Constructing and delineating a character to meet the author's needs can be accomplished by direct or indirect means. When done directly, the character is described by adjectives or by nouns, abstract or specific, but only when spoken by the most authoritative voice in the text. When indirect, characterization is accomplished by showing the reader – through one-time, non-routine actions such as murder or suicide, through the character's physical appearance, or by describing the physical surroundings – the city, village, river, house, or train – or the human landscape – the tribe, clan, family, and the like.[4]

It is true that the role of the character – its authority and credibility – derives from the status that the author chooses to accord it. One way of creating an authentic text is to have the story told from several points of view by various characters, à la Rashomon. Several such attempts were made in Western literature, such as *The Alexandria Quartet* (1957–60) by Lawrence Durrell (1912–90). In modern Arabic literatures as well, several attempts were made to construct a text, usually a novel, in which the author bestows credibility by presenting different points of view of the story. There are successful cases such as the quatrain by Fatḥī Ghānim, *al-Rajul Alladhī Faqada Ẓillahu* and less successful attempts, such as the novel *al-Safīna* by Jabrā Ibrāhīm Jabrā.

Credibility, authority, and the attitude of the author toward the characters in the narrative are integral to writing a persuasive and credible text, or alternatively where the author's voice and degree of closeness, sympathy or antipathy to a character are clearly expressed. To some extent, the voice and authority that appear in the text are of the implied author whose dialogue with the reader mediates between two parties who do not appear in the text – the author and the reader. Needless to say, the status and characterizations of the characters are derived not just from the creative powers of the writer, but also from the author's desire to convey preferences, dislikes, and distancing of a character from the spotlight in the narrative. Thus, the direct, straightforward characterization is not always most effective. Sometimes the opposite is true, i.e., pointing out what the character is missing may have a stronger effect than citing his or her negative qualities. The author can define the character without directly mentioning even one negative quality, but rather through descriptions of the voice, manner of speaking, surroundings, or personal appearance, thereby giving the reader full information about the author's attitude toward the character. Another fictional character in the text – one often in a key role – can also speak on the author's behalf.

One obvious example in contemporary Arabic literatures is the short story 'Za'balāwī' by Najīb Maḥfūẓ. In this work, author and reader encounter the world of Sheikh Qamar, the first station in the quest to find the wondrous character Za'balāwī, who is said to be able to cure illness. The uncompromising attitude of the author toward the *nouveaux riches* of Egypt – the opportunists and the career-driven who pursue personal interests – is expressed indirectly through the description of Sheikh Qamar's clothing, the location of his office, his clients and office furnishings. All these convey with precision the author's point of view about the situation in Egypt and this class of people. Thus we hear the voice of the author speaking through the narrator.[5]

Defining the Character

In the following I shall examine character development in the writing of al-Ṭayyib Ṣāliḥ. We, like the real author, begin with the assumption as stated above that the works of Ṣāliḥ, his novels and short stories combined, form one organic whole.[6] In this context, it is interesting to cite Khalīl al-Nu'aymī, who was asked in an interview if he considered the novels he wrote as one organic work, and said, 'I noticed this a short time ago. It's like someone building a house with dozens of rooms opening up into each other'.[7] Looking at the phenomenon of creating one large, undivided text, we note that most of the characters, whether central, secondary, or marginal, reappear in al-Ṭayyib Ṣāliḥ's writing in various roles, at various ages, and levels of emphasis.[8]

Themes as well as characters recur in the writing, such as the encounter between Western and Eastern culture, or the city and the village, the confrontation between the old and the new, and relationships between local residents and the government. Most of the action takes place in one location, the village of Wad Ḥāmid in the Marawī district of north Sudan. Even events partially repeat themselves in the course of several works. The author does not draw hard-and-fast distinctions between his various works, often using events that took place in one to suit his purposes in another. For example, the title of the short-short story 'Laka ḥattā al-Mamāt' (For You Until Death) from the collection *Dawmat Wad Ḥāmid* [9], written in 1962, later appears in the novel *Mawsim al-Hijra ilā al-Shamāl*, uttered by Isabella Seymour as she dedicates a picture to Muṣṭafā Sa'īd.[10]

Among motifs that recur in Ṣāliḥ's writing are miracles, dreams, and legends. The use of this literary device adds richness and variety to the world described by Ṣāliḥ. Examples are the miracles, dreams, and legends related to saints and righteous men such as Wad Ḥāmid ('Dawmat Wad Ḥāmid'), al-Ḥanīn (*'Urs al-Zayn*), Bandar Shāh (*Bandar Shāh: Ḍaw al-Bayt*), and Bilāl (*Bandar Shāh: Maryūd*).[11] Like other writers,[12] al-Ṭayyib Ṣāliḥ often writes about the relationship between the government of Sudan and villagers. For the villagers, the government is a negative element, evoking ridicule, hostility, and suspicion. These are the result of the villagers' bitter experiences with the government, and symbolize for them the city with its corruption and deprecation of rural values and beliefs.[13] Another key motif in the work of Ṣāliḥ is the natural environment – trees (palm, doum) and the river (Nile) – the latter representing a source of life and death as well as a channel to the outside world.[14] In addition to their practical uses, elements of nature embody the meaning of life for the *fallāḥ* (peasant-farmer).

Al-Ṭayyib Ṣāliḥ often writes of the changes in Sudanese villages, especially in the second half of the twentieth century. Much has changed, though the process of change and its acceptance has been gradual. We can follow the chronological sequence in Sālih's writing: In the first stage in the 1950s ('Dawmat Wad Ḥāmid'), the Sudanese governments attempted to force change on the village of Wad Ḥāmid. At this point, the villagers did not oppose the concept of change, but opposed the coercive methods used by the authorities.[15] In the second stage (*'Urs al-Zayn*),[16] modernization has just begun in the village with the government introducing water pumps rather than water wheels for agriculture, and voices of opposition were not yet heard from the inhabitants.[17] In the third stage (*Mawsim al-Hijra ilā al-Shamāl*),[18] attitudes to progress and agricultural projects have become more positive, cooperatives are formed, and water pumps are accepted for use. The villagers themselves direct the projects, led by Maḥjūb, one of the major characters in Ṣāliḥ's writings. The changes are now perceived in a positive light, in contrast with what was perceived in *'Urs al-Zayn.*[19] Nonetheless, the changes in the village are not sufficiently deep to transform the rural lifestyle or attitudes of the villagers toward the authorities, as indicated in Maḥjūb's words to the narrator:

> 'The world hasn't changed as much as you think', said Mahjoub. 'some things have changed – pumps instead of water-wheels, iron ploughs instead of wooden ones, sending our daughters to school, radios, cars, learning to drink whiskey and beer instead of arak and millet wine – yet even so everything's as it was'. Mahjoub laughed as he said, 'The world will really have changed when the likes of me become ministers in the government. And naturally that', he added still laughing, 'is an out-and-out impossibility'.[20]

However, Maḥjūb's belief that the change has been superficial does not stand the test of time. In a later work (*Bandar Shāh: Ḍaw al-Bayt*), we see young people of the village, headed by al-Ṭarīfī (Maḥjūb's nephew), bring about a local revolution by democratic means, toppling Maḥjūb and his friends from their positions of power. Now the change is profound, because revolution came about through the acceptance of democracy by the young people, who make it clear that progress cannot be halted.[21] This change becomes part of village life, although some villagers (especially the elders) are still reluctant to accept it (*Bandar Shāh: Maryūd*).[22]

In his works, al-Ṭayyib Ṣāliḥ creates an alternative world to the one in which he lives today in England, a world that he left as a young man, but which he internalized. Ṣāliḥ's most recent works give a detailed and in-depth portrait of the Sudanese village in which he was born and raised. This is clearly not a concocted world unconnected to reality. On the contrary, it is profoundly real and concrete, based on the actual village of Wad Ḥāmid in northern Sudan. However, the author, who cut himself off from that life, creates new layers that were not necessarily part of the original village, but are the fruit of his imagination.

The phenomenon of constructing a fictitious world to which the storyteller returns and focuses has parallels in Arabic and other modern literatures. In Arabic literature, we must note the Egyptian authors 'Abd al-Sattār Khulayyif and 'Abd al-Ḥakīm Qāsim. The descriptions of 'Abd al-Sattār Khulayyif also appear in his first three novels, creating one literary unity.[23] Here, too, one village provides the setting for the plot and most of the figures appear and reappear in the novels (Ibrāhīm al-Baḥrāwī, Zaydān Effendi, Raḍwān). Recurring motifs are class distinctions, exploitation of the villagers, the inferior status of women, and events, such as the theft of Ibrāhīm al-Baḥrawī's *jāmūsa* [female water buffalo]. Similarly, 'Abd al-Ḥakīm Qāsim[24] focuses on one world, the world of the village, the setting for most of his writings.[25] Qāsim weaves most of his plots around Bandara, his own village, and occasionally substitutes it for another (the village of his grandfather or uncle). Some of his characters are also protagonists in other works, especially 'Abd al-'Azīz, who bears several autobiographical features of the author. Themes recur in Qāsim's writing (transition from the village to the city, the protagonist's link with and disconnection from the villagers to whom he returns from time to time, foreignness, alienation).

The phenomenon of one character appearing in several works or as an iconographic figure is familiar from non-Arabic literature, notably in the works of Gabriel García Márquez, Honoré de Balzac and William Faulkner.[26] Neither the similarities nor the very existence of this phenomenon in al-Ṭayyib Ṣāliḥ's writing necessarily indicate the possible influence of these writers on Ṣāliḥ. Although, chronologically, it would be Balzac and, even more so, Faulkner who might have influenced him, but Ṣāliḥ's writings rather resemble those of García Márquez. Not that Márquez influenced Ṣāliḥ in the way that, for instance, Najīb Maḥfūẓ was influenced by García Márquez (in particular by the novel *One Hundred Years of Solitude*), evident in Maḥfūẓ's novel *Malḥamat al-Ḥarāfīsh* (The Harafish), both in the poetics of the writing and in the novel's thematic aspects.[27] The fact is that Ṣāliḥ wrote and published most of his short stories in the 1950s and early 1960s, and his novels *'Urs al-Zayn* and *Mawsim al-Hijra ilā al-Shamāl* were written in the first half of the 1960s, while García Márquez's major work, *One Hundred Years of Solitude*, was not published until 1967 and in Spanish. Although five other works by García Márquez had appeared earlier (1947–62),[28] he became known and his works were translated only after *One Hundred Years of Solitude* had appeared.

Let me illustrate this assumption from the writings of García Márquez because of the similarities between his work and that of al-Ṭayyib Ṣāliḥ, especially the thematic resemblance [29] The Colombian writer created a fantasy world in which most events transpire in the mythical village of Macondo.[30] In depicting this imaginary world, the author addresses issues such as politics, folk beliefs, agriculture, violence, sex, and the like. Similar to al-Ṭayyib Ṣāliḥ, García Márquez does not keep distinct the events and figures to each work, but uses them throughout his writings to construct an entire world, with events or episodes reappearing or undergoing development in other works. One example of this is the rebellion against the government and the civil war in the story 'No One Writes to the Colonel' (El Coronel No Tiene Quien Le Escriba, 1957), dealt with in much greater depth in the novel *One Hundred Years of Solitude*. We find the same characters reappearing in several works, the most striking is that of Colonel Aureliano Buendía, a key figure both in 'No One Writes to the Colonel' and again in *One Hundred Years of Solitude*. Of interest, too, are the similar attitudes toward the government and religion by the villagers in both Macondo and Wad Ḥāmid. Neither group appreciates the government or its representatives, and views them as unbidden and interfering in their internal lives.[31] As for religious officials, the residents of Wad Ḥāmid resent the preacher the government has sent, just as those of Macondo, led by José Arcadio Buendía, can not abide the priest that their government dispatched.[32]

Al-Ṭayyib Ṣāliḥ, too, makes extensive use of characters who repeatedly appear in novels and short stories, and when tracing these characters through his works one can follow their development and changing status. This becomes evident from examining the works of Ṣāliḥ in chronological order, which might provide the reader with a more coherent picture of the world created by Ṣāliḥ. The reappearance of characters sometimes helps clarify events and individuals in previous writings, and enables the reader to discern the changes that take place in the village such as: attitudes toward progress, relations between city-dwellers and villagers, and relations between Western and Eastern cultures.

An examination of the characters and their changing roles suggests that there are models according to which Ṣāliḥ created them. In each work, one character stands out prominently and others evoke reflections about him, or perhaps some are merely secondary and marginal characters that serve an illustrative role. For example, Muṣṭafā Sa'īd in *Mawsim al-Hijra ilā al-Shamāl* is the main protagonist, while figures like the narrator, Muṣṭafā's mother, and his wife Ḥusna comment on various aspects. Further, some characters like the Western women and Wad al-Rayyis, though distinctive, also fill an illustrative role.

The cast of Ṣāliḥ's characters is varied and not homogeneous in age, ethnic origin, gender, or features.[33] One particularly interesting phenomenon in Ṣāliḥ's effective portrayal of characters is their disappearance when he no longer has any use for them. There are central characters such as al-Zayn (*'Urs al-Zayn*), Muṣṭafā Sa'īd (*Mawsim al-Hijra ilā al-Shamāl*), and Ḍaw al-Bayt and Bandar Shāh (*Bandar Shāh: Ḍaw al-Bayt*) whom the narrator has chosen to place at the centre of action in one work, weaving an entire constellation of events around them, until he no longer needs them and they disappear from later writings (Muṣṭafā Sa'īd) or become secondary or even marginal characters (al-Zayn, Ḍaw al-Bayt, Bandar Shāh). The changing function of the characters is key to understanding the unity and coherence of the corpus of writing by al-Ṭayyib Ṣāliḥ.

Some of Ṣāliḥ's characters are symbolic and at times even archetypal, rather than real, personal, vital, and convincing. A brief examination of some of the characters will illustrate this, beginning with the narrator: undoubtedly, the character of the narrator, who appears in most of Ṣāliḥ's writing, provides a model for the persona of the educated Sudanese who began life in the village, left to further his education in the West, returned to his country, and now wanders between city and village. In some ways he feels like a stranger who functions in one community (the city), but does not belong to the community in which he longs to live (the village). In other words, this is the classic liminal character that will be discussed later. The grandfather is another key character who turns up frequently in Ṣāliḥ's writing. The grandfather symbolizes rootedness and stability, and he is the voice responding to issues of progress and modernization. He confronts these without flinching, earning the respect of the Sudanese intelligentsia (Muṣṭafā Sa'īd, the narrator). Another important model is that of Maḥjūb. More than any other character in Ṣāliḥ's writing, Maḥjūb represents the young villager who clings to his land and wins the admiration of the narrator, who probably even idealizes him.[34] Hence, transformation of this figure from a young, admired village leader to someone deprived of his powerful positions because of the march of progress (*Bandar Shāh: Ḍaw al-Bayt* and *Maryūd*) is crucial for understanding the changes that occur in the village and in Sudan in general.

Another recurring figure is the folk saint. Notable examples are al-Ḥanīn and al-Zayn (*'Urs al-Zayn*), who are admired by the villagers. Characters like these are the antithesis of official religious leaders whom the government appoints to serve in the village, such as the *imām*, who is not treated sympathetically by Ṣāliḥ.[35] The web of relations between al-Ḥanīn and al-Zayn contains a mystical spiritual quality,[36] the bond between teacher and pupil or father and son. A parallel relationship exists between Sheikh Naṣrallāh Wad Ḥabīb and Bilāl (*Bandar Shāh: Maryūd*). The figure of al-Zayn brims over with love, and in that sense is juxtaposed with al-Ṭāhir Wad al-Rawwāsī (*Bandar Shāh: Maryūd*) and counterpoised against the demonic figure of Muṣṭafā Sa'īd (*Mawsim al-Hijra ilā al-Shamāl*). In the category of legendary figures I might include Ḍaw al-Bayt, Bandar Shāh, and Maryūd. Unquestionably, al-Ṭayyib Ṣāliḥ is well aware that some of his characters are empowered with mythical qualities:

> I also tried in the novel *Bandar Shāh* to deal symbolically with the issue of government and the city, which is why I relied on the special features of the enviroment of northen Sudan, for no other reason than that I know them well. I represented them as ordinary people, farmers living in that environment, turning them into legendary figures. Thereupon, we find that Maḥjūb, 'Abd al-Ḥafīẓ, al-Ṭāhir Wad al-Rawwāsī, and others, are ordinary farmers, yet by the novel *Bandar Shāh* I have turned them into myth... into legend... and legend as I understand it, means giving reality broader dimensions in time, as Homer did. He took the Greeks and turned them into symbols that simultaneously interacted with a mythological world.[37]

And back to the Bandar Shāh family. This is a family that Ḍaw al-Bayt founded and Bandar Shāh raised to glory, but then Maryūd, the designated successor, is murdered by his uncles. Two comments about this family: one is that the relationship between Bandar Shāh and Maryūd (*Bandar Shāh: Ḍaw al-Bayt*, *Maryūd*) runs parallel to the relationship between the narrator and his grandfather (discussed below); and, second, that Ḍaw al-Bayt in some way evokes the figure of Muṣṭafā Sa'īd. On another level, Ḍaw al-Bayt can be seen as a reincarnation of Muṣṭafā Sa'īd (*Mawsim al-Hijra ilā al-Shamāl*), who comes from the river and disappears into it. Like Muṣṭafā Sa'īd, Ḍaw al-Bayt is a foreigner who lives in the village for a while, but his past and future are unknown. He marries a villager, begets children, and seemingly builds a family. Like Muṣṭafā Sa'īd and, to some extent, Bilāl (a major figure in *Bandar Shāh: Maryūd*), Ḍaw al-Bayt is also an outsider whose arrival in the village and his disappearance catalyze important changes there. Al-Ṭayyib Ṣāliḥ points this out in his semi-autobiography:

> There is a dialogue between me and myself; anyone following my writing, despite its paucity, will find the very same characters. I turn them to the left and to the right, sometimes I get rid of them and sometimes I perpetuate them. Thus, you'll notice that

> Muṣṭafā Sa'īd went with the waves. People ask: Where did he go? It does not matter. Years later or earlier, only God knows, Ḍaw al-Bayt comes out of the sea, and it was as if the energy itself reappeared in a different form and another time. That is what matters. What is important is that the energy reappears. Muṣṭafā Sa'īd, too, is veiled in ambiguity, like Ḍaw al-Bayt, but when Muṣṭafā Sa'īd arrives in the village, he gets a name, a status, and a history. The villagers didn't know it, but Muṣṭafā Sa'īd recounted his entire history to the narrator. In other words, he fixed him in time and place, but Ḍaw al-Bayt was fixed neither in time nor place.[38]

Another important set of characters in Ṣāliḥ's writing are the exceptional young village women. In depicting this group of characters, Ṣāliḥ renders an unrealistic portrayal of village life, but perhaps a reflection of his desire to change the reality.[39] These young women symbolize the hope for change in Sudanese society, especially in the village.[40] Prominent among them is Ni'ma (*'Urs al-Zayn*), an exceptional young woman who studied with boys and, unconventionally for Arab society and particularly the village, chooses al-Zayn as her husband without regard for the opinions of her father, mother, or brothers.[41]This is also somewhat true of Ḥusna (*Mawsim al-Hijra ilā al-Shamāl*), a young woman who dares to defy her father and brothers and turns down a marriage proposal from Wad al-Rayyis. When forced to accept him, Ḥusna kills her husband and commits suicide.[42] Fāṭima (*Bandar Shāh: Ḍaw al-Bayt*) is another remarkable young village woman, a tomboy who competes with boys her age and represents the development and progress of the Sudan. She is looked at askance by the villagers, because of their marriages to 'strangers' (Muṣṭafā and Ḍaw al-Bayt).[43] This is also true of Maryam (*Bandar Shāh: Maryūd*) who, like Ni'ma and Fāṭima, learns how to read and write with boys, believes in equality between the sexes, and introduces progress to the village.[44] Ḥawwā' (*Bandar Shāh: Maryūd*) closes the cast of female characters. This beautiful and intelligent young woman is courted by the village dignitaries but, like Ni'ma (*'Urs al-Zayn*), she turns down her suitors and hopes for someone different. And indeed, her marriage, like that of Ni'ma, is also exceptional and completely unexpected (to Bilāl), like the surprising match of Ni'ma and al-Zayn.[45] In addition, after Bilāl released Ḥawwā' from the ties of marriage she, like Ḥusna after Muṣṭafā Sa'īd's disappearance, refuses to be with another man, and exactly like Ḥusna, she devotes herself to raising her son.

In presenting this array of characters, the author generally takes an objective approach – if it is possible to speak of objectivity in the case of fiction – although in two cases he seems to express hostility. Ṣāliḥ, therefore, uses the implied author, who holds a dialogue through the text, not with the audience addressed by the narrator (the internal addressee), but with the actual reader, to clarify his position vis-à-vis these characters and to cast them in a negative light. One case is that of the *imām* of Wad Ḥāmid (*'Urs al-Zayn*), and the other is the school principal. Neither of these characters is given a name, which is an unusual phenomenon in the work in which they appear. Perhaps the author viewed them not as specific individuals, but as representatives of their institutions, iconographic figures, possible (though undesirable) models of an *imām* and a school principal. Both are figures who do not win the sympathy or respect of the villagers, and upon whom the author heaps ridicule.[46]

Fiction and Reality in the Figure of the Narrator

Although many characters reappear in al-Ṭayyib Ṣāliḥ's writings, the figure that appears in most of the works, one that develops and can shed light on Ṣāliḥ himself, is that of the narrator.[47] In most of his works, the narrator serves as a link connecting the 'real author' and implied author – in this case not identical, but very close – with the actual and the implied reader. The status, credibility, and authority of the narrator remain particularly high in most of the works in which he plays a role. We shall examine the character of the narrator in sequence of his chronological appearance.

The narrator present in most of al-Ṭayyib Ṣāliḥ's writings has autobiographical elements of the author himself. He appears from boyhood through maturity when he settles in the village of Wad Ḥāmid. I suggest that the evolution of the narrator reflects not only the evolution of the implied author, but also of the author. There are processes, however, that the real author has not yet experienced; these appear in the narrator and could be termed 'future writing', or perhaps 'utopian writing', or writing out of a desire to idealize time, place, and meaning which are no longer within the reach of the writer, the realistic part of his life. This occurs in the novel *Bandar Shāh: Maryūd*.

The changes that take place in the narrator at various stages are reflected in the works themselves. We first make the acquaintance of the narrator in the short story 'Ḥafnat Tamr' (written in 1957 and first published in 1967), where he is an older man who reflects upon the events of his childhood. This story is told simultaneously in the voice of a boy and an old man.[48] Clearly, using a boy to relate events limits both the credibility of the child-narrator and the messages he conveys to the reader. The narrator is depicted as a dreamy, sensitive youth who spends his childhood in the village. His relationship with his grandfather is a relationship that borders on adoration.

In the short story 'Risāla ilā Aylīn' (written in 1960 and first published in 1967), the narrator (again anonymous) is the writer of the letter to Aileen. Here the narrator returns to his village after having spent some time in the West where he married a young European woman. Upon returning, he feels ambivalent toward the village and its inhabitants. Although he loves the place and the people, he also senses that he has changed. He feels alienated in the village because of the gap that has opened between himself and the villagers and his family in particular. In this story, we find the alienation at the tragic core of the narrator's life, and this will grow in other writing (*Mawsim al-Hijra ilā al-Shamāl*) and reach even more tragic proportions with Muṣṭafā Sa'īd.

Another stage in the development of the narrator occurs in the story 'Dawmat Wad Ḥāmid' (1961). Unlike this figure in Ṣāliḥ's other works, here the young narrator, assigned more than a marginal role, assumes the role of the internal addressee who observes but is seemingly passive. Al-Ṭayyib Ṣāliḥ skillfully uses the technique of hearing and listening. The role of the listener is an old one, found in *Alf Layla wa-Layla* and, in Western literature, ever since *The Decameron* (1358) by Boccaccio through *The Ambassadors* (1903) by Henry James.[49]The narrator in our story is not necessarily the same narrator who appears in other works. In any event the questions asked by the young person, who actually serves as an external narrator, his profound empathy for the villagers and their struggle, and his sympathetic attitude toward the old man, who serves as an internal narrator, are all reminiscent of the web of relations between grandson and grandfather in Ṣāliḥ's other writing.

In 'Hākadhā Yā Sādatī' (1962), the character of the narrator develops further. When he encounters the West he realizes the alienation and abyss between himself and the villagers. This story is a kind of prologue to the division of the figure of the narrator into two – the narrator and Muṣṭafā Sa'īd. There are two voices here, and the struggle between them seems unresolved, passing on to *Mawsim al-Hijra ilā al-Shamāl*. In 'Hākadhā Yā Sādatī', the narrator deals with the West on two levels: internally, his burning hatred for the Western world is clear, while externally, he deals with the West according to how he is expected to behave, rather than how he feels. When these two levels are integrated, he bursts out in harsh criticism of his hosts,[50] which is merely a prologue to the great clash between the two cultures in *Mawsim al-Hijra ilā al-Shamāl*.

In 'Muqaddimmāt' (1966),[51] the figure of the narrator evolves through yet another stage. Here is a well-educated young man from the East who meets a young woman from the West, an encounter that can sometimes lead to marriage ('al-Ikhtibār' and 'Khuṭwa li'l-Amām') and sometimes ends with no results ('Ughniyat Ḥubb', 'Laka ḥattā al-Mamāt', and 'Sūzān wa-'Alī').[52] In these short-short stories, the narrator is presented as the other, who is constantly in touch with the local Europeans. These connections vary from simple friendship to marriage. In these works, al-Ṭayyib Ṣāliḥ expresses the full range of options for connections between East and West. The central Eastern figure is the same educated individual whose familiar attributes link him with the narrator in various works, and suggest to the reader autobiographical elements.

Mawsim al-Hijra ilā al-Shamāl (1966) is the first of Ṣāliḥ's long narrative texts in which the narrator is closer to the implied author than to the writer himself. The character of the narrator undergoes considerable development; he seems to be split in two, reflecting two options. One is embodied by the figure of his *Doppelgänger*, i.e., Muṣṭafā Sa'īd, while the second option is the narrator who represents the desired model for Easterners. This narrator seeks to provide objective, multi-dimensional evidence about the West, as opposed to the one-dimensional evidence suggested by Muṣṭafā Sa'īd. However, the narrator's attempts to appear objective are not persuasive, even though he knows quite well how to emphasize his shortcomings either to himself or to an Easterner who has spent considerable time in England.

Notwithstanding Muṣṭafā Sa'īd's central role in the plot, the narrator is the most important character in *Mawsim al-Hijra ilā al-Shamāl.* As in earlier works, here, too, the narrator remains unnamed, enabling the author to blur his identity, making it easier for him to converge with the figure of Muṣṭafā. The narrator is a key figure that is linked, or merged as some say, with the figure of Muṣṭafā Sa'īd.[53] Unlike Muṣṭafā Sa'īd, the narrator has honorable qualities and serves as a positive role model for the educated Sudanese. He is the antithesis of Muṣṭafā, a tragic character who symbolizes the alien not only in Europe but also in his own land. However, the narrator does not resolve all the problems faced by the educated Sudanese when he meets Western society, nor does he answer all the questions raised by these encounters. Rather, the narrator represents the second-generation educated Sudanese in addition to his academic Western education, who is searching for his identity and role in Eastern culture. He seeks to bridge the gap between his birthplace, its customs, tradition, and norms of Sudanese society, the village in particular, and Western values and norms. Throughout the entire novel, his efforts to integrate these two patently different cultures pit him against himself and the villagers, when – at the moment of truth – he is rejected by the villagers because he represents different norms.[54] Nevertheless, it is clear to the narrator that the village and its inhabitants are the core of his life not just in the past, but also in the present and will be in the future. His warmth toward the villagers contrasts sharply with his alienated attitude to places in the West where he once lived. The bond of the narrator with the villager may stem from his awareness that stability, security, and serenity can be found in the village, not the city. This is corroborated by the fact that he and his family choose to live in the village, despite his work in the city.[55] Thus he expresses his acknowledgment that his characteristic liminality, like many of his generation and of the previous and following generations, is a permanent and not a temporary condition of those who live in both societies. They are destined to be caught between two worlds, unable to exist unequivocally in one or the other.

Research into al-Ṭayyib Ṣāliḥ's works, particularly of *Mawsim al-Hijra ilā al-Shamāl*, has attempted to evaluate the influence on these by Western philosophers, psychologists, and writers such as Albert Camus in his *The Outsider* (1942) and *The Myth of Sisyphus* (1942), Sigmund Freud, Joseph Conrad in his *Heart of Darkness* (1902), *Lord Jim* (1900), 'Youth' (1902), *Chance* (1913), and *The Secret Sharer* (1912), William Shakespeare's *Othello* (1604) and *Hamlet* (1601), Stendhal's *The Red and the Black* and others.[56]For our purposes, it would be most useful to examine the 'connections' between Joseph Conrad (especially *Heart of Darkness*) and al-Ṭayyib Ṣāliḥ as reflected in the novel *Mawsim al-Hijra ilā al-Shamāl*.[57]

Let us examine the literary and, more precisely, philosophical perspective and its possible impact on al-Ṭayyib Ṣāliḥ. To which portions of the text does it apply? It seems that Muṣṭafā Sa'īd (*Mawsim al-Hijra ilā al-Shamāl*) like Meursault (*The Outsider*)[58] are depicted to a great extent as absurd heroes according to existentialist perceptions. We can expand on this subject and also restrict it: we can expand it by saying that Muṣṭafā Sa'īd is the more tragic hero, a prisoner of his destiny, and restrict it by saying that his absurdity is especilly evident during his stay in England. Muṣṭafā Sa'īd as a prisoner of his destiny is only one part of his life, while the other part is bound up in his attempts to rebel against his tragic fate, as in his Sisyphean efforts to free himself from both his destiny and from tragedy. True, these subjects existed prior to existentialism, and they contain elements of universal culture. Yet, it is difficult to ignore Camus' works that deal with man's attempts to rebel against his fate and existence, and also his Sisyphean experiences.[59] In general terms, three main points are common to Meursault, hero of *The Outsider*, and Muṣṭafā Sa'īd, hero of *Mawsim al-Hijra ilā al-Shamāl*. The first is the relationship between mother and son in both novels. In *The Outsider*, Meursault has lost his father and then loses his mother. His attitude towards his mother's death is shocking. Meursault does not remember the date of her death, he does not know how old she was, and he does not weep at her graveside. Furthermore, he smokes and drinks during the funeral, and scandalizes those around him. It should be remembered that while his mother was alive, his attitude towards her was one of alienation and indifference and was characterized by silence, the same silence that might be characteristic of relations between strangers. What is surprising (or perhaps not?) is that Meursault is conscious of his insensitive behaviour. In other words, that Meursault is alienated and indifferent and ignores his mother is due to man's absurd existence as experienced by Meursault, who is conscious of it, but cannot comprehend it. The relationship between Muṣṭafā Sa'īd and his mother exsists along similar lines. Here, too, the relationship is a non-relationship with the mother who wears a series of masks to eliminate any expression of emotion towards her son:

> When I think back, I see her clearly with her thin lips resolutely closed, with something on her face like a mask, I don't know – a thick mask, as though her face were the surface of the sea. Do you understand? It possessed not a single colour but a multitude, appearing and disappearing and intermingling.[60]

If silence marks the relationship between Meursault and his mother, Muṣṭafā Sa'īd's relationship with his mother is depicted by a glance, the kind of glance that highlights the lack of relationship and contact between the two. Thus, for example, when Muṣṭafā Sa'īd seeks to enrol at the school and needs her consent, it is expressed by him as follows:

> For a moment she glanced at me curiously, as though she wanted to hug me to her, for I saw that her face had momentarily lit up, that her eyes were bright and her lips had softened as though she wished to smile or to say something.[61]

The lack of emotional, contact and the mutual indifference between mother and son, reach a climax when he, her only son, takes his leave before going to high school in Cairo:

> That was our farewell: no tears, no kisses, no fuss. Two human beings had walked along a part of the road together, then each had gone his way [...] I packed up my belongings in a small suitcase and took the train. No one waved to me and I spilled no tears at parting from anyone.[62]

The fact that Muṣṭafā Sa'īd mentions that neither his mother nor anyone else waved him goodbye underlines the lack of emotion, just like the inability, or perhaps the lack of desire, to express emotion. Perhaps the author is hinting in a parody of the leave-taking related in Arabic novels (*al-Ḥayy al-Lātīnī* by Suhayl Idrīs, for example), between the hero and his family. In addition, we read in this description a completely opposite picture of Mrs Robinson's parting from Muṣṭafā in Alexandria when he left for his studies in England, like the description of her drying her tears and the high emotion expressed by her husband, all of which are diametrically opposed to what Muṣṭafā Sa'īd feels: 'However I was not sad'.[63] Muṣṭafā Sa'īd, like Meursault and the death experience, on the one hand, flees from death and is terrified by it, while on the other he is also attracted to it and is aware that he has no escape from it. And death, as in the case of Meursault, is connected to the mother. Muṣṭafā Sa'īd describes his feelings when he travels to London:

> The whole of the journey I savoured that feeling of being nowhere, alone, before and behind me either eternity or nothingness. The surface of the sea when calm is another mirage, ever changing and shifting, like the mask on my mother's face. Here, too, was a desert laid out in blue-green, calling me, calling me. The mysterious call led me to the coast of Dover, to London and tragedy.[64]

Like Meursault, Muṣṭafā Sa'īd receives the news of his mother's death with complete indifference. He, too, is drunk and with one of the British women when the news reaches him. Not only the way in which they both accept the death of their mothers, their only relative, but their sterile and alienated response, speaks volumes on the absurdity of and lack of meaning in their lives.

The second point linked to the two heroes and the two texts is the sun motif. This motif is employed as a kind of analogy for nature that is hostile towards the alienated hero, Camus' absurd man, and Sālih's hero as well. The sun appears in two contexts in *The Outsider*, both of which are connected with death. In the first instance, it is the death of the mother and her funeral. The sun gradually penetrates Meursault's consciousness and confuses him. There is a parallel between Meursault's heightened consciousness of the sun, its warmth and colour, and the fact that it, like nature and in contrast to what he thought, is foreign and hostile toward him. There is also a parallel between Meursault's fear of the sun and his fear of death. The second occasion on which Camus uses the sun in this clearly symbolic way is on the day of the murder. The sun beats down on him, confusing the workings of his soul, appearing to him as the fires of hell and becoming his enemy. Thus he finds himself disconnected from reality and living in another, illusory world in which he has neither control over his life and fate or the lives of others. All of nature, symbolized by the sun and the sea, conspire with the mother against Meursault, who claims in his defence that he had no intention of murdering the Arab, that the entire story is a fabrication and that it was all because of the sun. It is hard to ignore the great similarity between the second fateful occurrence of the sun in Camus' *The Outsider* and in al-Ṭayyib Ṣāliḥ's *Mawsim al-Hijra ilā al-Shamāl.* With Muṣṭafā Sa'īd, too, the sun and the sea, that is nature, conspire with the mother and lead him to destruction. Muṣṭafā Sa'īd's flight from death, from south to north, is no help, as nature, regardless of location, calls on him to carry out what he is destined to do: kill Jean Morris.

> I pursued her for three years. Every day the string of the bow became more taut. It was with air that my waterskins were distended; my caravans were thirsty, and the mirage shimmered before me in the wilderness of longing; the arrow's target had been fixed and it was inevitable the tragedy would take place.[65]

With Muṣṭafā Sa'īd the sun knows no peace, is merciless, and symbolizes his enemy. A certain absurdity is expressed here, for the sun in the east and/or the south is generally perceived as a part of nature, but as Muṣṭafā Sa'īd lives in an upside-down world, and as nature is alienated from and hostile towards him, he perceives it this way. Accordingly, Muṣṭafā Sa'īd must flee from the sun, or from the south to the north, but even there, too, he escapes the terrible heat, for Jean Morris's murder was committed in the heat and flames of hell, while outside it was bitterly cold. This is a complete contrast between Muṣṭafā's heat and the cold outside. The sun is joined by the sea, or the River Nile, that flows and finally reaches the north because that is nature's way, and the direction of its flow cannot be changed. The parallel with Muṣṭafā Sa'īd is completely clear. Muṣṭafā is led unwillingly (or perhaps not) to the north and in his case the north symbolizes tragedy and death. As we shall see later, the sun, the river and other forces of nature are not hostile towards the narrator, and he is not alienated from them, because he knows that they are the sources of his life's stability. In the end, and in contrast to the narrator, Muṣṭafā is lost in the river.

The subject of the sun and death in *Mawsim al-Hijra ilā al-Shamāl* merits the intervention of the real author, who conducts a dialogue with this subject as it appears in *The Outsider*, just as we can also see this issue as a solution different from that suggested by Camus. In one of the narrator's journeys to Khartoum, where he worked, he and the other travellers cross a desert and meet police officers in police car. They have come to arrest a Bedouin woman who has murdered her husband. The Bedouins, of course, keep silent for they all know the woman and it is unheard of a woman to murder her husband. In any event, we, the readers, witness the narrator's consciousness as he comments on death, the sun and the desert:

> An idea occurred to me; turning it over in my mind, I decided to express it and see what happened. I said to them that she had not killed him but he had died from sunstroke – just as Isabella Seymour had died, and Sheila Greenwood, Ann Hammond, and Jean Morris.[66]

The omniscient narrator is offering information, according to which it is not people killing one another, but nature, and in our case it is the sun that causes death. This may be a reference to, possibly even agreement with, Meursault, the hero of *The Outsider*, who claims in court that it was not he who killed the Arab, but the sun. Therefore, both Meursault and Muṣṭafā Sa'īd are not to be blamed for the murders they committed, and in the case of Muṣṭafa Sa'īd, he was not guilty of causing the suicides of his three English lovers. It was the sun.

The third point of similarity between Meursault and Muṣṭafā Sa'īd is the level of the individual and the collective, which, like their symbolism, is used as an analogy for the experience of the absurd in both novels. In *The Outsider*, the Algerian Arab not only threatens Meursault's identity by his silence, foreignness and alienation, he also symbolizes the problem of the Algerian collective, dominated by the French colonial collective. Meursault is divided: he is a Frenchman of Algerian extraction. Muṣṭafā Sa'īd, too, is divided, being a Muslim, black African Sudanese, who lives in the West, is Western educated, well-read in English poetry, and his principal relationships in the novel are with English women. It is Jean Morris who threatens Muṣṭafā Sa'īd just as the Algerian threatens Meursault. She, like Muṣṭafā Sa'īd, is violent and cruel and turns him from hunter into prey. They are both attracted to death and perceive it as a sanctuary, and both are afraid of it. The end for Jean Morris and the Algerian is death, wherease Meursault and Muṣṭafā's ends are obscure; whether they die or are saved remains unclear. Both, as may be expected of absurd heroes, seek relief from their fear of death by murdering the person who threatens their individual and collective identity, which destabilizes their mental state.

The pair of figures in this novel, the narrator and Muṣṭafā Sa'īd, and another pair of characters, Marlow and Kurtz, the two main protagonists in Joseph Conrad's *Heart of Darkness*, have much in common. Kurtz can be compared with Muṣṭafā Sa'īd,[67] while Marlow, the internal narrator, can be compared with the narrator of *Mawsim al-Hijra ilā al-Shamāl*. The relationship between Kurtz and Marlow also runs parallel in some ways to the relationship between Muṣṭafā Sa'īd and the narrator. Just as Muṣṭafā Sa'īd is the key figure in *Mawsim al-Hijra ilā al-Shamāl* – or perhaps it would be better to describe him as the major character, i.e., the figure serving as the pivot not only of the plot, but also of the novel's other characters – Kurtz is the key figure in *Heart of Darkness*, although he occupies less space in the book than Muṣṭafā Sa'īd. In both novels, however, the narrator and Marlow, who also serves as a narrator, are more complex and important figures, as well as more developed than those of Kurtz and Muṣṭafā Sa'īd. This may be attributed to their being highly aware, connecting links that closely express the implied authors. Therefore, their authority and credibility are particularly great. Moreover, their story is part of the framework story, which provides the main axis of the text. In other words, the story they tell, as credible and important as it may be, is not the full story of the actual narrator.

Kurtz leaves Western culture for Africa where he is idolized by the natives, but reaches the depths of moral and spiritual depravity, ultimately leading to his death. Muṣṭafā Sa'īd goes to the West where he is adored by women who worship him to death. Muṣṭafā is not corrupted by the West; he was cold, sterile, alienated, insensitive, and unable to love even before his arrival there. However, his experience in the West further damages his soul and accelerates his spiritual and moral decline. Furthermore, Muṣṭafā's mental makeup and his disposition, expressed negatively in Europe, is the outcome of latent traits encouraged and exacerbated by Western society. Ultimately, he does not find himself in the West and returns to Africa. But even there, peace eludes him and he disappears into the river. Muṣṭafā is more tragic than Kurtz because he remains isolated and alien both in the West and in his homeland.

Marlow, who serves as a narrator (internal) in *Heart of Darkness*, goes to Africa in search of Kurtz. His encounter with the heart of darkness does not lead to his death, but rather strengthens him like the narrator in *Mawsim al-Hijra ilā al-Shamāl* – although it tests him and he is frightened. Marlow returns to the West, his natural place; but thereafter he sees more clearly and critically the failings of the West. At the same time, he also recognizes the shortcomings of Africa. Marlow remains in the West, now aware of the imperfections of both the West and Africa.

The narrator in *Mawsim al-Hijra ilā al-Shamāl* is a Sudanese who spent several years in the West, learning both its positive and its negative qualities. Like Marlow, the narrator returns home and struggles to deal with the impact that Western culture has had upon him. And also like Marlow, who feels both attracted and repelled by Kurtz, the narrator feels attracted and repelled by Muṣṭafā Sa'īd, during Muṣṭafā's life and after his disappearance. The attraction felt by the narrator toward Ḥusna, Muṣṭafā's wife, exacerbates his struggle with his soul, bound up with his desire to rid himself of the dark internal forces. In this struggle, the narrator, like Marlow, emerges victorious.

In this connection, I must mention again the river, in which the narrator was purifed and where he undergoes a catharsis. The river was a source of strength for the narrator's inner struggles; for Muṣṭafā Sa'īd the river is where he disappeared or died. The narrator thus uses the river positively to overcome his crisis. Muṣṭafā Sa'īd uses it negatively. Perhaps al-Ṭayyib Ṣāliḥ was influenced by Faulkner, who inverted the symbolism of the river, using it as a source of impurity rather than purity, whereas in contrast to Christianity as well as Islam, Judaism, and other religions, the river is the source of purification.

In *Bandar Shāh: Ḍaw al-Bayt* (1971), Ṣāliḥ for the first time gives his narrator a name, that of Muḥaymīd. As in the previous works, the narrator is a key figure and takes an active key role in the novel. A turning point occurs in his life. The narrator had previously been absent from Wad Ḥāmid for only short intervals, but now an extended absence and return is followed by his decision never to leave the village again. The narrator, who had been immersed in his internal struggle and torn between two worlds – the village and the city, the old and the new – decides to return to the village after long periods of residence in the city. The narrator has extensive exposure in the novel, which sheds light on the author's life. The narrator wants to live out the remainder of his life in the village, to discover the truth and to live among his family, close to the earth and nature that he loves. His return was motivated by his clear objective to die in the village, as evidenced by his words: 'I've returned so as to be buried here. I swore I wouldn't give my body to any earth other than that of Wad Hamid'.[68]

In this novel the narrator is a more developed character as is obvious in the relationship with his grandfather. While in previous works, the narrator relates to his grandfather with respect ('Ḥafnat Tamr') or admiration (*Mawsim al-Hijra ilā al-Shamāl*), here we sense an undertone of criticism and bitterness concerning two issues related to his grandfather: one, his grandfather's earlier opposition to his marriage with Maryam, and two, his grandfather's demand that he study, completely disregarding his desire to be a farmer. These two events changed the course of the narrator's life, for which he blames his grandfather. Nonetheless, he has enough integrity to acknowledge his guilt for not standing up to his grandfather and thus leading a life at odds with his judgment and desires.[69]

In the short text 'al-Rajul al-Qubruṣī' (1973), the nameless narrator appears as the key figure. He lives for a while in Beirut, his trip to Cyprus is connected to the figure of al-Ṭāhir Wad al-Rawwāsī, and his trip to Wad Ḥāmid is related to the death of the narrator's father. The figure of Muḥaymīd comes up once again when the external narrator arrives at the village of Wad Ḥāmid, where he assumes the figure of Muḥaymīd. This figure, a composite of the narrator and Muḥaymīd, casts light on Ṣāliḥ the real author. The evidence of this is fragments of Ṣāliḥ's biography, his trips to Beirut and Sudan.[70]

The most recent long work (so far) in which the narrator is an integral part is the novel *Bandar Shāh: Maryūd* (1976–7). As in *Bandar Shāh: Ḍaw al-Bayt*, here too the character of the narrator develops more directly. The narrator documents life in Wad Ḥāmid where he chooses to live out the end of his days. He is aware that his extended absence from the village has weakened the bond he had with his childhood friends, as al-Ṭāhir Wad al-Rawwās notes: 'You were away, you were travelling. You'd be away for a year and come and stay with us for a month or two... The person who's with you isn't like the person who's far away, no matter what!'[71] Echoes of this in the author's private life occur in his semi-autobiography.[72]

In *Bandar Shāh: Maryūd*, the narrator searches his soul about himself and his grandfather while attempting to find the truth, as he had done in *Bandar Shāh: Ḍaw al-Bayt*. Events in the past and present cast light on the narrator's own history and future, including his ongoing search for the meaning of life.[73] The search is revealed in description of his love for Maryam, a love that his grandfather forbade, which forced him to leave the village. His feelings about his grandfather emerge clearly: he still loves his grandfather, but this love is for the first time mixed with resentment, sadness, and even hatred. Hatred is a foreign impulse to the narrator and derives from irreparable harm done to him by his grandfather. Since it is the end of the journey, not the beginning, for the narrator as well as the author, we should bear in mind that he wrote *Bandar Shāh: Maryūd* in his late 40s, after the decision to live in Europe had become fact.

In *Bandar Shāh: Maryūd*, we discern a blending of the personae of the narrator – Muḥaymīd and Maryūd[74] – into one persona, that of the grandson who carries on after his grandfather. Maryūd, who was murdered in *Bandar Shāh: Ḍaw al-Bayt*, reappears in the eponymous novel *Bandar Shāh: Maryūd*, and merges into the figure of the narrator and Muḥaymīd. Maryūd appears in the same two works as his grandfather (Bandar Shāh) and great-grandfather (Ḍaw al-Bayt). In his first appearance in *Bandar Shāh: Ḍaw al-Bayt*, he plays the key role of Bandar Shāh's grandson; he follows his orders and is designated the heir and successor. Maryūd is a legendary figure, idealized as the grandson by the author. And Maryūd ends up like his grandfather – murdered. In the novel *Bandar Shāh: Maryūd*, the grandson Maryūd reappears even though he was murdered in *Bandar Shāh: Ḍaw al-Bayt*. Ṣāliḥ resurrects this legendary figure and the complex and distinctive relationship between Maryūd and his grandfather Bandar Shāh. In this relationship, similar to that of the narrator and his grandfather, we see a latent competition between the two. I might suggest that the narrator in this novel is both Muḥaymīd and Maryūd, or the narrator is the grandson – Maryūd and Muḥaymīd integrated. He is the man who was restored to life so he could continue to tell the wonderful story of the remote village in Sudan, its past, present, and future.

The merging and splitting of several figures was meant to emphasize the contrasts as well as their uniqueness by juxtaposing them.[75] The figures take one course or several, but eventually merge into one. Therefore, the ties between the various options of the figures embodied by the narrator can be viewed as a possible realization of fantasy and imagination, which enrich and vary the writing. At times, the figures are close and sufficiently connected to be 'doubles'.[76]

As we pointed out earlier the phenomenon of a double or a *Doppelgänger* already occurred in the figure of Muṣṭafā Sa'īd and the narrator in *Mawsim al-Hijra ilā al-Shamāl*. The concept is not new in literature and derives from European 'romantic theories' of the eighteenth and nineteenth centuries. Such intertwining of figures can be also defined as binary oppositions and particularly complementary opposites. Therefore, possibly the narrator and Muṣṭafā changed from two characters, who started to play the role of binary oppositions, becoming later complementary opposites. This may be the case of the narrator and Maḥjūb who started to play their role on the stage of Wad Ḥāmid first as binary oppositions and then became increasingly two characters who assumed the role of complementary opposites.

In *Bandar Shāh: Maryūd*, the narrator confronts the world he had loved and his grandfather whom he had admired. This harsh confrontation ensues from the narrator's desire to find his place in the world, to understand it, and to search for the meaning of life. This may be regarded as stages of apprenticeship, the last stage being an internal search. Inner and external journeys of this kind are used by other Arab writers in their *Bildungsroman* (Maḥfūẓ, Ghānim, 'Abd al-Ḥakīm Qāsim), and poets (Adūnīs, Unsī al-Hājj, Fū'ad Rifqa, Badr Shākir al-Sayyāb, 'Abd al-Wahhāb al-Bayyātī and Jubrān Khalīl Jubrān) follow the literary Hellenist heritage.[77] Here, as elsewhere, one is struck by the parallels between the narrator, a literary invention, and al-Ṭayyib Ṣāliḥ, the author of the fictional work. However, while Ṣāliḥ moves back and forth between Europe and the Arab world, preferring to establish a home in the West, the narrator settles down in Wad Ḥāmid, which is at once the narrator's and the author's favoured village.[78] Is this perhaps the hidden desire of the real author, expressed through the narrator, to return some day to the village of his birth and to live out his remaining days there? From another perspective, we might consider this 'future or utopian writing', as noted earlier. It idealizes time (the past), place (Wad Ḥāmid, Sudan), and figures, both real characters who had accompanied the author in the past when he lived in Sudan, and fictitious figures created by the author, whether based on reality or not. Ṣāliḥ's novels imitate reality, are *mimesis* in the words of Auerbach, and may contain elements of both fiction and reality simultaneously. Imagination blends with fiction, and reality in his writings as well as in his life. In the novel *Bandar Shāh: Ḍaw al-Bayt*, the narrator states a similar desire to live in Wad Ḥāmid. But there the narrator is seventy years old, while Ṣāliḥ the real author, is currently about forty, suggesting that this might portend a wish that may yet be fulfilled; though probably not, since as observed earlier, Ṣāliḥ manoeuvres well between the real and the alternative worlds, managing to make the best of both. But with this we touch on questions of Eastern and Western cultures, to which Arab writers often reflect the time they had spent in the West in written texts, mostly novels. Al-Ṭayyib Ṣāliḥ is exceptional by preferring to remain in the West, while dealing in his literary works with the East. This encounter between Eastern and Western worlds shall be discussed in the next chapter.

CHAPTER FIVE

The Migration to the North/West: On East/South and West/North in the Works of al-Ṭayyib Ṣāliḥ

The conceptual framework of this chapter is based on issues of duality and complementary opposites, or perhaps on the better known term of 'binary oppositions'. This can be defined as follows:

> Binary opposition is the principle of contrast between two mutually exclusive terms: on/off, up/down, left/right etc; an important concept of structuralism which sees such distinction as fundamental to all language and thought. The theory of phonology developed by Roman Jakobson uses the concept of binary features, which are properties either present or absent in any phoneme: voicing, for example, is present in /z/ but not in /s/. This concept has been extended to anthropology by Claude Levi-Strauss (in such oppositions as nature/culture, raw/cooked, inedible/edible) and to narratology by A. J. Greimas.[1]

Between East/South and West/North in Modern Arabic Literatures

Encounters between Western culture, or better Western cultures and Eastern cultures, particularly Mediterranean cultures, did not begin in the modern era. As long ago as the pre-Islamic period, prior to the year 622, contacts existed between nomadic and non-nomadic Arabs and their Greek, Roman and Byzantine neighbours, and also with Persia. Encounters between Arab culture and those surrounding it continued after the birth of Islam, the appearance of the Prophet Muḥammad, and even later, during the periods of his successors, the Orthodox Caliphs (632–661), the Umayyad Caliphs (661–750) and the Abbasid Caliphs (750–1258), and in the course of the spread of the Ottoman empire, especially in the 15th and 16th centuries. These encounters, in times of peace as in times of war, took place in numerous spheres, in art, literature, music, and the like. In past periods, particularly during that of the Abbasid rule, there were reciprocal relations and influences between Greek and Jewish cultures and Arab culture, and there was also the great influence of Persian culture on that of the Arab. During periods of contact, the Arabs did not refrain from learning, translating and allowing themselves to be influenced by science, and especially in such fields as literature, philosophy, chemistry, mathematics, and astronomy.[2]

It seems that the turning point between Arab and Western cultures had its beginnings in 1096 with the first crusade, and was intensified due to the conquest of

Jerusalem by the Crusaders in 1099. Moreover, the conflict grew in subsequent crusades, especially the religious-political conflict over Jerusalem.[3] But even before the crusades there were wars between the Arabs and Western or non-Western nations such as the Persians, yet the crusades symbolize the religious-political overtones that would henceforth characterize the encounters between the Arabs and Europe.

Many scholars agree that the first significant encounter in the modern era between East and West took place when the French invaded Egypt in 1798.[4] Accordingly, this date, more than any other, marks the massive penetration of the Christian West into the greater part of the Muslim East. The tremendous gap between Western technology, science and military knowledge and their absence in the East continues to accompany the Mediterranean peoples to the present day. There can be no disputing the fact that the trauma caused by the French conquest at the end of the 18th century and other conquests during the 19th and at the beginning of the 20th centuries by France and Great Britain in the Arab world, has left its mark on Arabs and Muslims even at the beginning of the third millennium. Despite this traumatic encounter, numerous 19th and 20th century Arab intellectuals did not ignore its positive aspects. In several aspects, the initial contact between the two cultures in the contemporary era was a continuation of earlier contacts that had begun in the 19th century. The contacts between Western and Eastern cultures during this period were in Europe in the spheres of culture, language, art, society, science and technology, and consisted initially of delegations of students from Arab countries going to study European languages and Western sciences. In the main, these students were from the upper class of Egyptian society.[5] Thus an interesting process occurred in which, paradoxically, Western states, especially Great Britain and France, continued to conquer and dominate parts of the Maghrib and Mashriq countries in the course of the 19th century and the early 20th,[6] while on the other hand they were teaching science and languages to the students from those same countries that were under their colonial rule. This may not be a paradox since Arab intellectuals and statesmen do not distinguish between military and political conquest. Indeed, they assert that the cultural conquest of Arab countries by the West is of far greater consequence. This, together with the gradual internalization of the Western conquest, has led to a shift from a naive, simplistic attitude to increasing suspicion and belligerence.

The issue under discussion is the encounter between the culture of the East with that of the West, or in other words, between the colonizer and the colonized or the oppressor and the oppressed.[7] In modern Arabic literatures generally and in the works of al-Ṭayyib Ṣāliḥ in particular, the subject of the cultural encounter is discussed in one form or another by the majority of Arab authors in the Arab Mashriq and Maghrib. The hypothesis regarding Western materialism and the imperialist offensive against Eastern spiritualism recurs in the works of Eastern intellectuals like Jamāl al-Dīn al-Afghānī (1839–97), Aḥmad Amīn (1886–1954), ʻAbd al-Wahhāb ʻAzzām (1893–1959), and Manṣūr Fahmī (1886–1959).[8] In fact, like the Western offensive against Arab culture, in the words of Arab intellectuals, the intercultural encounter encompasses every sphere of life, from industry and agriculture to technology and science in the last two hundred years. New versus old, village versus city, women's rights and status, attitudes towards religion and the citizen, the relationship between tradition and change, and between education and urbanization, all are subjects engendered by the relationships with Western cultures from the beginning of the 19th century to the present day, the beginning of the third millennium. In one form or another, encounters with Western cultures are discussed by all major writers in every literary genre. Regarding poetry, brief mention should be made of the Syrian poet Adūnīs, which is the pseudonym of Aḥmad ʻAlī Saʻīd (b.1930), Lebanese poet Khalīl Ḥāwī (1919–82), Moroccan poet Muḥammad Bennīs (b.1947), Iraqi poet Badr Shākir al-Sayyāb (1926–64), and Egyptian poet Ṣalāḥ ʻAbd al-Ṣabūr (1931–81). For many prominent writers of fiction the cultural encounter is a central axis in their works. There are the Egyptian writers Tawfīq al-Ḥakīm, Ṭāhā Ḥusayn, Najīb Maḥfūẓ, Fatḥī Ghānim and Muḥammad Yūsuf al-Qaʻīd. From Syria, Ḥannā Mīna and ʻAbd al-Salām al-ʻUjaylī; from Lebanon, Suhayl Idrīs and Ḥanān al-Shaykh; from Iraq, Dhū al-Nūn Ayyūb and Muḥammad Khuḍayyir (b.1940). The Jordanian Palestinian Ibrāhīm Naṣrallāh, and Palestinian writers Jabrā Ibrāhīm Jabrā and Emīl Ḥabībī, are similarly important, as are the Maghribi writers, particularly al-Ṭāhir Waṭṭār from Algeria, and Muḥammad Zifzāf from Morocco. The Arab writer of Saudi extraction, ʻAbd al-Raḥmān Munīf occupies a respected place among them.

Even if there were not many writers among Arab intellectuals from the Mashriq and the Maghrib who travelled to Western countries in the 20th century to acquire an education, those who did became prominent. These writers often dealt with their impressions in novels bearing a clear autobiographical imprint that took the form of the heroes who journeyed to the West/North.[9] We should bear in mind that we are not discussing only Egyptian and Lebanese writers, for the encounter with the West also includes authors and poets from the Arab Mashriq and Maghrib.[10] The heroes of these works acted according to an almost standard formula: they travelled to a European country, usually France, like Ṭāhā Ḥusayn in his novel *Adīb* (Man of Letters, 1935), Tawfīq al-Ḥakīm in his novel *ʻUṣfūr min al-Sharq* (1938), Suhayl Idrīs in his novel *al-Ḥayy al-Lātīnī* (1954), ʻAbd al-Salām al-ʻUjaylī in his short novel *Raṣīf al-ʻAdhrā' al-Sawdā'* (Sidewalk of the Black Virgin, 1960), or the hero of the novel *Matāhat al-Raml* (The Sand's Labyrinth, 1994) by the Tunisian author al-Ḥabīb al-Sālimī. Among those who travelled to England there is Yaḥyā Ḥaqqī and his novel *Qindīl Umm Hāshim* (1944), or al-Ṭayyib Ṣāliḥ and the novel *Mawsim al-Hijra ilā al-Shamāl* (1966). The European scene is sometimes set in Germany, as in the novels *Badawī fī Ūrūbbā* (A Bedouin in Europe, 1977) by Jordanian author Jumʻa Ḥammād and *Qadar Yalhū* (Fate Plays, 1939) by the Syrian author Shakīb al-Jābirī, or in Scandinavia as in the novel by Fatḥī Ghānim, *al-Sākhin wa'l-Bārid* (The Hot and the Cold, 1960). In the new African literature there are writers who travelled not only to Europe but also to the United States, and who conveyed their impressions in novels.[11]

Common models may be distinguished in these literary works, as follows:

The literary category – In the main, the Arab writers who summarized the impressions of their journey to Europe cast them in the form of novels and less in other literary categories, such as short stories, plays or poetry.[12] The novels were usually written along autobiographical lines that spoke for the author rather than a fictional character of his creation. A parallel can be drawn here between this phenomenon and the corpus of village novels in modern Arabic literatures.[13] In these the writers constructed their text around their actual experiences, and therefore the autobiographical elements are a central part of the text.

The corpus of Arabic novels, which we shall call 'between East and West', can be divided into two main categories: The first includes those novels that meet the definition of the Eastern hero who leaves for the West and returns to his own country. The central plot of the novel takes place between East and West, the central character is Eastern, and the novel's subjects are related to the encounter between the two cultures. In this category there are novels like *Adīb, 'Usfūr min al-Sharq, Qadar Yalhū, Qindīl Umm Hāshim, al-Sākhin wa'l-Bārid, Mawsim al-Hijra ilā al-Shamāl, al-Mar'a wa'l-Warda* (1972), by Muḥammad Zifzāf, *Musāfir bilā Ḥaqā'ib* (1979) by Walīd Ḥajjār (b.1931) and *al-Marfūḍūn* (1981), by Ibrāhīm Saʻdī (b.1950). There are sub-categories in which the hero (or one of the principal characters) is not an Arab intellectual but a simple labourer (*al-Marfūḍūn, Matāhat al-Raml*) who travels to France seeking work,[14] or a Bedouin who goes to Germany (*Badawī fī Ūrūbbā)*, or a political exile in Paris as in the novel al-*Sayyid wa-Mar'atuh fī Bārīs*, by Bayram al-Tūnisī (1893–1961),[15] an official who travels to Austria under the pretence of a business trip but actually to pursue the local women, as in the novel *al-Sayyida Fiyinnā* (Lady Vienna, 1975), by Yūsuf Idrīs.[16] Or there are Syrian and Palestinian travellers to London for medical treatment as in the novel *Ḥamāma Zarqā' fī al-Suḥub* (Blue Doves in the Clouds) by Ḥannā Mīna.[17] The second category includes novels in which the subject of East and West is employed only as a partial axis of the plot. Among these are the novels *Fī al-Ṭufūla* (In Childhood, 1956), by the Moroccan author 'Abd al-Majīd Ibn Jallūn (1919–81), *Widā'an Yā Afāmiya* (Farewell, Afamiya, 1960), by Shakīb al-Jābirī, *al-Safīna* (1969), by Jabrā Ibrāhim Jabrā, *al-Ashjār wa-Ightiyāl Marzūq* and *Sharq al-Mutawassiṭ* (East of the Mediterranean, 1975), by 'Abd al-Raḥmān Munīf, *Fallāḥ Miṣrī fī Bilād al-Firanja* (An Egyptian Fellah in the Lands of the Franks, 1978), by Egyptian author Khayrī Shalabī (b.1938), *Qālat Ḍuḥā* (Duha Said, 1985), by Egyptian author Bahā' Ṭāhir (b.1935), and *'Ā'id ilā al-Quds*, (Returning to Jerusalem, 1998) by the Canadian Palestinian author and scholar 'Īsā Bullāṭa (b.1929).[18]

Two sub-categories of the second category are important: the first includes two novels in which the plot takes place in the East and it is the Western woman who comes there. In the first novel, the hero is Eastern – in this case Egyptian – the Western heroine is a Frenchwoman, the scene is Egypt, or more precisely an Egyptian village. In this novel, *Aṣwāt* (Voices, 1972) by Sulaymān Fayyāḍ (b.1929), the author has the Western woman confront the norms of the people of the East. In the second novel *Muḥāwala li'l-Khurūj* (An Attempt to Get Away, 1980), by 'Abd al-Ḥakīm Qāsim, Evelyn, a Swiss woman, comes to Egypt with a group of Swiss tourists and through her relationship with Ḥakīm, a villager who has moved to Cairo in an effort to become a writer, she discovers the personal differences between them.[19] The second sub-category includes the novel *Naham* (Greed, 1937),[20] by Shakīb al-Jābirī. This novel is unique for its plot takes place in Germany, all the characters are European and there are no Arab or Eastern characters. The author tells the story of a Russian émigré and his relationships with the local women in Berlin in the early twenties.

Male authors – On the face of it, it seems peculiar and even extraordinary that among the writers of these texts, there is not a single woman. The explanation is that in modern Arab societies, the student delegations that travelled to the West consisted usually of men, and women were not generally included. As a result of either necessity or choice, in the second half of the 20th century, particularly after the civil war in Lebanon (1976), Arab women writers reached the West and today they work in Europe, writing mainly in Arabic.[21] One of the most prominent Arab woman writers is Lebanese author Ḥanān al-Shaykh who lives in London. Her recent works and the translation of these into English are marked by European influences.[22]

Locale of the encounter – Generally speaking, in modern Arabic literatures an Eastern Muslim Arab man is depicted as arriving in the Christian European West where he meets a Christian Western woman. Hence in the novels we shall define as East-West novels, the hero is usually a man, the narrator; he is an Eastern man who goes to the West to study and excels in his studies: Adīb (*Adīb*), Ismā'īl (*Qindīl Umm Hāshim*) and Muṣṭafā (*Mawsim al-Hijra ilā al-Shamāl*). Accordingly, the European scene usually portrays characters who with the exception of the narrator are European, and the loved one or the fiancée is the one left behind in his homeland. The locale is the Western capital (Paris, London), which is an intentional choice as these are the capital cities of the imperialist countries in the heart of the great darkness.[23] Quite possibly, the capital city symbolizes the 'culture' and is intentionally employed as the antithesis of the Arab desert or African forest, and is a place in which man is destined to wander. While some of the Arab heroes reject the idea of Westernization from an ideological and religious standpoint, we find also cases where Western characters convert to Islam, as with Mr Robinson (*Mawsim al-Hijra ilā al-Shamāl*) and the Germans 'Abd Allāh and Maryam (*Badawī fī Ūrūbbā*).[24] The locale of the encounter dictates the language in which the Eastern man and the Western woman converse. In the Arabic novel, as in the African novel, or even in novels that are neither Arabic nor African, the dialogue between the hero who belongs to the conquered collective, and the European characters who belong to the conquering collective, therefore takes place on European soil and in a European language.

The character of the Western woman – In works dealing with the encounter between the Eastern man and the Western woman with whom he forms a relationship, even when Eastern women are linked to the Eastern man's past (*Qindīl Umm Hāshim, al-Ḥayy al-Lātīnī*), although in some cases Eastern women are also connected to his future (*Qindīl Umm Hāshim*). In these works the Western woman is usually presented in a negative light, like, for example, Eileen (*Adīb*), Suzy (*'Uṣfūr min al-Sharq*), Françoise (*al-Ḥayy al-Lātīnī*), Jean Morris (*Mawsim al-Hijra ilā al-Shamāl*) and Odèle and Anastasia (*Musāfir bilā Ḥaqā'ib*). Only infrequently are the positive aspects of these female characters presented, and then while noting their negative attributes as women who represent all that is negative in Europe, as for example, Marie (*Qindīl Umm Hāshim*), Janine (*al-Ḥayy al-Lātīnī*) and Julie (*al-Sākhin wa'l-Bārid*). But the exception proves the rule, and this can be found in the novel by Syrian author Shakīb al-Jābirī, *Qadar Yalhū*, in which the young German woman, Ilse, has positive attributes which, *inter alia*, lead the hero to marry her, but she dies a short time later. In other words, happiness and marriage must end. Aside from few exceptions, in no case does the relationship between the Eastern hero and the European woman end in a happy marriage. This possibly indicates the traditional view that rejects equality between men and women, and therefore women are portrayed as 'satanic' characters. There are certainly certain sectors of Muslim society which view the woman with suspicion, hence needing to restrict her and guard against her bringing disgrace upon those around her. Descriptions of the Western woman in these novels express not only hostility towards the West, but might also mark the Arab writer's commitment to his own collective, indicative of a type of engagé literature.[25]

The place of the novel in the author's corpus – An examination of authors who deal with the subject of the encounter between the two cultures shows that not in every case this is the writers' first text. The writers can be divided into two main categories: the first includes writers whose novel discusses East-West relations and which is not their first novel. In this category are Tawfīq al-Ḥakīm (*'Uṣfūr min al-Sharq*), who had previously published important novels like *'Awdat al-Rūḥ* (Return of the Spirit, 1933), and *Yawmiyyāt Nā'ib fī al-Aryāf* (The Maze of Justice, 1937).[26] The second is comprised of writers for whom this is their first novel, but not the first text they have written. It includes Suhayl Idrīs and his novel *al-Ḥayy al-Lātīnī*, which was preceded by collections of short stories.[27] Furthermore, in the majority of cases – if not all of them – those writers who wrote a novel about their encounter with the West had previously written short and/or long texts whose plots frequently dealt with this subject. Despite containing numerous autobiographical references, a novel of this type is extraordinary because only rarely have authors in this category written more than one novel on this subject. An exception is Shakīb al-Jābirī, who has written three novels on the subject.[28] Accordingly, the majority of the novels in this category are relatively mature works, as their authors had acquired experience in writing short and/or long texts which often restrained the emotional charge that was part of their experience.

The period of the novels' publication – The number of novels included in the various categories of encounter between cultures is approximately twenty, and they were published from the mid-thirties until the mid-nineties.[29] Five novels were published in the thirties (*Adīb, Naham, 'Uṣfūr min al-Sharq, Qadar Yalhū* and *al-Duktūr Ibrāhīm*) and four were published in the eighties (*Muḥāwala li'l-Khurūj, Ḥubb fī Cūpenhāgen, al-Marfūḍūn* and *Qālat Ḍuḥā*). The striking difference between the two periods is that while the five novels published in the thirties were written by Arab Mashriq writers, the four published in the eighties were written by three Arab writers from the Mashriq and two from the Maghrib. Moreover, in the two Maghribi novels, especially in the one by Sa'dī Ibrāhīm, *al-Marfūḍūn*, the hero is no longer an intellectual who seeks Western culture, but one of many Algerian workers who went to France to earn a living as a manual labourer. He symbolizes the acute problem of Maghribi workers in general who work in France.[30] One might have expected that with the process of modernization and great progress taking place in the Arab world, the subject of East-West encounter would either disappear or at least wane, but apparently it is not so. Indeed, the encounter between the two cultures not only continues and remains one of the central subjects in modern Arab literatures generally; thus the results of the encounter reverberate in many of Arab literary categories.

Images – The novels reveal how each party adheres to preconceptions and stigmas vis-à-vis the other.[31] Images of individuals or collectives in juxtaposition often depict the other party in a dehumanized way. The approach towards imperialism in terms of images was that on the one hand, the Westerner caused the Arab world to see the 'ugly face' of Europe, while on the other, imperialism took back to Europe an incorrect picture of the Arabs, namely of a primitive and barbaric world.[32] The image of Westerners in the eyes of the Eastern heroes living in Europe is on the whole negative. They perceive Europeans, particularly their women, as licentious, wanton, uninhibited and as heretics (*al-Sākhin wa'l-Bārid, Badawī fī Ūrūbbā, Mawsim al-Hijra ilā al-Shamāl, al-Ḥayy al-Lātīnī*). Easterners in the West see democracy, the value of human life, order and cleanliness, science, art and music (*'Uṣfur min al-Sharq, al-Sayyid wa-Mar'atuh fī Bārīs*), in a positive light, whereas the Westerners' attitude to Easterners is ambivalent. They retain the exotic image of the East and are attracted to the East and its people (*'Uṣfur min al-Sharq, Qindīl Umm Hāshim, Mawsim al-Hijra ilā al-Shamāl, al-Sākhin wa'l-Bārid, Raṣīf al-'Adhrā' al-Sawdā', al-Sayyida Fiyinnā, Qālat Ḍuḥā*). Obviously they were influenced by classical Eastern and Arab texts such as *Alf Layla wa-Layla* and *Rubā'iyyāt 'Umar al-Khayyām* that they read as outsiders, as the other.[33] On the other hand, Westerners view the Easterner as he is often portrayed in Europe: the wild, uneducated, inhuman Eastern hero; someone who has resisted all efforts to civilize him (*al-Sākhin wa'l-Bārid, Mawsim al-Hijra ilā al-Shamāl, al-Marfūḍūn*). The subject of mutual images is described most succinctly in the words of al-Ṭayyib Ṣāliḥ about *Mawsim al-Hijra ilā al-Shamāl*:

> There was always a thought in my mind on the imaginary relationship between our Muslim Arab world and Western or, more precisely, European culture. This relationship seemed to me through my interest and research, to be one that existed in the vain fancies held by both us and them. Vain fancies are first and foremost related to our notion of ourselves, then to what we think of our relationship with them, and then to their view of us from an imaginative viewpoint. Western Europe has imposed itself and its culture [upon us]. It has imposed itself upon our world for a long period and become part of our psychological and cultural entity, whether we want it or not.[34]

Elsewhere, and at another time, al-Ṭayyib Ṣāliḥ expands on the Arabs' dual-value approach to Europe:

> We are a people that does not know where it is in relation to the world. The strange thing is that we are aware of hating something we actually love: our current position regarding Europe, for example, is a strange one, for it is very clear from our behaviour that we are passionately in love with Europe, but in our debates and declarations we appear to hate it, and that is one of the strange contradictions in which we live. We have to completely understand our true feelings. If we love Europe, that's fine... but not that we should love something and then pretend to hate it, for in a situation like this we will never reach a solution.[35]

Nevertheless, we should bear in mind that because of the contradictory images of the Westerners as reflected in the novels of Arab authors, some Arab writers and artists try to present the characters of the other as 'normal people'. Therefore, when the narrator in al-Ṭayyib Ṣāliḥ's *Mawsim al-Hijra ilā al-Shamāl* is asked by the villagers for his impressions of the English on his return to his village after seven years in England, he replies simply:

> As best I could I had answered their many questions. They were surprised when I told them that Europeans were, with minor differences, exactly like them, marrying and bringing up their children in accordance with principles and traditions, that they had good morals and were in general good people.
>
> 'Are there any farmers among them? Mahjoub asked me.
>
> 'Yes, there are some farmers among them. They've got everything – workers and doctors and farmers and teachers, just like us'. I preferred not to say the rest that had come to my mind: that just like us they are born and die, and in the journey from the cradle to the

> grave they dream dreams some of which come true and some of which are frustrated; that they fear the unknown, search for love and seek contentment in wife and child; that some are strong and some are weak; that some have been given more than they deserve by life, while others have been deprived by it, but that the differences are narrowing and most of the weak are no longer weak [36]

The Sudanese artist Ibrāhīm al-Ṣalaḥī was sent to the U.K as a student with some Sudanese colleagues and expressed his surprise to find the English not as rulers as he used to see them in the Sudan, but as a regular people:

> And then I came to their country and we noticed, the first thing that we noticed was that the street sweeper was English! It was beyond our imagination! And in the restaurants the people who served us were English. Our imagination told us that there could not be English people who did this work since we knew them as rulers [...] I found them to be human beings just like us. Some are clever and some are stupid, some have an open mind and come to understand people, and some are racist, they have distinctions as well as shortcomings.[37]

Other images connected with the way that the Westerner used to see himself not in his country but rather in the East, occur in the works of the Egyptian-English author Ahdaf Soueif:

> There is also a kind of attachment that comes from a satisfaction with the European's own image of himself in the east, an image different from the one he has of himself in his own country and among his own people. Certain aspects of the European's personality which find no outlet in his own land, he allows to flourish while he is in the East.[38]

Foreignness and alienation – Many of the Eastern heroes in these novels have the common attributes of foreignness and alienation. From descriptions we learn of the Westerners' ambivalent attitude towards the Arabs. By the same token, those same Europeans who relate to people from the East fairly and liberally are not prepared to accept them into their society. The Eastern hero is on foreign territory where the people usually belong to a different religion (Christianity) and speak a different language (English, French, Swedish or German). For him, the differences between Europeans and Arabs underscore the fact that in their society he is different (*Badawī fī Ūrūbbā, al-Sākhin wa'l-Bārid, al-Marfūḍūn, Mawsim al-Hijra ilā al-*

Shamāl). The sense of foreignness and alienation experienced in Europe by someone from the East is understandable. The problem is, however, that this feeling frequently accompanies him on his return to his own soil. This is where the roots of these heroes' tragedy are firmly planted – on returning to their own country (*Qindīl Umm Hāshim, Mawsim al-Hijra ilā al-Shamāl, al-Marfūḍūn, Qālat Ḍuḥā*), even if their going back to the East and/or the South is explained as a return to their roots, the wellspring they abandoned for the West: Muḥsin (*'Uṣfūr min al-Sharq*), Ismā'īl (*Qindīl Umm Hāshim*), Muṣṭafā Sa'īd (*Mawsim al-Hijra ilā al-Shamāl*).[39]

East/South and West/North in the Works of al-Ṭayyib Ṣāliḥ

Al-Ṭayyib Ṣāliḥ's non-literary world, that is his personal life, plays a crucial role in his writing. He thus utilizes the contradictory or/and complementary worlds of his voluntary exile while writing in Arabic rather than in English on Sudanese, African and Muslim existence, and particularly that of his village. He writes about the Sudan on the one hand, and on the United Kingdom on the other, as two different societies, but also as two places where communities exist separately, although each has its own special character. He writes about a dual world.

Al-Ṭayyib Ṣāliḥ's life, who in his early twenties moved to England[40] and since then has wandered between Europe and Arab countries, finds expression in his works. In contrast to other authors of East-West novels, Ṣāliḥ went to the West and did not return to live in the East. It is therefore possible that his novel *Mawsim al-Hijra ilā al-Shamāl,* if not all his works, belong to a separate category of émigré or refugee literature. Émigré and/or refugee literature is a well known category in world literatures. There is, for example, the literature of Russian refugees or émigrés who fled their homeland at the beginning of the Russian Revolution and continued writing in France. Émigré literature also exists in modern Arabic literatures, be it in the *Mahjar* literature at the end of the 19th and beginning of the 20th centuries, in Palestinian works mainly after the 1948 war and the establishment of the State of Israel, in the emigration of Maghribi authors mainly to France and Canada, or in the literature of Arab political refugees and exiles in Europe and the United States (see Chapter One).

To return to al-Ṭayyib Ṣāliḥ: it seems that his life in England and his marriage to a Scottish woman intensified the cultural encounter in both his personal life and his works. The encounter between the two cultures in al-Ṭayyib Ṣāliḥ's works appears in two major books, *Dawmat Wad Ḥāmid* and *Mawsim al-Hijra ilā al-Shamāl.*[41] The subject is present in his other books in a more indirect manner, in the guise of the struggle between the old world and modernization, but not as directly and sharply as in those two works.[42]

A close examination of the works of al-Ṭayyib Ṣāliḥ shows the gradual emergence of his concept of encounter with the best and worst in Western culture as he saw it when he wrote these texts. Al-Ṭayyib Ṣāliḥ often expresses himself harshly and directly, but at times more gently. He first dealt with the subject of cultural encounter in some of his shorter works: 'Risāla ilā Aylīn', 'al-Shay' al-Ākhar', 'Idhā Jā'at', 'Hākadhā Yā Sādatī' and 'Muqaddimāt'.[43]

But unquestionably this subject reaches a climax of complexity directly and bluntly, as well as constituting one of the focal points, in the novel *Mawsim al-Hijra ilā al-Shamāl.* In this work the author portrays the cultural encounter in the most absolute way. Thus, as with other subjects, we can indicate some of his shorter works that constitute a kind of introduction to this long and important text. Encounters in his works take place in four central spheres: women, sex and violence – politics, nation and nationalism – edcation, culture and art – science and technology.

Women, Sex and Violence

It is very true that encounters between Eastern and Western cultures, the colonizer and the colonized, the oppressor and the oppressed, frequently revolve around the relationship between the Southern/Eastern man and the Northern/Western woman. Modern Arabic literatures frequently deal with these themes. Al-Ṭayyib Ṣāliḥ belongs to the category of those Arab authors and poets outside of the Arab world, such as Ḥanān al-Shaykh and Adūnīs among others. The problem is, however, that in contrast to the majority of these authors, in al-Ṭayyib Ṣāliḥ's texts encounters are accompanied by harsh feelings of violence and bitterness towards Western culture and its imperialist representatives. Some critics explain these feelings in reference to the colour of black skin in contrast to that of the 'white man'.[44] This can possibly be linked to al-Ṭayyib Ṣāliḥ's mention of acclimatization difficulties experienced by Sudanese outside the Sudan, in this case England, in contrast to other Arabs, like Egyptians, Lebanese and Palestinians.

In the works of al-Ṭayyib Ṣāliḥ an initial encounter between the Sudanese intellectual and the Western woman stands at the centre of several stories and novels such as 'Hākadhā Yā Sādatī'. In this story the man is an African Muslim and the women English Christian. The encounter that takes place on English soil, and the women, sex and violence are important characteristics in the relationships between the Eastern man and the Western women. From the moment the (unnamed) narrator enters the room and meets the hostess, to the moment of his exit with the girl whom he will eventually marry, his relationships with his hosts, particularly the hostesses, revolve around sex and violence. The feeling of foreignness and alienation that accompanied the narrator in 'Risāla ilā Aylīn' recurs here with greater intensity, and we can see it at the story's beginning: 'This girl doesn't smile at me. Is it because I'm a foreigner?'[45] His attitude towards the girl is like his attitude towards all other people in the house, and takes place on the internal, intimate level, in which he keeps his hostile attitude towards them to himself, and the external level in which he tries to ingratiate himself with them. This conflict accompanies him throughout the story and the two voices struggling within lead him to two different relationships: one with the hostess in which he fights the strong sexual urges she premeditatedly arouses in him, and even her words, 'Don't be afraid of me, I don't bite',[46] do not calm him. On the contrary, her provocations, particularly the sexual ones, confuse and embarrass him, but in the end he overcomes his embarrassment and with the help of the girl, who represents the second relationship, he overcomes his inner struggle and hesitancy. His feelings of foreignness and alienation dissipate slightly, his anger towards the English and their attitude towards him, as he feels them, diminishes, and he marries the girl as also occurs in some of his shorter works. But in other encounters that take place between an Eastern man and a Western woman, in the short-short stories, 'Muqaddimāt' (with the exception of 'Khuṭwa li'l-Amām'), the encounter does not culminate in marriage but is employed by the narrator to highlight the differences between him and the woman ('Laka ḥattā al-Mamāt', 'al-Ikhtibār', 'Sūzān wa-'Alī').

Such descriptions of the Sudanese intellectual hero's dual-value attitude, not only in his relationships with English women but also in the entire gamut of his relationships with English society, reach extreme and tragic proportions in *Mawsim al-Hijra ilā al-Shamāl* (1966). In this novel the author brings two male Muslim-African characters together with the West. The first is Muṣṭafā Sa'īd who symbolizes the first generation of Sudanese intellectuals that encounter Westerners on their own ground, while the second character is the narrator who represents the second generation of Sudanese intellectuals. The author poses two concepts regarding the West that are sometimes contrary and contradictory, sometimes integrative and sometimes parallel. The two concepts symbolize two different viewpoints, two different points of observation or two different prisms through which al-Ṭayyib Ṣāliḥ seeks to indicate all possible relationships between East and West. However, the subject in both cases is encounters other than those with which we are familiar from previous novels that dealt with this subject. In those novels the encounters were romantic, while in *Mawsim al-Hijra ilā al-Shamāl* the message is clear: not only the shattering of the romantic figure but a direct, harsh and trenchant confrontation between the two cultures and their representatives.[47] Furthermore, the other aspect of this encounter is the failure to reach a compromise between modernism (West) and tradition (East) as was the case of Muṣṭafā Sa'īd with the Western women, as well as the connection with Ḥusna and Wad al-Rayyis that ended in death.[48] Yet despite the fact that the author endeavours to present two concepts, he provides a more intensive treatment by placing Muṣṭafā Sa'īd at the centre because of his image in the eyes of the Western women. In other words, the West has a mistaken image of the African Arab's attitude towards sex, just as the Westerner has a mistaken image of the European woman, and in al-Ṭayyib Ṣāliḥ's words:

> What I have tried to do is use the European's mistaken image of the African Arab, because to this day Europeans think that the African Arab thrives on sexual fantasies, has no sense of responsibility and is a child in the cultural process [...] while on the other hand, and in the same way, I wanted the mistaken Arab image of the European woman to be a challenge for the Arab reader. It is clear that the sexual relations in the novel take place between the two parties on a mythological, not a realistic basis.[49]

Muṣṭafā Sa'īd, the novel's central yet not necessarily most important character, leaves the Sudan for Egypt and thence to England where he encounters English women, and this is potentially disastrous for both him and those women. A spiritual-dialectical process takes place here that recurs in various forms in all Muṣṭafā's relationships with English women. But they take on a new form in England; dark attributes that were only latent in the East materialize and bring catastrophe upon him, shattering his internal spiritual order.[50] This is true of those English women who had sexual relations with Muṣṭafā Sa'īd; within them, too, were the same latent dark attributes that Muṣṭafā, acting as a catalyst, helped to materialize, although these were not women who either loved him or whom he sought to destroy.[51] Therefore, the results of Muṣṭafā's encounters with English women were bad for both sides. Clearly the Europeans expected Muṣṭafā to behave in a specific way and he assumed the role they gave him, generally as well as vis-à-vis Western women. As in the story 'Hākadhā Yā Sādatī', here, too, Muṣṭafā Sa'īd does not completely reveal himself to the Europeans but uses a dual-value approach, just as they use with him. Women are an object of conquest for him and all is fair in achieving it, as he himself testifies: 'I would read poetry, talk of religion and philosophy, discuss paintings, and say things about the spirituality of the East. I would do everything possible to entice a woman to my bed. Then I would go after some new prey'.[52]

The women were not an end in themselves but only a means for Muṣṭafā to revenge himself on the imperialist English, the conquerors of his country, and he therefore uses women to liberate Africa. 'I will liberate Africa with [my penis]',[53] states Muṣṭafā bluntly. It is significant that Muṣṭafā, who seeks to settle accounts with the British and reaches England with a sense of being both invader and conqueror, does not wreak his vengeance on men but only on women. A possible explanation might be the similarity of women and cities. Cities, and London in particular, like mountains were objectives demanding conquest. The difference is that while a mountain symbolizes the wild and the anti-cultural, the city symbolizes culture and modernization.[54] In addition, the author described the relations between Muṣṭafā and the English women and especially the relationship with Jean Morris as a kind of a game, more precisely hunting games. Muṣṭafā is assigned the role of the hunter, but in the case of Jean Morris he became the hunted prey. Al-Ṭayyib Ṣāliḥ's perception of hunting was derived from three possible sources: the first source could be Africa; the second the Arabic tradition of hunting in classical and modern times; the third source could be from England where hunting is part and parcel of a long tradition. Whatever the source, as is true in many of his literary works, it may be a combination of 'his' and 'their' heritage.

Despite the background of his sterile relationships with English women, a notable fact is that with Ḥusna (although we do not know very much about their relationship) he had two children. Therefore, in contrast to sex for sex's sake, sex as a value in itself, or sex as a weapon in his struggle against the English, his relationships with southern/Eastern women were with one woman only, with sex as part of the relationship.

Muṣṭafā Sa'īd has relationships with four English women. Each of the four represents several aspects, not only herself, but is an archetypal character symbolizing a certain class of women in English society. They testify to the English attitude towards the East and the Arabs.[55] Through the character of Ann Hammond the author seeks to present Western intellectuals who view the East as an enchanted world. Ann Hammond's perception of the East is superficial and her familiarity with Muslim Arab reality is sketchy in the extreme. When Muṣṭafā meets her at a lecture he is giving on the classical Arabic poet, Abū Nuwās, she is part of the audience that the author succeeds in placing in a ludicrous light:

> After the lecture they all crowded round me: retired civil servants who had worked in the East, old women whose husbands had died in Egypt, Iraq and the Sudan, men who had fought with Kitchener and Allenby, orientalists, and officials in the Colonial Office and the Middle East section of the Foreign Office.[56]

The relationship between Muṣṭafā Sa‘īd and Ann Hammond begins with lies and ends in Ann's suicide. Both know their respective roles in the fabric of the relationship: he gives her the exoticism of the East that is enveloped in mendacity and treats her as a master would a slave. For her part, Ann is searching for an interest in life and she thinks that Muṣṭafā Sa‘īd is the man who will give her this and instil meaning into her life. No rules apply to the game they play and certainly no rules of fair play; they both perform as if on a theatre stage; both satisfy their curiosity and hunger and their sexual relationship is not only the means but also the end.

Just as Ann Hammond symbolizes the young, educated, Arabic-speaking English woman captivated by the exotic East, Sheila Greenwood symbolizes the English working class woman whom the author criticizes. The members of this class support socialism and communism and talk endlessly about equality, but according to al-Ṭayyib Ṣāliḥ they are prejudiced and their prejudices are not commensurate with their egalitarian ideology. The author succeeds in showing that Sheila Greenwood's prejudices are no different from those of her parents, especially their attitude to the colour of Muṣṭafā Sa‘īd's skin. Sheila and her parents address this fact each from his or her own viewpoint and the author places them all in the same category. After their relationship has become cemented, Sheila tells Muṣṭafā: 'My mother [...], would go mad and my father would kill me if they knew I was in love with a black man, but I don't care'.[57] Yet her own words reveal that Sheila Greenwood cares very much about the colour of Muṣṭafā's skin and that it plays a very important role in her sexual attraction to him: 'How marvellous your black colour is!' she would say to me, 'the colour of magic and mystery and obscenities'.[58] Like Ann Hammond, Sheila Greenwood's fate is suicide, but unlike the case of Ann Hammond we do not know how she took her own life, although she blamed Muṣṭafā Sa‘īd for her death.

According to the author the character of Isabella Seymour symbolizes the liberal, permissive Western women who circulate fearlessly in European society, frequently out of boredom or in search of stimulation and interest, as a result of their day-to-day way of life. Isabella Seymour thus represents a stereotypical Western female character, not only as the Eastern hero sees her, but even as the mothers and/or the Eastern people perceive her who protest vehemently when their sons leave for the

West. We should also bear in mind that Isabella Seymour's Spanish background plays a significant role in her relationship with Muṣṭafā Sa'īd. On the one hand, there is the conquest of Spain by Ṭāriq Ibn Ziyād in 711,[59] while on the other we might think that Muṣṭafā in the present became her conqueror through their sexual relations, since in the past Queen Isabella expelled the Muslims from Spain (1492). In this relationship too Muṣṭafā is intent on settling accounts between him (the East), and her (the West).[60]

The character of Isabella Seymour is the most tragic of the four English women. She is married, has two children and is a 'regular' churchgoer. Like Ann Hammond and Sheila Greenwood, Isabella has dark, latent drives that are revealed in her encounter with Muṣṭafā Sa'īd, or in the words of the novel, 'Then she met him and discovered deep within herself dark areas that had previously been closed'.[61] Unlike Ann Hammond, whose relationship with Muṣṭafā Sa'īd was based on mutual dishonesty, but like Sheila Greenwood, both Muṣṭafā's black skin and sex play an important role in Isabella's relationship with Muṣṭafā. She says, 'Ravish me, you African demon. Burn me in the fire of your temple, you black god. Let me twist and turn in your wild and impassioned rites'.[62] Muṣṭafā Sa'īd expresses the author's irony and criticism of two-faced English society that talks about equality, while on the other it in fact discriminates against people because of the colour of their skin or their origins. By means of Muṣṭafā the author transmits clear messages, for Isabella Seymour, too, is attracted to Muṣṭafā Sa'īd because of his colour and deifies him in a manner that irks the narrator:

> She denied her religion and worshipped a god like the calf of the Children of Israel. How strange! How ironic! Just because a man has been created on the Equator some mad people regard him as a slave, others as a god. Where lies the mean? Where the middle way?[63]

The relationships between Muṣṭafā Sa'īd and the three English women have been described in some detail, for all three constitute a preface to Muṣṭafā's relationship with Jean Morris.[64] It is she who expresses everything that is sick, distorted, deviant and evil in the West. Of the four women, she represents the lowest level of humanity. She subscribes to the ugliness, baseness and violence of Western society as the author views it, and brings the encounter between the Eastern man and the Western woman to a terrible, tragic climax from which death is the only escape. Muṣṭafā Sa'īd's relationship with Jean Morris is characterized by both violence and sick sexual relations.[65] Paradoxically, and perhaps even cynically, death brings them closer; it is not that Muṣṭafā becomes insane and murders her, but that she actively participates in the words and deeds leading to her death. With her last words she shocks the reader:

'Darling,' she said painfully, 'I thought you would never do this. I almost gave up hope of you.'[66]

Muṣṭafā is tried for the murder of Jean Morris. He feels that not only he alone is on trial but that all of Africa is in the dock with him, while England sits on the bench.[67] Muṣṭafā despises and mocks his defence counsel, the jury and the judge; he thinks that they are no better than he and therefore do not have the right to sit in judgement of him. Moreover, he views the West as the source of violence:

> They imported to us the germ of the greatest European violence, as seen on the Somme and at Verdun, the like of which the world has never previously known, the germ of a deadly disease that struck them more than a thousand years ago. Yes, my dear sirs, I came as an invader into your very homes: a drop of the poison which you have injected into the veins of history. 'I am no Othello. Othello was a lie.[68]

Muṣṭafā Sa'īd serves his sentence and returns to the East, after twenty-five years of having known the West and its women, and despairing of them. He returns to the Sudan and marries one of the village women, hoping to turn over a new leaf in life in which there is no room for Europe and its women. A comparison is appropriate with Ismā'īl, the protagonist of *Qindīl Umm Hāshim.* He, too, returns to Egypt from Europe, tries to abandon his beliefs and traditions, but realizing that there is no other way, accepts them and marries Fāṭima, his unassuming fiancée. The significant difference between Ismā'īl and Muṣṭafā however, is that while Ismā'īl rids himself of Europe, returns to Egypt and has a happy marriage, Muṣṭafā, though married to Ḥusna, does not manage to abandon Europe and find peace. Indeed, he transmits the germ he carries both to the narrator and Ḥusna, who is forced to marry Wad al-Rayyis, one of the villagers, after Muṣṭafā's disappearance in the Nile. Her marriage to Wad al-Rayyis ends in his murder and her suicide. In short, Muṣṭafā, brought to the Sudan the sex, violence and death that had accompanied him in Europe. The change that he brings about in Ḥusna, his wife, does not escape the villagers and especially Maḥjūb (the narrator's close friend).[69]

The final proof of Muṣṭafā's failure to rehabilitate himself is his disappearance in the Nile. Muṣṭafā's contagious disease with which he infects those closest to him is evident when his widow murders Wad al-Rayyis and subsequently commits suicide.[70] Curiously, the villagers ascribe Ḥusna's actions to the new era, and even Bint Majdhūb, that mischievous old woman, sums up Ḥusna's deeds in the words, 'It is something we have never seen or heard of in times past or present'.[71]

Al-Ṭayyib Ṣāliḥ did not leave the arena of encounters between East and West solely to Muṣṭafā Sa'īd. He describes this failed encounter with the West in bleak terms, but it should be remembered that this is only one possibility of an encounter. We shall call it 'the first possibility'. This 'first possibility', that represents the older generation's encounter with the West with tragic results, also exists in novels by other authors. In *al-Marfūḍūn* by Sa'dī Ibrāhīm, for example, Aḥmad (the major character) stands for the older generation while Majīd (a marginal character), the young Algerian, symbolizes the 'second possibility'. Aḥmad says to Majīd:

> My brother, we have drowned in the wadi. We are more or less finished. You, the youngsters may have a future. You just have to be men. Do not forget that we have suffered a lot for you. Never forget that.[72]

Al-Ṭayyib Ṣāliḥ's purpose is to show that an encounter of this kind need not exist between East and West.[73] The 'second possibility' which is, in my opinion, the more interesting, as I pointed out earlier, is introduced by the narrator. He is frequently described as someone who has learned the lessons of Muṣṭafā Sa'īd, and is employed as his antithesis. In direct contrast to Muṣṭafā Sa'īd, the narrator tackles his East-West problems by soberly considering the contradictions without abandoning, however, irony and cynicism. Regarding women, we hear nothing of the narrator's experiences with European women, even if he might have had some encounters with English women. Compared to Muṣṭafā Sa'īd, his time in England is only briefly depicted. Therefore, when the narrator returns to his village in the Sudan and is questioned by Wad al-Rayyis, like Bint Majdhūb expecting an answer in the form of stories, he is surprised to hear the narrator say, 'I wouldn't know'.[74] This sums up the main difference between the 'first possibility' presented by the author and the 'second possibility' concerning relationships between the Eastern man and the Western woman. The narrator's perspective on women can possibly be explained by the fact that both his family and clan are known in the village as people who do not take more than one wife. He seeks to continue the family tradition while the time he spent in the other culture has not changed his behaviour and family norms. It should be noted that Muṣṭafā Sa'īd, too, married no more than one Sudanese woman.

Politics, Nation and Nationality

The first military and political confrontation in the modern era between France and Egypt in 1798, mentioned above, and the conquests of Arab countries in the Mashriq and the Maghrib by European powers are evident in all spheres of life in the Arab world. Imperialism and European colonialism remain etched on the consciousness of Arab authors who have devoted an important portion of their works to both subjects at various periods of the 20th century. Numerous Arab authors have dealt with the political aspects of the East-West encounter as does also al-Ṭayyib Ṣāliḥ, who covers this subject in some of his short works as well as in the novel *Mawsim al-Hijra ilā al-Shamāl.*[75] The minor role he accords to the subject of politics in the confrontations he describes between the two cultures is not surprising. We have seen earlier that in some of his early works the author refers to this conflict, but the political aspect is not on his agenda. Although in the short short story 'al-Shay' al-Ākhar' he discusses the inter-cultural struggle from the political point of view, he does so only marginally. The Sudanese man who meets an English woman feels great bitterness towards the British, and when asked why he hates them, replies, 'Because they [the English] are imperialists'.[76]

The novel *Mawsim al-Hijra ilā al-Shamāl* is the only text, and certainly the only long text, in which al-Ṭayyib Ṣāliḥ deals intensively with the cultural encounter while discussing the political and national aspects of the two cultures. Although these aspects do find expression, they are neither intensively nor ideologically dealt with as they are in other Arabic novels such as *al-Ḥayy al-Lātīnī* and *al-Marfūḍūn*, in which this subject is the central axis of the plot.[77] Al-Ṭayyib Ṣāliḥ's political consciousness, like his national, patriotic and African consciousness,[78] is expressed through the personalities of Muṣṭafā Sa'īd and the narrator. It is also apparent in the city vis-à-vis village setting, for awareness of Western politics and the parliamentary system is greater in the city than in the village.

Despite the differences between Muṣṭafā Sa'īd and the narrator in the novel *Mawsim al-Hijra ilā al-Shamāl*, they both view Europeans, and in their particular case, the English, as foreign conquerors. The narrator as well as Muṣṭafā betray an uncommon intensity of feeling. The latter faces an English court on English soil charged with the murder of Jean Morris. His judges are English and he, a Sudanese African, believe that he cannot be judged by them; he does not see himself as the accused and them as his accusers. On the contrary, he considers their roles reversed.

The personal situation in which he finds himself reminds him of a political event in the history of the Sudan, when similar personal ramifications occurred:

> When Mahmoud Wad Ahmed was brought in shackles to Kitchener after his defeat at the Battle of Atbara, Kitchener said to him, 'Why have you come to my country to lay waste and plunder?' It was the intruder who said this to the person whose land it was, and the owner of the land bowed his head and said nothing.[79]

He later compares the two and concludes that the roots of political, national and religious history are not in either the present or the recent past, but rather go back to a distant past, to the beginning of the conflict between the two cultures.

While Muṣṭafā relates to present and past, the narrator, who represents the 'second possibility' in the encounter between East and West, addresses the present and future. He considers the conquest of the Sudan by the English as a passing phenomenon:

> The fact that they came to our land, I know not why, does that mean that we should poison our present and our future? Sooner or later they will leave our country, just as many people throughout history left many countries. The railways, ships, hospitals, factories and schools will be ours and we'll speak their language without either a sense of guilt or a sense of gratitude. Once again we shall be as we were – ordinary people – and if we are lies we shall be lies of our own making.[80]

It is quite likely that al-Ṭayyib Ṣāliḥ used these two contradictory mindsets not by chance: Muṣṭafā Sa'īd's pessimistic view brings in its wake a different account to be settled with Western culture, and a second, optimistic view that recalls the past but which seeks to view the present and the future as more important. If this is so, then the author sought to present two different worldviews, both of which, however, reject Western imperialism. Because the first approach is essentially unproductive, the author offers a second approach which clearly asserts that the open accounts with the other culture should be concluded for the sake of the present, and especially for a better future. The conclusion he draws, therefore, is that the Sudanese must develop their country with their own hands and make mistakes, but their own mistakes. There is no contradiction in the author's approach which, on the one hand, does not see anything wrong in using the English language and implicitly, Western culture, while calling for constructing Sudan's independence and future by the Sudanese, on the other.

How the European conquerors see this is worthy of note. Their viewpoint is, of course, completely different from that of the people of the East. They do not regard themselves as conquerors or imperialists but rather as those who brought the best of enlightened culture to the East. This is the position of the 'enlightened' members of the English intelligentsia. In *Mawsim al-Hijra ilā al-Shamāl,* Richard (I wonder if al-Ṭayyib Ṣāliḥ gave him this name at random, or whether he chose the name purposely, thinking of Richard Coeur de Lion and the Crusades), a young Englishman employed by the Ministry of Finance, who believes that:

> All this shows that you [the Sudanese] cannot manage to live without us. You used to complain about colonialism and when we left [the Sudan] you created the legend of neo-colonialism. It seems that our presence, in an open or undercover form, is as indispensable to you as air and water.[81]

Even though the words of this young, 'enlightened' and 'progressive' intellectual strike us as incongruous today, they do indicate the perspective of at least a portion of the English intelligentsia of the period.

Culture, Education and Art

In its broadest sense, culture enables us to encounter the world of a people about whom we seek to learn and know something. In the past, relations between Western and Eastern culture had their ups and downs with reciprocal influence on each other. In the modern era, the encounter between the two cultures took place at a time when Arab culture had increasingly declined, whereas Western culture developed since the 16th century and flourished. Clearly, when these two cultures confront one another it is quickly apparent that each has its own codes, and when the encounter takes place at a moment of cultural asymmetry, this has repercussions on the relationship.

Western cultures and their relations with Arab culture are at the centre of al-Ṭayyib Ṣāliḥ's works that deal with the encounter. The differences between both cultures are depicted by means of a sense of foreignness and alienation present in his early works, especially the stories 'Risāla ilā Aylīn' and 'Hākadhā Yā Sādatī. In the latter work we see the cultural differences in the Eastern man who behaves according to prevailing Western criteria in order to find favour in Western eyes. The problem is that deep down the Eastern character judges the culture in which he is living harshly:

'I have read their books, then saw them and found them saying one thing and doing another'.[82] The West's dual-value, and possibly double-faced, attitude does not characterize only al-Ṭayyib Ṣāliḥ's perspective, it is an attitude held by many Arab intellectuals. This is especially true of the value of human life. Arabs harshly criticize Westerners who talk about values, justice, morals and the like in their countries. Yet with regard to others – in this case the conquered people, the Arabs – the scale of values and codes by which they act change completely. In modern Arabic literatures this criticism occurs in a very early work by Egyptian author Maḥmūd Ṭāhir Ḥaqqī (1884–1964), *'Adhrā' Dinshawāy* (The Virgin of Dinshaway, 1906).[83] Aḥmad Amīn, one of the most prominent Egyptian intellectuals, spoke cuttingly of the value accorded to human life by the English in England and the French in France, but with regard to the countries they ruled, their scale of values changed. He writes:

> In general, the people of the East rejected Western teaching methods outright, and the difference they found in the Westerners' words possibly helped them in this. This is because they [the Westerners] frequently call for adherence to human principles at times of trouble, but they forget them when all is well. Thus, for example, Great Britain promises King Ḥusayn that she will grant independence to Arab countries after the [First World war], while at the same time she makes a secret agreement with France to divide up the Arab countries between them into spheres of influence. And should a British soldier disappear for one reason or another, the English turn into a tiger and threaten. And if the French kill thousands of Moroccans and Maghribis, they don't lift a finger. All this has caused the people of the East to lose their trust in the West, and just as they have lost it with regard to politics, they have lost their trust in them regarding culture, because trust cannot be divided.[84]

Possibly, in a conqueror-conquered relationship where there are conspicuous contrasts, the level of sensitivity to the difference between theory and practice is very high. The dual-value attitude of Arab intellectuals towards Western culture is focused on the desire to imitate the West, and the desire to distance themselves from the West's tremendous influence in order to develop the local culture. These considerations lead alienated Arab intellectuals onto the path of hesitancy when facing Western culture. The dilemma of Arab intellectuals derives from being torn between Western science and education, and religious beliefs, which are usually Muslim.[85]

In his early works al-Ṭayyib Ṣāliḥ deals with this subject very well, especially in the 'Muqaddimāt', which he later used as chapter headings as it were, for a more comprehensive overview in the novel *Mawsim al-Hijra ilā al-Shamāl*. In this book al-Ṭayyib Ṣāliḥ discusses the encounter between the cultures of East and West and indirectly addresses the myth of Eastern spiritual culture vis-à-vis the material culture of the West. In contrast to authors like Tawfīq al-Ḥakīm, who in his novel *'Uṣfūr min al-Sharq*, unrealistically elevated Eastern culture to spiritual culture versus material culture – an idealization based on wishful thinking – al-Ṭayyib Ṣāliḥ attacks the myth of 'Eastern spirituality' in an unprecedented way and shows how the Eastern man, in this case Muṣṭafā Sa'īd, 'sells' the myth to Westerners who are more than ready to 'buy' it.[86] Muṣṭafā exploits his knowledge in the literary and spiritual spheres solely as a means to conquer Western women. The education he has acquired is not adequate for seriously coping with Western culture, but like Muḥsin in Tawfīq al-Ḥakīm's *'Uṣfūr min al-Sharq*, he uses it to reach the Western woman. Although Muṣṭafā's English education enables him to penetrate deeper into foreign society and culture, he misuses his education. By the same token English society has a selfish interest in this education, as in this way it can flaunt the liberalism and equality emblazoned on its escutcheon.[87] Yet the author views education as a supreme value:

> I therefore feel that through the Aṣīla [Morocco] Festival, people understood the importance of education and that political and economic efforts must be accompanied by an educational effort, because education is the foundation as it is linked to an endless movement of time and it is this that links the past to the present and future.[88]

The question is, does al-Ṭayyib Ṣāliḥ view the encounter between the cultures as leading necessarily to changing Eastern culture by imitation born of denial? This is the conclusion drawn by Muḥsin in *'Uṣfūr min al-Sharq*:

> Yes, the East does not exist today, it is only a forest in whose trees there are apes wearing Western clothing without order, without organization, without perceptivity and without conception.[89]

Alternatively, does al-Ṭayyib Ṣāliḥ view the encounter between the two cultures as Aḥmad Amīn viewed it, that is, to take the best of both cultures, Eastern and Western, to discard the worst while fully observing the harmony between them, for otherwise it will lead to failure.[90] Apparently, al-Ṭayyib Ṣāliḥ expresses a perspective close to Aḥmad Amīn's view through the words of the narrator in *Mawsim al-Hijra ilā al-Shamāl.* The narrator, who was educated in the West, views education as a means, not an end; a means of making a living and not as a means of achieving other objectives.[91] The narrator is conscious of the two cultures and understands that in Western culture there are fields from which he can learn and benefit both personally and for the common good, but all that is on one condition: as a result, his people will not lose its identity and rid itself of everything linked to Sudanese culture while blindly imitating the West. Borrowing aspects of culture from the West must take place with the clear understanding that the people must remain as they are, not as the West would like them to be. Indeed, the narrator does not adopt a hypocritical attitude but preaches explicitly that the cultural standards and codes of the Sudanese must be continued and not be replaced by those of the English:

> By the standards of the European industrial world we are poor peasants, but when I embrace my grandfather I experience a sense of richness as though I am a note in the heartbeats of the very universe.[92]

It is obvious that the attitude of the narrator, like that of al-Ṭayyib Ṣāliḥ, toward Western culture reveals that he neither wants nor is able, to ignore this culture. This is where al-Ṭayyib Ṣāliḥ's approach is similar to that of Aḥmad Amīn who relates to Western culture using dual values, and who is unable (or perhaps does not want) to sever his ties with this culture. In deeds rather than words, al-Ṭayyib Ṣāliḥ confirms this concept totally. He made his home in Europe, married a European woman, works in Europe and frequently visits Arab countries, including the Sudan.[93] Accordingly, his attitude towards the West has remained truly one of dual values. He is conscious of the world in which he lives in relation to the world he left. His preference for one of those worlds does not constitute a verdict in favour of one or the other. Evidence of this is perhaps his preference for writing in Arabic. According to al-Ṭayyib Ṣāliḥ, Western culture is represented by England, which ruled the Sudan. But despite the pernicious elements in imperialism, they, the English, also did some positive things – first and foremost the superior education they gave him and his contemporaries.[94]

Science and Technology

In the modern era Western cultures has obviously made great strides in the scientific, technological, military and civil fields while the East became fossilized. Eastern culture, therefore, was forced to adopt Western science and technology in the 19th and 20th centuries, and later, in Iran, a non-Arab Muslim country with Islam as its national constitution, while not abandoning Western science and technology in the civil and religious spheres. Western scientific achievements were adopted by the rulers and social elites of Arab and non-Arab Muslim countries like Turkey and Iran. Conservative circles in the Muslim world, particularly among the clergy, tried to prevent, or at least slow down, the penetration of Western science and technology into the Eastern world. In the cities progress is greater than in the villages, yet there is no doubt that the Eastern way of life is changing. The difference is that in the West, progress growing from within became an integral part of society, while in the rest of the world, including the Arab and Muslim world, changes in all spheres of life were adopted only superficially and were not internalized. In Iran, the clergy reacted forcefully, leading to the fall of the Shah of Persia and the rise of Khomeini who imposed a fundamentalist Muslim regime on the country. A similar reaction occurred in the Sudan, especially at the end of the 1980s and the early 1990s with the rise of Ḥasan al-Turābī and the imposition of traditional Muslim rule. Likewise, in Turkey of 2002, the Islamic party won the general election and the party leader was appointed prime minister.

In the past, some Arab intellectuals, mostly Egyptian, like Aḥmad Amīn and Shawqī Dayf and some present-day Arab intellectuals held that Western science and technology should be adopted without adopting other cultural values. The works of Arab authors who have written on the cultural encounter devote considerable space to the cultural clash against the background of the adoption of Western technology. One of the first novels in which the question of adopting Western technology is discussed was *Qindīl Umm Hāshim*,[95] by Yaḥyā Ḥaqqī. In this novel, Ismā'īl, the Eastern hero, returns home after seven years of ophthalmology studies in England. But his attempts to cure his patients' ills solely with Western medical methods are doomed to failure, and he succeeds when he combines modern medicine with local folk belief. His professional success is, of course, a function of the inner balance he achieves following a nervous breakdown that accompanied his medical failure.[96]

Al-Ṭayyib Ṣāliḥ uses a different approach. He has a dual-value attitude towards Western scientific and technological achievements. In his opinion, 'regarding Western culture, science and the machine have become an end in themselves, while in our view it [science] is part of all that the universe entails'.[97] On the one hand, he believes that they can benefit the Sudan, while on the other, he is aware of the damage they can cause. This ambivalent approach is revealed by Muṣṭafā Sa'īd's attitude towards England's technological innovations which at worst cause the enslavement of the

Sudan by the English, and at best can indicate the relief and benefit of these innovations. The best proof of this view's salient points is that despite his reservations about the English and their technology, Muṣṭafā Sa'īd seeks to use them for the advancement of the village in which he has chosen to live.[98] Furthermore, he can see the benefit of science for the villagers. The narrator in *Mawsim al-Hijra ilā al-Shamāl* is caught in the trap of ambivalence to an even greater extent than Muṣṭafā Sa'īd. He has learned to understand both the positive and negative aspects of the West, and he understands that rejection of technology will put an end to the benefits he seeks for the villagers. Yet he is well aware of the heavy price Sudanese society, in this case rural society, will have to pay for individual and collective welfare. He is clearly in favour of change, but the question is how deeply should change go? Perhaps Maḥjūb, the novel's young village character, best expresses as this.[99]

Beyond the question of adopting Western science and technology and the degree of their adoption, the question of pace arises. At what pace should the changes be allowed to seep into Sudanese society? Can the penetration rate of progress be controlled? Al-Ṭayyib Ṣāliḥ discusses this important question in the story 'Dawmat Wad Ḥāmid' in which he places the traditional, rural, old world in confrontation with the progress and modernization.[100] The opposition is not against modernizing the village, but the extent of the changes and the pace of change are questioned. Even the old villager, who plays the role of internal narrator in this story, admits that modernization must come to the village, but he transmits the author's message with utter clarity: change can only be instituted with the agreement of the villagers and must be gradual. With the wisdom of his years he understands that in the struggle between the villagers and the authorities, who seek to cut down the doum tree of Wad Ḥāmid in order to construct an anchorage, there are no victors, only losers.[101]

In this chapter it was thought more appropriate to deal with the encounter between these two cultures in term of North/West and East/South rather than as a simple, though more commonly stipulated East/West encounter. Despite its beginnings as a military and economic conflict the encounter has become cultural and religious.

Some Arab authors and poets deal with encounter between cultures in their fictional or poetic works, constructing their narratives or poems around several focal areas such as politics, religion and gender. In several literary works and particularly in his *Mawsim al-Hijra ilā al-Shamāl*, al-Ṭayyib Ṣāliḥ has continued the modern Arab traditional perception of the 'other' culture(s). But he also has a broader view of this encounter, perhaps because he himself has become, in one way or another, part of the 'otherness' discussed in his fiction. Equally important in those fictional works, where he addresses questions of the cultural encounter, are issues of mutual misunderstandings that have led to stereotypical and skewed images on both sides. Aside from the question of the cultural encounter, the uniqueness of his work written for the greater part in Europe and in Arabic is a new phenomenon from both poetic and thematic perspectives.

EPILOGUE:
An Attempt at Evaluating al-Ṭayyib Ṣāliḥ's Writing

As our study has shown, al-Ṭayyib Ṣāliḥ is not merely another Arab author but rather a phenomenon in modern Arabic literatures. A significant part of his rather extraordinary status is the fact that he is a writer, and possibly first and foremost, a man who deviates from convention by not living in his own country. The aura surrounding him may derive from a number of factors that complement one another and which are sometimes even contradictory. Therefore, we consider al-Ṭayyib Ṣāliḥ and his literary works in terms of complementary opposites rather than representing binary oppositions. Yet it is these components that may shed some light on this author's unparalleled importance. As stated earlier, the fact that he left the Sudan for England at an early age (he was twenty-four) has far-reaching ramifications not only for him as a man and writer, but on the attitudes of readers, literary critics and, so it seems, also politicians. The fact that al-Ṭayyib Ṣāliḥ left the Sudan (voluntarily, not under duress) and settled in England would include him in the category of émigré authors and/or writers in exile. This phenomenon has a very long history in the annals of modern Arabic literatures, especially in the *Mahjar* literature created in the second half of the 19th century until the end of the first quarter of the twentieth. No doubt, however, *Mahjar* literature can be extended to the present day, for the incidence of Arab authors emigrating or being forced to leave their countries for other Arab countries, or the West, goes on to this day. Possibly we have here a category of post-*Mahjar* writers.

Four categories of writers come under consideration: in the first are writers who left their countries for political, cultural, religious or/and economic reasons, such as the well-known *Mahjar* authors Jubrān Khalīl Jubrān, Mīkhā'īl Nu'ayma (1899–1988), Īlyā Abū Māḍī (1889–1957). In the second category are Palestinian writers who were uprooted from their country in the wake of the 1948 war, like Ghassān Kanafānī, Samīra 'Azzām (1927–67), Jabrā Ibrāhīm Jabrā. The third category consists of writers from the Arab Maghrib who left their homeland, mainly voluntarily, for French-speaking countries, first and foremost France, and among these are Muḥammad Dīb (1920–2003), Kātib Yāsīn (1929–89), al-Ṭāhir Ibn Jallūn. In the fourth category are writers who left their homelands from the 1950s onwards for other Arab or Western lands.

It should be remembered that fifty and sixty years ago significant changes occurred in many spheres of the Arab world, first and foremost politically, but also in the social, cultural, economic, and religious spheres. These changes, which are continuing to this day, come in recurring waves, during which political and social activists as well as both intellectuals and writers are expelled. Yet it should be borne in mind that anyone who was exiled, or left of his own free will, did so from necessity, rarely by choice. Prominent writers who left the Arab Mashriq (like the Arab Maghrib) for other Arab countries or the West are citizens of many countries, like Egypt, Syria, Iraq, Lebanon or the Sudan. Among them are Syrian writers like Zakariyyā Tāmir (England), Salīm Barakāt (Sweden), Adūnīs (France), and Rafīq al-Shāmī (Germany). From Iraq there are poets like 'Abd al-Wahhāb al-Bayyātī (1926–99) who spent several years in the Soviet Union and settled there before moving to Amman, and Sargūn Būlus (1944–2000) who spent most of his life outside Iraq, especially in the United States and England. Women authors Ḥanān al-Shaykh (England) and Hudā Barakāt (France) hail from Lebanon. Regarding Sudanese writers, many left their homeland for Arab countries, like Mukhtār Ibrāhīm 'Ajūba and Ibrāhīm Isḥāq Ibrāhīm (Saudia). Others live in Western countries, such as al-Ṭayyib Ṣāliḥ, Aḥmad Muḥammad el-Badawī (England) and the late Ṣalāḥ Aḥmad Ibrāhīm (France).

The language in which the Arab writers in these four categories work in the West is of prime importance. *Mahjar* writers, particularly those of the first generation, write aside from Arabic also in the languages of their new home – English, Spanish and Portuguese. But the second-generation *Mahjar* writers shifted to the language of their new country while in many cases Arabic was either used selectively or disappeared entirely. The majority of Arab Mahgribi writers write in French, as is the case with Kātib Yāsīn, and al-Ṭāhir Ibn Jallūn. Other Maghribi writers who moved temporarily or permanently to another country write in two languages, French and Arabic, as do 'Abd al-Wahhāb Meddeb (b.1946) of Tunisia and al-Mu'ṭī Qabbāl (b.1954) of Morocco. Only very few Maghribi writers who moved to France continue to write solely in Arabic. In the category linked to the subject of our study we find Arab writers who fastidiously wrote, and write, in Arabic for which they have gained acclaim not only in the Arab world, but outside it too. Among these writers are al-Ṭayyib Ṣāliḥ, Adūnīs, Salīm Barakāt and Ḥanān al-Shaykh. Al-Ṭayyib Ṣāliḥ, whose English was fluent as a youth and who, by his own testimony, excelled in it, was able, after a very short time in England, to begin writing in English. He could have written in English, but chose not to. Apparently this is one of the central points when we try to understand the author's inner world; for according to him the objective of his works is not to describe his own life, as in his opinion it is of no interest and he has neither the need nor any vested interest in writing about it. Rather his literary output aims at his describing the world in which he lived in the past, that is to say that al-Ṭayyib Ṣāliḥ premeditatedly and consciously chose to describe the Sudan in his literary works in Arabic. A choice of this kind is no small matter and that it stems from the man's motivations may have something to do with the different circles in which Sudanese live, and the author's own roots.

The Sudan is, of course, an African country and we have seen that the African factor is of great importance. Apart from Western languages spoken in Africa – English and French – numerous local African dialects are spoken in addition to Arabic. Moreover, African folk literature, customs and beliefs have a significant place in African culture. As an African country, the Sudan is characterized not only by the Arabic language but also by other languages and dialects, similar to the various folk beliefs, Sufism and holy orders that constitute an important element in its social fabric. Hence despite the Sudan's usual portrayal as a Moslem country, not all of its inhabitants are Moslem, some are Christian and others pagan. Furthermore, Islam in the Sudan is not necessarily typical of other Moslem Arab countries because popular Islam enjoys an extraordinarily important status as a result of the country's social, political, and religious history. Also considered an Arab country, the Sudan's Arabism has different nuances than that of other Arab countries. Finally, not all Sudanese are happy with defining their country as 'Arab', so a dilemma of collective identity certainly exists despite (or possibly because of) the Sudan's special relationship with Egypt. These circles of Africanism, Islamism and Arabism have been, and still are, principal sources of inspiration for Sudanese authors, including al-Ṭayyib Ṣāliḥ.

And indeed, al-Ṭayyib Ṣāliḥ, in his literary as in his journalistic writings, makes extensive use of the different elements that make the Sudan unique. He draws on classical Arabic literature, especially its poetry, and the new Western literatures, especially English literature. In contrast to other Sudanese authors or those from other Arab countries that are not at the Arab world's cultural and/or literary centre, al-Ṭayyib Ṣāliḥ's works are only slightly influenced by modern Arabic literatures. He has great respect and affection for certain Arab authors like the Egyptian author Yaḥyā Ḥaqqī and the Lebanese Palestinian poet Tawfīq Ṣāyigh, but it is doubtful that they influence him. Western writers like Shakespeare, Yeats, Conrad, Faulkner and Camus have inspired him frequently, and Shakespeare, Conrad and Camus have also influenced his works in one form or another. Both Western and Eastern literary critics are aware of his sources of inspiration and have noted them, Arab literary critics addressed al-Ṭayyib Ṣāliḥ's works only rarely. Yet from the end of the sixties and the early seventies, the literary critics and particularly the Arab attitude to his works underwent a change. Two reasons account for this. First, a number of his works were published in 1966–7, particularly *Mawsim al-Hijra ilā al-Shamāl* which both readers and critics considered an extraordinary literary work. Second, al-Ṭayyib Ṣāliḥ's works appeared in translations into other languages.

He is one of the unique cases in the history of modern Arabic literatures where an Arab writer submitted for translation a text that is not a book, but a manuscript. According to both the author and his English translator, Denys Johnson-Davies, the latter translated *Mawsim al-Hijra ilā al-Shamāl* directly from the Arabic manuscript. The fact that some of al-Ṭayyib Ṣāliḥ's texts appeared in English translation in 1967 ('Dawmat Wad Ḥāmid'), 1968 (*'Urs al-Zayn*) and 1969 (*Mawsim al-Hijra ilā al-Shamāl*), the first French translation of *Mawsim al-Hijra ilā al-Shamāl* appearing in 1972, and the German and Italian translations of 'Dawmat Wad Ḥāmid' appeared in the same period, placed the author at the centre of the canon of modern Arabic literatures. The simultaneous appearance of his works in Arabic and their translations in the sixties led Arab critics to devote ever-increasing space to a discussion of his works.

The fact that al-Ṭayyib Ṣāliḥ was a Sudanese, Arab, Moslem, and African author living in England and writing in Arabic, doubtless also aroused the critics' curiosity. A combination of pride, envy and possibly even suspicion on the part of Arab critics played a role. Some wondered whether al-Ṭayyib Ṣāliḥ could be viewed as an Arab author since he did not live in the Arab world. Together with a few articles, al-Ṭayyib Ṣāliḥ has not published many literary works. He is not a prolific author like Yūsuf Idrīs, Najīb Maḥfūẓ or Muḥammad 'Abd al-Ḥalīm 'Abd Allāh (1913–71). He published a total of five slim volumes of prose that includes four novels, the majority of which may be seen as short novels or novellas – and a collection of short stories consisting of seven stories, and another two stories published later. Al-Ṭayyib Ṣāliḥ's last story, 'Yawm Mubārak 'alā Shāṭi' Umm Bāb', was published in 1993, while his previous text, *Bandar Shāh: Maryūd*, was published in book form in 1977. In other words, sixteen years elapsed between the publication of these two texts. This period of 'drought' is uncharacteristic of al-Ṭayyib Ṣāliḥ's literary activity in the sixties and seventies for which there are two possible explanations: First, an author's silence, even though prolonged, is not unusual when due to personal reasons; second, it could well be related to the fact that al-Ṭayyib Ṣāliḥ, who has gained worldwide recognition mainly because of the novel *Mawsim al-Hijra ilā al-Shamāl*, is aware of this reason, but he still prefers and appreciates more both parts of the novel *Bandar Shāh.* He has publicly acknowledged this fact and it is quite possible that the literary critics, who reviewed this novel but sparingly, were the cause of at least part of his creative silence.

The poetic world of al-Ṭayyib Ṣāliḥ is rich and variegated. The author's close familiarity with modern Western literatures on the one hand, and his deep knowledge of classical Arabic literature on the other, have contributed to the poetic richness and variety of his literary works. He has succeeded in internalizing the various components of the Western novel and short story as the leading literary genres of the past few centuries, together with the poetic components of classical Arabic literature. Thus the author's stream-of-consciousness texts abound with dialogue, monologue, and the technique of filling gaps, together with the use of the narrator-listener technique. In addition, he has borrowed formulae from the religious Moslem-Arab type of story known as *al-Faraj ba'd al-Shidda*. Clearly, al-Ṭayyib Ṣāliḥ pays much attention to important elements on the poetic side of the work such as title, exposition, ending, relation to place, time and space, and particularly to the characters.

Much time and thought are devoted to shaping his characters. Apart from the fact that portions of his works, and perhaps the majority, are texts in which the author seeks to transmit his social, political, philosophical and cultural messages, the characters are at the centre of his texts. Indeed, the characters in al-Ṭayyib Ṣāliḥ's fiction are of prime importance. The author himself has said that most of his characters are figures from Sudanese reality he experienced as a boy; to which he has added various strata of time, fiction and legend, for according to his perception they should express the world he seeks to present to the reader, not his own personal world. Again, according to the author, his own world is not so interesting as to warrant writing about it. In any event, in this study I have devoted two chapters to characters for they have a status and significance that call for extensive treatment. There are Eastern and Western men and women, children and old people, and central, minor and marginal characters. Some of these reappear in a number of his works. Central characters like the narrator, the grandfather, the narrator's cronies, and also some less important village characters reappear in a number of the author's works in varying degrees of centrality and importance. This is linked in turn to al-Ṭayyib Ṣāliḥ's views that his texts are a single large text. The plot in his work takes place in a fixed location (usually the Sudan, in Wad Ḥāmid village), at different times. Exceptions from the standpoint of the characters are stories like 'Yawm Mubārak 'alā Shāṭi' Umm Bāb', where the plot does not take place in the Sudan and where the characters are not familiar to us from previous texts. However, the extraordinary little girl, Rabāb, has female parallels in many of al-Ṭayyib Ṣāliḥ's other works. The air of mystery and Muslim mysticism that marks this short text exists in others ('Dawmat Wad Ḥāmid', *'Urs al-Zayn, Bandar Shāh: Ḍaw al-Bayt, Maryūd*). The Eastern characters are mostly Sudanese; they are convincing, even though they often verge on archetypicality. This differs from, and sometimes stands in contrast to Western characters who, aside from being often archetypal, are frequently not credible and sometimes unconvincing.

One character who reappears in the majority of works and passes through numerous metamorphoses, from childhood to aging, is the narrator. He is sometimes employed as the figure of Muḥaymīd or Maryūd (*Bandar Shāh: Ḍaw al-Bayt, Maryūd*), and he narrates either the story of the Sudan, or alternatively the story of the remote Sudanese village and the changes taking place in it, as well as the author's personal story. Thus, in contrast to his statement that the author's personal life is not sufficiently interesting to warrant writing about it, he constructs the character of the narrator. In one form or another he has autobiographical features, enabling him to relate both his personal and collective stories. The narrator, who constitutes an option or alternative of the second generation (not the one presented, for example, by Muṣṭafā Sa'īd), expresses the author's ideaistic world and endows the world in which the author has, and has not, a part with both fictitious and realistic layers. Like Plato's cave, the outside world is the realistic world, but is not necessarily so. There is an element of futuristic or Utopian writing, or idealization of place, time, space, and characters. The real author lives his life in England, not the Sudan, he visits the Sudan for short periods, gives his opinion in writing on the changes taking place in the Sudanese village, and it is on these that he builds layers of fiction. The use he makes of the character of the narrator is evidence of his desire to be involved in the events taking place in his former village and to try, through fiction, to return even partially to the paradise which, from his point of view, has been lost.

One of the expressions of the relationship between reality and fiction in the works of al-Ṭayyib Ṣāliḥ is the encounter between Western and Eastern characters, usually Sudanese men and English or Scottish women. We have already noted that al-Ṭayyib Ṣāliḥ's works are generally ideaistic. Portions of his life, mainly during the fifties and sixties, were infused with encounters between East and West and he gave these encounters literary expression ('Risāla ilā Aylīn', 'Hākadhā Yā Sādatī', 'Muqaddimāt', *Mawsim al-Hijra ilā al-Shamāl*). However, the Western characters are not properly treated by the author and are usually stereotypes and archetypes (which is also the case with some Eastern characters); not a single Western character seems either developed or convincing. Moreover, they are usually depicted in a negative and uncomplimentary light (this also applies to the characters of Mr and Mrs Robinson in *Mawsim al-Hijra ilā al-Shamāl*). Al-Ṭayyib Ṣāliḥ is no different here from Arab Mashriq and Maghrib authors who generally describe Western characters negatively. Yet the author successfully expresses his opinion with great precision on the cultural encounter between East and West. Like many Arab intellectuals he gives Western culture credit for technological progress and science, education and freedom. Westerners were, first and foremost, imperialists, and have remained so to this day. The political hostility towards the foreign conqueror, primarily the British, is wrathful and indignant, even by those of his characters who were educated by them, but mainly by those who lived and continue living among them. Violence and sex are the ugly face reflected in the British mirror, individually and collectively.

The backbone of al-Ṭayyib Ṣāliḥ's works was and is the Sudanese village. It is clearly difficult to reflect reality through art, in our case literature. The literary prism enables the writer to reflect at least part of the reality of the Sudanese village in the fictional text. In his works he depicts the individual and collective experience of people in a world that is changing, both in reality, and in fiction. The author cannot precisely describe the existence he left behind, not only in geographical terms, but also in distance of time. Yet he is able to describe events that are characteristic of the Sudanese village, its customs and tradition, and the legends and folk beliefs current among its inhabitants. Relations between the authorities and the villagers, the villagers' attitude towards life and death, or their attitude towards fate, education and death, are legitimate subjects for debate among the villagers. In the final accounting, the processes undergone by the village as a result of modernization are important. Sudanese society and particularly village society have experienced great changes over the past fifty years. By describing these he also casts light on his inner world. He feels his way between realism and fiction, both of which are not always under his control.

During these decades he has changed his views and opinions, which are reflected in the works he has written. In one way or another all writing is autobiographical. Elements like his life in a foreign country, his marriage to a non-Arab woman, have become part of his fictional narratives. That he never returned to the Sudan and to the village where he was born indicates that he chose not to return.

In contrast to his own life, his fictional characters do not exercise this choice. In al-Ṭayyib Ṣāliḥ's works, fiction and reality intertwine and fuse almost seamlessly. His personal and literary life form a whole, composed as it is of complementary opposites.

APPENDICES

A. Places and Dates of Publication of al-Ṭayyib Ṣāliḥ's Works[1]

'Nakhla 'alā al-Jadwal' (A Date Palm by the Stream)

- Written in London in 1953, it was first published in the Sudanese journal *al-Qiṣṣa* 10 (October 1960), pp. 11–15.[2]
- It first appeared in al-Ṭayyib Ṣāliḥ's collection, *'Urs al-Zayn, Riwāya wa-Sab' Qiṣaṣ*, Beirut, al-Dār al-Sharqiyya li'l-Ṭibā'a wa'l-Nashr, Kitāb *Ḥiwār* 3, 1967, pp. 9–19.
- Appears in all the editions of the collection of stories, *Dawmat Wad Ḥāmid, Sab' Qiṣaṣ*, published in Beirut by Dār al-'Awda. Thus, for example, the 3rd ed., 1970, pp. 7–18. The last edition to be published by this house was in 1984.
- Appears in all the editions of al-Ṭayyib Ṣāliḥ, *al-A'māl al-Kāmila*, Beirut, Dār al-'Awda, from 1972. Thus, for example, the 1996 edition, pp. 479–88.
- The story appears in an anthology edited by the Sudanese author 'Alī al-Makk, *Mukhtārāt min al-Adab al-Sūdānī*, 2nd ed., Khartoum, Dār Jāmi'at al-Kharṭūm li'l-Nashr, 1980 (1st ed. 1975), pp. 214–21.
- Appears in the collection edited by 'Ami El'ad[-Bouskila] *al-Ṭayyib Ṣāliḥ–Mivḥar Yetzirot* (Selected Works), Jerusalem, Academon, 1981, pp. 1–12 (Arabic and Hebrew).
- This story appears in the collection *Dawmat Wad Ḥāmid, Sab' Qiṣaṣ*, Beirut, Dār al-Jīl, 1997, pp. 7–19.

'Ḥafnat Tamr' (A Handful of Dates)

- Written in 1957.[3] First published in al-Ṭayyib Ṣāliḥ's book, *'Urs al-Zayn, Riwāya wa-Sab' Qiṣaṣ*, pp. 21–7.
- Published in the Sudanese weekly, *al-Ra'y al-'Āmm*, 117 (15 July 1968), p. 15.[4]
- The story appears in the Egyptian journal *al-Hilāl*, 10 (October 1969), pp. 106–9.
- Appears in all the editions of the collection *Dawmat Wad Ḥamid, Sab' Qiṣaṣ*, Beirut, Dār al-'Awda. Thus, for example, the 3rd ed., 1970, pp. 19–25.
- Appears in all the editions of al-Ṭayyib Ṣāliḥ, *al-A'māl al-Kāmila*, Beirut, Dār al-'Awda, from 1972. Thus, for example, the 1996 edition, pp. 489–94.
- The story is included in the collection edited by 'Ami El'ad[-Bouskila], *al-Ṭayyib Ṣāliḥ – Mivḥar Yetzirot*, pp. 13–19 (Arabic and Hebrew).
- This story appears in the collection of stories *Dawmat Wad Ḥāmid, Sab' Qiṣaṣ*, Beirut, Dār al-Jīl, 1997, pp. 20–6.

'Risāla ilā Aylīn' (A Letter to Aileen)

- Written in 1960. It was first published in al-Ṭayyib Ṣāliḥ's book, *'Urs al-Zayn, Riwāya wa-Sab' Qiṣaṣ*, pp. 29–34.
- Appears in all editions of the collection *Dawmat Wad Ḥāmid, Sab' Qisas*. Thus, for example, the 3rd ed., 1970, pp. 26–32.
- The story is included in all the editions of *al-Ṭayyib Ṣāliḥ, al-A'māl al-Kāmila* (1972). Thus, for example, the 1996 edition, pp. 495–500.
- The story appears under a different title, ''Azīzatī Aylīn', in the contents of 'Alī al-Makk's anthology, *Mukhtārāt min al-Adab al-Sūdānī*, but under the same title in pp. 210–13.
- The story is included in the collection edited by 'Ami El'ad [-Bouskila], *al-Ṭayyib Ṣāliḥ– Mivḥar Yetzirot*, pp. 20–6 (Arabic and Hebrew).
- This story appears in the collection *Dawmat Wad Ḥāmid, Sab' Qiṣaṣ*, Beirut, Dār al-Jīl, 1997, pp. 27–32.

'Dawmat Wad Ḥāmid' (The Doum Tree of Wad Hamid)

- Written in al-Dabba in the Sudan in 1960.[5] First published in the London journal *Aṣwāt*, 3 (1961), pp. 44–55.
- Included in al-Ṭayyib Ṣāliḥ's collection, *'Urs al-Zayn, Riwāya wa-Sab' Qisas*, pp. 35–52.
- Appeared in the Egyptian journal *al-Hilāl,* 8 (August 1969), pp. 6–17. It is worthy of note that this is a special issue on the Arabic short story, and al-Ṭayyib Ṣāliḥ's story was chosen to open it.
- Included in all editions of the collection *Dawmat Wad Ḥāmid, Sab' Qiṣaṣ*. Thus, for example, the 3rd ed., 1970, pp. 33–52.
- Appears in all the editions of *al-Ṭayyib Ṣāliḥ, al-A'māl al-Kāmila* (1972). Thus, for example, the 1996 edition, pp. 501–17.
- Included in the collection of stories edited by Mukhtār Ibrāhīm 'Ajūba, *Namādhij min al-Qiṣṣa al-Qaṣīra fī al-Sūdān*, pp. 130–42.
- Included in the collection edited by 'Ami El'ad [-Bouskila], *al-Ṭayyib Ṣāliḥ – Mivḥar Yetzirot*, pp. 27–46 (Arabic and Hebrew).
- Included in Wadād al-Qāḍī (ed.), *Mukhtārāt min al-Nathr al-'Arabī*, Beirut, al-Mu'assasa al-'Arabiyya li'l-Dirāsāt wa'l-Nashr, 1983, pp. 417–27.
- Included in the collection edited by 'Ami El'ad [-Bouskila], *HaSippur Ha'Aravi* HaQatzar (The Arabic Short Story), Jerusalem, Academon, 1983, pp. 143–59 (Arabic and Hebrew).

- Included in the anthology edited by ‘Ami El‘ad-Bouskila, *Aḍwā’ Dāniya: Mukhtārāt min al-Qiṣṣa al-‘Arabiyya al-Ḥadītha* (Near Lights: Selected Modern Arabic Short Stories), Jerusalem, Academon, 1991, pp. 68–78.
- This story is included in the collection of al-Ṭayyib Ṣāliḥ’s stories, *Dawmat Wad Ḥāmid, Sab‘ Qiṣaṣ*, Beirut, Dār al-Jīl, 1997, pp. 33–53.

‘Idhā Jā’at’ (If She Comes)

- Written in 1961. It was first published in al-Ṭayyib Ṣāliḥ’s collection, *‘Urs al-Zayn, Riwāya wa-Sab‘ Qiṣaṣ*, pp. 53–65.
- Included in all editions of the collection *Dawmat Wad Ḥāmid, Sab‘ Qiṣaṣ*. Thus, for example, the 3rd ed., 1970, pp. 53–68.
- Appears in all the editions of *al-Ṭayyib Ṣāliḥ, al-A‘māl al-Kāmila* (1972). Thus, for example, the 1996 edition, pp. 519–33.
- Included in the collection edited by ‘Ami El‘ad [-Bouskila], *al-Ṭayyib Ṣāliḥ – Mivḥar Yetzirot*, pp. 47–62 (Arabic and Hebrew).
- This story is included in the collection of al-Ṭayyib Ṣāliḥ’s stories, *Dawmat Wad Ḥāmid, Sab‘ Qiṣaṣ*, Beirut, Dār al-Jīl, 1997, pp. 54–71.

‘Hākadhā Yā Sādatī’ (That’s the Way It Is, Gentlemen)

- Written in 1961. It was first published in the Beirut journal *Adab*, 1:1 (Winter 1962), pp. 9–16.
- Included in the collection *‘Urs al-Zayn, Riwāya wa-Sab‘ Qiṣaṣ*, pp. 67–79.
- Appears in all editions of the collection *Dawmat Wad Ḥāmid, Sab‘ Qisas*. Thus, for example, the 3rd ed., 1970, pp. 53–68.
- Included in the collection edited by ‘Ami El‘ad [-Bouskila], *al-Ṭayyib Ṣāliḥ – Mivḥar Yetzirot*, pp. 63–76 (Arabic and Hebrew).
- Included in all the editions of *al-Ṭayyib Ṣāliḥ, al-A‘mal al-Kāmila* (1972). Thus, for example, the 1996 edition, pp. 535–47.
- This story appears in the collection of al-Ṭayyib Ṣāliḥ’s stories, *Dawmat Wad Ḥāmid, Sab‘ Qiṣaṣ*, Beirut, Dār al-Jīl, 1997, pp. 72–86.

‘Muqaddimāt’ (Preludes)

- Written in 1962. This title comprises six short short stories: ‘Ughniyat Ḥubb’, ‘Khuṭwa li’l-Amām’, ‘al-Shay’ al-Ākhar’, ‘Laka ḥattā al-Mamāt’, ‘al-Ikhtibār’ and ‘Sūzān wa-‘Alī’.
- The six stories of ‘Muqaddimāt’ first appeared in the Beirut journal *Ḥiwār*, 21 (March-April 1966), pp. 36–40.
- The ‘Muqaddimāt’ appear in all the other places as comprising only five short short stories. The story ‘al-Shay’ al-Ākhar’ (The Other Thing), that appeared in

Ḥiwār, 21 (March-April 1966), pp. 37–8, does not appear in the various editions of Dār al-'Awda or other journals.

- Included in the book *'Urs al-Zayn, Riwāya wa-Sab' Qiṣaṣ*, pp. 81–96.
- Included in all the Dār al-'Awda editions of the collection *Dawmat Wad Ḥāmid, Sab' Qiṣaṣ*. Thus the 2nd ed., 1969, pp. 83–91.
- Published in the Sudanese daily *al-Ra'y al-'Āmm,* 8458 (29 April 1969).
- Appeared in the Egyptian journal *al-Hilāl*, 9 (September 1969), pp. 34–9.
- Included in all the editions of *al-Ṭayyib Ṣāliḥ, al-A'māl al-Kāmila* (1972). Thus, for example, the 1996 edition, pp. 549–56.
- The story 'al-Ikhṭibār' was published in *al-Ayyām,* 9794 (31 August 1979).[6]
- Included in the collection edited by 'Ami El'ad [-Bouskila], *al-Ṭayyib Ṣāliḥ – Mivḥar Yetzirot*, pp. 77–87 (Arabic and Hebrew).
- These stories appear in the collection of al-Ṭayyib Ṣāliḥ's stories, *Dawmat Wad Ḥāmid, Sab' Qiṣaṣ*, Beirut, Dār al-Jīl, 1997, pp. 87–95.

'Urs al-Zayn (The Wedding of Zein)

- The novel was written at Lavanca near Cannes in 1960–62.[7] Two chapters appeared in the Beirut journal *Ḥiwār*, 10 (May-June 1964), pp. 40–51.[8]
- The entire novel was first published in the Sudanese journal *al-Kharṭūm*, 3 (December 1966), pp. 97–137.[9]
- The novel first appeared in book form under the title *'Urs al-Zayn, Riwāya wa-Sab' Qiṣaṣ*, Beirut, al-Dār al-Sharqiyya li'l-Ṭibā'a wa'l-Nashr, Kitāb *Ḥiwār* 3, 1967, pp. 97–170. The novel continued to appear in the three Dār al-'Awda editions. Last printing in 1998.
- It was published in Cairo by Dār al-Hilāl.[10]
- The novel is included in all the editions of *al-Ṭayyib Ṣāliḥ, al-A'māl al-Kāmila* (1972). See the 1996 edition, pp. 179–280.
- The novel appeared in Beirut, Dār al-Jīl, 1997.
- The novel appears in its entirety in the project 'Kitāb fī Jarīda' that includes 22 Arabic newspapers, *al-Ahrām,* 8 (3 June 1998), pp. 5–29.

Mawsim al-Hijra ilā al-Shamāl (Season of Migration to the North)

- The novel was written at Lavanca near Cannes, and London in 1962–6.[11] The novel was to be published with *'Urs al-Zayn* in 1965.[12]
- The novel was first published in the Beirut journal *Ḥiwār*, 24–5 (September-December 1966), pp. 5–87.
- First published in book form in Beirut, Dār al-'Awda, 1967.

- Published by the Egyptian publisher Dār al-Hilāl, Riwāyāt *al-Hilāl*, 245, May 1969.
- The novel has been included in all the editions of *al-Ṭayyib Ṣāliḥ, al-A'māl al-Kāmila* since 1972 and up to the last edition in 1996, pp. 9–177.
- It was published in Jerusalem, Manshūrāt Ṣalāḥ al-Dīn, 1976.
- The novel appeared in Acre, Dār al-Aswār, 1977.
- The book is included in the collection edited by 'Ami El'ad [-Bouskila], *al-Ṭayyib Ṣāliḥ – Mivḥar Yetzirot*, pp. 88–254 (Arabic and Hebrew).
- Published by Dār al-'Awda in fourteen editions, the last being published in 1987.
- The novel was published by the Tunisian publisher Dār al-Janūb, Silsilat 'Uyūn al-Mu'āṣara, 1992.
- It was published in Silsilat 'Mahrajān al-Qirā'a li'l-Jamī'', Wizārat al-Thaqāfa, Cairo, 1996.[13]
- The novel was published in Beirut, Dār al-Jīl, 1997.

Bandar Shāh: Ḍaw al-Bayt (Bandarshah Dau Al-Beit)

- The novel was written in 1967–70.
- One source asserts that by 1970 the novel was already in print.[14]
- The novel first appeared in Beirut, Dār al-'Awda, 1971.
- The novel appeared in book form in Cairo, Mu'assasat Rūz al-Yūsuf, al-Kitāb al-Dhahabī 194, September 1972.
- The novel has been included in all editions of *al-Ṭayyib Ṣāliḥ, al-A'māl al-Kāmila*, Beirut, Dār al-'Awda, since 1972. In the 1996 edition it appears on pages 281–401.
- The novel appeared in a second edition, Acre, Dār al-Aswār, n.d.
- The last Dār al-'Awda edition, 1996.
- The novel was published in Beirut, Dār al-Jīl, 1997.

Bandar Shāh: Maryūd (Bandarshah-Meryoud)

- The book was written in 1976. The author finished writing the novel in Greece.
- One chapter was published in the Iraqi journal *al-Aqlām*, 9 (1972), pp. 84–7.
- One chapter was published in the Beirut journal *al-Thaqāfa al-'Arabiyya*, (1976), pp. 84–6.
- The novel appeared in its entirety in a four-part series in the Sudanese weekly *al-Shabāb*, 205–9, (June-July 1976).[15]
- Initially, two chapters of the novel were published in the Cairo weekly *al-Hilāl*, the first (December 1976), pp. 62–9, and the second (January 1977), pp. 50–7.

- The novel appeared in its entirety in a four-part series in the Qatar journal *al-Dōḥa*: first Chapter, 19 (July 1977), pp. 67–77; second Chapter, 20 (August 1977), pp. 66–77; third Chapter, 21 (September 1977), pp. 66–75; forth Chapter, 22 (October 1977), pp. 66–75.
- The novel appeared in book form in a first edition, Beirut, Dār al-'Awda, 1977.[16]
- According to the author (1977), two out of five planned parts of the novel have already appeared.[17]
- The novel appeared in book form in Acre, 2nd ed., Maktab al-Aswār, 1979.
- Appeared in book form in Tunis, Dār al-Janūb li'l-Nashr, Silsilat 'Uyūn al-Mu'āṣara, 1986.
- The novel was not included in the Dār al-'Awda editions of *al-Ṭayyib Ṣāliḥ, al-A'māl al-Kāmila* 1972. It was included in the 1996 edition, pp. 403–73.
- The novel appeared in two editions by Dār al-'Awda. Last printing 1987.
- The novel was published in Beirut, Dār al-Jīl, 1997.

'al-Rajul al-Qubruṣī' (The Cypriot Man)

- Written in Beirut in the summer of 1972.
- First published in *al-Thaqāfa al-'Arabiyya*, 2 (October 1973), pp. 88–91.
- Published with a different opening and ending in the Qatar journal *al-Dōḥa*, 1 (January 1976), pp. 105–8.
- It was published in the Sudanese daily *al-Ayyām,* 7723 (19 March 1976), p. 7. The editor indicated that this story is published as it was in *al-Dōḥa*.
- The story was included in an anthology edited by al-Ṭāhir Aḥmad Makkī, *al-Qiṣṣa al-Qaṣīra, Dirāsa wa-Mukhtārāt*, 2nd ed., Cairo, Dār al-Ma'ārif, 1978, pp. 304–14 (1st ed. 1977). This is the version published in *al-Thaqāfa al-'Arabiyya*.
- The story was not included in the various editions of *al-Ṭayyib Ṣāliḥ, al-A'māl al-Kāmila.*

'Yawm Mubārak 'alā Shāṭi' Umm Bāb' (A Blessed Day on the Umm Bab Shore)

- The story was first published in the anthology *Mukhtārāt min al-Qiṣaṣ al-Qaṣīra fī 18 Baladan 'Arabiyyan,* Cairo, Markaz al-Ahrām li'l-Tarjama wa'l-Nashr, 1993, pp. 159–66.
- This story appeared in a special edition of the Sudanese journal *al-Kharṭūm*, 13 (October-December 1994), pp. 167–75.
- It was published in *Tūmā,* Majalla Thaqāfiyya Sūdāniyya, Alexandrria, 1996.[18]
- The story was not included in the 1996 edition of *al-Ṭayyib Ṣāliḥ, al-A'māl al-Kāmila.*

B. A Short Summary of his Works[19]

'Nakhla 'alā al-Jadwal' (A Date Palm by the Stream) – The story revolves around Maḥjūb, a Sudanese *fallāḥ*, who is in dire financial straits. Ḥusayn, a merchant, tries to exploit Maḥjub's situation to tempt him to sell his date palm for twenty pounds. Maḥjūb, who in the past was a successful young farmer, has become impoverished. He deliberates about accepting the merchant's tempting offer because the festival is approaching and he needs the money. He finally decides to place his trust in God and rejects Ḥusayn's offer. His great faith in God stands him in good stead and he receives some unexpected financial assistance from his son Ḥasan, who has emigrated to Egypt to work.

'Ḥafnat Tamr' (A Handful of Dates) – There are three principal characters at the centre of the story: the grandfather, the grandson, and Mas'ūd. The latter cultivates large parts of his land because he has to finance his numerous marriages. The grandfather buys a piece of Mas'ūd's land and hopes to purchase the rest during his lifetime. The story focuses on a single episode in which Mas'ūd's creditors divide his date yield among themselves. The grandson is shocked by the scene of his grandfather and the merchants receiving part of their debt, with no compassion for Mas'ūd. He feels that he is unable to eat Mas'ūd's dates, and vomits them.

'Risāla ilā Aylīn' (A Letter to Aileen) – This is the first story in which the meeting between an Eastern man and a Western woman is discussed. The story focuses on the narrator, a Sudanese villager who has left his village for London. In the big city he meets a Scottish woman named Aileen and a relationship is formed between them. They marry eight months after having met. He continues to visit his family in the Sudanese village, while she gives him support in maintaining contact with them. The author describes what happens to the hero on one of his visits to his homeland.

'Dawmat Wad Ḥāmid' (The Doum Tree of Wad Hamid). The narrator, whose name we do not know, tells the readers, through his young listener, the story of Wad Ḥāmid village in the Sudan. The narrator describes the beliefs, customs, and traditions that exist in the village, and also the attempts of those in power, to force modernization on the village during both the period of British rule and after the Sudan attained independence. The villagers oppose the way in which the authorities try to force progress on their village. The doum tree, named after a righteous man called Wad Ḥāmid, and which the authorities want to cut down to build an anchorage, becomes a symbol of the struggle between the two concepts. On the face of it, the struggle ends in the villagers' victory and the government leaves the doum tree in place. The problem is that the readers, the young listener, and the old narrator are all aware of the fact that this victory is only temporary and that they are unable to halt progress. Therefore, the old narrator asks his young listener to publish the story of the doum tree and the struggle over it wherever he goes. He should not judge the villagers too harshly, pleads the narrator.

'Idhā Jā'at' (If She Comes) – This story, which is the most ironic and critical written by the author, describes the attempts of a young woman, Sanā', and two young men, Bahā' and Amīn, to open and run a tourist travel agency. The three young people running the agency are unsuccessful in their efforts as they have no customers. Sanā' is the first to see how wrong and vain this foolish venture is, and she decides to close down the agency. Amīn hastens to support her opinion, while Bahā', the third partner, continues to interest himself only in women. The story has no central plot and it focuses on the criticism leveled by the author at the provincial young people who fail to understand the progress and modernization that have come to their country.

'Hākadhā Yā Sādatī' (That's the Way It Is, Gentlemen) – This story, one of those whose subject is East-West relations, revolves around one principal character, the Eastern narrator, who unfolds his story before us at a cocktail party in England. The story places East and West in direct confrontation as the narrator reveals the beliefs and prejudices of both. The Eastern hero, who has no name, meets two women at the party. One is a 40 year-old married woman who spares no effort to seduce him, but who makes him continue resenting the West and Westerners. The second is a young, not particularly pretty Englishwoman, who has a nice voice, who does everything in her power so as not to arouse in him feelings of hate and resentment towards the West. In the end they marry and have two daughters.

'Muqaddimāt' (Preludes) – This collection contains five short short stories that deal with relationships between the Eastern man and the Western woman. The sixth story, 'al-Shay' al-Ākhar', also deals with the subject of East and West, but from a different angle. These short short stories place the East-West encounter at their centre, an encounter that usually ends with the Eastern man returning to his homeland. The exception is the short short story 'Khuṭwa li'l-Amām', that ends in marriage. These short short stories are a kind of introduction or prelude to the author's most important work on this topic, *Mawsim al-Hijra ilā al-Shamāl* (Season of Migration to the North).

'Urs al-Zayn (The Wedding of Zein) – The novel *'Urs al-Zayn* is built on an apparently common event: a wedding. The story opens with the news that one of the villagers, al-Zayn, is getting married. The news spreads through the village, sending the villagers into a high state of excitement. Between the opening of the story in which we, like the villagers, hear the news of al-Zayn's wedding to Ni'ma, and the

novel's end when the wedding takes place, the author manages to tell a simple story describing the village and its inhabitants. The framework is, of course, the wedding of al-Zayn, but as in other works by the author, this is a novel of ideals and descriptions of the village, its way of life, customs and traditions. The escapades of al-Zayn, who is the major protagonist, shed light on the Sudanese village of the fifties, and also on the lives and deaths of its inhabitants.

Mawsim al-Hijra ilā al-Shamāl (Season of Migration to the North) – This novel is the story of both rural Sudan and the Sudan that encounters Western culture. The plot is conveyed to us through two characters: Muṣṭafā Sa'īd and the narrator. Muṣṭafā was born in Khartoum and lost his parents when he was still young. He was known as a brilliant elementary school pupil and moved to Cairo for high school studies, and later went to London for his higher education. He completes his doctorate and joins the university faculty as a lecturer. He forms relationships with English women, four in particular, three of whom commit suicide, while he marries and later kills the fourth. Muṣṭafā is sentenced to seven years in jail, and after his release wanders around Europe but realizes that if he wants to rehabilitate himself, he must return to his homeland. He goes back to Khartoum where he engages in commerce, but can find no peace. He therefore decides to live in a village and not the city. He chooses a remote Sudanese village where he purchases land, gets married and has two children. Five years after Muṣṭafā settled in the village, the narrator returns to the same village after a seven-year absence in Europe, where he completed his doctorate in poetry. He meets Muṣṭafā Sa'īd, and a complex relationship develops between the two until Muṣṭafā disappears in the river and no one knows whether he is alive or dead. His image continues to accompany and even persecute the narrator who decides to investigate Muṣṭafā Sa'īd's life story. He goes into Muṣṭafā's mysterious room where evidence of his past life is found. The narrator leaves the room agitated and horrified, and goes to the river in which Muṣṭafā disappeared. There he confronts Muṣṭafā's spirit, and himself. The conflict between life and death, North and South, city and village, choice and acceptance of authority, ends in the victory of life over death. The narrator, it might be assumed, has undergone a cathartic process, purged himself of Muṣṭafā Sa'īd, and turned over a new leaf. This is, however, only partially true, the novel concludes with a Muṣṭafā-like sentence that the narrator's purification and his desire to finally rid himself of Muṣṭafā, were only partly successful.

Bandar Shāh: Ḍaw al-Bayt – This is the first novel written after *Mawsim al-Hijra ilā al-Shamāl*. Intended originally as a trilogy or quintology, to date only two parts have been published, this being the first. The novel does not have a single plot but rather a number of plots and events that take place in Muḥaymīd's village. Muḥaymīd, who returns to his village after a long absence, is the narrator. He comes back to his childhood friends and describes the many changes that have taken place in the village. The most important change of all is the replacing of the older generation by the new, with the dismissal of Maḥjūb and his gang from village leadership. This is the same gang that accumulated great power in the previous novels (*'Urs al-Zayn* and *Mawsim al-Hijra ilā al-Shamāl*). The younger villagers, including Maḥjūb's children, conspire, and using democratic means they rebel against the prolonged rule of Maḥjūb and his gang. Muḥaymīd hears of the murders of his grandson Maryūd and Bandar Shāh by the sons of Bandar Shāh. The narrator learns about Bandar Shāh's family, which enjoyed special status in the village, and he, too, is harmed. The shift to dealing with this family introduces an atmosphere of mystery and legend. Ḍaw al-Bayt is apparently Bandar Shāh's father. Ḍaw al-Bayt's origins, his arrival in the village and his disappearance in the river are shrouded in mystery. One day he came from the river, from where no one knew. The villagers gave him the name Ḍaw al-Bayt, circumcised him as he was uncircumcised, married him to Fāṭima, and three months before the birth of his son, he disappeared in the river and no one knew what had become of him. Three months after his disappearance, his son, named 'Īsā, was born, but he was nicknamed Bandar Shāh. His life was a great sucsess and the legends about him were numerous. He had eleven children, but preferred his grandson, Maryūd, not only over his father but also over his uncles. The sons, who detested the rule of Bandar Shāh and Maryūd, attacked and murdered them. The villagers informed the authorities of the murder and the sons were arrested. The narrator is shocked by the story of the murder and realizes that the changes in the village are deeper than he first thought. Because of his absence from the village he was insufficiently aware of them. The novel concludes with recollections of Ḍaw al-Bayt by the old men of the village.

Bandar Shāh: Maryūd – This novel is the second part of *Bandar Shāh*. As in the first part of *Bandar Shāh*, it has no plot but a series of episodes. The obscurity, legend and mystery that characterize part of *Bandar Shāh: Ḍaw al-Bayt* are also present in this book. Maryūd, who was murdered by his uncles, has his identity in this novel linked to a number of similar points between the narrator and Maryūd on the one hand, and between Bandar Shāh and the grandfather on the other. The narrator is presented as Maryūd, not only as Muḥaymīd, describing his life as an old man who spends his time with his old friends. The text describes Muḥaymīd, Sa'īd 'Ashā al-Bāyitāt, al-Ṭāhir Wad al-Rawwāsī, part of the old gang, and with them the central heroes of the previous novel, Bandar Shāh and Ḍaw al-Bayt. The author adds details about Bandar Shāh which do not shed light on his history and origins, and heighten the obscurity, mystery and legends connected with them. By enlarging on the obscure, mystical strata of reality it is difficult to separate the legendary and realistic parts of the same village. The novel that began with a description of Muḥaymīd and the band of old men is concluded with Maryūd's description, his relationship with Maryam, Maḥjūb's sister whom Muḥaymīd loved, but never married in accordance with his grandfather's command. Maryam says some harsh words to him on his deathbed, and the narrator, Muḥaymīd and Maryūd, has no choice but to admit his mistake.

'al-Rajul al-Qubruṣī' (The Cypriot Man) – This story was written and published after the appearance of the first part of *Bandar Shāh* and prior to the publication of the second. The narrator, who is staying in Beirut with his wife and daughters, goes to Nicosia in the month of July to meet his old friend al-Ṭāhir Wad al-Rawwāsī. In his hotel he meets an elderly man, called by the author 'The Cypriot Man', who engages him in conversation. The latter embarrasses the narrator with obscene proposals and temptations and ideas that the narrator does not want. Accordingly, he returns to his village and to al-Ṭāhir Wad al-Rawwāsī in search of safety. Thus the secondary plot returns the narrator to Wad Ḥāmid village and its inhabitants, while he is presented as Muḥaymīd of the two books of *Bandar Shāh*. On his return to Beirut he is given the news of his father's death and rushes to get to Wad Ḥāmid, where to his surprise he finds The Cypriot Man who tells him that this time he has taken the narrator's father, but next time he will take the narrator's soul.

'Yawm Mubārak 'alā Shāṭi' Umm Bāb' (A Blessed Day on the Umm Bab Shore) – This story is the last text published by al-Ṭayyib Ṣāliḥ to date. It seemingly is a turning point in the author's writing; the characters and location are different from those we have encountered to date. Yet the mystical, obscure and legendary atmosphere is not new in the author's works. There are three principal characters at the centre of the story: Rabāb, her father and her mother. Rabāb is a nine year-old girl who is spending a 'blessed day' on the sea shore. She was born when her father was fifty and her mother forty. Rabāb came into the world after a seven-month pregnancy, and here the fact that she is different becomes apparent. She is shown as an extraordinary child who is clever, brilliant and erudite in literature and mystical Arabic literature in particular. On the day in question, the mother and daughter are swimming and move away from the shore. Rabāb swims back to the beach, lights a big bonfire and other children gather around her. She and her parents are very happy. They see a herd of camels, and single out one particular animal. The camels walk into the sea to bathe, they come out of the water, move away, and only the big camel remains on the hill. The father, mother and Rabāb go into the sea to bathe. They come out, get into their car, start it, switch on the lights, and only then the camel leaves and joins the herd.

C. Translations of his Works into Other Languages[20]

Short stories

'Nakhla 'alā al-Jadwal' (A Date Palm by the Stream)

- 'A Date Palm by the Stream' (trans. Denys Johnson-Davies), *Azure: The Review of Arabic Literature, Arts and Culture*, 8 (1981), pp. 21–4.

'Ḥafnat Tamr' (A Handful of Dates)

- 'A Handful of Dates' (trans. Denys Johnson-Davies), *Encounter*, 26 (January 1966), pp. 22–4. See also *Azure*, 1 (1977), pp. 44–6. The same translation reprinted in Tayeb Salih, *The Wedding of Zein and Other Stories* (1978, 1999), pp. 21–8. See in Chinua Achebe and C.L. Innes (eds), *African Short Stories*, Oxford, Heinemann, 1987, pp. 90–4.
- French translation 'Une Poignée de dates' (trans. Anne Wade Minkowski). Published in *Les Noces de Zeyn et autres récits*, Paris, Sindbad, 1996, pp. 103–8.
- Polish translation 'Garść Daktyli' (trans. Jolanta Jasińska), *Kontynenty*, 11 (1970), pp. 42–3.
- Dutch and Italian.[21]
- Hebrew translation 'Ḥofen shel Tmarim' (trans. David Sagiv), *Liqā' – Mifgash* 4–5 (8–9) (Winter 1986), p. 26. For another translation see 'Ḥofen Tmarim' (trans. Raḥel Ḥalabe) in *Zein Mitḥaten*, Tel Aviv, Andalus, 2001, pp. 23–9.

'Risāla ilā Aylīn' (A Letter to Aileen)

- 'A Letter to Aileen, by al-Ṭayyib Ṣāliḥ' (trans. N.S. Doniach), *Journal of Arabic Literature*, XI (1980), pp. 76–9.
- Hebrew translation 'Yaqirati Aylīn' (trans. Moshe Ḥakham), in Sasson Somekh (ed.), *'Anbar Lulu: Sippurei Ahava 'Arviyyim*, Tel-Aviv, 'Eked, 1995, pp. 49–51.

'Dawmat Wad Ḥāmid' (The Doum Tree of Wad Hamid)

- 'The Doum Tree of Wad Hamid' (trans. and ed. Denys Johnson-Davies), *Encounter*, 28 (November 1962), pp. 15–22. See also in *Modern Arabic Short Stories*, London, Oxford University Press, 1967, pp. 84–96. See also in *Modern Arabic Short Stories*, Heinemann, Washington, Three Continents Press, 1981, pp. 83–94 (1st ed. 1967). See Tayeb Salih, *The Wedding of Zayn and Other Stories*, 1978 (1999), pp. 1–20.

- It was translated from the English translation into German under the title 'Die Palm von Wadd Hamid' and published in the March 1969 issue of *Der Monat*.[22]
- It was also translated into German under the same title 'Die Palm von Wadd Hamid', Übers V. Wiebke, in Erkan Dungen, *17 Arabische Erzähler*, Berlin, 1971.[23]
- It was translated from the English into Italian in 1964 under the title *Le Più Belle Novelle di Tutti I Paesi*.[24] According to another source it was translated into Italian under the title 'II Dum di Wad Hamid', Pavia, *Lettera Internazionale* 26 (1990), pp. 18–22.[25]
- Translated into French by Anne Wade Minkowski, 'Le Doum de Wad Hamid', published in *Lettre Internationale*, 19 (Winter 1988–9). See also in Salih, *Les Noces de Zeyn*, 1996, pp. 87–101.
- Also translated into French as 'Le Palmier de Ouad Hamid' (trans. Mohamed Saad Eddin El Yamani), in *Serpent a plumes, récit & fictions courtes*, 29 (Autumn 1995), pp. 3–8.
- Translated into Polish, 'I w ten sam Sposób Panowie' in collection of short stories, *Ziemia Smutnej Pomarańczy*, Warsaw, 1983.
- Translated into Dutch.[26]
- Translated into Japanese, 'Wado Haamido no douma no ki' (trans. Nobuyuki Nutahara). Published in *Bungei*, 18:8 (1st August 1978), pp. 270–83.
- Translated into Hebrew, 'Etz HaDom shel Wad Ḥāmid' (trans. 'Ami El'ad-Bouskila) in idem (ed.), *Me'Ever LaOfeq HaQarov: Sippurim 'Arviyyim Bnei Yamyenu*, Jerusalem, Keter, 1989, pp. 231–40. Also published in the same translation, in *Liqā'-Mifgash*, 6 (Spring 1986), pp. 25–7. See also in Joseph Givony (ed.), *Makom 'al Pnei HaAdama* (A Place on the Earth), Jerusalem, The Van Leer Jerusalem Institute, 1986, pp. 124–35. For another translation see 'Dekel HaDom shel Wad Ḥamid' (trans. Raḥel Ḥalabe) in *Zein Mitḥaten*, Tel Aviv, Andalus, 2001, pp. 7–21.

'Idhā Jā'at' (If She Comes)

- 'If She Comes' (trans. Shakir Mustafa) in Peter Clark (ed.), *Sardines and Oranges: Short Stories from North Africa*, London, Banipal Books, 2005, pp. 141–9. This translation appeared in: *Banipal*, 22 (Spring 2005), pp. 32–6.[27]

'Hākadhā Yā Sādatī' (That's the Way It Is, Gentlemen)

- 'C'est ainsi messieurs' (trans. and ed. Paul and Laura Makarius), *Anthologie de la littérature arabe contemporaine, le roman et la nouvelle*, vol. I, Paris, Editions du Seuil, 1964, pp. 397–404.

- Translated into Polish, 'I w ten sam Sposób Panowie', in the collection of short stories entitled *Ziemia Smutnej Pomarańczy*, 1983.

'al-Rajul al-Qubruṣī' (The Cypriot Man)

- 'The Cypriot Man' (trans. Constance E. Berkley, ed., revised Osman Hassan Ahmed), *al-Dōḥa* (January 1976), pp. 105–8. This translation appeared in Constance E. Berkley, *The Roots of Consciousness*, pp.viii–xx. In *Pacific Moana Quarterly*, 6: 3–4 (July-October 1981), pp. 180–8. It was also published in Osman Hassan Ahmed (ed.), *Sixteen Short Stories*, Washington D.C., Office of the Cultural Counselor, Embassy of the Democratic Republic of Sudan, 1981, pp. 9–15.
- 'The Cypriot Man' (trans. Denys Johnson-Davies), first published in *Encounter*, (April, 1980), pp. 3–7. It was also published in *Azure*, 8 (1981), pp. 25–7. See also in Denys Johnson-Davies (ed. and trans.), *Arabic Short Stories*, London, Quartet Books, 1983, pp. 75–83.

'Yawm Mubārak 'alā Shāṭi' Umm Bāb' (A Blessed Day on the Umm Bab Shore)

- It was translated into Hebrew under the title 'Yom Mevorakh 'al Ḥof Umm Bab' (trans. 'Ami El'ad-Bouskila), *Ma'ariv* (15 May, 1994), pp. 36, 38.

Novels

'Urs al-Zayn (The Wedding of Zein)

- *The Wedding of Zein and Other Stories* (trans. Denys Johnson-Davies), first published in hardcover, London, Heinemann Educational Books, 1969. First published in African Writers Series, 47, 1969, rpt. 1971, 1975, 1978. Rpt. In Arab Authors Series, 13, London, Heinemann, 1970, 1978, pp. 29–120. Rpt. In *Season of Migration to the North: The Wedding of Zein*, London, Quartet Books, 1980, pp. 171–263. Published by Lynne Rienner publishers, A Three Continents Book, 1999, pp. 29–120.
- Translated into French, *Les Noces de Zeyn et autres récits* (trans. Anne Wade Minkowski), Paris, Sindbad/Acted Sud, 1996, pp. 11–85.
- Translated into German *Die Hochzeit des Zain* (trans. Stefan Reichmuth), Berlin, Orient, 1983.
- Translated into Dutch, *De roep van de Nijl* (trans. Richard van Leeuwen), Houten, Het Wereldvenster, 1987.
- Translated into Spanish, *La Boda de Zayn* in *Dos Novellas Sudanesas* (trans. Milagros Nuim), Madrid, Cantarabia, 1987, pp. 15–117.
- Translated into Polish by Jolanta Koziowska but never published as a book.

- Translated into Russian, see E. Shikova (ed.), *al-Ṭayyib Ṣāliḥ 'Urs al-Zayn, Mawsim al-Hijra ilā al-Shamāl, Bandar Shāh*, Moscow, Raduga, 1982, pp. 15–82.
- Translated into Japanese, *Zeen no kekkon* (trans. Seiji Takai). Published in the collection, *Modern Arabic Stories*, vol. 8 (Gendai araba shusetu zenshuu dai 8 kan), Kawadeshobou-Shinsha, Tokyo, 1978.
- Translated into Hebrew, *HaḤatuna* which includes the first chapter (trans. Peretz Dror-Banai), *Moznaim*, 72:8 (may 1998), pp. 54–8. For the full translation see *Zein Mitḥaten* (trans. Raḥel Ḥalabe), Tel Aviv, Andalus, 2001, pp. 31–101.

Mawsim al-Hijra ilā al-Shamāl (Season of Migration to the North)

- *Season of Migration to the North* (trans. Denys Johnson-Davies), first published in hardcover, London, Heinemann Educational Books, 1969. Arab Authors Series, 4, 1969 rpt. In paperback 1970 rpt. With corrections, 1976. Rpt. 1978, 1980 rpt. *Season of Migration to the North: The Wedding of Zein*, London, Quartet Books, 1980, pp. 1–169. African Authors Series, 66, London, Heinemann, 1977, rpt. 1978, 1980, 1981. Published by Lynne Rienner Publishers, A Three Continents Book, 1997.
- Translated into French, *Le Migrateur* (trans. Fadi Noum), Paris, Sindbad, La Bibliothèque Arabe, Litératures, 1972.
- Also translated into French by Fadi Noum and Abdel Wahab Meddeb, *Saison de la migration vers le nord*, Paris, Sindbad, 1983. 3rd ed. Babel/Sindbad, 1996.
- Translated into Italian, *La Stagione della Migrazione al Nord,* (trans. Francesco Leggio) Palermo, Sellerio, 1992.
- Translated into Dutch, *Seizoen van de Trek naar het Noorden* (trans. Kees Versteegh), Amsterdam, Meulenhof, 1985.
- Translated into Russian by Vladimir Shagal and published (1975) in *Inostrannaya Literatura* (Foreign Literature). Also published together with some of al-Ṭayyib Ṣāliḥ's stories in book form by 'Progress' Publishers, and later published in the anthology *Selected Works by Middle Eastern Writers*, also by 'Progress'.[28] See also E. Shikova (ed.), *al-Ṭayyib Ṣāliḥ's Novels*, Moscow, 1982, pp. 83–210.
- Translated into German, *Zeit Nordwanderung* (trans. Regina Karachouli), Basel, Lenos Verlag, 1998.
- Translated into Japanese, *Kitae uturiyuku toki* (trans. Toshio Kuroda). Published in the collection of *Modern Arabic Stories*, vol. 8 (Gendai araba shusetu zenshuu dai 8 kan), Kawadeshobou-Shinsha, Tokyo, 1978.
- Translated into Norwegian, Turkish, Bulgarian, Yugoslavian, Czechoslovakian, Hungarian and Chinese.[29]

- Hebrew translation, *'Onat HaNedida el HaTzafon* (trans. Tuvia Shamosh), Tel Aviv, 'Am 'Oved, 1973 (Hebrew).

Bandar Shāh: Ḍaw al-Bayt (Bandarshah: Dau Al-Beit)

- *Dau Al-Beit* in *Bandarshah* (trans. Denys Johnson-Davies), London and New York, Kegan Paul International, Paris, UNESCO Publishing, 1996, pp. 1–80.
- In 1981, Denys Johnson-Davies declared that '...*Meryoud* is shortly to be published, together with the other novella, *Bandar Shāh*, in English translation under the title, *The Season of Wad Hamid...*'[30]
- Translated into French *Daw el-Beyt* in *Bandarchâh, roman* (trans. Anne Wade Minkowski), Paris, Sindbad, La Bibliothèque Arabe, 1985, pp. 13–140.
- Translated into Spanish as *Bandar Shah* in *La Boda de Zayn: Bandar Shah* (trans. Milagros Nuim) in *Dos Novellas Sudanesas,* Madrid, Cantarabia, 1987, pp. 119–238.
- Translated into Russian, *al-Ṭayyib Ṣāliḥ's Novels*, Moscow, 1982, pp. 211–91.
- Translated also into Dutch and Yugoslavian.[31]

Bandar Shāh: Maryūd (Bandarshah: Meryoud)

- *Meryoud* in *Bandarshāh* (trans. Denys Johnson-Davies), London and New York, Kegan Paul International, Paris, UNESCO Publishing, 1996, pp. 81–122.
- *Meryoud* in *Bandarchâh* (trans. Anne Wade Minkowski), Paris, Sindbad, La Bibliothèque Arabe, 1985, pp. 141–211.
- Translated into Russian in *al-Ṭayyib Ṣāliḥ's Novels*, Moscow, pp. 292–335.

D. Dissertations, Theses and Diplomas about his Works

Doctoral Dissertations

- Berkley, Constance E., *The Roots of Consciousness Molding the Art of El-Tayeb Salih: A Contemporary Sudanese Writer*, Ph.D Dissertation, New York University, 1979 (Michigan, UMI Dissertation Information Services, 1989).
- Bushrā, Muḥammad al-Mahdī, *al-Fulklūr fī A'māl al-Ṭayyib Ṣāliḥ* (The Folklore in al-Ṭayyib Ṣāliḥ's Writing), Ph.D. Dissertation, Khartoum University, The Asian and African Institute, 1990.
- David, Margit, *Az Eszakarn van Dorlas Ideje*, Ph.D Thesis, Dept. of Arabic, University of Letters, Budapest, 1996.[32]
- Harb, Ahmed Musa, *Half Way between North and South, An Archetypal Analysis of the Fiction of Tayeb Salih*, Ph.D. Dissertation, University of Iowa, 1987.
- Al-Halool, Musa, *In Quest of Miranda: Towards A Postcolonial Semantic of Transitive Set* (Prospero-Caliban, Tayeb Salih, Andrew Salkey, Dany Laferrier,

Sudan, Jamaica, Haiti, Quebec). (Michigan, UMI Dissertation Services, 1999), Ph.D Dissertation, Pennsylvania State University, 1995.

- Hassan, Wail Seddiq, *Tayeb Salih: Culture, History, Memory*, (Ann Arbor, June 1999). Ph.D Dissertation, University of Illinois, Urbane, 1998.
- Kambal, Zaki El-Din Suleiman, *The Thematic Concerns* of *Al-Ṭayyib Ṣāliḥ: A Study of his Short stories and Novels*, Ph.D. Dissertation, The University of Exeter, 1984.
- Nehme, Raja', (= Ni'ma Rajā'), *Mawsim al-Hijra ilā al-Shamāl, Dirāsa fī al-Taḥlīl al-Nafsī li'l-Adab* (*Mawsim al-Hijra ilā al-Shamāl*: A Psychoanalytical Study of Literature), Ph.D. Dissertation, University of Saint Joseph, Beirut, 1984.
- Peters, Barbara Diane, *Power Relations and Conflict in Selected Works of Tayeb Salih: Implications For A New History, (*Michigan, UMI Dissertation Services, 1999). Ph.D. Dissertation, University of Wisconsin, 1989.
- Sa'd, Muḥammad Fā'iza, *Tayyār al-Wa'y fī Riwāyāt al-Ṭayyib Ṣāliḥ, Dirāsa fī al-Adab al-Muqāran* (Stream of Consciousness in al-Ṭayyib Ṣāliḥ's Novels, a Study in Comparative Literature), Ph.D. Dissertation, Jāmi'at 'Ayn Shams, Kulliyyat al-Alsun, 1996.
- Scott, Pauline Marie, *Writing, Rewriting, and Unwriting the Renaissance: Constructing 'Otherness' In Ariosto's 'Orlando Furioso', Shakespeare's 'Othello', Woolf's 'Orlando', and Salih's Season of Migration to the North* (Otherness, Ludovico Ariosto, Italy, Virginia Woolf, Tayeb Salih, Sudan). (Michigan, UMI Dissertation Services, 1999). Ph.D Dissertation, University of Wisconsin-Madison, 1994.
- Al-Yāzijī, Ḥalīm, *Al-Sūdān wa'l-Ḥaraka al-Adabiyya*, Jāmi'at al-Qiddīs Yūsuf, Beirut, 1978. This Ph.D. Dissertation was published as a book (see Bibliography).

Masters and/or Diploma Theses

- 'Ajūba, Mukhtār Ibrāhīm, *al-Qiṣṣa al-Qaṣīra wa-Taṭawwuruhā fī al-Adab al-Sūdānī al-Ḥadīth* (The Short Story and its Development in the Modern Sudanese Literature). A Master of Arts thesis, Cairo University, Faculty of Science, 1968. This thesis was published as a book (see Bibliography).
- Barjāndza, Jūrj, *Ḥawla Thulāthiyyat al-Ṭayyib Ṣāliḥ* (On the Trilogy of al-Ṭayyib Ṣāliḥ), University of Khartoum, Department of Arabic Literature, 1989.[33]
- Bou Najem, Michel, *L'Emploi du temps dans Mawsim... Essai de lecture globale* (The Use of Tenses in Mawsim...a Global Reading). A DEA Thesis, Sorbonne Nouvelle, Paris, 1980.[34]

- Dyouma, Babiker Ali, *Le Migrateur de Tayeb Salih, Les Themes, la forme et une compararison de la traduction francaise et anglaise avec le texte arabe pour l'obtention de la maîtrise en littérature comparée.* Travail dirigé par Mme. Magalimorsky, Paris 1978.
- El'ad-[Bouskila], 'Ami, '*Olamo shel al-Ṭayyib Ṣāliḥ* (The World of al-Ṭayyib Ṣāliḥ). A Master of Arts Thesis, The Hebrew University of Jerusalem, 1981 (Hebrew).
- Essafi, Wahid, *Mawsim al-Hijra…, Essai de lecture globale* (*Mawsim*, A Global Reading). A Master of Arts Thesis, Sorbonne Nouvelle, Paris, 1980.[35]
- Mazen, Rita, *Une Proposition de lecture du roman de Tayyib Sālih, Mawsim* (An Attempt at Interpretation). A Master of Arts Thesis, Sorbonne Nouvelle, 1980.[36]
- Al-Mūdin, Ḥasan, *Lā wa'y al-Naṣṣ fī Riwāyāt al-Ṭayyib Ṣāliḥ* (The Text's Unconciousness in al-Ṭayyib Ṣāliḥ's Novels), Diploma Degree, Jāmi'at Muḥammad al-Khāmis, Rabat, February 1996. (A summary of this work was published in *Faḍā'āt Mustaqbaliyya*, 2–3 (March 1996), pp. 54–6) (see Bibliography). This thesis was published as a book (see Bibliography).
- Nasr, Ahmed, *Popular Islam in al-Ṭayyib Ṣāliḥ.* A Master of Arts Thesis, University of Wisconsin, 1975. (Part of this thesis was published in *Journal of Arabic Literature*, XI (1980), pp. 88–103 (see Bibliography).
- Al-Ṣaffār, Fawziyya, *Azmat al-Ajyāl al-'Arabiyya al-Mu'āṣira* (The Crisis of Contemporary Arabic Generations). Diploma Degree (= Master of Arts). Tunis University. Faculty of Humanities and Social Science, 1980. This thesis was published as a book (see Bibliography).
- Tababi, Amar, *Analyse du roman Mawsim* (An Analysis of Mawsim). A Master of Arts Thesis, Sorbonne Nouvelle, Paris, 1979.[37]
- Torres, Carmen M., *Colonialism and Gender* in *Season of Migration to the North*, M.A. Thesis, University of California at Berkley, 1990.

E. Reviews, Introductions and Articles by al-Ṭayyib Ṣāliḥ

- 'Mashrū' al-Jazīra', book review on Arthur Gaitskell, *Gezira, A Story of Development in the Sudan*, Faber and Faber, *Aswāt*, 1 (1961), pp. 97–9.
- 'Budhūr al-Ḥadāra', book review on Roland Oliver, *The Dawn of African History*, Oxford University Press, *Aswāt*, 5 (1962), pp. 109–13.
- 'Ṣūra Ḥadītha li'l-Sūdān', book review on K.M. Barbour, *The Republic of the Sudan*, University of London, *Aṣwāt*, 10 (1963), pp. 103–4.
- 'Ḥadīth al-Shi'r wa'l-Shurūq', *al-Dōḥa*, 42 (June 1979), pp. 40–1.

- Writing 'al-Ṣafḥa al-Akhīra' (=Last Page) of the periodical *al-Majalla* between 1989–99.
- Introduction to al-Bashīr Khurayyif's *al-Daqla fī 'Arājīnihā*, Tunis, Dār al-Janūb li'l Nashr, 1990, pp. 7–20.
- Introduction in Ṣalāḥ Aḥmad Ibrāhīm, *Ghābat al-Ābanūs wa-Qaṣā'id Ukhrā*, Paris, Idfra, 1990, pp. 1–20.[38]
- Introduction to Ṭāriq al-Ṭayyib's *al-Jamal Lā Yaqif Khalf Ishāra Ḥamrā'*, Cairo, al-Ḥaḍāra li'l-Nashr, 1993, pp. 5–9.
- 'Naḥwa Ufuq Ba'īd', *al-Majalla*, 758 (21–27 August 1994), p. 78.
- 'Taqdīm wa-Ta'rif, Mughāmara Ma'rifiyya fī al-Tukhūm al-Janūbiyya', in Yūsuf al-Sharīf, *al-Sūdān wa-Ahl al-Sudān, Asrār al-Siyāsa wa-Khafāyā al-Mujtama'*, Cairo, Dār al-Hilāl, 1996, pp. 7–9.
- Introduction to Bashīr 'Awfī's *Marbat al-Jamal*, vol. 1, London, 2001, pp. 7–8.
- Introduction to Riyāḍ Baydas' *Ḥikāyat al-Dīk al-Faṣīḥ*, Ramallah, Manshūrāt Bayt al-Maqdis, 2001, pp. 7–11.

F. Films and Plays Based on his Works

'Urs al-Zayn

Adapted as a drama in Libya sometime in the late 1960s.[39]

Made into a film by the Kuwaiti director Khālid Ṣiddīq, who won an award for it at the Cannes Film Festival in 1977.[40]

In Lebanon the novel was staged as a play.[41]

Mawsim al-Hijra ilā al-Shamāl

Produced on stage by director Ya'qūb al-Shadrāwī in Beirut in the early 1970s.[42]

Performed on stage in Hebrew in Israel by the Palestinian actor Muḥammad Bakrī since the early 1990s.

Performed by Shaykh al-Islām Ḥājj Aḥmad in July 1996 at the Institute of Music and Theatre in the Sudan.[43]

A film version is being prepared by the Kuwaiti director Khālid Ṣiddīq.[44]

G. Interviews Conducted with al-Ṭayyib Ṣāliḥ

Adab,	'Ḥiwār fī Kull Shay' ma'a al-Ṭayyib Ṣāliḥ', *al-Fajr*, 94 (15 November 1976).[45]
El'ad-Bouskila, 'Ami,	'Muqābalāt ma'a al-Ṭayyib Ṣāliḥ fī Oxford', 24–5 April, 1998.

Elad-Bouskila, Ami — 'The Path and its Stations: An Interview with al-Ṭayyib Ṣāliḥ', London, 22 August 2000 (see Appendix H).

Fāḍil, Jihād, — 'Ḥiwār Ākhār ma'a al-Ṭayyib Ṣāliḥ', in idem, *As'ilat al-Riwāya*, pp. 38–43. (This article was first published in *al-Qabas*, 1 October 1987).

Fāḍil, Jihād, — 'Ma'a al-Ṭayyib Ṣāliḥ', in idem, *As'ilat al-Riwāya*, pp. 32–7. (This interview was first published in *al-Ḥawādith*, 21 July 1989).

Farghalī, Sayyid, — 'Liqā' ma'a al-Ṭayyib Ṣāliḥ fī Landan', *al-Hilāl*, 3 (March 1970), pp. 118–21. Rpt. In Muḥammadiyya (ed.), *al-Ṭayyib Ṣāliḥ*, pp. 204–11.

Al-Ḥaḍārī, Ḥasan, — 'Liqā' ma'a al-Ṭayyib Ṣāliḥ', *al-Ṣiḥāfa*, (17 September, 1981), p. 9.

Hijab, Nadia, — 'Meet the Maker of Modern Arab Mythology', *The Middle East*, 56 (June 1979), pp. 66–8.

al-Ḥilū, 'Īsā — 'Ḥiwār ma'a al-Ṭayyib Ṣāliḥ', *al-Ayyām*, 9226 (28 October 1977).[46]

al-Ḥilū, 'Īsā — 'Ḥiwār ma'a al-Ṭayyib Ṣāliḥ', *al-Ayyām*, 9232 (4 November 1977).[47] (For the English translation, see Berkley 79, pp. lxxii–lxxiii).

al-Ḥilū, 'Īsā — 'Ḥiwār ma'a al-Ṭayyib Ṣāliḥ', *al-Ayyām*, 9238 (11 November 1977).[48]

al-Ḥusaynī, Hudā, — 'al-Ṭayyib Ṣāliḥ fī Bayrūt: Hunāka Asrār Lam Udrikhā Ba'du', in Muḥammadiyya (ed.), *al-Ṭayyib Ṣāliḥ*, pp. 212–20.

Jamāl al-Dīn, Mu'āwiya, — 'Taḥqīq ma'a al-Ṭayyib Ṣāliḥ', *al-Kharṭūm*, al-juz' al-awwāl (19 June 1993), al-juz' al-thānī (20 June 1993).[49]

Al-Jazīra, — 'Muqābala ma'a al-Kātib al-Sūdānī al-Ṭayyib Ṣāliḥ bi Munāsabat Mahrajān al-Qiṣṣa al-Qaṣīra' (An interview with al-Ṭayyib Ṣāliḥ on the occasion of the Short Story Festival).

Jibrīl, Ṭalḥat, — 'al-Ṭayyib Ṣāliḥ li'l-*Wasaṭ*: Yurīdūna Waqf al-Baḥr bi Sudūd min al-Rimāl!', *al-Wasaṭ*, 239 (26 August 1996), pp. 52–4.

Jibrīl, Ṭalḥat, — 'al-Ṭayyib Ṣāliḥ: Malāmiḥ min Sīra Dhātiyya (1), al-Takwīn fī al-Qarya al-Sūdāniyya ab'ad min Khuṭūṭ 'alā al-Raml', *al-Ḥayāt*, 12251 (10 September 1996), p. 16.

Jibrīl, Ṭalḥat, 'al-Ṭayyib Ṣāliḥ: Malāmiḥ min Sīra Dhātiyya (2), Qalaq fī al-Mawqif min al-Jāmi'a wa-Ittijāh ilā Kasb al-'Aysh fī al-Sūdān', *al-Ḥayāt* 12252 (11 September 1996), p. 16.

Jibrīl, Ṭalḥat 'al-Ṭayyib Ṣāliḥ: Malāmiḥ min Sīra Dhātiyya (3), al-Takayyuf al-Ṣa'b fī Landan wa-Thalj *Mawsim al-Hijra ilā al-Shamāl*', *al-Ḥayāt* 12253 (12 September 1996), p. 16.

Jibrīl, Ṭalḥat 'al-Ṭayyib Ṣāliḥ: Malāmiḥ min Sīra Dhātiyya (4), Munākhāt Sharqiyya wa-Inṭilāqa Adabiyya min Bayrūt Yūsuf al-Khāl', *al-Ḥayāt*, 12254 (13 September 1996), p. 16.

Jibrīl, Ṭalḥat 'al-Ṭayyib Ṣāliḥ: Malāmiḥ min Sīra Dhātiyya (5), Mashhad al-Tasāmuḥ al-Sūdānī: Fusayfisā' Talawwun Waṭanan', *al-Ḥayāt*, 12255 (14 September 1996), p. 16.

Jibrīl, Ṭalḥat, 'al-Ṭayyib Ṣāliḥ: Malāmiḥ min Sīra Dhātiyya (6), 'An La'nat al-Kitāba wa'l-Abṭāl al-Ghāmiḍīn wa-Tawbīkh al-Shuhra', *al-Ḥayāt*, 12258 (17 September 1996), p. 20.

Jibrīl, Ṭalḥat, *'Alā al-Darb...ma'a al-Ṭayyib Ṣāliḥ: Malāmiḥ min Sīra Dhātiyya,* 1997 (see Bibliography).

John, Joseph, 'A Dialogue with Mr Tayeb Salih on *Season of Migration to the North*', *The Islamic Quarterly*, XXXVI:3 (1992), pp. 207–18.

Al-Khātim, 'Abd al-Quddūs and 'Abd al-Hādī Ṣadīq, 'Ḥiwār Idhā'ī ma'a al-Ṭayyib Ṣāliḥ', *al-Idhā'a al-Sūdāniyya*, 1982.[50]

MBC 'Masā' al-Khayr Yā 'Arab: Muqābala ma'a al-Ṭayyib Ṣāliḥ' (An Interview with al-Ṭayyib Ṣāliḥ), London, MBC, 3 June, 1998. [Published in Ḥasan Abbashir al-Ṭayyib (ed.), *al-Ṭayyib Ṣāliḥ*, pp. 101–12].

al-Muqābila, Sabīl, 'Ḥiwār ma'a al-Ṭayyib Ṣāliḥ' (An Interview with al-Ṭayyib Ṣāliḥ). Simultaneous interpretation by Osman Hassan Ahmed. Revised and edited by Constance E. Berkley, *Voice of the Arabs Cairo Broadcasting Service*, n.d. Office of the Cultural Counsellor, Embassy of the Democratic Republic of the Sudan, 18 April, 1978.[51]

al-Muqābila, Sabīl, and Muhis Ṣādiq, 'Liqā' ma'a al-Ṭayyib Ṣāliḥ', *al-Shabāb wa'l-Riyāda*, n.d.[52]

Naṣrallāh, Muḥammad Riḍā, 'Hadhā Huwa', MBC, 1993/4.[53]

Ni'ama, Rajā' 'Ḥiwār ma'a al-Ṭayyib Ṣāliḥ', *al-Fikr al-'Arabī al-Mu'āṣir*, 2 (June 1980), pp. 114–19.

Al-Qamarī, Bashīr, 'Hākadhā Ḥaddathanī al-Ṭayyib Ṣāliḥ ...Ashkur al-Nās Alladhīna Aḥabbū A'malī...', *Kitābāt Sūdāniyya*, 8 (June 1999), pp. 58–70. [This interview was conducted in *Aṣīla* in August 1994].

'Al-Qiṣṣa fī al-Waṭan al-'Arabī-Nadwa (1)', *al-Ma'rifa*, 138 (August 1973), pp. 161–9. (2), *al-Ma'rifa*, 138 (August 1973), pp. 170–9.

al-Sa'īd, 'Īsā, 'al-Ṭayyib Ṣāliḥ: Taftīt al-'Ālam', *al-Karmil*, 9 (1983), pp. 256–64.

Ṣāliḥ, al-Ṭayyib, 'Aḥtafī bi'l-Māḍī wa-Uṣāri'u al-Rāhin wa-Ajma' bayn al-Ithnayn', *al-Quds* (29 March 1998) p. 15. [Originally published in the Lebanese daily *al-Safīr*].

Salīm, 'Abd al-Mun'īm, 'Majhūd li'l-Rū'ya 'an Bu'd al-Ṭayyib Ṣāliḥ Ṣāḥib *Mawsim al-Hijra ilā al-Shamāl*', *al-Sharq*, 2;5 (October 1971), pp. 29–30.

al-Sāmarrā'ī, Mājid, 'Muqābala Adabiyya ma'a al-Ṭayyib Ṣāliḥ, Tafāṣīl fī 'Ālam al-Riwāya', *al-Ādāb* (January 1981), pp. 3–8.

al-Sāmarrā'ī, Mājid, 'Muqābalāt al-Ṭayyib Ṣāliḥ, Humūm al-Riwā'ī fī 'Aṣr Mutaghayyir', *al-Aqlām*, (April 1982), pp. 142–50.

al-Sayiḥ, Laylā 'Liqā', Kitābāt al-Ṭayyib Ṣāliḥ bayn al-Wāqi' wa'l-Usṭūra', *al-Anbā'*, (10 January 1978), pp. 13–15. (For the English translation, see Berkley, *The Roots of Consciousness*, pp. lxxxii–lxxxvii).

Shāhīn, Muḥammad, 'Ḥiwār ma'a al-Ṭayyib Ṣāliḥ: Raj' al-Ṣadā' (Jean Morris Shakhṣiyya fī Aṣlihā Ḥaqīqiyya), in idem, *Taḥawwulāt al-Shawq*, pp. 171–203.

Shaheen, Mohammed (= Muḥammad Shāhīn), 'Interview with Tayeb Salih', *Banipal, Magazine of Modern Arab Literature*, 10–11 (Spring-Summer 2001), pp. 82–4.

Sha'īr, Muḥammad, 'al-Ṭayyib Ṣāliḥ Yatakhayyal ma'anā: Mawsiman Jadīdan li'l-Hijra', *Akhbār al-Adab*, 523 (20 July 2003), pp. 6–7.

Ṣubḥī, Muḥyī al-Dīn and Khaldūn al-Sham'a, 'al-Ṭayyib Ṣāliḥ Riwā'iyyan wa-Nāqidan', *al-Mawqif al-Adabī*, 4–5 (August-September 1973), pp. 50–6 (For more information see Bibliography).

Uthmān, Fatḥī, 'Ḥiwār Ṭawīl ma'a Ṣāḥib *Mawsim al-Hijra ilā al-Shamāl* Alladhī Lā Yuḥibb al-Kitāba wa-Lākin...' (1), *al-Wasaṭ*, 345 (7 September 1998), pp. 48–52. (2), *al-Wasaṭ*, 346 (14 September 1998), pp. 56–7.

'Uthmān, Sibā'ī, 'Ḥiwār ma'a al-Ṭayyib Ṣāliḥ', *al-Madīna*, 5223 (27 May), 1981.

Wahaba, Zāhī, 'Muqābala ma'a al-Ṭayyib Ṣāliḥ' (An Interview with al-Ṭayyib Ṣāliḥ), Beirut, *al-Mustaqbal Channel*, 5 February 2002.

Yājzī, 'Ādil, 'Ḥiwār Maftūḥ ma'a al-Ṭayyib Ṣāliḥ', *al-Mawqif al-Adabī*, 193–194 (May-June 1987), pp. 146–56.

al-Ẓāhir, Muḥammad, 'Ḥiwār ma'a al-Ṭayyib Ṣāliḥ: Aktub li Takwīn Tayyār 'Arabī Wāḥid', *al-Aqlām*, 12 (August-October 1980), pp. 149–55.

Interview with al-Ṭayyib Ṣāliḥ on *The Voice of America* in Arabic (see the English translation, Berkley, *The Roots of Consciousness*, pp. xxxix–xxxx).

H. The Path and its Stations: An Interview with al-Ṭayyib Ṣāliḥ in London, 22 August 2000

Ami Elad-Bouskila: Thank you very much for agreeing to this interview.

Al-Ṭayyib Ṣāliḥ: Thank you, it is my pleasure.

A.E-B: Let's talk about reading.

T.S: Well, this is something I find very pleasurable when I read a poet or in fact a story. I like history too, and I read widely, not just literature, which clarifies things for me. And I think it's the kindred spirit, the boy inside admiring in English. Of course, people like Donne and the mystics, and I very much like Emerson, although he is not as prolific. I admire Thomas Hardy's poetry and I also admire the works of Robert Frost. I like his precision and the receptive simplicity in his poetry.

A.E-B: But not E.M. Forster.

T.S: Forster, no. Well, I read *A Passage to India.* I wouldn't know.

A.E-B: Do you really think that it's a good novel?

T.S: I think so. Yes.

A.E-B: Did you like it? This is a very interesting point, I think, since we're dealing with East-West relations, et cetera.

T.S: Well, I know that it is also a matter of one's mind. I've even seen the film. At the time, you know, when you put it in the context of time, it was quite pioneering, but he is not generally a writer. You know, the names do not come to me. There are quite a few… Dickens, I like Dickens very much.

A.E-B: Why is that? Because of the thematic issues in his work or in terms of the poetic manner of his writing?

T.S: You know, I think Dickens is far deeper than he is generally thought to be. Of course, as we know, he was a popular novelist, but I think many of his novels were actually allegories, and I think there are studies attesting to that. Dickens, for example, when I think there is somebody who got rich from selling rubbish. And I think the whole novel is allegory deep down, in fact, when you read his most popular novels.

A.E-B: You mean Great Expectations...

T.S: Yes, and then of course the sheer technical skill is unbelievable. I believe writers like Dostoyevsky admitted to being influenced by Dickens. What did I want to say? But I also read, I read history a great deal, and I think now I feel that if I had my time over again I'd be a historian. And I do say that I write like a historian, really. You know, I try to achieve the objectivity of a historian, or even an archaeologist, because in fiction you assemble, don't you, a world from bits and pieces. It's a construction like a historian does from little documents and this and that, or an archaeologist finding a bit of stone here, a piece of a utensil there, and then trying to construct the overall picture.

A.E-B: I used to think that in addition to archaeology, perhaps geology. We've mentioned it before, maybe you just try to cross everything we call *ṭabaqāt* (strata) or something like that, you know, that is close to the depths of our soul, of our society et cetera. So maybe it's not archaeology, but geology. I think that in a way it's a matter of geology.

T.S: I see your point, but I'd rather use the archaeology analogy because geology is more precise. They dig and they find the stratum, but they are not really interested in it. They are usually digging for something, water or oil, whereas an archaeologist is interested in every stratum, and it has this almost artistic element which is akin to fiction, that ultimately the whole world is based on assumptions, isn't it?

A.E-B: That's correct, and that's why I would like to stress one point. Since you mentioned archaeology and I know that your approach is very similar to this concept, I'm not quite sure that it was in your twenties, but I think in the last two decades, I think to compare it to archaeology, because I did come across the point that in fiction, in history and archaeology you face only the facts, while in fiction you can use both of them. I mean, in addition to the facts and the reality you can also use, at the same time, fiction. I found that fiction has a very strong presence in the way we think, the way we prefer to write, so in this sense, I think that fiction can give us a better angle than history because history is only the reality, in a way.

T.S: Or what they claim is reality. Yes I understand what you are saying and of course we will talk about fiction being more real than the real. You are actually…

A.E-B: Absolutely.

T.S: You are through an illusory world, isn't that so? You are aiming at discovering what's your hope. Is something true? Yes, I agree with you.

A.E-B: Yes. Because from time to time you can't make any differences ... I mean it's very hard to find the differences between fiction and reality because, you know, it's like dreams I mean, in a way, it's...

T.S: Well, actually, from the very beginning when I started writing, I understood that this is not real. It does not exist. When I say so-and-so did such-and-such and said such-and-such, this is a fiction of my imagination. This, believe me, was before the so-called Magical Realism.

A.E-B: Yes.

T.S: I gave myself total freedom to do what I like and that's why I made al-Zayn an imbecile, and made him marry the most beautiful girl. And this was in a time when in the Arab world, in Egypt especially, the predominant fiction was so-called Social Realism.

A.E-B: *al-wāqi'iyya al-ijtimā'iyya.*

T.S: *al-wāqi'iyya al-ijtimā'iyya.*

A.E-B: Right.

T.S: So you are right and...

A.E-B: So you see, you do have the freedom to do, I mean, to use your imagination, while in history and archaeology – and I am not trying to convince you – but what I'd like to stress is the point that in writing, in literature, the fictional element is very crucial not just to our writing but rather to our life, in a way.

T.S: Yes, I agree although, you know, in history, you are right. I mean they find little elements of reality, but then the assumptions, how they put it together, even something recent, like the French Revolution, I mean look at the hundreds, the thousands of interpretations, because each historian has got his or her own predetermined ideas, notions, the way of looking at history, whether he's a Marxist or a macro-historian or a micro-historian, or whatever.

A.E-B: A new historian?

T.S: A new historian, and the way they juggle facts, so-called, I find rather similar to the way a novelist juggles fictions which are presented as facts.

A.E-B: And then some of the critics prefer to use the term 'autobiographical elements' and then it's none of them. It is a bit of fiction and a bit of autobiographical elements, and it is, in fact, a mixture.

T.S: Yes, the technique I used in *Season of Migration to the North,* of using two narrators, was very deliberate. The reader is continuously confronted with the personal voice. Either the narrator or Muṣṭafā Sa'īd, and he will definitely, the reader will ultimately think that this is the writer telling him his life story. But it's a very objective novel, you know? Every historical fact is true. Every statement has got a counter-statement, and I wanted to create a world that was not stable, which was not certain.

A.E-B: Why is that, by the way? Why is that?

T.S: Because I was dealing with something I thought was an issue or a theme which people looked at in a prejudicial way. What was I saying?

A.E-B: About the two narrators and Muṣṭafā. About the readers' expectations and the autobiographical elements.

T.S: Oh, yes. I mean from my point of view the novel is very, very objective but it does create... you asked why, why I used that technique, because I wanted to dislodge deeply embedded ideas on both sides, and I felt it was no use preaching to the reader. I wanted the reader to be confused, at least, and then make up his or her own mind later on.

A.E-B: That's very interesting, because you didn't say that you were confused about this kind of relations et cetera. You said that your expectation was that the reader would be, in a way, confused. What is happening in these relations?

T.S: I may have been confused as well! But I think in this particular novel... I seem to have had a thesis, anyway, whether it be true or false, I started with a thesis and I did lots of reading. For example, people don't know that to render the trial of Muṣṭafā Sa'īd, I read so many murder cases. Men who killed their wives for love and similar situations. And I went to see the Old Bailey, but ultimately, I discarded the whole thing. I wrote at the beginning, I thought I would render the trial scene realistically. Then, I decided to discard it and kept a few sentences. And these sentences, spoken by the judge, for example, they have actually been said by a judge in a specific case, you see?

A.E-B: Yes. We shall come back to *Mawsim al-Hijra ilā al-Shamāl*, but since you mentioned your background, your educational background, your work at the BBC in the drama section, and I think that in your writing you did try to write, and I'm only asking, did you try to write drama? Or a scenario or maybe poetry? Because I'm very curious whether you ever tried to write a play? Or poetry? Because you mention *Season of Migration to the North* , *'Urs al-Zayn,* I mean 'The Wedding of Zein' as well, and 'Idhā Jā'at' and 'Hākadhā Yā Sādatī', and in a way, I can say that it's like a film, like a camera. It's like theatre in a way. And then you can say: Well, all our life is one big theatre. Maybe, I really don't know, but I would like to connect it, because you didn't publish ...I mean you did publish, at least, I really don't know if you did write, but you did publish fiction and I do have the feeling that you are very connected, as you pointed out, to poetry and drama and scenario and film and maybe to the camera, and I would like to ask if you could elaborate on these points.

T.S: I mean that's only true in my case ... I mean you can find ... these elements, visual elements for example, in other writers, but I think what I can say is first I love poetry. And when I love poetry I can progress... but I never wrote poetry.

A.E-B: Never?

T.S: Ever.

A.E-B: And plays?

T.S: Except, you know, in fun *ya'nī*, what are they called? limericks and things. And I wrote only a play or two for the BBC when I was working there.

A.E-B: In Arabic?

T.S: Yes. But not for my…

A.E-B: And you didn't publish it at the time?

T.S: No, no, nothing really serious. You know, a half hour thing for radio.

A.E-B: Yes.

T.S: And I translated some plays.

A.E-B: From English into Arabic?

T.S: Yes.

A.E-B: Can you mention some titles?

T.S: For example, I translated, as I told you, *Anthony and Cleopatra.* I translated a play by Montherlant, are you familiar with him?

A.E-B: No.

T.S: A very, very strange...

A.E-B: No, I haven't come across…

T.S: Montherlant was fashionable in the sixties and I translated a play called *La Reine morte.*

A.E-B: This was in the sixties or...?

T.S: Yes. That must have been in the sixties. But I must have been influenced by broadcasting, I'll tell you how, now that you mention it.

A.E-B: Yes, all right.

T.S: The economy ... the economy in radio, you know, the first time is very, very valuable.

A.E-B: The limits, yes.

T.S: And I think there isn't much, you know, what you call in English 'slack' in my writing.

A.E-B: Yes.

T.S: And this economy, and the technique of juxtaposition, I think I learned from radio.

A.E-B: Yes.

T.S: You know if in radio there's a scene of somebody talking to somebody on a farm, and then suddenly there is a shift in time and geography. Fluidity, I think, I must have learned from radio.

A.E-B: So there is influence concerning your educational background or your experience at the BBC.

T.S: Oh, yes.

A.E-B: So in a way...

T.S: This was a very important part in my life because it exposed me to so many influences. I read a lot, I went to the theatre. I saw films, music. And don't forget painting. There is a great Sudanese painter called Ibrāhīm al-Ṣalaḥī.

A.E-B: Ah, it's Ibrāhīm al-Ṣalaḥī, not al-Ṣulḥī?

T.S: No, Ṣalaḥī. We seem to influence each other. He had an exhibition in London in the early sixties which was a great revelation to me. And then he told me that my writing also influenced him. So it's, as you know, the question of influence is such a diffused subject.

A.E-B: I know that you don't like this issue, as I mentioned before, but I think that if you are aware of your background in terms of reading, for example, Ibsen, Yeats, Abū Nuwās, Al-Mutanabbī.

T.S: I forgot to mention Chekhov and Brecht, because for me the great dramatists are Euripides, Shakespeare, Chekhov and Brecht.

A.E-B: I'd like to move on to what I think a very interesting point, and that is language usage.

T.S: Yes.

A.E-B: And I'd like to ask you why you chose to write in Arabic. Because you did tell me that you had tried several times to write the 'Muqaddimāt', (Preludes) in English, but it didn't work. So the question is why? Because most of your writing is on the fifties and the sixties and that was very close to your moving from Khartoum to London, but after 20 years you had written *Bandar Shāh: Ḍaw al-Bayt*, that was in 1971, and 'al-Rajul al-Qubruṣī' in 1972, *Bandar Shāh-Maryūd* in 1976 and 'Yawm Mubārak 'alā Shāṭi' Umm Bāb' that was published in 1993. So I want...

T.S: Yes?

A.E-B: What? 'Yawm Mubārak' of course, which I translated into Hebrew and sent you, by the way, *ma'lesh* (never mind).

T.S: Oh, yes, of course.

A.E-B: Anyway it's interesting because I found 'Yawm Mubārak' to be a very fascinating story by the way. So, you know, 'al-Rajul al-Qubruṣī' is a very strong story; the presence of death. I didn't mention it but I compare 'al-Rajul al-Qubruṣī' – and maybe you'll think I'm crazy – to Ingmar Bergman's *The Seventh Seal.*

T.S: Good Lord!

A.E-B: Really, because it's the play of Death and all these forbidden games with the Other or with the devil or with the past. But anyway, I'd like to get back to language usage. Can you elaborate on this point?

T.S: I write in Arabic as a matter of principle.

A.E-B: Not for political, ideological or cultural reasons?

T.S: *Wala ishi* (none of the sort), actually I wrote 'al-Muqaddimāt' in English for fun, I was in Beirut.

A.E-B: And that was in the early sixties?

T.S: Yes. I was in Beirut and it just came to me in English and it worked, actually.

A.E-B: Really?

T.S: Yes.

A.E-B: But you didn't publish it in English.

T.S: No, I translated it into Arabic. I showed it to Tawfīq Ṣāyigh.

A.E-B: The editor of *Ḥiwār*?

*T.S:*_ Yes, at the time. He was a close friend of mine, a very nice man.

A.E-B: A very unique man, I think.

T.S: He liked them. I didn't think much of it. Although there is a serious idea behind these 'Muqaddimāt', I wanted to write stories of just skeletons, to strip off all the flesh. You know the men's clothes, he did this, he did that and… but I never seriously tried to write in English, because I wanted the language not to be an impediment ... I mean... there are enough problems in writing a novel without writing, you know, in a foreign language. I wanted to be totally free with the language and I think my Arabic is quite good and also…

A.E-B: It's excellent. It's not quite good, it's excellent!

T.S: And I also wanted to experiment with the language. You know, you must have noticed in *Ḍaw al-Bayt* the passive use toward the end, when *Ḍaw al-Bayt* comes out of the river. I use a colloquial Arabic which is almost like classical, and I use classical which is almost colloquial. Now, one cannot have this freedom with a foreign language. And there is another element I am aware of with writing in a language which is not one's mother tongue. There is an element of falsity from the very beginning. I mean, from the very beginning when you start to write in English, you feel false because this is not your language.

A.E-B: Even today you can't say...

T.S: Yes.

A.E-B: I mean you can't say that you can write freely, absolutely freely…

T.S: No. Well, this is the way I feel. I mean I know other writers may...

A.E-B: Like Conrad, by the way, who when only in his twenties, made a shift from Polish to English.

T.S: I know. I know.

A.E-B: That's very interesting because your English was excellent, I believe, when you were a student, even before you moved to England.

T.S: Oh, certainly better than Conrad's! (laughter). But Conrad, I think, used that very cleverly, wittingly. He used the fact that English was not his language to create ... with his fiction, and create this strange, alien atmosphere.

A.E-B: Right, right. Very ambiguous.

T.S: Ambiguity.

A.E-B: I think you like it, too.

T.S: Oh yes. I think *Nostromo* is a very good novel...But that`s the way I...

A.E-B: You still stress *Nostromo*, and since you didn't mention *Heart of Darkness,* and mind you, just bear in mind that I spent three or four pages in my manuscript comparing *Season of Migration* and *Heart of Darkness!*

T.S: I know and, as you'd say, do the same, and believe me, I read *Heart of Darkness* after I finished *Season*, and of course I saw the film before.

A.E-B: Really? Before *Season*?

T.S: Before I wrote it. But I read the novel afterwards. I knew *Lord Jim,* and what else?

A.E-B: *Nostromo*?

T.S: *Nostromo*, no. *Nostromo*...

A.E-B: *The Secret Agent*

T.S: *Nostromo*, no. *The Secret Agent* I haven't read until now.

A.E-B: Is that so?

T.S: Yes. You know, as they say in Arabic, *tawārud khawāṭir* (telepathy), but it looks as though… I brought in the influences because in *Season of Migration*, when I was drawing the character of Muṣṭafā Sa'īd…

A.E-B: Yes?

T.S: I was fascinated by Richard III and the study of evil in Richard III, and one can probably find elements there. Nobody ever made this point.

A.E-B: Richard III.

T.S: Yes.

A.E-B: Yes. It's very interesting, but you know the point I would like to stress is not... I don't think it's bad or good to be influenced, etc. I think it's in our mind, our background, in our unconsciousness, etc. We are not always aware of this point, I think. But I would just like to mention that when I asked Fatḥī Ghānim, the Egyptian writer, if he was influenced in his novel *al-Rajul Alladhī Faqada Ẓillahu* (The Man who Lost his Shadow) by, you know...

T.S: Durrell.

A.E-B: Durrell, and he said: 'Ami, believe me, I can swear that I didn't read it before'. Just it is when people say, 'Oh, you have been influenced by whatever, he said: 'I never read it. I can swear to it'.

T.S: I believe him. It's possible.

A.E-B: It is possible according to your...

T.S: It is possible, and of course the assumptions are different between, I mean, Conrad and myself.

A.E-B: In what way?

T.S: I think that in *Heart of Darkness*, if I remember correctly, Conrad was not condemning colonization, was he?

A.E-B: I don't think so. And in a way, your point of departure is the matter of the colonizer and the colonized, I mean you stress it very strongly.

T.S: I'll tell you why, because at the time I read Freud very, very closely, and the book which influenced me greatly, was called *Man Against Himself*, by a disciple of Freud's, a man called Miller, if I remember correctly. I read it again and again and again. I don't know whether I read Fanon before or after. But because I am ... you know ... I brought something of the scientific approach as well; history, sociology, psychology all probably influenced me consciously more than literature.

A.E-B: So, I mean, in a way it's a combination. Not just of literature but also other sources, as you mentioned, psychology, history, et cetera. So it's a combination. You mentioned before, and I would like to move on to multiglossia or diglossia, you know, *al-Fuṣḥā* (classical Arabic) and *al-'Āmmiyya* (colloquial Arabic) in Modern Arabic literature. And this is a question, because you stressed it several times, and we mentioned it earlier today, that you don't think that there is a vast difference between a Sudanese colloquial and a Tunisian colloquial, and in any case you think that Lebanese can manage with your literary works. Can you explain?

T.S: The whole southern band were searching, those from southern Libya, southern Tunisia, southern Algeria, southern Morocco and then Mauritania. There is a great similarity with Sudan and probably, I mean, I don't know, this is a hunch, it is the Yemenite element, Yemenite tribes in all cases. In

Syria, in Dér al-Zōr and these places, in Lebanon, strangely enough in the mountains. And the Maronites.

A.E-B: Oh, we are coming back to the Maronites! (Laughter)

T.S: The only difference you would have discovered, I am sure, is that first of all, certain words acquire slightly different usages in each environment. Secondly, certain words are more current in particular colloquialisms. For example we use *zōl* (person), and that is classical Arabic, *zōl.* It's in the dictionary.

A.E-B: So, we can find it in classical dictionaries.

T.S: You will find it in the...

A.E-B: In *Lisān al-'Arab.*

T.S: The Lebanese may use *zalameh.*

A.E-B: *zalameh, ṣaḥḥ.* Like the Palestinian one, yes?

T.S: The people in the Gulf say *riyāl-rigāl*

A.E-B: *rigāl,* yes.

T.S: Thirdly, the intonation. The Moroccans, for example, some people when you listen to them for the first time, they think this is not Arabic. It is Arabic, but they have a way of speaking, probably influenced by the Berbers which puts the emphasis at the beginning of the word. So the word becomes almost....

A.E-B: That's correct...

T.S: So, the words are more or less the same, and one of the reasons, almost a chauvinistic reason, why I use colloquial sometimes, is actually to put our colloquial in the marketplace with other peoples. Why do we read Egyptian colloquial and Syrian and Lebanese and God knows what else? I say all right, there is Sudanese colloquial. And I think... gradually people will get used to it like we got used to Egyptian and to Lebanese. Now, as you know, Lebanese and Egyptian colloquial are very, very current...

A.E-B: Because of Beirut and Cairo...I mean...

T.S: Because of films and television and radio…

A.E-B: And scenarios...

T.S: And the pretty actresses and so on.

A.E-B: So in a way you don't feel that there are any obstacles, I mean for Arab readers in different countries.

T.S: Oh, yes there is an obstacle. In *Bandar Shāh,* and honestly this is true, I am not just saying it as an afterthought, I sometimes used language to mystify, not to clarify, and if the reader doesn't understand the colloquial he's actually in the same boat as the Sudanese writer who would understand the words, but who would still find difficulties with the meaning. For me that is part of the technique.

A.E-B: So this was just in *Bandar Shāh: Maryūd* or also in *Bandar Shāh: Ḍaw al-Bayt?*

T.S: In both.

A.E-B: In both of them.

T.S: In both I used colloquial.

A.E-B: Right.

T.S: In 'The Wedding of Zein', the reason was different. The reason was dramatically I could not name Zayn in classical Arabic. He would lose all credibility.

A.E-B: So, in a way, to obtain this credibility in *Bandar Shāh: Ḍaw al-Bayt* and *Maryūd*, you created a very unique correlation between the themes, I mean, in terms of legend, in terms of moving back to the history of Sudan et cetera, on the one hand. While on the other hand you use a different technique to make it on the same level. So there is a correlation between the poetic and the thematic way of writing between the characters and the register of their speech.

T.S: Yes, you could say that.

A.E-B: Is that correct?

T.S: There is some, actually in *Ḍaw al-Bayt*, some *saj'* (rhymed prose) in the colloquial. And this... it opened the venues.

A.E-B: I think that as a reader I can say this... the reason... the options of readings, different readings because it's not only a way of reading, and I think in a way you come back to... in a way ... to *Season of Migration*, I mean that this ... I mean especially I think *Bandar Shāh* and *Mawsim,* but especially *Bandar Shāh,* I found it very attractive way, very attractive literary work since it's a question of ambiguity of unclearness in each. I mean, there is a message to the reader that says, 'Well, you, my dear reader, are supposed to make an effort if you would like to try to understand'. Is that correct?

A-T.S: That was very, very nice, your last remark.

A.E-B: About what?

T.S: Your last remark about asking the reader to make an effort. I believe that. I do not believe ... I assume the reader is intelligent and since he actually goes above the words, he's interested. And then he is supposed to interact.

A.E-B: Do you have the same feeling for 'al-Rajul al-Qubruṣī' and especially 'Yawm Mubārak 'alā Shāṭi' Umm Bāb'? Because this short story I found fascinating, maybe one of your best. I like it very much and...

T.S: 'Yawm Mubārak'?

A.E-B: I like it very much, you know. As I like *Maryūd,* by the way. And I would like to come to the point and see if I can combine these two questions before the last question.

T.S: These three things I like personally, these two short stories and *Maryūd,* and I am immeasurably happy that you like them.

A.E-B: I like them because I found them to be unique literary works.

T.S: In what terms?

A.E-B: In terms of that it's not clarified it's not readable... Because it forces me, especially 'Yawm Mubārak' and *Maryūd,* it forces me to make an effort to try and understand what the writer's intention is. Why is there so much Sufism in it, so much ambiguity. In a way it's a very confusing literary work, and you have to figure out how to deal with it, because it's not 'normal' literature. In what terms? In terms of that from your point of view I can see it as part and parcel of a long study, a long creative process or trying to create an epos, a *malḥama.* In a way it's a step-by-step process, it's one more stratum in your archaeology, or a level in your building. That's all.

T.S: Well, I like to think that.

A.E-B: Well, maybe you didn't intend to, but that is my interpretation.

T.S: It is part of the spiritual archeology. I first made a very profane mood, like in some parts of *Season of Migration* and then... But ... here ... this was a... you know, another kind of stratum in which I expressed the ... you know that 'al-Rajul al-Qubruṣī' was my *rithā'* elegy for my father? There are elements of truth in it. I was in Beirut and I heard the news that my father had died suddenly. And I went to Cyprus as I described and met a man there, as I described, but then the rest was... and I felt that the pain which I described, you know, and the rest, you know, I made up.

A.E-B: It's very interesting since you mention 'al-Rajul al-Qubruṣī' and because I would like to connect it with 'al-Rajul al-Qubruṣī'. You mentioned your father's death and I'm just wondering all the time, why did you mention the special connections, the special relations between you and your grandfather? I mean between the narrator and the grandfather. Why is that? Is it connected to the subtitle of *Bandar Shāh*, that the present, I mean the father is a victim of his son and his father. It means, that there is, in a way, a conspiracy, if we can put it like that, between the future and the past against the present. Can you agree with that?

T.S: Absolutely, absolutely. First of all, in realistic terms, my grandfather represented power. He was a tall, powerful man and he believed in power. He had nine sons. My father was the weakest one physically but I discovered later on that he was the nicest, full of love, you see, and maybe, as a child, I allied myself with my grandfather's power. And it is true that I had many, many talks with my grandfather. I always would come to him. I was sort of the favorite of his grandchildren. And I used the metaphor to explore the idea that we are continuously ransoming the present for the future, influenced by the past. In fact, the Sudan is literally in this situation is now. People will come and want to leave for the…, the Muslim state in Medina at the time of the prophet and they are preaching a Utopian future. Meanwhile now, what have you now for the people, you see? And this was the trigger of the work.

A.E-B: But you know what the trigger is? That we, I mean we and I stress this word 'we', we are constantly in the same position, because we, all the time, we have children and this is the future, and we as fathers, all the time, we are the sons of our fathers, of our parents, so in a way, every generation is in the same trap. So it's a trigger. In a way, because we can't say, 'Oh, we are the middle generation'. No. Everyone is the middle generation. Everyone is a 'victim'. I mean, this is the bottom line. Everyone is a 'victim' of the future and the past. For his next generation and the past generation.

T.S: This is true, but you know when this situation which passes from one generation to another becomes a whole philosophy, a social philosophy. Then, of course, it becomes legend, doesn't it?

A.E-B: Right. And in a way I just wonder if, because I find this very interesting, in a way I just want to try and understand the question of influence, the African legends, the Christian legends, the Muslim legends, the Sudanese legends. I mean, I found that the role of legends is very profound in your literary works and especially, and you can check it... I mean, *Bandar Shāh* of course, Rabāb in 'Yawm Mubārak 'alā Shāṭi' Umm Bāb'. So is it true? I mean, all this legendary background.

T.S: Yes of course. When I was living in this atmosphere where there were legends about various historical figures, from Islam and where the chanters went from village to village to sing the praises of the prophet, and actually they presented the prophet as a very attractive human being, not abstract, but actual flesh and blood, who said this and did that, and got angry and laughed, and I suppose all that seemed true to one.

A.E-B: So in a way that's also part and parcel of not just your writing, but your personality. I mean, all this legendary background, and you didn't differentiate between Muslim or African or Sudanese or Arabic. I think you didn't differentiate at all. Is that correct?

T.S: No, I didn't, because it all got mixed up. I mean, this part of the Sudan... where I come from... although it became the most Arab part, had been Christian for over six or seven hundred years when Islam came.

A.E-B: Right.

T.S: And Islam actually came on top.

A.E-B: So it's one more stratum?

T.S: Yes. There was no fight between these things in northern Sudan.

A.E-B: Yes. Why is that, because you can find them, in a way, in harmony between all the strata, can't you?

T.S: Well, I don't know. People just switch from one way to another, taking with them lots of the old ways. When we were pagans, you know, the Nubians, some people now claim that the worship of Amun began in Nubia, not in Egypt. And people just went on. Sometimes the same places were centres of worship for different religions for thousands of years, just going from one to the other and maybe the priests of the old religion went on to become the priests of another religion, you know. Probably these people have a deeper notion of reality than other people, because they feel that probably it all amounts ultimately to the same thing. You know, when *Ḍaw al-Bayt* comes from the river. By the way, this episode, from the beginning of the appearance of *Ḍaw al-Bayt* until he disappears, I think is the best thing I have written, for many reasons: for the language, for the fact that I hope I succeeded in presenting a complex notion in very simple terms. And you remember when he woke up after his illness and they started questioning him about his religion, he didn't even know his name. He didn't know where he came from. He didn't know his religion and they said, 'If we'd known what religion you were, we'd let you. But since you have no religion, for sheer practical reasons', they said, 'become Muslim like us and you could get married and life would become easy for you'. They did not present this as a higher truth. They didn't say, 'Our religion is better', but they said, 'For practical reasons it's better for you since you do not know any religion'. And then they give a name, they circumcise him and marry him off to the girl. All in the same day. I mean, it becomes a microcosm of the whole ritualistic reality.

A.E-B: But he was still regarded as a foreigner, an outsider, as *al-Lā muntamī*, and they mention it exactly like they mention it to Muṣṭafā Sa'īd in *Mawsim al-Hijra.*

T.S: No. He was not the same as Muṣṭafā Sa'īd.

A.E-B: No, Muṣṭafā was a foreigner, an outsider a colonizer an *al-Lā muntamī.* Now, in a way, Muṣṭafā...

T.S: No, but this man was embraced much more than Muṣṭafā Sa'īd by the villain. Muṣṭafā Sa'īd himself was keeping himself distant because of his history...

A.E-B: Right, his background ... his...

T.S: This man threw himself in…

A.E-B: Yes, but he still was regarded as a foreigner, wasn't he? I mean, they said, well, your becoming Muslim is a good way, it's one thing, but to marry? I mean...

T.S: Well... this was one of them when he asked to get married.

A.E-B: I don't remember if it's Ḥasab al-Rasūl.

T.S: This man... He was thinking himself, because that was a traumatic time. They had never before given a daughter in marriage to somebody they didn't know much about.

A.E-B: So this is just the basis to compare him with Muṣṭafā, I mean with Ḥusna.

T.S: Yes, that is a...

A.E-B: Of course, of course, what you say about the continuity of energies et cetera. I think that it's absolutely right. By the way, it's also Rabāb that... in terms of, you know, of reader or sea, she is all the time, I mean, this dealing with water, it's very interesting. I found it very interesting because it's part and parcel of your environment in a way.

T.S: I actually say in *Maryūd,* you know, Maryam tells him or the spirit of Maryam, *āyatuka mā'* (your sign is water) and I don't know why I wrote that, but there must be something fatal about water as far as I'm concerned.

A.E-B: And now, before we finish, I'd like to ask you, al-Ṭayyib, about the question of *Bandar Shāh.* You have said on several occasions, I think, and you even mentioned to me that you consider *Bandar Shāh* far more important than *Season of Migration,* and *Season of Migration to the North,* on the other hand, is your most well known work, and as you mention and stress, the most translated work, into more than 20 languages. So why do you think that it's so well known? And why do you think that *Bandar Shāh* is so important to you, in terms of closeness to you.

T.S: I think I wrote *Mawsim al-Hijra…* it came out in 1966, right?

A.E-B: Yes, December 1966.

T.S: And I believe the Arab defeat by Israel suddenly shook the certainties in Arab minds. Because it became much better known after that, in the Arab world, anyway. And of course, it brought in the element of anti-colonialism, which probably appeals to the readers' resentments. And it is written in a condensed dramatic way, technically. And it has certain sensational elements: little obscenities, little erotic ideas, and I think the murder of Husna, of Wad al-Rayyis and herself, is the most obscene scene in Arabic literature, at least. I don't know about... it's very shocking...

A.E-B: In terms of violence, maybe...

T.S: And she castrates the old man. She castrates the man, by the way, years before the incident in America. Remember? When there was actually a lady who cut off…

A.E-B: Yes, right, yes.

T.S: And it was then, in various places and at various times, that always adds to the reputation of a work. It was done in Egypt, in Sudan, in Jordan, in Morocco. *Bandar Shāh* is written in a quieter way and there are no fireworks. There are no fireworks.

A.E-B: It's a matter of age, I think, too. I mean, you wrote *Bandar Shāh* when you were around 40 years old, and *Mawsim al-Hijra* when you were in your thirties. I think it's a difference of... maybe, maybe...

T.S: Yes, that's true. I was also, I mean, my experience is in observation and reading and so on, and I was exploring an idea without consciously trying to make an effect, to make an impact. And I think it's much more relevant in many ways. And then the experimentation with the language and with shifting from various levels, and this ambiguity you're talking about, it's an ambiguous work even to me, not only to the writer.

A.E-B: Not only to the reader, you mean.

T.S: I mean not only to the reader (laughter). In other words, I am actually exploring, and as I say, if I am confused, then I express my confusion and to that extent I think it will probably gain, inasmuch as literature will remain, it may gain in influence and importance.

A.E-B: And you did mention the question of *Bandar Shāh* meaning the city and the king?

T.S: This is the eternal problem with us, anyway.

A.E-B: When you use the term 'us', do you mean just the Sudanese or do you mean, broadly speaking, the Arabs? Or the Africans or the Muslims?

T.S: Well, I'm talking about the area in general. You know, the Sudan and her neighbours. I think it's a problem in Black Africa, in the Third World in general, wouldn't you say?

A.E-B: My last question is about *ba'īd 'annā* (far apart from us), on death. You stress several times that according to your perception, death is part and parcel of our life. Can you elaborate on this?

T.S: You see, this is probably due to my early life in the village. You know, in the village everything is transparent. Death and all the other rituals of life and death. A person is born – the whole village actually participates in the birth. And if there is a circumcision, everybody goes. There is a wedding... and I described that, I think, in ... probably better in *Bandar Shāh* than in 'The Wedding of Zein'. And when a person dies, they take him and they go upwards at the edge of the desert where there are tombs of the holy men, and they bury him and come back. Of course they are sad and there is wailing and so on, but it's an integral, organic, almost organic part of life. It's very simple. It happens simply. Not like in a big city. And sometimes they use undertakers and God knows what. This is the same people living and dying in unison. And everybody knows about it. And I have always been struck by that personally because I remember the death of my grandmother, on my mother's side, when I was very young, maybe four years old, and the other people, other relatives and so on, and then how the whole community comes together and how they gradually bury this memory in themselves. They mention the person occasionally in talk, and life goes on like the river, the flood and then it goes down. I mean it's a sort of natural rhythm in life.

A.E-B: So do you think it's this way today too? Is this your perception? Is it your attitude towards death and life, or have you changed your mind?

T.S: Well, no, I don't know, quite honestly. Since I wrote that, many things have happened. I don't know. For one thing, it no longer looks as though it's a simple act as part of the fabric of life itself. But I don't know. I think I tried to… I made a tension in 'Yawm Mubārak' about this, didn't I?

A.E-B: That's why I'm asking you. Because you still considered death, I think, as part and parcel of our life. That's why I'm asking you, because I didn't realize that there is a shift in your approach to...

T.S: No, not a shift. I said I don't know because is it that simple? Maybe it's still the same? I don't know. But if I sit down and start exploring deep into myself, God knows whether I'll come to the same conclusion.

A.E-B: I'd like to ask you if there are any differences between your journalistic writing and your fictional writing?

T.S: Yes, of course. Although I brought to what you call journalistic writing some of the fictional techniques, I was not actually writing journalism as such. I was writing, I think, what is known in this country as literary journalism. I would take a topic or a poet or a writer or a philosopher or a historian, and go a little deeper into the subject than is usually done in journalism. And some of the products I feel rather proud of. For example the articles of Dhū al-Rumma, as you know is a poet of the Umayyad period, from *Najd,* who dedicated himself to describing the desert and its animals and dunes and love for a lady called Mayya. He also chants praising the princes. He hardly said any poems in praise of princes and I, before he was forty, I found his poetry really beautiful. He is not often discussed, even by academicians. There are very few references to him in modern Arabic. And I also wrote on al-Mutanabbī where I argued with Ṭāhā Ḥusayn. You know Ṭāhā Ḥusayn wrote a book in the thirties probably, about al-Mutanabbī and he said from the very beginning that he hated al-Mutanabbī, you see? And I wondered why he bothered. I admire al-Mutanabbī very much, and I think, of course it's a great… *iddi'ā'* what's the word in English… It's a great (pretense) to argue with a man like Ṭāhā Ḥusayn, but I said that he failed, in some cases, even to understand some of al-Mutanabbī's poetry because he was blinded by hatred. And I think it's interesting. I also wrote about al-Ma'arrī.

A.E-B: Whom you also like very much.

T.S: I like him very much. I wrote about Braudel and so on. So this was journalism where I liked to present ideas, you know, slightly...

A.E-B: Not through fiction, but through...

T.S: Not fiction. I sometimes use the technique of fiction in describing situations. I describe my travels in America, in Germany, in various other places, and so on.

A.E-B: Thank you very much.

NOTES

Notes to Chapter One:
The Author's World: The Case of al-Ṭayyib Ṣāliḥ

1. Ṭalḥat Jibrīl, 'al-Ṭayyib Ṣāliḥ: Malāmiḥ min Sīra Dhātiyya (1), al-Takwīn fī al-Qarya al-Sūdāniyya Ab'ad min al-Khuṭūṭ 'alā al-Raml', *al-Ḥayāt*, 12251 (September 1996), p. 16. Idem, 'al-Ṭayyib Ṣāliḥ: Malāmiḥ min Sīra Dhātiyya (2), Qalaq fī al-Mawqif min al-Jāmi'a wa-Ittijāh ilā Kasb al-'Aysh fī al-Sūdān', *al-Ḥayāt*, 12251 (September 11, 1996), p. 16. Idem, 'al-Ṭayyib Ṣāliḥ: Malāmiḥ min Sīra Dhātiyya (3), al-Takayyuf al-Ṣa'b fī Landan wa-Thalj *Mawsim al-Hijra ilā al-Shamāl*', *al-Ḥayāt*, 12253 (September 12, 1996), p. 16. Idem, 'al-Ṭayyib Ṣāliḥ: Malāmiḥ min Sīra Dhātiyya (4), Munākhāt Sharqiyya wa-Inṭilāqa Adabiyya min Bayrūt Yūsuf al-Khāl', *al-Ḥayāt*, 12254 (September 13, 1996), p. 16. Idem, 'al-Ṭayyib Ṣāliḥ: Malāmiḥ min Sīra Dhātiyya (5), Mashhad al-Tasāmuḥ al-Sūdānī: Fusayfisā' Talawwun al-Waṭan', *al-Ḥayāt*, 12255 (September 14, 1996), p. 20. Idem, 'al-Ṭayyib Ṣāliḥ: Malāmiḥ min Sīra Dhātiyya (6), 'An La'nat al-Kitāba wa'l-Abṭāl al-Ghāmiḍīn wa-Tawbīkh al-Shuhra', *al-Ḥayāt*, 12258 (September 17, 1996), p. 20. Idem, *'Alā al-Darb... ma'a al-Ṭayyib Ṣāliḥ, Malāmiḥ min Sīra Dhātiyya*, Rabat, Tōb li'l-Istithmār wa'l-Khadamāt, Cairo, Markaz al-Dirāsāt al-Sūdāniyya, 1997. In interviews such as in literary evenings, we can comprehend the main concept of the author. Therefore we can indicate: Sayyid Faghalī, 'Liqā' ma'a al-Ṭayyib Ṣāliḥ fī Landan', in Aḥmad Sa'īd Muḥammadiyya (ed.), *al-Ṭayyib Ṣāliḥ 'Abqarī al-Riwāya al-'Arabiyya*, Beirut, Dār al-'Awda, 1976, pp. 204–11. Muḥyī al-Dīn Ṣubḥī and Khaldūn al-Sham'a, 'al-Ṭayyib Ṣāliḥ Riwā'iyyan wa-Nāqidan', in Muḥammadiyya (ed.), *al-Ṭayyib Ṣāliḥ*, pp. 118–36. Rajā' Ni'ma, 'Ḥiwār ma'a al-Ṭayyib Ṣāliḥ', *al-Fikr al-'Arabī al-Mu'āṣir*, 2 (June 1980), pp. 114–19. Muḥammad al-Ẓāhir, 'Ḥiwār ma'a al-Ṭayyib Ṣāliḥ, Aktub li Takwīn Tayyār 'Arabī Wāḥid', *al-Aqlām*, 12 (August-October 1980), pp. 149–55. Qāsim 'Uthmān Nūr, 'al-Ṭayyib Ṣāliḥ, Dirāsa Bībliyūgrāfiyya', *al-Thaqāfa al-Sūdāniyya*, 19 (November 1981), pp. 122–9. Mājid al-Sāmarrā'ī, 'Muqābala: al-Ṭayyib Ṣāliḥ, Humūm al-Riwā'ī fī 'Ālam Mutaghayyir', *al-Aqlām* (April 1982), pp. 142–50. Idem, 'Muqābala Adabiyya ma'a al-Ṭayyib Ṣāliḥ, Tafāṣīl fī 'Ālam al-Riwāya', *al-Ādāb*, 1–2 (January 1981), pp. 3–8. Murtaḍā Miqdād, 'As'ila ilā al-Ṭayyib Ṣāliḥ, hal Ṣaḥīḥ anna al-Ḥayawāniyya al-Baḥta Hiya min Naṣīb 'al-Waḥsh' al-Sharqī?' *al-Nahār al-'Arabī wa'l-Duwalī*, 307 (March 21–7, 1983), pp. 60–1. Muḥammad Shāhīn, 'Ḥiwār ma'a al-Ṭayyib Ṣāliḥ', in idem, *Taḥawwulāt al-Shawq fī Mawsim al-Hijra ilā al-Shamāl, Dirāsa Naqdiyya Muqārina*, Beirut, al-Mu'assasa al-'Arabiyya li'l-Dirāsāt wa'l-Nashr, 1993, pp. 171–203. al-Ṭayyib Ṣāliḥ, 'Naḥwa Ufuq Ba'īd', *al-Majalla*, 758 (August 21–7, 1994), p. 78. Talḥat Jibrīl, 'al-Ṭayyib Ṣāliḥ li'l-*Wasaṭ*: Yurīdūn Waqf al-Baḥr bi Sudūd al-Rimāl!', *al-Wasaṭ*, 239 (August 26, 1996), pp. 52–4. Ḥasan Abbashir al-Ṭayyib (ed.), *al-Ṭayyib Ṣāliḥ: Dirāsāt Naqdiyya*, Beirut, Riyāḍ al-Rayyis li'l-Kutub wa'l-Nashr, 2001. See also Appendix G. Unless noted otherwise, all excerpts given in English of the works of al-Ṭayyib Ṣāliḥ are taken from translations made by Denys Johnson-Davies, hence transliterations in these excerpts may differ in some respects from transliterations used elsewhere in the text.
2. For further details on the history of al-Dabba and Marawī see Nā'ūm Shuqayr, *Ta'rīkh al-Sūdān*, 2nd ed., Beirut, Dār al-Jīl, 1981, pp. 33–45, 875–7. Fatḥī 'Uthmān, 'Ḥiwār Ṭawīl ma'a Ṣāḥib *Mawsim al-Hijra ilā al-Shamāl* Alladhī lā Yuḥibb al-Kitāba, wa-Lākin...(1)', *al-Wasaṭ*, 345 (7 September 1998), pp. 48–52.
3. The biographical details on al-Ṭayyib Ṣāliḥ were derived from the following sources: Muḥammad Zaghlūl Salām, *al-Qiṣṣa fī al-Adab al-Sūdānī al-Ḥadīth*, Cairo, Ma'had al-Buḥūth wa'l Dirāsāt al-'Arabiyya, 1970, p. 110. al-Ṭayyib Ṣāliḥ, *Bandar Shāh: Ḍaw al-Bayt*, Beirut, Dār al-'Awda, 1971, p. 5. Muḥammadiyya (ed.), *al-Ṭayyib Ṣāliḥ*, pp. 7–8. 'Ami El'ad[-Bouskila], 'al-Ṭayyib Ṣāliḥ wa'l-Adab al-Sūdānī al-Jadīd', *Liqā'*, 6 (Spring 1987), pp. 22–4. Jibrīl, 'al-Ṭayyib Ṣāliḥ: Malāmiḥ min Sīra Dhātiyya (1–6)', *al-Ḥayāt*, 12251–8 (September 10–14, 17, 1996). Idem, *'Alā al-Darb*. Shāhīn,

Taḥawwulāt al-Shawq, pp. 198–9. Aḥmad Muḥammad el-Badawī, *al-Ṭayyib Ṣāliḥ: Sīrat Kātib wa-Naṣṣ*, Cairo, al-Dār al-Thaqāfiyya li'l-Nashr, 2000, pp. 9–44. Tayeb Salih, *Season of Migration to the North* (trans. Denys Johnson-Davies), London, Heinemann, 1978 (1st ed. 1969). Idem, 'Profile: The World of Tayeb Salih', *Azure: The Review of Arab Literature and Culture*, 8 (1981), pp. 15–20. Idem, *Bandarshah* (trans. Denys Johnson-Davies), London and Paris, Kegan Paul International, UNESCO Publishing, 1996. Roger Allen (ed.), *Modern Arabic Literature*, New York, The Ungar Publishing Company, 1987, pp. 264–70. Ami Elad-Bouskila, 'Al-Ṭayyib Ṣāliḥ: The Author and his Works' in Ami Elad-Bouskila and Ahmed Al-Shahi (eds), *Al-Ṭayyib Ṣāliḥ: Seventy Candles, Edebiyât*, 10:1 (1999), pp. 5–32. Constance Berkley, *The Roots of Consciousness Molding the Art of El Tayeb Salih: A Contemporary Sudanese Writer*, Michigan, UMI Dissertation Information Service, 1979, pp. 26–9. Idem, 'El Tayeb Salih, An Introductory Essay in Appreciation', *Pacific Moana Quarterly, African Writing Today*, 6:3/4 (July-October 1981), pp. 176–9.

4. Jibrīl, *'Alā al-Darb*, pp. 79–89.
5. Ibrāhīm Isḥāq Ibrāhīm, *Ḥadath fī al-Qarya*, Khartoum, Jāmi'at al-Kharṭūm, Dār al-Ta'līf wa'l-Tarjama wa'l-Nashr, 1969. Idem, *A'māl al-Layl wa'l-Balda*, Khartoum, Jāmi'at al-Kharṭūm, Dār al-Ta'līf wa'l-Nashr, 1971. Idem, *Wabāl fī Klīmindū*, Cairo and Khartoum, Markaz al-Dirāsāt al-Sūdāniyya, 2001. Idem, *Akhbār al-Bint Mayākāyā*, Cairo and Khartoum, Markaz al-Dirāsāt al-Sūdāniyya, 2001. Aḥmad Muḥammad el-Badawī, *Laban al-Ābanūs Yā Zōl, Riwaya Sūdāniyya*, Cairo, Markaz al-Buḥūth al-'Arabiyya, 1992. Needless to say, what we have indicated earlier does not contradict the seniority status of the city in modern Arabic literature, see: M.M. Badawi, 'The City in Modern Egyptian Literature', in idem, *Modern Arabic Literature and the West*, London, Ithaca Press, 1985, pp. 26–43. Sasson Somekh, *The Changing Rhythm: A Study of Najīb Maḥfūẓ's Novels*, Leiden, Brill, 1973, pp. 65–136, 156–90. R.C. Ostle, 'The City in Modern Arabic Literature', *Bulletin of the School of Oriental and African Studies*, XLIX: 1 (1986), pp. 193–202. Mona N. Mikhail, 'The City as Metaphor: Loss and Alienation', in idem, *Studies in the Short Fiction of Mahfouz and Idris*, New York, New York University Press, 1992, pp. 97–103. Mona Takieddine Amyuni, 'The Image of the City: Wounded Beirut', in Ferial J. Ghazoul and Barbara Harlow (eds), *The View From Within: Writers and Critics on Contemporary Arabic Literature*, Cairo, The American University in Cairo Press, 1994, pp. 53–76.
6. al-Ṭayyib Ṣāliḥ, 'Nakhla 'alā al-Jadwal', in *Dawmat Wad Ḥāmid, Sab' Qiṣaṣ*, 3rd ed., Beirut, Dār al-'Awda, 1970, pp. 7–18 (1st ed. 1967). 'Ḥafnat Tamr', *Dawmat Wad Ḥāmid*, pp. 19–25. 'Dawmat Wad Ḥāmid', *Dawmat Wad Ḥāmid*, pp. 33–55. *'Urs al-Zayn*, 3rd ed., Beirut, Dār al-'Awda, 1970 (1st ed. 1967). *Bandar Shāh: Maryūd*, 2nd ed., Beirut, Dār al-'Awda, 1978. 'Risāla ilā Aylīn', *Dawmat Wad Ḥāmid*, pp. 26–32. *Mawsim al-Hijra ilā al-Shamāl*, 2nd ed., Beirut, Dār al-'Awda, 1969 (1st ed., 1967). 'al-Rajul al-Qubruṣī', in al-Ṭāhir Aḥmad Makkī (ed.), *al-Qiṣṣa al-Qaṣīra, Dirāsa wa-Mukhtārāt*, 2nd ed., Cairo, Dār al-Ma'ārif, 1978, pp. 367–79. For this perception see also Bashīr al-Qamarī, 'Shi'riyyat al-Ṭayyib Ṣāliḥ: al-Naṣṣ, al-Sard, al-Alīghūryā-Madkhal 'Āmm', in idem, *Majāzāt: Muqārabāt Naqdiyya fī al-Ibdā' al-'Arabī al-Mu'āṣir*, Beirut, Dār al-Ādāb, 1999, p. 140.
7. The Sudanese critic and writer Aḥmad Muḥammad el-Badawī provides evidence for al-Ṭayyib Ṣāliḥ's knowledge and information on the reality of rural Sudan in particular and on Sudan in general on the one hand, and his erudition in English history and literature on the other, on England in general and especially on London. See: el-Badawī, *Qirā'a Jadīda fī Riwāyat Mawsim al-Hijra ilā al-Shamāl*, Manchester, al-Zōl, 1992, pp. 45–51.
8. For more details on the characters in Ṣāliḥ's writing see Ami Elad-Bouskila, 'Shaping the Cast of Characters: The Case of al-Ṭayyib Ṣāliḥ', *Journal of Arabic Literature*, XXIX:2 (July 1998), pp. 59–84.
9. This is the way of Ṣāliḥ's expressions in some interviews that he gave, see for example, al-Sāmarrā'ī, 'al-Ṭayyib Ṣāliḥ', *al-Aqlām*, p. 143.

10. al-Ṭayyib Ṣāliḥ demonstrates this, as cited in Jibrīl, *'Alā al-Darb*, pp. 9–10.
11. Note the correlation between the rural world which al-Ṭayyib Ṣāliḥ left and his childhood which he spent in his Sudanese village. See his words: 'The [literary] work itself may be the search after the lost childhood [. . .] When the man grows up and enters life's difficulties, the childhood world seems to him as a beautiful paradise', Jibrīl, *'Alā al-Darb*, p. 12. See also Ibid., pp. 33, 35. See also: Ḥalīm al-Yāzijī, *al-Sūdān wa'l-Ḥaraka al-Adabiyya*, Beirut, Manshūrāt al-Jāmi'a al-Lubnāniyya, Qism al-Dirāsāt al-Insāniyya, 1985, pp. 919–21.
12. Jibrīl, 'al-Ṭayyib Ṣāliḥ: Malāmiḥ min Sīra Dhātiyya (6)', *al-Ḥayāt*, p. 20.
13. al-Ṭayyib Ṣāliḥ, 'Yawm Mubārak 'alā Shāṭi' Umm Bāb', in *Mukhtārāt min al-Qiṣaṣ al-Qaṣīra fī 18 Baladan 'Arabiyyan*, 159–63.
14. Ṭāhā Ḥusayn, *Adīb*, Cairo, Dar al-Ma'ārif, 1962 (1st ed. 1935). For the French translation see *Adib, ou l'Aventure occidentale* (trans. Amina and Moenis Taha-Hussein), Cairo, Dar al-Ma'ārif , 1960. Tawfīq al-Ḥakīm, *'Uṣfūr min al-Sharq*, Cairo, al-Maṭba'a al-Namūdhajiyya, n.d. (1st ed. 1938). For the English translation see *Bird from the East* (trans. R. Bayly Winder), Beirut, Khayat, 1966. Yaḥyā Ḥaqqī, *Qindīl Umm Hāshim*, Cairo, al-Hay'a al-Miṣriyya al-'Āmma li'l-Kitāb, 1990 (1st ed. 1944). For the English translation see *The Saint's Lamp and Other Stories* (trans. M.M. Badawi), Leiden, E.J. Brill, 1973. Suhayl Idrīs, *al-Ḥayy al-Lātīnī*, Beirut, Dār al-Ādāb, 1981 (1st ed. 1954). Muḥammad Zifzāf, *al-Mar'a wa'l-Warda*, Rabat, al-Sharika al-Maghribiyya li'l-Nāshirīn al-Muttaḥidīn, 1981 (1st ed., 1972). Sa'dī Ibrāhīm, *al-Marfūḍūn, Riwāya*, Algiers, al-Sharika al-Waṭaniyya li'l-Nashr wa'l-Tawzī', 1981.
15. Some researchers assert that the only parameter which defines the cultural and literary belonging of the writer is the writing language of his works. See Jihād Fāḍil, *al-Adab al-Ḥadīth fī Lubnān, Naẓra Mughāyira*, London, Riyāḍ al-Rayyis li'l-Kutub wa'l-Nashr, 1996, pp. 45–53. For a different and more theoretical and comparative approach, see Florian Coulmas, 'Language Masters: Defying Linguistic Materialism', *International Journal of the Sociology of Language*, 137 (1999), pp. 33–8.
16. For further information on the Maghrib in literature and the question of the language's writing, see Albert Memmie (ed.), *Écrivains Francophones du Maghreb, Anthologie*, Paris, Editions Segkers, 1985, pp. 7–17. Jacqueline Kaye (ed.), *Maghreb, New Writing From North Africa*, York, Talus Editions and University of York, 1992, pp. 5–7. Jacqueline Kaye and Abedlhamid Zoubir, *The Ambiguous Compromise: Language, Literature and National Identity in Algeria and Morocco*, London, Routledge, 1990. Ami Elad-Bouskila, 'En deux langues, La littérature moderne d'Afrique du Nord', in Erez Biton and Ami Elad-Bouskila (eds), *Le Maghreb, Litterature et Culture, Apirion*, 28 (1993), pp. 86–7. Layla Ibnlfassi and Nicki Hitchcot (eds), *African Francophone Writings, A Critical Introduction*, Oxford, Berg, 1996, pp. 1–6, 33–43. Aida A. Bamia, 'The North African Novel: Achievement, and Prospects', in Issa Boullata (ed.), *The Arabic Novel Since 1950*, Cambridge, Mass., Dar Mahjar, 1992, pp. 61–88. *The Hybrid Literary Text: Arab Creative Authors Writing in Foreign Languages, Alif*, 20 (2000). 'Abd al-Raḥmān Yāghī, 'Mubdi'ūn bi ghayr Lughatihim al-Umm' in idem, *al-Baḥth 'an Īqā' Jadīd fī al-Riwāya al-'Arabiyya*, Beirut, Dār al-Fārābī, 1999, pp. 105–43. For more details of Lebanese literature in French see Fāḍil, *al-Adab al-Ḥadīth fī Lubnān*, pp. 45–53. Maḥmūd Qāsim, *al-Adab al-'Arabī al-Maktūb bi'l-Faransiyya*, Cairo, al-Hay'a al-Miṣriyya al-'Āmma li'l-Kitāb, 1996, pp. 70–97.
17. This is the opinion of the Palestinian author Emīl Ḥabībī (1921–96), as he indicated in the course of our discussion in the early nineties. Possibly this statement is connected to other considerations. See also the article's title of M.M. Badawi, 'Two Novelists from Iraq: Jabrā and Munīf', *Journal of Arabic Literature*, XXIII: 2 (1992), pp. 140–54. In addition to the fact that Jabrā is Palestinian, his literary works belong to Iraqi but also to Palestinian literature. This is the opinion of the Iraqi literary critic Najm 'Abd Allāh Kāẓim, *al-Riwāya fī al-'Irāq 1965-1980 wa-Ta'thīr al-Riwāya al-Amrīkīyya fīhā*, Baghdad, Dār al-Shu'ūn al-Thaqāfiyya al-'Āmma, 1987, pp. 8–9, 133. For a similar opinion see

Mu'jam al-Bābaṭīn li'l-Shu'arā' al-'Arab al-Mu'āṣirīn, Kuwait, Mu'assasat Jā'izat 'Abd al-'Azīz Sa'ūd al-Bābaṭīn li'l-Ibdā' al-Shi'rī, 1995, vol. 1, p. 642.

18. Ami Elad-Bouskila, *Modern Palestinian Literature and Culture*, London and Portland, Frank Cass, 1999, pp. 32–62.

19. Some literary critics regard al-Ṭayyib Ṣāliḥ as a *Mahjarī* writer, comparing him respectfully to *Mahjarī* writers, especially because of his erudition in the Arabic language and its heritage. See Maḥmūd Aḥmad Haykal, '*Bandar Shāh*', *al-Dōḥa*, 2 (February 1976), p. 131. For further information on the *Mahjar* literature see 'Īsā al-Nā'ūrī, *Adab al-Mahjar*, 3rd ed., Cairo, Dār al-Ma'ārif, 1977. Muḥammad 'Abd al-Mun'im al-Khafājī, *Qiṣṣat al-Adab al-Mahjarī*, Beirut, Dār al-Kitāb al-Lubnānī, 1986. Barbara Young, *This Man From Lebanon*, New York, Knopf, 1959. Joseph P. Ghougassian, *Khalil Gibran: Wings of Thought*, New York, Philosophical Library, 1973. M.M. Badawi (ed.), *The Cambridge History of Arabic Literature, Modern Arabic Literature*, Cambridge, Cambridge University Press, 1992, pp. 96–8.

20. Only few literary critics relate to this interesting point. See for example John E. Davidson, 'In Search of a Middle Point: The Origins of Oppression in Tayeb Sālih's *Season of Migration to the North*', *Research in African Literature*, 20 (1989), pp. 386, 398.

21. For more details see Fuad Ajami, *The Dream Palace of the Arabs, A Generation's Odyssey*, New York, Pantheon Books, 1998, pp. 297–304. 'Adab al-Muhajjarīn al-Judud', *Ibdā'*, 11 (November 1999), pp. 40–2. Shams al-Dīn Mūsā, 'Ash'ār wa-Mawādd Adabiyya fī Majallāt Mughtariba', *Ibdā'*, 11 (November 1999), pp. 70–3. Sulaymān al-Azra'ī 'Ẓāhirat al-Mahjariyya al-Jadīda: Fī Tashkhīṣ al-Ẓāhira', in *al-Kitāba wa'l Mutakkayyil, al-Mahjariyya al-Jadīda, al-Adab al-Nisawyyī*, Beirut, al-Mu'assasa al-'Arabiyya li'l-Dirāsāt wa'l Nashr, 1999, pp. 31–8. Muḥsin Jāsim Mūsawī, *Infirāṭ al-'Aqd al-Muqaddas: Mun'aṭafāt al-Riwāya al-'Arabiyya ba'd Maḥfūẓ*, Cairo, al-Hay'a al-Miṣriyya al-'Āmma li'l-Kitāb, 1999, pp. 223–55, 329–92. For critical works which deal with the question of limits of freedom in modern Arabic literature see Marina Stagh, *The Limits of Freedom of Speech: Prose Literature and Prose Writing in Egypt under Nasser and Sadat*, Stockholm, Almqvist Wiksel International, 1993. Isabella Camera d'Afflitto 'Prison Narratives: Autobiography and Fiction', in Robin Ostle, Ed de Moor, and Stefan Wild (eds), *Writing the Self: Autobiography Writing in Modern Arabic Literature*, London, Saqi Books, 1998, pp. 148–56. Robin Ostle (ed.), *The Quest of Freedom in Modern Arabic Literature*, *Journal of Arabic Literature*,xxvi:1–2 (March-June 1995). Samāḥ Idrīs, *al-Muthaqqaf al-'Arabī wa'l-Sulṭa, Baḥth fī Riwāyāt al-Tajriba al-Nāṣiriyya*, Beirut, Dār al-Ādāb, 1992. Ḥalīm Barakāt, 'al-Kātib al-'Arabī wa'l-Sulṭa', *Mawāqif*, 12 (1070), pp. 28–48. 'Abd al-Salām Muḥammad al-Shādhilī, *Shakhṣiyyat al-Muthaqqaf fī al-Riwāya al-'Arabiyya al-Ḥadītha*, Beirut, Dār al-Ḥadātha li'l-Ṭibā'a wa'l-Nashr wa'l-Tawzī', 1985.

22. al-Ṭayyib Ṣāliḥ professed that before he left Khartoum for London (1953), he had writen two short stories but as he was not happy with them so he tore the two drafts up and threw them away. See Jibrīl, *'Alā al-Darb*, p. 13. In another place he indicates that when he studied in high school some pupils, including himself, published a 'wall newspaper'. al-Ṭayyib Ṣāliḥ took part in this enterprise but was not one of its prominent initiators. See al-Sāmarrā'ī, 'Muqābala Adabiyya ma'a al-Ṭayyib Ṣāliḥ', *al-Ādāb*, p. 3. According to al-Ṭayyib Ṣāliḥ, he wrote a short story called 'Nawma Ḥālima' (Beauty Sleep), see al-Ṭayyib Ṣāliḥ, 'Aḥtafī bi'l-Māḍī wa-Uṣāri' al-Rāhin wa Ajma' bayn al-Ithnayn', *al-Quds* (March 29, 1998), p. 15.

23. al-Ṭayyib Ṣāliḥ told me in Oxford on April 24, 1998, that he wrote his 'Muqaddimāt' in English but he was not happy with it, therefore he rewrote it in Arabic.

24. On the one hand, this experiment of writing the 'Muqaddimāt' in English can indicate the language choice as a typical characteristic of the *Mahjar* and post-*Mahjar* literature. On the other hand when al-Ṭayyib Ṣāliḥ was asked in an interview if he has ever thought of writing in English his answer was:

'No, never. Never. It is a matter of principle' See Mohammed Shaheen, 'Interview with Tayeb Salih', *Banipal*, 10–11 (Spring-Summer 2001), p. 83.

25. For more details on Abū Nuwās see Ewald Wagner, *The Encyclopaedia of Islam*, New Edition, Leiden, E.J. Brill, vol. I, 1986, pp. 143–4. For more details on al-Mutanabbī see R. Blachère (Ch. Pellat), *The Encyclopaedia of Islam*, vol. VII, 1993, pp. 769–72. On the significance of al-Mutanabbī and his influence on al-Ṭayyib Ṣāliḥ, see the speech of Ghāzī b. 'Abd al-Raḥmān al-Quṣaybī, Ambassador of Saudi Arabia in Great Britain, in honor of al-Ṭayyib Ṣāliḥ, at a 'literary evening' which was held for him in London, December 1, 1992. I thank Aḥmad el-Badawī for giving me this information.

26. For further discussion of this issue see Muḥammad Khayr 'Uthmān, 'al-Āfāq al-Ba'īda aw Istirāḥat al-Muḥārib', in Ḥasan Abbashir al-Ṭayyib (ed.), *al-Ṭayyib Ṣāliḥ*, pp. 243–53. al-Ṭayyib Ṣāliḥ expressed this perception several times: see the interview that was conducted on MBC on 3 June 1998 (see Appendix G). See also Ḥasan Abbashir al-Ṭayyib (ed.), *al-Ṭayyib Ṣāliḥ*, pp. 105–6. 'Ami El'ad-Bouskila, 'Muqābalāt ma'a al-Ṭayyib Ṣāliḥ fī Oxford' (24–25 April 1998). Idem, 'The Path and its Stations: An Interview with al-Ṭayyib Ṣāliḥ', London, 22 August 2000 (see Appendix H). Between 1989–99 al-Ṭayyib Ṣāliḥ published in *al-Majalla* hundreds of literary journalistic articles. In addition, al-Ṭayyib Ṣāliḥ contributed some critiques and introductions written between 1961–2001 (see Appendix E).

27. Elad-Bouskila, 'The Path and its Stations', (see Appendix H).

28. On modern Sudanese literature, see Aḥmad Abū Sa'd, *al-Shi'r wa'l-Shu'arā' fī al-Sūdān 1900–1958, Dirāsa wa-Mukhtārāt*, Beirut, Dār al-Ma'ārif, 1959. 'Abd al-Majīd 'Ābdīn, *Ta'rīkh al-Thaqāfa al-'Arabiyya fī al-Sūdān mundhu Nash'atihā ilā al-'Aṣr al-Ḥadīth*, 2nd ed., Beirut, Dār al-Thaqāfa, 1967. Salām, *al-Qiṣṣa fī al-Adab al-Sūdānī al-Ḥadīth*. Mukhtār Ibrāhīm 'Ajūba, *al-Qiṣṣa al-Ḥadītha fī al-Sūdān*, Kharṭoum, Jāmi'at al-Kharṭūm, Dār al-Ta'līf wa'l-Tarjama wa'l-Nashr, 1972. Muḥammad Ibrāhīm al-Shūsh, *al-Shi'r al-Ḥadīth fī al-Sūdān*, 2nd ed., Khartoum, Jāmi'at al-Kharṭum, 1972. Ibrāhīm Isḥāq Ibrāhīm, 'Ḥawla al-Qiṣṣa al-Qaṣīra fī al-Sūdān', *al-Thaqāfa al-Sūdāniyya*, 10 (May 1979), pp. 20–4. 'Alī al-Makk (ed.), *Mukhtārāt min al-Adab al-Sūdānī*, 2nd ed., Khartoum, Dār Jāmi'at al-Kharṭūm li'l-Nashr, 1980. Sayyid Ḥāmid al-Nassāj, *Bānūrāmā al-Riwāya al-'Arabiyya al-Ḥadītha*, Cairo, Dār al-Ma'ārif, 1980, pp. 231–52. 'Abd al-Ḥamīd Muḥammad Aḥmad, *al-Shi'r wa'l-Mujtama' fī al-Sūdān, Qirā'āt fī al-Shi'r al-Sūdānī al-Ḥadīth wa'l-Mu'āṣir*, Khartoum, Dār al-Wa'y li'l-Ṭibā'a wa'l-Nashr wa'l-Tawzi', 1987. Mu'āwiya al-Bilāl, *al-Shakl wa'l-Ma'sāt: Dirāsa fī al-Qiṣṣa al-Qaṣīra al-Sūdāniyya*, Cairo, al-Sharika al-'Ālamiyya li'l-Ṭibā'a wa'l-Nashr, 2000. Idem, *al-Kitāba fī Muntaṣaf al-Dā'ira*, Cairo, al-Sharika al-'Ālamiyya li'l-Ṭibā'a wa'l-Nashr, 2000. Muḥammad al-Mahdī Bushrā, 'al-Wajh wa'l-Qinā', Ibdā' al-Unthā Mir'at al-Dākhil', in *al-Mar'a wa'l-Ibdā' fī al-Sūdān*, Cairo and Khartoum, Markaz al-Dirāsāt al-Sūdāniyya, 2001, pp. 188–218. Osman Hassan Ahmed (ed.), *Sixteen Sudanese Short Stories*, Washington, D.C., Office of the Cultural Counselor, Embassy of the Democratic Republic of the Sudan, 1981, pp. 1–5. Berkley, *The Roots of Consciousness Molding*, pp. 105–42.

29. For further information on this concept see 'Ami El'ad-Bouskila, *Sifrut 'Aravit bi Levush 'Ivri* (Arabic Literature in Hebrew Dress), Jerusalem, Ministry of Education, Culture and Sport, 1995, pp. 14–25 (Hebrew). Idem (ed.), *Writer, Culture, Text: Studies in Modern Arabic Literature*, Fredericton, York Press, 1993, pp. 5–8. Idem, *The Village Novel in Modern Egyptain Literature*, Berlin, Klaus Schwarz, 1994, pp. 7–13. Iḥsān 'Abbās, 'Naẓra fī Milaff al-Adab al-Sūdānī', *al-Ādāb*, 4 (April 1975), pp. 110–12.

30. On Sudanese dialects see 'Awn al-Sharīf Qāsim, *Qāmūs al-Lahja al-'Āmmiyya fī al-Sūdān*, 2nd ed., Cairo, al-Maktab al-Miṣrī, 1985, pp. 13–25. 'Ābdīn, *Ta'rīkh al-Thaqāfa al-'Arabiyya fī al-Sūdān*, pp. 11–23. Ḥasan Abbashir al-Ṭayyib, 'al-'Arabiyya fī al-Sūdān, Mu'allaf al-Marḥūm al-Shaykh 'Abd Allāh 'Abd al-Raḥmān al-Amīn', *al-Kharṭūm*, 8 (May 1969), pp. 40–7. 'Abd al-Ḥayy 'Abd al-Ḥaqq,

'Dirāsāt Sūdāniyya, al-Lahajāt al-'Arabiyya fī Darfūr', *al-Kharṭūm*, 8 (May 1969), pp. 54–7. G. S. Burton, *Sudan Arabic Note-Book*, London, McCorquodule, 1934. Awn al-Sharif Gasim, 'Some Aspects of Sudanese Colloquial Arabic', *Sudan Notes and Records*, XLVI (1965), pp. 40–9. P. E. Hair, 'A Layman's Guide to the Languages of the Sudan Republic', *Sudan Notes and Records*, XLVII (1966), pp. 65–78. Alan S. Kaye, *Chadian and Sudanese in the Light of Comparative Arabic Dialectology*, The Hague, Mouton, 1976, pp. 1–90. Arlette Roth-Laly, *Lexique des Parlers Arabes Tchado-Sudanais (An Arabic-English-French Lexicon of the Dialects Spoken in the Chad-Sudan Area)*, Paris, Edition du Centre National de la Recherche Scientifique, 1969–72.

31. Gabriel R. Warburg, *Historical Discord in the Nile Valley*, London, Hurst and Company, 1992, pp. 125–53. 'Abd al-Rahim Muddathir, 'Arabism, Africanism and Self-Identification in the Sudan', *Journal of African Studies*, 8:2 (July 1970), pp. 233–49. P.M. Holt, *A Modern History of the Sudan*, London, Weldenfeld and Nicholson, 1961, pp. 139–68.
32. 'Īsā al-Ḥilū, 'Qirā'āt fī al-Qiṣṣa al-Sūdāniyya al-Qaṣīra', *al-Ādāb*, 4 (April 1975), p. 39. 'Abd Allāh Ḥāmid al-Amīn, 'al-Rasm al-Bayānī li'l-Riwāya al-Sūdāniyya', *al-Ādāb*, 4 (April 1975), p. 55.
33. For more details on poetry in the Sudan see 'Abd al-Ḥamīd Muḥammad Aḥmad, *al-Shi'r wa'l-Mujtama' fī al-Sūdān*. al-Shūsh, *al-Shi'r al-Ḥadīth fī al-Sūdān*. Muḥammad Muṣṭafā Haddāra, *Tayyār al-Shi'r al-'Arabī al-Mu'āṣir fī al-Sūdān*, Beirut, Dār al-Thaqāfa, 1972. Ḥasan Abbashir al-Ṭayyib, *Fī al-Adab al-Sūdānī al-Mu'āṣir*, Beirut and Khartoum, Dār al-Fikr and al-Dār al-Sūdāniyya, 1971, pp. 12–146. Ḥalīm al-Yāzijī, *al-Sūdān wa'l-Ḥaraka al-Adabiyya*, Beirut, Manshūrāt al-Jāmi'a al-Lubnāniyya, Qism al-Dirāsāt al-Insāniyya, 1985, pp. 805–12. al-Ṭāhir Muḥammad 'Alī al-Bashīr, *al-Adab al-Ṣūfī al-Sūdānī*, [Khartoum], al-Dār al-Sūdāniyya, 1970, pp. 21–40, 84–264. 'Ābdīn, *Ta'rīkh al-Thaqāfa al-'Arabiyya fī al-Sūdān*, pp. 181–308.
34. al-Makk (ed.), *Mukhtārāt min al-Adab al-Sūdānī al-Ḥadīth*, pp. 2–3, 5–6, 13. Salām, *Dirāsāt fī al-Qiṣṣa al-'Arabiyya al-Ḥadītha*, p. 375. 'Ābdīn, *Ta'rīkh al-Thaqāfa al-'Arabiyya fī al-Sūdān*, pp. 151–4. 'Abd al-Raḥmān Abū 'Awf, *al-Baḥth 'an Ṭarīq Jadīd li'l-Qiṣṣa al-Qaṣīra al-Miṣriyya*, Cairo, al-Hay'a al-Miṣriyya al-'Āmma li'l-Ta'līf wa'l-Nashr, 1971, p. 135. al-Ḥilū, 'Qirā'āt', *al-Ādāb*, 4 (April 1975), p. 37. al-Amīn, 'al-Rasm al-Bāyanī', al-*Ādāb*, pp. 52–3. Fuḍaylī Jammā', *Qirā'a fī al-Adab al-Sūdānī al-Ḥadīth*, Oman, 1991, pp. 155–7. al-Yāzijī, *al-Sūdān wa'l-Ḥaraka al-Adabiyya*, pp. 769–75, 814–26, 857–9. Muhammad 'Abdul-Hai, *Conflict and Identity, the Cultural Poetics of Contemporary Sudanese Poetry*, Khartoum, University of Khartoum, 1976, pp. 4–26. Heather J. Sharkey, 'A Century in Print: Arabic Journalism and Nationalism in Sudan, 1899–1999', *International Journal of Middle East Studies*, 31 (1999), pp. 537–40. For conclusive information of the four main stages of the Sudanese Arabic press development between 1899–1999, see idem, pp. 544–5.
35. 'Ami El'ad [-Bouskila], 'al-Ṭayyib Ṣāliḥ wa'l-Adab al-Sūdānī al-Ḥadīth', *Liqā'*, 6 (Spring 1987), pp. 22–3. al-Yāzijī, *al-Sūdān wa'l-Ḥaraka al-Adabiyya*, pp. 785–92, 857–9.
36. Muṣṭafā Muḥammad Aḥmad al-Ṣāwī, 'al-Riwāya al-'Arabiyya fī al-Sūdān (1948–97)', *Kitābāt Sūdāniyya*, 13 (September 2000), pp. 27–46. al-Makk (ed.), *Mukhtārāt min al-Adab al-Sūdānī al-Ḥadīth*, pp. 2–3, 5–6, 13. Salām, *Dirāsāt fī al-Qiṣṣa al-'Arabiyya al-Ḥadītha*, p. 375. Abū 'Awf, *al-Baḥth 'an Ṭarīq Jadīd*, p. 135. al-Ḥilū, 'Qirā'āt', *al-Ādāb*, p. 37. 'Ābdīn, *Ta'rīkh al-Thaqāfa al-'Arabiyya fī al-Sūdān*, pp. 333–45. al-Amīn, 'al-Rasm al-Bāyanī', *al-Ādāb*, pp. 52–3. Jammā', *Qirā'a fī al-Adab al-Sūdānī al-Ḥadīth*, pp. 155–7. al-Yāzijī, *al-Sūdān wa'l-Ḥaraka al-Adabiyya*, pp. 857–91. al-Bilāl, *al-Shakl wa'l-Ma'sāt*, pp. 5–8, 46–52, 142–53. Abdul-Hai, *Conflict and Identity*, pp. 4–26 Stepanov, 'Between the Past and the Future', in Shikova (ed.), *Al-Ṭayyib Ṣāliḥ's Three Novels*, Moscow, Raduga, 1982, pp. 4–5.
37. For further details on the second stage see 'Ajūba, *al-Qiṣṣa al-Ḥadītha fī al-Sūdān*, pp. 15–16, 95–111. Salām, *Dirāsāt fī al-Qiṣṣa al-'Arabiyya al-Ḥadītha*, pp. 386–97, 446–50. al-Nassāj, *Bānūrāmā al-Riwāya al-'Arabiyya al-Ḥadītha*, pp. 232–4. Abū 'Awf, *al-Baḥth 'an Ṭarīq Jadīd*, pp. 135–6. al-Amīn, 'al-Rasm al-Bayānī', *al-Ādāb*, p. 53. Ibrāhīm Isḥāq Ibrāhīm, 'Ḥawla al-Qiṣṣa al-Qaṣīra fī al-

Sūdān', *al-Thaqāfa al-Sūdāniyya*, pp. 20–1. Jammā', *Qirā'a fī al-Adab al-Sūdānī al-Ḥadīth*, pp. 157–9. al-Yāzijī, *al-Sūdān wa'l-Ḥaraka al-Adabiyya*, pp. 767–84, 891–904. al-Bilāl, *al-Shakl wa'l-Ma'sāt*, pp. 8, 112–19. Abdul-Hai, *Conflict and Identity*, pp. 31–48. Sharkey, 'A Century in Print', *International Journal of Middle East Studies*, pp. 542–3. Muddathir, 'Arabism', *Journal of African Studies*, pp. 245–6. Douglas A. Boyd, *Broadcasting in the Arab World: A Survey of Radio and Television in the Middle East*, Philadelphia, Temple University Press, 1982, pp. 51–2. William A. Rugh, *The Arab Press: New Media and Political Process in the Arab World*, 2nd ed. Syracuse, New York, Syracuse University Press, 1987, pp. 54–5. J.C.M. Starkey, 'Appendix IV, Staff of the Education Department', in Ina Beasley, *Before the Wind Changed: People, Places and Education in the Sudan*, Ed. Janet Starkey, Oxford, Oxford University Press, 1992, pp. 420–1.

38. On the third stage see 'Ajūba, *al-Qiṣṣa al-Ḥadītha fī al-Sūdān*, pp. 112–277. Salām, *Dirāsat fī al-Qiṣṣa al-'Arabiyya al-Ḥadītha*, pp. 395–405. Al-Nassāj, *Bānūrāmā al-Riwāya al-'Arabiyya*, pp. 234–52. Abū 'Awf, *al-Baḥth 'an Ṭarīq Jadīd*, pp. 136–43. Ibrāhīm, Isḥāq Ibrāhīm, 'Ḥawla al-Qiṣṣa al-Qaṣīra fī al-Sūdān', *al-Thaqāfa al-Sūdāniyya*, pp. 21–4. al-Ḥilū, 'Qirā'āt', *al-Ādāb*, pp. 53–5. Muḥammad al-Mahdī Bushrā, 'Qiṣṣat al-Fajī'a wa'l-Kāritha, Dirāsa li'l-Qiṣṣa al-Qaṣīra fī al-Sab'īnāt', al-Juz' al-awwal, al-*Thaqāfa al-Sūdāniyya*, 19 (November 1981), pp. 38–47. al-Yāzijī, *al-Sūdān wa'l-Ḥaraka al-Adabiyya*, pp. 900–19. Jammā', *Qirā'a fī al-Adab al-Sūdānī al-Ḥadith*, pp. 159–73. al-Bilāl, *al-Shakl wa'l-Ma'sāt*, pp 9–10, 12–28, 29–45, 119–41, 171–85, 200–15. Abdul-Hai, *Conflict and Identity*, pp. 47–54. Sharkey, 'A Century in Print', *International Journal of Middle East Studies*, pp. 543–5. Stepanov, 'Between the Past and the Future', pp. 5–6.

39. On Sudanese periodicals and broadcasting in the third stage see: Qāsim 'Uthmān Nūr, 'al-Ṭayyib Ṣāliḥ, Dirāsa Bībliyūghrāfiyya' *al-Thaqāfa al-Sūdāniyya*, 19 (November 1981), pp. 128–9. Sharkey, 'A Century in Print', *International Journal of Middle East Studies*, pp. 543–5. al-Yāzijī, *al-Sūdān wa'l-Ḥaraka al-Adabiyya*, pp. 782–4, 818–19. Rugh, *The Arab Press*, pp. 58, 64–5, 67, 115, 117–18, 120–1. Boyd, *Broadcasting in the Arab World*, pp. 52–64.

40. al-Ṭayyib Zarrūq and Abū Bakr Khālid, *Qiṣaṣ Sūdāniyya*, Cairo, Dār al-Nashr al-Miṣriyya, 1957. al-Ṭayyib Zarrūq, *al-Arḍ al-Ṣafrā'*, Cairo, Maṭba'at al-Baramān, 1961. Idem, *al-Shay' Alladhī Ḥadath, Qiṣaṣ Sūdāniyya*, [Cairo], al-Hay'a al-Miṣriyya al-'Āmma li'l-Ta'līf wa'l-Nashr, 1970. 'Alī al-Makk, *Fī Qarya*, Beirut, Maktabat al-Ḥayāt, 1961. 'Īsā al-Ḥilū, *Rīsh al-Babaghā'*, Beirut, Maktabat al-Ḥayāt, 1967. For further information on these authors and their literary works see 'Ajūba, *al-Qiṣṣa al-Ḥadītha fī al-Sūdān*, pp. 172–88, 197–9. al-Makk (ed.), *Mukhtārāt min al-Adab al-Sūdānī*, pp. 273–4. Jammā', 'al-Taḥlīl al-Nafsī fī Qiṣaṣ 'Isā al-Ḥilū', in idem, *Qirā'a fī al-Adab al-Sūdānī al-Ḥadīth*, pp. 163–8. Aḥmad 'Abd al-Mukarram, 'al-'Unṣur al-Muhayman fī al-Khitāb al-Qaṣaṣī li 'Alī al-Makk (2)', *Kitābāt Sūdāniyya*, 9 (September 1999), pp. 137–48. al-Bilāl, *al-Shakl wa'l-Ma'sāt*, pp. 16–23, 52–66, 116–123, 154–70, 185–99.

41. Abū Bakr Khālid, *al-Nab' al-Murr, Riwāya Sudāniyya*, Cairo, Dār al-Kātib al-'Arabī li'l-Ṭibā'a wa'l-Nashr, n.d. [1967]. Ibrāhīm Isḥāq Ibrāhīm, *Ḥadath fī al-Qarya* (1969), and *A'māl al-Layl wa'l-Balda* (1971). For further information on this prominent author and his works see Aḥmad 'Abd al-Mukarram and al-Khalīfa Wahhāb Ḥasan, 'al-Mubdi' Ibrāhīm Isḥāq Ibrāhīm, 'Alāma Bāriza li 'Abqariyyat al-Riwāya fī Thaqāfatinā', *al-Kharṭūm*, 759 (December 15, 1994), pp. 4–5. al-Amīn, 'al-Rasm al-Bayānī', *al-Ādāb*, p. 55. Jammā', 'Ibrāhīm Isḥāq… Iḍāfa Jādīda li'l-Riwāya al-Sūdāniyya', in idem, *Qirā'a fī al-Adab al-Sūdānī al-Ḥadīth*, pp. 169–73. 'Umar Khalīl, 'Naẓarāt fī Sardiyyāt Ibrāhīm Isḥāq Ibrāhīm, Tajliyāt al-Jānib al-Usṭūrī (1)', *al-Kharṭūm*, 2494 (17 August 2000), p. 5. Naṣṣār al-Ḥājj, 'Tajribat Ibrāhīm Isḥāq Ibrāhīm', *Kitābāt Sūdāniyya*, 20 (June 2002), pp. 97–100.

42. Muḥammad al-Mahdī al-Majdhūb, *Diwān Nār al-Majādhīb*, Khartoum, Lajnat al-Ta'līf wa'l-Nashr bi Wizārat al-I'lām, 1969. Ṣalāḥ Aḥmad Ibrāhīm, *Ghābat al-Ābanūs wa-Qaṣā'id Ukhrā*, Paris, Idfira, 1990.

43. Aḥmad el-Badawī, *al-Qahr al-Thaqāfī wa'l-Isti'lā'*, Manchester, al-Zōl, n.d., pp. 8–21. 'Abd al-Hādī al-Ṣiddiq, 'al-Azal al-Makānī li'l-Shi'r al-Sūdānī', *al-Ādāb*, 4 (April 1975), pp. 18–25.
44. On African literatures and the written language see Kenneth W. Harrow (ed.), *Faces of Islam in African Literature*, London, James Currey, 1991. Idem (ed.), *Marbout and the Muse, New Aspects of Islam in African Literature*, London, James Currey, 1996. Elder Durosimi Jones (ed.), 'The Question of Language in African Literature Today', *African Literature Today*, 17 (1991). Jeremy Harding, 'African Countries', in John Sturrock (ed.), *The Oxford Guide to Contemporary Writing*, Oxford, Oxford University Press, 1996, pp. 1–21.
45. Tayeb Salih, 'A Handful of Dates' (trans. Denys Johnson-Davies) in Chinua Achebe and C.L. Innes (eds), *African Short Stories*, Oxford, Heinemann, 1987, pp. 90–4.
46. Muḥammad Miftāḥ al-Faytūrī, *Aghānī Ifrīqiyā, Shi'r*, Beirut, Dār al-'Awda, n.d. (1st ed. 1956). Idem, *'Āshiq min Ifrīqiyā, Shi'r*, Beirut, Dār al-Ādāb, 1964. Idem, *Aḥzān Ifrīqiyā, Sulārā*, Cairo, al-Hay'a al-Miṣriyya al-'Āmma li'l-Ta'līf wa'l-Nashr, 1969 (1st ed. 1966). Idem, *Udhkurīnī Yā Ifrīqiyā*, Beirut, Dār al-'Awda, 1970.
47. Muḥammad 'Abd al-Ghanī al-Bayyūmī, 'al-Aṣāla wa'l-Tajdīd fī al-Riwāya al-Ifrīqiyya', *al-Kharṭūm*, 6 (March 1969), pp. 29–35.
48. For further details on this issue see Patrick William and Chrismas Laura (eds), *Colonial Discourse and Post-Colonial Theory: A Reader*, London, Harvester Wheatsheaf, 1994. Michael Parker and Roger Starkey (eds), *Postcolonial Literatures Achebe, Ngugi, Desai, Wakott*, London, Macmillan Press, 1995. Bruce King (ed.), *New National and Post-Colonial Literatures, An Introduction*, Oxford, Oxford University Press, 1996.
49. al-Ṭayyib Ṣāliḥ's point of view toward this issue was expressed to Aḥmad Sa'īd Muḥammadiyya, 'al-Ṭayyib Ṣāliḥ Yad'ū ilā al-Ifāda min al-Turāth al-Sha'bī', *Shi'r*, 44 (Fall 1970), pp. 143–4. Muḥammad al-Mahdī Bushrā, 'Taḥdīd al-Jins al-Fūlklūrī fī Ibdā' al-Ṭayyib Ṣāliḥ', in Ḥasan Abbashir al-Ṭayyib (ed.), *al-Ṭayyib Ṣāliḥ*, pp. 313–45. Some literary critics connected al-Ṭayyib Ṣāliḥ's success not just to his talent and skill but also to his knowledge and erudition in classical Arabic literature and culture on the one hand, and in modern and classical European literature on the other, in addition to his impressive erudition in the Arabic language. See Haykal, '*Bandar Shāh*', *al-Dōḥa*, p. 127. 'Abd al-Mun'im Salīm, 'Majhūd li'l-Rū'ya 'an Bu'd al-Ṭayyib Ṣāliḥ *Mawsim al-Hijra ilā al-Shamāl*', *al-Sharq*, 2:5 (October 1971), p. 30. Fāṭima Mūsā, ''Uṣfūr min al-Janūb aw 'Ālam al-Ṭayyib Ṣāliḥ', *al-Majalla*, 164 (August 1970), p. 95.
50. For further discussion on the influence of the existentialism in modern Sudanese literature since the beginning of the fifties onwards, see 'Ajūba, *al-Qiṣṣa al-Ḥadītha fī al-Sūdān*, pp. 225–77.
51. Ami Elad [-Bouskila], 'Mahfūz's Za'balāwī: Six Stations of a Quest', *International Journal of Middle East Studies*, 26 (1994), pp. 631–44. Menahem Milson, 'Najīb Maḥfūẓ and the Quest for Meaning', *Arabica*, 17 (1970), pp. 155–86. Somekh, *The Changing Rhythm*, pp. 45, 121, 185.
52. Najīb Maḥfūẓ, *Malḥamat al-Ḥarāfīsh*, Cairo, Maktabat Miṣr, n.d. (1st ed. 1977). For the English translation, see *The Harafish* (trans. Catherine Cobham), Cairo, The American University in Cairo Press, 1994. Gabriel García Márquez, *One Hundred Years of Solitude* (trans. Gregory Rabassa), London, Penguin Books, 1970.
53. Muḥammad Yūsuf al-Qa'īd, *Yaḥduth fī Miṣr al-Ān*, 2nd ed., Beirut, Dār Ibn Rushd, 1979 (1st ed. 1977). On this novel and the influence of the *nouveau roman* on al-Qa'īd see Fadwā Mālṭī-Dūglās, 'Yūsuf al-Qa'īd wa'l-Riwāya al-Jadīda', *Fuṣūl*, 4:3 (April-June 1984), pp. 190–202. Elad [-Bouskila], *The Village Novel*, pp. 113–44.
54. al-Ṭayyib Ṣāliḥ is aware of the resemblance and connection of some works of Latin-American literature, and the difference between himself and them: 'I have noticed that the Latin-American writers, in particular Gabriel García Márquez, were greatly occupied by the issue of government, especially in *One Hundred Years of Solitude*. But I think government occupied them from the

historical and mythical aspect'. Jibrīl, 'al-Ṭayyib Ṣāliḥ: Malāmiḥ min Sīra Dhātiyya (6)', *al-Ḥayāt*, p. 20.

55. Jibrīl, 'al-Ṭayyib Ṣāliḥ: Malāmiḥ min Sīra Dhātiyya (6)', *al-Ḥayāt*, p. 20. Achebe and Innes (eds), *Contemporary African Short Stories*, p. 5.

56. On the connection between al-Ṭayyib Ṣāliḥ and classical Arabic poetry, especially the *Jāhiliyya* poetry as reflected in *Mawsim al-Hijra ilā al-Shamāl*, see el-Badawī, *Qirā'a Jadīda*, pp. 53–65, 69–71. Idem, *al-Ṭayyib Ṣāliḥ*, pp. 130–4. For more details on the connection of the real author and the Koran as reflected in *Bandar Shāh-Ḍaw al-Bayt*, see Sayyid Aḥmad Bilāl, 'Qirā'a Jadīda fī Riwāyat *Bandar Shāh-Ḍaw al-Bayt*', *Kitābāt Sūdāniyya*, 3 (April 1993), pp. 78–9. And as it is reflected in *Mawsim al-Hijra ilā al-Shamāl*, see Ṣāliḥ Ibrāhīm, *al-Mar'a fī Adab al-Ṭayyib Ṣāliḥ*, Beirut, Ma'had al-Dirāsāt al-Nisā'iyya fī al-'Ālam al-'Arabī, al-Jāmi'a al-Lubnāniyya al-Amirīkiyya, 1997, p. 18n. 36, 37.

57. For more details on this literary genre see Ch. Pellat, *The Encyclopaedia of Islam*, New Edition, Leiden, E.J. Brill, vol. VII, 1993, p. 857. On *al-Faraj ba'd al-Shidda* in the context of 'Dawmat Wad Ḥāmid', see Ami Elad [-Bouskila], 'Fiction and Reality', in idem, *Writer, Culture, Text*, p. 69. Sara Sviri, 'On Trees, Dreams, and Holy Men', in Elad-Bouskila and Al-Shahi (eds), *Al-Ṭayyib Ṣāliḥ, Edebiyât*, p. 113.

58. For more details on 'Antara b. Shaddād see R. Blachére, *The Encyclopaedia of Islam*, New Edition, Leiden, E.J. Brill, vol. I, 1986, pp. 521–2. On al-Shahrazūrī, see P. Lory, *The Encyclopaedia of Islam*, New Edition, Vol. IX, 1997, pp. 219–20. On Ibn al-Fārid, see R.A. Nicholson (J. Pedersen), *The Encyclopaedia of Islam*, New Edition Vol. III, 1986, pp. 763–4. On Rābi'a al-'Adawiyya, see Margaret Smith (Ch. Pellat), *The Encyclopaedia of Islam*, New Edition Vol. VIII, 1995, pp. 354–6.

59. Muḥammadiyya (ed.), *al-Ṭayyib Ṣāliḥ*, pp. 6, 119–120, 215. al-Sāmarrā'ī, 'al-Ṭayyib Ṣāliḥ', *al-Aqlām*, p. 149. al-Ẓāhir, 'Ḥiwār ma'a al-Ṭayyib Ṣāliḥ', *al-Aqlām*, pp. 153–4. Jibrīl, 'al-Ṭayyib Ṣāliḥ: Malāmiḥ min Sīra Dhātiyya (6)', *al-Ḥayāt*, p. 20. Muḥammad Rushdī Ḥasan 'Alī, *al-Ibdā' al-Fannī fī Qiṣaṣ al-Ṭayyib Ṣāliḥ*, Cairo, Maṭba'at al-Ma'rifa, 1980, pp. 22, 60–61, 78, 80. Manṣūr Qaysūma, '*Mawsim al-Hijra ilā al-Shamāl* aw al-Kidhb al-Ḥaqīqa', in idem, *al-Anā wa'l-Ākhar fī al-Riwāya al-'Arabiyya al-Ḥadītha*, Tunis, Dār Saḥar, 1994, pp. 110–11, 125–6, 140, 15–151. Ḥilmī Muḥammad al-Qā'ūd, *Mawsim al-Baḥth 'an Huwiyya, Dirāsāt fī al-Riwāya wa'l-Qiṣṣa*, Cairo, al-Hay'a al-Miṣriyya al-'Āmma li'l-Kitāb, 1987, p. 19. Bushrā, 'Taḥdīd al-Jins al-Fūlklūrī fī Ibdā' al-Ṭayyib Ṣāliḥ', in Ḥasan Abbashir al-Ṭayyib (ed.), *al-Ṭayyib Ṣāliḥ*, pp. 313–45. Mona Takieddine Amyuni, *La Ville Source d'Inspiration, Le Caire, Khartoum, Beyrouth, Paola Scola Chez Quelques, Ecrivains Arabes Contemporains*, Beirut, Beiruter Texter und Studien, Stuttgart, Steiner Verlag, 1998, p. 73.

60. Jibrīl, 'al-Ṭayyib Ṣāliḥ: Malāmiḥ min Sīra Dhātiyya (6)', *al-Ḥayāt*, p. 20. See also 'Īsā al-Sa'īd, 'al-Ṭayyib Ṣāliḥ: Taftīt al-'Ālam', *al-Karmil*, 9 (1983), p. 259. For detailed discussion on this issue see Muḥammad al-Makkī Ibrāhīm, 'Fitnat al-Ṭayyib Ṣāliḥ bi Abī al-Ṭayyib', in Ḥasan Abbashir al-Ṭayyib (ed.), *al-Ṭayyib Ṣāliḥ*, pp. 187–95.

61. al-Sāmarrā'ī, 'al-Ṭayyib Ṣāliḥ', *al-Aqlām*, p. 146.

62. al-Ẓāhir, 'Ḥiwār ma'a al-Ṭayyib Ṣāliḥ', *al-Aqlām*, p. 151.

63. Muḥammadiyya (ed.), *al-Ṭayyib Ṣāliḥ*, pp. 208–10, 219–20. al-Ẓāhir, 'Ḥiwār ma'a al-Ṭayyib Ṣāliḥ', *al-Aqlam*, p. 153. Muḥammad Rushdī Ḥasan 'Alī, *al-Ibdā' al-Fannī*, p. 5. Ṣāliḥ, 'Aḥtafī bi'l-Māḍī wa-Uṣāri'u; al-Rāhin', *al-Quds*, p. 15. Jihād Fāḍil, 'Ma'a al-Ṭayyib Ṣāliḥ', in idem, *As'ilat al-Riwāya*, Tunis, al-Dār al-'Arabiyya li'l-Kitāb, 1993, pp. 33–4. 'al-Qiṣṣa fī al-Waṭan al-'Arabī-Nadwa (2)', *al-Ma'rifa*, 138 (August 1973), pp. 171–2, 178. el-Badawī, *al-Ṭayyib Ṣāliḥ*, pp. 93–5.

64. Muḥammadiyya (ed.), *al-Ṭayyib Ṣāliḥ*, p. 6. Farghalī, 'Liqā' ma'a al-Ṭayyib Ṣāliḥ', *al-Hilāl*, p. 119. 'Abd al-Raḥmān Abū 'Awf, 'Bu'd al-Wāqi' fī Adab al-Ṭayyib Ṣāliḥ', *al-Ṭalī'a*, 6 (June 1976), p. 154. el-Badawī, *Qirā'a Jadīda*, pp. 49–51. 'Abd al-Raḥmān al-Khānjī, *Ru'yat al-Mawt fī 'Ālam al-Ṭayyib Ṣāliḥ al-Riwā'ī min Khilāl Riwāyatay* Mawsim al-Hijra ilā al-Shamāl wa-Bandar Shāh, *Ḥawliyyāt Kulliyyat al-Ādāb*, 15 (1995), pp. 69, 76–7. 'Abd al-Quddūs al-Khātim, 'al-Ṭayyib Ṣāliḥ bayn al-Ramz

wa'l-Iqtibās' *al-Ayyām*, 7723 (19 March 1976), p. 7. Salīm, 'Majhūd li'l-Rū'ya', *al-Sharq*, p. 30. Fatḥī 'Uthmān, 'Ḥiwār Ṭawīl (1)', *al-Wasaṭ*, p. 52. Johnson-Davies, 'Profile: The World of Tayeb Salih', *Azure*, 8 (1981), p. 16. M.M. Badawi, *A Short History of Modern Arabic Literature*, Oxford, Oxford University Press, 1993, p. 230. Mona Takieddis Amyuni (ed.), *Tayeb Salih's Season of Migration to the North: A Casebook*, Beirut, The American University of Beirut, 1985, p. 15. Davidson, 'In Search of a Middle Point', *Research in African Literatures*, 20 (1989), pp. 385–6. al-Ṭayyib Ṣāliḥ mentions the possible sources of influence on his writing on the one hand, but on the other he criticizes the issue of possible influence on modern Arabic literature and particularly on his writing. According to his concept, this issue of influence is embarrassing and boring in Arabic literary criticism. See the interview of the *al-Jazīra* channel with al-Ṭayyib Ṣāliḥ (Appendix G). In addition, it is also very interesting to mention that al-Ṭayyib Ṣāliḥ did read some English literature written in English by Arab intellectuals such as Edward Atiyah. For more details on al-Ṭayyib and his writing see Geoffrey P. Nash, *The Arab Writer in English*, Brighton and Portland, Sussex Academic Press, 1998, pp. 94–119. On the status of Shakespeare in modern Arabic literatures and his influence see Ghālī Shukrī, 'Shaksbīr fī al-'Arabiyya', in idem, *Thawrat al-Fikr fī Adabinā al-Ḥadīth*, Cairo, al-Maktaba al-Anglū al-Miṣriyya, 1954, pp. 53–71. M.M. Badawi, 'The Arabs and Shakespeare', in idem, *Modern Arabic Literature and the West*, pp. 191–204. Muhammad Abdul-Hai, *Tradition and English and American Influence in Arabic Romantic Poetry*, Oxford, The Middle East Centre, St. Antony's College, London, Ithaca Press, 1982, pp. 16–24.

65. al-Ẓāhir, 'Ḥiwār ma'a al-Ṭayyib Ṣāliḥ', *al-Aqlām*, pp. 153–4. Elad-Bouskila, 'Al-Ṭayyib Ṣāliḥ: The Author and his Works' in Elad-Bouskila and Ahmed Al-Shahi (eds), *Al-Ṭayyib Ṣāliḥ, Edebiyât*, pp. 5–32. Qaysūma, '*Mawsim al-Hijra ilā al-Shamāl* aw al-Kidhb al-Haqīqa', in idem, *al-Anā wa'l-Ākhar*, pp. 108–9.

66. Shāhīn, *Taḥawwulāt al-Shawq*, pp. 12–14, 19, 22, 30–1, 43–56. Muḥammad Khalafallāh 'Abd Allāh, ''*Urs al-Zayn* Namūdhajan li'l-Ḥiwāriyya al-Naṣṣiyya', *Mawāqif*, 72 (June-September 1993), pp. 84–95.

67. Muḥyī al-Dīn Ṣubḥī, 'Mawsim al-Hijra ilā al-Shamāl bayn 'Uṭayil wa-Mīrsū'', in idem, *Abṭāl fī al-Ṣayrūra, Dirāsāt fī al-Riwāya al-'Arabiyya wa'l-Mu'arraba*, Beirut, Dār al-Ṭalī'a li'l-Ṭibā'a wa'l-Nashr, 1980, pp. 8–32. Qaysūma, *al-Anā wa'l-Ākhar*, pp. 142, 147. Ḥāmid Badawī, 'Qirā'a Jadīda fī Riwāyat *Mawsim al-Hijra ilā al-Shamāl* (1)', *al-Ayyām*, 9426 (9 June 1978) p. 6. Ghassān Ziyāda, *Qirā'āt fī al-Adab wa'l-Riwāya, Innahu Nidā' al-Janūb*, Beirut, Dār al-Muntakhab al-'Arabī, 1995, p. 175.

68. Many books and articles have been written on this issue. See Jāk Tājir, *Ḥarakat al-Tarjama fī Miṣr Khilāl al-Qarn al-Tāsi' 'Ashar*, Cairo, Dār al-Ma'ārif, 1945. Laṭīfa al-Zayyāt, *Ḥarakat al-Tarjama al-Adabiyya min al-Injlīziyya ilā al-'Arabiyya fī Miṣr fī al-Fatra mā bayn 1882–1925*, Cairo, Jāmi'at al-Qāhira, 1975 (Ph.D. Dissertation, unpublished). Mohammad Bakir Alwan, 'A Bibliography of Modern Arabic Fiction in English Translation', *Middle East Journal*, 26 (1972), pp. 195–200. Idem, 'A Bibliography of Modern Arabic Poetry in English Translation', *Middle East Journal*, 27 (1973), pp. 373–81. Salih Al-Toma, *Modern Arabic Literature: A Bibliography of Articles, Books, Dissertations and Translations in English*, Bloomington, Indiana University, 1975. Idem, *Modern Arabic Poetry in English Translation, A Bibliography*, Tangier, Abdelmalek Essaâdi University, Publications of the King Fuad School of Translation, 1993. Muhammad Abdul-Hai, 'A Bibliography of Arabic Translations of English and American Poetry (1830–1970)', *Journal of Arabic Literature*, VII (1976), pp. 120–50. Matti Moosa, *The Origins of Modern Arabic Fiction*, 2nd ed., Boulder and London, Three Continents Books, Lynne Rienner Publishers, 1997, pp. 91–110. Pierre Cachia, 'The Age of Translation and Adaptation, 1850–1914', in idem, *An Overview of Modern Arabic Literature*, Edinburgh, Edinburgh University Press, 1990, pp. 29–42. Trevor Le Gassick, 'The Arabic Novel in English Translation', in Boullata (ed.), *The Arabic Novel Since 1950*, pp. 47–60. Denys Johnson-

Davies, 'On Translating Arabic Literature', in Ferial J. Ghazoul and Barbara Harlow (eds), *The View from Within*, pp. 272–82. Peter Clark, 'Translation Without Translators', *Banipal*, 2 (June 1998), pp. 74–5.

69. According to Ṭalḥat Jibrīl, Ṣāliḥ's works have been translated into twenty languages. See Jibrīl: 'al-Ṭayyib Ṣāliḥ li'l-*Wasaṭ*', *al-Wasaṭ*, p. 52. According to other sources Ṣāliḥ's works have been translated into more than fifteen languages; see the back of the book, al-Ṭayyib Ṣāliḥ, *Bandar Shāh: Maryūd*, Tunisia, Dār al-Janūb li'l-Nashr, 1986. al-Ṭayyib Ṣāliḥ mentioned to me that *Mawsim al-Hijra ilā al-Shamāl* has been translated into twenty languages as follows: Bulgarian, Chinese, Czech, Danish, Dutch, English, Finnish, French, German, Greek, Hebrew, Italian, Japanese, Norwegian, Polish, Rumanian, Russian, Spanish, Swedish and Turkish (see Appendix C). For comparison between the Arabic texts and the English translation see el-Badawī, *al-Ṭayyib Ṣāliḥ*, pp. 194–5.

70. I use the term 'novels' although it may be more precise to define them as short novels or even novellas. On the term 'novella' as a genre and its place in modern Arabic literatures, see Roger Allen, 'The Novella Genre in Arabic: A Study in Fictional Genres', *International Journal of Middle East Studies*, 18:4(1986), pp. 473–84. For the reference to Ṣāliḥ's novellas see pp. 474, 477–9. al-Ṭayyib Ṣāliḥ published very few literary works because he did not want to devote himself to writing belle-lettres for two reasons: the first because he regards himself as a lazy person in this sense, and the second reason is because he prefers to devote himself to his family and he has not enough time to write since he needs to support his family while the writing process takes too much time and compels him to change his way of life. See 'Ami El'ad-Bouskila, 'Muqābalāt ma'a al-Ṭayyib Ṣāliḥ fī Oxford', 24–25 April 1998. Fāḍil, 'Ma'a al-Ṭayyib Ṣāliḥ' in idem, *As'ilat al-Riwāya*, pp. 36–7.

71. For details on al-Ṭayyib Ṣāliḥ's writings in translation, see Appendix C. Clearly, there are modern Arabic authors like Najīb Maḥfūẓ who is the most translated Arabic author into English, but it is mainly his novels, not all his works, that have been translated. For a detailed list of translations of Maḥfūẓ's literary works, see Māhir Shafīq Farīd, 'Najīb Maḥfūẓ fī al-Injlīziyya', *Fuṣūl*, 2:2 (January-March 1987), pp. 312–19, and Rasheed El-Enany, *Naguib Mahfouz: the Pursuit of Meaning*, London and New York, Routledge, 1993, pp. 256–7.

72. Tayeb Salih, *Season of Migration to the North* (trans. Denys Johnson-Davies), London, Heinemann, 1969. For criticism of the English translation, see Mahmud Husein Salih and Naser Y. Al-Hassan Athamneh, 'Silence in Arabic-English Translation: The Case of Salih's *Season of Migration to the North*', *Babel*, 41:4 (1995), pp. 216–33. Peter Nazareth, 'The Narrator as Artist and the Reader as Critic', in Amyuni (ed.), Tayeb Salih's Season of Migration to the North, p. 126 n. 6. Rotraud Wielandt, 'The Problem of Cultural Identity in the Writing of al-Ṭayyib Ṣāliḥ', in Wadad al-Qadi (ed.), *Studia Arabica and Islamica: Festschrift for Ihsan Abbas on his Sixtieth Birthday*, Beirut, Imprimerie Catholique, 1981, p. 495 n. 32. Ali Abdallah Abbas, 'Notes on Tayeb Salih: *Season of Migration to the North* and *The Wedding of Zein*', *Sudan Notes and Records*, LV (1974), p. 46.

73. We might note that some literary critics count among the reasons for the success of Ṣaliḥ's works in translation especially into English, elements connected with quality, authenticity and originality. See the introduction of Iḥsān 'Abbās in Shāhīn's *Taḥawwulāt al-Shawq*, p. 9. Ṣubḥī, *Abṭāl fī al-Ṣayrūra*, p. 33. On the acceptance of this novel despite the mistaken criticism, see al-Shūsh, *Adab wa-Udabā'*, pp. 29–30, 53–8. The Egyptian researcher Sīzā Qāsim explains the success of *Mawsim al-Hijra ilā al-Shamāl* in the connection between the text itself, which explores the East in a charming and simple light, and the connections that the reader's imagination creates with the interaction of the text. See Qāsim, 'Tajriba Naqdiyya: *Mawsim al-Hijra ilā al-Shamāl*', *Fuṣūl*, 1:1 (January-March 1981), pp. 224–9. For more reasons see Ziyāda, *Qirā'āt fī al-Adab wa'l-Riwāya*, pp. 69, 75–7.

74. Jūrj Shāmī, 'Rā'iḥat al-Laban wa-Rā'iḥat al-Tamr', *Shi'r*, 35 (Summer 1967), pp. 90–2. Rajā' al-Naqqāsh, ''Abqariyya Jadīda fī Samā' al-Riwāya al-'Arabiyya', *al-Muṣawwar* (February 2, 1968). See also Rajā' al-Naqqāsh, ''Āṣifa Adabiyya lahā Ta'rīkh', *al-Waṭan al-'Arabī*, 1214 (9 June 2000),

pp. 49. Jalāl al-'Asharī, 'Zūrbā al-Sūdānī aw al-Baḥth 'an al-Dhāt al-Ifrīqiyya', *al-Fikr al-Mu'āṣir*, 45 (November 1968), pp. 68–78. Jabrā Ibrāhīm Jabrā, *al-Riḥla al-Thāmina, Dirāsa Naqdiyya*, Sidon-Beirut, al-Maktaba al-'Aṣriyya, 1968, p. 99 n. 1. Ṣiddīq Ḥasan Ibrāhīm, 'Kutub: al-Ṭayyib Ṣāliḥ, *Mawsim al-Hijra ilā al-Shamāl*', *al-Kharṭūm*, 11 (August 1969), pp. 153–9. Idem, 'Dirāsāt 'an al-Ṭayyib Ṣāliḥ fī Riwāyat *Mawsim al-Hijra ilā al-Shamāl* bayn al-Riwāya wa-Muṣṭafā Sa'īd', *al-Kharṭūm*, 1 (October 1969), pp. 52–61. Tawfiq Ḥannā, 'Muqaddimāt al-Ṭayyib Ṣāliḥ, Muḥāwala li Taqdīm Tajriba Jadīda', *al-Hilāl*, 11 (November 1969), pp. 81–5. Muḥammad al-Ḥasan Fāḍil al-Mawlā, 'Naḥnu wa'l- Ṭayyib Ṣāliḥ wa'l-Ākharūn', in Muḥammadiyya (ed.), *al-Ṭayyib Ṣāliḥ*, pp. 191–7. al-Ṭayyib Ṣāliḥ praised this contribution of Rajā' al-Naqqāsh, see the interview conducted by Bashīr al-Qamarī, 'Hākadhā Ḥaddathanī al-Ṭayyib Ṣāliḥ...Ashkur al-Nās Alladhīna Aḥabbū 'Amalī...', *Kitābāt Sūdāniyya*, 8 (June 1999), pp. 68–9.

75. Portions of al-Ṭayyib Ṣāliḥ's first novel were published in the Lebanese periodical *Ḥiwār*, 10 (May-June 1964), pp. 40–51. The first publication of the full text appeared in the Sudanese periodical *al-Kharṭūm*, 3 (December 1966), pp. 97–137. As a book it was published as *'Urs al-Zayn, Riwāya wa-Sab' Qiṣaṣ*, Beirut, al-Dār al-Sharqiyya li'l-Ṭiba'a wa'l-Nashr, Kitāb *Ḥiwār* 3, 1967. The second edition was published in 1969, *'Urs al-Zayn*, Beirut, Dār al-'Awda, 1969. The novel *Mawsim al-Hijra ilā al-Shamāl* was published several times by different publishers in the 1960s as follows: first in the Lebanese periodical *Ḥiwār*, 24–5 (September-December 1966), pp. 5–87. As a book it was first published in Beirut, Dār al-'Awda, 1967. The second edition appeared in 1969, and in the same year in Cairo, Dār al-Hilāl, Riwāyāt *al-Hilāl* 245, May 1969. The collection of his short stories *Dawmat Wad Ḥāmid* was published first in Beirut as part of *'Urs al-Zayn, Riwāya wa-Sab' Qiṣaṣ*, 1967. Some stories were published from the 1960s onwards: 'Dawmat Wad Ḥāmid', in London in the Arabic periodical *Aṣwāt*, 3 (1961), pp. 44–55. It was published once more in the Egyptian weekly *al-Hilāl*, 8 (August 1969), pp. 6–17. It also appeared in 'Ajūba, *Namādhij min al-Qiṣṣa al-Qaṣīra fī al-Sūdān*, pp. 130–42. See also 'Ami El'ad-Bouskila (ed.), *Aḍwā' Dāniya, Mukhtārāt min al-Qiṣṣa al-'Arabiyya al-Ḥadītha*, Jerusalem, Academon, 1991, pp. 68–78. 'al-Muqaddimāt' was published in the Lebanese periodical *Ḥiwār*, 21 (March-April 1966), pp. 36–40. 'al-Muqaddimāt' contains six short-short stories and not five. The sixth short-short story 'al-Shay' al-Ākhar' was published in *Ḥiwār*, 21 (March-April 1966), pp. 37–8. 'al-Muqaddimāt' was also published in the Egyptian weekly *al-Hilāl*, 9 (September 1969), pp. 34–9, as well as in the Sudanese periodical *al-Ra'y al-'Āmm*, 8458 (April 29, 1969) cited in Nūr, 'al-Ṭayyib Ṣāliḥ', *al-Thaqāfa al-Sūdāniyya*, p. 125. The short story 'Ḥafnat Tamr' from the collection *Dawmat Wad Ḥāmid* was published in *al-Hilāl*, 10 (October 1969), pp. 106–9. The short story 'Hākadhā Yā Sādatī' was published, in addition to *Dawmat Wad Ḥāmid*, in the Lebanese periodical *Adab*, 1:1 (Autumn 1962), pp. 9–16. It also appeared in the Sudanese periodical *al-Ra'y al-'Āmm*, 117 (July 15, 1968), p. 15, as cited in Nūr, 'al-Ṭayyib Ṣāliḥ', *al-Thaqāfa al-Sūdāniyya*, p. 125. The short story 'Risāla ilā Aylīn' was published also in al-Makk (ed.), *Mukhtārāt min al-Adab al-Sūdānī*, pp. 210–13. The short story 'Nakhla 'alā al-Jadwal' was printed in al-Makk (ed.), *Mukhtārāt min al-Adab al-Sūdānī*, pp. 214–21, and in the Sudanese periodical *al-Qiṣṣa*, 10 (October 10, 1960), pp. 11–15, as cited in Nūr, 'al-Ṭayyib Ṣāliḥ', *al-Thaqāfa al-Sūdāniyya*, p. 125. For more details see Appendix A.

76. The fact is that the Egyptian edition of *Mawsim al-Hijra ilā al-Shamāl* (10,000 copies!) was not restricted only to Egypt, but to the Arab world in general. Moreover, in the Sudan itself many copies of this edition were snatched up. The Sudanese monthly *al-Kharṭūm* reported in August 1969 that all the copies of this novel had been sold out since July. See Ṣiddīq Ḥasan Ibrāhīm, 'Kutub: al-Ṭayyib Ṣāliḥ, *Mawsim al-Hijra ilā al-Shamāl*', *al-Kharṭūm*, p. 153. al-Naqqāsh, ''Āṣifa Adabiyya lahā Ta'rīkh', *al-Waṭan al-'Arabī*, pp. 48–9.

77. Tayeb Salih, *The Wedding of Zein and Other Stories*, London, 1978, pp. 29–120 (1st ed. 1968). The story 'A Handful of Dates' (Ḥafnat Tamr) was published in the same book, pp. 21–8, the story 'The

Doum Tree of Wad Hamid' (Dawmat Wad Ḥāmid), pp. 1–20. This story appeared earlier, see Denys Johnson-Davies (ed. and trans.), *Modern Arabic Short Stories*, London, Heinemann, 1981, pp. 83–94 (1st ed 1967).

78. The 1960s were the turning point in the development of fictional genres in modern Arabic literatures. In the second half of the 1960s, especially between 1966–7, when Ṣāliḥ's first three books (*Dawmat Wad Ḥāmid, 'Urs al-Zayn, Mawsim al-Hijra ilā al-Shamāl*) were published in the Arab world especially in the Mashriq, very important novels were published in 1966, such as *Tharthara fawq al-Nīl* (Adrift on the Nile, trans. Frances Liardet, New York, Doubleday, 1993) by Najīb Maḥfūẓ. *Tilka al-Rā'iḥa* (The Smell of It, trans. Denys Johnson-Davies, London, Heinemann, 1971) by the Egyptian writer Ṣun'allāh Ibrāhīm (b.1937), and *al-Shirā' wa'l-'Āṣifa* (The Sail and the Storm) by the Syrian writer Ḥannā Mīna (b.1924).

79. For more details of '*Ḥiwār*'s Scandal' see Maḥmūd Shrīḥ, *Tawfīq Ṣāyigh, Ṣūrat Shā'ir wa-Manfā*, London, Riyāḍ al-Rayyis li'l-Kutub wa'l-Nashr, 1989, pp. 113–57. Fāḍil, *al-Adab al-Ḥadīth fī Lubnān*, pp. 359–67. el-Badawī, *al-Ṭayyib Ṣāliḥ*, pp. 85–8. al-Naqqāsh, ''Āṣifa Adabiyya lahā Ta'rīkh', *al-Waṭan al-'Arabī*, pp. 48–9.

80. al-Naqqāsh, 'al-Ṭayyib Ṣāliḥ 'Abqariyya Riwā'iyya Jadīda', in Muḥammadiyya (ed.), *al-Ṭayyib Ṣāliḥ*, p. 100. al-Ṭayyib Ṣāliḥ indicates that the Egyptian critic Rajā' al-Naqqāsh succeeded in convincing the Egyptian publishing house Dār al-Hilāl to re-publish the novel *Mawsim al-Hijra ilā al-Shamāl*, see Jibrīl, *'Alā al-Darb*, p. 103.

81. al-Ḥusaynī, 'al-Ṭayyib Ṣāliḥ fī Bayrūt', in Muḥammadiyya (ed.), *al-Ṭayyib Ṣāliḥ*, pp. 219–20.

82. At the end of the 1960s and the beginning of the 1970s, some cultural circles in the Sudan voiced self-accusations, namely that in the Arab world as in the West al-Ṭayyib Ṣāliḥ's talent is recognized while in the Sudan his literary works are still not read and very little is written in the Sudanese press. These views were reflected by the Sudanese literary critic Ṭalḥat Jibrīl, who wrote that his contemporary colleagues read *Mawsim al-Hijra ilā al-Shamāl* only in the 1970s, see Jibrīl, *'Alā al-Darb*, p. 10. During the 1970s, 1980s and 1990s a great number of books, essays and articles were published in the Arab world and outside of it. For a detailed discussion of Arab and Sudanese critics see Khālid Mūsā Daf'allāh, 'al-Manhajiyya al-Naqdiyya al-Ḥadītha li A'māl al-Ṭayyib Ṣāliḥ Wafq Ru'ya 'Arabiyya' in idem, *al-Lā Muntamī fī Adab al-Ṭayyib Ṣāliḥ*, Khartoum, Dār Jāmi'at al-Kharṭūm li'l-Nashr, 1993, pp. 35–56.

83. M.M. Badawi, 'Tayeb Salih: *Bandarshah*. Translated from the Arabic by Denys Johnson-Davies, London and New York: Kegan Paul International; Paris: UNESCO Publishing, 1996'. *Bulletin of the School of Oriental and African Studies*, 61:2(1998), pp. 339–40. Bilāl, 'Qirā'a Jadīda' *Kitābāt Sūdāniyya*, 3 (April 1993), p. 72.

84. The various editions of Ṣāliḥ's books in the Lebanese publishing house Dār al-'Awda, in addition to Dār al-Jīl, and especially *Mawsim al-Hijra ilā al-Shamāl*, which was published in its fourteenth edition (1987), as a general editing of Ṣāliḥ's books in Dār al-'Awda: al-Ṭayyib Ṣāliḥ, *al-Āthār al-Kāmila* (*Mawsim al-Hijra ilā al-Shamāl, 'Urs al-Zayn, Ḍaw al-Bayt (Bandar Shāh), Maryūd (Bandar Shāh), Dawmat Wad Ḥāmid*, Beirut, Dār al-'Awda, 1996. In addition, there are two stories by al-Ṭayyib Ṣāliḥ which are not included in his collection *Dawmat Wad Ḥāmid*. The first is 'al-Rajul al-Qubruṣī' (The Cypriot Man), which was written in 1972 and was published in 1973. The other story is 'Yawm Mubārak 'alā Shāṭi' Umm Bāb' (A Blessed Day on Umm Bab's Shore), published in 1993. See Appendix A.

85. On interviews and research theses and dissertations, see, Appendices D, G. In addition, see Amyuni, Tayeb Salih's Season of Migration to the North, pp. 172–3. el-Badawī, *al-Ṭayyib Ṣāliḥ*, pp. 169, 175–6. Between 1976–2001 several books and special issues on al-Ṭayyib Ṣāliḥ and his literary works were published, as follows: Aḥmad Sa'īd Muḥammadiyya (ed.), *al-Ṭayyib Ṣāliḥ, 'Abqarī al-Riwaya al-'Arabiyya*, Beirut, Dār al-'Awda, 1976. Muḥammad Rushdī Ḥasan 'Alī, *al-Ibdā' al-Fannī fī Qiṣaṣ al-*

Ṭayyib Ṣāliḥ, Cairo, al-Ma'rifa, 1980. Fawziyya al-Ṣaffār, Azmat al-Ajyāl al-'Arabiyya al-Mu'āṣira, Dirāsa fī Riwāyat Mawsim al-Hijra ilā al-Shamāl, Tunisia, Mu'assasat 'Abd al-Karīm Ghallāb, 1980, 2nd ed. 1997. Yūsuf Nūr 'Awaḍ, *al-Ṭayyib Ṣāliḥ fī Manẓūr al-Naqd al-Bunyawī*, Jedda, Maktabat al-'Ilm, 1983. 'Abd al-Raḥmān al-Khānjī, *Qirā'a Jadīda fī Riwāyāt al-Ṭayyib Ṣāliḥ*, Omdurman, Jāmi'at Umm Durmān al-Islāmiyya li'l-Ṭibā'a wa'l-Nashr, 1983. Idem, Ru'yat al-Mawt wa-Dalālatuhā fī 'Ālam al-Ṭayyib Ṣāliḥ min Khilāl Riwāyatay Mawsim al-Hijra ilā al-Shamāl wa-Bandar Shāh, *Ḥawliyyāt Kulliyat al-Ādāb*, 15 (1995). Afnān al-Qāsim, Mawsim al-Hijra ilā al-Shamāl aw Wahm 'Alāqat al-Sharq wa'l-Gharb (*'Amaliyyat Naqd wa-Naqḍ li'l-Riwāya*), Casablanca, Mu'assasat bin Bishāra li'l-Ṭibā'a wa'l-Nashr, 1984. Mona Takieddin Amyuni (ed.), Tayeb Salih's Season of Migration to the North: A Casebook, Beirut, The American University of Beirut, 1985. Rajā' Ni'ma, Ṣirā' al-Maqhūr ma'a al-Sulṭa, Dirāsa fī al-Taḥlīl al-Nafsī li Riwāyat Mawsim al-Hijra ilā al-Shamāl, Beirut, 1986. Muḥammad Shāhīn, *Taḥawwulāt al-Shawq fī* Mawsim al-Hijra ilā al-Shamāl, Beirut, al-Mu'assasa al-'Arabiyya li'l-Dirāsāt wa'l-Nashr, 1993. Ami Elad-Bouskila and Ahmed Al-Shahi (eds), *Al-Ṭayyib Ṣāliḥ, Seventy Candles, Edebiyât*, 10:1 (1999). Aḥmad Muḥammad el-Badawī, *al-Ṭayyib Ṣāliḥ: Sīrat Kātib wa-Naṣṣ*, Cairo, al-Dār al-Thaqāfiyya li'l-Nashr, 2000. Ḥasan Abbashir al-Ṭayyib (ed.), *al-Ṭayyib Ṣāliḥ: Dirāsāt Naqdiyya*, Beirut, Riyāḍ al-Rayyis li'l-Kutub wa'l-Nashr, 2001.

86. Seven of the text books which were mentioned in the previous note deal in general with al-Ṭayyib Ṣāliḥ, while the other six books mentioned deal especially with *Mawsim al-Hijra ilā al-Shamāl*. This is also true of the articles, theses, dissertations and interviews.

87. al-Naqqāsh, ''Abqariyya Jadīda fī Samā' al-Riwāya al-'Arabiyya', *al-Muṣawwar* (February 2, 1968). Idem, 'al-Ṭayyib Ṣāliḥ 'Abqariyya Riwā'iyya Jadīda', in Muḥammadiyya (ed.), *al-Ṭayyib Ṣāliḥ*, pp. 78–100. Idem, *Udabā' Mu'āṣirun*, Cairo, Maktabat al-Anglū-al-Miṣriyya, 1968, p. 125. Ghāda al-Sammān, 'al-Ṭayyib Ṣāliḥ: Adīb Sayakhlud', in idem, *al-Jasad Ḥaqībat Safar*, Beirut, Manshūrāt Ghāda al-Sammān, 1979, p. 212. The literary critic Muḥammadiyya (1976) defines the title of the book that he edited as the name *'Abqarī al-Riwāya al-'Arabiyya* (The Genius of the Arabic Novel). 'Azmī Khālis, *Ḥikāyat al-Adab al-'Arabī al-Mu'āṣir*, Baghdad, Maṭba'at Shafīq, 1970, p. 152. Daf'allāh, *al-Lā Muntamī fī Adab al-Ṭayyib Ṣāliḥ*, p. 71. Furthermore, the Egyptian literary critic 'Abd al-Raḥmān Abū 'Awf did include the term *malḥama*, not only because of *Mawsim al-Hijra ilā al-Shamāl*, but all al-Ṭayyib Ṣāliḥ's novels which used the term *Malḥama Riwā'iyya* (novelist's epos). See 'Abd al-Raḥmān Abū 'Awf, 'al-Baḥth 'an Ṭarīq Jadīd li'l-Riwāya al-Miṣriyya wa'l-'Arabiyya al-Mu'āṣira', *al-Ādāb* (June 1980), p. 36. It is worth mentioning the harsh criticism of the Palestinian critic and author Afnān al-Qāsim (b.1938) on al-Ṭayyib Ṣāliḥ, *Mawsim al-Hijra ilā al-Shamāl* and the literary critics and their compliments about this novel. See al-Qāsim, *Mawsim al-Hijra ilā al-Shamāl*', pp. 45–8.

88. Jabrā, *al-Riḥla al-Thāmina*, p. 99.

89. Jibrīl, 'al-Ṭayyib Ṣāliḥ: Malāmiḥ min Sīra Dhātiyya (6)', *al-Ḥayāt*, p. 20. For a similar concept, see *Majallat al-Ḥayāt al-Thaqāfiyya al-Tūnisiyya*, 4:1 (1979), p. 42, as cited in 'Abd Allāh Ibrāhīm, 'Maghzā al-Mawt fī Adab al-Ṭayyib Ṣāliḥ al-Riwā'ī', *al-Ṭalī'a al-Adabiyya*, 2 (February 1980), p. 31, n. 5, p. 32, n. 2. Fāḍil, 'Ḥiwār Ākhar ma'a al-Ṭayyib Ṣāliḥ', in idem, *As'ilat al-Riwāya*, p. 38. Bilāl, 'Qirā'a Jadīda fī Riwāyat *Bandar Shāh-Ḍaw al-Bayt*', *Kitābāt Sūdāniyya*, p. 72. This is is also the appreciation of the Egyptian author and critic Idwār al-Kharrāt, 'The Mashriq', in Robin Ostle (ed.), *Modern Literature in the Near and Middle East 1850–1970*, London, Routledge, 1991, p. 192, and the Sudanese critic and translator Bilāl, 'Qirā'a Jadīda fī Riwāyat *Bandar Shāh-Ḍaw al-Bayt*', *Kitābāt Sūdāniyya*, p. 72. See also the interview that *al-Jazīra* held with al-Ṭayyib Ṣāliḥ (Appendix G).

90. Muḥammadiyya (ed.), *al-Ṭayyib Ṣāliḥ*, pp. 99–100, 215, 144–51. Ni'ma, *Ṣirā' al-Maqhūr ma'a al-Sulṭa*, 1986. Muhammad Siddiq, 'The Process of Individuation in al-Ṭayyib Ṣāliḥ's Novel *Season of Migration to the North*', *Journal of Arabic Literature*, IX (1978), pp. 67–104. Joseph John and Yosif Tarawneh, 'Quest of Identity: The Thou Imbroglio in Tayeb Salih's *Season of Migration to the*

North', *Arab Studies Quarterly*, 8:2 (Spring 1986), pp. 161–77. Yosif Tarawneh and Joseph John, 'Tayeb Salih and Freud: The Impact of Freudian Ideas on *Season of Migration to the North*', *Arabica*, 35 (1988), pp. 328–49.

91. Johnson-Davies, 'On Translating Arabic Literature', in Ghazoul and Harlow (eds), *The View From Within*, p. 228. Idem, 'The World of al-Tayeb Salih', *Azure*, p. 16. See also the interview with al-Ṭayyib Ṣāliḥ by Bashīr al-Qamarī, 'Hākadhā Ḥaddathanī al-Ṭayyib Ṣāliḥ', *Kitābāt Sūdāniyya*, pp. 66–7. Hānz-Bīter Kūnsh, 'al-Injlīzī al-Aswad 'alā Ḍifāf al-Nīl, *Mawsim al-Hijra ilā al-Shamāl* li'l-Ṭayyib Ṣāliḥ, Riwāya Klasīkiyya li Adab mā ba'd al-Kūlūnyāliyya Tuktashaf min Jadīd' (trans. Ḥāmid Faḍl Allāh and Amīr Ḥamd), *Kitābāt Sūdāniyya*, 8 (June 1999), p. 89. Here I want to point out that the Sudanese critic and author, Aḥmad el-Badawī, supported al-Ṭayyib Ṣāliḥ's treatment of sex in his novel *Mawsim al-Hijra ilā al-Shamāl* by stating that it is not exceptional with regard to accepted norms in the Arab/Muslim/Sudanese societies. Furthermore, el-Badawī holds that the issue of sex was treated in Arab classical poetry, in modern Arabic literature, as well as in modern African literatures and is discussed in Sudanese society. See el-Badawī, *Qirā'a Jadīda*, pp. 73–6.

92. Jibrīl, 'al-Ṭayyib Ṣāliḥ li'l-*Wasaṭ*', *al-Wasaṭ*, pp. 52–4. Adūnīs, 'Taḥiyya ilā Idwār Sa'īd wa'l-Ṭayyib Ṣāliḥ', *al-Ḥayāt*, 12246 (September 5, 1996), p. 16. 'Muntadā al-Ḥurriyyāt Yuṣdir Nidā'an 'Ālamiyyan li'l-Taḍāmun ma'a al-Ṭayyib Ṣāliḥ wa-Idānat Qarār al-Kharṭūm', *al-Ittiḥādī*, 220 (September 3, 1996), p. 1. Muḥammad Ḥarbī, 'al-Ṭayyib Ṣāliḥ fī Risāla Jāmi'iyya', *al-Ahrām* (October 4, 1996), p. 19. Usāma al-Khawwād, 'al-Ṭayyib Ṣāliḥ: Ārā' fī al-Siyāsa wa'l-Hujna al-Thaqāfiyya', *Kitābāt Sūdāniyya*, 8 (June 1999), pp. 82–3. el-Badawī, *al-Ṭayyib Ṣāliḥ*, pp. 83–5. After the scandal that occurred in the American University in Cairo, when Samia Mehrez was not allowed to teach the Moroccan author Muḥammad Shukrī's (1935–2003) novel *al-Khubz al-Ḥāfī* (1982) (For Bread Alone 1973), the immediate result of this scandal was the removal from the shelves of the AUC Bookstore of works which were considered damaging to public morals or injurious to good taste. In addition, the AUC seriously considered removing al-Ṭayyib Ṣāliḥ's novel *Season of Migration to the North* from its reading list for the following semester. See Internet of AUC's book banning blues updated: 2 February 1994. For details on the perception of Ḥasan al-Turābī see Mohamed Elhachmi Hamdi, *The Making of an Islamic Political Leader: Conversations with Hasan al-Turabi* (trans. Ashur A. Shamis), Boulder, Colorado, Westview Press, 1998.

93. Sasson Somekh, *Genre and Language in Modern Arabic Literature*, Wiesbaden, Otto Harrassowitz, 1991. Sāṭi' al-Ḥuṣrī, *Ārā' wa-Aḥādīth fī al-Lugha wa'l-Adab*, Beirut, Dār al-'Ilm li'l-Malā'īn, 1958. Nafūsa Zakariyya Sa'īd, *Ta'rīkh al-Da'wa ilā al-'Āmmiyya wa-Atharuhā fī Miṣr*, Cairo, Dār al-Ma'ārif, 1964. al-Sa'īd Muḥammad Badawī, *Mustawayāt al-'Arabiyya al-Mu'āṣira fī Miṣr*, Cairo, Dār al-Ma'ārif, 1973.

94. 'Ami El'ad[-Bouskila], *Shinuyei Girsa'ot BeSipurav HaKtzarim shel Maḥmūd Taymūr* (The Arabic Various Versions of Maḥmūd Taymūr's Short Stories), Jerusalem, 1981 (unpublished paper) (Hebrew). Matityahu Peled, *al-Uqṣūṣa al-Taymūriyya fī Marḥalatayn*, Tel Aviv, Jāmi'at Tel Aviv, Acre, Dār al-Nashr al-'Arabī, 1977. Somekh, *Genre and Language in Modern Arabic Literature*, pp. 93–107.

95. al-Ṭayyib Ṣāliḥ, 'Muqaddimāt', *al-Hilāl*, 9 (September 1969), pp. 34–9.

96. Ibid., 'Muqaddimāt', *Ḥiwār*, 21 (March-April 1966), pp. 36–40.

97. Ṣāliḥ, 'al-Shay' al-Ākhar', *Ḥiwār*, 21 (March-April 1966), pp. 37–8.

98. Ṣāliḥ, *'Urs al-Zayn*, *Ḥiwār*, 10 (May-June 1964), pp. 40–51.

99. Ibid., p. 40.

100. Ibid., *al-Kharṭūm*, 3 (December 1969), pp. 97–137.

101. On the opinion of al-Ṭayyib Ṣāliḥ about the current rulers in the Sudan, see his words as cited in Jibrīl, *'Alā al-Darb*, pp. 80–2. Idem, 'al-Ṭayyib Ṣāliḥ li'l-*Wasaṭ*', *al-Wasaṭ*, pp. 52–4.

102. Laylā Ba'labakkī, *Safīnat Ḥanān ilā al-Qamar, Qiṣaṣ Qaṣīra*, Beirut, al-Maktab al-Tijārī li'l-Ṭibā'a wa'l-Tawzī' wa'l-Nashr, 1964, pp. 5–26. Muṣṭafā 'Awaḍ Allāh Bishāra, *Aḍwā' al-Naqd, Dirāsāt fī al-Qiṣṣa wa'l-Shi'r wa'l-Naqd*, Khartoum, al-Dār al-Sūdāniyya li'l-Ṭibā'a wa'l-Nashr wa'l-Tawzī', 1977, pp. 90–6.
103. al-Ṭayyib Ṣāliḥ, 'al-Rajul al-Qubruṣī', *al-Thaqāfa al-'Arabiyya*, 2 (October 1973), pp. 88–91. *al-Dōḥa*, 2 (January 1976), pp. 105–8. *al-Ayyām*, 7723 (19 March 1976), p. 7. *al-Ayyām*'s version is exactly like *al-Dōḥa's*, while the version of Makkī (ed.), *al-Qiṣṣa al-Qaṣīra, Dirāsa wa-Mukhtārāt*, pp. 304–14, identical to *al-Thaqāfa al-'Arabiyya*.
104. Ṣāliḥ, *al-Dōḥa*, 2 (January 1976), p. 105.
105. Ibid., p. 108.
106. For more details see Berkley, *The Roots of Consciousness*, pp. 170–1. Ṣāliḥ, 'al-Rajul al-Qubruṣī', *al-Thaqāfa al-'Arabiyya*, p. 91; *al-Dōḥa*, p. 108.
107. Ṣāliḥ, *Bandar Shāh: Ḍaw al-Bayt*, p. 7. *al-Dōḥa*, 2 (January 1976), p. 105.
108. Ṣāliḥ, *Bandar Shāh: Maryūd*, 2nd ed., Dār al-'Awda, Beirut, 1978. *Bandar Shāh: Maryūd*, Tunisia, Dār al-Janūb li'l-Nashr, 1986. *Maryūd*, Chapter one, *al-Hilāl* (December 1976), pp. 63–9. Chapter two, *al-Hilāl* (January 1977), pp. 50–7. Chapter one, *al-Dōḥa*, 19 (July 1977), pp. 67–77. Chapter two, *al-Dōḥa*, 20 (August 1977), pp. 66–77. Chapter three, *al-Dōḥa*, 21 (September 1977), pp. 66–75. Chapter four, *al-Dōḥa*, 22 (October 1977), pp. 66–75. The four chapters were published in the Sudanese weekly *al-Shabāb*, 205–9 (June-July 1976), as cited in Nūr, 'al-Ṭayyib Ṣāliḥ', *al-Thaqāfa al-Sūdāniyya*, p. 125.
109. *al-Hilāl* (December 1976), p. 63.
110. Ṣāliḥ, *Bandar Shāh: Maryūd*, Tunisia, 1986, pp. 152–7. These pages include sixty-six footnotes that explain and clarify words, terms and names in colloquial Sudanese.

Notes to Chapter Two: Poetic Elements in al-Ṭayyib Ṣāliḥ's Works

1. On the relationship between literature and biography, see: René Wellek and Austin Warren, *Theory of Literature*, Harmondsworth, Penguin Books, 1982, pp. 75–80; Joseph T. Shipley, *Dictionary of World Literature*, Totowa, New Jersey, Littlefield and Adams, 1972, pp. 39–41; Jenny Stringer, (ed.), *The Oxford Companion to Twentieth Centrury Literature in English*, Oxford, Oxford University Press, 1996, pp. 66–7.
2. For a detailed discussion on various titles in world literature see Gérard Genette, *Seuils*, Paris, Seuil, 1987, pp. 54–97. Jean-Pierre Goldenstein, *Entrées en Literature*, Paris, Hachette, 1990, pp. 67–84. Vincet Jouve, *La Poétique du Roman*, Paris, Sedes, 1997, pp. 13–16, 121–2. Jonathan Culler, *Structuralist Poetic: Structuralism Linguistics and the Study of Literature*, London and Henley, Routledge and Kegan Paul, 1975, p. 211. In modern Arabic literatures, see Tetz Rooke, *In My Childhood: A Study of Arabic Autobiography*, Stockholm, Almqvist and Wiksell International, 1997, pp. 57–8.
3. There is a long discussion about what is canon and non-canon in world literature. See Harold Bloom, *The Western Canon, the Books and School of the Ages*, London, Macmillan, 1995.
4. Miguel de Cervantes, *Don Quixote* (trans. Barton Raffel), New York and London, W.W. Norton, 1995. Honoré de Balzac, *Père Goriot* (trans. Barton Raffel), New York and London, W.W. Norton, 1994 (1st ed. 1835). Thomas Hardy, *Tess of the D'Urbervilles, A Pure Woman*, Middlesex, Penguin Books, 1983 (1st ed. 1891). James Joyce, *Ulysses*, London, Everyman's Library, 1994 (1st ed. 1922).
5. Muḥammad Ḥusayn Haykal, *Zaynab, Manāẓir wa-Akhlāq Rīfiyya*, Cairo, Dār al-Ma'ārif, 1979 (1st ed.1914). For the English translation see *Zainab* (trans. John Mohammed Grinsted), London, Darf, 1989. Edwār al-Kharrāt, *Rāma wa'l-Tinnīn*, 2nd ed., Beirut, al-Mu'assasa al-'Arabiyya li'l-Dirāsāt wa'l-Nashr, 1980 (1st ed. 1979). For the English translation see *Rama and the Dragon* (trans. Ferial

Ghazoul and John Verlenden), Cairo, The American University in Cairo Press, 2002. Jabrā Ibrāhīm Jabrā, *al-Baḥth 'an Walīd Mas'ūd*, 2nd ed., Beirut, Dār al-Ādāb, 1981 (1st ed. 1978); Ḥannā Mīna, *Ma'sāt Dymītrīyū*, Beirut, Dār al-Ādāb, 1985; Dhū al-Nūn Ayyūb, *al-Duktūr Ibrāhīm*, Baghdad, Maṭba'at Umm al-Rib'iyyīn, 1939; al-Ṭayyib Ṣāliḥ, *Bandar Shāh: Maryūd*, 2nd ed., Beirut, Dār al-'Awda, 1978. For the English translation see *Bandarshah*, (trans. Denys Johnson-Davies), Kegan Paul International/UNESCO Publishing, 1996, pp. 81–122.

6. Muḥammad Taymūr, 'Fi al-Qiṭār', *al-Sufūr*, 107 (June 7, 1917), p. 3; Jabrā Ibrāhīm Jabrā, *al-Safīna*, 3rd ed., Beirut, Dār al-Ādāb, 1981 (1st ed. 1969). For the English translation, see *The Ship* (trans. Adnan Haydar and Roger Allen), Washington, D.C., Three Continents, 1985. Muḥammad 'Izz al-Dīn al-Tāzī, *Raḥīl al-Baḥr*, Beirut, al-Mu'assasa al-'Arabiyya li'l-Dirāsāt wa'l-Nashr, 1983; Najīb Maḥfūẓ, *Bayt Sayyi al-Sum'a*, Cairo, Maktabat Miṣr, n.d. (1st ed. 1965); 'Abd al-Ḥakīm Qāsim, *Qadar al-Ghuraf al-Muqbiḍa*, Cairo, Maṭbū'āt al-Qāhira, 1982; Sa'īd al-Kafrāwī, *Madīnat al-Mawt al-Jamīl*, Cairo, Dār Kutub Khāna li'l-Nashr wa'l-Tawzī', 1985; Najīb Maḥfūẓ, *al-Qāhira al-Jadīda*, Cairo, Maktabat Miṣr, n.d. (1st ed. 1946); Maḥmūd Ṭāhir Lāshīn, 'Ḥadīth al-Qarya', *al-Jadīd*, 32 (November 19, 1928), p. 225; Muḥammad Yūsuf al-Qa'īd, *Akhbār 'Izbat al-Manīsī*, Cairo, al-Hay'a al-Miṣriyya al-'Āmma li'l-Ta'līf wa'l-Nashr, 1971.

7. Emily Naṣrallāh, *Ṭuyūr Aylūl, Riwāya*, Beirut, Dār al-Makshūf, 1967 (1st ed. 1962). Najīb Maḥfūẓ, *Yawm Qutila al-Za'īm*, Cairo, Maktabat Miṣr, n.d. (1st ed. 1988). For the English translation, see *The Day the Leader was Killed* (trans. Malak Hashim), Cairo, General Egyptian Book Organization, 1989. Yūsuf Abū Rayya, *al-Ḍuḥā al-'Ālī*, Cairo, Dār Shuhdī li'l-Nashr wa'l-Tawzī', 1985; 'Abd al-Ḥakīm Qāsim, 'Layla Shatawiyya', Idem, *al-Ashwāq wa'l-Āsā*, Cairo, al-Hay'a al-Miṣriyya al-'Āmma li'l Kitāb, Mukhtārāt *Fuṣūl* 10, 1984, pp. 25–34; Sa'īd al-Kafrāwī, 'Kull Tilka al-Fuṣūl', *al-Karmil*, 26 (1987), pp. 137–41.

8. Sasson Somekh, 'Za'balāwī: Author, Theme and Technique', *Journal of Arabic Literature*, I (1970), pp. 24–35; Elad[-Bouskila], 'Mahfuz's 'Za'balāwī'', *International Journal of Middle East Studies*, pp. 631–44. On the meaning of the name 'Za'balāwī', see Muḥammad bin al-Zubayr, *Mu'jam Asmā' al-'Arab*, Beirut, Musqat, Maktabat Lubnān, Jāmi'at al-Sulṭān Qābūs, vol.1, 1991, p. 722.

9. Muṣṭafā al-Misnāwī, 'al-Ūṭūrūṭ', in idem, *Ṭāriq Alladhī Lam Yaftaḥ al-Andalus, Qiṣaṣ*, Beirut, al-Mu'assasa al-'Arabiyya li'l-Dirāsāt wa'l-Nashr, 1979, pp. 72–81.

10. al-Ṭayyib Ṣāliḥ, *Dawmat Wad Ḥāmid, Sab' Qiṣaṣ*, 3rd ed., Dār al-'Awda, 1970 (1st ed. 1967).

11. Ṣubḥī and al-Sham'a, 'al-Ṭayyib Ṣāliḥ Riwā'iyyan wa-Nāqidan', in Muḥammadiyya (ed.), *al-Ṭayyib Ṣāliḥ*, p. 122; Elad[-Bouskila], 'Fiction and Reality', in idem (ed.), *Writer, Culture, Text*, pp. 63–4.

12. Ṣāliḥ, *Dawmat Wad Ḥāmid*, pp. 7–18.

13. Jibrīl, 'al-Ṭayyib Ṣāliḥ: Malāmiḥ min Sīra Dhātiyya (6)', *al-Ḥayāt*, p. 20.

14. The palm tree is used in titles of works in modern Arabic literature as in the collection of stories by Tunisian author Ibrāhīm al-Daghūthī (b.1955), *al-Nakhl Yamūt Wāqifan*, Tunis, Ṣāmid li'l-Nashr wa'l-Tawzī', 1989. There are texts in which the name of a tree is used as a title, for example, the vine in the story by Palestinian-Israeli author Zakī Darwīsh (b.1944), 'al-Karma lā Tamūt'. We find a tree in the singular as a metaphor in Egyptian author Ṭāhā Ḥusayn, *Shajarat al-Bu's*, Cairo, Dār al-Ma'ārif, 1944; another in the plural as a metaphor in the Saudi author 'Abd al-Raḥmān Munīf's, *al-Ashjār wa-Ightiyāl Marzūq*, 5th ed., Beirut, al-Mu'assasa al-'Arabiyya li'l-Dirāsāt wa'l-Nashr, 1987 (1st ed. 1973).

15. Ṣāliḥ, 'Nakhla 'alā al-Jadwal', in idem, *Dawmat Wad Ḥāmid*, p. 18. 'Ḥafnat Tamr', in idem, *Dawmat Wad Ḥāmid*, pp. 22–4. Idem, 'Dawmat Wad Ḥāmid', in *Dawmat Wad Ḥāmid*, pp. 38–40, 44, 46.

16. Ṣāliḥ, *Dawmat Wad Ḥāmid*, pp. 19–25.

17. Ibid., pp. 26–32.

18. On Correspondence Literature (*al-Rasā'il*) see A. Arazi and H. Ben-Shammay, *Risāla, The Encyclopaedia of Islam*, New Edition, E.J. Brill, vol. VIII, 1995, pp. 532–9. In classical Arabic

literature see *Risālat al-Ghufrān* by Abū al-'Alā' al-Ma'arrī (973–1057). In modern Arabic literatures see the Palestinian poets Maḥmūd Darwīsh (b.1941) and Samīḥ al-Qāsim (b.1939), *al-Rasā'il*, Haifa, Dār 'Arabesk, 1989.

19. Ṣāliḥ, *Dawmat Wad Ḥāmid*, pp. 33–52.
20. Sviri, 'On Trees, Dreams, and Holy Men', in Elad-Bouskila and Al-Shahi (eds) *Al-Ṭayyib Ṣāliḥ, Edebiyât*, pp. 110–18. Fadwā Mālṭī-Dūglās, 'al-'Anāṣir al-Turāthiyya fī al-Adab al-'Arabī al-Mu'āṣir, al-Aḥlām fī Thalāth Qiṣaṣ', (trans. 'Iffat al-Sharqāwī), *Fuṣūl*, 2:2 (January-March 1982), pp. 21–9. Shāmī, 'Rā'iḥat al-Laban wa-Rā'iḥat al-Tamr', *Shi'r*, p. 90. In this context it is note worthy that the tree as a symbol and a central motif appears in additional Arabic works. A good example is the story by Egyptian author Yūsuf Idrīs, 'Sirruhu al-Bāti'', in idem, *Ḥādithat Sharaf*, 3rd ed., Cairo, Dār Miṣr, n.d. pp. 100–58 (1st ed. 1958). For further details see 'Ajūba, *al-Qiṣṣa al-Ḥadītha fī al-Sūdān*, pp. 220–1; Elad[-Bouskila], 'Fiction and Reality', in idem (ed.), *Writer, Culture, Text*, p. 73. Patricia Gessey, 'Culture Hybridity and Contamination in Tayeb Salih's *Mawsim al-Hijra ilā al-Shamāl* (Season of Migration to the North)', *Reasearch in African Literature*, 28 (Fall 1997), p. 128. On the legendary *al-tabaldī* tree (monkey bread) see Khalīl, 'Naẓarāt fī Sardiyyāt Ibrāhīm Isḥāq Ibrāhīm', *al-Kharṭūm*, p. 5.
21. Fernand Braudel has indicated in this context that every city (in our case we are dealing with a village), does have a real or mythical establisher, hero or holy character. See idem, *La Méditerranée: l'espace et l'histoire*, Paris, Flammarion, 1985, p. 147.
22. Ṣāliḥ, *Bandar Shāh: Maryūd*, pp. 56–7.
23. Ṣāliḥ, *Dawmat Wad Ḥāmid*, pp. 53–68.
24. Ibid., pp. 69–82.
25. An example of a similar title can be found in the book written by Palestinian intellectual Khalīl al-Sakākīnī (1878–1953), *Kadhā Anā Yā Dunyā, Yawmiyyāt Khalīl al-Sakākīnī*, Jerusalem, al-Maṭba'a al-Tijāriyya, 1955.
26. al-Ṭayyib Ṣāliḥ says that this story is a kind of sketch for *Mawsim al-Hijra ilā al-Shamāl*, see Jibrīl, *'Alā al-Darb*, p. 69.
27. Ṣāliḥ, *Dawmat Wad Ḥāmid*, pp. 83–93.
28. Ṣāliḥ, 'al-Rajul al-Qubruṣī' in Makkī (ed.), *al-Qiṣṣa al-Qṣīra*, pp. 367–79. For the English translation, see 'The Cypriot Man' (trans. Denys Johnson-Davies), *Azure*, 8 (1981), pp. 25–7.
29. These two works, particularly the second, contain a resolute (but indirect) reply to the scholars who speculated as to whether al-Ṭayyib Ṣāliḥ could write texts that would be unrelated to Wad Ḥāmid village, such as Yūsuf Nūr 'Awaḍ, *al-Ṭayyib Ṣāliḥ fī Manẓūr al-Naqd al-Bunyawī*, p. 206. In the collection *Dawmat Wad Ḥāmid*, there are short stories that are not related to the village: 'Idhā Jā'at', 'Hākadhā Yā Sādatī'.
30. The most notable example is that of the Egyptian author Fatḥī Ghānim (1924–99) in his tetralogy *al-Rajul Alladhī Faqada Ẓillahu*, Cairo, Kitāb *al-Jumhūriyya*, 1969 (1st ed. 1962). For details on Fatḥī Ghānim and his works, see Ami Elad[-Bouskila], 'Ideology and Structure in Fatḥī Ghānim's *al-Jabal*', *Journal of Arabic Literature*, XX, 2 (1989), pp. 168–86.
31. *Mukhtārāt min al-Qiṣaṣ al-Qaṣīra fī 18 Baladan 'Arabiyyan*, pp. 159–66.
32. On differences between this work and other texts by al-Ṭayyib Ṣāliḥ, and on difficulties in comprehending the story, see *Mukhtārāt min al-Qiṣaṣ al-Qaṣīra fī 18 Baladan 'Arabiyyan*, pp. 45–50. Ṭāriq al-Ṭayyib, 'al-Ightirāb 'inda al-Ṭayyib Ṣāliḥ', in Ḥasan Abbashir al-Ṭayyib (ed.), *al-Ṭayyib Ṣāliḥ*, pp. 277–80.
33. Jibrīl, *'Alā al-Darb*, pp. 64–7.
34. al-Ṭayyib Ṣāliḥ, *'Urs al-Zayn, Riwāya wa-Sab' Qiṣaṣ*, 3rd ed., Beirut, Dār al-'Awda, 1970 (1st ed. 1967). For the English translation see *The Wedding of Zein* (trans. Denys Johnson-Davies), London, Quartet Books, 1980.

35. ‘Awn al-Sharīf Qāsim, *Qāmūs al-Lahja al-‘Āmmiyya fī al-Sūdān*, pp. 514–15; Salām, *Dirāsāt fī al-Qiṣṣa al-‘Arabiyya al-Ḥadītha*, pp. 416, 424. There is a partially common meaning in the Sudanese colloquial between *al-Zayn* and *al-Ṭayyib*. See ‘Īsā al-Sa‘īd, ‘al-Ṭayyib Ṣāliḥ: Taftīt al-‘Ālam’, *al-Karmil*, p. 264. ‘Awn al-Sharīf Qāsim, *Qāmūs al-Lahja al-‘Āmmiyya fī al-Sūdān*, pp. 730–1.
36. Examples of titles of this kind can be found in the book by Algerian author al-Ṭāhir Waṭṭār, *‘Urs Baghl*, Algiers, al-Sharika al-Waṭaniyya li'l-Nashr wa'l Tawzī‘, 1982 (1st ed. 1978). See also Syrian author Adīb Naḥawī (b.1926), *‘Urs Filasṭīnī*, Beirut, Dār al-‘Awda, n.d. (1st ed. 1971).
37. al-Ṭayyib Ṣāliḥ, *Mawsim al-Hijra ilā Shamāl*, 2nd ed., Beirut, Dār al-‘Awda 1969 (1st ed. 1967). For the English translation see *Season of Migration to the North* (trans. Denys Johnson-Davies), London, Heinemann, 1978 (1st ed. 1969).
38. On the term ‘binary oppositions’ see Chris Baldick, *Oxford Concise Dictionary of Literary Terms*, Oxford and New York, Oxford University Press, 1996, p. 24. Culler, *Structuralist Poetics*, pp. 14–16, 75–95, 126–7, 177–8, 225–7.
39. For the term *mawsim*, see A. J. Wensink [C. E. Bosworth], *The Encyclopaedia of Islam*, New Edition, Leiden, E.J. Brill, vol. VI, 1991, p. 903; Edward William Lane, *An Arabic-English Lexicon*, Beirut, Librairie du Liban, vol. 8, 1968, p. 3054.
40. Mattityahu Peled, ‘Portrait of an Intellectual’, *Middle Eastern Studies*, XIII, 2 (1977), pp. 218–28.
41. Shāhīn, *Taḥawwulāt al-Shawq*, pp. 80–3.
42. al-Ṣaffār, *Azmat al-Ajyāl al-‘Arabiyya al-Mu‘āṣira*, p. 151.
43. For the term *hijra* see W. Montgomery Watt, *The Encyclopaedia of Islam*, New Edition, Leiden, E.J. Brill, vol. III, 1986, pp. 366–7; Lane, *An Arabic-English Lexicon*, vol. 8, 1968, pp. 2879–81. In *hijra* as in *riḥla* (travel, journey) we have one or several stops or stages. The stops or stages of Muṣṭafā Sa‘īd and the narrator are connected with *marḥala* (pl. *marāḥil*) which means not only stage (or stages) but also a long journey in his protracted travel. For this perception see also Aḥmad al-Zu‘bī, *Fī al-Īqā‘ al-Riwā'ī*, Beirut, Dār al-Manā'il, 1995 pp. 73–90.
44. This phenomenon of the Sudanese migration to al-Jazīra and other places, especially for economic reasons, is reflected not only in research books and articles but also in fictional work. al-Ṭayyib Ṣāliḥ himself, in his short story ‘Nakhla ‘alā al-Jadwal’, describes how Maḥjūb was yearning for his daughter Āmina who was married to his nephew, who had taken her to al-Jazīra, while his son, Ḥasan had left their village for Egypt five years ago. Ṣāliḥ, ‘Nakhla ‘alā al-Jadwal’ in idem, *Dawmat Wad Ḥāmid*, pp. 11–12.
45. On this subject, see the statement by al-Ṭayyib Ṣāliḥ and Ṭalḥat Jibrīl, *‘Alā al-Darb*, pp. 24–6, 31–2. On internal migration seasons in the Sudan, see ‘Abd al-‘Azīz Kāmil, *Dirāsāt fī al-Jughrāfiya al-Bashariyya li'l-Sūdān*, Cairo, Dār al-Ma‘ārif, 1972, pp. 71–5. On the migration of Sudanese intellectuals in search of knowledge, see al-Sāmarrā‘ī, ‘Muqābala Adabiyya ma‘a al-Ṭayyib Ṣāliḥ’, *al-Ādāb*, p. 4. For the connection between migration (*hijra*) and travel (*riḥla*) as a traditional Arabic phenomenon, including the Sudanese one, see Ḥasan al-Mūdin, ‘Lā Wā‘ī al-Naṣṣ fī Riwāyāt al-Ṭayyib Ṣāliḥ’, *Faḍā'āt Mustaqbaliyya*, 2–3 (March 1996), pp. 56–7. For more details on the Sudanese Mahdi's *hijra* to Qadīr see P.M Holt, *The Mahdist State in the Sudan, 1881–1898*, Oxford, Oxford University Press, 1958, pp. 47–50.
46. For a similar concept see Manṣūr Qaysūma, ‘al-Riwāya al-‘Arabiyya wa-Thunā'iyyat al-Naṣṣ al-Muta‘addid *Mawsim al-Hijra ilā al-Shamāl Namūdhajan*’, in idem, *al-Riwāya al'Arabiyya al-Ishkāl wa'l-Tashakkul*, Tunis, Dār Saḥar li'l-Nashr, 1995, pp. 157–8.
47. al-Ṭayyib Ṣāliḥ notes that in the long term, the Arab must migrate into himself as such a migration will reveal to him the fountainhead of his culture and will thus enable him to create a world with its special components, a world that will allow him to belong to it. al-Ẓāhir, ‘Ḥiwār ma‘a al-Ṭayyib Ṣāliḥ’, *al-Aqlām*, p. 150.

48. A novel of this kind is a *Bildungsroman,* as is, for example in Western literature: *A Portrait of the Artist as a Young Man* (1916), by James Joyce. On this term, see Baldick (ed.), *Oxford Concise Dictionary of Literary Terms*, p. 24. In modern Arabic literatures, there is the novel *Ayyām al-Insān al-Sab'a* by 'Abd al-Ḥakīm Qāsim. On the *Bildungsroman* and autobiographical writing connected to the journey in Modern Arabic literatures, see Nedal Al-Mousa, 'The Arabic Bildungsroman: A Generic Appraisal', *International Journal of Middle East Studies*, 25 (1993), pp. 223–40. Robin Ostle, Ed de Moor and Stefan Wild (eds), *Writing the Self, Autobiographical Writing in Modern Arabic Literature*, London, Saqi Books, 1998. Tetz Rooke, *In My Childhood: A Study of Arabic Autobiography*, Stockholm, Almquist Wiksell International, Stockholm University, 1992. Muhammed Khalafalla 'Abdalla, 'Muṣṭafā's Migration from the Ṣa'īd: An Odyssey in Search of Identity', in Elad-Bouskila and Al-Shahi (eds), *Al-Ṭayyib Ṣāliḥ, Edebiyât*, pp. 43–61.
49. Ṣāliḥ, *Mawsim al-Hijra ilā al-Shamāl*, p. 170.
50. For further details on this concept, see the literary critic Jūrj Ṭarābīshī, *Sharq wa-Gharb, Rujūla wa-Unūtha, Dirāsa fī Azmat al-Jins wa'l-Ḥaḍāra fī al-Riwāya al-'Arabiyya*, 2nd ed., Beirut, Dār al-Ṭalī'a, 1979, pp. 142–4.
51. A partially similar concept may be found in Barbara Harlow, 'Othello's Season of Migration', *Edebiyât*, 4 (1979), pp. 162–3, 172.
52. Francis Joseph Steingass, *A Comprehensive Persian-English Dictionary*, London, Kegan Paul, Trench, Trubner, 1930, pp. 202, 762. Ibn Manẓūr, *Lisān al-'Arab*, Cairo, al-Mu'assasa al-Miṣriyya al-'Āmma li'l Ta'līf wa'l-Anbā' wa'l-Nashr, n.d., vol. 8, p. 147. 'Awn al-Sharīf Qāsim, *Qāmūs al-Lahja al-'Āmmiyya fī al-Sūdān*, p. 130.
53. Muḥammadiyya (ed.), *al-Ṭayyib Ṣāliḥ*, p. 220. It is interesting to note that in another place he expands and changes this point: '*Bandar* hints at "city" and *Shāh* at "sovereign", and this novel might therefore have been entitled "The Sovereign and the City" as this is an expression for a mould into which I have tried to cast the entire story'. Jibrīl, 'al-Ṭayyib Ṣāliḥ: Malāmiḥ min Sīra Dhātiyya' (6), *al-Ḥayāt*, p. 20. In addition, the title and the sub-title indicate the connections not only between the present on the one hand and the future on the other, and between the father and the grandfather and grandchild, but also between the rulers of Wad Ḥāmid village and the other characters. In other words, the changes in Wad Ḥāmid are connected with modernity and the differences between generations and classes. For this perception see Muḥammad 'Abd al-Khāliq Bakrī, 'Shabaḥ al-Mu'allif Yatajawwal ḥawla al-Ma'nā, Qaḍiyyat al-Sulṭa wa'l-Madīna fī *Bandar Shāh', Kitābāt Sūdāniyya*, 8 (June 1999), pp. 43–57.
54. Muḥammadiyya (ed.), *al-Ṭayyib Ṣāliḥ*, p. 220. According to the Lebanese literary critic Mona Takieddine Amyuni, the search is for a good ruler and city. See idem, 'Literary Creativity and Social Change: What has happened to the Arab Psyche since the Sixties? A Study in a New Literary Masks', in Kamal Abdel-Malek and Wael Hallaq (eds), *Tradition, Modernity and Post Modernity in Arabic Literature*, Leiden, E.J. Brill, 2000, p. 101.
55. Muḥammadiyya (ed.), *al-Ṭayyib Ṣāliḥ*, p. 220.
56. For a more detailed discussion of this type of period novel in the context of *Bandar Shāh: Ḍaw al-Bayt*, see Yūsuf Nūr 'Awaḍ, *al-Ṭayyib Ṣāliḥ fī Manẓūr al-Naqd al-Bunyawī*, pp. 182–3, 195.
57. On the relationship, not only in the Biblical and Koranic stories of Joseph and his brothers, but rather in *Joseph and his Brothers*, by Thomas Mann, see Wielandt, 'The Problem of Cultural Identity', in al-Qadi (ed.), *Studia Arabica and Islamica*, 512–14.
58. Egyptian author Ṭāhā Ḥusayn, *Ḥadīth al-Arbi'ā'*, 12th ed., Cairo, Dār al-Ma'ārif, 1965. Egyptian author Suhayr al-Qalamāwī (1911–97), *Aḥādīth Jaddatī*, Cairo, Maṭba'at Lajnat al-Ta'līf wa'l-Tarjama wa'l-Nashr, 1935.
59. For a similar perception see the Sudanese critic Daf'allāh, *al-Lā Muntamī fī Adab al-Ṭayyib Ṣāliḥ*, pp. 80–1. Mūdin, 'Lā Wa'y al-Naṣṣ', *Faḍā'āt Mustaqbaliyya*, pp. 57–8.

60. Muḥammadiyya (ed.), *al-Ṭayyib Ṣāliḥ*, p. 220. For references to the meaning of the name Maryūd, see 'Awn al-Sharīf Qāsim, *Qāmūs al-Lahja al-'Āmmiyya fī al-Sūdān*, p. 482. al-Ṭayyib Ṣāliḥ, *Maryūd*, first Chapter, *al-Hilāl* (December 1976), p. 63. According to the Sudanese literary critic Khālid Mūsa Daf'allāh, the word is *al-rīda* which means 'love'. See Daf'allāh, *al-Lā Muntamī fī Adab al-Ṭayyib Ṣāliḥ*, p. 80. The title 'beloved' exists in some novels in world literature. See for example Toni Morrison (b.1931) *Beloved*, 1987.
61. Muḥammadiyya (ed.), *al-Ṭayyib Ṣāliḥ*, p. 220.
62. The Lebanese poet and critic 'Iṣām Maḥfūẓ (b.1939) says in this context: 'al-Ṭayyib [Ṣāliḥ] told me in a conversation that took place a long time ago that the new culture is temporary, despite its stable appearance'. See 'Iṣām Maḥfūẓ, *al-Riwāya al-'Arabiyya al-Ṭalī'iya wa'l-Shāhida*, Beirut, Dār Ibn Rushd, 1982, p. 78.
63. For more details on various dedications in world literatures see Genette, *Seuils*, pp. 110–33.
64. We find notable examples of this usage by the Moroccan author Muṣṭafā al-Misnāwī's story 'al-Ūṭūrūṭ', see idem, *Ṭāriq Alladhī Lam Yaftaḥ al-Andalus*, pp. 72–81. See also Egyptian author al-Qa'īd in his novel *Yaḥduth fī Miṣr al-Ān*. Palestinian author Emīl Ḥabībī in his novel *al-Waqā'i' al-Gharība fī Ikhtifā' Sa'īd Abī al-Naḥs al-Mutashā'il*, 3rd ed., Jerusalem, Manshūrāt Ṣalāḥ al-Dīn, 1977 (1st ed. 1974), for the English translation, see *The Secret Life of Saeed, the Ill-Fated Pessoptimist* (trans. Salma Khadra Jayyusi and Trevor Le Gassick), New York, Vantage Press, 1982.
65. Jibrīl, *'Alā al-Darb*, pp. 87, 97–8. el-Badawī, *al-Ṭayyib Ṣāliḥ*, pp. 12, 21.
66. The full names of his parents and siblings are: his father, who died close to the writing of *Bandar Shāh: Maryūd*, Muḥammad Ṣāliḥ Aḥmad; his mother: 'Ā'isha Aḥmad Zakariyyā, who died in 1988; his brother, Basīhr Muḥammad Ṣāliḥ; his sister married Tāj al-Sirr Muḥammad Nūr. See, Jibrīl, *'Alā al-Darb*, pp. 21, 30, 94–6; Ṣāliḥ, *Bandar Shāh: Maryūd*, p. 5.
67. el-Badawī, *Qirā'a Jadīda*, p. 65. al-Khānjī, *Qirā'a Jadīda fī Riwāyāt al-Ṭayyib Ṣāliḥ*, pp. 72–3.
68. For details on al-Faytūrī and his works, see *Mu'jam al-Bābaṭīn li'l-Shu'arā' al-'Arab al-Mu'aṣirīn*, Kuwait, Dār al-Qabas li'l-Ṣiḥāfa wa'l-Ṭibā'a wa'l-Nashr, vol. 3, 1995, pp. 272–3. Robert B. Kambel, *A'lām al-Adab al-'Arabī al-Mu'aṣir, Siyar wa-Siyar Dhātiyya*, Beirut, al-Ma'had al-Almānī li'l-Abḥāth al-Sharqiyya, 1996, vol. 2, pp. 1070–4.
69. al-Ṭayyib Ṣāliḥ does not quote accurately the verse taken from Abū Nuwās. See the Egyptian critic Muḥammad Rushdī Ḥasan 'Alī, *al-Ibdā' al-Fannī*, p. 68, n. 1.
70. I wholeheartedly concur with Yūsuf Nūr 'Awaḍ (*al-Ṭayyib Ṣāliḥ fī Manẓūr al-Naqd al-Bunyawī*, pp. 196–8) who argues that in the novel *Maryūd*, there is a philosophical stratum in the literary works of al-Ṭayyib Ṣāliḥ, and hence the use made of quotations from Abū Nuwās and *Kalīla wa-Dimna*. But at the same time I disagree with him. It should be made clear that the earlier works indeed contain philosophical strata for this is one of the most important components in both al-Ṭayyib Ṣāliḥ's stories and novels. On the philosophical and mythological aspects, see also Egyptian critic Rajā' al-Naqqāsh, 'Qaṣīda fī al-'Ishq wa'l-Maḥabba', in al-Ṭayyib Ṣāliḥ, *Bandar Shāh: Maryūd*, Tunis, 1986, pp. 9–10. See also specific statements made by the author in this context, Jibrīl, *'Alā al-Darb*, p. 121.
71. 'Abd Allāh b. al-Muqaffa', *Kalīla wa-Dimna*, 2nd ed., Beirut, Dār al-Āfāq al-Jadīda, 1979. For the English translation, see Jill Sanchia Cowen, *Kalila wa Dimna, An Animal Allegory of the Mongol Court*, New York, Oxford University Press, 1989.
72. For more details on Ḥabībī's works see Ami Elad-Bouskila, *Modern Palestinian Literature and Culture*, London and Portland, Frank Cass, 1999, pp. 23–7, 38–9. Maḥmūd Ghanā'im, *Fī Mabnā al-Naṣṣ, Dirāsa fī Riwāyat Emīl Ḥabībī* al-Waqā'i' al-Gharība fī Ikhtifā' Sa'īd Abī al-Naḥs al-Mutashā'il, Jatt, Manshūrāt al-Yasār, 1987.
73. It is noteworthy that the real author explains his choice of this paragraph from *Kalīla wa-Dimna*, by refering to two worlds: the first is the world of the rulers and the other is the world of love and lovers. See 'Īsā al-Sa'īd, 'al-Ṭayyib Ṣāliḥ', *al-Karmil*, pp. 263–4. According to the literary critic Muḥammad

'Abd al-Khāliq Bakrī, al-Ṭayyib Ṣāliḥ prefered to use these parts of *Kalīla wa-Dimna* to open various options of interpretations. See idem, ''Ibr Majrā al-Ta'rīkh fī Wad Ḥāmid al-Muthqala: Baḥth fī Shajarat Ansāb Shakhsiyyāt al-'Ālam al-Riwā'ī', *al-Kharṭūm*, 1796 (9 May 1998), p. 6.

74. Johnson-Davies, 'Profile: The World of Tayeb Salih', *Azure*, p. 20.
75. For more details on the expositions in Arabic literature see Qaysūma, 'al-'Awda ilā al-Fātiḥa al-Ḥikā'iyya' in idem, *al-Riwāya al-Arabiyya*, pp. 104–6. For a detailed discussion on this issue see my article: 'The Expositions in al-Ṭayyib Ṣāliḥ's Writing', in Elad-Bouskila and Al-Shahi (eds), *Al-Ṭayyib Ṣāliḥ, Edebiyât*, pp. 85–103.
76. For a detailed discussion of this novel and other works by al-Qa'īd, see Elad[-Bouskila], *The Village Novel*, pp. 113–44. Māltī-Dūglās, 'Yūsuf al-Qa'īd wa'l-Riwāya al-Jadīda', *Fuṣūl*, pp. 190–202.
77. Muḥammad Yūsuf al-Qa'īd, *Fī al-Usbū' Sab'at Ayyām*, Cairo, al-Hay'a al-Miṣriyya al-'Āmma li'l-Kitāb, 1975, pp. 5–16.
78. Muḥammad Mustajāb, *Min al-Ta'rīkh al-Sirrī li Nu'mān 'Abd al-Ḥāfiẓ*, Cairo, Maktabat al-Munīl, 1982. For a detailed discussion of this novel, see Fadwā Māltī-Dūglās, '*Min al-Ta'rīkh al-Sirrī li Nu'mān 'Abd al-Ḥāfiẓ* wa-Tadmīr Ṭuqūs al-Ḥayāt wa'l-Lugha', *Ibdā'*, 6 (June-July 1983), pp. 86–92; Muḥammad Barrāda, *La'bat al-Nisyān*, 3rd ed., Rabat, Dār al-Amān li'l-Nashr wa'l-Tawzī', 1995 (1st ed. 1987); al-Misnāwī, 'al-Ūṭūrūṭ', in idem, *Ṭāriq Alladhī Lam Yaftaḥ al-Andalus*, pp. 72–81.
79. On the term *Tawakkul*, see L. Lewisohn, *The Encyclopaedia of Islam*, New Edition, E.J. Brill, vol. X, 2000, pp. 376–8; Annemarie Schimmel, *Mystical Dimensions of Islam*, Chapel Hill, The University of North Carolina Press, 1995, pp. 117–20.
80. For the term *al-Faraj ba'd al-Shidda* see Ch. Pellat, *The Encyclopaedia of Islam*, E.J. Brill, vol. VII, 1993, p. 857. al-Ṭayyib Ṣāliḥ uses *al-Faraj ba'd al-Shidda* in some of his literary works such as 'Dawmat Wad Ḥāmid'. See Elad [-Bouskila], 'Fiction and Reality', in idem, *Writer, Culture, Text*, p. 69. Sviri, 'On Trees, Dreams and Holy Men', in Elad-Bouskila and Al-Shahi (eds), *Al-Ṭayyib Ṣāliḥ, Edebiyât*, pp. 112–13.
81. Najīb Maḥfūẓ, 'Za'balāwī', *Dunyā Allāh*, Cairo, Maktabat Miṣr, n.d. (1st ed. 1963), pp. 135–50. For the English translation, see *God's World* (trans. Akef Abadir and Roger Allen), Minneapolis: Bibliotheca Islamica, 1973.
82. There are indeed some critics who noted these words not only as key words but as the pivot of the entire story. See Yūsuf Nūr 'Awaḍ, *al-Ṭayyib Ṣāliḥ fī Manẓūr al-Naqd al-Bunyawī*, pp. 121–5. Muḥammad Rushdī Ḥasan 'Alī, *al-Ibdā' al-Fannī*, pp. 12–13. Daf'allāh, *al-Lā Muntamī fī Adab al-Ṭayyib Ṣāliḥ*, pp. 62–3.
83. A less successful attempt at using a child to relate village events was made in the novel *al-Arḍ* (The Earth, 1954) by the Egyptian author 'Abd al-Raḥmān al-Sharqāwī. 'Abd al-Raḥmān al-Sharqāwī, *al-Arḍ*, 3rd ed., Cairo, Dār al-Kātib li'l Ṭibā'a wa'l-Nashr, 1968 (1st ed. 1954). For the English translation, see *Egyptian Earth* (trans. Desmond Stewart), Delhi, Hind Pocket Books, 1972 (1st ed. 1962).
84. In another place in this story the author uses the same phrase *aghlab al-ẓann* which means 'it is very likely', when the old storyteller tells the young listener the story of the doum tree of Wad Ḥāmid, that no one knew who had planted this particular doum and when. In so doing he could conclude that 'it is very likely (*aghlab al-ẓann*) nobody planted it' (*Dawmat Wad Ḥāmid*, p. 38). For the same meaning of this phrase see also 'Idhā Jā'at' in idem, *Dawmat Wad Ḥāmid*, p. 57.
85. *The Book of a Thousand Nights and a Night* (trans. Richard F. Burton), London, H.S. Nichols, 1897.
86. al-Ṭayyib Ṣāliḥ, 'al-Shay' al-Ākhar', *Ḥiwār*, 21 (March-April 1966), pp. 37–8.
87. al-Ṭayyib Ṣāliḥ, 'al-Rajul al-Qubruṣī', in Makkī (ed.), *al-Qiṣṣa al-Qaṣīra, Dirāsa wa-'Mukhtārāt*, p. 367
88. Ṣāliḥ, 'Yawm Mubārak 'alā Shāṭi' Umm Bāb', in *Mukhtārāt min al-Qiṣaṣ al-Qaṣīra fī 18 Baladan 'Arabiyyan*, p. 159

89. Āmina is the name of the author's maternal aunt who died a short time before his mother. See Jibrīl, *'Alā al-Darb*, p. 95.
90. Ṣāliḥ, *'Urs al-Zayn*, pp. 5–9.
91. Sudanese literary critic 'Alī 'Abd Allāh 'Abbās notes al-Ṭayyib Ṣāliḥ's impressive exposition in this novel and discusses the cinematic technique employed by the real author. According to him, the roaming camera enables the author to move from scene to scene and delineate the characters, the plot, the events and the place. See 'Notes on Tayeb Salih's *Season of Migration to the North* and *The Wedding of Zein*', *Sudan Notes and Records*, LV (1974), pp. 54–5. The literary critic Muḥammad Ḥasan 'Abd Allāh adds to the use of the cinematic technique the option of the television drama technique and stresses the flashback as a typical means of this exposition, see Muḥammad Ḥasan 'Abd Allāh, *'al-Rīf al-Sūdanī, Ṣuwar Khāṣṣa'*, in idem, *al-Rīf fī al-Riwāya al-'Arabiyya*, Kuwait, al-Majlis al-Waṭanī li'l-Thaqāfa wa'l-Funūn wa'l-Ādāb, Silsilat 'Ālam al-Ma'rifa, 1989, p. 305.
92. Another Sudanese author, Ibrāhīm Isḥāq Ibrāhīm, in his novel *Ḥadath fī al-Qarya* (1969), bases the novel's plot on an extraordinary event: the appearance of a crocodile in a local wadi. This news excites the inhabitants of the village and changes their way of life during that period.
93. Popular legends mention people who are extraordinary from the time of their birth. See Nājī Najīb, 'al-Huwiyya al-Dhātiyya fī al-Mujtama' al-Taqlīdī wa-Bu'd al-Hijra ilā al-Shamāl', *Fikr wa-Funūn*, 38 (1983), p. 64. An interesting example is the birth of Baykās in the novel *Fuqahā' al-Ẓalām* (1985) by the Syrian author and poet Salīm Barakāt (b.1951).
94. Ṣāliḥ, *Mawsim al-Hijra ilā al-Shamāl*, pp. 5–6. Similarly, it is interesting to compare the condensed exposition of the entire book with James Joyce's novel, *Portrait of the Artist as a Young Man*. See also the exposition of Emily Brontë, *Wuthering Heights* (1847). For the latter comparison see Muḥammad Shāhīn, *al-Adab wa'l-Usṭūra*, Beirut, al-Mu'assasa al-'Arabiyya li'l-Dirāsāt wa'l-Nashr, 1996, p. 111.
95. For the *ḥakawātī* interpretation with regard to the exposition see Saree S. Makdisi, 'The Empire Renarrated: *Season of Migration to the North*', *Critical Inquiry*, 18 (Summer 1992), pp. 814–15. el-Badawī, *al-Ṭayyib Ṣāliḥ*, p. 100.
96. For this concept see the Tunisian critic Manṣūr Qaysūma, '*Mawsim al-Hijra ilā al-Shamāl* al-Kidhb al-Ḥaqīqa', in idem, *al-Anā wa'l-Ākhar*, pp. 110–16. al-Mūdin, 'Lā Wa'y al-Naṣṣ', *Faḍā'āt Mustaqbaliyya*, pp. 56–7.
97. Note the similarity, which might not be coincidental, and the verse 'Wa-ayna al-Tamāsīḥ min Lamḥa, Yamūt min al-Bard Ḥītānūhā', from the noted Egyptian poet Aḥmad Shawqī, as cited by el-Badawī, *Qirā'a Jadīda*, p. 70, n. 18.
98. Jibrīl, 'al-Ṭayyib Ṣāliḥ: Malāmiḥ min Sīra Dhātiyya (3)', *al-Ḥayāt*, p. 16.
99. Ṣāliḥ, *Bandar Shāh: Ḍaw al-Bayt*, pp. 9–10.
100. On the struggle between the different generations in this novel, see the literary critic Khālida Sa'īd, 'al-Riwāya al-'Arabiyya bayn 1920–72', *Mawāqif* (Summer 1974), p. 84.
101. Ṣāliḥ, *Bandar Shāh: Maryūd*, pp. 13–14.
102. Idem, *Maryud*, first Chapter, *al-Hilāl* (December 1976), pp. 63–9. Second Chapter, *al-Hilāl* (December 1976), pp. 50–7. *Maryūd*, first Chapter, *al-Dōḥa*, 19 (July 1977), pp. 67–77. Second Chapter, *al-Dōḥa*, 20 (August 1977), pp. 66–77. Third Chapter, *al-Dōḥa*, 21 (September 1977), pp. 66–75. Fourth Chapter, *al-Dōḥa*, 22 (October 1977), pp. 66–77.
103. For a detailed discussion on endings in modern literature see Guy Larroux, *Le Mot de la fin: la clôture romanesque en question*, Paris, Nathan, 1995. Ann Amherst and Katherine Astbury (eds), *Endings*, Exeter, Elm Bank Publications, 1999. For a detailed discussion on endings in Modern Arabic Literature and especially in Najīb Maḥfūẓ's novels see Mahmud Ghanayim, 'Characters Narrate their own Tragic Ends: a Study of Endings of Five Novels by Najīb Maḥfūẓ', *Arabic and Middle Eastern Literature*, 2:2 (July 1999), pp. 177–88.

104. On the status of the reader and the critic regarding al-Ṭayyib Ṣāliḥ's texts, see the statement by the author as cited by Sudanese literary critic Ibrāhīm al-Shūsh, *Adab wa-Udabā'*, Khartoum, Jāmi'at al-Kharṭūm, Dār al-Ta'līf wa'l-Tarjama wa'l-Nashr, 1973, p. 45.
105. *Mukhtārāt min al-Qiṣaṣ al-Qaṣīra fī 18 Baladan 'Arabiyyan*, pp. 45–50.
106. Afnān al-Qāsim feels that the narrator did not truly choose life. According to him, the narrator, in contrast to Muṣṭafā Sa'īd, did not want to disappear or drown in the river, He did not choose life in the sense of an overall human struggle, but if there was a choice here at all, he would choose the life of a petit bourgeois. The choice of life was derived from a fear of death and the desire to hold on to the life chosen for him. See al-Qāsim, *Mawsim al-Hijra ilā al-Shamāl*, pp. 44–5.
107. Ṣāliḥ, *Mawsim al-Hijra ilā al-Shamāl*, pp. 170–1. Ṣāliḥ, *Season of Migration to the North*, p. 169. The same words, i.e., 'Help! Help!' appeared at the end of Chapter Five of Joseph Conrad's (1857–1924) *Lord Jim* (1900), Ware, Wordsworth Classics, 1993, p. 34.
108. In the course of this study, I frequently discuss the dialogue between author and reader, with the mediation of the narrator. In this novel, the reader plays a very important role as the author involves him from the opening sentence on. He does not allow him to sink back into his own tranquil world. Therefore, the ending of the novel shocks him and obliges him to be an active critic who interprets the text. On this concept especially ital., see Peter Nazareth, 'The Narrator as Artist and the Reader as Critic in *Season of Migration to the North*', in Amyuni (ed.), Tayeb Salih's Season of Migration to the North, pp. 123–4. Sāmī Suwīdān, 'Min Dalālat al-Ma'nā fī *Mawsim al-Hijra ilā al-Shamāl*', in idem, *Abḥāth fī al-Naṣṣ al-Riwā'ī al-'Arabī*, Beirut, Mu'assasat al-Abḥāth al-'Arabiyya, 1986, p. 129.
109. Peled, 'Portrait of an Intellectual', *Middle Eastern Studies*, p. 228. Siddiq, 'The Process of Individuation', *Journal of Arabic Literature*, pp. 103–4.
110. Arieh Sachs, *The Essence of the Theatre*, Tel Aviv, Ministry of Defence Publications, Broadcast University (1989), p. 10 (Hebrew). Christopher S. Nassar indicates that 'This sentence connects the narrator with Beckett's clownlike characters in *Waiting for Godot*, who spent much of Act 2 on the stage floor shouting for help and waiting despairingly for salvation that will never come'. See Nassar, 'Beckett's *Waiting for Godot* and Salih's *Season of Migration to the North*', *The Explicator*, 56 (Winter 1998), p. 105.
111. Joseph Conrad, *Heart of Darkness*, London, Everyman's Library, 1993, pp. 98, 105, 109. (1st ed. 1902). For a detailed discussion of the words 'The Horror! The Horror', and their various interpretations see Carola M. Kaplan, 'Colonizers, Cannibals, and the Horror of Good Intentions in Joseph Conrad's *Heart of Darkness*', *Studies in Short Fiction*, 34:3 (Summer 1997), pp. 331–2. James Ellis, 'Kurtz's Voice: The Intended as "The Horror", *English Literature in Transition 1880–1920*', 19 (1976), pp. 105–10.
112. For different interpretations of the ending of the novel, see Peled, 'Portrait of a Sudanese Intellectual', p. 223; Tawfīq Bakkār, 'al-Thābit wa'l-Mutaḥawwil', in al-Ṭayyib Ṣāliḥ, *Mawsim al-Hijra ilā al-Shamāl*, Tunis, Dār al-Janūb li'l-Nashr, 1992, p. 9; Sīzā Qāsim, 'Tajriba Naqdiyya: *Mawsim al-Hijra ilā al-Shamāl*', *Fuṣūl*, p. 227; 'Iṣām Bahī, 'Aydiyūlūjīyyā al-Muṣālaḥa fī *Qindīl Umm Hāshim* wa-*Mawsim al-Hijra ilā al-Shamāl*', *Fuṣūl*, 5:4 (July-September 1985), p. 196; Siddiq, 'The Process of Individuation', *Journal of Arabic Literature*, pp. 103–4; Berkley, *The Roots of Consciousness*, pp. 273–4. Nassar, 'Beckett's *Waiting for Godot* and Salih's *Season of Migration to the North*', *The Explicator*, pp. 105–7. Amyuni, 'Literary Creativity and Social Change', in Abdel-Malek and Hallaq (eds), *Tradition, Modernity and Post Modernity in Arabic Literature*, p. 101.
113. It is interesting that some literary critics view the two books of *Bandar Shāh* (*Ḍaw al-Bayt, Maryūd*) together with the novel '*Urs al-Zayn*, as a trilogy. It may be assumed that the reasons for this are related to the characters, events, time, place and space. See Afnān al-Qāsim, Mawsim al-Hijra ilā al-Shamāl, p. 1.
114. Ṣāliḥ, *Bandar Shāh: Ḍaw al-Bayt*, p. 135. Ṣāliḥ, *Bandarshah*, p. 80.

115. Ibid., p. 88.
116. Ibid., p. 83.
117. See Chapter Four, n. 75. For a partly similar perception see also Daf'allāh, *al-Lā Muntamī fī Adab al-Ṭayyib Ṣāliḥ*, pp. 81–4
118. Examples of works of this kind in modern Arabic literatures can be found in Lebanese author Laylā Ba'labakkī in her novel *Anā Aḥyā* (1958); for the French translation see *Je Vis!* (trans. Michel Barbot) Paris, Seuil, 1961; Egyptian authors Najīb Maḥfūẓ in his novel *al-Liṣṣ wa'l-Kilāb*, (1961); for the English translation see Naguib Mahfouz, *The Thief and the Dogs*, (trans. Trevor Le Gassick and M.M. Badawi, revised by John Rodenbeck), Cairo, The American University in Cairo Press, 1984); Fatḥī Ghānim in his novel *al-Rajul Alladhī Faqada Ẓillahu*, (1962); for the English translation Fathy Ghanem, *The Man who Lost his Shadow* (trans. Desmond Stewart), London, Heinemann, 1966. 'Abd al-Ḥakīm Qāsim in his novel *Ayyām al-Insān al-Sab'a* (1969); for the English translation see Abdel-Hakim Kassem, *The Seven days of Man* (trans. Joseph N. Bell), Cairo, General Egyptian Book Organization, 1989. Also significant are al-Ṭayyib Ṣāliḥ in his novel *Mawsim al-Hijra ilā al-Shamāl*, (1966) and Palestinian author Ghassān Kanafānī in his short novel *Mā Tabaqqā Lakum*, (1966); for the English translation, see *All That I Left to You* (trans. May Jayyusi and Jeremy Reed), Austin, University of Texas Press, 1998.
119. For a detailed discussion of these subjects, see Somekh, *Genre and Language in Modern Arabic Literature* (1991); al-Sa'īd Muḥammad Badawī, *Mustawayāt al-'Arabiyya al-Mu'āṣira fī Miṣr* (1973); Nafūsa Zakariyyā Sa'īd, *Ta'rīkh al-Da'wa ilā al-'Āmmiyya wa-Atharuhā fī Miṣr* (1964); al-Ḥuṣrī, *Ārā' wa-Aḥādīth fi al-Lugha wa'l-Adab* (1958).
120. On al-Ṭayyib Ṣāliḥ's perception of the use of dialogues between literary Arabic and popular Sudanese dialect, see 'Īsā al-Ḥilū, 'Ḥiwār ma'a al-Ṭayyib Ṣāliḥ (2)', *al-Ayyām* (4 November 1977). As cited and translated into English in Berkley, *The Roots of Consciousness*, pp. xii–xiv. On the use made by the author of the popular Sudanese dialect in his home village, see 'Uthmān Ḥasan Aḥmad, 'al-Qarya fī *'Urs al-Zayn* hiya al-Sūdān bi Qabā'ilihā al-Mutanāfira' in Muḥammadiyya (ed.), *al-Ṭayyib Ṣāliḥ*, p. 180; 'Ajūba, *al-Qiṣṣa al-Ḥadītha fī al-Sūdān*, p. 217; al-Ḥilū, 'Qirā'āt fī al-Qiṣṣa al-Sūdāniyya al-Qaṣīra', *al-Ādāb*, p. 39. Johnson-Davies, 'Profile: The World of Tayeb Salih', *Azure*, p. 17. For praise on the clever and convincing use made by al-Ṭayyib Ṣāliḥ of both literary Arabic and Sudanese dialect, see Maḥmūd Aḥmad Haykal, '*Bandar Shāh*', *al-Dōḥa*, p. 131. On the use made by the author of Sudanese dialect expressions, see el-Badawī, *Qirā'a Jadīda*, p. 66.
121. Ṣāliḥ, *Dawmat Wad Ḥāmid*, p. 52. Salih, 'The Doum Tree of Wad Hamid' in idem, *The Wedding of Zein*, pp. 19–20.
122. The literary critic Rajā' al-Naqqāsh expresses a similar opinion and compares the use of dialogues by al-Ṭayyib Ṣāliḥ to those of Najīb Maḥfūẓ in his works. See al-Naqqāsh, 'al-Ṭayyib Ṣāliḥ...'Abqariyya Riwā'iyya Jadīda', in Muḥammadiyya (ed.), *al-Ṭayyib Ṣāliḥ*, pp. 94–5. However, literary critics who praised the Sudanese atmosphere of al-Ṭayyib Ṣāliḥ's works also criticised his use of popular Sudanese dialect, and there were those who suggested sacrificing something of the 'local colour' for the benefit of a wider audience. See S.M., 'Riḥlat al-Ṭayyib Ṣāliḥ min al-Majāl al-Sūdānī ilā al-Majāl al-'Arabī', *al-Usbū' al-'Arabī* (June 1967), p. 53. al-Qamarī, 'Hākadhā Ḥaddathanī al-Ṭayyib Ṣāliḥ', *Kitābāt Sūdāniyya*, pp. 63–4.
123. Ṣāliḥ, *Mawsim al-Hijra ilā al-Shamāl*, p. 21. Salih, *Season of Migration to the North*, pp. 17–18.
124. S.M., 'Riḥlat al-Ṭayyib Ṣāliḥ', *al-Usbū' al-'Arabī*, p. 53. Ṣāliḥ, *Bandar Shāh: Ḍaw al-Bayt*. Ṣāliḥ, *Bandar Shāh: Maryūd*, in both the Tunisian edition and in the four chapters of the novel published in the Qatari journal *al-Dōḥa* (see Bibliography). M.M. Badawi, 'Tayeb Salih: *Bandarshah*', *Bulletin of the School of Oriental and African Studies*, p. 340. Ibrāhīm Isḥāq Ibrāhīm, *Ḥadath fī al-Qarya* (1969). Idem, *A'māl al-Layl wa'l-Balda* (1971). el-Badawī, *Laban al-Ābanūs, Yā zōl, (*1992).

125. On Sudanese dialects, see Chapter One n. 30 and 'Awn al-Sharīf Qāsim, *Dirāsāt fī al-'Āmmiyya*, Kharṭoum, al-Dār al-Sūdāniyya, 1974, pp. 25–77. Spencer Trimingham, *Sudan Colloquial Arabic*, Oxford, Oxford University Press, 1946; Gasim, 'Some Aspects of Sudanese Colloquial Arabic', *Sudan Notes and Records*, pp. 40–9.

126. al-Ṭayyib Ṣāliḥ comments on this point as follows: first, the principal language of expression and thought is indeed literary Arabic; second, it is impossible to imagine al-Zayn speaking in anything but the popular dialect of the Sudan, and the third aspect is linked to his assertion that it is indeed possible to understand any popular Arabic dialect without any particular difficulty. See, al-Ẓāhir, 'Ḥiwār ma'a al-Ṭayyib Ṣāliḥ', *al-Aqlām*, p. 153. See also the interview conducted by the *al-Jazīra* channel with al-Ṭayyib Ṣāliḥ who raised this issue in terms of adequacy between the different characters, their background, education and the roles they play in the text (Appendix G).

127. Ṣāliḥ, *'Urs al-Zayn*, pp. 5–6. Salih, *The Wedding of Zein*, p. 31.

128. Ibid., p. 67. Ibid., pp. 80–1.

129. Reactions to the difficulties likely to occur due to the extensive use of popular Sudanese dialect, as pursued by al-Ṭayyib Ṣāliḥ, are voiced by literary critic Muḥammad Rushdī Ḥasan 'Alī, *al-Ibdā' al-Fannī*, pp. 64–5.

130. Ṣāliḥ, *Bandar Shāh: Ḍaw al-Bayt*, p. 22. Salih, *Bandarshah*, p. 11.

131. Ibid., p. 35. Ibid., *Bandarshah*, p. 95.

132. Barrāda, *La'bat al-Nisyān* (1987). For the English translation see Mohamed Berrada, *The Game of Forgetting* (trans. Issa J. Boullata), (1996); Salīm Barakāt, *Fuqahā' al-Ẓalām* (1985); Munīf, *al-Ashjār wa-Ightiyāl Marzūq* (1973); Ibrāhīm Naṣrallāh, *Barārī al-Ḥummā*, *Riwāya*, 2nd ed., Amman, Dār al-Shurūq li'l-Nashr wa'l-Tawzī', 1992 (1st ed. 1985). For the English translation, see *Prairies of Fever* (trans. May Jayyusi and Jeremy Reed), New York, Interlink Books, 1993; al-Ṭāhir Waṭṭār, *al-Zilzāl (Riwāya min al-Jazā'ir)*, Beirut, Dār al-'Ilm li'l-Malāyīn, 1974 (1st ed. 1974).

133. Ṣāliḥ, *Dawmat Wad Hāmid*, p. 55.

134. In her collection of stories *Safīnat Ḥanān ilā al-Qamar* (1963) (Spaceship of Tenderness to the Moon), Laylā Ba'labakkī uses parentheses extensively, mainly to express the heroine's interior world either through interior monologue or with the objective of highlighting the fantastic sections of the text in order to differentiate them from the realistic parts of the story.

135. Ṣāliḥ, *Mawsim al-Hijra ilā al-Shamāl*, pp. 23–48.

136. Ibid., pp. 52–3. Salih, *Season of Migration to the North*, p. 49.

137. Ṣāliḥ, *'Urs al-Zayn*, p. 59. Salih, *The wedding of Zein*, p. 75.

138. Ibid., p. 103.

139. Rajā' al-Naqqāsh, *Aṣwāt Ghāḍiba fī al-Adab wa'l-Naqd*, Beirut, Dār al-Ādāb, 1970, p. 127; Idem. *Udabā' Mu'āṣirūn*, Cairo, Maktabat al-Anglū al-Miṣriyya, 1968, p. 54; Muḥammadiyya (ed.), *al-Ṭayyib Ṣāliḥ*, p. 37; al-Amīn, 'al-Rasm al-Bayānī li'l-Riwāya al-Sūdāniyya', *al-Ādāb*, p. 54; Salīm 'Abd al-Mun'im, 'Majhūd li'l-Ru'ya 'an Bu'd al-Ṭayyib Ṣāliḥ Ṣāḥib *Mawsim al-Hijra ilā al-Shamāl*', *al-Sharq*, 5 (October 1971), p. 29

140. Ṣāliḥ, *Mawsim al-Hijra ilā al-Shamāl*, p. 5.

141. Ibid., p. 8.

142. Ibid., p. 103, and compare terms and words taken from the popular Sudanese dialect, such as *nimitte* and *wad* in *Dawmat Wad Ḥāmid*, (p. 33), in which the dialogues, as in *Mawsim al-Hijra ilā al-Shamāl*, are held in literary Arabic.

143. Ṣāliḥ, *Dawmat Wad Hāmid*, pp. 7, 16. 'Awn al-Sharīf Qāsim, *Qāmūs al-Lahja al-'Āmmiyya fī al-Sūdān*, pp. 439, 512. El-Said Badawi and Martin Hinds, *A Dictionary of Egyptian Arabic*, Beirut, Librairie du Liban, 1986, pp. 327–8.

144. Najīb Maḥfūẓ, *Kifāḥ Ṭība*, Cairo, Maktabat Misr, n.d. (1st ed. 1944); Munīf, *al-Ashjār wa- Ightiyāl Marzūq* (1973). For the English translation see *Thebes at War* (trans. Humphrey Davies), Cairo, The American University in Cairo Press, 2003.
145. Elad [-Bouskila], *The Village Novel*, pp. 14–53.
146. Muḥammad Taymūr, 'Fī al-Qiṭār', *al-Sufūr*, p. 3; Najīb Maḥfūẓ, *Mīrāmār*, Cairo, Maktabat Miṣr, 1967. For the English translation, see *Miramar* (trans. Fatma Moussa-Mahmoud), Cairo, American University in Cairo Press, 1978. Jabrā, *al-Safīna* (1969).
147. al-Ḥakīm, *'Uṣfūr min al-Sharq*, (1938); Suhayl Idrīs, *al-Ḥayy al-Lātīnī* (1954); Yaḥyā Ḥaqqī, *Qindīl Umm Hāshim*, (1944).
148. On the village of Wad Ḥāmid as a framework for the works of al-Ṭayyib Ṣāliḥ, in which there is room for all, see the article by the Jordanian literary scholar Muhammad Shaheen, 'Tayeb Salih and Wad Hamid: An Alternation of Vision', *Arab Journal for the Humanities*, 5:17 (Winter 1985), pp. 276–86. See also Mūrīs Abū Nādir, *al-Alsuniyya wa'l-Naqd al-Adabī fī al-Naẓariyya wa'l-Mumārasa*, Beirut, Dār al-Nahār, 1979, pp. 135–9.
149. al-Ṭayyib Ṣāliḥ has used time and again the number seven years in several works: in *Bandar Shāh, Ḍaw al-Bayt*, Sa'īd al-Būm (one of the secondary characters) had worked for seven years to marry the headmaster's daughter (p. 29). In *Bandar Shāh: Maryūd*, the grandfather throws his Muḥaymīd to swim in the Nile (p. 19).
150. Rabāb was born when her mother was in her seventh month of pregnancy. See Ṣāliḥ, 'Yawm Mubārak 'alā Shāṭi' Umm Bāb', in *Mukhtārāt min al-Qiṣaṣ al-Qaṣīra fī 18 Baladan 'Arabiyyan*, p. 161. Sa'diyya (Ni'ma's mother) has seven brothers. See *'Urs al-Zayn*, p. 31.
151. On the importance of the number seven and the legends linked with it, see Smith Thompson, *Motive Index of Folk Literature*, Indiana, Indiana University Press, 1958, vol. VI, pp. 688–9; Maria Leach, *The Standard Dictionary of Folklore Mythology and Legend*, New York, Funk and Wagnalls, 1950. vol. II, p. 999. In Muslim tradition as in the Koran and Sufism we find a wide usage. Notable examples are the Seven Heavens; the *Fātiḥa* has seven sentences; the Koran has seven canonical ways of recitation; the Muslim pilgrim circles the Kaaba seven times and he runs between al-Ṣafā and Marwa. For more details see Annemarie Schimmel, *Sab'a, The Encyclopaedia of Islam*, New Edition, Leiden, E.J Brill, vol. viii, 1995, pp. 662–3.
152. 'Izz al-Dīn Ismā'īl, *al-Qaṣaṣ al-Sha'bī fī al-Sūdān*, Cairo, al-Hay'a al-Miṣriyya al-'Āmma li'l-Ta'līf wa'l-Nashr, 1971, pp. 201–4; Murād Kāmil, *Qiṣaṣ Sūdāniyya*, Cairo, Dār al-Ma'ārif, 1973, pp. 7, 12, 65. In modern literature, too, we find the number seven. Thus, for example, in the novel by Nigerian author Chinua Achebe (b.1930), *Things Fall Apart* (1958), the hero Okanako is forced to leave his village for seven years as punishment for accidentally killing one of the young men of the village.
153. 'Abd al-Ḥakīm Qāsim, *Ayyām al-Insān al-Sab'a* (1969); Muḥammad Yūsuf al-Qa'īd, *Fī al-Usbū' Sab'at Ayyām*, Cairo, al-Hay'a al-Miṣriyya al-'Āmma li'l-Kitāb, 1975.
154. Yaḥyā Ḥaqqī, *Qindīl Umm Hāshim*, pp. 83, 117.
155. Sa'dī Ibrāhīm, *al-Marfūḍūn, Riwāya*, Algiers, al-Sharika al-Waṭaniyya li'l-Nashr wa'l-Tawzī', 1981, pp. 176–7.
156. Ṣāliḥ, *Dawmat Wad Ḥāmid*, pp. 42–3. *'Urs al-Zayn*, p. 43. *Mawsim al-Hijra ilā al-Shamāl*, pp. 91, 103. Salih, *The Wedding of Zein*, pp. 9, 6, 15. *Season of Migration to the North*, pp. 88, 100.
157. Ṣāliḥ, *Mawsim al-Hijra ilā al-Shamāl*, pp. 5, 6, 54. The Lebanese literary critic, Rajā' Ni'ma, gives a slightly different series of dates in *Ṣirā' al-Maqhūr ma'a al-Sulṭa*, pp. 48–9, 58. Also in the Sudanese literary critic and author Aḥmad Muḥammad el-Badawī, *Qirā'a Jadīda*, pp. 22–3, 31.
158. On the political significance of this date, see P.M. Holt, *A Modern History of the Sudan from the Funj Sultanate to the Present Day*, 2nd ed., London, Weidenfeld and Nicholson, 1963, pp. 75–108. Muddathir 'Abd al-Raḥim, *al-Imbiryāliyya wa'l-Qawmiyya fī al-Sūdān*, Beirut, Dār al-Nahār li'l-Nashr, 1971, pp. 21–40. On the symbolism and cultural and psychological reality of this date, see

'Abd al-Raḥīm Muḥammad 'Abd al-Raḥīm, 'al-Shakl wa'l-Ramz fī Riwāyat al-Ṭayyib Ṣāliḥ *Mawsim al-Hijra ilā al-Shamāl*', *al-Qāhira*, 115 (August-September 1991), pp. 19, 25; Ni'ma, *Ṣirā' al-Maqhūr ma'a al-Sulṭa*, pp. 175–7. Tarawneh and John, 'Tayeb Salih and Freud', *Arabica*, p. 332.

159. Ṣāliḥ, *Mawsim al-Hijra ilā al-Shamāl*, p. 22
160. Ibid., p. 28
161. Ibid., p. 36.
162. Ibid., p. 33
163. Ibid., pp .33, 38.
164. Ibid., p. 122.
165. Ibid., pp. 124, 125, 129, 134. Compare Ṣāliḥ, *Bandar Shāh: Maryūd*, pp. 29, 42–3. Compare 'The old days were good, better than these days', 'Abd al-Raḥmān Munīf, *Mudun al-Milh, al-Tīh*, 2nd ed., Beirut, al-Mu'assasa al-'Arabiyya li'l-Dirāsāt wa'l-Nashr, 1986, p. 20. For the English translation, see Abdelrahman Munif, *Cities of Salt* (trans. Peter Theroux), London, Jonathan Cape, 1988, p. 14.
166. For a similar concept see Qaysūma, *al-Anā wa'l-Ākhar*, p. 118, and for a different concept see 'Abd al-Ṣamad Zāyid, *Mafhūm al-Zaman wa-Dalālātuhu fī al-Riwāya al-'Arabiyya al-Mu'āṣira*, Libya-Tunis, al-Dār al-'Arabiyya li'l-Kitāb, 1988, pp. 221–8.
167. For more details of the meaning of *al-ḍuḥā* and *Sūrat al-Ḍuḥā* (the chapter of al-Ḍuḥa) see Lane, *An Arabic-English Lexicon*, vol. V, pp. 1773–4. This word is mentioned in the Koran three times as follows: *Sūra* (chapter in the Koran) 7, *Āya* (Koranic verse) 98; *Sūra* 20, *Āya* 59, *Sūra* 93, *Āya* 1. For more details of Ṣalāt al-Ḍuḥā, the five daily prayers, see G. Monnot, *The Encyclopaedia of Islam*, E.J. Brill, vol. VIII, 1995, pp. 925–34.
168. Ṣāliḥ, 'Dawmat Wad Ḥāmid', in idem, *Dawmat Wad Ḥāmid*, p. 37. *Bandar Shāh: Ḍaw al-Bayt*, pp. 21–5, 73–4, 97–8, *Bandar Shāh: Maryūd*, pp. 83–8. 'Dawmat Wad Ḥāmid', in idem, *Dawmat Wad Ḥāmid*, p. 42. *'Urs al-Zayn*, p. 24. *Bandar Shāh: Maryūd*, p. 24. *Bandar Shāh: Ḍaw al-Bayt*, pp. 87–8. *Bandar Shāh: Maryūd*, p. 32. *'Urs al-Zayn*, pp. 5, 30. *Bandar Shāh: Ḍaw al-Bayt*, pp. 93–4, 105–6, 110–12, 122–3. *Bandar Shāh: Maryūd*, pp. 27–8, 80. *Bandar Shāh: Ḍaw al-Bayt*, pp. 55–6, 68, 122. *Bandar Shāh: Maryūd*, p. 49.
169. Ṣāliḥ, *Mawsim al-Hijra ilā al-Shamāl*, pp. 20, 49–50, 117, 136–7, 164, 168. *Bandar Shāh: Ḍaw al-Bayt*, pp. 25, 48, 65, 67, 93, 95, 101, 122. *Bandar Shāh: Maryūd*, pp. 19, 35–6, 39, 55, 80.
170. Ṣāliḥ, *Mawsim al-Hijra ilā al-Shamāl*, pp. 52–3. *Bandar Shāh: Ḍaw al-Bayt*, pp. 101–35. *Bandar Shāh: Maryūd*, pp. 48–9, 83–5.
171. Ṣāliḥ, *Mawsim al-Hijra ilā al-Shamāl*, pp. 108–17. On this subject see, Ni'ma, *Ṣirā' al-Maqhūr ma'a al-Sulṭa*, pp. 88–95.
172. Ṣāliḥ, *Dawmat Wad Ḥāmid*, pp. 17–18.
173. On these events, see 'Abd al-Majīd 'Ābdīn, *Bayn al-Ḥabasha wa'l-'Arab*, Cairo, Dār al-Fikr al-'Arabī, 1947, pp. 209–11; Idem., *Ta'rīkh al-Thaqāfa al-'Arabiyya fī al-Sūdān*, pp. 31–2, 45; Holt, *The Mahdist in the Sudan*, pp. 117–247.
174. Ṣāliḥ, *Bandar Shāh: Maryūd*, pp. 50–5.
175. Jibrīl, 'al-Ṭayyib Ṣāliḥ: Malāmiḥ min Sīra Dhātiyya (6)', *al-Ḥayāt*, p. 20.

Notes to Chapter Three: Status of the Characters in al-Ṭayyib Ṣāliḥ's Works

1. Erich Auerbach, *Mimesis: The Representation of Reality in Western Literature* (trans. William R. Trask), New York, Doubleday Anchor Books, 1957, p. 166. For a detailed discussion of the character's function see Ḥasan Baḥrāwī, *Bunyat al-Shakl al-Riwā'ī*, Beirut, al-Markaz al-Thaqāfī al-'Arabī, 1990, pp. 207–21.
2. E.M. Forster, *Aspects of the Novel*, San Diego, New York, London, Harcourt Brace and Company, 1955, pp. 67–78.

3. These categories are based on Shlomith Rimmon-Kenan, *Narrative Fiction, Contemporary Poetics*, London, Routledge, 1966, pp. 29–42, 59–70. Joseph Ewen, *HaDemut BaSipporet* (Character in Narrative), Tel Aviv, Sifriyat HaPo'alim, 1980, pp. 45–95 (Hebrew).
4. William Faulkner, *The Sound and the Fury*, London, Picador, 1993 (1st ed. 1929). Idem, *Absalom, Absalom!*, London, Vintage, 1985 (1st ed. 1935).
5. For further information on Sudanese authors who aspired to enlarge their public readership and who clarified words and terms from colloquial Sudanese in written Arabic, see al-Ṭayyib Ṣāliḥ in his novels *Bandar Shāh: Ḍaw al-Bayt*, (1971) and *Bandar Shāh: Maryūd*, 2nd ed., (1978); Aḥmad Muḥammad el-Badawī, in his novel *Laban al-Ābanūs Yā Zōl* (1992). Another Sudanese writer who preferred not to clarify the dialogues in his novels, which, in my opinion, was the cause, among other reasons, for his works not reaching a wider readership despite his talent, is Ibrāhīm Isḥāq Ibrāhīm, in his novels *Ḥadath fī al-Qarya* (1969), *A'māl al-Layl wa'l-Balda* (1971), and *Wabāl fī Klīmindū* (2001).
6. Stendhal (Henri Beyle), *The Red and the Black* (1981) (trans. Catherine Slater), Oxford, Oxford University Press, 1991 (1st ed. 1830).
7. Fathī Ghānim, *al-Rajul Alladhī Faqada Ẓillahu* (1962). For the English translation see Fathy Ghanem, *The Man who Lost his Shadow* (1966).
8. Maḥfūẓ's short story 'Za'balāwī' was first published in the Cairene daily *al-Ahrām* (12 May 1961), p. 12.
9. Najīb Maḥfūẓ, *Awlād Ḥāratinā*, 5th ed., Beirut, Dār al-Ādāb, 1986 (1st ed. 1967). This novel was serialized in the Cairene daily *al-Ahrām* between 21 September and 25 December 1959. For the English translation see Naguib Mahfouz, *Children of Gebelawi* (trans. Philip Stewart), London, Heinemann, 1981. For detailed discussion of this novel see Somekh, *The Changing Rhythm*, pp. 137–55. Rasheed El-Enany, *Naguib Mahfouz the Pursuit of Meaning*, London and New York, Routledge, 1993, pp. 141–4. Menahem Milson, *Najib Mahfuz: The Novelist-Philosopher of Cairo*, New York, St. Martin's Press, Jerusalem, The Magnes Press, 1998, pp. 101–3, 125–6, 133–6.
10. Ṣabrī Mūsā, *Fasād al-Amkina*, Cairo, al-Hay'a al-Miṣriyya al-'Āmma li'l-Kitāb, 1987, pp. 119–390. For the English translation see Sabri Moussa, *Seeds of Corruption* (trans. Mona Mikhail), Boston, Houghton Mifflin, 1980. Salīm Barakāt, *Fuqahā' al-Ẓalām* (1985). Khalīl al-Nu'aymī, *Tafrīgh al-Kā'in*, Cairo, Dār Sharqiyyāt li'l-Nashr wa'l-Tawzi', 1995. Sa'd al-Khādim, *Thulāthiyyat 'Ūlayis*, Fredericton, York Press, 1988. This novel has been translated into English: Saad el-Khadem, *Avant-Garde Egyptian Fiction: The Ulysses Trilogy* (trans. Saad el-Gabalawy), Fredericton, New Brunswick, York Press, 1988.
11. For further details on the character in al-Ṭayyib Ṣāliḥ's works see 'Ami El'ad [-Bouskila], 'Taṭawwur al-Shakhṣiyya fī A'māl al-Ṭayyib Ṣāliḥ', *al-Karmil*, 10 (1989), pp. 7–26. Idem, 'Shaping the Cast of Characters: The Case of al-Ṭayyib Ṣāliḥ', *Journal of Arabic Literature*, XXIX:2 (July 1998), pp. 59–84. Ḥasan Abbashir al-Ṭayyib, 'al-Ṭayyib Ṣāliḥ Riwā'iyyan wa-Shā'iran Mubdi'an', *Ibdā'*, pp. 27–33. 'Abd al-Mun'im 'Ajab Alfiyā, 'Qirā'a fī Kitāb *al-Lā Muntamī fī Adab al-Ṭayyib Ṣāliḥ*', *Kitābāt Sūdāniyya*, 19 (March 2002), pp. 128–30.
12. Muḥammad al-Makhazanjī, 'al-Bashar al-Thalātha', in idem, *Rashq al-Sikkīn*, Cairo, al-Hay'a al-Miṣriyya al-'Āmma li'l-Kitāb, Mukhtārāt *Fuṣūl* 8, 1984, pp. 34–6.
13. 'Azmī Khālis, *Ḥikāyat al-Adab al-'Arabī al-Mu'āṣir*, Baghdad, Maṭba'at Shafīq, 1970. al-Naqqāsh, 'al-Ṭayyib Ṣāliḥ, 'Abqariyya Riwā'iyya Jadīda', in Muḥammadiyya (ed.), *al-Ṭayyib Ṣāliḥ*, pp. 102–8, 109–11. El'ad [-Bouskila] 'Taṭawwur al-Shakhṣiyya fī A'māl al-Ṭayyib Ṣāliḥ', *al-Karmil*, pp. 7–26.
14. Ṭalḥat Jibrīl conducted an interview with al-Ṭayyib Ṣāliḥ, 'al-Ṭayyib Ṣāliḥ, Malāmiḥ min Sīra Dhātiyya (6)', *al-Ḥayāt*, p. 20.
15. We would like to note that in Maḥjūb's character it is possible to find inspiration for some realistic characters, as the author has testified. al-Ṭayyib Ṣāliḥ has indicated that in Dalqa in the al-Jazīra

region of the Sudan, the village of his student colleague, 'Abd al-Wahhāb Mūsā, that Mūsā's family could have symbolized the Sudanese citizens in their rootedness. One can therefore find such characters as Maḥjūb. See Jibrīl, *'Alā al-Darb*, p. 100.

16. Maḥfūẓ, *Dunyā Allāh*, p. 136. Johnson-Davies (ed.), *Modern Arabic Short Stories*, p. 136.
17. al-Sharqāwī, *al-Arḍ* (1954). For the English translation see A.R. Sharkawi, *Egyptian Earth* (1962).
18. 'Abd al-Muḥsin Ṭāhā Badr, *al-Riwā'ī wa'l-Arḍ*, 2nd ed., Cairo, Dār al-Ma'ārif, 1979, pp. 163–71 (1st ed. 1971). Ṭāhā Wādī, *Ṣūrat al-Mar'a fī al-Riwāya al-Mu'āṣira*, 2nd ed., Cairo, Dār al-Ma'ārif, 1980, p. 342. al-Sa'īd al-Waraqī, *Ittijāhāt al-Riwāya al-'Arabiyya al-Mu'āṣira*, Alexandria, al-Hay'a al-Miṣriyya al-'Āmma li'l-Kitāb, 1982, pp. 163–4. Elad [-Bouskila], *The Village Novel*, pp. 88–90.
19. The grandfather was a stranger even forty years earlier. Therefore, it is a very interesting way for this character to open the gate to other strangers to the village of Wad Ḥāmid throughout several works of al-Ṭayyib Ṣāliḥ, such as Muṣṭafā Sa'īd, the grandfather, partly the narrator (*Mawsim al-Hijra ilā al-Shamāl*), Bandar Shāh, Ḍaw al-Bayt (*Bandar Shāh: Ḍaw al-Bayt*) and Bilāl (*Bandar Shāh: Maryūd*). Nevertheless, this outsider is always part and parcel of the legendary world of al-Ṭayyib Ṣāliḥ. See also Fāṭima Mūsā, 'al-Gharīb fī Riwāyāt al-Ṭayyib Ṣāliḥ', in idem, *Fī al-Riwāya al-'Arabiyya al-Mu'āṣira*, vol. I, Cairo, al-Hay'a al-Miṣriyya al-'Āmma li'l-Kitāb, 1997, pp. 264–80.
20. Jibrīl, 'al-Ṭayyib Ṣāliḥ: Malāmiḥ min Sīra Dhātiyya (1)', *al-Ḥayāt*, p. 16.
21. Exaggeration as an element emphasizing strangeness appears in the relationship between 'Ā'isha and Kamāl in Maḥfūẓ's novel *Bayn al-Qaṣrayn*, Cairo, Maktabat Miṣr, n.d., p. 301. For the English translation see Naguib Mahfouz, *Palace Walk*, volume one of *The Cairo Trilogy* (trans. William M. Hutchins and Olive E. Kenny), Cairo, The American University in Cairo Press, 1990.
22. In an interview with Muḥyī al-Dīn Ṣubḥī and Khaldūn al-Sham'a, al-Ṭayyib Ṣāliḥ indicated that he thought that people in Arab society – in our case Sudanese society – change with modernity. There are as well other complicated and difficult issues, such as using irony which allows them to simultaneously hint at refusal and acceptance of solutions they do not agree with. See Ṣubḥī and al-Sham'a, 'al-Ṭayyib Ṣāliḥ Riwā'iyyan wa-Nāqidan' in Muḥamadiyya (ed.), *al-Ṭayyib Ṣāliḥ*, p. 122.
23. The real author likes to attribute importance to irony as part and parcel of Arab culture and as it was expressed by classical writers like al-Jāḥiz or modern writers like the Egyptians 'Abd al-Qādir al-Māzinī and Yaḥyā Ḥaqqī, the Sudanese-Egyptian Ṭāriq al-Ṭayyib, and the Tunisian writer al-Bashīr Khurayyif. See Ṣubḥī and al-Sham'a, 'al-Ṭayyib Ṣāliḥ Riwā'iyyan wa-Nāqidan', in Muḥamadiyya (ed.), *al-Ṭayyib Ṣāliḥ*, pp. 120–1. See also the introduction by al-Ṭayyib Ṣāliḥ to Ṭāriq al-Ṭayyib's *al-Jamāl Lā Yaqif Khalf Ishāra Ḥamrā'*, Cairo, al-Ḥaḍāra li'l-Nashr, 1993, pp. 8–9. See also Ṣāliḥ's introduction to al-Bashīr Khurayyif's *al-Daqla fī 'Arājīnihā*, Tunis, Dār al-Janūb li'l-Nashr, 1990, p. 20.
24. Ṣāliḥ, *'Urs al-Zayn*, 3nd ed., Beirut, Dār al-'Awda, 1970, pp. 73–4, 79–80. This novel has been translated into several languages. Ṭāhā Ḥusayn, *al-Ayyām*, Cairo, Dār al-Ma'ārif, vol.1, pp. 80–7 (1st ed. 1929). For the English translation see Taha Hussein, *An Egyptian Childhood*, vol. 1 (trans. E.H. Paxton), London, Heinemann, 1981 (1st ed. 1932). al-Shārqawī, *al-Arḍ*, pp. 8–9. Elad [-Bouskila], *The Village Novel*, p. 85.
25. Ṣāliḥ Ibrāhīm, *al-Mar'a fī Adab al-Ṭayyib Ṣāliḥ*, Beirut, Ma'had al-Dirāsāt al-Nisā'iyya fī al-'Ālam al-'Arabī, al-Jāmi'a al-Lubnāniyya al-Amīrikiyya, 1997, pp. 50–1, 55.
26. Ṣāliḥ, 'al-Shay' al-Ākhar', *Ḥiwār*, 21 (March-April 1966), pp. 37–8. 'Muqaddimāt', *al-Hilāl*, 9 (September 1989), pp. 34–9.
27. Jibrīl, 'al-Ṭayyib Ṣāliḥ: Malāmiḥ min Sīra Dhātiyya' (4), p. 16.
28. For a detailed discussion of this film see Melvyn Bragg, *The Seventh Seal*, London, British Film Institute, 1993.
29. For details on prose literature and Sufism in a wider context see Caesar E. Farah, 'The Prose Literature of Sufism' in M.J.L. Young, J.D. Latham and R.B. Serjeant (eds), *The Cambridge History*

of Arabic Literature, Religion, Learning and Science in the 'Abbadid Period, Cambridge, Cambridge University Press, 1990, pp. 56–75.

30. Salām, *Dirāsāt fī al-Qiṣṣa al-'Arabiyya al-Ḥadītha*, p. 422.
31. For a comprehensive and detailed analysis of the character of al-Zayn, especially in the Sufi context, see Aḥmad Shams al-Dīn al-Ḥaggāgī, *Ṣāni' al-Usṭūra, al-Ṭayyib Ṣāliḥ*, Cairo, al-Hay'a al-Miṣriyya al-'Āmma li'l-Kitāb, al-Maktaba al-Thaqāfiyya 460, 1990. For the English version see Ahmad Shams al-Din al-Haggagi, 'The Mythmaker: Tayeb Salih' in Ghazoul and Harlow (eds), *The View From Within*, pp. 99–133. Kenneth W. Harrow, 'Camara Laye, Cheikh Hamidou Kame and Tayeb Salih: The Sufi Author', in idem (ed.), *Faces of Islam in African Literature*, London, James Currey, 1991, pp. 278–85. Ibrāhīm Muḥammad Zayn, 'Taṭawwur Shakl al-Ta'bīr al-Dīnī fī Riwāyāt al-Ṭayyib Ṣāliḥ (4): al-Zayn Muharrij am Rajul Ṣāliḥ', *al-Multaqā* (1 May 1993), p. 41. Muḥammad Khalafallāh 'Abd Allāh, 'Khiṭāb al-Darāwīsh Tanqīb 'an al-Wajh al-Ākhar li'l-Ablah fī Riwāyat *'Urs al-Zayn*' (1), *al-Kharṭūm* 857 (13 April 1995, p. 4; (2), *al-Kharṭūm*, 859 (15 April 1995), p. 4; (3) *al-Kharṭūm*, 860 (16 April 1995), p. 4. Ṣalāh Ḥasan 'Abd Allāh, ''An al-Usṭūra fī Adab al-Ṭayyib Ṣāliḥ, *'Urs al-Zayn Namūdhajan*', *Kitābāt Sūdāniyya*, 8 (June 1999), pp. 78–81. Muḥammd Ibrāhīm al-Shūsh, 'al-Athar al-Dīnī al-Ṣūfī fī A'māl al-Ṭayyib Ṣāliḥ', in Ḥasan Abbashir al-Ṭayyib (ed.), *al-Ṭayyib Ṣāliḥ*, pp. 163–4. Muḥammad al-Mahdī Bushrā, 'Taḥdīd al-Jins al-Fūlklūrī fī Ibdā' al-Ṭayyib Ṣāliḥ', in Ḥasan Abbashir al-Ṭayyib (ed.), *al-Ṭayyib Ṣāliḥ*, pp. 323–4.
32. Muḥammadiyya (ed.), *al-Ṭayyib Ṣāliḥ*, pp. 124–5. 'Abd al-Mun'im, 'Majhūd li'l-Ru'ya 'an Bu'd al-Ṭayyib Ṣāliḥ', *al-Sharq*, p. 30.
33. Other writers who have used the motif of 'the village idiot', 'the court jester' or the characters of 'the retard', 'the idiot' and 'the fool' in world literatures are William Shakespeare (*King Lear, Macbeth*), Dostoyevsky (*The Idiot*), and Faulkner (*The Sound and the Fury*). For further details see Khalafallāh 'Abd Allāh, 'Khiṭāb al-Darāwīsh', *al-Khartūm*, 857, 859–60, p. 4. al-Shaykh Muḥammad al-Shaykh, *al-Insān wa'l-Taḥlīl al-Fā'ilī, Taḥlīl al-Shakhṣiyya al-Sūdāniyya min khilāl* Mawsim al-Hijra ilā al-Shamāl wa-'Urs al-Zayn, [Khartoum], 1989, pp. 24, 31. See also Emīl Ḥabībī, (*al-Waqā'i' al-Gharība fī Ikhtifā' Sa'īd Abī al-Naḥs al-Mutashā'il*), Salīm Barakāt (*Fuqahā' al-Ẓalām*) and 'Abd al-Raḥmān al-Sharqāwī (*al-Arḍ*).
34. The Sudanese critic al-Shaykh Muḥammad al-Shaykh has supported this theory, see *al-Insān wa'l-Taḥlīl al-Fā'ilī*, pp. 4, 13, 30.
35. For a comprehensive concept of these different worlds between which al-Zayn compromises, see the Sudanese literary critic Ibrāhīm al-Shūsh, *Adab wa-Udabā'*, pp. 23–8.
36. The author mentions that in *'Urs al-Zayn* he drew his inspiration for the dominant characters in his village from the village of al-Biryāb in al-Jazīra, the village of his best friend Fatḥ al-Raḥmān al-Bashīr. See Jibrīl, *'Alā al-Darb*, p. 97.
37. Abbas, 'Notes on Tayeb Salih', *Sudan Notes and Records*, pp. 57–8.
38. Ṣāliḥ, *'Urs al-Zayn*, pp. 25, 27. 'Alī al-Rā'ī, 'Zaghrūda Ṭawīla li'l-Ḥayāt', *al-Hilāl*, 7 (July 1970), p. 28. Muḥammadiyya (ed.), *al-Ṭayyib Ṣāliḥ*, p. 168. Najīb, 'al-Ḥayāt Tuṣbiḥ Mahrajān', *al-Muṣawwar*, pp. 86–7. Muḥammad Khalafallāh 'Abd Allāh, 'Fī Ṣuḥbat al-Zayn, Qirā'a Naqdiyya: Fī Tajsīr al-Huwwa bayn al-Ṣakhāb wa'l-Shawq', *al-Ittiḥādī al-Duwaliyya*, 65616 (6 July 1998), p. 6. Īnās Mamdūḥ Ṭāhā, 'Ṣūrat al-Qarya fī al-Riwāya al-'Arabiyya', *al-Mustaqbal al-'Arabī*, 48 (February 1983), pp. 62–3.
39. Ṣāliḥ, *Mawsim al-Hijra ilā al-Shamāl*, p. 124. Salih, *Season of Migration to the North*, p. 123.
40. Ṣāliḥ, *'Urs al-Zayn*, pp. 88, 92–3.
41. Ibid., pp. 37–9. See Ṣāliḥ Ibrāhīm, *al-Mar'a fī Adab al-Ṭayyib Ṣāliḥ*, pp. 22, 40–1.
42. Salām, *Dirāsāt fī al-Qiṣṣa al-'Arabiyya al-Ḥadītha*, p. 422.
43. Ṭāhā Ḥusayn, *al-Ayyām*, pp. 31–62. Idem, *Shajarat al-Bu's*, p. 72.

44. For this concept see also Muḥammad 'Azzām, *al-Baṭal al-Ishkālī fī al-Riwāya al-'Arabiyya al-Mu'āṣira,* Damascus, al-Ahālī li'l-Ṭibā'a wa'l-Nashr wa'l-Tawzī', 1992, pp. 41–4.
45. Although he is aware of Muṣṭafā's dominant role, al-Ṭayyib Ṣāliḥ does not consider Muṣṭafā Sa'īd to be the main character, but rather the narrator. See al-Ẓāhir, 'Ḥiwār ma'a al-Ṭayyib Ṣāliḥ', *al-Aqlām*, p. 154. Ḥāmid Badawī, 'Qirā'a Jadīda li Riwāyat *Mawsim al-Hijra ilā al-Shamāl*', *al-Ayyām* (1), 9426 (9 June 1978), p. 6. Joseph John, 'A Dialogue with Mr Tayeb Salih on *Season of Migration to the North*', *The Islamic Quarterly*, XXXVI:3 (1992), pp. 213–14, 216–17. Ali Abdallah Abbas, 'The Strangled Impulse: The Role of the Narrator in Tayeb Salih's *Season, Sudan Notes and Records*', LX (1979), pp. 56–85. Idem, 'The Father of Lies: The Role of Mustafa Sa'eed as Second Self in *Season of Migration to the North*', in Amyuni (ed.), Tayeb Salih's Season of Migration to the North, pp. 27–37. Mona Takieddine Amyuni, 'Tayeb Salih's *Season*, an Interpretation', *Arab Studies Quarterly*, II:` (Winter 1980), pp. 1–17. Asa'd E. Khairallah, 'The Traveling Theatre or the Art of Entertaining, a Doomed Caravan with Amusing Stories', in Amyuni (ed.), Tayeb Salih's Season of Migration to the North, pp. 95–111. A different concept is expressed by other literary critics who do not consider the narrator to be a central or leading character, but a minor one such as Maḥjūb, Wad al-Rayyis, Ḥusna and even the European women. See for example Muḥammad Rushdī Ḥasan 'Alī, *al-Ibdā' al-Fannī*, p. 42.
46. This with *Qindīl Umm Hāshim* by Yaḥyā Ḥaqqī, in which the protagonist, Ismā'īl, comes back from England after seven years of study. On the one hand, it may be considered as part of Yaḥyā Ḥaqqī's influence on al-Ṭayyib Ṣāliḥ, as Ṣāliḥ himself has indicated, see Farghalī, 'Liqā' ma'a al-Ṭayyib Ṣāliḥ fī Landan', *al-Hilāl*, p. 118, while on the other, this possibly indicates that both were influenced by the same sources, i.e., the number seven, which bears importance and blessings in Muslim Arab culture as it does in other cultures such as Judaism and Christianity (see Chapter Two).
47. Jibrīl, 'al-Ṭayyib Ṣāliḥ: Malāmiḥ min Sīra Dhātiyya (6)', *al-Ḥayāt*, p. 20. See also Jibrīl, *'Alā al-Darb*, pp. 39, 44–5.
48. We might note that in *Mawsim al-Hijra ilā al-Shamāl* the narrator teaches *Jāhilī* Arab literature in high school, and this is the author's best-liked literature and is closest to his heart. This should also be compared with the author who taught in high school and at a teachers' training college, see Jibrīl, *'Alā al-Darb*, pp. 45–7.
49. Ṣāliḥ, *Dawmat Wad Ḥāmid*, p. 31. N. S. Doniach, 'A Letter to Aileen', *Journal of Arabic Literature*, XI (1980), pp. 78–9.
50. Muḥammadiyya (ed.), *al-Ṭayyib Ṣāliḥ*, pp. 145–51, 215. Ni'ma, *Ṣirā' al-Maqhūr ma'a al-Sulṭa*, pp. 99–105. Siddiq, 'The Process of Individuation', *Journal of Arabic Literature*, pp. 81–5.
51. Salām, *Dirāsāt fī al-Qiṣṣa al-'Arabiyya al-Ḥadītha*, pp. 433–44. Siddiq, 'The Process of Individuation', *Journal of Arabic Literature*, p. 87. Abbas, 'The Father of Lies', in Amyuni (ed.), Tayeb Salih's Season of Migration to the North , pp. 27–37.
52. Faulkner, *The Sound and the Fury* (1929).
53. Jūrj Ṭarābīshī, *Sharq wa-Gharb, Rujūla wa-Unūtha, Dirāsa fī Azmat al-Jins wa'l-Ḥaḍāra fī al-Riwāya al-'Arabiyya*, 2nd ed., Beirut, Dār al-Ṭalī'a, 1974, pp. 182–5. See also *al-Fajr* (15 November 1976), as cited by Berkley, *The Roots of Consciousness*, pp. XXXIII–XXXXIV.
54. Fāṭima Mūsa, ''Uṣfūr min Janūb aw 'Ālam al-Ṭayyib Ṣāliḥ', *al-Majalla*, 164 (August 1970), p. 98. Siddiq, 'The Process of Individuation', *Journal of Arabic Literature*, 1978, p. 98.
55. See *al-Fajr* (15 November 1976) as cited in Berkley, *The Roots of Consciousness*, p. XXXXIII.
56. In this context we can mention Emīl Ḥabībī's novel *al-Mutashā'il* (1974). We draw a parallel line between the usage of the name Sa'īd, the major character in both novels. While Muṣṭafā was selected by al-Ṭayyib Ṣāliḥ to be the most unhappy character in the novel, Emīl Ḥabībī chose the character of Sa'īd as the *naḥs* (misfortune) character of the most tragic, comic, ironic character that is mocked not only by the author, the readers and his friends, but first and foremost by himself. Sa'īd is also the first

name of Sa'īd Mahrān in *al-Liṣṣ wa'l-Kilāb* by Najīb Maḥfūẓ and Sa'īd S. in *'Ā'id ilā Ḥayfā* (Return to Haifa, 1969) by Ghassān Kanafānī. al-Muṣṭafā is also the hero in *The Prophet* (1923) by Jubrān Khalīl Jubrān (1883–1931) and the connection between the Prophet Muḥammad and Jubrān's prophet is clear. For more details on names and their meaning see Milson, *Najib Mahfuz*, pp. 159–277.

57. Philip Vellacott, *Sophocles and Oedipus, A Study of Oedipus Tyrannus*, Ann Arbor, University of Michigan Press, 1971.

58. Ṣāliḥ, *Mawsim al-Hijra ilā al-Shamāl*, p. 110. *'Urs al-Zayn*, p. 27. Muḥammadiyya (ed.), *al-Ṭayyib Ṣāliḥ*, pp. 125–6. al-Shūsh, *Adab wa-Udabā'*, pp. 50–2. Najīb, 'al-Ḥayāt Tuṣbiḥ Mahrajān', *al-Muṣawwar*, p. 86. For an interesting comparison between al-Zayn and Muṣṭafā Sa'īd see the Sudanese literary critic Ḥasan Abbashir al-Ṭayyib, 'al-Ṭayyib Ṣāliḥ Riwā'iyyan wa-Shā'iran Mubdi'an', *Ibdā'*, pp. 27–8, 33. The Egyptian critic Muḥammad Ḥasan 'Abd Allāh ('al-Rīf al-Sūdānī, Ṣuwar Khāṣṣa' in idem, *al-Rīf fī al-Riwāya al-'Arabiyya*, p. 334, n. 10), indicates that *al-Nabiyy al-Khaḍir* occupies a very important place in many Sudanese village novels and plays the role of harmony blessing and helpful place. al-Yāzijī, *al-Sūdān wa'l-Ḥaraka al-Adabiyya*, p. 943. Daf'allāh, *al-Lā Muntamī fī Adab al-Ṭayyib Ṣāliḥ*, pp. 72, 114–22. Nassar, 'Beckett's *Waiting for Godot*', *The Explicator*, pp. 105–8. Abbas, 'Sense of Proportion in *Season of Migration to the North*', in Amyuni (ed.), Tayeb Salih's Season of Migration to the North , p. 42. Qaysūma, 'al-Riwāya al-'Arabiyya wa-Thunā'iyat al-Naṣṣ al-Muta'ddid *Mawsim al-Hijra ilā al-Shamāl* Namūdhajan' in idem, *al-Riwāya al-'Arabiyya, al-Ishkāl wa'l-Tashakkul*, p. 165. el-Badawī, *al-Ṭayyib Ṣāliḥ*, p. 130.

59. Ṣāliḥ, *Mawsim al-Hijra ilā al-Shamāl*, pp. 26, 55. For more details of *Mu'jizāt* and *Karāmāt* see L. Gardet, 'Karāma', *The Encyclopaedia of Islam*, New Edition, Leiden, E.J. Brill, vol. IV, 1990, pp. 615–16. A.J. Wensinck, 'Mu'jiza', *The Encyclopaedia of Islam*, New Edition, Leiden, E.J. Brill, vol. VII, 1993, p. 295. On terms and other Sufi elements in al-Ṭayyib Ṣāliḥ's writing see al-Rā'ī, 'Zaghrūda Ṭawīla li'l-Ḥayāt', in Muḥammadiyya (ed.), *al-Ṭayyib Ṣāliḥ*, pp. 111–12. Ahmad Nasr, 'Popular Islam in al-Ṭayyib Ṣāliḥ', *Journal of Arabic Literature*, XI (1980), pp. 88–104. Elad [Bouskila], 'Fiction and Reality' in idem, *Writer, Culture, Text*, pp. 62–73. Sviri, 'On Trees, Dreams and Holy Men', in Elad-Bouskila and Al-Shahi (eds), *Al-Ṭayyib Ṣāliḥ, Edebiyât*, pp. 103–22.

60. For further details on this issue see Ṭarābīshī, *Sharq wa-Gharb*, pp. 144–77. Ibrāhīm al-Sa'afīn, '*Mawsim al-Hijra ilā al-Shamāl*, Dirāsa fī Wujhat al-Naẓar' in idem, *Taḥawwulāt al-Sard: Dirāsāt fī al-Riwāya al-'Arabiyya*, Amman, Dār al-Shurūq li 'l-Nashr wa'l-Tawzi', 1996, pp. 206–18. Joseph John, 'The Life and Death of Mustafa Sa'eed: Riddles, Paradoxes and Ambiguities', *Abhath al-Yarmouk*, 5:1 (1987), pp. 55–61.

61. There are prophets like Moses in Judaism, Jesus in Christianity and Muḥammad in Islam who grew up fatherless and thus had a childhood that influenced not only their personal lives, but also their communities. al-Ṭayyib Ṣāliḥ, who uses in his literary works some popular elements from classical and local fairy tales and legends, hints in Muṣṭafā's orphanhood in popular Arab and Eastern stories such as 'Alā' al-Dīn in *Alf Layla wa-Layla*. See al-Shaykh Muḥammad al-Shaykh, *al-Insān wa'l-Taḥlīl al-Fā'ilī*, pp. 4, 13. Qaysūma, *al-Anā wa'l-Ākhar*, p. 141. In addition to being orphaned influencing him, the influence of the slave origin of his mother's family and their blackness is significant. See Bakrī, ''Ibr Majrā al-Ta'rīkh (1)', *al-Kharṭūm*, 1796 (9 May 1998), p. 6. (2), *al-Kharṭūm*, 1828 (15 June 1998), p. 4. (3), *al-Kharṭūm*, 1829 (16 June 1998), p. 6. Heather Sharkey, 'The Sudan's Ex-Slaves: A Study of Tayeb Salih's *The Wedding of Zein*', *Sudan Studies*, 11 (1992), pp. 18–23.

62. Aḥmad al-Zu'bī, 'al-Riwā'ī fī *Mawsim al-Hijra ilā al-Shamāl*' in idem, *Fī al-Īqā' al-Riwā'ī, naḥwa Manhaj Jadīd fī Dirāsat al-Bunya al-Riwā'iyya*, Amman, Dār al-Amal, 1986, pp. 57–74. Compare with other stages in the life of the hero in Modern Arabic Literatures such as the hero in Maḥfūẓ's 'Za'balāwī', see Elad [-Bouskila], 'Mahfūz's "Za'balāwī": Six Stations of a Quest', *International Journal of Middle East Studies*, pp. 631–44.

63. This is the concept of some literary critiques, see for example, Ḥasan al-Mānī'ī, *Nafaḥāt 'an al-Adab wa'l-Fann*, Beirut, Dār al-Āfāq al-Jadīda, 1981, pp. 9–10.
64. Muṣṭafā Sa'īd's disappearance in the Nile is interpreted by some scholars as suicide, see al-Shaykh Muḥammad al-Shaykh, *al-Insān wa'l-Taḥlīl al-Fā'ilī*, pp. 16–20.
65. Echoes of this concept of purity and harmony with the river and a rebirth of energies can be found in al-Ṭayyib Ṣāliḥ's interview with Ṣubḥī and al-Sham'a, 'al-Ṭayyib Ṣāliḥ Riwā'iyyan wa-Nāqidan', in Muḥammadiyya (ed.), *al-Ṭayyib Ṣāliḥ*, p. 20. See also the Egyptian literary critic Rajā' al-Naqqāsh, 'al-Ṭayyib Ṣāliḥ, 'Abqariyya Riwā'iya Jadīda', in Muḥammadiyya (ed.), *al-Ṭayyib Ṣāliḥ*, p. 93. For a different concept accompanied by a physiological explanation see Tarawneh and John, 'Tayeb Salih and Freud', *Arabica*, pp. 340–2.
66. Ambiguity in *Mawsim al-Hijra ilā al-Shamāl*, is part and parcel of al-Ṭayyib Ṣāliḥ's literary devices, and Muṣṭafā Sa'īd's disappearance is evidence of this. See John, 'A Dialogue with Mr Tayeb Salih', *The Islamic Quarterly*, pp. 207–9. el-Badawī, *al-Ṭayyib Ṣāliḥ*, pp. 110–11.
67. 'Alī al-Shar', 'al-Baḥth 'an al-Shakhṣiyya al-Jadīda fī *Mawsim al-Hijra ilā al-Shamāl*', *Abḥāth al-Yarmūk*, 5:2 (1987), pp. 21–9.
68. Muḥammadiyya (ed.), *al-Ṭayyib Ṣāliḥ*, p. 126.
69. 'Ḥiwār Maftūḥ fī Kull Shay' ma'a al-Ṭayyib Ṣāliḥ', *al-Fajr* (15 November 1976), as cited by Berkley, *The Roots of Consciousness*, p. XXXXIII. In another interview al-Ṭayyib Ṣāliḥ indicated, on the one hand, that Muṣṭafā is part and parcel of the real author, but on the other he is not part and parcel of himself. See al-Qamarī, 'Hākadhā Ḥaddathanī al-Ṭayyib Ṣāliḥ', *Kitābāt Sūdāniyya*, pp. 65–6.
70. Muḥyī al-Dīn Ṣubḥī, *Abṭāl fī al-Ṣayrūra*, Beirut, Dār al-Ṭalī'a, 1980, pp. 27–32. Laṭīfa al-Zayyāt, *Min Ṣuwar al-Mar'a fī al-Qiṣaṣ wa'l-Riwāyāt al-'Arabiyya*, Cairo, Dār al-Thaqāfa al-Jadīda 1989, pp. 84–6, 121. Shāhīn, *Taḥawwulāt al-Shawq*, pp. 19–23. 'Abd Ghallāb, '*Mawsim al-Hijra ilā al-Shamāl*', in Muḥammadiyya (ed.), *al-Ṭayyib Ṣāliḥ*, pp. 125–7.
71. The question of rootlessness exists in al-Ṭayyib Ṣāliḥ 's literary works and is expressed especially in *Mawsim al-Hijra ilā al-Shamāl* by the narrator, but more so by Muṣṭafā Sa'īd, as the literary critic Muḥammad 'Abd al-Khāliq Bakrī indicates in his article ''Ibr Majrā al-Ta'rīkh (4)', *al-Kharṭūm*, p. 6. (5), *al-Khartūm*, p. 5.
72. Muḥammadiyya (ed.), *al-Ṭayyib Ṣāliḥ*, p. 128.
73. Jibrīl, 'al-Ṭayyib Ṣāliḥ: Malāmiḥ min Sīra Dhātiyya (6)', *al-Ḥayāt*, p. 20. See also Nasr, 'Popular Islam in al-Ṭayyib Ṣāliḥ', *Journal of Arabic Literature*, pp. 100–1.
74. William Shakespeare, *Othello* (ed. Norman Sandors), Cambridge, Cambridge University Press, 1995 (1st ed. 1604). Albert Camus, *The Outsider* (trans. Joseph Laredd), London, Penguin Books, 1983 (1st ed. 1942).
75. Muḥyī al-Dīn Ṣubḥī, '*Mawsim al-Hijra ilā al-Shamāl* bayn 'Uṭayil wa-Mirsū', in Muḥammadiyya (ed.), *al-Ṭayyib Ṣāliḥ*, pp. 39–77. El'ad [-Bouskila], 'Taṭawwur al-Shakhṣiyya fī A'māl al-Ṭayyib Ṣāliḥ', *al-Karmil*, pp. 7–26. Shāhīn, *Taḥawwulāt al-Shawq*, pp. 43–120. Harlow, 'Othello's Season of Migration', *Edebiyât*, pp. 157–75. Idem, 'Sentimental Orientalism: Season of Migration to the North and Othello', in Amyuni (ed.), Tayeb Salih's Season of Migration to the North, pp. 75–9. Mohammad Shaheen, 'Tayeb Salih's Mustafa Sa'eed: The Southern Invader in Icy Battlefield', *Arab Journal for the Humanities*, 4:16 (Fall 1984), pp. 281–92. Pauline Marie Scott, 'Writing Back to Othello in Season of Migration to the North', in idem, Writing, Rewriting, and Unwriting the Renaissance: Constructing 'Otherness' In Ariosto's 'Orlando Furioso', Shakespeare's Othello, Woolf's Orlando and Salih's Season of Migration to the North *(Otherness, Ludorico, Aristo, Itlay, Virginia Woolf, Tayeb Salih, Sudan)* (Ph.D. Dissertation), Michigan, UMI Dissertation Services, 1999, pp. 166–206.
76. Muḥammadiyya (ed.), *al-Ṭayyib Ṣāliḥ*, pp. 132–3. Shāhīn, *Taḥawwulāt al-Shawq*, pp. 145–51, 160–1. Ṭarābīshī, *Sharq wa-Gharb*, pp. 171–2. John, 'A Dialogue with Mr Tayeb Sālih', *The Islamic*

Quarterly, pp. 211–12. Another perception might provide another option which holds that Muṣṭafā was a lie, but since he assumes that the lie is the truest of all, we can conclude that Muṣṭafā was not a lie but the truth. In other words, since it is very difficult to differentiate between reality and fiction, falseness and truth, everything is possible. See for example, Qaysūma, *al-Anā wa'l-Ākhar*, pp. 142–77. We also should bear in mind that al-Ṭayyib Ṣāliḥ alludes to Shakespeare not only in *Mawsim al-Hijra ilā al-Shamāl*, but also in his short story 'Risāla ilā Aylīn', when Aylīn responds to the narrator who proposes marriage and reminds him in this context of Shakespeare's words: 'Cupid is a knavish lad' (*Dawmat Wad Ḥāmid*), p. 28.

77. For further information on Ṣāliḥ's concept and some other elements in the comparison between these two characters, see al-Ḥilū, 'Ḥiwār ma'a al-Ṭayyib Ṣāliḥ (2)', *al-Ayyām*, as cited by Berkley, *The Roots of Consciousness*, pp. LXVII–LXIX.
78. The author has testified that since he grew to maturity he realized that his seventy year-old grandfather was still working in the fields. He has mentioned elsewhere that his grandfather died in 1966 when he was very old and had nine sons and one daughter. His grandfather married a second wife when he was already an old man, and had three children. See Jibrīl, *'Alā al-Darb*, pp. 28, 94–6.
79. Shams al-Dīn Mūsā, *al-Mar'a al-Unmūdhaj fī al-Riwāya al-'Arabiyya al-Ḥadītha*, Cairo, al-Hay'a al-Miṣriyya al-'Āmma li'l-Kitāb, 1985, pp. 58–65. Ḥasan al-Māni', *Nafaḥāt 'an al-Adab wa'l-Fann*, pp. 19–20. Ṣāliḥ Ibrāhīm, *al-Mar'a fī Adab al-Ṭayyib Ṣāliḥ*, pp. 46–9. al-Shar', 'al-Baḥth 'an al-Shakhṣiyya al-Jadīda', *Abḥāth al-Yarmūk*, p. 25.
80. We might note that the narrator's crisis, which derived especially from Muṣṭafā Sa'īd in his life as in his death, is part and parcel of the narrator's crisis circle created by the author and which includes quite a few characters (Muṣṭafā, Ḥusna, the English women), see Ni'ma, *Ṣirā' al-Maqhūr ma'a al-Sulṭa*, pp. 167–287. Ṣubḥī and al-Sham'a, 'al-Ṭayyib Ṣāliḥ Riwā'iyyan wa-Nāqidan', in Muḥammadiyya (ed.), *al-Ṭayyib Ṣāliḥ*, pp. 126–8.
81. The Egyptian writer and literary critic Latīfa al-Zayyāt explains the background of Ḥusna's rebellion against Wad al-Rayyis' efforts to take her by force, and indicates that his violence created even more violence and that the villagers did not support her, but rather the narrator. See al-Zayyāt, *Min Ṣuwar al-Mar'a*, pp. 65–7. Ni'ma in *'Urs al-Zayn* did not want to get married to several men courting her such as Aḥmad and Idrīs, and her father had not forced her. Furthermore, when the headmaster did want to marry Ni'ma, her father did not agree, and stressed the age difference between the headmaster and Ni'ma (p. 70).
82. The similarity between Muṣṭafā Sa'īd and Wad al-Rayyis might be mentioned, especially with regard to women, sex and wildness, and the fact that Ḥusna was the wife of both. Muṣṭafā shows a particular interest in Wad al-Rayyis and the proof of this is that the narrator did not find many pictures of the villagers in Muṣṭafā's room, but Wad al-Rayyis is honoured by eight different ones. Also, Muṣṭafā pursued Jean Morris for three years, the same period of time that Wad al-Rayyis waited to marry the widow Ḥusna. In addition, Wad al-Rayyis had waited two weeks after his marriage to Ḥusna to sleep with her (pp. 126–7) but she rejected him, while Muṣṭafā had waited two months after his marriage to Jean Morris to sleep with her, but she also rejected him (pp. 160–1). See al-Ṣaffār, *Azmat al-Ajyāl al-'Arabiyya al-Mu'aṣira*, pp. 44–9. al-Khānjī, *Ru'yat al-Mawt fī 'Ālam al-Ṭayyib Ṣāliḥ al-Riwā'ī*, pp. 27–9. John, 'A Dialogue with Mr Tayeb Salih', *The Islamic Quarterly*, pp. 214, 217. al-Shar', 'al-Baḥth 'an al-Shakhṣiyya al-Jadīda', *Abḥāth al-Yarmūk*, pp. 18–21. For further details on the psychological meaning of the two murders see Tarawneh and John, 'Tayeb Salih and Freud', *Arabica*, pp. 337, 339.
83. Bilāl, 'Qirā'a Jadīda', *Kitābāt Sūdāniyya*, p. 75.
84. Muḥammadiyya (ed.), *al-Ṭayyib Ṣāliḥ*, p. 128.

85. Jibrīl, 'al-Ṭayyib Ṣāliḥ: Malāmiḥ min Sīra Dhātiyya (6)', *al-Ḥayāt*, p. 20. See also the Egyptian literary critic 'Abd al-Raḥmān Abū 'Awf, 'Bu'd al-Wāqi' fī Adab al-Ṭayyib Ṣāliḥ', *al-Ṭalī'a*, 6 (June 1976), pp. 152–3.
86. It is true that Ḍaw al-Bayt in the perception of the real author signified light, but he also might signify the search for meaning and the pure and positive world. See also Bilāl, 'Qirā'a Jadīda', *Kitābāt Sūdāniyya*, p. 75.
87. Steingass, *A Comprehensive Persian-English Dictionary*, pp. 202, 726.
88. Muḥammadiyya (ed.), *al-Ṭayyib Ṣāliḥ*, p. 220.
89. 'Ābdīn, *Ta'rīkh al-Thaqāfa al-'Arabiyya fī al-Sūdān*, pp. 24–6.
90. Muḥammadiyya (ed.), *al-Ṭayyib Ṣāliḥ*, p. 220. Bilāl, 'Qirā'a Jadīda', *Kitābāt Sūdāniyya*, pp. 73, 75, 77.
91. Ṣāliḥ, *Bandar Shāh: Ḍaw al-Bayt*, p. 19. Idem, *Mawsim al-Hijra ilā al-Shamāl*, pp. 18, 52, 60, 124–5, 134, 135.
92. The meaning of the name 'Maryūd' in colloquial Sudanese is 'the beloved', see 'Awn al-Sharīf Qāsim, *Qāmūs al-Lahja al-'Āmmiyya fī al-Sūdān*, p. 482. Ṣāliḥ, *Maryūd*, *al-Hilāl* (December 1976), p. 63.
93. Muḥammadiyya (ed.), *al-Ṭayyib Ṣāliḥ*, p. 220.
94. For this thesis see 'Īsā al-Sa'īd, 'al-Ṭayyib Ṣāliḥ: Taftīt al-'Ālam', *al-Karmil*, p. 262. Bakrī, ''Ibr Majrā al-Ta'rīkh', *al-Kharṭūm*, p. 6.
95. Ṣāliḥ, *Dawmat Wad Ḥāmid*, p. 36.
96. Ṣāliḥ, *Bandar Shāh: Ḍaw al-Bayt*, pp. 21, 76. *Bandar Shāh: Maryūd*, pp. 15, 16. *Dawmat Wad Ḥāmid*, p. 20. Māhir Ḥasan Fahmī, 'Maryūd aw Humūm al-Muthaqqafīn', in idem, *Qaḍāyā fī al-Adab wa'l-Naqd*, Doha, Dār al-Thaqāfa, 1986, pp. 326–33.
97. Ṣāliḥ, *Bandar Shāh: Maryūd*, pp. 50–6.
98. al-Naqqāsh, 'Qaṣīda fī al-'Ishq wa'l-Maḥabba', in al-Ṭayyib Ṣāliḥ, *Bandar Shāh: Maryūd*, pp. 33–6.
99. On the term 'Bilāl' see W. 'Arafat, The *Encyclopaedia of Islam*, New Edition, E.J. Brill, Leiden, vol.1, 1986, p. 1215. We should bear in mind that some of Ṣāliḥ's characters have a similar background of slavery and in some case of blackness like Muṣṭafā's mother, Fāṭima 'Abd al-Ṣādiq (*Mawsim al-Hijra ilā al-Shamāl*). Wad Ḥāmid the holy man was a slave of a godless person ('Dawmat Wad Ḥāmid') and Mūsā (a marginal character in *'Urs al-Zayn*) who was the slave of a rich man in the village who, when the government freed the slaves, preferred to stay with his master. For more details on the phenomenon of slavery in the Sudan with its connection to Ṣāliḥ's works see Bakrī, ''Ibr Majrā al-Ta'rīkh', *al-Kharṭūm*, 1831, p. 5. Usāma al-Khawwād, 'al-Ṭayyib Ṣāliḥ: Ārā' fī al-Siyāsa wa'l Hujna al-Thaqāfiyya', *Kitābāt Sūdāniyya*, 8 (June 1994), pp. 82–8. el-Badawī, *al-Ṭayyib Ṣāliḥ*, pp. 66–9.
100. Jibrīl, 'al-Ṭayyib Ṣāliḥ: Malāmiḥ min Sīra Dhātiyya (6)', *al-Ḥayāt*, p. 20.
101. El'ad-[Bouskila], 'Taṭawwur al-Shakhṣiyya fī A'māl al-Ṭayyib Ṣāliḥ', *al-Karmil*, pp. 7–26. Idem, 'Shaping the Cast of Characters', *Journal of Arabic Literature*, pp. 59–84.

Notes to Chapter Four:
Development of the Characters in al-Ṭayyib Ṣāliḥ's Writing

1. This chapter is based on two of my earlier articles: the first is an earlier and shortened version which appeared in Arabic: 'Taṭawwur al-Shakhṣiyya fī A'māl al-Ṭayyib Ṣāliḥ', *al-Karmil*, Haifa, 10 (1989), pp. 7–26. The second is in English; 'Shaping the Cast of Characters: The Case of al-Ṭayyib Ṣāliḥ', *Journal of Arabic Literature*, XXIX:2 (July 1998), pp. 59–84.
2. For a clear and thorough discussion of the status of the character, see Rimmon-Kenan, *Narrative Fiction*, pp. 29–42.

3. Salīm Barakāt, *Fuqahā' al-Ẓalām*, 1985; Barrāda, *La'bat al-Nisyān*, 1987. Ibrāhīm Naṣrallāh, *Barārī al-Hummā*, 1985. See Samira Aghacy 'The Use of Autobiography in Rashīd al-Ḍa'īf's *Dear Mr Kawabata*', in Ostle, De Moor and Wild (eds) *Writing the self*, pp. 217–28. Rashīd al-Ḍa'īf, *'Azīzī al-Sayyid Kawābātā*, 2nd ed., Beirut, Riyāḍ al-Rayyis li'l-Kutub wa'l-Nashr, 2001 (1st ed. 1995). For the English translation see *Dear Mr Kawabata* (trans. Paul Starkey), Northampton, MA, Interlink, 2000. Ilyās Khūrī, *Abwāb al-Madīna*, Beirut, Dār Ibn Rushd, 1981. For the English translation see Elias Khoury, *Gates of the City* (trans. Paula Haydar), Minneapolis, University of Minnesota Press, 1993.
4. Rimmon-Kenan, *Narrative Fiction*, pp. 59–70. Ewen, *HaDemut BaSipporet*, pp. 45–135. (Hebrew).
5. Maḥfūẓ, *Dunyā Allāh*, pp. 122–3. Johnson-Davies (ed.), *Modern Arabic Short Stories*, p. 136.
6. I take issue here with the Sudanese scholar 'Abd al-Raḥmān al-Khānjī, who views the novels alone as one organic unit and does not include the short stories. See his important work *Qirā'a Jadīda fī Riwāyat al-Ṭayyib Ṣāliḥ*, 1980. For my thesis see El'ad [-Bouskila], 'Taṭawwur al-Shakhṣiyya fī A'māl al-Ṭayyib Ṣāliḥ', *al-Karmil*, pp. 7–26. Idem, 'Shaping the Cast of Characters', *Journal of Arabic Literature*, pp. 59–84. Shaheen, 'Tayeb Salih and Wad Hamid', *Arab Journal for Humanities*, pp. 276–86. Bakrī, ''Ibr Majrā al-Tā'rīkh', al-Kharṭūm, p. 6. al-Qamarī, *Majāzāt*, pp. 137–45. The real author relates in one text to another work as we, the readers, should keep in mind that all of his literary works are indeed a single work. Therefore, we can find in *Bandar Shāh: Ḍaw al-Bayt* (pp. 19, 25, 26, 32) hints and comments which the author relates to his other works like 'Ḥafnat Tamr', *'Urs al-Zayn* and *Mawsim al-Hijra ilā al-Shamāl*. See also al-Qamarī, 'Hākadhā Ḥaddathanī al-Ṭayyib Ṣāliḥ', *Kitābāt Sūdāniyya*, p. 63.
7. Bassām Manṣūr interviewed Khalīl al-Nu'aymī upon publication of his new novel *Tafrīgh al-Kā'in*: 'Khalīl al-Nu'aymī: ḥattā law Karrartu Nafsī ayna al-Mushkila?' *Barīd al-Janūb*, 73 (September 16, 1996), pp. 14–15.
8. For this perception see also Ḥasan Abbashir al-Ṭayyib, 'al-Ṭayyib Ṣāliḥ Riwā'iyyan wa-Shā'iran Mubdi'an', *Ibdā'*, pp. 27–32. Below is a list of characters that reappear in al-Ṭayyib Ṣāliḥ's writing, divided into two main categories: The first includes main characters and the second secondary characters that are not developed, that do not advance the reader in understanding the text or other characters, but whose role is to serve as backdrop to the village of Wad Ḥāmid.

   The first category includes the following characters: the narrator (the grandson and Muḥaymīd): 'Ḥafnat Tamr', 'Risāla ilā Aylīn', 'Dawmat Wad Ḥāmid', 'Hākadhā Yā Sādatī', 'Muqaddimāt', *Mawsim al-Hijra ilā al-Shamāl, Bandar Shāh: Ḍaw al-Bayt*, 'al-Rajul al-Qubruṣī', *Bandar Shāh: Maryūd*. The grandfather: 'Ḥafnat Tamr', 'Dawmat Wad Ḥāmid', *Mawsim al-Hijra ilā al-Shamāl, Bandar Shāh: Ḍaw al-Bayt*. Ḍaw al-Bayt: *Bandar Shāh: Ḍaw al-Bayt, Maryūd*. Bandar Shāh: *Bandar Shāh: Ḍaw al-Bayt, Maryūd*. Sa'īd 'Ashā al-Bāyitāt (Sa'īd al-Būm): *'Urs al-Zayn, Bandar Shāh: Ḍaw al-Bayt, Maryūd*. al-Ṭāhir al-Rawwāsī (al-Ṭāhir Wad al-Rawwās, al-Ṭāhir Wad al-Rawwāsī): *'Urs al-Zayn, Mawsim al-Hijra ilā al-Shamāl, Bandar Shāh: Ḍaw al-Bayt, Maryūd*. 'Abd al-Ḥafīẓ: *'Urs al-Zayn, Bandar Shāh: Ḍaw al-Bayt, Maryūd*. Wad al-Baṣīr: *Mawsim al-Hijra ilā al-Shamāl, Bandar Shāh: Ḍaw al-Bayt*. Sayf al-Dīn: *'Urs al-Zayn, Bandar Shāh: Ḍaw al-Bayt*. Ibrāhīm Wad Ṭāhā: *'Urs al-Zayn, Bandar Shāh: Ḍaw al-Bayt, Maryūd*. al-Ṭarīfī: *'Urs al-Zayn, Bandar Shāh*. Wad al-Rayyis: *Mawsim al-Hijra ilā al-Shamāl, Bandar Shāh: Ḍaw al-Bayt*. al-Ḥanīn: *'Urs al-Zayn, Bandar Shāh: Ḍaw al-Bayt*.

   In the second category are the following characters: the father: *Mawsim al-Hijra ilā al-Shamāl*, 'al-Rajul al-Qubruṣī', *Bandar Shāh: Maryūd*. Ḥusayn the merchant: 'Nakhla 'alā al-Jadwal', 'Ḥafnat Tamr'. Mas'ūd the neighbor: 'Ḥafnat Tamr', *Bandar Shāh: Ḍaw al-Bayt*. Sa'īd al-Qānūnī: *'Urs al-Zayn, Mawsim al-Hijra ilā al-Shamāl, Bandar Shāh: Ḍaw al-Bayt*. Fāṭima (Faṭṭūma): *'Urs al-Zayn*, 'al-Rajul al-Qubruṣī', *Bandar Shāh: Ḍaw al-Bayt, Maryūd*. Sheikh 'Alī: *'Urs al-Zayn, Bandar Shāh: Ḍaw al-Bayt*. Aḥmad Abū al-Banāt: *Bandar Shāh: Ḍaw al-Bayt, Maryūd*. Maryam (Maryūm):

Bandar Shāh: Ḍaw al-Bayt, 'al-Rajul al-Qubruṣī', *Bandar Shāh: Maryūd*. Ḥāmid Wad Ḥalīma: *Bandar Shāh: Ḍaw al-Bayt, Maryūd*. Wad al-Shā'ib: *Bandar Shāh: Ḍaw al-Bayt, Maryūd*. Mukhtār Ḥasab al-Rasūl: *Bandar Shāh: Ḍaw al-Bayt, Maryūd*.

9. Ṣāliḥ, *Dawmat Wad Ḥāmid*, pp. 87–9.
10. Ṣāliḥ, *Mawsim al-Hijra ilā al-Shamāl*, p. 141.
11. Ṣāliḥ, *Dawmat Wad Ḥāmid*, pp. 39–40, 44–6; *'Urs al-Zayn*, pp. 46–50, 58, 67; *Bandar Shāh: Ḍaw al-Bayt*, pp. 47–50, 64–8; *Maryūd*, pp. 55–8. Also on this subject, see the article by Mālṭī-Dūglās, 'al-'Anāṣir al-Turāthiyya fī al-Adab al-'Arabī al-Mu'āṣir', *Fuṣūl*, pp. 21–9.
12. This appears widely in the village novels of modern Arabic literatures, especially Egyptian literature. See Elad [-Bouskila], *The Village Novel*, pp. 94–8. See also other Arab writings such as Salīm Barakāt in *Fuqahā' al-Ẓalām*, el-Badawi in *Laban al-Ābanūs Yā Zōl*, or Munīf, in *al-Ashjār wa-Ightiyāl Marzūq*.
13. Ṣāliḥ, *Dawmat Wad Ḥāmid*, pp. 37, 42, 48; *'Urs al-Zayn*, p. 62; *Mawsim al-Hijra ilā al-Shamāl*, pp. 68, 119–20. *Bandar Shāh: Ḍaw al-Bayt*, p. 61; *Maryūd*, p. 75.
14. Ṣāliḥ, *Dawmat Wad Ḥāmid*, pp. 7, 19, 22, 30, 42, 44. *Mawsim al-Hijra ilā al-Shamāl*, pp. 6, 49, 53, 66, 105; *Bandar Shāh: Ḍaw al-Bayt*, p. 92; *Maryūd*, pp. 13, 17, 19.
15. Ṣāliḥ, *Dawmat Wad Ḥāmid*, pp. 37–8, 42–3, 48, 50.
16. The novel *'Urs al-Zayn* was written in 1962. Two of its chapters were published in *Ḥiwār*, 10 (May-June 1964), pp. 40–51. The novel was first published in its entirety in the Sudanese journal *al-Kharṭūm*, 3 (December 1966), pp. 98–139. *'Urs al-Zayn* was first published as a book in 1967 (see Appendix A).
17. Ṣāliḥ, *'Urs al-Zayn*, pp. 62–3.
18. The novel *Mawsim al-Hijra ilā al-Shamāl* was written, according to the author, only after he had written the novel *'Urs al-Zayn*. See Jibrīl, 'al-Ṭayyib Ṣāliḥ: Malāmiḥ min Sīra Dhātiyya (6)', *al-Ḥayāt*, p. 20. However, in an interview, he indicated that he began to write the first third of the novel in a small village near Cannes in the southeast of France in 1960 or 1962 (he does not remember exactly). He completed it in London four years later. See al-Sāmarrā'ī, 'Muqābala Adabiyya ma'a al-Ṭayyib Ṣāliḥ', *al-Ādāb*, pp. 7–8. The text first appeared in the journal *Ḥiwār*, 24–5 (September-December 1966), pp. 5–87. It was first published as a book in 1967 (see Appendix A).
19. Ṣāliḥ, *Mawsim al-Hijra ilā al-Shamāl*, pp. 103–5.
20. Ibid., p. 103. Salih, *Season of Migration to the North*, p. 100.
21. Ṣāliḥ, *Bandar Shāh: Ḍaw al-Bayt*, pp. 9–11, 43–6, 88–91.
22. Ṣāliḥ, *Bandar Shāh: Maryūd*, pp. 29–30, 43.
23. 'Abd al-Sattār Khulayyif, *al-Baḥth 'an Bunduqiyya*, Cairo, al-Hay'a al-Miṣriyya al-'Āmma li'l-Kitāb, 1978; *Gharīb bayn al-Diyār*, Cairo, al-Hay'a al-Miṣriyya al-'Āmma li'l-Kitāb, 1980; *al-Musāfirūn*, Cairo, Dār al-Ma'ārif, 1982.
24. The following works of 'Abd al-Ḥakīm Qāsim were translated into English: 'The Trial of the Small Black Woman', in Denys Johnson Davies (trans. and ed.), *Arabic Short Stories*, London, Quartet Books, 1983, pp. 137–42. *The Seven Days of Man* (trans. Joseph N. Bell), Cairo, General Book Organization, 1989; and *Rites of Assent: Two Novellas* (trans. Peter Theroux), Philadelphia, Temple University Press, 1995.
25. 'Abd al-Ḥakīm Qāsim, *Ayyām al-Insān al-Sab'a*, 1969. *al-Mahdī, al-Safīr* (July 9, 1978), p. 8; (July 16, 1978), p. 8; (July 23, 1978), p. 8; *Qadar al-Ghuraf al-Muqbiḍa*, Cairo, Maṭbū'āt al-Qāhira, 1982.
26. Honoré de Balzac is among writers whose central and even secondary characters reappear in other works, especially *La Comédie Humaine*. Most of William Faulkner's works are set in an American locale he created – the remote town of Jefferson in Yoknapatawpha County in the deep South (*The Sound and the Fury*, *Light in August*, *Absalom, Absalom!*, *The Bear*, and *Requiem for a Nun*), and various characters reappear in other roles and changing importance. Faulkner's themes are also

repeated in some of his writing, most notably the gap between blacks and whites and the fear of the stranger, always represented by someone with at least some black blood. This encounter of the stranger with local society – in *Light in August*, for example – leads to violent outbursts between them. We see some parallels with Ṣāliḥ's *Mawsim al-Hijra ilā al-Shamāl* in Muṣṭafā Sa'īd's encounter with Western society.

27. Maḥfūẓ, *Malḥamat al-Ḥarāfīsh*, 1977. For the English translation, see *The Harafish*, 1994. Nedal al-Mousa, 'The Nature and Uses of the Fantastic in the Fictional World of Naguib Mahfouz', *Journal of Arabic Literature*, XXIII (1992), pp. 36–48.
28. The five works are 'Eye of a Blue Dog', 1947, *Leaf Storm*, 1955, *No One Writes to the Colonel*, 1958, *In Evil Hour*, 1962, and 'Big Mama's Funeral', 1962.
29. al-Ṭayyib Ṣāliḥ is aware of the resemblance and connection with literary works of Latin-American writers, and the difference between himself and them: 'I have noticed that the Latin-American writers, in particular Gabriel García Márquez, were greatly occupied by the issue of government, in particular in *One Hundred Years of Solitude*. But I think government occupied them from the historic, not the mythical aspect'. Jibrīl, 'al-Ṭayyib Ṣāliḥ, Malāmiḥ min Sīra Dhātiyya (6)', *al-Ḥayāt*, p. 20. See also al-Qamarī, 'Hākadhā Ḥaddathanī al-Ṭayyib Ṣāliḥ', *Kitābāt Sūdāniyya*, pp. 60–1.
30. It is interesting to note that al-Ṭayyib Ṣāliḥ, unlike Gabriel García Márquez who invented a village named Macondo, preferred an existing community, a village in northern Sudan. Sālih's choice gives his writing a more credible dimension, and enables him to move freely between the real and the fictional worlds, similar to other Arab and Western writers. A particularly striking example in Western literature is the English writer Thomas Hardy, in his book published over a century ago – *Tess of the D'Urbervilles*, 1891.
31. Ṣāliḥ, *Dawmat Wad Ḥāmid*, pp. 37, 42, 48. *'Urs al-Zayn*, p. 62; *Mawsim al-Hijra ilā al-Shamāl*, pp. 68, 119–20; *Bandar Shāh: Ḍaw al-Bayt*, p. 61. *Maryūd*, p. 75. García Márquez, *One Hundred Years of Solitud.*
32. Ṣāliḥ, *Dawmat Wad Ḥāmid*, p. 36; García Márquez, *One Hundred Years of Solitude.*
33. Abū Nādir, *al-Alsuniyya wa'l-Naqd al-Adabī fī al-Naẓariyya wa'l-Mumārasa*, pp. 139–43.
34. Ṣāliḥ, *Mawsim al-Hijra ilā al-Shamāl*, pp. 101–2 and compare with al-Sharqāwī, *al-Arḍ*, p. 290. Idem, *Qulūb Khāliya*, Cairo, al-Dār al-Qawmiyya li'l-Ṭibā'a wa'l-Nashr, 1965, p. 26 (1st ed. 1957). Muḥammad Khalīl Qāsim, *al-Shamandūra*, Cairo, Dār al-Kātib li'l-Ṭibā'a wa'l-Nashr, 1968, p. 164. Ghānim, *al-Jabal*, pp. 91–4.
35. Ṣāliḥ, *'Urs al-Zayn*, pp. 73–4, 79–80. Compare with Ṭāhā Ḥusayn, *al-Ayyām*, vol. 1. al-Sharqāwī, *al-Arḍ*, pp. 8–9. See Elad [-Bouskila], *The Village Novel*, p. 85. About official and popular Islam and the Sufi orders in Sudan, see John Spencer Trimingham, *Islam in the Sudan*, London, Frank Cass, 1965, pp. 105–241.
36. For research on the role of mysticism in modern life in contemporary Arab literatures, especially in the Sudan and Egypt, see Menahem Milson, 'Reality, Allegory and Myth in the Work of Najīb Maḥfūẓ', *Asian and African Studies*, 11:2 (1976), pp. 157–79. Nasr, 'Popular Islam in al-Ṭayyib Ṣāliḥ', *Journal of Arabic Literature*, pp. 88–103. al-Haggagi, 'The Mythmaker: Tayeb Salih' in Ghazoul and Harlow (eds), *The View from Within*, pp. 94–133. Hamdi Sakkut, 'Naguib Mahfouz and the Sufi Way' (translated from the Arabic by Noha Radwan), in Ghazoul and Harlow (eds), *The View from Within*, pp. 90–8; Elad [-Bouskila], 'Fiction and Reality', in idem, *Writer, Culture, Text*, pp. 62–73. Idem, 'Mahfuz's "Za'balāwī": Six Stations of a Quest', *International Journal of Middle East Studies*, pp. 631–44
37. Jibrīl, 'al-Ṭayyib Ṣāliḥ: Malāmiḥ min Sīra Dhātiyya (6)', *al-Ḥayāt*, p. 20.
38. Ibid.

39. For more information on women in the Sudanese society during the period in which the real events in al-Ṭayyib Ṣāliḥ's writing took place see Ḥalīm al-Yāzijī, *al-Sūdān wa'l-Ḥaraka al-Adabiyya*, pp. 763–7.
40. Delineating characters of village women who actually represent the writer's idealized or wishful thinking is a common phenomenon in modern Egyptian literature. For example, Zaynab in the novel *Zaynab, Manāẓir wa-Akhlāq Rīfiyya* by Muḥammad Ḥusayn Haykal or Waṣīfa in the novel *al-Arḍ* by al-Sharqāwī. See Elad [-Bouskila], *The Village Novel*, pp. 66–7, 90–2. See also Ṣāliḥ Ibrāhīm, *al-Mar'a fī Adab al-Ṭayyib Ṣāliḥ*, pp. 52–6. For a similar role of young women as exceptional characters in modern Palestinian literature see for example characters such as Ikhtayya and Sarwa in Emīl Ḥabībī, *Ikhtayya*, Nicosia, Mu'assasat Bīsān Press, 1985. See also the character of Nawāl in Anṭōn Shammās' *'Arabesqot*, Tel Aviv, 'Am 'Oved, 1986, pp. 46–7 (Hebrew). For the English translation see idem, *Arabesques* (trans. Vivian Eden), New York, Harper and Row, 1988.
41. Ṣāliḥ, *'Urs al-Zayn*, pp. 31–2, 37–8. See Ṣāliḥ Ibrāhīm, *al-Mar'a fī Adab al-Ṭayyib Ṣāliḥ*, p. 22. Ḥalīm al-Yāzijī, *al-Sūdān wa'l-Ḥaraka al-Adabiyya*, pp. 941–2.
42. Ṣāliḥ, *Mawsim al-Hijra ilā al-Shamāl*, pp. 99, 102–4. Shams al-Dīn Mūsā, *al-Mar'a al-'Unmūdhaj fī al-Riwāya al-'Arabiyya al-Ḥadītha*, pp. 58–65.
43. Ṣāliḥ, *Bandar Shāh: Ḍaw al-Bayt*, pp. 109–10. See Ṣāliḥ Ibrāhīm, *al-Mar'a fī Adab al-Ṭayyib Ṣāliḥ*, pp. 22, 49–50.
44. Ṣāliḥ, *Bandar Shāh: Maryūd*, pp. 20, 75.
45. Ibid., pp. 63–5.
46. Ṣāliḥ, *'Urs al-Zayn*, pp. 5–6, 99–100; compare with the uncomplimentary description of the preacher in 'Dawmat Wad Ḥāmid' in the collection by the same name, p. 36.
47. El'ad [-Bouskila], 'Taṭawwur al-Shakhṣiyya fī A'māl al-Ṭayyib Ṣāliḥ', *al-Karmil*, pp. 18–25. Idem, 'Shaping the Cast of Characters', *Journal of Arabic Literature*, pp. 59–84. Mona Takieddine Amyuni, 'The Arab Artist's Role in Society: Three Case Studies: Naguib Mahfouz, Tayeb Salih and Elias Khoury', *Arabic and Middle Eastern Literatures*, 2:2 (1999), p. 209.
48. A similar use of this literary device can be found in modern Arabic literatures, e.g., *al-Arḍ* by al-Sharqāwī, or the novel *Ayyām al-Insān al-Sab'a* by 'Abd al-Ḥakīm Qāsim, or the short story 'Arḍ al-Burtuqāl al-Ḥazīn' in the collection ot short stories of that name, 1963 by Kanafānī. For the English translation, see 'The Land of Sad Oranges', in Kanafani, *Men in the Sun* (trans. and ed. Hilary Kilpatrick), London, Heinemann, 1978, pp. 57–62.
49. *The Book of a Thousand Nights and a Night* (trans. Richard F. Burton), London, H.S Nichols, 1897. Giovanni Boccaccio, *The Decameron* (trans. Guido Waldman), Oxford, Oxford University Press, 1993, and Henry James, *The Ambassadors*, 2nd ed., A Norton Critical Edition, New York, W.W. Norton, 1994 (1st ed. 1903).
50. Ṣāliḥ, *Dawmat Wad Ḥāmid*, pp. 77–81.
51. 'Muqaddimāt' includes five short-short stories in the collection *Dawmat Wad Ḥāmid*, pp. 83–93. Note that an earlier version of 'Muqaddimāt' in *Ḥiwār* comprises six stories! The short-short story 'al-Shay' al-Ākhar' was published in *Ḥiwār*, 21 (March-April 1966), pp. 37–8. This story differs from the other five stories of 'Muqaddimāt' mainly in that it does not repeat the same formula – bringing together a young Eastern man with a young Western woman.
52. Ṣāliḥ, *Dawmat Wad Ḥāmid*, pp. 85–6, 87–9, 90–1, 93.
53. Siddiq, 'The Process of Individuation', *Journal of Arabic Literature*, pp. 85–9; Peled, 'Portrait of an Intellectual', *Middle Eastern Studies*, pp. 218–28.
54. Ṣāliḥ, *Mawsim al-Hijra ilā al-Shamāl*, pp. 89–90, 100–1, 133–4.
55. The feelings of an author who returns to his village and wants to prove to his fellow villagers – but above all to himself – that he is still part of the village and not a stranger, can be found in modern Arabic literatures such as al-Ṭayyib Ṣāliḥ's, *Bandar Shāh: Ḍaw al-Bayt*, p. 86; al-Sharqāwī, *al-Arḍ*,

pp. 3–4; ʻAbd al-Wahhāb al-Aswānī, *Salmā al-Aswāniyya*, Cairo, al-Hay'a al-Miṣriyya al-ʻĀmma li'l-Ta'līf wa'l-Nashr, 1970, p. 16. Alfred Faraj, *Ḥikāyāt al-Zaman al-Ḍā'i' fī Qarya Miṣriyya*, Cairo, Dār al-Mustaqbal al-ʻArabī, 1983, p. 10. However, there are also examples in modern Arabic literatures of writers who returned to their villages only to discover that they do not belong, becoming aware of their foreignness and even mocking the village: for example, al-Sharqāwī in his novel *al-Fallāḥ*, 1968. Ḥasan Muḥassib in his novel *Ḥulm al-Layl wa'l-Nahār*, Cairo, Dār al-Maʻārif, 1979, p. 21, and al-Qaʻīd in *Yaḥduth fī Miṣr al-Ān*, pp. 110–11.

56. Muḥammadiyya (ed.), *al-Ṭayyib Ṣāliḥ ʻAbqarī al-Riwāya al-ʻArabiyya*, 1976. al-Ṣaffār, *Azmat al-Ajyāl al-ʻArabiyya al-Muʻāṣira*, 1980; Ṣubḥī, *Abṭāl fī al-Ṣayrūra*, 1980. Amyuni (ed.), Tayeb Salih's Season of Migration to the North, 1985. Niʻma, *Ṣirāʻ al-Maqhūr maʻa al-Sulṭa*, 1986; Shāhīn, *Taḥawwulāt al-Shawq*, 1993, and Siddiq, 'The Process of Individuation', *Journal of Arabic Literature*, pp. 67–104.

57. Conrad, *Heart of Darkness*, 1902. As al-Ṭayyib Ṣāliḥ tried in some respects to rewrite *Othello*, he also tried to rewrite Conrad's *Heart of Darkness*. That is to say that Muṣṭafā possibly expected to find the heart of light in the cultural center of Europe, i.e., London, but actually discovered the ugly face of Europe or in other words the real 'Heart of Darkness'. As far as the narrator is concerned, he did not expect to find the heart of light in Europe and therefore did not find the 'Heart of Darkness', but the point of balance between them. See also Shāhīn, *al-Adab wa'l-Usṭūra*, 1996, Edward W. Said, 'The Politics of Knowledge', in David H. Riechter (eds), *Falling into Theory: Conflicting Views on Reading Literature*, Boston, Bedford Books of St. Martin's Press, 1994, p. 200.

58. Camus, *The Outsider*, 1942.

59. Albert Camus, *The Rebel* (trans. Anthony Bower), London, Penguin Books, 1971 (1st ed. 1951). Idem, *The Myth of Sisyphus* (trans. Justin O'Brien), London, Penguin Books, 1975 (1st ed. 1955).

60. Ṣāliḥ, *Mawsim al-Hijra ilā al-Shamāl*, p. 23; See also p. 27. Salih, *Season of Migration to the North*, p. 19.

61. Ibid., p. 25. Ibid., p. 21.

62. Ibid., p. 27. ibid., p. 23.

63. Ibid., p. 30.

64. Ibid., p. 31. Salih, *Season of Migration to the North*, p. 27.

65. Ibid., p. 37. Ibid., p. 33.

66. Ibid., p. 113. Ibid., pp. 110–11. For more information see Ṣalāḥ Ṣāliḥ, *al-Riwāya al-ʻArabiyya wa'l-Ṣaḥrā'*, Damascus, Manshūrāt Wizārat al-Thaqāfa, 1996, pp. 120–8, 168–9.

67. For this perception see also John, 'The Life and Death of Mustafa Saʻeed', *Abhath al-Yarmouk*, p. 62.

68. Ṣāliḥ, *Bandar Shāh: Ḍaw al-Bayt*, p. 86. Salih, *Bandarshah: Dau Al-Beit*, p. 53.

69. Ibid., pp. 83, 86.

70. Part of the semi-autobiography edited by the Sudanese journalist Talḥat Jibrīl was published serially under the title 'al-Ṭayyib Ṣāliḥ: Malāmiḥ min Sīra Dhātiyya (1–6)', *al-Ḥayāt*, 12251–5, 12258 (September 10–14, 17, 1996), and later in idem, *ʻAlā al-Darb*, 1997. For a critical review of this book see Aḥmad Maḥmūd, 'Nūstāljyā al-Ṭayyib Ṣāliḥ wa'l-Ittikā' ʻalā al-Dhākira, Qirā'a fī al-Sīra al-Dhātiyya', *Kitābāt Sūdāniyya*, 8 (June 1999), pp. 71–7.

71. Ṣāliḥ, *Bandar Shāh: Maryūd*, p. 41. Salih, *Bandarshah: Meryoud*, p. 98.

72. Jibrīl, 'al-Ṭayyib Ṣāliḥ: Malāmiḥ min Sīra Dhātiyya (1)', *al-Ḥayāt*, p. 16.

73. The search for the meaning of life is a central theme in many works of modern Arab literatures in the twentieth century. The focus and method of the search are influenced both by the Western way of life and modernization, education, and technology, and by the influence that Western writers and philosophers – especially existentialists such as Jean Paul Sartre, Albert Camus, and Franz Kafka – have had on Arab writers, primarily in the 1960s. From Egypt, we can mention Najīb Maḥfūẓ in his novels *al-Liṣṣ wa'l-Kilāb*, 1961. *al-Summān wa'l-Kharīf*, 1962. For the English translation, see

Autumn Quail (trans. Roger Allen, revised by John Rodenbeck), Cairo, The American University in Cairo Press, 1985. *al-Ṭarīq,* 1964. For the English translation, see *The Search* (trans. Mohamed Islam; ed. Magdi Wahba), Cairo, The American University in Cairo Press, 1987. a*l-Shaḥḥādh*, 1965. For the English translation, see *The Beggar* (trans. Kristin Walker Henry and Nariman Khales Naili al-Warraki), Cairo, The American University in Cairo Press, 1986. *Tharthara fawq al-Nīl,* 1966. For the English translation, see *Adrift on the Nile* (trans. Frances Liadet), Cairo, The American University in Cairo Press, 1993. Also see Ghānim in his novels *al-Rajul Alladhī Faqada Ẓillahu,* 1962 and *al-Afyāl,* 1981. From Saudi Arabia, 'Abd al-Raḥmān Munīf in his novels *al-Ashjār wa-Ightiyāl Marzūq,* 1973, *al-Nihāyāt,* 1977. For the English translation, of the latter novel see *Endings* (trans. Roger Allen), London, Quartet Books, 1988, and *Mudun al-Milḥ,* 1984–9. For the English translation, see *Cities of Salt* (trans. Peter Theroux), London, Jonathan Cape, 1988 (1st ed. 1987). *The Trench* (trans. Peter Theroux), New York, Pantheon Books, 1991; *Variations on Night and Day* (trans. Peter Theroux), New York, Vintage Books, 1994 (1st ed. 1993. From Syria, Mīna in the novel *al-Yāṭir,* 1975. From Morocco, Barrāda in his novel *La'bat al-Nisyān,* 1987. The Palestinian Ḥabībī in his novel *al-Mutashā'il,* 1974.

74. 'Maryūd' means 'the beloved'. See 'Awn al-Sharīf Qāsim, *Qāmūs al-Lahja al-'Āmmiyya fī al-Sūdān,* p. 482. Ṣāliḥ dedicated the book to his father: 'To the spirit of my father, Muḥammad Ṣāliḥ Aḥmad – rich in his poverty and strong in his weakness; he lived his life loving and beloved, and died satisfied and connected' (p. 5). This name reflects the relationship between Bandar Shāh and Maryūd, the grandfather and the grandson. The name alludes to the fact that Bandar Shāh – like the grandfather – prefers the grandson to the sons. See also L. Stepanov, 'Between the Past and the Future' (trans. from Russian into English by Ella London), in the Russian translation of several of al-Ṭayyib Ṣāliḥ's novels, p. 11 (see Appendix C).
75. In modern world literature, there are writers who juxtapose opposite characters in a single work, such as Stephen Dedalus and Bloom in *Ulysses,* 1922 by James Joyce or the novella *Tonio Kröger,* 1903 by Thomas Mann, in which an introverted, suffering artist is contrasted with his simple and uncomplicated childhood friend. See Ewen, *HaDemut BaSipporet*, pp. 114–17 (Hebrew).
76. Theories about the 'double' in eighteenth and nineteenth century European literature are exemplified by writers such as E.T. Hoffman (1776–1822) and F.M. Dostoyevsky (1821–81). Furthermore it is not just a double and dualism in terms of characters but also in terms of attributes such as reality and fiction, true and false, freedom and slavery, beauty and ugliness, male and female, black and white, townsmen and villagers, colonized and colonizer, in short 'binary oppositions' or rather 'complementary opposites'. For this concept see also Qaysūma, 'al-Riwāya al-'Arabiyya wa-Thunā'iyyat al-Naṣṣ al-Muta'addid *Mawsim al-Hijra ilā al-Shamāl* Namūdhajan', in idem, *al-Riwāya al-'Arabiyya al-Ishkāl wa'l-Tashakkul*, pp. 159–60. Berta al-Nabr, 'al-'Unf fī Riwāyat *Mawsim al-Hijra ilā al-Shamāl*', in idem, *al-'Unf fī al-Qiṣṣa al-'Arabiyya al-Ḥadītha* [Beirut], 1991, pp. 114–15. Mona Amyuni, 'Images of Arab Women in *Middaq Alley* by Naguib Mahfouz and *Season of Migration to the North* by Tayeb Salih', *International Journal of Middle East Studies*, 17 (1985), p. 25.
77. Muhammed Khalafallah 'Abdalla, 'Muṣṭafā Migration from the Ṣa'īd: An Odyssey in Search of Identity' in Elad-Bouskila and Al-Shahi (eds), *Al-Ṭayyib Ṣāliḥ, Edebiyât*, pp. 43–61. Mousa, 'The Arabic Bildungsroman: A Generic Appraisal', *International Journal of Middle East Studies*, 25 (1993), pp. 223–40. Asa'd E. Khairallah, 'The Greek Cultural Heritage and the Odyssey of Modern Arab Poets', in Issa J. Boullata and Terri DeYoung (eds), *Tradition and Modernity in Arabic Literature*, Arkansas, Arkansas University Press, 1997, pp. 43–61.
78. A partial list of Arab authors who wrote a novel about time they had spent living in Europe includes writers from various Arab countries, especially Egypt, such as Ṭāhā Ḥusayn, *Adīb,* 1935; Tawfīq al-Ḥākīm, *'Uṣfur min al-Sharq,* 1938. Yaḥyā Ḥaqqī, *Qindīl Umm Hāshim,* 1944. Fatḥī Ghānim, *al-*

Sākhin wa'l-Bārid, 1960; Lewis 'Awaḍ (1915–90), *Mudhakkirāt Ṭālib Ba'tha,* 1965. 'Abd al-Ḥakīm Qāsim, *Muḥāwala li'l-Khurūj,* 1980. From Lebanon: Suhayl Idrīs, *al-Ḥayy al-Lātīnī,* 1954. From Syria, Shakīb al-Jābirī (b.1912), *Qaws Quzaḥ,* 1946. From Jordan: Jum'a Ḥammād, *Badawī fī Ūrūbbā,* 1977. From Morocco: Muḥammad Zifzāf, *al-Mar'a wa'l-Warda,* 1972. (see Chapter Five).

Notes to Chapter Five: The Migration to the North/West

1. Baldick, *Oxford Concise Dictionary of Literary Terms*, p. 24. For a detailed definition and discussion of this term see J.A. Cuddon, *The Penguin Dictionary of Literary Terms and Literary Theory*, 4th ed., London, Penguin Books, 1999, pp. 82–3. Culler, *Structuralist Poetic,* pp. 14–16, 75–95, 126–7, 177–8, 225–7.
2. Reynold A. Nicholson, *A Literary History of the Arabs,* Cambridge, Cambridge University Press, 1956, pp. 282–3, 358–64. Gustav Von Grunebaum, *Islam: Essays in the Nature and Growth of a Cultural Tradition,* 2nd ed., London, Routledge and Kegan Paul, 1961, pp. 237–45. Idem, *Modern Islam: The Search for Cultural Identity,* New York, Vintage Books, 1964, pp. 32–3. Bernard Lewis, *The Muslim Discovery of Europe,* London, Weidenfeld and Nicholson, 1982, pp. 221–3. A.F.L. Beeston et al. (eds), *The Cambridge History of Arabic Literature: Arabic Literature to the End of the Umayyad Period,* Cambridge, Cambridge University Press, 1983, pp. 460–82, 483–96, 497–501. Young et al. (eds), *The Cambridge History of Arabic Literature,* pp. 76–87, 248–423.
3. Gustav von Grunebaum 'The Sacred Character of Islamic Cities', in 'Abd al-Rahman Badawi (ed.), *Mélanges Taha Husain,* Cairo, Dar al-Maarif, 1942, pp. 25–37. Shlomo Dov Goitien, 'The Sanctity of Jerusalem and Palestinians in the Early Islam', in idem, *Studies in Islamic History and Institutions,* Leiden, E.J. Brill, 1966, pp. 135–48. Franz Rosenthal, *A History of Muslim Historiography,* 2nd ed., Leiden, E.J. Brill, 1968. Herbert Busse, 'The Sanctity of Jerusalem in Islam', *Judaism,* xvii (1968), pp. 441–68. Emmanuel Sivan, 'The Beginnings of Fadā'il al-Quds Literature', *Israel Oriental Studies,* I (1979), pp. 263–71. Isaac Hasson, 'Muslim Literature in Praise of Jerusalem: Faḍā'il al-Bayt al-Maqdis', *The Jerusalem Cathedra,* I (1981), pp. 168–84. Elad-Bouskila, *Modern Palestinian Literature and Culture,* pp. 127–38 . Idem, 'Symbol of Confrontation: Jerusalem in the Israeli-Arab Literature During the Intifāḍa', in Judith Rosenhouse and Ami Elad-Bouskila (eds), *Linguistic and Cultural Studies in Arabic and Hebrew*, Wiesbaden, Harrassowitz Verlag, 2001, pp. 255–75.
4. Hamilton A.R. Gibb and Harold Bowen, *Islamic Society and the West,* Oxford, Oxford University Press, vol. I, 1950, vol. II, 1957. Bernard Lewis, *The Middle East and the West,* London, Weidenfeld and Nicholson, 1982, pp. 28–46. Israel Gershoni and James R. Jankowski, *Egypt, Islam and the Arabs: The Search for Egyptian Nationhood 1900–1930,* Oxford, Oxford University Press, 1986, pp. 3–39. 'Abd al-Raḥmān al-Jabartī, *Al-Jabartī's Chronicle of the First Seven Months of the French Occupation of Egypt* (trans. by Shmuel Moreh), Leiden, E.J. Brill, 1993. Abdel-Aziz Abdel-Meguid, *The Modern Arabic Short Story: Its Emergence, Development and Form,* Cairo, Dar Al-Maaref Press, n.d. [1956], pp. 52–61. Malcolm Yapp, 'Modernism and Literature in the Middle East 1850–1914', in Robin Ostle (ed.), *Modern Literature in the Near and Middle East 1850–1970,* London, Routledge, 1991, pp. 3–16. Derek Hopwood, *Sexual Encounter in the Middle East: the British, the French and the Arabs*, Reading, Ithaca Press, 1999, pp. 51–122. Muḥammad Ḥusayn Haykal, *al-Sharq al-Jadīd,* Cairo, Dār al-Ma'ārif, 1987, pp. 222–34. Albert Memmi, *The Colonizer and the Colonized* (trans. Howard Greenfeld), Boston, Beacon Press, 1991, pp. 19–76, 90–118.
5. Shawqī Ḍayf, *al-Adab al-'Arabī al-Mu'āṣir fī Miṣr,* 5th ed. Cairo, Dār al-Ma'ārif, 1974, pp. 14. One of the most outstanding characters in Egypt during that period was Rifā'a Rāfi' al-Ṭahṭāwī (1801–73), who was sent to Paris and wrote his impressions in his book *Takhlīṣ al-Ibrīz ilā Talkhīṣ Bārīz* (1834). Literary critics disagree about the definition of the text's genre between novel, essay and travel literature. See Ṣadūq Nūr al-Dīn, *al-Gharb fī al-Riwāya al-'Arabiyya, Qindīl Umm Hāshim*

Namūdhajan, Casablanca, Dār al-Thaqāfa, 1995, pp. 16–23. This is also true of the book written by Muḥammad al-Muwayliḥī (1858–1930), *Ḥadīth 'Īsā Ibn Hishām (*1907*).* About these literary works see Shujā' Muslim al-'Ānī, *al-Riwaya al-'Arabiyya wa'l-Ḥadāra al-Urūbbiyya,* Baghdad, Manshūrāt Wizārat al-Thaqāfa wa'l-Funūn, 1979, pp. 6–27. Mohammed Ali Shawabkeh, *Arabs and the West: A Study in the Modern Arabic Novel (1935–1985),* Karak, Mu'ta University, 1992, pp. 25–35.

6. Albert Hourani, *A History of the Arab Peoples,* Cambridge, Massachusetts, the Belknap Press of Harvard University Press, 1991, pp. 265–332. Ajami, *The Dream Palace of the Arabs,* pp. 114–17, 124–30. Menahem Milson, 'Medieval and Modern Intellectual Traditions in the Arab World', *Daedalus,* 101 (Summer 1972), pp. 22–34.
7. The question of 'other' and 'otherness' concerning our debate in terms of the colonized/oppressed conquest and the colonizer/oppressor/conqueror from a theoretical point of view is discussed widely by several scholars such as Homi Bhabha in his book *The Location of Culture*, London and New York, Routledge, 2001, pp. 66–84, 108–17. See also 'Ami El'ad-Bouskila in his book *HaOr HaKalush: Itzugim ve Tadmiyot shel Demut HaAkher BaSifruyot Ha'Araviyot HaModerniyot (The Dim Light: Representations and Images of the Other in Modern Arabic Literatures)*, Tel Aviv, The Tami Steinmetz Center for Peace Research, Tel Aviv University, 2005, pp. 11–27 (Hebrew).
8. Aḥmad Amīn, *al-Sharq wa'l-Gharb*, Cairo, Maṭba'at Lajnat al-Ta'līf wa'l-Tarjama wa'l-Nashr, 1955, pp. 136–46. Grunebaum, *Modern Islam, The Search for Cultural Identity,* p. 187. Milson, 'Medieval and Modern Intellectual Traditions in the Arab World', *Daedolus,* pp. 17–37. Giora Eliraz, *Intelektualim Mitzriyyim mul Masoret ve Shinouy 1919–1939* (Egyptian Intellectuals in the Face of Tradition and Change 1919–1939), Ph.D. Dissertation, the Hebrew University of Jerusalem, 1980, pp. 23–5 (Hebrew). Manṣūr Fahmī, 'al-Sharq wa'l-Ḥaḍāra al-Gharbiyya', *al-Muqtaṭaf,* 77, (October 1930), pp. 257–63. Hamilton A.R. Gibb, *Studies on the Civilization of Islam,* Princeton, New Jersey, Princeton University Press 1982, pp. 228–32. Hisham Sharabi, *Arab Intellectuals and the West: The Formative Years 1875–1914,* Baltimore: The Johns Hopkins Press, 1970, pp. 46–7. Mīkhā'īl Nu'ayma has a different point of view since he stresses that Eastern and Western Cultures are intertwined, East is not just East and West is not just West. He concluded that sometime in the future the two cultures will achieve a balance between them. Mīkhā'īl Nu'ayma, 'Ḥikāyat al-Sharq wa'l-Gharb', *al-Hilāl,* 55:6 (June 1947), pp. 49–51.
9. M.M. Badawi, 'The Lamp of Umm Hashim: The Egyptian Intellectual Between East and West', *Journal of Arabic Literature,* I (1970), pp. 145–61. Fatma Moussa-Mahmoud, *The Arabic Novel in Egypt 1914–1970,* Cairo, The Egyptian General Book Organization, 1973, pp. 31–8. Issa Boullata, 'Encounter Between East and West: A Theme in Contemporary Arabic Novels', *The Middle East Journal,* 30: 1 (winter 1976), pp. 49–62. Allen, *The Arabic Novel,* pp. 88–90. Hopwood, *Sexual Encounter in the Middle East: the British, the French and the Arabs*, pp. 245–76. Shawabkeh, *Arabs and the West*, pp. 16–189. Rasheed El-Eneny, 'Tawfīq al-Hakīm and the West: A New Assessment of the Relationship', *British Journal of Middle Eastern Studies*, 27:2 (November 2000), pp. 165–75. Nūr al-Dīn, *al-Gharb fī al-Riwāya al-'Arabiyya,* pp. 13–49. Khālid al-Karakī, *al-Riwāya fī al-Urdunn, Muqaddima,* Amman, al-Jāmi'a al-Urdunniyya 1986, pp. 129–32. Aḥmad Bahī, *al-Riḥla ilā al-Gharb fī al-Riwāya al-'Arabiyya al-Ḥadītha,* Cairo, al-Hay'a al-Miṣriyya al-'Āmma li'l-Kitāb, 1991. Ṭarābīshī, *Sharq wa-Gharb,* 1977. Aḥmad Ibrāhīm al-Hawwārī, 'al-Raḥīl ilā al-A'māq: Qirā'a Naqdiyya fī Qiṣaṣ Yaḥyā Ḥaqqī', *Fuṣūl,* 2:4 (July-September), pp. 59–61. Ḥilmī Muḥammad al-Qā'ūd, *Mawsim al-Baḥth 'an Huwiyya, Dirāsāt fī al-Riwāya wa'l-Qiṣṣa*, Cairo, al-Hay'a al-Miṣriyya al-'Āmma li'l-Kitāb, 1987, pp. 9–13, 156. al-Shar', 'al-Baḥth 'an al-Shakhṣiyya al-Jadīda', *Abḥāth al-Yarmūk,* pp. 7–9. Ḥasan Abbashir al-Ṭayyib, 'al-Ṭayyib Ṣāliḥ Riwā'iyyan wa- Shā'iran Mubdi'an', *Ibdā',* pp. 33–4. Al-Mousa, 'The Arabic Bildungsroman', *International Journal of Middle East Studies,* pp. 223–40. Ḥusām Abū al-'Alā, 'Samīr Amīn wa-Yaḥyā al-Ṭāhir, Ḥikāyāt 'an Ṣirā' al-Sharq wa'l-Gharb', *Fuṣūl,* 12:2 (Summer 1993), pp. 204–14. Muṣṭafā 'Abd al-Ghanī, *Qaḍāyā al-Riwāya al-*

'Arabiyya, Cairo, al-Dār al-Miṣriyya al-Lubnāniyya, 1999, pp. 39–51, 83–93. Salīm al-Ma'ūsh, *Ṣūrat al-Gharb fī al-Riwāya al-'Arabiyya*, Beirut, Mu'ssasat al-Riḥāb al-Ḥadītha, 1998, pp. 158–403. Muḥammad Najīb al-Talāwī, *al-Dhāt wa'l-Mihmāz: Dirāsat al-Ṭaqāṭub fī Ṣirā' Riwāyāt al-Muwājaha al-Ḥaḍāriyya*, Cairo, al-Hay'a al-Miṣriyya al-'Āmma li'l-Kitāb, 1998. Aḥmad al-Hawwārī, Naqd al-Mujtama' fī Ḥadīth 'Isā Ibn Hishām, Cairo, 'Ayn li'l Dirāsāt wa'l-Buḥūth al-Insāniyya wa'l-Ijtimā'iyya, 1993, pp. 130–2. Muḥammad Ḥasan 'Abd Allāh, *al-Wāqi'iyya fī al-Riwāya al-'Arabiyya*, Cairo, Dār al-Ma'ārif, 1971, pp. 400–21. 'Abd al-'Azīz al-Maqāliḥ, *Aṣwāt min al-Zaman al-Ḥadīth, Dirāsāt fī al-Adab al-'Arabī al-Mu'āṣir*, Beirut, Dār al-'Awda, 1980, pp. 89–101. Muṣṭafā 'Abd al-Ghanī, *al-Ittijāh al-Qawmī al-'Arabī fī al-Riwāya*, Cairo, al-Hay'a al-Miṣriyya al-'Āmma li'l-Kitāb, 1998, pp. 95–131. Maḥmūd Ḥanafī Kassāb, 'al-Baḥth 'an al-Wajh al-Ḍā'i' fī Riwāyat *Ḥubb fī Kūbenhāgen* li'l-Riwā'ī Muḥammad Jalāl', *al-Kātib*, 219 (July 1979), pp. 90–3. Aḥmad 'Abd al-Mu'ṭī Ḥijāzī, '*Mawsim al-Hijra ilā al-Shamāl*', in Ḥasan Abbashir al-Ṭayyib (ed.), *al-Ṭayyib Ṣāliḥ*, pp. 197–201.

10. A partial list of novels that includes different categories concerning East and West encounters is: Egypt – Ṭāhā Ḥusayn, *Adīb*, 1935, Tawfīq al-Ḥakīm, *'Uṣfūr min al-Sharq*, 1938, Yahyā Ḥaqqī, *Qindīl Umm Hāshim*, 1944, Fatḥī Ghānim, *al-Sākhin wa'l-Bārid*, 1960, Luwīs 'Awaḍ, *Mudhakkirāt Ṭālib Ba'tha*, 1965, Yūsuf Idrīs, *al-Sayyida Fiyinnā*, 1975, 'Abd al-Ḥakīm Qāsim, *Muḥāwala li'l-Khurūj*, 1980, Muḥammad Jalāl (b.1929), *Ḥubb fī Cūpenhāgen*, 1975, Bahā' Ṭāhir, *Qālat Duḥā* (1985). From Syria, Shakīb al-Jābirī, in his novels: *Naham*, 1937, *Qadar Yalhū*, 1939 [a revised version of this book was published in 1980], *Qaws Quzaḥ*, 1946, 'Abd al-Salām al-'Ujaylī, *Raṣīf al-'Adhrā' al-Sawdā'*, 1960 and Walīd Ḥajjār, *Musāfir bilā Ḥaqā'ib*, 1979. From Lebanon: Suhayl Idrīs, *al-Ḥayy al-Lātīnī*, 1954. From Jordan: Jum'a Ḥammād, *Badawī fī Ūrūbbā*, 1977, 'Īsā al-Nā'ūrī, (1918–85), *Layla fī al-Qiṭār*, 1974, Muḥammad 'Īd, *al-Mutamayyiz* (1978). From Iraq: Dhū al-Nūn Ayyūb, *al-Duktūr Ibrāhīm*, 1939. From Sudan: al-Ṭayyib Ṣāliḥ, *Mawsim al-Hijra ilā al-Shamāl*, 1966. From Morocco: Muḥammad Zifzāf, *al-Mar'a wa'l-Warda*, 1972. From Algeria: Sa'dī Ibrāhīm, *al-Marfūḍūn*, 1981. From Tunis: al-Ḥabīb al-Sālimī, *Matāhat al-Raml*, 1994, from Saudi Arabia Ghālib Ḥamza Abū al-Faraj, *Sanawāt al-Ḍay'a*, 1980.
11. From Ghana; Ayi Kwei Armah, *Why Are We So Blest?* See: Frank M. Birbalsingh, 'Season of Migration to the West: The Fiction of Tayeb Salih and Ayi Kwei Armah' in Amyuni (ed.) Tayeb Salih's Season of Migration to the North, pp. 62–72.
12. With regard to the short stories, we can list a number of books: from Syria, Ṣabāḥ Muḥyī al-Dīn (1926–62), *al-Sinfūnya al-Nāqiṣa*, 1958. Fu'ād al-Shā'ib (1911–70), *Aḥlām Yūlānd* ,1937. From Egypt, Bahā' Ṭāhir, *Bi'l-Ams Ḥalamt bik*, 1975. From the Sudan, Laylā Abū al-'Alā' in her short story 'al-Mutḥaf'; As cited by Bashīr al-Bakrī, 'Sūdāniyya Tumnaḥ al-Jā'iza al-'Ālamiyya li Kuttāb Ifrīqiyā', *al-Kharṭūm*, 2494 (17 August 2000), p. 8. With regard to plays, from Egypt: the dramatist 'Alī Sālim (b.1936), *Awlādunā fī Landan: Trājīdiyā bilā Dumū'*, 1975. With regard to poetry, the Lebanese poet Khalīl Ḥāwī, his poem '*al-Majūs fī Urūbbā*', 1972. For further details see Ṭarābīshī, *Sharq wa-Gharb*, pp. 48–70, 113–23. Nūr al-Dīn, *al-Gharb fī al-Riwāya al-'Arabiyya*, p. 41. Bahī, *al-Riḥla ilā al-Gharb*, p. 228. Sophie Bennet, 'Transcendence and Immanence: Self and Other in Bahā' Ṭāhir's Short Stories', *Arabic and Middle Eastern Literatures*. 1:1 (January 1998), pp. 75–85.
13. Elad [-Bouskila], *The Village Novel in Modern Egyptian Literature*, 1994.
14. This is typical of the Maghribi emigrants in France who being far away from their homeland, are considered foreigners and are treated very badly by French citizens as well as the local authorities. For more information see 'Abd al-Fattāḥ 'Uthmān, *al-Riwāya al-'Arabiyya al-Jazā'iriyya*, Cairo, al-Hay'a al-Miṣriyya al-'Āmma li'l-Kitāb, 1994, pp. 221–44.

15. Bayram al-Tūnisī, *al-Sayyid wa-Mar'atuh fī Bārīs,* Sidon-Beirut, n.d.. (1st ed. 1923). For more about the author and his work see: Marilyn Booth, *Bayram al-Tunisi's Egypt: Social Criticism and Narration Strategies,* Oxford, The Middle East Centre, St. Anthony's College, Exeter, Ithaca Press, 1990.
16. Yūsuf Idrīs, *al-Sayyida Fiyinnā,* Beirut, Dār al-'Awda, 1977 (1st ed. 1975).
17. Ḥannā Mīna, *Ḥamāma Zarqā' fī al-Suḥub*, Beirut, Dār al-Ādāb, 1988. For discussion on Mīna's novels see M.M Badawi, *A Short History of Modern Arabic Literature*, Oxford, Clarendon Press, 1993, pp. 210–11, 215–20. For a discussion about this novel with a connection between East and West society see Riyāḍ Kāmil, 'Riwāyat Ḥannā Mīna *Ḥamāma Zarqā' fī al-Suḥub*: Liqā' al-Sharq bi'l-Gharb fī Iṭār Jadīd', *al-Jadīd,* 40:9 (September 1991), pp. 35–46.
18. Shakīb al-Jābirī, *Widā'n Yā Afāamiyā,* Damascus, Dār al-Hilāl, 1960. Jabrā, *al-Safīna*, 1969. Munīf, *al-Ashjār wa-Ightiyāl Marzūq,* 1973. Ibid., *Sharq al-Mutawassiṭ*, 1975. Khayrī Shalabī, *Fallāḥ Miṣrī fī Bilād al-Firanja,* Cairo, Dār al-Ma'ārif, 1978. Bahā' Ṭāhir, *Qālat Ḍuḥā, Majmū'at al-A'māl,* Cairo, Dār al-Hilāl, 1992, pp. 307–414 (1st ed. 1985). 'Īsā Bullāṭa, *'Ā'id ilā al-Quds*, 1998.
19. Shakīb al-Jābirī, *Naḥam,* Aleppo, al-Maṭba'a al-'Ilmiyya, n.d. (1st ed. 1937).
20. Sulaymān Fayyāḍ, *Aṣwāt,* 2nd ed., Cairo, Kutub 'Arabiyya, 1977 (1st ed. 1972). For the English translation, see *Suleiman Fayyad, Voices: A Novel* (trans. Hosan Abdoul-Ela), London, Marion Boyars, 1993. 'Abd al-Ḥakīm Qāsim, *Muḥāwala li'l-Khurūj*, 1980.
21. Three Arab women have written novels dealing with East and West. The plots take place in both Arab and European countries. The first is an Iraqi author living in England, Samīra al-Māni' (b.1935) in her novel *al-Sābiqūn wa'l-Lāḥiqūn*, 1972. The plot takes place mainly in London, the relationship is between Salīm, an Iraqi student studying at Cambridge, and Munā, an ex-teacher who followed her lover from Iraq to London, where she works in the Iraqi Embassy. For more information about this novel, see al-'Ānī, *al-Riwāya al-'Arabiyya wa'l-Ḥadāra al-Urūbbiyya,* pp. 105–13. The second is the Algerian author Aḥlām Mustaghānimī (b.1953) in her novel *Dhākirat al-Jasad* (Memory in the Flesh), 1993, most characters are Eastern and are part of the plot set partly in Paris and mostly in Algeria. Mustaghānimī insisted on writing her novel in Arabic and not in French. For more details on Mustaghānimī's literary works see Buthayna Sha'bān, *100 'Ām min al-Riwāya al-Nisā'iyya al-'Arabiyya*, Beirut, Dār Ādāb, 1999, pp. 194–9. The third case is that of an Egyptian-English author, Ahdaf Soueif (b.1950). Her novel, *In the Eye of the Sun*, 1992, was written in English. The story is about the relationship between two cultures and the main character is Asian, an Egyptian woman married to an Egyptian man, who travels to England. Her husband, Saif Madi, does not understand her, he humiliates her and physically abuses her. Her English friend, Gerald, does not understand her either. She returns to Egypt and finds peace there. Ahdaf Soueif, *In the Eye of the Sun,* London, Bloomsbury, 1992.
22. Ḥanān al-Shaykh has published ten books to date, seven of which are novels. The first is *Intiḥār Rajul Mayyit,* 1970. The most recent novel is *Imra'tān 'alā Shāṭi' al-Baḥr,* 2003. Her first book of short stories is *Wardat al-Ṣaḥrā',* 1982, and the last is *Ukannis al-Shams 'an al-Suṭūḥ*, 1994. A play: *Anā Waḥdī,* 1992. Ḥanān al-Shaykh's works have been translated into a number of languages, mainly English: for example, *Women of Sand and Myrrh (*trans. Catherine Cobham), London and New York, Quartet Books, 1989. *Beirut Blues* (trans. Catherine Cobham), London, Chatto and Windus, 1995. For further information about Ḥanān al-Shaykh and her works, see Joseph T. Zeidan, *Arab Women Novelists, The Formative Years and Beyond,* State University of New York Press, New York, 1995, pp. 205–17, 227–9. Allen, *The Arabic Novel*, pp. 231–44. Miriam Cooke, *Women Claim Islam*, New York and London, Routledge, 2001, pp. 22, 24–5, 27–8. Sha'bān, *100 'Ām min al-Riwāya al-Nisā'iyya al-'Arabiyya*, pp. 168–78.
23. A similar view can be found from the literary critic, Ṭarābīshī, *Sharq wa-Gharb,* pp. 12–13.

24. For further information on the term 'the rejection of the Westernization process', see the work of Egyptian literary critic, 'Iṣām Bahī, *al-Riḥla ilā al-Gharb*, pp. 23–6.
25. Eliraz, *Intelektualim Mitzryyim mul Masoret ve Shinuy*, pp. 75–114. M.M. Badawi, 'Commitment in Contemporary Arabic Literature', in idem, *Modern Arabic Literature and the West*, London, Ithaca Press, 1985, pp. 1–25.
26. Prior to the publication of *'Uṣfūr min al-Sharq*, Tawfīq al-Ḥakīm wrote five books, the most famous of which is *'Awdat al-Rūḥ*, Cairo, al-Maṭba'a al-Namūdhajiyya, n.d. (1st ed. 1933). The book was translated into Russian (1935) and French (1937). The English translation, *Return of the Spirit* (trans. William Hutchins), was published in Washington D.C. 1985. The novel *Yawmiyyāt Nā'ib fī al-Aryāf* (1937), was translated under the title: *Maze of Justice* (1947). For further reading on Tawfīq al-Ḥakīm and his works, see Ismā'īl Adham and Ibrāhīm Nājī, *Tawfīq al-Ḥakīm*,Cairo, Dār Miṣr li'l-Ṭibā'a wa'l-Nashr, 1945. Ḍayf, *al-Adab al-'Arabī al-Mu'āṣir fī Miṣr*, pp. 288–94. Ghālī Shukrī, *Thawrat al-Mu'tazil, Dirāsa fī Adab Tawfīq al-Ḥakīm*, 3rd ed. Beirut, Dār Ibn Rushd, 1973. Salām, *Dirāsāt fī al-Qiṣṣa al-'Arabiyya al-Ḥadītha*, pp. 156–65. Paul Starkey, *From the Ivory Tower: A Critical Biography*, London, Ithaca Press, 1982. The novel, *'Uṣfūr min al-Sharq*, was translated into French (1946), 2nd ed. 1960. The English translation, *Bird from the East* (1967). For an interesting comparison between the novel *'Uṣfūr min al-Sharq* and *Mawsim al-Hijra ilā al-Shamāl* from the standpoint of poetic writing and shaping of the characters, but especially from the thematic point of view, and the different ideologies of al-Ḥakīm and Ṣāliḥ, see Shāhīn, *Taḥawwulāt al-Shawq*, pp. 121–40.
27. The novel *al-Ḥayy al-Lātīnī*, was published after three previous collections of short stories: *Ashwāq*, 1947, *Nīrān wa-Thulūj*, 1948, *Kulluhunn Nisā'*, 1949. For more details about Suhayl Idrīs and his work, see 'Alī Najīb 'Aṭawī, *Taṭawwur Fann al-Qiṣṣa al-Lubnāniyya al-'Arabiyya ba'd al-Ḥarb al-'Ālamiyya al-Thāniya*, Beirut, Dār al-Āfāq al-Jadīda, 1982, pp. 159–67, 179–87. Badawi, *A Short History of Modern Arabic Literature*, pp. 16–17, 155, 183–4.
28. For further reading about his life and his works, see Ḥusām al-Khatīb, *Riwāyāt Taḥt al-Mijhar, Dirāsat Nuhūḍ al-Riwāya al-Sūriyya*, Damascus, Manshūrāt Ittiḥād al-Kuttāb al-'Arab, 1983, pp. 37–73. Roger Allen, 'The Mature Arabic Novel Outside Egypt', in Badawi (ed.), *The Cambridge History of Arabic Literature: Modern Arabic Literature*, Cambridge, Cambridge University Press, 1992, p. 195. Badawi, *A Short History of Modern Arabic Literature*, p. 210.
29. In this definition we have not considered those literary works which were first published in the second half of the 19th century and in the first third of the 20th century. We should mention that these works dealing with East and West are not only novels, but refer to other literary genres too. See Nūr al-Dīn, *al-Gharb fī al-Riwāya al-'Arabiyya*, pp. 15–30.
30. For detailed discussion of these Maghribi novels see 'Abd al-Ghānī, *Qaḍayā al-Riwāya al-'Arabiyya*, pp. 83–93. Bahī, *al-Riḥla ilā al-Gharb*, pp. 95–112.
31. For more details of the Western image in modern Arabic fiction and thought see 'Abd Allāh Abū Hayf, *al-Qiṣṣa al-'Arabiyya al-Ḥadītha wa'l-Gharb*, Damascus, Manshūrāt Ittiḥād al-Kuttāb al-'Arab, 1993, pp. 19–24. Muḥammad Rajab al-Bāridī, *Shakhṣ al-Muthaqqaf fī al-Riwāya al-'Arabiyya al-Mu'āṣira*, Tunis, al-Dār al-Tūnisiyya li'l-Nashr, 1993, pp. 289–307. Bashīr Buwyjara Muḥammad, 'al-Shakhṣiyya al-Ajnabiyya', in idem, *al-Shakhṣiyya fī al-Riwāya al-Jazā'iriyya*, Algiers, Diwān al-Maṭbū'āt al-Jāmi'iyya, 1986, pp. 183–98.
32. Ḥalīm al-Yāzijī, *al-Sūdān wa'l-Ḥaraka al-Adabiyya*, pp. 944–5, 948–51. Amyuni, 'Literary Creativity and Social Literary Masks', in Abdel-Malek and Hallaq (eds), *Tradition, Modernity and Postmodernity in Arabic Literature*, pp. 99, 101.
33. *Alf Layla wa-Layla*, Beirut, al-Maṭba'a al-Kathūlīkiyya, 1888–90. For the English translation see *The Book of a Thousand Nights and a Night* (1897). 'Umar al-Khayyām, *Rubā'iyyāt 'Umar al-Khayyām* (Arabicising by Wadī' al-Bustānī), Cairo, Dār al-'Arab li'l-Bustānī, 1994. For the English translation

see *Rubāiyāt of Omar Khayyām* (trans. Edward Fitzgerald), New York, Garden City Books, 1952. For a similar concept see the Jordanian critic Ibrāhīm al-Sa'āfīn in his book *Taḥawwulāt al-Sard,* pp. 205–7, 227–8.

34. Ṣubḥī and al-Sham'a, 'al-Ṭayyib Ṣāliḥ Riwā'iyyan wa-Nāqidan', in Muḥammadiyya (ed.), *al-Ṭayyib Ṣāliḥ,* p. 125.
35. al-Sāmarrā'ī, 'al-Ṭayyib Ṣāliḥ', *al-Aqlām,* p. 147. For a similar approach of other Arab intellectuals see Anouar Abdel-Malek (ed.), *Contemporary Arab Political Thought* (trans. Michael Pallis), London, Zed Books, 1983, pp. 89–92, 104–7.
36. Ṣāliḥ, *Mawsim al-Hijra ilā al-Shamāl,* 2nd ed., Beirut, Dār al-'Awda, 1969, p. 7. Salih, *Season of Migration to the North,* p. 3.
37. Fatḥī Muḥammad 'Uthmān, 'Ḥiwār ma'a Ibrāhīm al-Ṣalaḥī' (2), *Kitābāt Sūdāniyya,* 4 (November 1993), pp. 113, 116.
38. Ahdaf Soueif, *The Map of Love,* London, Bloomsbury, 1999, p. 482.
39. Jalāl al-'Asharī, 'Zūrbā al-Sūdānī aw al-Baḥth 'an al-Dhāt al-Ifrīqiyya', in Muḥammadiyya (ed.), *al-Ṭayyib Ṣāliḥ,* p. 163. al-Ṭayyib Ṣāliḥ's words to Ṣubḥī and al-Sham'a, 'al-Ṭayyib Ṣāliḥ Riwā'iyyan wa-Nāqidan' in Muḥammadiyya (ed.), *al-Ṭayyib Ṣāliḥ,* p. 133. al-Naqqāsh, 'al-Ṭayyib Ṣāliḥ 'Abqariyya Riwā'iyya Jadīda', in Muḥammadiyya (ed.), *al-Ṭayyib Ṣāliḥ,* p. 83
40. Jibrīl, 'al-Ṭayyib Ṣāliḥ: Malāmiḥ min Sīra Dhātiyya (3)', *al-Ḥayāt,* p. 16.
41. Ṣāliḥ, *Dawmat Wad Ḥāmid* (1967). Idem, *Mawsim al-Hijra ilā al-Shamāl* (1966). The novel has been translated into various languages (see Appendix C).
42. For a detailed discussion of the encounter and of cultural identity see Wielandt, 'The Problem of Cultural Identity in the Writings of al-Tayyib Salih', in al-Qadi (ed.), *Studia Arabica and Islamica,* pp. 487–515.
43. Ṣāliḥ, 'Risāla ilā Aylīn', in idem, *Dawmat Wad Ḥāmid,* pp. 26–32. Written 1960. (trans. N.S. Doniach), 'A Letter to Ayleen', *Journal of Arabic Literature,* XI (1980), pp. 76–9. 'al-Shay' al-Ākhar', *Ḥiwār,* 21 (March-April 1966), pp. 37–8. 'Idhā Jā'at'', in idem, *Dawmat Wad Ḥāmid,* pp. 53–68. This story was written in 1961. Ṣāliḥ, 'Hakadhā Yā Sādatī', in idem, *Dawmat Wad Ḥāmid,* pp. 69–82. Two different versions explain when the story was written. According to the first, the story was written in the second half of the fifties and first published in the Lebanese journal *Adab,* 1958. See Jibrīl, 'al-Ṭayyib Ṣāliḥ: Malāmiḥ min Sīra Dhātiyya (4)', *al-Ḥayāt,* p. 16. The second version is that the story was written in 1961, see: Ṣāliḥ, *'Urs al-Zayn, Riwāya wa-Sab' Qiṣṣaṣ,* p. 5. In any case the story was first published in the Lebanese journal *Adab,* 1:1 (Winter 1961), pp. 9–16. 'Muqaddimāt', in idem, *Dawmat Wad Ḥāmid,* pp. 83–93. These short-short stories included in these 'Muqaddimāt' were written in 1962. In this collection of short stories, the short short story 'al-Shay' al-Ākhar' is not included (see Appendix A).
44. al-Naqqāsh, 'al-Ṭayyib Ṣāliḥ 'Abqariyya Riwā'iyya Jadīda', in Muḥammadiyya (ed.), *al-Ṭayyib Ṣāliḥ,* pp. 80–2. 'Abd al-Jalāb, '*Mawsim al-Hijra ilā al-Shamāl*', in Muḥammadiyya (ed.), *al-Ṭayyib Ṣāliḥ,* p. 139. al-'Asharī, '*Zūrbā al-Sūdānī*', in Muḥammadiyya (ed.), *al-Ṭayyib Ṣāliḥ,* pp. 155–61. Ṭarābīshī, *Sharq wa-Gharb,* pp. 154, 171. Ḥasan al-Māni', *Nafaḥāt 'an al-Adab wa'l-Fann,* pp. 10–11, 15–17. Najīb, 'Ru'ya Jadīda fī Adab al-Ṭayyib Ṣāliḥ (2)', *al-Muṣawwar,* p. 56. al-Khānjī, *Ru'yat al-Mawt wa-Dalālatuhā fī 'Ālam al-Ṭayyib Ṣāliḥ al-Riwā'ī, Ḥawliyyāt Kulliyyat al-Ādāb,* pp. 12–16, 29. Aḥmad al-Zu'bī, 'Thalāthat Wujūh li Muṣṭafā Sa'īd, Dirāsa fī Riwāyat al-Ṭayyib Ṣāliḥ *Mawsim al-Hijra ilā al-Shamāl*', *Ibdā',* 3:1 (January 1985), pp. 111–14. al-Maqāliḥ, *Aṣwāt min al-Zaman al-Ḥadīth,* pp. 81–2. For more details about this issue in general, see Frantz Fanon, *Black Skin White Masks,* (translated from the French by Charles Lam Macramann), New York, Grove Press, 1968, pp. 63–82. Edward W. Said, *Orientalism,* New York, Pantheon Books, 1978, pp. 226–54. For a different opinion, see Yūsuf Nūr 'Awaḍ, *al-Ṭayyib Ṣāliḥ fī Manẓūr al-Naqd al-Bunyawī,* pp. 74–5. Daf'allāh, *al-Lā Muntamī fī Adab al-Ṭayyib Ṣāliḥ,* pp. 37–9. al-Shūsh, *Adab wa-Udabā',* p. 54. The Sudanese

literary critic Khālid Mūsā Daf'allāh rejects any connection between blackness and whiteness in terms of the African and Western struggle, but holds that it is part of the Arabic and European cultural struggle. See Daf'allāh, *al-Lā Muntamī fī Adab al-Ṭayyib Ṣāliḥ*, pp. 98–101, 106. Taysīr al-Sabūl, '*Mawsim al-Hijra ilā al-Shamāl* li'l-Ṭayyib Ṣāliḥ', in idem, *Taysīr al-Sabūl: al-A'māl al-Kāmila*, 2nd ed., Amman, Dār Azminat li'l-Nashr wa'l-Tawzī', 1997, pp. 277–8.

45. Ṣāliḥ, *Dawmat Wad Ḥāmid*, p. 69.
46. Ibid., p. 73.
47. For the main assumptions of this concept as expressed by the real author, see Ṣubḥī and al-Sham'a, 'al-Ṭayyib Ṣāliḥ Riwā'iyyan wa-Nāqidan', in Muḥammadiyya (ed.), *al-Ṭayyib Ṣāliḥ*, , pp. 129–30. Bakrī, ''Ibr Majrā al-Ta'rīkh (4)', *al-Kharṭūm*, p. 6. (5), *al-Kharṭūm*, p. 5.
48. This is the message that al-Ṭayyib Ṣāliḥ and some other critics pointed out. For this concept see Jalāl Amīn, 'al-Aṣāla wa'l-Mu'āṣara: Yaḥyā Ḥaqqī wa'l-Ṭayyib Ṣāliḥ', *al-Hilāl*, 101:1 (January 1993), pp. 110–12. Stephan G. Meyer, *The Experimental Arabic Novel*, New York, State University of New York Press, 2001, pp. 141–3.
49. Shāhīn, *Taḥawwulāt al-Shawq*, pp. 177–8. Echoes of these words can be found in the Tunisian literary critic Manṣūr Qaysūma, 'al-Riwāya al-'Arabiyya wa-Thunā'iyyat al-Naṣṣ al-Muta'addid', in idem, *al-Riwāya al-'Arabiyya al-Ishkāl wa'l-Tashakkul*, pp. 162–73. For reinforcement of this concept we can indicate the words of Masha the Viennese woman to the Aleppian character about the Middle Eastern attitude towards women. See Muḥyī al-Dīn, 'al-Sinfūniyya al-Nāqiṣa', *al-Ādāb*, 9 (September 1956) p. 45.
50. For the psychological concept in this novel and especially in relation to Muṣṭafā Sa'īd, see the discussion of the Sudanese Association of Psychology: 'Hijra bilā Mawsim', in Muḥammadiyya, (ed.), *al-Ṭayyib Ṣāliḥ*, pp. 144–51. Siddiq, 'The Process of Individuation', *Journal of Arabic Literature*, pp. 67–104.
51. Miriam Cooke, *War's Other Voices, Women Writers on the Lebanese Civil War*, Cambridge, Cambridge University Press, p. 77. al-Shaykh Muḥammad al-Shaykh, *al-Insān wa'l-Taḥlīl al-Fā'ilī*, pp. 14–15.
52. Ṣāliḥ, *Mawsim al-Hijra ilā al-Shamāl*, p. 33.
53. Ibid., p. 122.
54. For a detailed discussion of this issue, see Ni'ma, *Ṣirā' al-Maqhūr ma'a al-Sulṭa*, pp. 35, 230–3. A similar concept is held by al-Naqqāsh, 'al-Ṭayyib Ṣāliḥ, 'Abqariyya Riwā'iyya Jadīda', in Muḥammadiyya (ed.), *al-Ṭayyib Ṣāliḥ*, pp. 85–6. Ṭarābīshī, *Sharq wa-Gharb*, pp. 9–17, 150–4. Ṣāliḥ Ibrāhim, *al-Mar'a fī Adab al-Ṭayyib Ṣāliḥ*, pp. 13–18.
55. 'Azzām, *al-Baṭal al-Ishkālī fī al-Riwāya al-'Arabiyya al-Mu'āṣira*, pp. 32–40.
56. Ṣāliḥ, *Mawsim al-Hijra ilā al-Shamāl*, p. 144.
57. Ibid., p. 140.
58. Ibid., p. 141. In connection with skin colour, the author's own words should be noted: 'Colour doesn't symbolize a problem for me and I don't have any inferiority complex in this regard. We in the Sudan, because of the relative isolation we live in, used to consider ourselves the most beautiful Arabs and the most Arab of Arabs [...] In *Mawsim al-Hijra*, I did use the skin colour to connect the hero of the novel with his African roots. We should note that Muṣṭafā Sa'īd exploited the colour of his skin for his own benefit, which did not symbolize for him an inferiority complex. On the contrary, it was a characteristic that he exploited in his love affairs and tied up his personality with that of Othello from the literary aspect'. See Jibrīl, *'Alā al-Darb*, p. 11. But on the other hand, Ṣāliḥ himself pointed out that the Lebanese or the Egyptian in Europe can be considered European, but the Sudanese or the Yemeni or the Mauritanian cannot be so regarded. See the interview conducted by the *al-Jazīra* channel with al-Ṭayyib Ṣāliḥ (see Appendix E).

59. For more details of Ṭāriq Ibn Ziyād, see L. Molina, *The Encyclopaedia of Islam*, New Edition, Leiden, E.J. Brill, vol. X, 2000, pp. 242–3.
60. In the novel *al-Ḥayy al-Lātīnī* by Suhayl Idrīs, the mother cautions her son who is about to leave for studies in France, against '…the West who has taken him from them, the West and its women, its girls and its female students'. In the short novel *Qindīl Umm Hāshim* by Yaḥyā Ḥaqqī, Sheikh Rajab 'Abd Allāh warns his son, who his leaving to study ophthalmology in England: 'Take care lest the women of Europe tempt you, for they are not for you and you are not for them', Suhayl Idrīs, *al-Ḥayy al-Lātīnī,* p. 209. Yahyā Ḥaqqī, *Qindīl Umm Hāshim,* p. 78.
61. Ṣāliḥ, *Mawsim al-Hijra ilā al-Shamāl,* p. 141.
62. Ibid., p. 109.
63. Ibid., p. 111.
64. For more details on al-Ṭayyib Ṣāliḥ's connection with a real woman named Jean Morris, see Shāhīn, *Taḥawwulāt al-Shawq,* pp. 199–200. For a psychological analysis of Muṣṭafā Sa'īd's relationship with Jean Morris and three other European women, see Ni'ma, *Ṣirā' al-Maqhūr ma'a al-Sulṭa,* pp. 124–39.
65. For more details on violence and crime in the works of al-Ṭayyib Ṣāliḥ, see 'Abd al-Mun'im al-Jadawī, 'al-Jarīma fi Qiṣaṣ al-Ṭayyib Ṣāliḥ', *al-Dōḥa,* 17 (May 1977), pp. 78–81.
66. Ṣāliḥ, *Mawsim al-Hijra ilā al-Shamāl,* p. 167.
67. The case of a man sitting in the dock on the collective level as in the individual is not exceptional in world literature. It is quite possible that al-Ṭayyib Ṣāliḥ read (see Chapter One) some of these novels, such as E.M. Foster, *A Passage to India* (1924). Albert Camus, in the novel *The Outsider* (1942).
68. Ṣāliḥ, *Mawsim al-Hijra ilā al-Shamāl,* p. 98. Salih, *Season of Migration to the North,* p. 95.
69. Ibid., p. 104.
70. That violence is a Western import and not locally Eastern is related to us by Muṣṭafā Sa'īd. Indeed, this germ infected Eastern characters such as the narrator, Ḥusna and to some extent, also Maḥjūb. That is to say that there are some literary critics who idealize the Sudan and especially the village of Wad Ḥāmid as a paradise in which modern inventions were the cause of all the serious troubles. This is the main thesis of al-Nabr, 'al-'Unf fī Riwāyat *Mawsim al-Hijra ilā al-Shamāl*', in idem, *al-'Unf fī al-Qiṣṣa al-'Arabiyya al-Ḥadītha,* pp. 116–22.
71. Ṣāliḥ, *Mawsim al-Hijra ilā al-Shamāl,* p. 126; see also pp. 124, 125.
72. Sa'dī Ibrāhīm, *al-Marfūḍūn,* p. 33.
73. The failed encounter between the Eastern man and the Western woman is extensively described in other novels such as (*Adīb, Qindīl Umm Hāshim, al-Sākhin wa'l-Bārid, al-Ḥayy al-Lātīnī*).
74. Ṣāliḥ, *Mawsim al-Hijra ilā al-Shamāl,* p. 83.
75. al-'Ānī, '*Mawsim al-Hijra ilā al-Shamāl*' in idem, *Fī Adabinā al-Qaṣaṣā al-Mu'āṣir,* pp. 101–3.
76. Ṣāliḥ, 'al-Shay' al-Ākhar', *Ḥiwār,* 21, (March-April 1966), p. 37.
77. For a detailed comparison between *Mawsim al-Hijra ilā al-Shamāl* and *al-Ḥayy al-Lātīnī,* see Daf'allāh, 'Bunyawiyāt al-Ṣirā' al-Ḥaḍārī bayn *Mawsim al-Hijra ilā al-Shamāl* wa *al-Ḥayy al-Lātīnī, Dirāsa Muqārina*', in idem, *al-Lā Muntamī fī Adab al-Ṭayyib Ṣāliḥ,* pp. 85–106.
78. In addition to the most important components of the Sudanese entity, i.e. Arabism and Islamism, the element of Africanism is also significant. Therefore, we would like to indicate that African literature is written not only in Arabic, but also in European languages such as English, French and Portuguese. See Osman Hassan Ahmad (ed.), *Sixteen Sudanese Short Stories,* Washington DC., Office of the Cultural Counselor, Embassy of the Democratic Republic of Sudan, 1981. Chinua Achebe and Innes, C. L. (eds), *African Short Stories, Twenty Short Stories From Across the Continent,* Oxford, Heinemann, 1987. Abdulrazak Gurnah (ed.), *Essays on African Writing,* 1: *A Re-Evaluation,* Oxford, Heinemann, 1993.
79. Ṣāliḥ, *Mawsim al-Hijra ilā al-Shamāl,* p. 97. Salih, *Season of Migration to the North,* p. 94.

80. Ibid., p. 53. Ibid., pp. 49–50. The Sudanese at that time viewed the English as rulers who dressed and behaved as masters. Hence, when Sudanese students spent time in England, they 'surprisingly' found that the English did ordinary work and even served them in restaurants as waiters. See, for example, the interview with the Sudanese artist Ibrāhīm al-Ṣalaḥī in 'Uthmān, 'Ḥiwār ma'a al-Fannān al-Ṣalaḥī', *Kitābāt Sūdāniyya*, p. 113.
81. Ṣāliḥ, *Mawsim al-Hijra ilā al-Shamāl*, p. 64. Salih, *Season of Migration to the North*, p. 60.
82. Ṣāliḥ, *Dawmat Wad Ḥāmid*, p. 78.
83. Maḥmūd Ṭāhir Ḥaqqī, *'Adhrā' Dinshawāy*, Cairo, al-Maktaba al-'Arabiyya, 1964 (1st ed. 1906). For the English translation see *The Virgin of Dinshaway* (trans. Saad el-Gabalawy), in idem, *Three Pioneering Egyptain Novels*, Fredericton, York Press, 1986, pp. 17–48.
84. Aḥmad Amīn, *al-Sharq wa'l-Gharb*, pp. 64–5.
85. This concept stands at the centre of the theses, as in the title of the article by Māhir Ḥasan Fahmī, 'Maryūd aw Humūm al-Muthaqqafīn li'l-Ṭayyib Ṣāliḥ', *Ḥawliyyāt Kulliyyat al-Insāniyyāt wa'l-'Ulūm al-Ijtimā'iyya*, 1 (1979), pp. 7–27.
86. Ṣāliḥ, *Mawsim al-Hijra ilā al-Shamāl*, pp. 61–4.
87. Ibid., p. 62.
88. Jibrīl, *'Alā al-Darb*, p. 78.
89. al-Ḥakīm, *'Uṣfūr min al-Sharq*, p. 190.
90. Amīn, *al-Sharq wa'l-Gharb*, pp. 20–2.
91. Ṣāliḥ, *Mawsim al-Hijra ilā al-Shamāl*, p. 53. A different expression of this concept can be found in an interview with al-Ṭayyib Ṣāliḥ, see Jibrīl, 'al-Ṭayyib Ṣāliḥ: Malāmiḥ min Sīra Dhātiyya (6)', *al-Hayāt*, p. 20.
92. Ṣāliḥ, *Mawsim al-Hijra ilā al-Shamāl*, p. 77.
93. For details on the reasons why al-Ṭayyib Ṣāliḥ did not go back to live in the Sudan, see Jibrīl, 'al-Tayyib Ṣāliḥ: Malāmiḥ min Sīra Dhātiyya (5)', *al-Ḥayāt*, p. 20.
94. Shāhīn, *Taḥawwulāt al-Shawq*, pp. 135–6, 182–3.
95. For a comprehensive study of this novel, see Nūr al-Dīn, *al-Gharb fī al-Riwāya al-'Arabiyya*, pp. 51–106. Miriam Cooke, *The Anatomy of an Egyptian Intellectual: Yahya Haqqi*, Washington, DC, Three Continents Press, 1984. Boullata, 'Encounter between East and West', *The Middle East Journal*, pp. 50–3.
96. Badawi, '*The Lamp of Umm Hashim*', *Journal of Arabic Literature*, pp. 145–61. Karīm al-Wā'ilī, 'al-Ṭabīb Walī wa'l- Maqām 'Iyāda?!. Zawāj al-'Ilm, bi'l-Khurāfa fī Qiṣṣat *Qindīl Umm Hāshim*', *al-Nāqid*, 57 (March 1993), pp. 38–41.
97. Laylā al-Ṣā'igh, 'Kitābāt al-Ṭayyib Ṣāliḥ bayn al-Wāqi' wa'l-Usṭūra', *al-Anbā'* (January 10, 1978), p. 13.
98. Ṣāliḥ, *Mawsim al-Hijra ilā al-Shamāl*, pp. 98, 104.
99. Ibid., p. 103.
100. Elad [-Bouskila], 'Fiction and Reality', in idem (ed.), *Writer, Culture, Text*, pp. 62–73.
101. Ṣāliḥ, *Dawmat Wad Ḥāmid*, p. 52.

Notes to Appendices

1. Ami Elad-Bouskila, 'Appendix A: Places and Dates of Publication of al-Ṭayyib Ṣāliḥ's Work and Translations into Other Languages', in Elad-Bouskila and Ahmed Al-Shahi (eds), *Al-Ṭayyib Ṣāliḥ, Edebiyât*, pp. 127–35.
2. According to the Sudanese literary critic Aḥmad Muḥammad el-Badawī, this story was published in 1953 by the Lebanese journal *al-Aḥad*. See el-Badawī, *al-Ṭayyib Ṣāliḥ*, pp. 47, 160. Unfortunately, I was unable to find this periodical.

3. According to another version it was written in the mid-fifties. See Berkley, *The Roots of Consciousness*, p. 143. While el-Badawī has mentioned 1960 or 1961, see idem, *al-Ṭayyib Ṣāliḥ*, pp. 50, 160.
4. As cited by Nūr, 'al-Ṭayyib Ṣāliḥ: Dirāsa Bībliyūgrāfiyya', *al-Thaqāfa al-Sūdāniyya*, p. 125, in Ḥasan Abbashir al-Ṭayyib (ed.), *al-Ṭayyib Ṣāliḥ*, p. 408.
5. al-Sāmarrā'ī, 'Muqābala Adabiyya ma'a al-Ṭayyib Ṣāliḥ', *al-Ādāb*, p. 3.
6. As cited in Nūr, 'al-Ṭayyib Ṣāliḥ: Dirāsa Bībliyūgrāfiyya', *al-Thaqāfa al-Sūdāniyya*, p. 125.
7. According to al-Tayyib Ṣāliḥ, he finished writing the last third of the novel in 1960 or 1962, but does not remember which of the two dates is correct. See: al-Sāmarrā'ī, 'Muqābala Adabiyya ma'a al-Ṭayyib Ṣāliḥ', *al-Ādāb*, p. 7. Further evidence provided by the author in the context of '*Urs al-Zayn*, reinforces this:
    a. The author indicated that he finished writing the novel in 1962. see Fatḥī 'Uthmān, 'Ḥiwār Ṭawīl (1)', *al-Wasaṭ*, 345 (7 September 1998), p. 50.
    b. He says he wrote the novel as early as the fifties and that it was published in the early sixties. Interview granted by al-Ṭayyib Ṣāliḥ to Sabīl al-Muqābila cited in Berkley, *The Roots of Consciousness*, p. xxxiii.
    c. He says he wrote the novel in the early sixties, see 'Īsā al-Ḥilū, 'Ḥiwār ma'a al-Ṭayyib Ṣāliḥ (2)', *al-Ayyām* (4 November 1977), cited in Berkley, *The Roots of Consciousness*, p. lxvi.
    d. The author says that during one month in the summer of 1960, he finished the last part of the novel in a small village near Cannes. See Amyuni (ed.) Tayeb Salih's Season of Migration to the North, p. 15.
    e. He says that the novel '*Urs al-Zayn* was in his head before he had decided to become a writer. Ṣubḥī and al-Sham'a, 'al-Ṭayyib Ṣāliḥ Riwā'iyyan wa-Nāqidan', in Muḥammadiyya (ed.), *al-Ṭayyib Ṣāliḥ*, p. 123.
    f. According to al-Ṭayyib Ṣāliḥ, he wrote '*Urs al-Zayn* after the story 'Dawmat Wad Ḥāmid'. He left off writing the novel, and the book was published only in 1964. See: Jibrīl, '*Alā al-Darb*, p. 115.
8. According to this source [*Ḥiwār*, 10 (May-June, 1964), p. 40], the novel was to be published the following year, i.e., 1965.
9. The novel appeared as a series in the Egyptian journal *Rūz al-Yūsuf*, as cited in *Ḥiwār*, 21 (March-April, 1966), p. 2, but we did not find it. According to al-Ṭayyib Ṣāliḥ it appeared as a series in the Egyptian periodical *al-Idhā'a wa'l-Telifisyūn* See Jibrīl, *'Alā al-Darb*, p. 104, and 'Abd al-Mun'im Salīm, 'al-Liqā' al-Awwal ma'a al-Ṭayyib Ṣāliḥ 'Ām 1962 wa-*Mawsim al-Hijra* 'Ām 1966', in Ḥasan Abbashir al-Ṭayyib (ed.), *al-Ṭayyib Ṣāliḥ*, p. 74.
10. See Ḥusayn 'Alī Muḥammad, *Jamāliyyāt al-Qiṣṣa al-Qaṣīra*, Cairo, al-Sharika al-'Arabiyya li'l-Nashr wa'l-Tawzi', 1996, p. 149.
11. According to al-Ṭayyib Ṣāliḥ, he wrote the first third of the novel in 1960 or 1962, but does not recall the exact date. He completed the remaining two thirds four years later. See al-Sāmarrā'ī, 'Muqābala Adabiyya ma'a al-Ṭayyib Ṣāliḥ', *al-Ādāb*, p. 7. Elsewhere he says that he wrote a third of the novel in one month in the summer of 1960, and then took a break of four years. See Amyuni (ed.), Tayeb Salih's Season of Migration to the North, p. 15. In another interview he indicated 1962, see Fatḥī 'Uthmān, 'Ḥiwār Ṭawīl', *al-Wasaṭ*, p. 50, and Salīm, 'al-Liqā al-Awwal', in Ḥasan Abbashir al-Ṭayyib (ed.), *al-Ṭayyib Ṣāliḥ*, pp. 71–3.
12. See *Ḥiwār*, 10 (May-June 1964), p. 40. But we did not find a shred of evidence.
13. See el-Badawī, *al-Ṭayyib Ṣāliḥ*, p. 162.
14. al-Ṭayyib Ṣāliḥ, '*Urs al-Zayn*, 3rd ed., Beirut, Dār al-'Awda, 1970, p. 129 (unpaginated).

15. As cited by Nūr, 'al-Ṭayyib Ṣāliḥ: Dirāsa Bībliyūgrāfiyya', *al-Thaqāfa al-Sūdāniyya*, p. 125 and in Ḥasan Abbashir al-Ṭayyib (ed.), *al-Ṭayyib Ṣāliḥ*, p. 408.
16. Amyuni (ed.), Tayeb Salih's Season of Migration to the North, p. 158. I have not found the 1st edition which some claim was published in 1977. See Wielandt, F., 'The Problem of Cultural Identity', in al-Qadi (ed.), *Studia Arabica and Islamica*, p. 487. According to the Egyptian journal *al-Hilāl* (December 1976), p. 63: 'The great Arab artist and writer al-Ṭayyib Ṣāliḥ has finished writing his new novel *Maryūd*, and it is shortly to be published as a book'. In its January 1977 issue, p. 50, the editor of this journal writes as follows: 'In its previous issue, *al-Hilāl* announced that the first chapter of the novel *Maryūd*, which the great Arab author al-Ṭayyib Ṣāliḥ has completed and will be published as a book in the next few weeks'. In the Qatar journal *al-Dōḥa*, 1 (January 1976), p. 108, al-Ṭayyib Ṣāliḥ is close to completing his novel *Maryūd*. In an interview granted to Sabīl al-Muqābila, al-Ṭayyib Ṣāliḥ says that he has been writing *Maryūd* for the past three years, as cited in Berkley, *The Roots of Consciousness*, p.xxxvii. The Egyptian literary critic, 'Abd al-Raḥmān Abū 'Awf analyses the novel *Maryūd* in June 1976. See idem, 'Bu'd al-Wāqi' fī Adab al-Ṭayyib Ṣāliḥ', *al-Ṭalī'a*, pp. 148–54. According to Kamal al-Nagar and Salah Hassan, the novel was ready in December 1977, see 'Tayeb Salih, Patterns and Ambiguities', *Sudanow*, 77 (December 1977), p. 51. According to another source, the novel was not published by Dār al-'Awda but by al-Mu'assasa al-'Arabiyya li'l-Dirāsāt wa'l-Nashr, see 'Abd Allāh Ibrāhīm, 'Maghzā al-Mawt fī Adab al-Ṭayyib Ṣāliḥ al-Riwā'ī', *al-Ṭalī'a al-Adabiyya*, 2 (February 1980), p. 33, n. 31. al-Nabr, 'al-'Unf fī Riwāyat *Mawsim al-Hijra ilā al-Shamāl*', in idem, *al-'Unf fī al-Qiṣṣa al-'Arabiyya al-Ḥadītha*, pp. 108–9, n.1.
17. In an interview granted by al-Ṭayyib Ṣāliḥ to 'Īsā al-Ḥilū:, 'Ḥiwār ma'a al-Ṭayyib Ṣāliḥ (3)', *al-Ayyām* (11 November 1977), cited in Berkley, *The Roots of Consciousness*, p. lxxix. One version has it that the novel would comprise three parts, see Ahmed (ed.), *Sixteen Sudanese Short Stories*, p. 77.
18. As cited in el-Badawī, *al-Ṭayyib Ṣāliḥ*, p. 162.
19. Ami Elad-Bouskila, 'Appendix B: A Short Summary of al-Ṭayyib Ṣāliḥ's Works', in Elad-Bouskila and Al-Shahi (eds), *Al-Ṭayyib Ṣāliḥ*, pp. 135–43.
20. Elad-Bouskila, 'Appendix A: Places and Dates', in Elad-Bouskila and Al-Shahi (eds), *Al-Ṭayyib Ṣāliḥ, Edebiyât*, pp. 127–35. See Johnson-Davies, 'Profile: The World of Tayeb Salih', *Azure*, p. 16. His books have been translated into more than twenty languages including Chinese, English, French, German, Italian, Japanese, Norwegian, Polish and Russian. See Ṣāliḥ, *Bandar Shāh: Maryūd*, Tunis, Dār al-Janūb li'l-Nashr, 1986, on the back cover. el-Badawī, *al-Ṭayyib Ṣāliḥ*, pp. 163–9. See *Ḥiwār*, 21 (March-April 1966), p. 2. Constance E. Berkley, 'El Tayeb Salih', p. 177.
21. See el-Badawī, *al-Ṭayyib Ṣāliḥ*, p. 164.
22. Farghalī, 'Liqā' ma'a al-Ṭayyib Ṣāliḥ', *al-Hilāl*, p. 118. See also *Global Voices: Contemporary Literature from the Non-Western World*, A.W. Biddle (ed.), Englewood Cliffs, Prentice Hall, 1995, pp. 512–22. Tayeb Salih, as cited by Johnson-Davies in Salih, *The Wedding of Zein and Other Stories*, London, Heinemann, 1978.
23. el-Badawī, *al-Ṭayyib Ṣāliḥ*, p. 163.
24. Farghalī, 'Liqā' ma'a al-Ṭayyib Ṣāliḥ', *al-Hilāl*, p. 118. Johnson-Davies in Salih, *The Wedding of Zein and Other Stories*. L. Stepanov, '*Between the Past and the Future*', p. 7.
25. See Stepanov, '*Between the Past and the Future*', p. 7. Http://helios-unive.it/-arabic/biblio.htm Bibliografia Arabo-Islamistica in Italian.
26. According to el-Badawī, *al-Ṭayyib Ṣāliḥ*, p. 164.
27. I would to thank Peter Clark for providing me with this information.
28. As cited by L. Stepanov, 'Between the Past and the Future', in the Russian translation of al-Ṭayyib Ṣāliḥ's novels, pp. 3–4. My thanks to Ella London who translated this information from Russian into English. Vlādīmīr Shāgāly 'Limādhā Turjimat *Mawsim al-Hijra ilā al-Shamāl* ilā al-Rūsiyya' (trans. 'Abd al-Karīm 'Abd al-Ṣamad), *al-Mawqif al-Adabī*, 220–1 (August-September 1989), pp. 59–64.

29. See el-Badawī, *al-Ṭayyib Ṣāliḥ*, pp. 167–8. al-Ṭayyib Ṣāliḥ, 'Naḥwa Ufuq Ba'īd, Ayyām fī Ūslū (1)', *al-Majalla*, 875 (23 November 1996), p. 78.
30. See Johnson-Davies, 'Profile: The World of Tayeb Salih', *Azure*, p. 17.
31. el-Badawī, *al-Ṭayyib Ṣāliḥ*, p. 169.
32. Ibid., p. 168.
33. Ibid., p. 169. According to *Kitābat Sūdāniyya*, 8 (June 1999), p. 97, this thesis was published in 1988.
34. Amyuni, (ed.), Tayeb Salih's Season of Migration to the North, p. 172.
35. Ibid.
36. Ibid.
37. Ibid.
38. It was also published in *Kitābāt Sūdāniyya*, 20 (June 2000), pp. 78–85. A critical review on this introduction was made by Muḥammad al-Rabī' Ṣāliḥ, ''Itābāt al-Naṣṣ wa-Jamāliyyāt al-Istijāba: Ḥafriyyāt fī Muqaddimat al-Ṭayyib Ṣāliḥ li Diwān *Ghābat al-Abanūs* li Ṣalāḥ Aḥmad Ibrāhīm', in *Kitābāt Sūdāniyya*, 12 (June 2000), pp. 67–77.
39. Amyuni (ed.), Tayeb Salih's Season of Migration to the North, p. 157. Berkley, *The Roots of Consciousness*, p. 8.
40. According to other source, it was in 1976, see Berkley, 'El Tayeb Salih', *Pacific Moana Quarterly*, p. 177. On the relationship between the film and the novel, see 'Iṣām Maḥfūẓ, *al-Riwāya al-'Arabiyya al-Ṭalī'iyya wa'l-Shahāda*, pp. 75, 77–8. Fārūq 'Abd al-Azīz, '*'Urs al-Zayn*', *al-'Arabī*, 233 (April 1978), pp. 124–30. el-Badawī, *al-Ṭayyib Ṣāliḥ*, pp. 71–2. For al-Ṭayyib Ṣāliḥ's opinion of this film, see al-Qamarī, 'Hākadhā Ḥaddathanī al-Ṭayyib Ṣāliḥ', *Kitābāt Sūdāniyya*, p. 69. al-Khawwāḍ, 'al-Ṭayyib Ṣāliḥ: Ārā' fī al-Siyāsa wa'l-Hujna al-Thaqāfiyya', *Kitābāt Sūdāniyya*, pp. 84–5.
41. See L. Stepanov, 'Between the Past and the Future' in Shikova (eds), *al-Ṭayyib Ṣāliḥ's Novels*, p. 7.
42. Amyuni (ed.), Tayeb Salih's Season of Migration to the North, p. 158. el-Badawī, *al-Ṭayyib Ṣāliḥ*, p. 90.
43. See *al-Ra'y al-Ākhar*; II :11 (August 1996), p. 8.
44. Amyuni (ed.), Tayeb Salih's Season of Migration to the North, p. 158. There is no indication of this information in Munā al-Bundārī, Maḥmūd Qāsim and Ya'qūb Wahbā (eds), *Mawsū'āt al-Aflām al-'Arabiyya*, Cairo, Bayt al-Ma'rifa, 1994.
45. For the English translation, see Berkley, *The Roots of Consciousness*, pp. xxxxi–xxxxviii.
46. For the English translation, see Ibid., pp. lii–lx.
47. For the English translation, see Ibid., pp. lxii–lxxiii.
48. For the English translation, see Ibid., pp. lxxv–lxxx.
49. As cited in Aḥmad Amīn al-Bashīr, 'al-Ṭayyib...wa-Ṣalāḥ wa-Hawiyuun 'Azza', in Ḥasan Abbashir al-Ṭayyib (ed.), *al-Ṭayyib Ṣāliḥ*, p. 297.
50. See Muḥammad al-Mahdī Bushrā, 'Taḥdīd al-Jins al-Fūlklūrī fī Ibdā'al-Ṭayyib Ṣāliḥ', in Ḥasan Abbashir al-Ṭayyib (ed.), *al-Ṭayyib Ṣāliḥ*, p. 345.
51. For the English translation, see Berkley, *The Roots of Consciousness*, pp. xxvi–xxxviii.
52. Ibid., p. 304.
53. Ṭāriq al-Ṭayyib, 'al-Ightirāb 'inda al-Ṭayyib Ṣāliḥ', in Ḥasan Abbashir al-Ṭayyib (ed.), *al-Ṭayyib Ṣāliḥ*, p. 283.

BIBLIOGRAPHY

Arabic and Hebrew

Abāẓa, Fārūq, 'Ṭuyūr al-Shamāl wa-Riḥlat al-Hijra ilā al-Janūb', *al-Muṣawwar*, 3093 (20 January 1984), 62–5.

'Abbās, Iḥsān, 'Naẓra fī Milaff al-Adab al-Sūdānī', *al-Ādāb*, 4 (April 1975), 110–15.

'Abd al-'Azīz, al-Fārūq, ''*Urs al-Zayn*, Naḥwa Sīnamā 'Arabiyya Jadīda', *al-'Arabī*, 233 (April 1978), 124–30.

'Abd al-Bāqī, Muḥammad 'Abd al-Ḥakam, 'Riḥlat al-Baṭal al-Riwā'ī fī Ḍaw Thunā'iyyat al-Qarya wa'l-Madīna wa-Ṭabī'at al-Mu'ālaja al-Fanniyya', *al-Majalla al-'Arabiyya li'l-'Ulūm al-Insāniyya*, 61 (Winter 1998), 8–50.

'Abd al-Ghanī, Muṣṭafā, *al-Ittijāh al-Qawmī al-'Arabī fī al-Riwāya*, Cairo, al-Hay'a al-Miṣriyya al-'Āmma li'l-Kitāb, 1998.

'Abd al-Ghanī, Muṣṭafā, *Qaḍāyā al-Riwāya al-'Arabiyya*, Cairo, al-Dār al-Miṣriyya al-Lubnāniyya, 1999.

'Abd al-Ḥaqq, 'Abd al-Ḥayy, 'Dirāsāt Sūdāniyya, al-Lahja al-'Arabiyya fī Darfūr', *al-Kharṭūm*, 8 (May 1969), 54–7.

'Abd al-Khāliq, Muḥammad, 'Qānūn kishāfat al-Ṭayyib Ṣāliḥ fī Riwāyātihi, al-Istiqlāl Ḥulm Mustaḥīl', *al-Ahrām al-'Arabī*, 14 (23 June 1977).

'Abd Allāh, 'Abd al-Badī', *al-Riwāya al-Ān*, Cairo, Dār al-Ādāb, 1990.

'Abd Allāh, Muḥammad Ḥasan, *al-Wāqi'iyya fī al-Riwāya al-'Arabiyya*, Cairo, Dār al-Ma'ārif, 1971.

'Abd Allāh, Muḥammad Ḥasan, *al-Rīf fī al-Riwāya al-'Arabiyya*, Kuwait, al-Majlis al-Waṭanī li'l-Thaqāfa wa'l-Funūn wa'l-Ādāb, Silsilat 'Ālam al-Ma'rifa, 1989.

'Abd Allāh, Muḥammad Khalafallāh, ''Urs al-Zayn Namūdhajan li'l-Ḥiwāriyya al-Naṣṣiyya', Mawāqif, 72 (June-September 1993), 84–95. [This article was published under the same title in the Sudanese newspaper al-Kharṭūm, (1) 878 (7 May 1995), 4; (2) 879 (8 May 1995), 4. It was also published under the title: ''Urs al-Zayn, Namūdhajan li'l-Ḥiwāriyya al-Naṣṣiyya (Dirāsa Naqdiyya Muqārana)', part 1, Kitābāt Sūdāniyya, 8 (June 1999), 33–42].

'Abd Allāh, Muḥammad Khalafallāh, 'Khiṭāb al-Darāwīsh Tanqīb 'an al-Wajh al-Ākhar li'l-Ablah fī Riwāyat '*Urs al-Zayn* (1)', *al-Kharṭūm*, 857 (13 April 1995), 4; (2), 859 (15 April 1995), 4; (3), 860 (16 April 1995), 4. [This article was published under the title ''*Urs al-Zayn* Namūdhajan li'l-Ḥiwāriyya al-Naṣṣiyya, Khiṭāb al-Darwīsh (Dirāsa Naqdiyya Muqārana)', part 2, *Kitābāt Sūdāniyya*, 9 (September 1999), 149–60].

'Abd Allāh, Muḥammad Khalafallāh, 'Fi Ṣuḥbat al-Zayn, Qirā'a Naqdiyya: Fī Tajsīr al-Huwwa bayn al-Ṣakhab wa'l-Shawq', *al-Ittiḥādī al-Duwaliyya*, 656 (July 1998), 6.

'Abd Allāh, Ṣalāḥ Ḥasan, ''An al-Usṭūra fī Adab al-Ṭayyib Ṣāliḥ, '*Urs al-Zayn* Namūdhajan', *Kitābāt Sūdāniyya*, 8 (June 1999), 78–81.

'Abd al-Mukarram, Aḥmad, 'al-'Unṣur al-Muhaymin fī al-Khitāb al-Qaṣaṣī li 'Alī al-Makk (1)', *Kitābāt Sūdāniyya*, 7 (March 1999), 130–40; (2), *Kitābāt Sūdāniyya*, 9 (September 1999), 137–48;

'Abd al-Mukarram, Aḥmad and al-Khalīfa 'Abd al-Wahhāb Ḥasan, 'al-Mubdī' Ibrāhīm Isḥāq, 'Alāma Bāriza li 'Abqariyyat al-Riwāya fi Thaqāfatinā', *al-Kharṭūm*, 759 (15 December 1994), 4–5.

'Abd al-Mun'im, Salīm, 'Majhūd li'l-Ru'ya 'an Bu'd, al-Ṭayyib Ṣāliḥ Ṣāḥib *Mawsim al-Hijra ilā al-Shamāl*', *al-Sharq*, 5 (October 1971), 29–30.

'Abd al-Qādir, Fārūq, 'Fī al-Riwāya al-Sūdāniyya (1): al-Ṭayyib Ṣāliḥ, Hāmish Saghīr 'an al-Ḥubb', *al-Muṣawwar*, 3997 (18 May 2001), 48–50.

'Abd al-Raḥīm, 'Abd al-Raḥīm Muḥammad, 'al-Shakl wa'l-Ramz fī Riwāyat al-Ṭayyib Ṣāliḥ, *Mawsim al-Hijra ilā al-Shamāl*', *al-Qāhira*, 115 (August-September 1991), 18–25.

'Abd al-Raḥīm, Muddathir, *al-Imbiryāliyya wa'l-Qawmiyya fī al-Sūdān, Dirāsa li'l-Taṭawwur al-Dustūrī wa'l-Siyāsī, 1899–1965*, Beirut, Dār al-Nahār, 1971.

'Abd al-Raḥmān, 'Ā'isha (Bint al-Shāṭi'), *Sayyid al-'Izba, Qiṣṣat Imra'a Khāṭi'a*, Cairo, Maṭba'at al-Ma'ārif wa-Maktabuhā, 1944.

'Ābdīn, 'Abd al-Majīd, *Bayn al-Ḥabasha wa' l-'Arab*, Cairo, Dār al-Fikr al-'Arabī, 1947.

'Ābdīn, 'Abd al-Majīd, *Ta'rīkh al-Thaqāfa al-'Arabiyya fī al-Sūdān mundhu Nash'atihā ilā al-'Aṣr al-Ḥadīth*, 2nd ed., Beirut, Dār al-Thaqāfa, 1967 (1st ed. 1953).

Abkar, al-Nūr 'Uthmān, 'Riwāya mā ba'd al-Istiqbāl: al-Baḥth 'an Huwiyya Ta'rīkhiyya Ḥadāriyya 'inda al-Ṭayyib Ṣāliḥ wa- Ibrāhīm Isḥāq', *al-Ayyām* (18 February, 1977). Reprinted in *al-Thaqāfa al-Sūdāniyya* (3 May 1977), 26–50.

Abū al-'Alā, Ḥusām, 'Ḥikāyāt 'an Ṣirā' al-Sharq wa'l-Gharb', *Fuṣūl*, 12:2 (Summer 1993), 204–14.

Abū 'Awf, 'Abd al-Raḥmān, *al-Baḥth 'an Ṭarīq Jadīd li'l-Qiṣṣa al-Qaṣīra al-Miṣriyya, Dirāsāt Naqdiyya*, Cairo, al-Hay'a al-Miṣriyya al-'Āmma li'l-Ta'līf wa'l-Nashr, 1971.

Abū 'Awf, 'Abd al-Raḥmān, 'Bu'd al-Wāqi' fī Adab al-Ṭayyib Ṣāliḥ', *al-Ṭalī'a*, 6 (June 1976), 148–54. [This article appeared under the title 'Bu'd al-Wāqi' wa'l-Usṭūra fī Adab al-Ṭayyib Ṣāliḥ', in idem, *Taḥawwulāt al-Riwāya al-'Arabiyya*, 19–38. It also appeared under the same title in idem, *Qirā'a fī al-Riwāya al-'Arabiyya al-Mu'āṣira*, 117–32].

Abū 'Awf, 'Abd al-Raḥmān, 'al-Baḥth 'an Ṭarīq Jadīd li'l-Riwāya al-Miṣriyya wa'l-'Arabiyya al-Mu'āṣira', *al-Ādāb*, 6 (June 1980), 36–9.

Abū 'Awf, 'Abd al-Raḥmān, *Taḥawwulāt al-Riwāya al-'Arabiyya*, Cairo, Dār al-Ghad li'l-Nashr wa'l-Di'āya wa'l-I'lān, Kitāb al-Ghad 21, 1990.

Abū 'Awf, 'Abd al-Raḥmān, *Qirā'a fī al-Riwāya al-'Arabiyya al-Mu'āṣira*, Cairo, al-Hay'a al-Miṣriyya al-'Āmma li'l-Kitāb, 1995.

Abū al-Faraj, Ghālib Ḥamza, *Sanawāt al-Ḍay'a*, Tunis, al-Dār al-Tūnisiyya li'l-Nashr, 1980.

Abū Hayf, 'Abd Allāh, *al-Qiṣṣa al-'Arabiyya al-Ḥadītha wa'l-Gharb*, Damascus, Manshūrāt Ittiḥād al-Kuttāb al-'Arabī, 1994.

Abū Ḥamdān, Samīr, 'al-Ṭayyib Ṣāliḥ: Azmat al-Makān', in idem, *al-Naṣṣ al-Marṣūd, Dirāsāt fī al-Riwāya*, Beirut, al-Mu'assasa al-Jāmi'iyya li'l-Dirāsāt wa'l-Nashr wa'l-Tawzī', 1990, 97–107.

Abū Nādir, Mūrīs, *al-Alsuniyya wa'l-Naqd al-Adabī fī al-Naẓariyya wa'l-Mumārasa*, Beirut, Dār al-Nahār li'l-Nashr, 1979.

Abū Rayya, Yūsuf, *al-Duḥā al-'Ālī*, Cairo, Dār Shuhdī li'l-Nashr wa'l-Tawzī', 1985.

Abū Sa'd, Aḥmad, *al-Shi'r wa'l-Shu'arā' fī al-Sūdān 1900–1958, Dirāsa wa-Mukhtārāt*, Beirut, Dār al-Ma'ārif, 1959.

'Adab al-Muhajjarīn al-Judud', *Ibdā'*, 11 (November 1999), 40–2.

Adham, Ismā'īl and Ibrāhīm Nājī, *Ṭawfīq al-Hakīm*, Cairo, Dār Miṣr li'l-Ṭibā'a wa'l-Nashr, 1945.

Adūnīs, 'Taḥiyya ilā Edwār Sa'īd wa'l-Ṭayyib Ṣāliḥ', *al-Ḥayāt*, 12246 (5 June 1996), 16.

Aghāsī, Eliyāhū, 'Mashākil al-Hijra ilā al-Shamāl', *al-Sharq*, 5–7 (October-December 1975), 45–8.

Aḥmad, 'Abd al-Ḥamīd Muḥammad, *al-Shi'r wa'l-Mujtama' fī al-Sūdān, Qirā'āt fī al-Shi'r al-Sūdānī al-Ḥadīth wa'l-Mu'āṣir*, Khartoum, Dār al-Wa'y li'l-Ṭibā'a wa'l-Nashr wa'l-Tawzī', 1987.

Aḥmad, Muḥammad al-Ḥasan, 'Fī Ṣuḥbat al-Ṭayyib al-Insān', in Ḥasan Abbashir al-Ṭayyib (ed.), *al-Ṭayyib Ṣāliḥ*, 65–7.

Aḥmad, 'Uthmān Ḥasan, 'Mujarrad Wujhat Naẓar', *al-Ṣiḥāfa* (August 1969).

Aḥmad, 'Uthmān Ḥasan, 'al-Qarya fī *'Urs al-Zayn* Hiya al-Sūdān bi Qabā'ilihā al-Mutanāfira', in Muḥammadiyya (ed.), *al-Ṭayyib Ṣāliḥ*, 180–90.

'Ajūba, Mukhtār [Ibrāhīm], 'Kitāb al-Shahr, al-Ṣiḥāfa al-Adabiyya wa-Taṭawwur al-Kitāba al-Nathriyya fī al-Sūdān 1898–1945', *al-Kharṭūm*, 3 (December 1969), 107–19.

'Ajūba, Mukhtār [Ibrāhīm], 'Fann al-Qiṣṣa al-Qaṣīra', *al-Kharṭūm*, 5:8 (May 1970), 36–40.

'Ajūba, Mukhtār Ibrāhīm, 'Dirāsa 'an al-Ṭayyib Ṣāliḥ', *al-Kharṭūm*, 5:8 (May 1970), 63–70.

'Ajūba, Mukhtār Ibrāhīm (ed.), *Namādhij min al-Qiṣṣa al-Qaṣīra fī al-Sūdān*, Khartoum, Jāmi'at al-Kharṭum, Dār al-Ta'līf wa'l-Tarjama wa'l-Nashr, 1972.

'Ajūba, Mukhtār Ibrāhīm, *al-Qiṣṣa al-Ḥadītha fī al-Sūdān*, Khartoum, Jāmi'at al-Kharṭūm, Dār al-Ta'līf wa'l-Tarjama wa'l-Nashr, 1972. 2nd ed., Cairo, Markaz al-Dirāsāt al-Sūdāniyya, 2000.

Alf Layla wa-Layla, Beirut, al-Maṭba'a al-Kāthūlīkiyya, 1888–90.

Alfiyā, 'Abd al-Mun'im 'Ajab, 'Qirā'a fī Kitāb *al-Lā Muntamī fī Adab al-Ṭayyib Ṣāliḥ*', *Kitābāt Sūdāniyya*, 19 (March 2002), 125–30.

'Alī, Badr al-Dīn Ḥasan, 'Ra'y Sarī' 'an Masīrat al-Masraḥ fī al-Sūdān', *al-Ādāb*, 4 (April 1975), 59–62.

'Alī, Muḥammad Rushdī Ḥasan, *al-Ibdā' al-Fannī fī Qiṣaṣ al-Ṭayyib Ṣāliḥ*, Cairo, Maṭba'at al-Ma'rifa, 1980.

Allāh, 'Imād al-'Abd, 'al-Riwāya al 'Arabiyya wa'l-Sulṭa, 'An Istiḥālat al-Fann al-Riwā'ī fī al-Anẓima al-Istibdādiyya', *al-Nāqid*, 58 (April 1993), 24–7.

Allāh, 'Imād al-'Abd, *al-Arḍ al-Ḥarām, al-Riwāya wa'l-Istibdād fī Bilād al-'Arab*, London, Riyāḍ al-Rayyis li'l-Kutub wa-li'l-Nashr, 1997.

Allen, Roger, ''Urs al-Zayn li'l-Ṭayyib: al-Turāth wa'l-Taghyīr', in Ḥasan Abbashir al-Ṭayyib (ed.), *al-Ṭayyib Ṣāliḥ*, 233–41.

'Allūsh, Sa'īd, 'al-Wāqi' wa'l-Muḥtamal fī al-Riwāya al-'Arabiyya', *al-Ādāb*, 28:2–3 (February-March 1980), 69–71.

Al-Amīn, 'Abd Allāh Ḥāmid, 'al-Rasm al-Bayānī li'l-Riwāya al-Sūdāniyya', *al-Ādāb*, 4 (April 1975), 52–55.

Amīn, Aḥmad, *al-Sharq wa'l-Gharb*, Cairo, Maṭba'at Lajnat al-Ta'līf wa'l-Tarjama wa'l-Nashr, 1955.

Amīn, Jalāl, 'al-Aṣāla wa'l-Mu'āṣara bayn Yaḥyā Ḥaqqī wa'l-Ṭayyib Ṣāliḥ', *al-Hilāl*, 101:1 (January 1993), 106–13.

Amīn, Jalāl, *Kutub lahā Ta'rīkh*, Cairo, Dār al-Hilāl, 2003.

Amyūnī, Munā Taqī al-Dīn (Trans. 'Alī Khalīl Ḥāmid), Dirāsa fī Mawsim al-Hijra ilā al-Shamāl, Nablus, Manshūrāt al-Waḥda, n.d.

Al-'Ānī, Shujā' Muslim, 'Mawsim al-Hijra ilā al-Shamāl', in idem, *Fī Adabinā al-Qaṣaṣī al-Mu'āṣir*, Baghdad, Dār al-Shu'ūn al-Thaqāfiyya al-'Āmma, 1989, 95–105. [This article was published in *al-Kalima*, 5 (May 1969)].

Al-'Ānī, Shujā' Muslim, *al-Riwāya al-'Arabiyya wa'l-Ḥaḍāra al-'Ūrubbiyya*, Baghdad, Manshūrāt Wizārat al-Thaqāfa wa'l-Funūn, 1979.

Al-'Aqqād, 'Abbās Maḥmūd, *Sāra*, Cairo, Maktabat Gharīb, n.d. (1st ed. 1938).

Al-'Arwī, 'Abd Allāh, *al-Ghurba wa'l-Yatīm*, 2nd ed., Casablanca, al-Markaz al-Thaqāfī al-'Arabī; Beirut, Dār al-Fārābī, 1980 (1st ed. 1972).

Al-'Asharī, Jalāl, 'Zūrbā al-Sūdānī aw al-Baḥth 'an al-Dhāt al-Ifrīqiyya', in Muḥammadiyya (ed.), *al-Ṭayyib Ṣāliḥ*, 152–79. [This article was published under the same title in the Egyptian monthly *al-Fikr al-Mu'āṣir*, 45 (November 1968), 68–78].

Al-'Asharī, Jalāl, *Thaqāfatunā bayn al-Aṣāla wa'l-Mu'āṣara*, Beirut, Dār al Ma'rifa, n.d.

'Āshūr, Raḍwā, *al-Riḥla: Ayyām Ṭāliba Miṣriyya fī Amirīkā*, Beirut, Dār al-Ādāb, 1983.

Al-Aswānī, 'Abd al-Wahhāb, *Salmā al-Aswāniyya*, Cairo, Dār al-Hay'a al-Miṣriyya al-'Āmma li'l-Ta'līf wa'l-Nashr, 1970.

'Aṭawī, 'Alī Najīb, *Taṭawwur Fann al-Qiṣṣa al-Lubnāniyya al-'Arabiyya ba'd al-Ḥarb al-'Ālamiyya al-Thāniya*, Beirut, Dār al-Āfāq al-Jadīda, 1982.

'Awaḍ, Luwīs, *Mudhakkirāt Ṭālib Ba'tha*, Cairo, al-Hay'a al-Miṣriyya al-'Āmma li'l-Kitāb, 1991 (1st ed. 1965).

'Awaḍ, Yūsuf Nūr, *al-Ṭayyib Ṣāliḥ fī Manẓūr al-Naqd al-Bunyawī*, Jedda, Maktabat al-'Ilm, 1983.

'Ayyād, Shukrī, *al-Ru'yā al-Muqayyada, Dirāsāt fī al-Tafsīr al-Ḥaḍārī li'l-Adab*, Cairo, al-Hay'a al-Miṣriyya al-'Āmma li'l-Kitāb, 1978.

'Ayyāsh, 'Abd al-Qādir, *Mu'jam al-Mu'allifīn al-Sūriyyīn fī al-Qarn al-'Ishrīn*, Damascus, Dār al-Fikr, 1985.

Ayyūb, Dhū al-Nūn, *al-Duktūr Ibrāhīm*, Baghdad, Maṭba'at Umm al-Rib'iyyīn, 1939.

Al-Azra'ī, Sulaymān, 'Ẓāhirat al-Mahjariyya al-Jadīda fī Tashkhīṣ al-Ẓāhira', in *al-Kitāba wa'l-Mutakhayyil al-Mahjariyya al-Jadīda, al-Adab al-Nisawī*, Beirut, al-Mu'assasa al-'Arabiyya li'l-Dirāsāt wa'l-Nashr, 1999, 31–8.

'Azzām, Muḥammad, *al-Baṭal al-Ishkālī fī al-Riwāya al-'Arabiyya al-Mu'āṣira*, Damascus, al-Ahālī li'l-Ṭibā'a wa'l-Nashr wa'l-Tawzī', 1992.

Badawī, 'Abduh, *al-Shi'r al-Ḥadīth fī al-Sūdān, 1840–1953*, Cairo, al-Majlis al-A'lā li'l-Hay'at al-Funūn wa'l-Ādāb wa'l-'Ulūm al-Ijtimā'iyya, 1964.

El-Badawī, Aḥmad Muḥammad, *Laban al-Ābanūs Yā Zōl, Riwāya Sūdāniyya*, Cairo, Markaz al-Buḥūth al-'Arabiyya, 1992.

El-Badawī, Aḥmad Muḥammad, *Qirā'a Jadīda fī Riwāyat Mawsim al-Hijra ilā al-Shamāl*, Cairo, al-Zōl, 1992.

El-Badawī, Aḥmad Muḥammad, *al-Qahr al-Thaqāfī wa'l-Isti'lā'*, Manchester, al-Zōl, n.d.

El-Badawī, Aḥmad Muḥammad, *al-Ṭayyib Ṣāliḥ: Sīrat Kātib wa-Naṣṣ*, Cairo, al-Dār al-Thaqāfiyya li'l-Nashr, 2000.

Badawī, Ḥāmid, 'Qirā'a Jadīda li Riwāyat *Mawsim al-Hijra ilā al-Shamāl* (1)', *al-Ayyām*, 9426 (9 June 1978), 6; (2), 9432 (16 June 1978), 6; (3), 9443 (30 June 1978), 6; (4), 9449 (7 July 1978), 7.

Badawī, Muḥammad, *al-Riwāya al-Jadīda fī Miṣr, Dirāsa fī al-Tashkīl wa'l-Idiyūlūjiyyā*, Beirut, al-Mu'assasa al-Jāmi'iyya li'l-Dirāsāt wa'l-Nashr wa'l-Tawzī', 1993.

Badawī, al-Sa'īd Muḥammad, *Mustawayāt al-'Arabiyya al-Mu'āṣira fi Miṣr*, Cairo, Dār al-Ma'ārif, 1973.

Badr, 'Abd al-Muḥsin Ṭāhā, *al-Riwā'ī wa'l-Arḍ*, 2nd ed. Cairo, Dār al-Ma'ārif, 1979. (1st ed. 1971).

Bahī, 'Iṣām, 'Idiūlūjiyyā al-Muṣālaḥa fī *Qindīl Umm Hāshim* wa-*Maswim al-Hijra ilā al-Shamāl*', *Fuṣūl*, 5:4 (July-September 1985), 177–202.[This article was published without the introduction and under a different title in Bahī, *al-Riḥla ilā al-Gharb*, 57–93, 162–83].

Bahī, 'Iṣām, *al-Riḥla ilā al-Gharb fī al-Riwāya al-'Arabiyya al-Ḥadītha*, Cairo, al-Hay'a al-Miṣriyya al-'Āmma li'l-Kitāb, 1991.

Baḥrāwī, Ḥasan, *Bunyat al-Shakl al-Riwā'ī*, Beirut, al-Markaz al-Thaqāfī al-'Arabī, 1990.

Bakhīt, Ja'far, 'al-Shakhṣiyya al-Sūdāniyya wa'l-Ḥukm al-Ajnabī', *Ḥiwār*, 10 (May-June 1964), 21–30.

Bakkār, Tawfīq, 'al-Thābit wa'l-Mutaḥawwil', in al-Ṭayyib Ṣāliḥ, *Mawsim al-Hijra ilā al-Shamāl*, Tunis, Dār al-Janūb li'l-Nashr, 1992, 9–28.

Bakrī, Bashīr, 'Sūdāniyya Tumnaḥ al-Jā'iza al-'Ālamiyya li Kuttāb Ifrīqiyā', *al-Kharṭūm*, 2494 (17 August 2000), 8.

Bakrī, Muḥammad 'Abd al-Khāliq, ''Ibr Majrā al-Ta'rīkh fī Wad Ḥāmid al-Muthqala: Baḥth fī Shajarat Ansāb Shakhṣiyyāt al-'Ālam al-Riwā'ī (1)', *al-Kharṭūm*, 1795 (7 May 1998), 4–5; (2), 1796 (9 May 1998), 6; (3), 1828 (15 June 1998), 4; (4), 1829 (16 June 1998), 6; (5), 1831 (18 June 1998), 5.

Bakrī, Muḥammad 'Abd al-Khāliq, 'Shabaḥ al-Mu'allif Yatajawwal ḥawla al-Ma'nā, Qaḍiyyat al-Sulṭa wa'l-Madīna fī *Bandar Shāh*', *Kitābāt Sūdāniyya*, 8 (June 1999), 43–57.

Ba'labakkī, Laylā, *Anā Aḥyā*, 2nd ed., Beirut, al-Maktab al-Tijārī li'l-Ṭibā'a wa'l-Tawzī' wa'l-Nashr, 1964 (1st ed. 1958).

Ba'labakkī, Laylā, *Safīnat Ḥanān ilā al-Qamar, Qiṣaṣ Qaṣīra*, Beirut, Dār al-Maktaba al-Tijāriyya li'l-Ṭibā'a wa'l-Tawzī' wa'l-Nashr, 1964 (1st ed. 1963).

Ballas, Shim'on, 'Masraḥiyyat *al-Sudd* li Maḥmūd al-Mas'adī wa-Ab'āduhā al-Wujūdiyya', *al-Karmil*, 2 (1981), 1–29.

Al-Baqlī, Muḥammad Qindīl, *Adab al-Darāwīsh*, Cairo, Maktabat al-Anglo al-Miṣriyya, 1970.

Barakāt, Ḥalīm, 'al-Kātib al-'Arabī wa'l-Sulṭa', *Mawāqif*, 12 (1970), 28–48.

Barakāt, Halīm, *al-Mujtama' al-'Arabī al-Mu'āṣir*, Beirut, Markaz Dirāsāt al-Waḥda al-'Arabiyya, 1991.

Barakāt, Salīm, *Fuqahā' al-Ẓalām*, Nicosia, Manshūrāt Mu'assasat Bīsān Press, 1985.

Al-Bāridī, Muḥammad Rajab, *Shakhṣ al-Muthaqqaf fī al-Riwāya al-'Arabiyya al-Mu'āṣira*, Tunis, al-Dār al-Tūnisiyya li'l-Nashr, 1993.

Barrāda, Muḥammad (ed.), *Lughat al-Ṭufūla wa'l-Ḥulm, Qirā'a fī Dhākirat al-Qiṣṣa al-Maghribiyya*, Rabat, al-Sharika al-Maghribiyya li'l-Nāshirīn al-Muttaḥidīn, 1986.

Barrāda, Muḥammad, *La'bat al-Nisyān*, 3rd ed., Rabat, Dār al-Amān li'l-Nashr wa'l-Tawzī', 1995 (1st ed. 1987).

Al-Bārūdī, Muḥammad, *Ḥannā Mīna, Riwā'ī al-Kifāḥ wa'l-Faraḥ*, Beirut, Dār al-Ādāb, 1993.

Al-Bashīr, Aḥmad al-Amīn, 'al-Ṭayyib...wa-Ṣalāḥ wa-Hawiyyun 'Azza', in Ḥasan Abbashir al-Ṭayyib (ed.), *al-Ṭayyib Ṣāliḥ*, 285–97.

Al-Bashīr, al-Ṭāhir Muḥammad 'Alī, *al-Adab al-Ṣūfī al-Sūdānī*, [Khartoum], al-Dār al-Sūdāniyya, 1970.

Al-Batayawī, Ḥātim, 'al-Ṭayyib Ṣāliḥ Yuwaddi' Aṣīla bi'l-Raqṣ 'alā Īqā' Ifrīqī', *al-Sharq al-Awsaṭ*, 5740 (19 August 1994), 1, 4.

Al-Bayyūmī, Muḥammad 'Abd al-Ghanī, 'al-Aṣāla wa'l-Tajdīd fī al-Riwāya al-Ifrīqiyya', *al-Kharṭūm*, 6 (March 1969), 29–35.

Bayyūmī, Muḥammad 'Abd al-Hānī, 'Mulāḥaẓāt ḥawla Ittijāh al-Shi'r al-Ifrīqī al-Ḥadīth', *al-Kharṭūm*, 10 (July 1969), 93–107.

Al-Bilāl, Mu'āwiya, *al-Kitāba fī Muntaṣaf al-Dā'ira*, Cairo, al-Sharika al-'Ālamiyya li'l-Ṭibā'a wa'l-Nashr, 2000.

Al-Bilāl, Mu'āwiya, *al-Shakl wa'l-Ma'sāt: Dirāsa fī al-Qiṣṣa al-Qaṣīra al-Sūdāniyya*, Cairo, al-Sharika al-'Ālamiyya li'l-Ṭibā'a wa'l-Nashr, 2000.

Bilāl, Sayyid Aḥmad, 'Qirā'a Jadīda fī Riwāyat *Bandar Shāh-Ḍaw al-Bayt*', *Kitābāt Sūdāniyya*, 3 (April 1993), 72–3.

Bin 'Īsā, Muḥammad, 'Takrīm al-Riwā'ī al-Sūdānī al-Ṭayyib Ṣāliḥ', al-Muntadā al-Thaqāfī al-'Arabī al-Ifrīqī, Muntadā Aṣīla, al-Dawra 13, Asila, 13–14 August, 1994 (two pages manuscript). Also published under the title: 'Sayyidī al-Ṭayyib... al-Ḥushūm al-Waqūr', in Ḥasan Abbashir al-Ṭayyib (ed.), *al-Ṭayyib Ṣāliḥ*, pp. 19–22.

Bishāra, Dālya, 'al-Ṭayyib Ṣāliḥ wa'l-Mas'ala al-Nisā'iyya', *Kull al-'Arab*, 354 (23 September 1994), 16.

Bishāra, Muṣṭafā 'Awaḍallāh, *Aḍwā' al-Naqd, Dirāsāt fī al-Qiṣṣa wa'l-Shi'r wa'l-Naqd*, [Khartoum], al-Dār al-Sūdāniyya li'l-Ṭibā'a wa'l-Nashr wa'l-Tawzī', 1977.

Bullāṭa, 'Īsā, *'Ā'id ilā al-Quds*, Beirut, Dār al-Ittiḥād li'l-Ṭibā'a wa'l-Nashr, 1998.

Al-Bundārī, Munā, Maḥmūd Qāsim and Ya'qūb Wahbā (eds), *Mawsū'at al-Aflām al-'Arabiyya*, Cairo, Bayt al-Ma'rifa, 1994.

Bushrā, Muḥammad al-Mahdī, 'al-Tajrīd fī al-Qiṣṣa al-Qaṣīra fī al-Sab'īnāt', al-juz' al-awwal, *al-Thaqāfa al-Sūdāniyya*, 19 (November 1979), 38–43.

Bushrā, Muḥammad al-Mahdī, 'Qiṣṣat al-Fājī'a wa'l-Kāritha, Dirāsa li'l-Qiṣṣa al-Qaṣīra fī al-Sūdān', *al-Thaqāfa al-Sūdāniyya*, al-juz' al-awwal, 19 (November 1981), 38–43; al-juz' al-thānī, 20 (December 1981).

Bushrā, Muḥammad al-Mahdī, 'al-Wajh wa'l-Qinā', Ibdā' al-Unthā Mir'at al-Dākhil', in *al-Mar'a wa'l-Ibdā' fī al-Sūdān*, Cairo and Khartoum, Markaz al-Dirāsāt al-Sūdāniyya, 2001, 188–218.

Bushrā, Muḥammad al-Mahdī, 'Taḥdīd al-Jins al-Fūlklūrī fī Ibdā'al-Ṭayyib Ṣāliḥ', in Ḥasan Abbashir al-Ṭayyib (ed.), *al-Ṭayyib Ṣāliḥ*, 313–45.

Daf'allāh, Khālid Mūsā, *al-Lā Muntamī fī Adab al-Ṭayyib Ṣāliḥ, Muqaddimāt Ru'ya li Mashrū' 'Aṣr al-Intiqāl*, Khartoum, Dār Jāmi'at al-Kharṭūm li'l-Nashr, 1993.

Al-Da'if, Rashīd, *'Azīzī al-Sayyid Kawābātā*, 2nd ed., Beirut, Riyāḍ al-Rayyis li'l-Kutub wa'l-Nashr, 2001 (1st ed. 1995).

Darghūthī, Ibrāhīm, *al-Nakhl Yamūt Wāqifan*, Tunis, Ṣāmid li'l-Nashr wa'l-Tawzī', 1989.

Darwīsh, Zakī, *Shitā' al-Ghurba wa-Qiṣaṣ Ukhrā*, Jerusalem, al-Sharq, 1970.

Darwīsh, Zakī, *Aḥmad, Maḥmūd wa'l-Akharūn*, 2nd ed., Nicosia, Mu'assasat Bīsān Press, 1989.

Ḍayf, Shawqī, *al-Adab al-'Arabī al-Mu'āṣir fī Miṣr*, 5th ed., Cairo, Dār al-Ma'ārif, 1974.

Duwāra, Fu'ād, *'Ashara Udabā' Yataḥaddathūn*, Cairo, Dār al-Ma'ārif, 1964.

El'ad [-Bouskila], 'Ami (ed.), *al-Ṭayyib Ṣāliḥ – Mivḥar Yetzirot*, Jerusalem, Academon, 1981 (Arabic and Hebrew).

El'ad[-Bouskila], 'Ami, *Shinuyei Girsa'ot BeSipurav HaKtzarim shel Maḥmūd Taymūr* (The Arabic Various Versions of Maḥmūd Taymūr's Short Stories), Jerusalem, 1981 (unpublished paper) (Hebrew).

El'ad [-Bouskila], 'Ami (ed.), *al-Qiṣṣa al-'Arabiyya al-Qaṣīra*, Jerusalem, Academon, 1984 (Arabic and Hebrew).

El'ad [-Bouskila], 'Ami, 'al-Ṭayyib Ṣāliḥ wa'l-Adab al-Sūdānī al-Jadīd', *Liqā'*, 6 (Spring 1987), 22–4.

El'ad [-Bouskila], 'Ami, 'Taṭawwur al-Shakhṣiyya fī A'māl al-Ṭayyib Ṣāliḥ', *al-Karmil*, Haifa, 10 (1989), 7–26.

El'ad-Bouskila, 'Ami (ed.), *Aḍwā' Dāniya, Mukhtārāt min al-Qiṣṣa al-'Arabiyya al-Ḥadītha*, Jerusalem, Academon, 1991.

El'ad-Bouskila, *Sifrut 'Aravit bi Levush 'Ivri* (Arabic Literature in Hebrew Dress), Jerusalem, Ministry of Education, Culture and Sport, 1995 (Hebrew).

El'ad-Bouskila, 'Ami, 'Infitāḥ wa-Inghilāq al-Mujtama' al-Isrā'īlī fī al-Sharq al-Awsaṭ fī Zaman al-Salām', *Mashārif*, 10 (August 1996), 35–43.

El'ad-Bouskila, 'Ami, 'Al-Wāqi' wa'l-Khayāl fī Qiṣṣat al-Ṭayyib Ṣāliḥ, 'Dawmat Wad Ḥāmid'', *Mashārif*, 13 (January 1997), 120–38.

El'ad-Bouskila, 'Ami, *HaOr HaKalush: Itzugim ve Tadmiyot shel Demut HaHakher BaSifruyot Ha'Araviyot HaModerniyot (The Dim Light: Representations and Images of the Other in Modern Arabic Literatures)*, Tel Aviv, The Tami Steinmetz Center for Peace Research, Tel Aviv University, 2005.

Eliraz, Giora, *Intelectualim Mitzriyyim mul Masoret ve Shinūy 1919–1939* (Egyptian Intellectuals in the Face of Tradition and Change 1919–1939), Ph.D. Thesis, The Hebrew University of Jerusalem, 1980 (Hebrew).

Ewen, Joseph, *HaDemut BaSipporet* (Character in Narrative), Tel Aviv, Sifriyat HaPo'alim, 1980 (Hebrew).

Fāḍil, Jihād, *As'ilat al-Riwāya, Ḥiwār ma'a al-Riwā'iyyīn al-'Arab*, Tunis, al-Dār al-'Arabiyya li'l-Kitāb, 1993.

Fāḍil, Jihād, *al-Adab al-Ḥadīth fī Lubnān*, London, Beirut, Riyāḍ al-Rayyis li'l-Kutub wa-li'l-Nashr, 1996.

Fāḍil al-Mawlā, Muḥammad al-Ḥasan, *Lamaḥāt min al-Naqd al-Adabī al-Ḥadīth*, Beirut, Dar al-'Awda, 1969.

Fāḍil al-Mawlā, Muḥammad al-Ḥasan, 'Naḥnu wa'l-Ṭayyib Ṣāliḥ wa'l-Ākharūn', in Muḥammadiyya (ed.), *al-Ṭayyib Ṣāliḥ*, 191–7. [This article was published under the same title in Fāḍil al-Mawlā, *Lamaḥāt min al-Adab al-'Arabī al-Ḥadīth*, 132–5. Published under the same title in *al-Idhā'a al-Sūdāniyya* (22 July 1968), 4–5].

Fahmī, Māhir Ḥasan, 'Maryūd, aw Humūm al-Muthaqqafīn' li'l-Ṭayyib Ṣāliḥ', in idem, *Qaḍāyā fī al-Adab wa'l-Naqd*, Doha, Dār al Thaqāfa, 1986, 311–33 [Published as an article under the title 'Maryūd aw Humūm al-Muthaqqafīn li'l-Ṭayyib Ṣāliḥ', in *Ḥawliyyāt Kuliyyat al-Insāniyyāt wa'l-'Ulūm al-Ijtimā'iyya*, 1 (1979), 7–27].

Fahmī, Manṣūr, 'al-Sharq wa'l-Ḥaḍāra al-'Arabiyya', *al-Muqtaṭaf*, 77 (October 1930), 257–63.

Faḥs, Hānī, *al-Tawḥīd al-Thaqāfī: al-Mar'a Mithālan*, Beirut, Dār al-Ahālī li'l-Ṭibā'a wa'l-Nashr wa'l-Tawzī', 1988.

Faraj, Alfred, *Ḥikāyāt al-Zaman al-Ḍā'i' fī Qarya Miṣriyya*, Cairo, Dar al-Mustaqbal al-'Arabī, 1983.

Farghalī, Sayyid, 'Liqā' ma'a al-Ṭayyib Ṣāliḥ fī Landan', *al-Hilāl*, 3 (March 1970), 118–21. [This interview was published under the same title in Muḥammadiyya (ed.) *al-Ṭayyib Ṣāliḥ*, 204–11].

Farīd, Māhir Shafīq, 'Najīb Maḥfūẓ fī al-Injlīziyya', *Fuṣul*, 2:2 (anuary-March 1987), 312–19.

Al-Faytūrī, Muḥammad Miftāḥ, *Aghānī Ifrīqiyā, Shi'r*, Beirut, Dār al-'Awda, n.d. (1st ed. 1956).

Al-Faytūrī, Muḥammad Miftāḥ, *'Āshiq min Ifrīqiyā, Shi'r*, Beirut, Dār al-Ādāb, 1964.

Al-Faytūrī, Muḥammad Miftāḥ, *Aḥzān Ifrīqiyā, Sulārā*, Cairo, al-Hay'a al-Miṣriyya al-'Āmma li'l-Ta'līf wa'l-Nashr, 1969 (1st ed. 1966).

Al-Faytūrī, Muḥammad Miftāḥ, *Udhkurīnī Yā Ifrīqiyā*, Beirut, Dār al-'Awda, 1970.

Fayyāḍ, Sulaymān, *Aṣwāt*, 2nd ed., Cairo, Kutub 'Arabiyya, 1977 (1st ed. 1972).

Fu'ād, Ni'mat Aḥmad, *al-Nīl fī al-Adab al-Miṣrī*, Cairo, Dār al-Ma'ārif, 1962.

Ghālib, Edwār, *al-Mawsū'a fī 'Ulūm al-Ṭabī'a*, Beirut, al-Maktaba al-Kathūlīkiyya, 1965.

Ghanāyīm, Maḥmūd, *Fī Mabnā al-Naṣṣ, Dirāsa fī Riwāyat Emīl Ḥabībī* al-Waqā'i' al-Gharība fī Ikhtifā' Sa'īd Abī al-Naḥs al-Mutashā'il, Jatt, Manshūrāt al-Yasār, 1987.

Ghanāyīm, Maḥmūd, *Tayyār al-Wa'y fī al-Riwāya al-'Arabiyya al-Ḥadītha, Dirāsa Uslūbiyya*, Beirut, Dār al-Jīl', Cairo, Dār al-Hudā, 1992.

Ghānim, Fatḥī, *al-Jabal*, Cairo, Dār al-Hilāl, Riwāyāt *al-Hilāl* 199, 1965 (1st ed. 1959).

Ghānim, Fatḥī, *al-Sākhin wa'l-Bārid*, Cairo, Mu'assasat Rūz al-Yūsuf, 1960.

Ghānim, Fatḥī, *al-Rajul Alladhī Faqada Ẓillahu*, Cairo, Kutub *al-Jumhūriyya*, 1969 (1st ed. 1962).

Ghānim, Fatḥī, *al-Afyāl*, Cairo, Maktabat Rūz al-Yūsuf, 1981.

Gharīb, Rūz, *Tamhīd fī al-Naqd al-Ḥadīth*, Beirut, Dār al-Makshūf, 1971.

Gharīb, Rūz, *Aḍwā' 'alā al-Ḥaraka al-Nisā'iyya al-Mu'āṣira*, Beirut, Markaz al-Dirāsāt al-Nisā'iyya fī al-'Ālam al-'Arabī, al-Jāmi'a al-Lubnāniyya al-Amirīkiyya, 1988.

Al-Ghīṭānī, Jamāl, *Awrāq Shābb 'Āsha mundhu Alf 'Ām*, 3rd ed., Cairo, Maktabat Madbūlī, n.d. (1st ed. 1969).

Ḥabībī, Emīl, *al-Waqā'i' al-Gharība fī Ikhtifā Sa'īd Abī al-Naḥs al-Mutashā'il*, 3rd ed., Jerusalem, Manshūrāt Ṣalāḥ al-Dīn, 1977 (1st ed. 1974).

Ḥabībī, Emīl, *Ikhtayya*, Nicosia, Mu'assasat Bīsān Press, 1985.

Ḥabībī, Emīl, 'Ifrīqiya Marta' al-Khayāl mundhu Ayyām Ibn Baṭṭūta', *al-Sharq al-Awsaṭ*, 5744 (20 August 1994), 22.

Al-Ḥadārī, Ḥasan, 'Liqā' ma'a al-Ṭayyib Ṣāliḥ', *al-Ṣiḥāfa* (17 September, 1981), 9

Haddāra, Muḥammad Muṣṭafā, *Tayyār al-Shi'r al-'Arabī al-Mu'āṣir fī al-Sūdān*, Beirut, Dār al-Thaqāfa, 1972.

Ḥāfiz, Ṣabrī, 'Aqāṣīṣ'Arabiyya Ḥadītha', *al-Majalla*, 137 (May 1968), 38–40, 59.

Al-Ḥājj, Naṣṣār, 'Tajribat Ibrāhīm Isḥāq Ibrāhīm', *Kitābāt Sūdāniyya*, 20 (June 2002), 97–100.

Al-Ḥajjājī [Al-Ḥaggāgī], Aḥmad Shams al-Dīn, *Ṣāni' al-Usṭūra al-Ṭayyib Ṣāliḥ*, Cairo, al-Hay'a al-Miṣriyya al-'Āmma li'l-Kitāb, al-Maktaba al-Thaqāfiyya, 460, 1990.

Ḥajjār, Walīd, *Musāfir bilā Ḥaqā'ib*, Damascus, 1979.

Al-Ḥakīm, Tawfīq, *'Awdat al-Rūḥ*, Cairo, al-Maṭba'a al-Namūdhajiyya, n.d. (1st ed. 1933).

Al-Ḥakīm, Tawfīq, *Yawmiyyāt Nā'ib fī al-Aryāf*, Cairo, al-Maṭba'a al-Namūdhajiyya, n.d. (1st ed. 1937).

Al-Ḥakīm, Tawfīq, *'Uṣfūr min al-Sharq*, Cairo, al-Maṭba'a al-Namūdhajiyya, n.d. (1st ed. 1938).

Ḥammād, Jum'a, *Badawī fī Ūrūbbā*, Amman, Maṭābi' al-Mu'assasa al-Ṣuḥufiyya al-Urdunniyya, 1977.

H.N., '*Mawsim al-Hijra* bayn al-Sharq wa'l-Gharb', *al-Kifāḥ al-'Arabī* (1 March 1993).

Ḥannā, Tawfīq, 'Muqaddimāt al-Ṭayyib Ṣāliḥ, Muḥāwala li Taqdīm Tajriba Jadīda', *al-Hilāl*, 11 (November 1969), 81–5.

Ḥanūn, 'Abd al-Majīd, *Ṣūrat al-Faransī fī al-Riwāya al-Maghribiyya*, Algiers, Dīwān al-Maṭbū'āt al-Jāmi'iyya, 1986.

Ḥaqqī, Maḥmūd Ṭāhir, *'Adhrā' Dinshawāy*, Cairo, al-Maktaba al-'Arabiyya, 1964 (1st ed. 1906).

Ḥaqqī, Yaḥyā, *Qindīl Umm Hāshim*, Cairo, al-Hay'a al-Miṣriyya al-'Āmma li'l-Kitāb, 1990 (1st ed. 1944).

Ḥarbī, Muḥammad, 'al-Ṭayyib Ṣāliḥ fī Risāla Jāmi'iyya Miṣriyya', *al-Ahrām* (4 October 1996), 16.

Al-Ḥardalū, Sayyid Aḥmad, *Mal'ūn Abūki Balad*, 3rd ed., Beirut, Dār al-'Awda, n.d. (1st ed. 1965).

Al-Ḥardalū, Sayyid Aḥmad, 'Ismuka Ṣār Waṭanan', in Ḥasan Abbashir al-Ṭayyib (ed.), *al-Ṭayyib Ṣāliḥ*, 55–8.

Ḥarīz, Sayyid Ḥāmid, 'Judhūr al-Adab al-Sha'bī al-Sūdānī', *al-Ādāb*, 4 (April 1975), 27–31.

Ḥasan, Yūsuf Fāḍil (ed.), *Kitāb al-Ṭabaqāt fī Khuṣūṣ al-Awliyā' wa'l-Ṣāliḥīn wa'l-Shu'arā' fī al-Sūdān li Muḥammad al-Nūr Ibn Dayfallāh*, al-Khartoum, Dār Jāmi'at al-Kharṭūm li'l-Nashr, Maṭba'at Jāmi'at al-Kharṭūm, 1971.

Ḥassūna, Muḥammad Amīn, *Rāwiya (Rajul al-Mu'jizāt), Qiṣṣa Rīfiyya*, Cairo, Maṭba'at Jarīdat al-Ṣabāḥ, 1956.

Ḥāwī, Khalīl, *Dīwān Khalīl Ḥāwī*, Beirut, Dār al-'Awda, 1972.

Al-Hawwārī, Aḥmad Ibrāhīm, 'al-Raḥīl ilā al-A'māq: Qirā'a Naqdiyya fī Qiṣaṣ Yaḥyā Ḥaqqī', *Fuṣūl*, 2:4 (July-September 1982), 59–72.

Al-Hawwārī, Aḥmad, Naqd al-Mujtama' fī Ḥadīth 'Īsā Ibn Hishām, Cairo, 'Ayn li'l-Dirāsāt wa'l-Buḥūth al-Insāniyya wa'l-Ijtimā'iyya, 1993.

Ḥaydarī, Buland, 'al-Ṭayyib Ṣāliḥ fī Ghurbatihi wa-Ibdā'ātihi', in Ḥasan Abbashir al-Ṭayyib (ed.), *al-Ṭayyib Ṣāliḥ*, 59–64.

Haykal, Muḥammad Aḥmad, '*Bandar Shāh*', *al-Dōḥa*, 2 (February 1976), 126–31.

Haykal, Muḥammad Aḥmad, 'al-Qiṣṣa fī al-Adab al-'Arabī', *al-Dōḥa*, (May 1976), 127–31.

Haykal, Muḥammad Ḥusayn, *Zaynab, Manaẓir wa-Akhlāq Rīfiyya*, Cairo, Dār al-Ma'ārif, 1979 (1st ed. 1914).

Ḥijāzī, Aḥmad 'Abd al-Mu'ṭī, '*Mawsim al-Hijra ilā al-Shamāl*', in Ḥasan Abbashir al-Ṭayyib (ed.), *al-Ṭayyib Ṣāliḥ*, 197–210.

Ḥijāzī, Muṣṭafā, *al-Takhalluf al-Ijtimā'ī*, 4th ed., Beirut, Ma'had al-Inmā' al-'Arabī, 1986.

Al-Ḥilū, 'Īsā, *Rīsh al-Babaghā'*, Beirut, Maktabat al-Ḥayāt, 1967.

Al-Ḥilū, 'Īsā, 'Qirā'āt fī al-Qiṣṣa al-Sūdāniyya al-Qaṣīra', *al-Ādāb*, 4 (April 1975), 37–9.

Al-Ḥilū, 'Īsā, 'Ḥiwār ma'a al-Ṭayyib Ṣāliḥ (1)' *al-Ayyām*, (23 October 1977); (2), (4 November 1977); (3), (11 November 1977).

Ḥusayn, Ṭāhā, *al-Ayyām*, vol. 1, Cairo, Dār al-Ma'ārif, 1973 (1st ed. 1929).

Ḥusayn, Ṭāhā, *Adīb*, Cairo, Dār al-Ma'ārif, 1962 (1st ed. 1935).

Ḥusayn, Ṭāhā, *al-Ḥubb al-Ḍā'i'*, Cairo, Maṭba'at al-Ma'ārif, 1943.

Ḥusayn, Ṭāhā, *Shajarat al-Bu's*, Cairo, Dār al-Ma'ārif, 1944.

Al-Ḥusaynī, Hudā, 'Al-Ṭayyib Ṣāliḥ fī Bayrūt: Hunāka Asrār Lam Udrikhā Ba'du', in Muḥammadiyya (ed.), *al-Ṭayyib Ṣāliḥ*, 212–20.

Al-Ḥuṣrī, Sāṭi', *Ārā' wa-Aḥādīth fī al-Lugha wa'l-Adab*, Beirut, Dār al-'Ilm li'l-Malā'īn, 1958.

Ibn Dhurayl, 'Adnān, *Adab al-Qiṣṣa fī Sūriya*, Damascus, Manshūrāt Dār al-Fann al-Ḥadīth al-'Ālamī, n.d.

Ibn Jallūn, 'Abd al-Majīd, *Fī al-Ṭufūla*, Rabat, Maktabat al-Ma'ārif, 1975 (1st ed. 1956).

Ibn Manẓūr, Jamāl al-Dīn al-Anṣārī, *Lisān al-'Arab*, Cairo, al-Mu'assasa al-Miṣriyya al-'Āmma li'l-Ta'līf wa'l-Anbā' wa'l-Nashr, n.d.

Ibn al-Muqaffa', 'Abd Allāh, *Kalīla wa-Dimna*, 2nd ed., Beirut, Dār al-Āfāq al-Jadīda, 1979.

Ibn al-Zubayr, Muḥammad (ed.), *Mu'jam Asmā' al-'Arab*, Beirut, Muscat, Maktabat Lubnān, Jāmi'at al-Sulṭān Qābūs, 1991.

Ibrāhīm, 'Abd Allāh, 'Maghzā al-Mawt fī Adab al-Ṭayyib Ṣāliḥ al-Riwā'ī', *al-Ṭalī'a al-Adabiyya*, Baghdad, 2 (February 1980), 21–33.

Ibrāhīm, Ibrāhīm Isḥāq, *Ḥadath fi al-Qarya*, Khartoum, Jāmi'at al-Kharṭūm, Dār al-Ta'līf wa'l-Tarjama wa'l-Nashr, 1969.

Ibrāhīm, Ibrāhīm Isḥāq, *A'māl al-Layl wa'l-Balda*, Khartoum, Jāmi'at al-Kharṭūm, Dār al-Ta'līf wa'l-Tarjama wa'l-Nashr, 1971.

Ibrāhīm, Ibrāhīm Isḥāq, *Mahrajān al-Madrasa al-Qadīma* [Khartoum], Wizārat al-Thaqāfa wa'l-I'lām, 1976.

Ibrāhīm, Ibrāhīm Isḥāq, 'Ḥawla al-Qiṣṣa al-Qaṣīra fī al-Sūdān', *al-Thaqāfa al-Sūdāniyya*, 10 (May 1979), 20–4.

Ibrāhīm, Ibrāhīm Isḥaq, *Akhbār al-Bint Mayākāyā*, Cairo, Khartoum, Markaz al-Dirāsāt al-Sūdāniyya, 2001.

Ibrāhīm, Ibrāhīm Isḥāq, *Wabāl fī Klīmindū*, Cairo, Khartoum, Markaz al-Dirāsāt al-Sūdāniyya, 2001.

Ibrāhīm, Muḥammad al-Makkī, 'Fitnat al-Ṭayyib bi Abī al-Ṭayyib', in Ḥasan Abbashir al-Ṭayyib (ed.), *al-Ṭayyib Ṣāliḥ*, 187–95.

Ibrāhīm, Nabīla, *Ashkāl al-Ta'bīr fī al-Adab al-Sha'bī*, Cairo: Dār al-'Ālam al-'Arabī, n.d.

Ibrāhīm, Sa'dī, *al-Marfūḍūn, Riwāya*, Algiers, al-Sharika al-Waṭaniyya li'l-Nashr wa'l-Tawzī', 1981.

Ibrāhīm, Ṣalāḥ Aḥmad, *Ghābat al-Ābanūs wa-Qaṣā'id Ukhrā*, Paris, Idfara, 1990.

Ibrāhīm, Ṣāliḥ, *al-Mar'a fī Adab al-Ṭayyib Ṣāliḥ*, Beirut, Ma'had al-Dirāsāt al-Nisā'iyya fī al-'Ālam al-'Arabī, al-Jāmi'a al-Lubnāniyya al-Amīrikiyya, 1997.

Ibrāhīm, Ṣiddīq Ḥasan, 'Kutub: al-Ṭayyib Ṣāliḥ, *Mawsim al-Hijra ilā al-Shamāl*', *al-Kharṭūm*, 11 (August 1969), 103–8.

Ibrāhīm, Ṣiddīq Ḥasan, 'Dirāsāt 'an al-Ṭayyib Ṣāliḥ fi Riwāyat *Mawsim al-Hijra ilā al-Shamāl*, bayn al-Riwāya wa-Muṣṭafā Sa'īd', *al-Kharṭūm*, 1 (October 1969), 52–61.

'Īd, Muḥammad, *al-Mutamayyiz*, Amman, Maṭba'at al-Sharq, 1978.

Al-'Īd, Yumnā, 'Tamalluk al-Waṭan wa-Mu'ādalat al-Jins wa'l-Ḥaḍāra (Mu'ānāt fī al-Ta'rīkh fī Riwāyat *Mawsim al-Hijra ilā al-Shamāl*)', *al-Ṭarīq*, 3–4 (August 1981), 98–130. [Published under the title 'Zaman al-Sard al-Riwā'ī fī Intājihi Dalālāt al-Tamalluk li'l-Waṭan fī Riwāyat *Mawsim al-Hijra ilā al-Shamāl*', in idem, *Fī Ma'rifat al-Naṣṣ*, 225–70.]

Al-'Īd, Yumnā, *Fī Ma'rifat al-Naṣṣ, Dirāsāt fī al-Naqd al-Adabī*, 3rd ed., Beirut, Dār al-Āfāq, 1985.

Al-'Īd, Yumnā, 'Bunyat al-Mawqi'ayn fī *Mawsim al-Hijra ilā al-Shamāl*', in idem, *al-Rāwī al-Mawqi' wa'l-Shakl, Baḥth fī al-Sard al-Riwā'ī*, Beirut, Mu'assasat al-Abḥāth al-'Arabiyya, 1986, 107–13.

Idrīs, Samāḥ, *al-Muthaqqaf al-'Arabī wa'l-Sulṭa, Baḥth fī Riwāyāt al-Tajriba al-Nāṣiriyya*, Beirut, Dār al-Ādāb, 1992.

Idrīs, Suhayl, *Ashwāq*, Beirut, Dār al-Ādāb, 1947.

Idrīs, Suhayl, *Nirān wa-Thulūj*, Beirut, Dār al-Ādāb, 1948.

Idrīs, Suhayl, *Kulluhunn Nisā*, Beirut, Dār al-Ādāb, 1949.

Idrīs, Suhayl, *Al-Ḥayy al-Lātīnī, Riwāya*, 8th ed., Beirut, Dār al-Ādāb, 1981 (1st ed. 1954).

Idrīs, Suhayl, *Al-Khandaq al-Ghamīq*, 2nd ed., Beirut, Dār al-Ma'ārif, 1972 (1st ed. 1958).

Idrīs, Yūsuf, *Ḥādithat Sharaf*, Beirut, Dār al-'Awda, n.d. (1st ed. 1958).

Idrīs, Yūsuf, *Lughat al-Āy Āy*, Beirut, Dār al-'Awda, n.d. (1st ed. 1965)

Idrīs, Yūsuf, *al-Sayyida Fiyinnā*, Beirut, Dār al-'Awda, 1977 (1st ed. 1975).

Ismā'īl, Ismā'īl Fahd, *al-Nīl Yajrī Shamālan: al-Bidāyāt*, Beirut, Dār al-'Awda, 1981.

Ismā'īl, 'Izz al-Dīn, *al-Shi'r al-Qawmī fī al-Sūdān*, Beirut, Dār al-'Awda, 1968.

Ismā'īl, 'Izz al-Dīn, *al-Qaṣaṣ al-Sha'bī fī al-Sūdān, Dirāsa Fanniyat al-Ḥikāya al-Sūdāniyya*, Cairo, al-Hay'a al-Miṣriyya al-'Āmma li'l-Ta'līf wa'l-Nashr, 1970.

'Izzat, Adīb, Samar Ruḥī al-Fayṣal and Ḥasan Ḥamīd (eds), *A'ḍā' Ittiḥād al-Kuttāb al-'Arab fī al-Quṭr al-'Arabī al-Sūrī wa'l-Waṭan al-'Arabī*, Damascus, Manshūrāt Ittiḥād al-Kuttāb al-'Arab, 1995.

Al-Jābirī, Shakīb, *Naham, ilā al-Nāhilīn min al-Lujaj al-Hamrā'*, Aleppo, al-Maṭba'a al-'Ilmiyya, n.d. (1st ed. 1937).

Al-Jābirī, Shakīb, *Qadar Yalhū, Ṣiyāgha Jadīda*, Beirut, Dār al-Nahār li'l-Nashr, 1980 (1st ed. 1939).

Al-Jābirī, Shakīb, *Qaws Quzaḥ*, Damascus, Dār al-Yakẓa, 1946.

Al-Jābirī, Shakīb, *Widā'an Yā Afāmiya*, Damascus, Dār al-Hilāl, 1960.

Jabrā, Jabrā Ibrāhīm, *al-Riḥla al-Thāmina, Dirāsāt Naqdiyya*, Sidon, Beirut, al-Maktaba al-'Aṣriyya, 1967.

Jabrā, Jabrā Ibrāhīm, *al-Safīna*, 3rd ed., Beirut, Dār al-Ādāb, 1983 (1st ed. 1969).

Jabrā, Jabrā Ibrāhīm, *al-Ghuraf al-Ukhrā*, Cairo, al-Hay'a al-Miṣriyya al-'Āmma li'l-Kitāb, Mukhtārāt *Fuṣūl* 54, 1988 (1st ed. 1986).

Jabrā, Jabrā Ibrāhīm, '*Mawsim al-Hijra*, Riwāya bayn al-Sharq wa'l-Gharb', *al-Kifāḥ al-'Arabī*, 761 (1 March 1993), 54.

Al-Jadawī, 'Abd al-Mun'im, 'al-Jarīma fī Qisas al-Ṭayyib Ṣāliḥ', *al-Dōḥa*, 17 (May 1977), 78–81.

Jalāl, Muḥammad, *Ḥubb fi Cūbenhāgen, al-A'māl al-Kāmila*, Cairo, al-Hay'a al-Miṣriyya al-'Āmma li'l-Kitāb, 1992, 137–287 (1st ed. 1975).

Jallāb, 'Abd, '*Mawsim al-Hijra ilā al-Shamāl*', in Muḥammadiyya (ed.), *al-Ṭayyib Ṣāliḥ*, 137–43.

Jammā', Fuḍaylī, *Qirā'a fī al-Adab al-Sūdānī al-Ḥadīth*, Oman, Maṭābi' Jarīdat 'Umān, 1991.

Al-Jazūlī, Ḥasan, 'Idā'a li Qirā'a Jadīda fī *Mawsim al-Hijra ilā al-Shamāl*', *al-Kharṭūm* (28 April 1993).

Jibrīl, Ṭalḥat, 'Muqābala: al-Riwā'ī al-Ṭayyib Ṣāliḥ', *al-Sharq al-Awsaṭ* (15 October 1983), 13.

Jibrīl, Ṭalḥat, 'al-Ṭayyib Ṣāliḥ li'l-*Wasaṭ*: Yuirīdūn Waqf al-Baḥr bi Sudūd min al-Rimāl!', *al-Wasaṭ*, 239 (26 August 1996), 52–4.

Jibrīl, Ṭalḥat, 'al-Ṭayyib Ṣāliḥ: Malāmiḥ min Sīra Dhātiyya (1), al-Takwīn fī al-Qarya al-Sūdāniyya ab'ad Min Khuṭūṭ 'alā al-Raml', 12251 (10 September 1996), 16; (2), 'Qalaq fī al-Mawqif min al-Jāmi'a wa-Ittijā'h ilā 'Kasb al-'Aysh fī al-Sudān'', 12252 (11 September 1996), 16; (3), 'al-Takkayyuf al-Ṣa'b fī Landan wa-Thalj *Mawsim al-Hijra ilā al-Shamāl*', 12253 (12 September 1996), 16; (4), 'Munākhāt Sharqiyya wa-Inṭilāqa Adabiyya min Bayrūt Yūsuf al-Khāl', 12254 (13 September 1996), 16; (5), 'Mashhad al-Tasāmuḥ al-Sūdānī: Fusayfisā' Talawwun Waṭanan', 12255 (14 September 1996), 20; (6), ''An la'nat al-Kitāba wa'l-Abṭāl al-Ghāmiḍīn wa-Tawbīkh al-Shuhra', *al-Ḥayāt*, 12258 (17 September 1996), 20.

Jibrīl, Ṭalḥat, *'Alā al-Darb . . . ma'a al-Ṭayyib Ṣāliḥ, Malāmiḥ min Sīra Dhātiyya*, Rabat, Tōb li'l-Istithmār wa'l-Khadamāt, Cairo, Markaz al-Dirāsāt al-Sūdāniyya, 1997.

Al-Jizawī, Sa'd al-Dīn, 'al-Adab al-Sūdānī wa-mā Yajib an Yakūna 'alayhi', *al-Kharṭūm*, 6 (March 1976), 58–64.

Al-Kafrāwī, Sa'īd, *Madīnat al-Mawt al-Jamīl*, Cairo, Dār Kutub Khāna li'l-Nashr wa'l-Tawzī', 1985.

Al-Kafrāwī, Sa'īd, 'Kull Hādhihi al-Fuṣūl', *al-Karmil*, 26 (1987), 137–41.

Kambel, Robert B., *A'lām al-Adab al-'Arabī al-Mu'āṣir, Siyar wa-Siyar Dhātiyya*, Beirut, al-Ma'had al-Almānī li'l-Abḥāth al-Sharqiyya, 1996.

Kāmil, 'Abd al-'Azīz, *Dirāsāt fi al-Jughrāfiya al-Bashariyya li'l-Sūdān*, Cairo, Dār al-Ma'ārif, 1972.

Kāmil, 'Ādil, *Millīm al-Akbar*, Cairo, Maktabat Miṣr wa-Maṭba'atuhā, 1944.

Kāmil, Murād, *Qiṣaṣ Sūdāniyya*, Cairo, Dār al-Ma'ārif, 1973.

Kāmil, Riyāḍ, 'Riwāyat Ḥannā Mīna *Ḥamāma Zarqā' fī al-Suḥub*: Liqā' al-Sharq bi'l-Gharb fī Iṭār Jadīd', *al-Jadīd*, 40:9 (September 1991), 35–46.

Kanafānī, Ghassān, *Arḍ al-Burtuqāl al-Ḥazīn*, 3rd ed., Beirut, Mu'assasat al-Abḥāth al-'Arabiyya, 1983, 73–80 (1st ed. 1963).

Kanafānī, Ghassān, *Mā Tabaqqā Lakum*, 3rd ed., Beirut, Mu'assasat al-Abḥāth al-'Arabiyya, 1983 (1st ed. 1966).

Al-Karakī, Khālid, *al-Riwāya fī al-Urdunn, Muqaddima*, Amman, al-Jāmi'a al-Urdunniyya, 1986.

Kassāb, Maḥmūd Ḥanafī, 'al-Baḥth 'an al-Wajh al-Ḍā'i' fī Riwāyat' *Ḥubb fī Kūbenhāgen* li'l-Riwā'ī Muḥammad Jalāl, *al-Kātib*, 219 (July 1979), 90–3.

Al-Kattānī, Muḥammad, *al-Ṣirā' bayn al-Qadīm wa'l-Jadīd fī al-Adab al-'Arabī al-Ḥadīth*, 2 vols. Casablanca, Dār al-Thaqāfa, 1982.

Kāẓim, Najm 'Abd Allāh, *al-Riwāya fī al-'Irāq 1965–1980 wa-Ta'thīr al-Riwāya al-Amrīkiyya fīhā*, Baghdad, Dār al-Shu'ūn al-Thaqāfiyya wa'l-'Āmma, 1987.

Al-Khādim, Sa'd, *Ajniḥa min Raṣāṣ*, Cairo, Dār al-Ma'ārif, 1971.

Al-Khādim, Sa'd, *Thulāthiyyat 'Ūlayis*, Fredericton, York Press, 1988.

Khaḍir, Muḥammad Ṣāliḥ, 'al-Ṭayyib Ṣāliḥ, Rajul min Karamkūl', in Ḥasan Abbashir al-Ṭayyib (ed.), *al-Ṭayyib Ṣāliḥ*, 299–305.

Khafājī, Muḥammad 'Abd al-Mun'im, *Qiṣṣat al-Adab al-Mahjarī*, Beirut, Dār al-Kitāb al-Lubnānī, 1986.

Khālid, Abū Bakr, *al-Nab' al-Murr, Riwāya Sūdāniyya*, Cairo, Dār al-Kitāb al-'Arabī li'l-Ṭiba'a wa'l-Nashr, n.d. [1967].

Khalīl, 'Umar, 'Naẓarāt fī Sardiyyāt Ibrāhīm Isḥāq Ibrāhīm, Tajliyāt al-Jānib al-Usṭūrī (1)', *al-Kharṭūm*, 2494 (17 August 2000), 5; (2), 2497 (20 August 2000), 5.

Khālis, 'Azmī, *Ḥikāyat al-Adab al-'Arabī al-Mu'āṣir*, Baghdad, Maṭba'at Shafīq, 1970.

Al-Khānjī, 'Abd al-Raḥmān, 'al-Lugha...al-Zaman... Dā'irat al-Fawḍā', *Fuṣūl*, 2:2 (January-March 1982), 261–5. [This article appears in al-Khānjī, *Qirā'a Jadīda fī Riwāyāt al-Ṭayyib Ṣāliḥ*, 68–84].

Al-Khānjī, 'Abd al-Raḥmān, *Qirā'a Jadīda fī Riwāyāt al-Ṭayyib Ṣāliḥ*, Omdurman, Dār Jāmi'at Umdurmān al-Islāmiyya, 1983.

Al-Khānjī, 'Abd al-Raḥmān, *Ru'yat al-Mawt wa-Dalālatuhā fī 'Ālam al-Ṭayyib Ṣāliḥ al-Riwā'ī min Khilāl Riwāyātay: Mawsim al-Hijra ilā al-Shamāl* wa-*Bandar Shāh*, *Ḥawliyyāt Kulliyyat al-Ādāb*, 15 (1995).

Al-Kharrāt, Edwār, *Rāma wa'l-Tinnīn*, 2nd ed., Beirut, al-Mu'assasa al-'Arabiyya li'l-Dirāsāt wa'l-Nashr, 1980 (1st ed. 1979).

Al-Khaṭīb, Ḥikmat Ṣabaq, *Dirāsāt al-Naṣṣ fī al-Naqd al-Adabī*, Beirut, Dār al-Āfāq al-Jadīda, 1983.

Al-Khaṭīb, Ḥusām, *Riwāyāt Taḥt al-Mijhar, Dirāsāt fī Nuhūḍ al-Riwāya al-Sūriyya*, Damascus, Manshūrāt Ittiḥād al-Kuttāb al-'Arab, 1983.

Al-Khātim, 'Abd al-Quddūs, 'al-Ṭayyib Ṣāliḥ bayn al-Ramz wa'l-Iqtibās', in idem, *Maqālāt Naqdiyya* [Published first under the same title in the Sudanese daily *al-Ayyām*, 7723 (19 March 1976), 7; it was also published in the Sudanese weekly *al-Sūdān al-Jadīd*, 48 (5 November 1976), as cited in Nūr, "al-Ṭayyib Ṣāliḥ: Dirāsa Bibliyūgrāfiyya', *al-Thaqāfa al-Sūdāniyya*, 127].

Al-Khātim, 'Abd al-Quddūs, *Maqālāt Naqdiyya*, Khartoum, al-Tamaddun, 1977.

Al-Khawwāḍ, Usāma, 'al-Ṭayyib Ṣāliḥ: Ārā' fī al-Siyāsa wa'l-Hujna al-Thāqāfiyya', *Kitābāt Sūdāniyya*, 8 (June 1999), 82–8.

Al-Khayyām, 'Umar, *Rubā'iyyāt 'Umar al-Khayyām* (Arabicizing by Wadī' al-Bustānī), 2nd ed., Cairo, Dār al-'Arab li'l-Bustānī, 1994.

Khuḍayyir, Muḥammad, *Baṣrayātha, Ṣūrat Madīna, Riwāya*, Damascus, Dār al-Madā li'l-Thaqāfa wa'l-Nashr, 1996.

Khulayyif, 'Abd al-Sattār, *al-Baḥth 'an Bunduqiyya*, Cairo, al-Hay'a al-Miṣriyya al-'Amma li'l-Kitāb, 1978.

Khulayyif, 'Abd al-Sattār, *Gharīb bayn al-Diyār*, Cairo, al-Hay'a al-Miṣriyya al-'Amma li'l-Kitāb, 1980.

Khulayyif, 'Abd al-Sattār, *al-Musāfirūn*, Cairo, Dār al-Ma'ārif, 1982.

Khurayyif, al-Bashīr, *al-Dikla fī 'Arājīnihā*, Tunis, al-Dār al-Tūnisiyya li'l-Nashr, 1969.

Al-Khūrī, Fu'ād Isḥāq, *al-Dhihniyya al-'Arabiyya*, Beirut, Dār al-Sāqī, 1993.

Khūrī, Ilyās, *Abwāb al-Madīna*, Beirut, Dār Ibn-Rushd, 1981.

Khūrī, Ilyās, *al-Baḥth 'an Tajribat Ufuq*, Beirut, Mu'asasat al-Abḥāth al-'Arabiyya, 1984.

Al-Kinānī, Jamāl, 'Maryūd, Marsūm al-Kalimāt', *al-Dōḥa*, 38 (February 1979).

Kūnsh, Hānz-Bīter, 'al-Injlīzī al-Aswad 'alā Ḍifāf al-Nīl, *Mawsim al-Hijra ilā al-Shamāl* li'l-Ṭayyib Ṣāliḥ, Riwāya Klāsikiyya li Adab mā ba'd al-Kūlūnyāliyya Tuktashaf min Jadīd' (trans. Ḥāmid Faḍl Allāh and Amīr Ḥamad), *Kitābāt Sūdāniyya*, 8 (June 1999), 89–92.

Kuraydī, Mūsā (ed.), *Qiṣaṣ Mukhtāra min Adabinā al-Qawmī al-Ishtirākī*, Baghdad, Dār al-Ḥurriyya li'l-Ṭibā'a, 1977.

'Kutub, *Dawmat Wad Ḥāmid*, al-Ṭayyib Ṣāliḥ', *al-Kharṭūm*, 5 (February 1970), 113–17.

Lāshīn, Maḥmūd Ṭāhir, 'Ḥadīth al-Qarya', *al-Jadīd*, 32 (19 November 1926), 225.

Al-Lawzī, Salīm, *al-Muhājirūn*, Cairo, Beirut, Dār al-Shurūq, n.d.

Madanī, Muḥammad Maḥmūd, 'al-Wa'y al-Jadīd fī al-Thaqāfa al-Sūdāniyya', *al-Ṣiḥāfa*, (18 December 1966).

Madanī, Muḥammad Maḥmūd, '*Bandar Shāh:* Dirāsa (1)', *al-Ayyām*, (7 October, 1977); (2) (14 October 1977).

Māḍī, Shukrī, 'al-Riwāya al-Sūriyya 1865–1980', *Fuṣūl*, 2:2 (January-March 1982), 329–30.

Maḥfūẓ, 'Iṣām, *al-Riwāya al-'Arabiyya al-Ṭalī'iyya wa'l-Shahāda*, Beirut, Dār Ibn Khaldūn, 1982.

Maḥfūẓ, 'Iṣām, *al-Riwāya al-'Arabiyya al-Shāhida*, Damascus, Dār al-Madā li'l-Thaqāfa wa'l-Nashr, 2000 (This book and the chapter concerning al-Ṭayyib Ṣāliḥ's writing is the same as 'Iṣām Maḥfūẓ 1982).

Maḥfūẓ, Najīb, *Kifāḥ Ṭība*, Cairo, Maktabat Miṣr, n.d. (1st ed. 1944).

Maḥfūẓ, Najīb, *al-Qāhira al-Jadīda*, Cairo, Maktabat Miṣr, n.d. (1st ed. 1945).

Maḥfūẓ, Najīb, *Zuqāq al-Midaqq*, Cairo, Maktabat Miṣr, n.d. (1st ed. 1947).

Maḥfūẓ, Najīb, *Bayn al-Qaṣrayn, Qaṣr al-Shawq, al-Sukkariyya*, Cairo, Maktabat Miṣr, n.d. (1st ed. 1956–7).

Maḥfūẓ, Najīb, 'Za'bālawī', *al-Ahrām* (12 May 1961), 12.

Maḥfūẓ, Najīb, *al-Liṣṣ wa'l-Kilāb*, Cairo, Maktabat Miṣr, 1977 (1st ed. 1961).

Maḥfūẓ, Najīb, *al-Summān wa'l-Kharīf*, Cairo, Maktabat Miṣr, n.d. (1st ed. 1962).

Maḥfūẓ, Najīb, *Dunyā Allāh*, Cairo, Maktabat Miṣr, n.d (1st ed. 1963).

Maḥfūẓ, Najīb, *al-Ṭarīq*, Cairo, Maktabat Miṣr, 1974 (1st ed. 1964).

Maḥfūẓ, Najīb, al-Shaḥḥādh, Cairo, Maktabat Miṣr, 1977 (1st ed. 1965).

Maḥfūẓ, Najīb, *Bayt Sayyi' al-Sum'a*, Cairo, Maktabat Miṣr, n.d. (1st ed. 1965).

Maḥfūẓ, Najīb, *Tharthara Fawq al-Nīl*, Cairo, Maktabat Miṣr, n.d. (1st ed. 1966).

Maḥfūẓ, Najīb, *Mīrāmār*, Cairo, Maktabat Miṣr, n.d. (1st ed. 1967)

Maḥfūẓ, Najīb, *Malḥamat al-Ḥarāfīsh*, Cairo, Maktabat Miṣr, n.d. (1st ed. 1977).

Maḥfūẓ, Najīb, *Yawm Qutila al-Za'īm*, Cairo, Maktabat Miṣr, n.d. (1st ed. 1985).

Maḥmūd, Aḥmad, 'Nūstāljya al-Ṭayyib Ṣāliḥ wa'l-Ittikā' 'alā al-Dhākira, Qirā'a fī al-Sīra al-Dhātiyya', *Kitābāt Sūdāniyya*, 8 (June 1999), 71–7.

Al-Majdhūb, Muḥammad al-Mahdī, *Diwān Nār al-Majādhīb*, Khartoum, Lajnat al-Ta'līf wa'l-Nashr bi Wizārat al-I'lām, 1969.

Al-Makhzanjī, Muḥammad, Rashq al-Sikkīn, Cairo, al-Hay'a al-Miṣriyya al-'Āmma li'l-Kitāb, Mukhtārāt *Fuṣul* 8, 1984.

Al-Makk, 'Alī, *Fī Qarya*, Beirut, Maktabat al-Ḥayāt, 1961.

Al-Makk, 'Alī (ed.), *Mukhtārāt min al-Adab al-Sūdānī*, 2nd ed., Khartoum, Dār Jāmi'at al-Kharṭūm li'l-Nashr, 1980 (1st ed. 1975).

Makkī, Al-Ṭāhir Aḥmad, *al-Qiṣṣa al-Qaṣīra, Dirāsa wa-Mukhtārāt*, 2nd ed., Cairo, Dār al-Ma'ārif, 1978 (1st ed. 1977).

Mālṭī-Dūglās, Fadwā (Trans. 'Iffat al-Sharqāwī), 'al-'Anāṣir al-Turāthiyya fī al-Adab al-'Arabī al-Mu'āṣir, al-Aḥlām fī Thalāth Qiṣaṣ', *Fuṣūl*, 2:2 (January-March 1982), 21–9.

Mālṭī-Dūglās, Fadwā, 'Min al-Ta'rīkh al-Sirrī li-Nu'mān 'Abd al-Ḥāfiẓ wa-Tadmīr Ṭuqūs al-Ḥayāt wa'l-Lugha', *Ibdā'*, 6 (June 1983), 86–94.

Mālṭī-Dūglas, Fadwā, 'Yūsuf al-Qa'īd wa'l-Riwāya al-Jadīda', *Fuṣūl*, 3:4 (April-June 1984), 190–202.

Al-Mānī', Ḥasan, *Nafaḥāt 'an al-Adab wa'l-Fann*, Beirut, Dār al-Āfāq al-Jadīda, 1981.

Al-Mānī', Samīra, *al-Sābiqūn wa'l-Lāḥiqūn*, Beirut, Dār al-'Awda, 1972.

Manṣūr, Bassām, 'Khalīl al-Nu'aymī: ḥattā Law Karrartu Nafsī ayna al-Mushkila?', *Barīd al-Janūb*, 73 (16 September 1996), 14–15.

Al-Maqāliḥ, 'Abd al-'Azīz, *Aṣwāt min al-Zaman al-Ḥadīth, Dirāsāt fī al-Adab al-'Arabī al-Mu'āṣir*, Beirut, Dār al-'Awda, 1980.

Al-Mas'adī, Maḥmūd, *al-Sudd*, 2nd ed., Tunis, al-Dār al-Tūnisiyya li'l-Nashr, 1974 (1st ed. 1955).

Al-Ma'ūsh, Sālim, *Ṣūrat al-Gharb fī al-Riwāya al-'Arabiyya*, Beirut, Mu'assasat al-Riḥāb al-Ḥadītha, 1998.

Al-Māzinī, Ibrāhīm, *Ibrāhīm al-Kātib*, Cairo, Maṭba'at Dār al-Turkī, 1931.

Mīna, Ḥannā, *al-Yāṭir*, Beirut, Dār al-Ādāb, 1975.

Mīna, Ḥannā, *Ma'sāt Dīmitrīyū*, Beirut, Dār al-Ādāb, 1985.

Mīna, Ḥannā, *Ḥamāma Zarqā' fī al-Suḥub*, Beirut, Dār al-Ādāb, 1988.

Miqdād, Murtaḍā, 'As'ila ilā al-Ṭayyib Ṣāliḥ, hal Ṣaḥīḥ anna al-Ḥayawāniyya al-Baḥta hiya min Naṣīb 'al-Waḥsh' al-Sharqī?', *al-Nahār al-'Arabī wa'l-Duawlī*, 307 (21–27 March 1983), 56–8.

Al-Misnāwī, Muṣṭafā, *Ṭāriq Alladhī Lam Yaftaḥ al-Andalus*, *Qiṣaṣ*, Beirut, al-Mu'assasa al-'Arabiyya li'l-Dirāsāt wa'l-Nashr, 1979.

Moreh, Shmuel and Menaḥem Milson, *Maṣādir li Dirāsat al-Adab al-'Arabī al-Ḥadīth wa- A'lāmihā 1800–1980*, Jerusalem, Academon, 1993.

Al-Mūdin, Ḥasan, 'Lā Wa'y al-Naṣṣ fī Riwāyāt al-Ṭayyib Ṣāliḥ', *Faḍā'āt Mustaqbaliyya*, 2–3 (March 1996), 54–8.

Al-Mūdin, Ḥasan, *al-Kitāba wa'l-Taḥawwul, Taḥawwulāt al-Dāll wa'l-Madlūl fī al-Sard al-'Arabī al-Jadīd*, Rabat, Manshūrāt Ittiḥād Kuttāb al-Maghrib, 2001.

Al-Muḥāddīn, 'Abd al-Ḥamīd, 'al-Jawānib al-Ghaybiyya fī A'māl al-Ṭayyib Ṣāliḥ', *Kitābāt*, 2 (July 1976), 8–38.

Muḥammad, Bashīr Buwayjara, *al-Shakhṣiyya fī al-Riwāya al-Jazā'iriyya 1970–1983*, Algiers, Diwān al-Maṭbū'āt al-Jāmi'iyya, 1986.

Muḥammad, Ḥusayn 'Alī, *Jamāliyyāt al-Qiṣṣa al-Qaṣīra, Dirāsa Naṣṣiyya*, Cairo, al-Sharika al-'Arabiyya li'l-Nashr wa'l-Tawzī', 1996.

Muḥammadiyya, Aḥmad Sa'īd, 'al-Ṭayyib Ṣāliḥ Yad'ū ilā al-Ifāda min al-Turāth al-Insānī Kullihi', *Shi'r*, 44 (Fall 1970), 134–5.

Muḥammadiyya, Aḥmad Sa'īd (ed.), *al-Ṭayyib Ṣāliḥ 'Abqarī al-Riwāya al-'Arabiyya*, Beirut, Dār al-'Awda, 1976.

Muḥassib, Ḥasan, *Ḥulm al-Layl wa'l-Nahār*, Cairo, Dār al-Ma'ārif, 1979.

Muḥyī al-Dīn, Ṣabāh, 'al-Sinfūniyyā al-Nāqisa', *al-Ādāb*, 9 (September 1956), 43–9.

Muḥyī al-Dīn, Ṣabāh, *al-Sinfūniyyā al-Nāqisa*, *Majmū'at Qiṣaṣ*, Beirut, Dār al-Ādāb, 1958.

Mu'jam al-Bābaṭīn li'l-Shu'arā' al-'Arab al-Mu'āṣirīn, Kuwait, Mu'assasat Jā'izat 'Abd al-'Azīz Sa'ūd al-Bābaṭīn li'l-Ibdā' al-Shi'rī, 1995.

Mukhtārāt min al-Qiṣaṣ al-Qaṣīra fī 18 Baladan 'Arabiyyan, Beirut, Markaz al-Ahrām li'l-Tarjama wa'l-Nashr, 1993.

Munīf, 'Abd al-Raḥmān, *al-Ashjār wa-Ightiyāl Marzūq*, 5th ed., Beirut, al-Mu'assasa al-'Arabiyya li'l-Dirāsāt wa'l-Nashr, 1987 (1st ed. 1973).

Munīf, 'Abd al-Raḥmān, *Sharq al-Mutawassiṭ*, 6th ed., Beirut, al-Mu'assasa al-'Arabiyya li'l-Dirāsāt wa'l-Nashr, 1987 (1st ed. 1975).

Munīf, 'Abd al-Raḥmān, *al-Nihāyāt*, Cairo, Mu'assasat Dār al-Hilāl, 1986 (1st ed. 1977).

Munīf, 'Abd al-Raḥmān, *Mudun al-Milḥ, al-Tīh*, 2nd ed., Beirut, al-Mu'assasa al-'Arabiyya li'l-Dirāsāt wa'l-Nashr, 1985 (1st ed. 1984). *Al-Ukhdūd*, 2nd ed., Beirut, al-Mu'assasa al-'Arabiyya li'l-Dirāsāt wa'l-Nashr, 1986 (1st ed. 1985). *Taqāsīm al-Layl wa'l-Nahār*, Beirut, al-Mu'assasa al-'Arabiyya li'l-Dirāsāt wa'l-Nashr, 1989. *Al-Munbatt*, Beirut, al-Mu'assasa al-'Arabiyya li'l-Dirāsāt wa'l-Nashr, 1989. *Bādiyāt al-Ẓulumāt*, Beirut, al-Mu'assasa al-'Arabiyya li'l-Dirāsāt wa'l-Nashr, 1989.

Munīf, 'Abd al-Raḥman, *al-Kātib wa'l-Manfā, Humūm wa-Āfāq al-Riwāya al-'Arabiyya*, Beirut, Dār al-Fikr al-Jadīd, 1992.

Munīf, 'Abd al-Raḥmān, *Sīrat Madīna, 'Ammān fī al-Arba'īnāt*, Beirut, al-Mu'assasa al-'Arabiyya li'l-Dirāsāt wa'l-Nashr, 1994.

'Muntadā al-Ḥurriyāt Yuṣdir Nidā'an 'Ālamiyyan li'l-Taḍāmun ma'a al-Ṭayyib Ṣāliḥ wa-Idānat Qarār Niẓām al-Kharṭūm', *al-Ittiḥādī*, 220 (3 September 1996), 1.

'Muqābala ma'a al-Ṭayyib Ṣāliḥ', *al-Sharq al-Awsaṭ* (13 October 1983).

Mūsā, 'Abd al-Wahhāb, 'al-Baḥth 'an al-Amān fī Adab al-Ṭayyib Ṣāliḥ', in Ḥasan Abbashir al-Ṭayyib (ed.), *al-Ṭayyib Ṣāliḥ*, 307–12.

Mūsā, Fāṭima, ''Uṣfūr min al-Janūb aw 'Ālam al-Ṭayyib Ṣāliḥ', *al-Majalla*, 164 (August 1970), 95–102. [Published under the same title in idem, *Fī al-Riwāya al-'Arabiyya al-Mu'āṣira*, vol. I, Cairo, al-Hay'a al-Miṣriyya al-'Āmma li'l-Kitāb, 1997, 239–58].

Mūsā, Fāṭima, *Fī al-Riwāya al-'Arabiyya al-Mu'āṣira*, Cairo, al-Hay'a al-Miṣriyya al-'Āmma li'l-Kitāb, 1997. (1st ed. 1972).

Mūsā, Ṣabrī, *Fasād al-Amkina*, Cairo, al-Hay'a al-Miṣriyya al-'Āmma li'l-Kitāb, 1987, 190–390 (1st ed. 1973).

Mūsā, Shams al-Dīn, *al-Mar'a al-Unmūdhaj fī al-Riwāya al-'Arabiyya al-Ḥadītha*, Cairo, al-Hay'a al-Miṣriyya al-'Āmma li'l-Kitāb, 1985.

Mūsā, Shams al-Dīn, 'Ash'ār wa-Mawādd Adabiyya fī Majallāt Mughtariba', *Ibdā'*, 11 (November 1999), 70–3.

Al-Mūsawī, Muḥsin, 'al-Nuhūḍ al-Thawrī fī al-Riwāya al-'Arabiyya', *al-Aqlām*, 12 (1973), 24–7.

Al-Mūsawī, Muḥsin, 'Ḥawla Mafhūmay al-Shakhṣiyya wa'l-Buṭūla fī al-Riwāya al-'Arabiyya al-Mu'āṣira', *al-Mawqif al-Adabī*, 104–5 (December 1979 – January 1980), 168–87.

Al-Mūsawī, Muḥsin Jāsim, *Alf Layla wa-Layla fī Naẓariyyat al-Adab al-Inklīzī, al-Wuqū' fī Dā'irat al-Siḥr*, 2nd ed., Beirut, Manshūrāt Markaz al-Inmā' al-Qawmī, 1986.

Al-Mūsawī, Muḥsin Jāsim, *Infirāṭ al-'A*qd *al-Muqaddas: Mun'āṭafāt al-Riwāya al-'Arabiyya ba'd Maḥfūẓ*, Cairo, al-Hay'a al-Miṣriyya al-'Āmma li'l-Kitāb, 1999.

Mustaghānimī, Aḥlām, *Dhākirat al-Jasad*, 9th ed., Beirut, Dār al-Adāb, 1998 (1st ed. 1993).

Mustajāb, Muḥammad, *Min al-Ta'rīkh al-Sirrī li Nu'mān 'Abd al-Ḥāfiẓ*, Cairo, Maktabat al-Munīl, 1982.

Mu'tamar al-Udabā' al-'Arab al-Tāsi', 'al-Qiṣṣa fī al-Waṭan al-'Arabī', al-juz' al-awwal, *al-Ma'rifa*, 138 (August 1973), 161–9.

Al-Muwayliḥī, Muḥammad, *Ḥadīth 'Īsā Ibn Hishām aw Fatra min al-Zaman*, Tunis, Dār al-Janūb li'l-Nashr, n.d. (1st ed. 1907).

Al-Nabr, Bertā, *al-'Unf fī al-Qiṣṣa al-'Arabiyya al-Ḥadītha*, [Beirut], 1991.

Naḥawī, Adīb, *'Urs Filasṭīnī*, Beirut, Dār al-'Awda, n.d. (1st ed. 1971).

Najīb, Nājī, 'al-Huwiyya al-Dhātiyya fī al-Mujtama' al-Taqlīdī wa-Bu'd *al-Hijra ilā al-Shamāl*', *Fikr wa-Funūn*, 38 (1983), 62–7.

Najīb, Nājī, 'Ru'ya Jadīda fī Adab al-Ṭayyib Ṣāliḥ (1): al-Ḥayāt Tuṣbiḥ Mahrajānan', *al-Muṣawwar*, 3101 (16 March 1984), 85–7; (2), 'al-Raḥīl min al-Janūb ilā al-Shamāl', 3102 (23 March 1984), 56–8.

Al-Naqqāsh, Rajā', 'al-Ṭayyib Ṣāliḥ, 'Abqariyya Riwā'iyya Jadīda', in Muḥammadiyya (ed.), *al-Ṭayyib Ṣāliḥ*, 78–100. [Appeared in al-Ṭayyib Ṣāliḥ, *Bandar Shāh*, Cairo, Mu'assasat Rūz al-Yūsuf, 1972, 7–18. Also published under the title ''Abqariyya Jadīda fī Samā' al-Riwāya al-'Arabiyya', *al-Muṣawwar* (2 February 1968)].

Al-Naqqāsh, Rajā', *Udabā' Mu'āṣirūn*, Cairo, Maktabat al-Anglū al-Miṣriyya, 1968.

Al-Naqqāsh, Rajā', *Aṣwāt Ghāḍiba fī al-Adab wa'l-Naqd*, Beirut, Dār al-Ādāb, 1970.

Al-Naqqāsh, Rajā', 'Bayn Aḥmad Bahā' al-Dīn wa'l-Ṭayyib Ṣāliḥ', *al-Dōḥa*, 7 (July 1976), 26–9.

Al-Naqqāsh, Rajā', 'Khawāṭir ḥawla Qiṣṣa fī al-'Ishq wa'l-Maḥabba', *al-Dōḥa*, 28 (April 1978), 83.

Al-Naqqāsh, Rajā', 'Qaṣīda fī al-'Ishq wa'l-Maḥabba', in al-Ṭayyib Ṣāliḥ, *Bandar Shāh: Maryūd*, Tunis, Dār al-Janūb li'l-Nashr, 1986, 7–46. [Also published in Ḥasan Abbashir al-Ṭayyib (ed.), *al-Ṭayyib Ṣāliḥ*, 211–31].

Al-Naqqāsh, Rajā', ''Āṣifa Adabiyya lahā Ta'rīkh', *al-Waṭan al-'Arabī*, 1214 (9 June 2000), 48–9.

Narrāyis, Ḥasan, *al-Ḍiḥk wa'l-Ākhar: Ṣūrat al-'Arabī fī al-Fukāha al-Faransiyya*, Casablanca, Ifrīqiyā al-Sharq, 1996.

Naṣrallāh, Emily, *Ṭuyūr Aylūl, Riwāya*, 2nd ed., Beirut, Dār al-Makshūf, 1967 (1st ed. 1962).

Naṣrallāh, Ibrāhīm, *Barārī al-Ḥummā*, 2nd ed., Amman, Dār al-Shurūq li'l-Nashr wa'l-Tawzī', 1992 (1st ed. 1985).

Al-Nassāj, Sayyid Ḥāmid, *Dalīl al-Qiṣṣa al-Miṣriyya al-Qaṣīra, Ṣuḥuf wa-Majmū'āt 1910–1961*, Cairo, al-Hay'a al-Miṣriyya al-'Āmma li'l-Kitāb, 1972.

Al-Nassāj, Sayyid Ḥāmid, *Bānūrāmā al-Riwāya al-'Arabiyya al-Ḥadītha*, Cairo, Dār al-Ma'ārif, 1980.

Al-Nā'ūrī, 'Īsā, *Layla fī al-Qiṭār*, Amman, Manshūrāt Dār Filādilfiyā, 1974.

Al-Nā'ūrī, 'Īsā, *Adab al-Mahjar*, 3rd ed., Cairo, Dār al-Ma'ārif, 1977.

Ni'ma, Rajā', 'Ḥiwār ma'a al-Ṭayyib Ṣāliḥ', *al-Fikr al-'Arabī al-Mu'āṣir*, 2 (June 1980), 114–19.

Ni'ma, Rajā', *Ṣirā' al-Maqhūr ma'a al-Sulṭa, Dirāsa fī al-Taḥlīl al-Nafsī li Riwāyat al-Ṭayyib Ṣāliḥ* Mawsim al-Hijra ilā al-Shamāl, Beirut, 1986.

Ni'ama, Rajā', 'Riwāyāt al-Ṭayyib Ṣāliḥ Talta'im fī Rubā'iyyat al-Arḍ... wa'l-Hijra', *al-Ḥayāt*, 14200 (3 February 2002), 16.

Nu'ayma, Mīkhā'īl, 'Ḥikāyāt al-Sharq wa'l-Gharb', *al-Hilāl*, 55:6 (June 1947), 49–51.

Nu'aymī, Aḥmad Ḥamad, 'Ṣūrat al-Zayn Fī (*'Urs al-Zayn*) li'l-Ṭayyib Ṣāliḥ', in idem, *al-Baḥr wa'l-Mir'a, Qirā'āt fī al-Qiṣṣa wa'l-Riwāya*, Beirut, al-Mu'assasa al-'Arabiyya li'l-Dirāsāt wa'l-Nashr, 2002, 27–35.

Al-Nu'aymī, Khalīl, *Tafrīgh al-Kā'in*, Cairo, Dār Sharqiyyāt li'l-Nashr wa'l-Tawzī', 1995.

Nūr, Qasīm 'Uthmān, 'al-Ṭayyib Ṣāliḥ, Dirāsa Bībliyūgrāfiyya', *al-Thaqāfa al-Sūdāniyya*, 19 (November 1981), 122–9.

Nūr al-Dīn, Ṣadūq, *al-Gharb fī al-Riwāya al-'Arabiyya*, Qindīl Umm Hāshim *Namūdhajan*, Casablanca, Dār al-Thaqāfa li'l-Nashr wa'l-Tawzi', 1995.

Peled, Matityahu, *al-Uqṣūṣa al-Taymūriyya fī Marḥalatayn*, Tel Aviv, Jāmi'at Tel Aviv; Acre, Dār al-Nashr al-'Arabī, 1977.

Qabalān, Hiyām Muṣṭafā, 'Yawm Mubārak 'alā Shāṭi' Umm Bāb', *al-Sinnāra* (17 December 1999), 13.

Al-Qa'īd, Muḥammad Yūsuf, *Akhbār 'Izbat al-Manīsī*, Cairo, al-Hay'a al-Miṣriyya al-'Āmma li'l-Ta'lif wa'l-Nashr, 1971.

Al-Qa'īd, Muḥammad Yūsuf, *Fī al-Usbū' Sab'at Ayyām*, Cairo, al-Haya' al-Miṣriyya al-'Āmma li'l Kitāb, 1975.

Al-Qa'īd, Muḥammad Yūsuf, *Yaḥduth fī Miṣr al-Ān*, 2nd ed., Beirut, Dār Ibn Rushd, 1979 (1st ed. 1977).

Al-Qāḍī, Wadād (ed.), *Mukhtārāt min al-Nathr al-'Arabī*, Beirut, al-Mu'assasa al-'Arabiyya li'l-Dirāsāt wa'l-Nashr, 1983.

Al-Qalamāwī, Suhayr, *Aḥādīth Jaddatī*, Cairo, Maṭba'at Lajnat al-Ta'līf wa'l-Tarjama wa'l-Nashr, 1935.

Al-Qamarī, Bashīr (ed.), *Takrīm al-Riwā'ī al-Sūdānī al-Ṭayyib Ṣāliḥ fī Mahrajān Aṣīla, Majmū'at Maqālāt*, Asila, 1994.

Al-Qamarī, Bashīr, 'Hākadha Ḥaddathanī al-Ṭayyib Ṣāliḥ... Ashkur al-Nās alladhīna Aḥabbū 'Amalī...', *Kitābāt Sūdāniyya*, 8 (June 1999), 58–70. [Published under the title 'al-Insān Yaḥmil fī Dākhilihi ma'lamyhi', in Ḥasan Abbashir al-Ṭayyib (ed.), *al-Ṭayyib Ṣāliḥ*, 87–99].

Al-Qamarī, Bashīr, *Majāzāt*: *Muqārabāt Naqdiyya fī al-Ibdā' al-'Arabī al-Mu'āṣir*, Beirut, Dār al-Ādāb, 1999.

Al-Qamḥāwī, 'Izzat, 'Aṣīla Taḥtafī bi'l-Ṭayyib', *Kull al-'Arab*, 59 (28 August 1994), 13.

Qāsim, 'Abd al-Ḥakīm, *Ayyām al-Insān al-Sab'a*, Cairo, Dār al-Kātib al-'Arabī li'l-Ṭibā'a wa'l-Nashr, 1969.

Qāsim, 'Abd al-Ḥakīm, *Muḥāwala li'l-Khurūj*, Cairo, al-Hay'a al-Miṣriyya al-'Āmma li'l-Kitāb, 1987 (1st ed. 1980).

Qāsim, 'Abd al-Ḥakīm, *Qadar al-Ghuraf al-Muqbiḍa*, Cairo, Maṭbū'āt al-Qāhira, 1982.

Qāsim, 'Abd al-Ḥakīm, *al-Ashwāq wa'l-Āsā*, Cairo, al-Hay'a al-Miṣriyya al-'Āmma li'l-Kitāb, Mukhtārāt *Fuṣūl* 10, 1984.

Al-Qāsim, Afnān, Mawsim al-Hijra ilā al-Shamāl *aw Wahm 'Alāqat al-Sharq wa'l-Gharb* (*'Amaliyyat Naqd wa-Naqḍ li'l-Riwāya*), Casablanca, Mu'assasat bin Bishāra li'l-Ṭibā'a wa'l-Nashr, 1984.

Qāsim, 'Awn al-Sharīf, *Dirāsāt fī al-'Āmmiyya*, Khartoum, al-Dār al-Sūdāniyya, 1974.

Qāsim, 'Awn al-Sharīf, *Qāmūs al-Lahja al-'Āmmiyya fī al-Sūdān*, 2nd ed., Cairo, al-Maktab al-Miṣrī al-Ḥadīth, 1985.

Qāsim, Maḥmūd, *al-Adab al-'Arabī al-Maktūb bi'l-Faransiyya*, al-Hay'a al-Miṣriyya al-'Āmma li'l-Kitāb, 1996.

Qāsim, Sīzā, 'Tajriba Naqdiyya, *Mawsim al-Hijra ilā al-Shamāl*', *Fuṣūl*, 2:2 (January-March 1981), 224–9.

Al-Qā'ūd, Ḥilmī Muḥammad, *Mawsim al-Baḥth 'an Huwiyya, Dirāsāt fī al-Riwāya wa'l-Qiṣṣa*, Cairo, al-Hay'a al-Miṣriyyia al-'Āmma li'l-Kitāb, 1987.

Qaysūma, Manṣūr, *al-Anā wa'l-Ākhar fī al-Riwāya al-'Arabiyya al-Ḥadītha*, Tunis, Dār Saḥar li'l-Nashr, 1994.

Qaysūma, Manṣūr, *al-Riwāya al-'Arabiyya al-Ishkāl wa'l-Tashakkul*, Tunis, Dār Saḥar li'l-Nashr, 1997.

'Al-Qiṣṣa fi al-Waṭan al-'Arabī – Nadwa', *al-Ma'rifa*, 138 (August 1973), 161–79.

Al-Quṣaybī, Ghāzī, 'al-Kalima Allatī Quddima bihā al-Adīb al-Ṭayyib Ṣāliḥ fī al-Nadwa Allatī 'Uqīmat bi Landan', *Saudi Arabian Embassy in London*, 1 December 1992 (two printed papers).

Al-Quṭṭ, 'Abd al-Qādir, *Fī al-Adab al-'Arabī al-Ḥadīth*, Cairo, Dār Gharīb li'l-Ṭibā'a wa'l-Tawzi', 2001.

Al-Rā'ī, 'Alī, 'Zaghrūda Ṭawīla li'l-Ḥayāt' in Muḥammadiyya (ed.), *al-Ṭayyib Ṣāliḥ*, 101–17. [Published in the Egyptian weekly *al-Hilāl*, 7 (July 1970), 24–31 and in the Israeli monthly *al-Sharq*, 1:5 (October 1970), 22–5. It was also published in al-Rā'ī, *al-Riwāya fī al-Waṭan al-'Arabī*, 527–34].

Al-Rā'ī, 'Alī, *al-Riwāya fī al-Waṭan al-'Arabī, Namādhij Mukhtāra*, Cairo, Dār al-Mustaqbal al-'Arabī, 1991.

Al-Rakhāwī, Yaḥyā, 'Tāqat al-Ibdā' wa-Ḥikāyat al-'Udwān', *Fuṣūl*, 10: 3:4 (January 1992), 50–6.

Al-Rifā'ī, 'Abd al-Raḥīm, 'Akram al-Nās', in Ḥasan Abbashir al-Ṭayyib (ed.), *al-Ṭayyib Ṣāliḥ*, 49–53.

Al-Sa'āfīn, Ibrāhīm, '*Mawsim al-Hijra ilā al-Shamāl*, Dirāsa fī Wujhat al-Naẓar', in idem *Taḥawwulāt al-Sard, Dirāsāt fī al-Riwāya al-'Arabiyya*, Amman, Dār al-Shurūq li'l-Nashr wa'l-Tawzī', 1996, 203–28.

Al-Sabūl, Taysīr, '*Mawsim al-Hijra ilā al-Shamāl*', in idem, '*al-A'māl al-Kāmila*', Beirut, Dār Ibn Rushd, 1980, 257–63. 2nd ed., Amman, Dār Azminat li'l-Nashr wa'l-Tawzī', 1998.

Sa'd, Fā'iza Muḥammad, *Tayyār al-Wa'y fī Riwāyāt al-Ṭayyib Ṣāliḥ, Dirāsa fī al-Adab al-Muqāran*, Ph.D. Dissertation, Jāmi'at 'Ayn-Shams, Kulliyyat al-Alsun, 1996.

Al-Ṣaffār, Fawziyya, *Azmat al-Ajyāl al-'Arabiyya al-Mu'āṣira, Dirāsa fī Riwāyat* Mawsim al-Hijra ilā al-Shamāl, Tunis, Mu'assasat 'Abd al-Karim bin 'Abd Allāh, 1980. For the new edition under the same title, see Fawziyya al-Ṣaffār al-Zāwiq, Maṭba'at al-Wafā', 1997.

Al-Sa'īd, 'Īsā, 'al-Ṭayyib Ṣāliḥ, Taftīt al-'Ālam', *al-Karmil*, 9 (1983), 256–64.

Sa'īd, Khālida, 'al-Riwāya al-'Arabiyya bayn 1920–1972', *Mawāqif* (Summer 1974), 75–89. [Published under the same title but in a shorter version in idem, *Ḥarakiyyat al-Ibdā', Dirāsāt fī al-Adab al-'Arabī al-Ḥadīth*, Beirut, Dār al-'Awda, 1979, 203–29].

Sa'īd, Naffūsa Zakariyyā, *Ta'rīkh al-Da'wa ilā al-'Āmmiyya wa-Atharuhā fī Miṣr*, Cairo, Dār al-Ma'ārif, 1964.

Al-Sā'idī, 'Abd Jāsim, *al-Dhākira wa'l-Ḥanīn fī al-Qiṣṣa al-'Irāqiyya al-Qaṣīra fī al-Manfā*, London, Mu'assasat al-Rāfid li'l-Nashr wa'l-Tawzī', 1996.

Al-Sakākīnī, Khalīl, *Kadhā Anā Yā Dunyā, Yawmiyyāt Khalīl al-Sakākīnī*, Jerusalem, al-Maṭba'a al-Tijāriyya, 1955.

Al-Sakkūt, Ḥamdī, *al-Riwāya al-'Arabiyya, Bibliyūghrāfiyā wa-Madkhal Naqdī 1865–1995*, 6 vols., Cairo, New York, al-Jāmi'a al-Amrīkiyya bi'l-Qāhira, 2000.

Ṣalaḥī, Ibrahīm, 'al-Ṣadīq al-Kātib – Nab' al-Ṣafā' wa'l-Mawadda wa'l-Ḥikma', in Ḥasan Abbashir al-Ṭayyib (ed.), *al-Ṭayyib Ṣāliḥ*, 23–39.

Salām, Muḥammad Zaghlūl, *al-Qiṣṣa fī al-Adab al-Sūdānī al-Ḥadīth*, Cairo, Ma'had al-Buḥūth wa'l-Dirāsāt al-'Arabiyya, 1970.

Salām, Muḥammad Zaghlūl, *Dirāsāt fī al-Qiṣṣa al-'Arabiyya al-Ḥadītha*, Alexandria, Munsha'at al-Ma'ārif, n.d. [1973].

Ṣāliḥ, Aḥmad Muḥammad Ṣalāḥ, 'Ṣadīq al-Ṭayyib', in Ḥasan Abbashir al-Ṭayyib (ed.), *al-Ṭayyib Ṣāliḥ*, 41–7.

Ṣāliḥ, Muḥammad al-Rabī' Muḥammad, ''Itābāt al-Naṣṣ wa-Jamāliyyāt al-Istijāba: Ḥafriyyāt fī Muqaddimāt al-Ṭayyib Ṣāliḥ li Diwān *Ghābat al-Ābanūs* li Ṣalāḥ Aḥmad Ibrāhīm', *Kitābāt Sūdāniyya*, 12 (June 2000), 67–77.

Ṣāliḥ, Ṣalāḥ, *al-Riwāya al-'Arabiyya wa'l-Ṣaḥrā'*, Damascus, Manshūrāt Wizārat al-Thaqāfa, 1996.

Ṣāliḥ, al-Ṭayyib, 'Mashrū' al-Jazīra', Book review on Arthur Gaitskell, *Gezira, A Story of Development in the Sudan*, Faber and Faber, *Aṣwāt*, 1 (1961), 97–9.

Ṣāliḥ, al-Ṭayyib, 'Dawmat Wad Ḥāmid', *Aṣwāt*, 3 (1961), 44–5.

Ṣāliḥ, al-Ṭayyib, 'Budhūr al-Ḥaḍāra', Book review on Roland Oliver (ed.), *The Dawn of African History*, Oxford University Press, *Aṣwāt*, 5 (1962), 109–13.

Ṣāliḥ, al-Ṭayyib, 'Hākadhā Yā Sādatī', *Adab*, 1:1 (Winter 1962), 9–16.

Ṣāliḥ, al-Ṭayyib, 'Ṣūra Ḥadītha li'l-Sūdān', Book review on K.M. Barbour, *The Republic of Sudan*, University of London, *Aṣwāt*, 10 (1963), 103–4.

Ṣāliḥ, al-Ṭayyib, *'Urs al-Zayn, Ḥiwār*, 10 (May-June 1964), 41–50.

Ṣāliḥ, al-Ṭayyib, 'al-Shay' al-Ākhar', *Ḥiwār*, 21 (March-April 1966), 37–8.

Ṣāliḥ, al-Ṭayyib, 'Muqaddimāt', *Ḥiwār*, 21 (March-April 1966), 36–40.

Ṣāliḥ, al-Ṭayyib, 'Risāla bi dūn Radd', *al-Ra'y al-'Āmm al-Usbū'ī*, 58 (19 May 1966).

Ṣāliḥ, al-Ṭayyib, *'Urs al-Zayn, Kitāb al-Shahr, al-Kharṭūm*, 3 (December 1966), 97–137.

Ṣāliḥ, al-Ṭayyib, *'Urs al-Zayn, Riwāya wa-Sab' Qiṣaṣ*, Beirut, al-Dār al-Sharqiyya li'l-Ṭibā'a wa'l-Nashr, Kitāb *Ḥiwār* 3, 1967.

Ṣāliḥ, al-Ṭayyib, 'Ḥafnat Tamr', *al-Ra'y al-'Āmm*, 117 (15 July 1968), 15.

Ṣāliḥ, al-Ṭayyib, 'Muqaddimāt', *al-Ra'y al-'Āmm*, 8458 (29 March 1969).

Ṣāliḥ, al-Ṭayyib, *Mawsim al-Hijra ilā al-Shamāl*, 2nd ed., Beirut, Dār al-'Awda, 1969.

Ṣāliḥ, al-Ṭayyib, 'Dawmat Wad Ḥāmid', *al-Hilāl*, 8 (August 1969), 6–17.

Ṣāliḥ, al-Ṭayyib, 'Muqaddimāt', *al-Hilāl*, 9 (September 1969), 34–9.

Ṣāliḥ, al-Ṭayyib, 'Ḥafnat Tamr', *al-Hilāl*, 10 (October 1969), 106–9.

Ṣāliḥ, al-Ṭayyib, *'Urs al-Zayn, Riwāya*, 3rd ed., Beirut, Dār al-'Awda, 1970.

Ṣāliḥ, al-Ṭayyib, *Dawmat Wad Ḥāmid, Sab' Qiṣaṣ*, 3rd ed., Beirut, Dār al-'Awda, 1970.

Ṣāliḥ, al-Ṭayyib, *Bandar Shāh: Ḍaw al-Bayt*, Beirut, Dār al-'Awda, 1971.

Ṣāliḥ, al-Ṭayyib, *Bandar Shāh, Qiṣṣa*, Cairo, Mu'assasat Rūz al-Yūsuf, al-Kitāb al-Dhahabī 194, 1972.

Ṣāliḥ, al-Ṭayyib, *al-Āthār al-Kāmila (Mawsim al-Hijra ilā al-Shamāl, 'Urs al-Zayn, Dawmat Wad Ḥāmid, Bandar Shāh, Ḍaw al-Bayt)*, Beirut, Dār al-'Awda, 1972.

Ṣāliḥ, al-Ṭayyib, 'al-Rajul al-Qubruṣī', *al-Thaqāfa al-'Arabiyya*, 2 (October 1973), 88–91.

Ṣāliḥ, al-Ṭayyib, 'al-Rajul al-Qubruṣī', *al-Dōḥa*, 2 (January 1976), 105–8.

Ṣāliḥ, al-Ṭayyib, 'al-Rajul al-Qubruṣī', *al-Ayyām*, 7723 (19 March 1976), 7.

Ṣāliḥ, al-Ṭayyib, 'Riḥla ilā Bārīs al-Shamāl', *al-Dōḥa*, 6 (June 1976), 10–13.

Ṣāliḥ, al-Ṭayyib, 'Maryūd', *al-Shabāb*, 205–9 (June-July 1976).

Ṣāliḥ, al-Ṭayyib, *Mawsim al-Hijra ilā al-Shamāl*, Jerusalem, Manshūrāt Ṣalāḥ al-Dīn, 1976.

Ṣāliḥ, al-Ṭayyib, *Maryūd*, First Chapter, *al-Hilāl* (December 1976), 62–9.

Ṣāliḥ, al-Ṭayyib, *'Urs al-Zayn, Riwāya*, Acre, Dār al-Aswār, 1977.

Ṣāliḥ, al-Ṭayyib, *Maryūd*, Second Chapter, *al-Hilāl* (January 1977), 50–7.

Ṣāliḥ, al-Ṭayyib, *Bandar Shāh: Maryūd*, First Chapter, *al-Dōḥa*, 19 (July 1977), 67–77.

Ṣāliḥ, al-Ṭayyib, *Maryūd*, Second Chapter, *al-Dōḥa*, 21 (September 1977), 66–75.

Ṣāliḥ, al-Ṭayyib, *Maryūd*, Third Chapter, *al-Dōḥa*, 22 (October 1977), 66–75.

Ṣāliḥ, al-Ṭayyib, *Bandar Shāh: Maryūd*, 2nd ed., Beirut, Dār al-'Awda, 1978 (1st ed. 1977).

Ṣāliḥ, al-Ṭayyib, 'al-Rajul al-Qubruṣī', in Makkī (ed.), *al-Qiṣṣa al-Qaṣīra, Dirāsāt wa-Mukhtārāt*, 304–14.

Ṣāliḥ, al-Ṭayyib, 'Maḥjūb al-Shā'ir', *al-Dōḥa*, 39 (March 1979), 42. (= *Aḍwā'*, 4 (July 1980), 42–4.

Ṣāliḥ, al-Ṭayyib, 'Ḥadīth al-Shi'r wa'l-Shurūq', *al-Dōḥa*, 42 (June 1979), 40.

Ṣāliḥ, al-Ṭayyib, *Maryūd*, 2nd ed., Acre, Maktab al-Aswār, 1979.

Ṣāliḥ, al-Ṭayyib, 'Ḥadith al-Sharq wa'l-Shurūq', *al-Dōḥa*, 42 (June 1979), 40–1.

Ṣāliḥ, al-Ṭayyib, 'Naḥwa Khalq Mithūlūjiya 'Arabiyya' (Trans. Sāmī Muḥammad), *al-Jumhūriyya* [Iraq], (7 June 1979).

Ṣāliḥ, al-Ṭayyib, 'Ḥadīth al-Shi'r', *Aḍwā'*, 2 (August 1979), 38–9.

Ṣāliḥ, al-Ṭayyib, 'al-Ikhtibār', *al-Ayyām*, 9794 (31 August 1979).

Ṣāliḥ, al-Ṭayyib, *Bandar Shāh: Maryūd*, Tunis, Dār al-Janūb li'l-Nashr, 1986.

Ṣāliḥ, al-Ṭayyib, *Mawsim al-Hijra ilā al-Shamāl*, Tunis, Dār al-Janūb li'l-Nashr, 1992.

Ṣāliḥ, al-Ṭayyib, 'Yawm Mubārak 'alā Shāṭi' Umm Bāb', in *Mukhtārāt min al-Qiṣaṣ al-Qaṣīra fī 18 Baladan 'Arabiyyan*, 159–66.

Ṣāliḥ, al-Ṭayyib, *al-A'māl al-Kāmila (Mawsim al-Hijra ilā al-Shamāl, 'Urs al-Zayn, Ḍaw al-Bayt (Bandar Shāh), Maryūd (Bandar Shāh), Dawmat Wad Ḥāmid)*, Beirut, Dār al-'Awda, 1996.

Ṣāliḥ, al-Ṭayyib, 'Qal'a Muhaddama Tarfuḍ al-Istislām', *Mashārif*, 9 (June 1996), 41–2.

Ṣāliḥ, al-Ṭayyib, 'Naḥwa Ufuq Ba'īd, Ayyām fī Uslū', *al-Majalla*, 875 (23 November 1996), 78.

Ṣāliḥ, al-Ṭayyib, 'Aḥtafī bi'l-Maḍī wa-Uṣāri' al-Rāhin wa-Ajma' bayn al-Ithnayn', *al-Quds* (29 March 1998), 15. [Published in the Lebanese journal *al-Safīr*].

Ṣāliḥ, al-Ṭayyib, 'Lamaḥāt min al-Sīra al-Dhātiyya', in Ḥasan Abbashir al-Ṭayyib (ed.), *al-Ṭayyib Ṣāliḥ*, 115–53.

Ṣāliḥ, al-Ṭayyib, 'Dawmat Wad Ḥāmid', in El'ad [-Bouskila] (ed.), *Aḍwā' Dāniya*, 68–78.

Ṣāliḥ, al-Ṭayyib, 'Muqaddima', in Ṣalāḥ Aḥmad Ibrāhīm, *Ghābat al-Ābanūs wa-Qaṣā'id Ukhrā*, 1–20.

Ṣāliḥ, al-Ṭayyib, 'Nakhla 'alā al-Jadwal', in al-Makk (ed.), *Mukhtārāt min al-Adab al-Sūdānī*, 214–21.

Ṣāliḥ, al-Ṭayyib, 'Risāla ilā Aylīn', in al-Makk (ed.), *Mukhtārāt min al-Adab al-Sūdānī*, 210–13.

Ṣāliḥ, al-Ṭayyib, 'Taqdīm wa-Ta'rīf Mu'āmara Ma'rifiyya fī al-Tukhūm al-Janūbiyya', in al-Sharīf, *al-Sūdān wa-Ahl al-Sūdān*, 7–9.

Ṣāliḥ, al-Ṭayyib, *Bandar Shāh*, 2nd ed., Acre, Dār al-Aswār, n.d.

Ṣāliḥ, al-Ṭayyib, 'Taqdīm', in Ṭāriq al-Ṭayyib, *al-Jamal Lā Yaqif Khalf Ishāra Ḥamrā'*, 5–9.

Salīm, 'Abd al-Mun'im, 'Majhūd li'l-Rū'ya 'an Bu'd al-Ṭayyib Ṣāliḥ Ṣāḥib *Mawsim al-Hijra ilā al-Shamāl*', *al-Sharq*, 2:5 (October 1971), 29–30.

Salīm, 'Abd al-Mun'im, 'al-Liqā' al-Awwal ma'a al-Ṭayyib Ṣāliḥ 'Ām 1962 wa-*Mawsim al-Hijra* 'Ām 1966', in Ḥasan Abbashir al-Ṭayyib (ed.), *al-Ṭayyib Ṣāliḥ*, 71–4.

Sālim, 'Alī, *Awalādunā fī Landan: Trājīdiyā bilā Dumū'*, Cairo, Mu'assasat Dār al-Sha'b, 1975.

Sālim, Jūrj, *Mughāmarat al-Riwāya al-'Arabiyya*, Damascus, Maṭābi' Alīf Bā, al-Adīb, 1973.

Al-Sālimī, al-Ḥabīb, *Matāhat al-Raml*, Beirut, al-Mu'assasa al-'Arabiyya li'l-Dirāsāt wa'l-Nashr, 1994.

Al-Sāmarrā'ī, Aḥmad, 'Ta'ṣīl al-Sard, al-Ṭayyib Ṣāliḥ Unmūdhajan', in idem, *Fī Naẓariyyat al-Uqṣūṣa*, Safaqus, al-Tafsīr al-Fannī, 2003, 133–46.

Al-Sāmarrā'ī, Mājid, 'Muqābala Adabiyya ma'a al-Ṭayyib Ṣāliḥ, Tafāṣil fī 'Ālam al-Riwā'ī', *al-Ādāb*, 1–2 (January 1981), 3–8.

Al-Sāmarrā'ī, Mājid, 'Muqābalat al-Ṭayyib Ṣāliḥ, Humūm al-Riwā'ī fī 'Aṣr Mutaghayyir', *al-Aqlām*, (April 1982), 142–50.

Al-Sammān, Ghāda, *al-Jasad Ḥaqībat Safar*, Beirut, Manshūrāt Ghāda al-Sammān, 1979.

Al-Ṣāwī, Muṣṭafā Muḥammad Aḥmad, 'al-Riwāya al-'Arabiyya fī al-Sūdān 1948–1967', *Kitābāt Sūdāniyya*, 13 (September 2000), 27–46.

Al-Sāyiḥ, Laylā, 'Kitābāt al-Ṭayyib Ṣāliḥ bayn al-Wāqi' wa'l-Usṭūra', *al-Anbā'* (10 January 1978), 12–14.

Sha'bān, Buthayna, *100 'Ām min al-Riwāya al-Nisā'iyya al-'Arabiyya (1899–1999)*, Beirut, Dār al-Ādāb, 1999.

Al-Shādhilī, 'Abd al-Salām, *Shakhṣiyyat al-Muthaqqaf fī al-Riwāya al-'Arabiyya al-Ḥadītha*, Beirut, Dār al-Ḥadātha, 1985.

Shāgāly, Vlādīmīr, 'Limādhā Turgimat *Mawsim al-Hijra ilā al-Shamāl* ilā al-Rūsiyya?' (trans. 'Abd al-Karīm 'Abd al-Ṣamad), *al-Mawqif al-Adabī*, 220–1 (August-September 1989), 59–64.

Shāhīn, Muḥammad, *Taḥawwulāt al-Shawq fī* Mawsim al-Hijra ilā al-Shamāl, *Dirāsa Naqdiyya Muqārina*, Beirut, al-Mu'assasa al-'Arabiyya li'l-Dirāsāt wa'l-Nashr, 1993.

Shāhīn, Muḥammad, *al-Adab wa'l-Usṭūra*, Beirut, al-Mu'assasa al-'Arabiyya li'l-Dirāsāt wa'l-Nashr, 1996.

Al-Shā'ib, Fu'ād, *Ta'rīkh Jurḥ*, Beirut, Dār al-Makshūf, 1944.

Shalabī, Khayrī, *Fallāḥ Miṣrī fī Bilād al-Firanja*, Cairo, Dār al-Ma'ārif, 1978.

Shamās, Anṭōn, *'Arabesqot*, Tel Aviv, 'Am 'Oved, 1986 (Hebrew).

Shāmī, Jūrj, 'Rā'iḥat al-Laban wa-Rā'ihat al-Tamr', *Shi'r*, 35 (summer 1967), 90–2.

Shamīs, 'Abd al-Mun'im, *al-Jinn wa'l-'Afārīt fī al-Adab al-Sha'bī al-Miṣrī*, Cairo, al-Hay'a al-Miṣriyya al-'Āmma li'l-Kitāb, 1976.

Shaqīr, Maḥmūd, *Tawfīq Ṣāyigh: Sīrat Shā'ir wa-Manfā*, London, Dār Riyāḍ al-Rayyis li'l-Kitāb wa'l-Nashr, 1989.

Al-Shar', 'Alī, 'al Baḥth 'an al-Shakhṣiyya al-Jadīda fī *Mawsim al-Hijra ilā al-Shamāl*', *Abḥāth al-Yarmūk*, 5:2 (1987), 7–33.

Al-Sharīf, Yūsuf, *al-Sūdān wa-Ahl al-Sūdan, Asrār al-Siyāsa wa-Khafāyā al-Mujtama'*, Cairo, Dār al-Hilāl, 1996.

Al-Sharqāwī, 'Abd al-Raḥmān, *al-Arḍ*, 3rd ed., Cairo, Dār al-Kātib li'l-Ṭibā'a wa'l-Nashr, 1968 (1st ed. 1954).

Al-Sharqāwī, 'Abd al-Raḥmān, *Qulūb Khāliya*, Cairo, al-Dār al-Qawmiyya li'l-Ṭibā'a wa'l-Nashr, 1965 (1st ed. 1957).

Al-Sharqāwī, 'Abd al-Raḥmān, *al-Fallāḥ*, Cairo, 'Ālam al-Kutub, 1968.

Shāwūl, Būl, *'Alāmāt min al-Thaqāfa al-Maghribiyya al-Ḥadītha*, Beirut, al-Mu'assasa al-'Arabiyya li'l-Dirāsāt wa'l-Nashr, 1979.

Al-Shaykh, Aḥmad, *al-Nās fī Kafr 'Askar (Awlād 'Awf)*, Cairo, al-Hay'a al-Miṣriyyia al-'Āmma li'l-Kitāb, 1979.

Al-Shaykh, Ḥanān, *Faras al-Shayṭān*, Beirut, Dār-al-Nahār, 1971.

Al-Shaykh, Ḥanān, *Intiḥār Rajul Mayyit*, Beirut, Dār al-Nahār li'l-Nashr, 1980.

Al-Shaykh, Ḥanān, *Ḥikāyat Zahra*, 2nd ed., Beirut, Dār al-Ādāb, 1989 (1st ed. 1980).

Al-Shaykh, Ḥanān, *Misk al-Ghazāl*, Beirut, Dār al-Ādāb, 1988.

Al-Shaykh, Ḥanān, *Ukannis al-Shams 'an al-Suṭūḥ*, Beirut, Dār al-Ādāb, 1994.

Al-Shaykh, Ḥanān, *Innahā Landan Yā 'Azīzī*, Beirut, Dār al-Ādāb, 2001.

Al-Shaykh, Ḥanān, *Imra'tān 'alā Shāṭi' al-Baḥr*, Beirut, Dār al-Ādāb, 2003.

Al-Shaykh, Muḥammad al-Shaykh, *al-Insān wa'l-Taḥlīl al-Fā'ilī*, Taḥlīl al-Shakhṣiyya al-Sūdāniyya min Khilāl Mawsim al-Hijra ilā al-Shamāl wa-'Urs al-Zayn, [Khartoum], 1989. 2nd ed. Cairo, Markaz al-Dirāsāt al-Sūdāniyya, 2000.

Al-Shidyāq, Aḥmad Fāris, *Kashf al-Mukhabbā fī Funūn Urūbbā, al-Wasīṭa fī Ma'rifat Aḥwāl Mālṭa*, 2nd ed., Constantinople, Maṭba'at al-Jawā'ib, 1299 (AH), (1st ed. 1854).

Shukrī, Ghālī, *Thawrat al-Fikr fī Adabinā al-Ḥadīth*, Cairo, Maktabat al-Anglū al-Miṣriyya, 1965.

Shukrī, Ghālī, *Thawrat al-Mu'tazil, Dirāsa fī Adab Tawfīq al-Ḥakīm*, 3rd ed. Beirut, Dār Ibn Rushd, 1973.

Shukrī, Ghālī, *Azmat al-Jins fī al-Qiṣṣa al-'Arabiyya*, 3rd ed., Beirut, Dār al-Āfāq al-Jadīda, 1978.

Shukrī, Ghālī, *Mir'āt al-Manfā, As'ila fī Thaqāfat al-Naft wa'l-Ḥarb*, London, Riyāḍ al-Rayyis li'l-Kitāb wa'l-Nashr, 1989.

Shukrī, Muḥammad, *al-Khubz al-Ḥāfī*, 4th ed., London, Dār al-Sāqī, 1996 (1st ed. 1982).

Shuqayr, Na'ūm, *Ta'rīkh al-Sūdān*, 2nd ed., Beirut, Dār al-Jīl, 1981.

Al-Shūsh, Muḥammad Ibrāhīm, *al-Shi'r al-Ḥadīth fī al-Sūdān*, 2nd ed., Khartoum, Dār Jāmi'at al-Kharṭūm, 1972 (1st ed. 1962).

Al-Shūsh, Muḥammad Ibrāhīm, *Adab wa-Udabā'*, Khartoum, Jāmi'at al-Kharṭūm, Dār al-Ta'līf wa'l-Tarjama wa'l-Nashr, 1973.

Al-Shūsh, Muḥammad Ibrāhīm, 'al-Ṭayyib Ṣāliḥ wa-Usṭūrat *Bandar Shāh*', *al-Nāqid*, 14 (August 1989), 40–2.

Al-Shūsh, Muḥammad Ibrāhīm, 'al-Makān Yattasi' li'l-Jamī', Qirā'a fī Adab al-Ṭayyib Ṣāliḥ', *al-'Arabī*, 405 (August 1992), 134–9.

Al-Shūsh, Muḥammad Ibrāhīm, 'al-Athar al-Dīnī al-Ṣūfī fī A'māl al-Ṭayyib Ṣāliḥ', in Ḥasan Abbashir al-Ṭayyib (ed.), *al-Ṭayyib Ṣāliḥ*, 157–67.

Sibā'ī, 'Uthmān, 'Ḥiwār ma'a al-Ṭayyib Ṣāliḥ', *al-Madīna*, 5224 (27 May 1981), 9.

Al-Ṣiddīq, 'Abd al-Hādī, 'al-Kharīf fī Shi'r al-Ḥardalū', *al-Kharṭūm*, 8 (May 1968), 48–53.

Al-Ṣiddīq, 'Abd al-Hādī, 'al-Azal al-Makānī li'l-Shi'r al-Sūdānī', *al-Ādāb*, 4 (April 1975), 18–25.

S.M., 'Riḥlat al-Ṭayyib Ṣāliḥ min al-Majāl al-Sūdānī ilā al-Majāl al-'Arabī', *al-Usbū' al-'Arabī* (June 1967), 52–3.

Stebanof, L., 'Muqaddima li Tarjamat Thulāthiyyat al-Ṭayyib Ṣāliḥ ilā al-Rūsiyya. Radugha, Moscow 1983, Taqdīm Nasīm 'Awn', *Jarīdat al-Nidā'* (13 February 1983).

Ṣubḥī, Muḥyī al-Dīn, '*Mawsim al-Hijra ilā al-Shamāl* bayn 'Uṭayl wa-'Mīrsū'', *al-Ma'rifa*, 138 (August 1973), 39–60. [Published under the same title in Muḥammadiyya (ed.), *al-Ṭayyib Ṣāliḥ*, 39–77, and in Ṣubḥī, *Abṭāl fī al-Ṣayrūra*, 8–32].

Ṣubḥī, Muḥyī al-Dīn, *Abṭāl fī al-Sayrūra, Dirāsāt fī al-Riwāya al-'Arabiyya wa'l-Mu'arraba*, Beirut, Dār al-Ṭalī'a, 1980.

Ṣubḥī, Muḥyī al-Dīn, 'Aqāṣīṣ al-Ṭayyib Ṣāliḥ', in idem, *Abṭāl fī al-Ṣayrūra*, 33–53. [Published in Muḥammadiyya (ed.), *al-Ṭayyib Ṣāliḥ*, 9–38].

Ṣubḥī, Muḥyī al-Dīn and Khaldūn al-Sham'a, 'al-Ṭayyib Ṣāliḥ Riwā'iyyan wa-Nāqidan', in Muḥammadiyya (ed.), *al-Ṭayyib Ṣāliḥ*, 118–36. [First published in the periodical *al-Mawqif al-Adabī*, 4–5 (August-September 1973), 50–6].

Summāq, Fayṣal, *al-Riwāya al-Sūriyya, Nash'atuhā wa-Taṭawwuruhā wa-Madhāhibuhā*, Damascus, Maṭābi' al-Idāra al-Siyāsiyya, 1984.

Suwaydān, Sāmī, 'Min Dalālat al-Ma'nā fī *Mawsim al-Hijra ilā al-Shamāl*' li'l-Ṭayyib Ṣāliḥ', in Idem, *Abḥāth fī al-Naṣṣ al-Riwā'ī al-'Arabī*, 121–30. 2nd ed., Dār al-Ādāb, 2000, 107–15.[Published in *al-Nahār al-'Arabī wa'l-Duwalī*, 341 (14–20 November 1983), 52–4].

Suwaydān, Sāmī, *Abḥāth fī al-Naṣṣ al-Riwā'ī al-'Arabī*, Beirut, Mu'assasat al-Abḥāth al-'Arabiyya, 1986.

Suwaydān, Sāmī, 'al-Waṣf fī *Mawsim al-Hijra ilā al-Shamāl* li'l-Ṭayyib Ṣāliḥ: Awḍā'uhā wa-'Alaqātuhā, Waẓā'ifuhā wa-Dalālātuhā', in Idem, *Abḥāth fī al-Naṣṣ al-Riwā'ī al-'Arabī*, 131–76. 2nd ed., Dār al-Ādāb, 2000, 116–57.

Suwayratī, Muḥammad, *al-Naqd al-Bunyawī wa'l-Naṣṣ al-Riwā'ī: Namādhij Taḥlīlīyya min al-Naqd al-'Arabī*, 2nd ed., Casablanca, Ifrīqiyā al-Sharq, 1994.

Ṭāhā, Iynās Mamdūḥ, 'Ṣūrat al-Qarya fī al-Riwāya al-'Arabiyya', *al-Mustaqbal al-'Arabī*, 48 (February 1983), 50–65.

Ṭāhā, Muḥammad 'Alī, *Jisr 'alā al-Nahr al-Ḥazīn, Majmū'a Qaṣaṣiyya*, Nazareth, Manshūrāt al-Ṣadāqa, 1978.

Ṭāhir, Bahā', *Bi'l-Ams Ḥalamt bik*, Cairo, al-Hay'a al-Miṣriyya al-'Āmma li'l-Kitab, 1984.

Ṭāhir, Bahā', *Qālat Ḍūḥā, Majmū'āt al-A'māl*, Cairo, Dār al-Hilāl, 1992, 307-414 (1st ed. 1985).

Al-Ṭahṭāwī, Rifā'a, *Takhlīṣ al-Ibrīz ilā Talkhīṣ Bārīz*, Dār al-Taqaddum, Cairo 1905 (1st ed. 1834).

Tājir, Jāk, *Ḥarakat al-Tarjama fī Miṣr Khilāl al-Qarn al-Tāsi' 'Ashar*, Cairo, Dār al-Ma'ārif, 1945.

Al-Talāwī, Muḥammad Najīb, *al-Dhāt wa'l-Mihmāz: Dirāsat al-Taqāṭub fī Ṣirā' Riwāyāt al-Muwājaha al-Ḥaḍāriyya*, Cairo, al-Hay'a al-Miṣriyya al-'Āmma li'l-Kitāb, 1998.

Ṭarābīshī, Jūrj, *La'bat al-Ḥulm wa'l-Wāqi', Dirāsa fī Adab Tawfīq al-Ḥakīm*, Beirut, Dār al-Ṭalī'a, 1972.

Ṭarābīshī, Jūrj, *Sharq wa-Gharb, Rujūla wa-Unūtha, Dirāsa fī Azmat al-Jins wa'l-Ḥaḍāra fī al-Riwāya al-'Arabiyya*, 2nd ed., Beirut, Dār al-Ṭalī'a, 1979.

Ṭarābīshī, Jūrj, *Min al-Nahḍa ilā al-Ridda: Tamazzuqāt al-Thaqāfa al-'Arabiyya fī 'Aṣr al-'Awlama*, Beirut, London, Dār al-Sāqī, 2000.

Taymūr, Maḥmūd, *al-Shaykh Jum'a wa-Aqāṣīṣ Ukhrā*, 2nd ed., Cairo, al-Maṭba'a al-Salafiyya wa-Maktabatuhā, 1927 (1st ed. 1925).

Taymūr, Maḥmūd, *al-Shaykh Sayyid al-'Abīṭ wa-Aqāṣīṣ Ukhrā*, Cairo, al-Maṭba'a al-Salafiyya wa-Maktabatuhā, 1926.

Taymūr, Maḥmūd, *al-Ḥājj Shalabī wa-Aqāṣīṣ Ukhrā*, Cairo, Maṭba'at al-I'timād, 1930.

Taymūr, Muḥammad, 'Fī al-Qiṭār', *al-Sufūr*, 107 (7 June 1917), 3.

Taymūr, Muḥammad, *Mā Tarāhu al-'Uyūn*, 2nd ed., Cairo, al-Maṭba'a al-Salafiyya wa-Maktabatuhā, 1927.

Al-Ṭayyib, Ḥasan Abbashir, 'al-'Arabiyya fī al-Sūdān, Mu'allaf al-Marḥūm al-Shaykh 'Abd Allāh 'Abd al-Raḥmān al-Amīn', *al-Kharṭūm*, 8 (May 1968), 40–7.

Al-Ṭayyib, Ḥasan Abbashir, *Fī al-Adab al-Sūdānī al-Mu'āṣir*, Beirut, Dār al-Fikr, Khartoum, al-Dār al-Sūdāniyya, 1971.

Al-Ṭayyib, Ḥasan Abbashir, 'al-Ṭayyib Ṣāliḥ Riwā'iyyan wa-Shā'iran Mubdi'an', *Ibdā'*, 9–10 (September-October 2000), 21–35. [Published under the same title in idem (ed.), *al-Ṭayyib Ṣāliḥ*, 169–86].

Al-Ṭayyib, Ḥasan Abbashir (ed.), *al-Ṭayyib Ṣāliḥ: Dirāsāt Naqdiyya*, Beirut, Riyāḍ al-Rayyis, 2001.

Al-Ṭayyib, Ṭāriq, *Mudun bilā Nakhīl*, Kolonia, Manshūrāt al-Jamal, 1992.

Al-Ṭayyib, Ṭāriq, *al-Jamal Lā Yaqif Khalf Ishāra Ḥamrā', Majmū'at Qiṣaṣ*, Cairo, al-Ḥaḍāra li'l-Nashr, 1993.

Al-Ṭayyib, Ṭāriq, 'al-Ightirāb 'inda al-Ṭayyib Ṣāliḥ', in Ḥasan Abbashir al-Ṭayyib (ed.), *al-Ṭayyib Ṣāliḥ*, 255–83.

Al-Tāzī, Muḥammad 'Izz al-Dīn, *Raḥīl al-Baḥr*, Beirut, al-Mu'assasa al-'Arabiyya li'l-Dirāsāt wa'l-Nashr, 1983.

Al-Tūnisī, Bayram, *al-Sayyid wa-Mar'atuh fī Bārīs*, Sidon-Beirut, al-Maktaba al-'Aṣriyya, n.d. (1st ed. 1923).

'Ubayyid, 'Alī, *Fī al-Riwāya al-'Arabiyya*, Safasqus, Dār Muḥammad 'Alī li'l-Nashr, 2003.

Al-'Ujaylī, 'Abd al-Salām, *Raṣīf al-'Adhrā' al-Sawdā'*, Beirut, Dār al-Ṭalī'a li'l-Ṭibā'a wa'l-Nashr, 1960.

'Uryān, 'Abd al-Mun'im, 'Ta'rīkh al-Qiṣṣa al-Qaṣīra fī al-Sūdān', *al-Kharṭūm*, 12 (September 1967), 23–5.

'Uthmān, 'Abd al-Fattāḥ, *al-Riwāya al-'Arabiyya al-Jazā'iriyya,* Cairo, al-Hay'a al-Miṣriyya al-'Āmma li'l-Kitāb, 1994.

'Uthmān, Fatḥī Muḥammad, 'Ḥiwār ma'a al-Fannān Ibrāhīm al-Ṣalaḥī (1)', *Kitābāt Sūdāniyya*, 2 (April 1993), 53–71; (2), 3 (November 1993), 113–39.

'Uthmān, Fatḥī, 'Ḥiwār Ṭawīl ma'a Ṣāḥib *Mawsim al-Hijra ilā al-Shamāl* Alladhī Lā yuḥibb al-Kitāba wa-Lākin…(1)', *al-Wasaṭ*, 345 (7 September 1998), 48–52; (2), *al-Wasaṭ*, 345 (14 September 1998), 56–7.

'Uthmān, Muḥammad Khayr, 'al-Āfāq al-Ba'īda aw Istirāḥat al-Muḥārib', in Ḥasan Abbashir al-Ṭayyib (ed.), *al-Ṭayyib Ṣāliḥ*, 243–53.

Wādī, Ṭāhā, 'Adab wa-Funūn', *Sayyidatī*, 4:157 (18 March 1984), 42.

Wahba, Majdī, and Kāmil al-Muhandis, *Mu'jam al-Muṣṭalaḥāt al-'Arabiyya fī al-Lugha wa'l Adab*, Beirut, Maktabat Lubnān, 1979.

Wahīd, 'Alā' al-Dīn, *Wujūh Qaṣaṣiyya Qadīma wa-Jadīda*, Cairo, Dār al-Ma'ārif, Iqra' 439, 1979.

Al-Wā'lī, Karīm, '*Mawsim al-Hijra ilā al-Shamāl*', *Majallat al-Jāmi'a*, Jāmi'at al-Mūṣul, 3 (1979), 65.

Al-Wā'lī, Karīm, 'al-Ṭabīb Walī wa'l-Maqām 'Iyāda?! Zawāj al-'Ilm bi'l-Khurāfa fī Qiṣṣat *Qindīl Umm Hāshim*', *al-Nāqid*, 57 (March 1993), 38–41.

Waqī' Allāh, 'Uthmān, 'Ilā Abī Zaynab', in Ḥasan Abbashir al-Ṭayyib (ed.), *al-Ṭayyib Ṣāliḥ*, 69.

Al-Waraqī, al-Sa'īd, *Ittijāhāt al-Riwāya al-'Arabiyya al-Mu'āṣira*, Alexandria, al-Hay'a al-Miṣriyya al-'Āmma li'l-Kitāb, 1982.

Waṭṭār, al-Ṭāhir, *al-Lāz*, Algiers, al-Sharika al-Waṭaniyya li'l-Nashr wa'l-Tawzī', 1974.

Waṭṭār, al-Ṭāhir, *al-Zilzāl (Riwāya min al-Jazā'ir)*, Beirut, Dār al-'Ilm li'l-Malāyīn, 1974.

Waṭṭār, al-Ṭāhir, *'Urs Baghl, Riwāya*, Algiers, al-Sharika al-Waṭaniyya li'l-Nashr wa'l-Tawzī', 1982 (1st ed. 1978).

Al-Yabūrī, Aḥmad, *Dīnāmiyyat al-Naṣṣ al-Riwā'ī*, Rabat, Manshūrāt Ittiḥād Kuttāb al-'Arab, 1993.

Al-Yabūrī, Aḥmad, *Fī al-Riwāya al-'Arabiyya, al-Takawwun wa'l-Inshighāl*, Casablanca, Sharikat al-Nashr wa'l-Tawzī', al-Madāris, 2000.

Yāghī, 'Abd al-Raḥmān, *al-Baḥth 'an Īqā' Jadīd fī al-Riwāya al-'Arabiyya*, Beirut, Dār al-Fārābī, 1999.

Yāzijī, 'Ādil, 'Ḥiwār Maftūḥ ma'a al-Ṭayyib Ṣāliḥ', *al-Mawqif al-Adabī*, 193–4 (May-June 1987), 146–56.

Al-Yāzijī, Ḥalīm, *al-Sūdān wa'l-Ḥaraka al-Adabiyya*, Beirut, Manshūrāt al-Jāmi'a al-Lubnāniyya, Qism al-Dirāsāt al-Insāniyya, 1985.

Yūnis, 'Abd al-Ḥamīd, *Difā' 'an al-Fūlklūr*, Cairo, al-Hay'a al-Miṣriyya al-'Āmma li'l-Kitāb, 1973.

Yūsuf, 'Abd al-Wāḥid 'Abd Allāh, 'al-Ṭayyib Ṣāliḥ: al-Insān al-Nabīl al-'Āshiq li Waṭanihi', in Ḥasan Abbashir al-Ṭayyib (ed.), *al-Ṭayyib Ṣāliḥ*, 75–83.

Al-Yūsuf, Yusūf, 'al-'Uqad al-Jinsiyya fī *Mawsim al-Hijra ilā al-Shamāl*', *al-Ma'rifa*, 150 (August 1974), 73–85.

Al-Ẓāhir, Muḥammad, 'Ḥiwār ma'a al-Ṭayyib Ṣāliḥ, 'Aktub li Takwīn Tayyār 'Arabī Wāḥid', *al-Aqlām*, 12 (August-October 1980), 148–55.

Zakī, 'Abd al-'Azīz, 'Yaḥyā Ḥaqqī wa-Ṣūrat al-Muthaqqafīn', *al-Fikr al-Mu'āṣir*, 62 (April 1970), 86–95.

Zarrūq, Ḥasan al-Ṭāhir, *'Abd al-Ṣamad wa-Bahiyya, Qiṣaṣ Sūdāniyya*, Cairo, Dār al-Kātib al-'Arabī, 1967.

Zarrūq, al-Ṭayyib, *al-Arḍ al-Ṣafrā'*, Cairo, Maṭba'at al-Baramān, 1961.

Zarrūq, al-Ṭayyib, *al-Shay' Alladhī Ḥadath, Qiṣaṣ Sūdāniyya*, [Cairo], al-Hay'a al-Miṣriyya al-'Amma li'l-Ta'līf wa'l-Nashr, 1970.

Zarrūq, al-Ṭayyib and Abū Bakr Khālid, *Qiṣaṣ Sūdāniyya*, Cairo, Dār al-Nashr al-Miṣriyya, 1957.

Zaydān, Joseph, *Maṣādir al-Adab al-Nisā'ī fī al-'Ālam al-'Arabī al-Ḥadīth (1800–1996)*, Beirut, al-Mu'ssasa al-'Arabiyya li'l-Dirāsāt wa'l-Nashr, 1999.

Zāyid, 'Abd al-Ṣamad, *Mafhūm al-Zaman wa-Dalālātuhu fī al-Riwāya al-'Arabiyya al-Mu'āṣira*, Libya-Tunis, al-Dār al-'Arabiyya li'l-Kitāb, 1988.

Al-Zayyāt, Laṭīfa, *Ḥarakat al-Tarjama al-Adabiyya min al-Inklīziyya ilā al-'Arabiyya fī Miṣr fī al-Fatra mā bayn 1882–1925*, Cairo, Jāmi'at al-Qāhira, 1957 (Ph.D., Diss. unpublished).

Al-Zayyāt, Laṭīfa, *Min Ṣūwar al-Mar'a fī al-Qiṣaṣ wa'l-Riwāyāt al-'Arabiyya*, Cairo, Dār al-Thaqāfa al-Jadīda, 1989.

Zayn, Ibrāhīm Muḥammad, 'Taṭawwur Shakl al-Ta'bīr al-Dīnī fī Riwāyāt al-Ṭayyib Ṣāliḥ: (4), al-Zayn Muharrij am Rajul Ṣāliḥ?!', *al-Multaqā* (1 May 1993), 38–41.

Zifzāf, Muḥammad, *al-Mar'a wa'l-Warda*, Rabat: al-Sharika al-Maghribiyya li'l-Nāshirīn al-Muttaḥidīn, 1981 (1st ed. 1972).

Ziyāda, Ghassān, *Qirā'āt fī al-Adab wa'l-Riwāya, Innahu Nidā' al-Janūb*, Beirut, Dār al-Muntakhab al-'Arabī, 1995.

Al-Zu'bī, Aḥmad, 'Thalāthat Wujūh li Muṣṭafā Sa'īd: Dirāsa fī Riwāyat al-Ṭayyib Ṣāliḥ *Mawsim al-Hijra ilā al-Shamāl*', *Ibdā'*, 3:1, (January 1985), 111–14.

Al-Zu'bī, Aḥmad, *Dirāsāt Naqdiyya*, Amman, Maktabat 'Ammān, 1985.

Al-Zu'bī, Aḥmad, '*Fī al-Īqā' al-Riwā'ī* fī [*Mawsim al-Hijra ilā al-Shamāl*]', in idem, *Fī al-Īqā' al-Riwā'ī, naḥwa Manhaj Jadīd fī Dirāsat al-Bunya al-Riwā'iyya*, Amman, Dār al-Amal, 1986, 57–74. [Published under the same title and under the same book's title: see Aḥmad al-Zu'bī, *Fī al-Īqā' al-Riwā'ī, naḥwa Manhaj Jadīd fī Dirāsat al-Bunya al-Riwā'iyya*, Beirut, Dār al-Manāhil li'l-Ṭibā'a wa'l-Nashr wa'l-Tawzi', 1995, 71–90. Published also as an article under the same title 'al-Īqā' al-Riwā'ī fī *Mawsim al-Hijra ilā al-Shamāl*', *al-Ma'rifa*, 306–7 (1988), 34–51].

Other Languages

Abbas, Ali Abdallah, 'Notes on Tayeb Salih: *Season of Migration to the North* and *The Wedding of Zein*', *Sudan Notes and Records*, LV (1974), 46–60.

Abbas, Ali Abdallah, 'The Strangled Impulse: The Role of the Narrator in Tayeb Salih's *Season...*', *Sudan Notes and Records*, LX (1979), 56–85.

'Abd al-Rahim, Muddathir, *Imperialism and Nationalism in the Sudan*, Oxford, Oxford University Press, 1969.

'Abd al-Rahim, Muddathir, 'Arabism, Africanism and Self-Identification in the Sudan', *Journal of African Studies*, 8:2 (July 1970), 233–49.

'Abdalla, Muhammed Khalafalla, 'Muṣṭafa Migration from the Ṣa'īd: An Odyssey in Search of Identity', in Elad-Bouskila and al-Shahi (eds), *Al-Ṭayyib Ṣāliḥ, Edebiyât*, 43–61.

Abdel-Malek, Anouar (ed.), *Contemporary Arab Political Thought* (trans. Michael Pallis), London, Zed Books, 1983.

Abdel-Malek, Kamal, 'The Khawāja Then and Now: Images of the West in Modern Egyptian Zajal', *Journal of Arabic Literature*, XIX, 2 (1988), 162–78.

Abdel-Malek, Kamal and Wael Hallaq (eds), *Tradition, Modernity and Postmodernity in Arabic Literature, Essays in Honor of Professor Issa Boullata*, Leiden, Boston, Köln, Brill, 2000.

Abdel-Meguid, Abdel-Aziz, *The Modern Arabic Short Story: Its Emergence, Development and Form*, Cairo, Dar al-Maarif, n.d. [1956].

Abdul-Hai, Muhammad, *Conflict and Identity: The Cultural Poetics of Contemporary Sudanese Poetry*, Khartoum, Institute of African and Asian Studies, University of Khartoum, African Seminar Series No. 26, 1976.

Abdul-Hai, Muhammad, 'A Bibliography of Arabic Translations of English and American Poetry (1830–1970)', *Journal of Arabic Literature*, VII (1976), 120–50.

Abdul-Hai, Muhammad, *Tradition and English and American Influence in Arabic Romantic Poetry: A Study in Comparative Literature*, Oxford, The Middle East Centre, St Antony's College, London, Ithaca Press, 1982.

Accad, Evelyn, *Sexuality and War: Literary Masks of the Middle East*, New York, New York University Press, 1990.

Achebe, Chinua, *Things Fall Apart*, London, Everyman's Library, 1992 (1st ed. 1958).

Achebe, Chunua, *A Man of the People*, 2nd ed. Oxford, Heineman, 1988 (1st ed. 1966).

Achebe, Chinua, and C.L. Innes (eds), *African Short Stories: Twenty Short Stories from Across the Continent*, Oxford, Heinemann, 1987 (1st ed. 1985).

Achebe, Chinua and C.L. Innes (eds), *Contemporary African Short Stories*, Oxford, Heinemann, 1992.

Adonis, *An Introduction to Arab Poetics* (trans. Catherine Cobham), London, Saqi Books, 1990.

Aghacy, Samira, 'The Use of Autobiography in Rashīd al-Ḍa'īf's *Dear Mr Kawabata*', in Ostle, De Moor and Wild (eds), *Writing the Self*, 217–28.

Ahmed, Osman Hassan (ed.), *Sixteen Sudanese Short Stories*, Sudanese publication series (No. 6), Washington, D.C., Office of the Cultural Counselor, Embassy of the Democratic Republic of the Sudan, 1981.

Ajami, Fouad, *The Dream Palace of the Arabs: A Generation's Odyssey*, New York, Pantheon Books, 1998.

Ali, Muhsin Jassim, 'The Socio-Aesthetics of Contemporary Arabic Fiction: An Introduction', *Journal of Arabic Literature*, XIV (1983), 67–84.

Allen, Roger, 'The Novella in Arabic: A Study in Fictional Genres', *International Journal of Middle East Studies* 18:4 (1986), 473–84.

Allen, Roger, *Modern Arabic Literature*, New York, The Ungar Publishing Company, 1987.

Allen, Roger, *The Arabic Novel: An Historical and Critical Introduction*, Manchester, University of Manchester, 1982. 2nd ed., Syracuse, New York, Syracuse University Press, 1995.

Allen, Roger, 'Sindbad the Sailor and the Early Arabic Novel', in Abdel-Malek and Hallaq (eds), *Tradition, Modernity and Postmodernity in Arabic Literature*, 78–86.

Alwan, Mohamad Bakir, 'A Bibliography of Modern Arabic Fiction in English Translation', *Middle East Journal*, 26 (1972), 195–200.

Alwan, Mohamad Bakir, 'A Bibliography of Modern Arabic Poetry in English Translation' *Middle East Journal*, 27 (1973), 373–81.

Amherst, Ann and Katherine, Astbury, (eds), *Endings*, Exeter, Elm Bank Publications, 1999.

Amireh, Amal, 'Publication in the West: Problems and Prospects for Arab Women Writers', *al-Jadid*, 10 (August 1996), 10–11, 23.

Amyuni, Mona Takieddine, 'Tayeb Salih's *Season of Migration to the North*: An Interpretation', *Arab Studies Quarterly*, 2:1 (1980), 1–18.

Amyuni, Mona Takieddine, 'Images of Arab Women in *Midaq Alley* by Naguib Mahfouz, and *Season of Migration to the North by Tayeb Salih*', *International Journal of Middle East Studies*, 17:1 (1985), 25–36.

Amyuni, Mona Takieddine (ed.) Tayeb Salih's Season of Migration to the North: A Casebook, Beirut, The American University of Beirut, 1985.

Amyuni, Mona Takieddine, 'Tayeb Salih's *Bandarshah*: An Attempt at Interpretation' in el-Badawi, M. and Sconyers, D. (eds), *Sudan Studies Association*, Selected Conference Papers, 1982–84, vol. I, Washington D.C, 1986, 68–83.

Amyuni, Mona Takieddine, 'Women in Contemporary Arabic and Francophone Fiction', *Feminist Issue*, 2:2 (Fall 1992), 2–19.

Amyuni, Mona Takieddine, 'The Image of the City' in Ferial J. Ghazoul and Harlow (eds), *The View from Within*, 53–76.

Amyuni, Mona Takieddine, *La Ville Source d'Inspiration, Le Caire, Khartoum, Beyrouth, Paola Scola Chez Quelques Ecrivains Arabes Contemporains*, Beirut, Beiruter Texte und Studien, Stuttgart, Steiner Verlag, 1998.

Amyuni, Mona Takieddine, 'The Arab Artist's Role in Society. Three Case Studies: Najuib Mahfouz, Tayeb Salih and Elias Khoury', *Arabic and Middle Eastern Literatures*, 2:2 (1999), 203–22.

Amyuni, Mona Takieddine, 'Literary Creativity and Social Change: What has Happened to the Arab Psyche since the Sixties? A Study in a Few Literary Masks', in Abdel-Malek and Hallaq (eds), *Tradition, Modernity and Postmodernity in Arabic Literature*, 94–112.

Andrzejewski, B. W., S. Piaszewicz and W. Tyloch (eds), *Literatures in African Languages, Theoretical Issues and Sample Surveys*, Cambridge, Cambridge University Press, 1985.

Al-'Aqqād, 'Abbās Maḥmūd [= El Akkad, Abbas Mahmoud], *Sara* (trans. M.M. Badawi), Cairo, General Egyptian Book Organization, 1978.

Armah, Ayi Kwei, *Why Are We So Blest?* 2nd ed., Garden City, Doubleday, 1974 (1st ed. 1972).

Ashtiany, Julia et al. (eds), *The Cambridge History of Arabic Literature: 'Abbasid Belles-Lettres*, Cambridge, Cambridge University Press, 1990.

Ashur, Radwa, *The Obsessive Encounter: Tawfiq al-Hakim, al-Tayeb Salih and Bahaa Taher*, Cairo, 'Ayn Shams University, 1985.

Atiyah, Edward Selim, *Black Vanguard*, London, Peter Davies, 1952.

Auerbach, Erich, *Mimesis: The Representation of Reality in Western Literature* (trans. William Trask), New York, Doubleday Anchor Books, 1957.

Badawi, 'Abd al-Rahman (ed.), *Mélanges Taha Husain*, Cairo, Dar al-Maarif, 1942.

Badawi, M.M., 'The Lamp of Umm Hashim: The Egyptian Intellectual Between East and West', *Journal of Arabic Literature*, I (1970), 145–61.

Badawi, M.M., *Modern Arabic Literature and the West*, London, Ithaca Press, 1985.

Badawi, M.M ,.*Modern Arabic Drama in Egypt*, Cambridge, Cambridge Univrsity Press, 1987.

Badawi, M.M., 'Two Novelists from Iraq: Jabrā and Munīf', *Journal of Arabic Literature*, XXIII, 2 (1992), 140–54.

Badawi, M.M. (ed.), *The Cambridge History of Arabic Literature: Modern Arabic Literature*, Cambridge, Cambridge University Press, 1992.

Badawi, M.M., *A Short History of Modern Arabic Literature*, Oxford, Oxford University Press, 1993.

Badawi, M.M., 'Tayeb Salih: *Bandarshah,* Translated from the Arabic by Denys Johnson-Davies, London and New York: Kegan Paul International, Paris: UNESCO Publishing, 1996', *Bulletin of the School of Oriental and African Studies*, 61:2 (1998), 339–40.

Badawi, El-Said and Martin Hinds, *A Dictionary of Egyptian Arabic, Arabic-English*, Beirut, Librairie du Liban, 1986.

Baines, J., *Joseph Conrad: A Critical Background*, London, Weidenfeld and Nicholson, 1960.

Bakhtin, Mikhail M., *Speech Genres and Other Late Essays* (trans. Vern W. McGee), edited by Caryl Emerson and Michael Holquist, Austin, Texas University Press, 1986.

Baldick, Chris (ed.) *Oxford Concise Dictionary of Literary Terms*, Oxford and New York, Oxford University Press, 1996 (1st ed. 1990).

Balzac, Honoré de, *Pére Goriot* (trans. Barton Raffel), New York, London, W.W. Norton, 1994.

Barakat, Halim, *Visions of Social Reality in the Contemporary Arab Novel*, Washington, D.C., Georgetown University Center for Contemporary Arab Studies, 1977.

Barrāda, Muḥammad [=Berrada Mohamed], *The Game of Forgetting* (trans. Issa J. Boullata), Austin, University of Texas at Austin, 1996.

Al-Bazzaz, Saad (ed.), *Modern Arab Stories*, London, UR/Magazine, Iraqi Cultural Centre, London, 1980.

Beasley, Ina, *Before the Wind Change: People, Places and Education in the Sudan*, Ed. Janet Starkey, Oxford, Oxford University Press, 1992.

Beaugrande, Robert de, Abdulla Shunnaq and Mohamed H. Kheliel (eds), *Language, Discourse and Translation in the West and Middle East*, Amsterdam/Philadelphia: John Benjamins Publishing Company, 1994.

Bečka, Jiři (ed.), *Dictionary of Oriental Literatures*, London, Allen and Unwin, 1974.

Beeston, A.F.L. et al. (eds), *The Cambridge History of Arabic Literature: Arabic Literature to the End of the Umayyad Period*, Cambridge, Cambridge University Press, 1983.

Bennet, Sophie, 'Transcendence and Immanence: Self and Other in Baha' Tahir's Short Stories', *Arabic and Middle Eastern Literatures*, 1:1 (January 1998), 75–85.

Berg, E. Nancy, *Exile from Exile: Israeli Writers from Iraq*, New York, State University of New York Press, 1996.

Berkley, Constance E.G., *The Roots of Consciousness Molding the Art of El Tayeb Salih: A Contemporary Sudanese Writer*, Michigan, UMI Dissertation Information Service, 1979 [Ph.D. Diss., New York University, 1979].

Berkley, Constance E.G., 'Review Article: El Tayeb Salih, *The Wedding of Zein*', *Journal of Arabic Literature,* XI (1980), 105–14.

Berkley, Constance E.G., 'El Tayeb Salih: An Introductory Essay in Appreciation', *Pacific Moana Quarterly, African Writing Today*, 6:3/4 (July-October, 1981), 176–9.

Berkley, Constance E.G., 'Systems of Thought in El-Tayeb Salih's al-Rajul al-Qubrosi' (The Cypriot Man), *The Search*, 4 i-ii (1983), 77–89.

Bhabha, Homi K, *The Location of Culture*, London and New York, Routledge, 2001 (1st ed. 1994).

Birbalsingh, Frank M., '*Season of Migration to the West*: The Fiction of Tayeb Salih and Ayi Kwei Armah', in Amyuni (ed.), Tayeb Salih's Season of Migration to the North, 65–73.

Bleuchot, Herve, Christian Delnet and Derek Hopwood (eds), *Sudan: History, Identity, Ideology*, Aix-en Provence and Oxford, Ireman and the Middle East Centre, St Antony's College, 1991.

Bloom, Harold, *The Western Canon, the Books and School of the Ages*, London, Macmillan, 1995.

Boccaccio, Giovanni, *The Decameron* (trans. Guido Waldman), Oxford, Oxford University Press, 1993.

The Book of a Thousand Nights and a Night (trans. Richard F. Burton), London, H.S. Nichols, 1897.

Booth, Marilyn, *My Grandmother's Cactus: Stories by Egyptian Women*, London, Quartet Books, 1992.

Booth, Marilyn, *Bayram al-Tunisi's Egypt: Social Criticism and Narrative Strategies*, Oxford, The Middle East Centre, St Antony's College, Exeter, Ithaca Press, 1990.

Boullata, Issa J., 'Encounter Between East and West: A Theme in Contemporary Arabic Novels', *The Middle East Journal*, 30:1 (Winter 1976), 49–62. [Published as a chapter under the same title, in Idem, *Critical Perspectives on Modern Arabic Literature*, 1980].

Boullata, Issa J. (ed.), *Critical Perspectives on Modern Arabic Literaure: Critical Essays, Interviews and Bibliography*, Washington, Three Continents Press, 1980.

Boullata, Issa J., 'Contemporary Arab Writers and the Literary Heritage', *International Journal of Middle East Studies*, 15 (1983), 111–19.

Boullata, Issa J., 'Tayeb Salih's *Season of Migration to the North: A Casebook*', *Middle East Journal*, 40;3 (Summer 1986), 532–3.

Boullata, Issa J., (ed.) 'The Arabic Novel Since 1950', *Mundus Arabicus*, 5, Cambridge, MA, Dar Mahjar, 1992.

Boullata, Issa and Terri De Young (eds), *Tradition and Modernity in Arabic Literature*, Arkansas, Arkansas University Press, 1997.

Boyd, Douglas A., *Broadcasting in the Arab World, A Survey of Radio and Television in the Middle East*, Philadelphia, Temple University Press, 1982.

Bragg, Melvyn, *The Seventh Seal*, London, British Film Institute, 1993.

Braudel, Fernand, *La Méditerranée: l'espace et l'histoire*, Paris, Flammarion, 1985.

Brontë, Emily, *Wuthering Heights*, London, Everyman's Library, 1991 (1st ed. 1847).

Buck, Claire (ed.), *Women's Literature A-Z*, London, Bloomsbury, 1994 (1st ed. 1992).

Bürgel, Jean Christoph, 'Tradition and Modernity in the Work of the Tunisian Writer al-Mas'adī', in Smart (ed.), *Tradition and Modernity in Arabic Language and Literature*, 165–85.

Burton, G.S., *Sudan Arabic Note-Book*, London, McCorquodale, 1934.

Busse, Heribert, 'The Sanctity of Jerusalem in Islam', *Judaism*, XVII (1968), 441–68.

Cachia, Pierre, *An Overview of Modern Arabic Literature*, Edinburgh, Edinburgh University Press, 1990.

Calvino, Italo, *Invisible Cities* (trans. William Weaver), New York, A Harvest Book, 1974.

Calvino, Italo, *If on a Winter's Night a Traveler* (trans. William Weaver), London, Minerva, 1997 (1st ed. 1981).

Camus, Albert, *The Outsider* (trans. by Joseph Laredo), London, Penguin Books, 1983 (1st ed. 1942).

Camus, Albert, *The Rebel* (trans. Anthony Bower), London, Penguin Books, 1971 (1st ed. 1951).

Camus, Albert, *The Myth of Sisyphus* (trans. Justin O'Brien), London, Penguin Books, 1975 (1st ed. 1955).

Cervantes, Miguel de, *Don Quixote* (trans. Barton Raffel), New York, London, W.W. Norton, 1995 (1st ed. 1605).

Chaucer, Geoffrey, *The Canterbury Tales*, London, Everyman, 1994 (1st ed. 1390).

Clark, Peter, 'Translation without Translators', *Banipal*, 2 (June 1998), 74–5.

Clark, Peter, (ed.), *Sardines and Oranges: Short Stories from North Africa*, London, Banipal Books, 2005.

Conrad, Joseph, *Heart of Darkness*, London, Everyman's Library, 1993 (1st ed. 1902).

Conrad, Joseph, 'Youth: A Narrative', in idem, *Selected Short Stories*, Ware, Wordsworth Classics, 1997, 69–94 (1st ed. 1902).

Conrad, Joseph, *Lord Jim*, Ware, Wordsworth Classics, 1993 (1st ed. 1902).

Conrad, Joseph, 'The Secret Sharer', in idem, *Selected Short Stories*, Ware, Wordsworth Classics, 1997, 171–205 (1st ed. 1912).

Conrad, Joseph, *Chance, A Tale in Two Parts*, London, Methuen, 1946.

Cooke, Miriam, *The Anatomy of an Egyptian Intellectual: Yahya Haqqi*, Washington, D.C., Three Continents Press, 1984.

Cooke, Miriam, *War's Other Voices: Women Writers on the Lebanese Civil War*, Cambridge, Cambridge University Press, 1988.

Cooke, Miriam, *Women Claim Islam: Creating Islamic Feminism through Literature*, New York and London, Routledge, 2001.

Coulmai, Florian, 'Language Masters: Defying Linguistic Materialism', *International Journal of Sociology of Language*, 137 (1999), 27–38.

Crowfoot, J. M., 'Wedding Customs in Northern Sudan', *Sudan Notes and Records*, v (1927), 1–28.

Cuddon, J. A, *The Penguin Dictionary of Literary Terms and Literary Theory*, 4th ed., London, Penguin Books, 1999.

Culler, Jonathan, *Structuralist Poetics: Structuralism Linguistics and the Study of Literature*, London and Henley, Routledge and Kegan Paul, 1975.

Al-Ḍa'īf, Rashīd [=Al-Da'if, Rashid], *Dear Mr Kawabata*, (trans, Paul Starkey), Northampton, MA, Interlink, 2000.

D'Alonzo, Robert William, *Displacing National Literature: Consequences of Diaspora for the Monumental Idea of Egypt in Albert Cossery, Radwa Ashour and Ahdaf Souef*, Michigan, UMI Diss., 1999.

Daly, M.W. (ed.), *Sudan*, World Bibliographical Series, vol. 40, Oxford, Clio Press, 1992.

Davidson, John. E., 'In Search of a Middle Point: The Origins of Oppression in Tayeb Salih's *Season of Migration to the North*', *Research in African Literatures*, 20 (1989), 385–400.

De Voogd, Lourina, 'Arabic Literature in North Africa', in Schipper (ed.), *Unheard Works*, 91–113.

Durrell, Lawrence, *The Alexandria Quartet*, London, Faber and Faber, 1968 (1st ed. 1957–60).

Eco, Umberto, *The Open Work* (trans. Anna Carcogni), Cambridge, Massachusetts, Harvard University Press, 1989.

Elad [-Bouskila], Ami, 'Ideology and Structure in Fatḥī Ghānim's *al-Jabal*', *Journal of Arabic Literature*, XX, 2 (1989), 168–86.

Elad-Bouskila, Ami, 'Le Doum de Wad Hamid: Une lecture de Tayeb Salih', *Levant*, 3 (1990), 129–34.

Elad [-Bouskila], Ami (ed.), *Writer, Culture, Text: Studies in Modern Arabic Literature*, Fredericton, York Press, 1993.

Elad [-Bouskila], Ami, 'Fiction and Reality in al-Ṭayyib Ṣāliḥ's *Dawmat Wad Ḥāmid*', in Idem (ed.), *Writer, Culture, Text*, 62–73.

Elad [-Bouskila], Ami, *The Village Novel in Modern Egyptian Literature*, Berlin, Klaus Schwarz, 1994.

Elad [-Bouskila], Ami, 'Mahfūz's 'Za'balāwī': Six Stations of a Quest', *International Journal of Middle East Studies*, 26 (1994), 631–44.

Elad-Bouskila, Ami, 'Shaping the Cast of Characters: The Case of al-Ṭayyib Ṣāliḥ', *Journal of Arabic Literature*, XXIX:2 (July 1998), 59–84.

Elad-Bouskila, Ami, 'Al-Ṭayyib Ṣāliḥ: The Author and His Works', in Elad-Bouskila and Al-Shahi (eds), *Al-Ṭayyib Ṣāliḥ, Edebiyât*, 7–34.

Elad-Bouskila, Ami, 'The Expositions in al-Ṭayyib Ṣāliḥ's Writing', in Elad-Bouskila and Al-Shahi (eds), *Al-Ṭayyib Ṣāliḥ, Edebiyât*, 85–103.

Elad-Bouskila, Ami, 'Appendices: Writing by and on al-Ṭayyib Ṣāliḥ', in Elad-Bouskila and Al-Shahi (eds), *Al-Ṭayyib Ṣāliḥ, Edebiyât*, 10:1 (1999), 127–48.

Elad-Bouskila, Ami and Ahmed Al-Shahi (eds), *Al-Ṭayyib Ṣāliḥ: Seventy Candles, Edebiyât*, special issue, 10:1 (1999).

Elad-Bouskila, Ami, *Modern Palestinian Literature and Culture*, London and Portland, Frank Cass, 1999.

Elad-Bouskila, Ami, 'Symbol of Confrontation: Jerusalem in Israeli-Arab Literature During the *Intifāḍa*', in Rosenhouse and Bouskila (eds), *Linguistic and Cultural Studies in Arabic and Hebrew*, Essays Presented to Professor Moshe Piamenta for his Eighties Birthday, 255–75.

Eliot, T.S., *The Complete Poems and Plays of T.S. Eliot*, London, Book Club Associates, 1977.

Ellis, James, 'Kurtz's Voice: The Intended as "the Horror"', *English Literature in Transition*, 19:2 (1976), 105–10.

El-Enany, Rasheed, *Naguib Mahfouz the Pursuit of Meaning*, London and New York, Routledge, 1993.

El-Enany, Rasheed, 'Tawfīq al-Hakīm and the West: A New Assessment of the Relationship', *British Journal of Middle Eastern Studies*, 27:2 (2000), 165–75.

Encyclopaedia of Islam, First Edition, Leiden, E.J. Brill, 1913–36.

Encyclopaedia of Islam, New Edition, Leiden, E.J. Brill, 1986–2002.

Farah, Caesar E, 'The Prose Literature of Sufism', in M.J.L Young et al. (eds), *The Cambridge History of Arabic Literature, Religion, Learning and Science in the 'Abbasid Period*, 56–75.

Farmer, Penelope, *Beginnings: Creation Myth of the World*, London, Chatto and Windus, 1978.

Faulkner, William, *The Sound and the Fury*, London, Picador, 1993 (1st ed. 1929).

Faulkner, William, *Light in August*, London, Picador, 1993 (1st ed. 1932).

Faulkner, William, *As I Lay Dying*, London, Vintage, 1996 (1st ed. 1935).

Faulkner, William, *Absalom, Absalom!*, London, Vintage, 1985 (1st ed. 1935).

Faulkner, William, *Requiem For a Nun*, London, Vintage, 1996 (1st ed. 1956).

Faulkner, William, *Collected Stories*, London, Vintage, 1995.

Fayyād, Sulaymān [= Fayyad, Suleiman], *Voices: A Novel* (trans. Hosam Aboul-Ela), London, Marion Boyars, 1992.

Forster, Edward Morgan, *Aspects of the Novel*, San Diego, New York, London, Harcourt Brace and Company, 1955 (1st ed. 1927).

Frazer, James, *The Golden Bough: A History of Myth and Religion*, London, Chancellor Press, 1924.

El-Gabalawy, Saad, *Three Pioneering Egyptian Novels*, Fredericton, York Press, 1986.

Galin, Müge, *Between East and West: Sufism in the Novels of Doris Lessing*, New York, State University of New York Press, 1997.

García Márquez, Gabriel, *No One Writes to the Colonel* (trans. J.S. Bernstein), London, Penguin Books, 1996 (1st ed. 1968).

García Márquez, Gabriel, 'Big Mama's Funeral' (trans. Gregory Rabassa and J.S. Bernstein), *Collected Stories*, London, Penguin Books, 1996, 90–185 (1st ed. 1968).

García Márquez, Gabriel, *One Hundred Years of Solitude* (trans. Gregory Rabassa), London, Penguin Books, 1970.

García Márquez, Gabriel, *Leaf Storm* (trans. Gregory Rabassa), London, Penguin Books, 1996 (1st ed. 1972).

García Márquez, Gabriel, *The Autumn of the Patriarch* (trans. Gregory Rabassa), London, Penguin Books, 1996 (1st ed. 1976).

García Márquez, Gabriel, *Innocent Eréndira and Other Stories* (trans. Gregory Rabassa), London, Penguin Books, 1978.

García Márquez, Gabriel, *In Evil Hour* (trans. Gregory Rabassa), London, Penguin Books, 1996 (1st ed. 1979).

García Márquez, Gabriel, *Chronicle of a Death Foretold* (trans. Gregory Rabassa), London, Penguin Books, 1996 (1st ed. 1982).

García Márquez, Gabriel, *Love in the Time of Cholera* (trans. Edith Grossman), London, Penguin Books, 1988.

García Márquez, Gabriel, *The General in His Labyrinth* (trans. Edith Grossman), London, Penguin Books, 1990.

García Márquez, Gabriel, 'Eye of a Blue Dog' (trans. Gregory Rabassa and J.S. Bernstein), in *Collected Stories*, London, Penguin Books, 1991, 1–89.

García Márquez, Gabriel, *Strange Pilgrims* (trans. Edith Grossman), London, Penguin Books, 1993.

García Márquez, Gabriel, *Of Love and Other Stories* (trans. Edith Grossman), London, Penguin Books, 1995.

Gasim, Awn al-Sharif, 'Some Aspects of Sudanese Colloquial Arabic', *Sudan Notes and Records*, XLVI (1965), 40–9.

Geesey, Patricia, 'Cultural Hybridity and Contamination in Tayeb Salih's *Mawsim al-Hijra ila al-Shamal* (Season of Migration to the North)', *Research in African Literature*, 28 (Fall 1997), 128–40.

Gershoni, Israel and James R. Jankowski, *Egypt, Islam and the Arabs: The Search for Egyptian Nationhood, 1900–1930*, Oxford, Oxford University Press, 1980.

Ghanaim, Mahmud, 'Characters Narrate Their Own Tragic Ends: A Study of the Endings of Five Novels by Najīb Mahfūz', *Arabic and Middle Eastern Literature*, 2:2 (July 1999), 177–88.

Ghānim, Fatḥī [= Ghanem, Fathy], *The Man who Lost his Shadow* (trans. Desmond Stewart), London, Heinemann, 1966.

Ghattas-Soliman, Sonia, 'The Two-Sided Image of Women in *Season of Migration to the North*', in Harrow (ed.), *Faces of Islam in African Literature*, 91–103.

Ghazoul, Ferial J. and Barbara Harlow (eds), *The View from Within: Writers and Critics on Contemporary Arabic Literature*, Cairo, The American University in Cairo Press, 1994.

Ghougassian, Joseph P., *Khalil Gibran: Wings of Thought*, New York, Philosophical Library, 1973.

Gibb, Hamilton A.R. and Harold Bowen, *Islamic Society and the West*, Oxford, vol. I, 1950; vol. II, 1957.

Gibb, Hamilton A.R., *Studies on the Civilization of Islam*, Princeton, Princeton University Press, 1982.

Gibson, Walker, 'Authors, Speakers, Readers, and Mock Readers', in Tompkins (ed.), *Reader-Response Criticism*, 1–6.

Gilsman, Michael, *Saint and Sufi in Modern Egypt: An Essay in the Sociology of Religion*, Oxford, Oxford University Press, 1973.

Gohlman, Susan A., 'Women as Cultural Symbols in Yahyā Hāqqī's *Saint's Lamp*', *Journal of Arabic Literature*, X (1979), 117–27.

Goitein, Shlomo Dov, 'The Sanctity of Jerusalem and the Palestinians in Early Islam', in idem, *Studies in Islamic History and Institutions*, Leiden, E.J. Brill, 1966, 135–48.

Gordon, Haim, *Naguib Mahfouz's Egypt: Existential Themes in His Writings*, Westport, Greenwood Press, 1990.

Goving, Rosemary (ed.), *Larousse Dictionary of Writers*, Edinburgh, Larousse, 1994.

Grunebaum, Gustav von, 'The Sacred Character of Islamic Cities', in 'Abd al-Rahman Badawi (ed.), *Mélanges Taha Husain*, 25–37.

Grunebaum, Gustav von, *Modern Islam: The Search for Cultural Identity*, New York, Vintage Books, 1964.

Gurnah, Abdulrazak (ed.), *Essays on African Writing: 1: A Re-Evaluation*, Oxford, Heinemann, 1993.

Gurnah, Abdulrazak (ed.), *Essays on African Writing: 2: Contemporary Literature*, Oxford, Heinemann, 1993.

Ḥābībī, Emīl [= Habibi, Emile], *The Secret Life of Saeed, the Ill-Fated Pessoptimist* (trans. Salma Khadra Jayyusi and Trevor Le Gassick), New York, Vantage Press, 1982.

Hafez, Sabry, 'The Egyptian Novel in the Sixties', *Journal of Arabic Literature*, VII (1976), 68–84.

Hafez, Sabry, 'A Complete Bibliography of Collections of Egyptian Short Stories (1921–70)', *Journal of Arabic Literature*, XI (1980), 123–38.

Hafez, Sabry, *The Genesis of Arabic Narrative Discourse: A Study in the Sociology of Modern Arabic Literature*, London, Saqi Books, 1993.

Hafez, Sabry and Catherine Cobham (eds), *A Reader of Modern Arabic Short Stories*, London, Saqi Books, 1988.

Al-Haggagi, Ahmad Shams al-Din, 'The Mythmaker: Tayeb Salih' (trans. Omaima Abou-Bakr) in Ghazoul and Harlow (eds), *The View from Within*, 94–133.

Hair, P.E.H., 'A Layman's Guide to the Languages of the Sudan Republic', *Sudan Notes and Records*, XLVII (1966), 65–78.

Al-Ḥakīm, Tawfīq [= Al-Hakim, Tawfiq], *Bird from the East* (trans. R. Bayly Winder), Beirut, Khayyat, 1967.

Al-Ḥakīm, Tawfīq [= Al-Hakim, Tawfiq], *The Maze of Justice: Diary of a Country Prosecutor* (trans. by Abba Eban), London: Saqi Books, 1981 (1st ed. 1947).

Hamdi, Mohamed Elhachmi, *The Making of an Islamic Political Leader: Conversations with Hasan al-Turabi* (trans. Ashur A. Shamis), Boulder, Colorado, Westview press, 1998.

Hamilton, Edith, *Mythology*, Boston, Little, Brown and Company, 1942.

Ḥaqqī, Yaḥyā [=Haqqi, Yahya], *The Saint's Lamp and Other Stories* (trans. M.M. Badawi), Leiden, E.J. Brill, 1973.

Ḥaqqī, Yaḥyā [=Haqqi, Yahya], *Good Morning! And Other Stories* (trans. Miriam Cooke), Washington, Three Continents Press, 1987.

Hardy, Thomas, *Tess of the Durbervilles*, Middlesex, Penguin Books, 1983 (1st ed. 1891).

Harlow, Barbara, 'Othello's Season of Migration', Edebiyât, 4:2 (1979), 157–75. [A short version of this article was published under a different title, 'Sentimental Orientalism: Season of Migration to the North and Othello', in Amyuni (ed.), Tayeb Salih's Season of Migration to the North, 75–9.]

Harrow, Kenneth W., 'The Power and the Word: L'Aventure ambiguë and *the Wedding of Zein*', *African Studies Review*, 30;1 (March 1987), 63–78.

Harrow, Kenneth W. (ed.), *Faces of Islam in African Literature*, Oxford, James Currey Publishers, 1991.

Harrow, Kenneth W., 'Camara Laye, Cheikh Hamidou Kane, and Tayeb Salih: Three Sufi Authors', in idem (ed.), *Faces of Islam in African Literature*, 261–97.

Harrow, Kenneth W. (ed.), *The Marabout and the Muse New Approaches to Islam in African Literature*, London, James Currey Publishers, 1996.

Hassan, Awad, 'Novelist Tayeb Salih: The Writer's Mandate', *Sudanow* (March 1983), 48.

Hasson, Isaac, 'Muslim Literature in Praise of Jerusalem: *Faḍā'il al-Bayt al-Maqdis*', *The Jerusalem Cathedra*, I (1981), 168–84.

Haykal, Muhammad Husayn [= Haikal, Mohammed Hussein], *Zainab* (trans. John Mohammed Grinsted), London, Darf Publishers, 1989.

Haywood, John A., *Modern Arabic Literature 1800–1970*, New York, St. Martin's Press, 1971.

Hijab, Nadia, 'Meet the Maker of Modern Arab Mythology', *Middle East* 56 (June 1979), 66–8.

Hillelson, Sigmar, *Sudan Arabic Texts with Translation and Glossary*, Cambridge, Cambridge University Press, 1935.

Hobsbawm, Eric J. and Terence Ranger, *The Invention of Tradition*, Cambridge, Cambridge University Press, 1992.

Holt, P.M., *The Mahdist State in the Sudan, 1881–1898*, Oxford, Oxford University Press, 1958.

Holt, P.M., *A Modern History of the Sudan from the Funj Sultanate to the Present Time*, 2nd ed., London, Weidenfeld and Nicholson, 1963.

Hopwood, Derek, *Sexual Encounters in the Middle East: the British, the French and the Arabs*, Reading, Ithaca Press, 1999.

Hourani, Albert, *Arabic Thought in the Liberal Age 1798–1939*, Cambridge, Cambridge University Press, 1962.

Hourani, Albert, *Islam in European Thought*, Cambridge, Cambridge University Press, 1996 (1st ed. 1991).

Hout, Syrine Chafiq, *Viewing Europe from Outside: Cultural Encounters and European Culture Critique in Eighteenth-Century Pseudo-Oriental Travelogue and the Nineteenth-Century* '*Voyage en Orient*', New York, Peter Lang, 1997.

Hunwick, John O (ed.), *The Writing of Central Sudanic Africa, Arabic Literature of Africa*, vol. II, Leiden, New York, Koln, E.J Brill, 1995.

Ḥusayn, Ṭāhā [= Hussein, Taha], *An Egyptian Childhood*, vol. I (trans. E.H. Paxton), London, Heinemann, 1981 (1st ed. 1932); *The Stream of Days*, vol. II (trans. Hilary Wament), Cairo, Anglo-Egyptian, 1943; *A Passage to France*, vol. III (trans. Kenneth Cragg), Leiden, E.J. Brill, 1976.

Ibnlfasi, Laïla and Nicki Hitchcott (eds), *African Francophone Writing: A Critical Introduction*, Oxford, Berg, 1996.

Iser, Wolfgang, *The Act of Reading: A Theory of Aesthetic Response*, Baltimore and London, The Johns Hopkins University Press, 1980 (1st ed. 1978).

Al-Jabartī, 'Abd al-Raḥmān, *Al-Jabartī's Chronicle of the First Seven Months of the French Occupation of Egypt* (trans. Shmuel Moreh), Leiden, E.J. Brill, 1985.

Jabrā, Jabrā Ibrāhīm, 'Modern Arabic Literature and the West', *Journal of Arabic Literature*, 2 (1971), 76–91.

Jabrā, Jabrā Ibrāhīm [= Jabra, Jabra Ibrahim], *The Ship* (trans. Adnan Haydar and Roger Allen), Washington, D.C., Three Continents Press, 1985.

Jad, Ali B., *Form and Technique in the Egyptian Novel 1922–1971*, London, Ithaca Press, 1983.

James, Henry, *The Ambassadors*, 2nd ed., A Norton Critical Edition, New York, W.W. Norton, 1994 (1st ed. 1903).

Jayyusi, Salma Khadra, *Trends and Movements in Modern Arabic Poetry*, Leiden, E.J. Brill, 1977.

Jayyusi, Salma Khadra (ed.), *Modern Arabic Poetry: An Anthology*, New York, Columbia University Press, 1987.

Jayyusi, Salma Khadra and Roger Allen (eds), *Modern Arabic Drama: An Anthology*, Bloomington and Indianapolis, Indiana University Press, 1995.

John, Joseph, 'The Life and Death of Mustafa Saeed: Riddles Paradoxes, and Ambiguities', *Abhāth al-Yarmouk*, 5:1 (1987), 51–66.

John, Joseph, 'Mustafa Sa'eed's Othello Complex: An Analysis', *The Islamic Quarterly*, xxxiv:4 (1990), 260–78.

John, Joseph, 'A Dialogue with Mr Tayeb Salih on Season of Migration to the North', *The Islamic Quarterly*, xxxvi:3 (1992), 207–18.

John, Joseph and Yosif Tarawneh, 'Quest for Identity: The I-Thou Imbroglio in Tayeb Salih's *Season of Migration to the North*', *Arab Studies Quarterly*, 8:2 (spring 1986), 161–77.

Johnson-Davies, Denys (ed. and trans.), *Modern Arabic Short Stories*, London, Oxford University Press, 1967. reprinted in London, Heinemann, 1981.

Johnson-Davies, Denys, 'Profile: The World of Tayeb Salih', *Azure: The Review of Arab Literature, Arts and Culture*, 8 (1981), 15–20.

Johnson-Davies, Denys, (ed. and trans.), *Arabic Short Stories*, London, Melbourne and New York, Quartet Books, 1983.

Johnson-Davies, Denys, 'On Translating Arabic Literature: An Interview', in Ghazoul and Harlow (eds), *The View from Within*, 272–82.

Johnson-Davies, Denys, 'Translation is First and Foremost an Art and not a Science', *Banipal*, 9 (Autum 2000), 38–41.

Jones, Elder Durosimi (ed.), 'The Question of Language in African Literature Today', *African Literature Today*, 17 (1991).

Jordan, Elaine (ed.), *Joseph Conrad*, London, Macmillan, 1996.

Joyce, James, *A Portrait of the Artist as a Young Man*, London, Everyman's Library, 1991 (1st ed. 1916).

Joyce, James, *Ulysses*, London, Everyman's Library, 1994 (1st ed. 1922).

Kadi, Joanna (ed.), *Food for our Grandmothers: Writing by Arab-American and Arab-Canadian Feminists*, Boston, South End Press, 1994.

Kalila wa Dimna, An Animal Allegory of the Mongol Court (trans. and ed. Jill Sanchia Cowen), New York and Oxford University Press, 1989.

Kambal, Zaki El-Din, *The Thematic Concerns of Al-Ṭayyib Ṣāliḥ: A Study of his Short Stories and Novels*, University of Exeter, Ph.D. Dissertation, 1984.

Kambal, Zaki, 'The Process of Transfomation in al-Tayyib Salih's The Cypriot Man (al-Rajul al-Qubrusi)', *Gombak Review*, 1 ii (1996), 108–17.

Kanafānī, Ghassān [= Kanafani, Ghassan], *Men in the Sun and Other Palestinian Stories* (trans. Hilary Kilpatrick), Washington, D.C., Three Continents Press, 1978.

Kanafānī, Ghassān [= Kanafani, Ghassan], 'The Land of Sad Oranges' (trans. Hilary Kilpatrick) in Kanafani, *Men in the Sun* (trans. and ed. Hilary Kilpatrick), London, Heinemann, 1978, 57–62.

Kanafānī, Ghassān [= Kanafani, Ghassan], *All that Left to You* (trans. May Jayyusi and Jeremy Reed), Austin, University of Texas Press, 1990.

Kaplan, Carola M., 'Colonizers, Cannibals, and the Horror of Good Intentions in Joseph Conrad's *Heart of Darkness*', *Studies in Short Fiction*, 34:3 (Summer 1997), 331–2.

Kapteijns, Lidwien, *Mahdist Faith and Sudanic Tradition: The History of the Masālīt Sultanate 1870–1930*, London, Kegan Paul, 1985.

Karrar, Ali Salih, *The Sufi Brotherhoods in the Sudan*, London, C. Hurst, 1992.

Kaye, Alan S., *Chadian and Sudanese in the Light of Comparative Arabic Dialectology*, The Hague, Mouton, 1976.

Kaye, Jacqueline (ed.), *Maghreb: New Writing from North Africa*, York, Talus Editions and University of York, 1992.

Kaye, Jacqueline and Abdelhamid Zoubir, *The Ambiguous Compromise: Language, Literature and National Identity in Algeria and Morocco*, London, Routledge, 1990.

El Khadem, Saad, *Avant-Garde Egyptian Fiction: The Ulysses Trilogy* (trans. by Saad el-Gabalawy), Fredericton, New Brunswick, York Press, 1988.

Khairallah, As'ad E., 'The Traveling Theatre or the Art of Entertaining A Doomed Caravan with Amusing Stories' in Amyuni (ed.), Tayeb Salih's Season of Migration to the North, 95–111.

Khairallah, As'ad E., 'The Greek Cultural Heritage and the Odyssey of Modern Arab Poets', in Boullata and De Young (eds), *Tradition and Modernity in Arabic Literature*, 43–61.

Khairi, Awad H., 'The Writer's Mandate', *Sudanow* (March 1983), 48.

Khan, Ruqayya Y, 'Childhood and Modern Arabic Literature: The Initiation Story', *Arabic and Middle Eastern Literatures*, 4:2 (2001), 167–78.

Al-Khanji, Abd al-Rahman, 'Significance of Love in the World of Tayeb Salih', *Majallat Kulliyyat al-Ādāb*, Jāmi`at Umm Durmān al-Islāmiyya, 2 (1984–5).

Al-Kharrāṭ, Edwār [=Al-Kharrat, Edwar], *Rama and the Dragon* (trans. Ferial Ghazoul and John Verlender), Cairo, The American University in Cairo Press, 2002.

Khayyām, Omar, *Rubāiyāt of Omar Khayyām* (trans. Edward Fitzgerald), New York, Garden City Books, 1952.

Al-Khozai, Mohamed A., *The Development of Early Arabic Drama (1867–1900)*, London, Longman, 1984.

Khūrī, Ilyās [= Khoury, Elias], *Gates of the City* (trans. Paula Haydar), Minneapolis, University of Minnesota Press, 1993.

Kilpatrick, Hilary, 'Women and Literature in the Arab World, the Arab East', in Schipper (ed.), *Unheard Works*, 72–90.

King, Bruce (ed.), *New National and Post-Colonial Literatures: An Introduction*, Oxford, Oxford University Press, 1996.

Klein, Leonard S. (ed.), *Encyclopedia of World Literature in the 20th Century*, New York, Frederich Ungar Publishing, 1984.

Krishnan, R.S, 'Reinscribing Conrad: Tayeb Salih's *Season of Migration to the North*', *International Fiction Review*, 23:1–2 (1996), 7–15.

Lane, Edward William, *Arabic-English Lexicon*, Beirut, Librairie du Liban, 1968 (1st ed. 1863).

Larroux, Guy, *Le Mot de la fin: La clôture romanesque en question*, Paris, Nathan, 1995.

Le Gassick, Trevor, 'The Arabic Novel in English Translation' in Boullata (ed.). *The Arabic Novel since 1950*, 47–60.

Leach, Maria, *The Standard Dictionary of Folklore, Mythology and Legend*, New York, Funk and Wagnalls, 1950.

Lee, Robert A. (ed.), *William Faulkner: The Joknapatawpha Fiction*, London, Vision Press, New York, St. Martin's Press, 1990.

Lewis, Bernard, *The Middle East and the West*, London, Weidenfeld and Nicholson, 1964.

Lewis, Bernard, *The Muslim Discovery of Europe*, London, Weidenfeld and Nicholson, 1982.

Liyong, T.L., 'Tayeb Salih's concluded *Season of Migration to the North*: An Exercise in a Subjective, Development Oriented Approach to African (and third world) Literary Discussion' in Ismail H. Abdalla with D.S. Conyers (eds), *Perspectives and Challenges in the Development of Sudanese Studies*, Lewiston, Queenston and Lampeter, Edwin Mellen Press, 1993, 265–85.

MacLean, Katrina, 'Poetic Themes in Yahyā Hāqqī's *Qindil Umm Hāshim*', *Journal of Arabic Literature*, XI (1980), 80–7.

Maḥfūẓ, Najīb [= Mahfouz, Naguib], *Middaq Alley* (trans. Trevor Le Gassick), Beirut, Khayyat, 1966.

Maḥfūẓ, Najīb [= Mahfouz, Naguib], *God's World (Short Stories)* ((trans. Akef Abadin and Roger Allen), Minneapolis and Chicago, Bibliotheca Islamica, 1973.

Maḥfūẓ, Najīb [= Mahfouz, Naguib], *Miramar* (trans. Fatma Moussa-Mahmoud), Cairo, General Egyptian Book Organization, 1978.

Maḥfūẓ, Najīb [= Mahfouz, Naguib], *Children of Gebelawi* (trans. Philip Stewart), London, Heinemann, 1981.

Maḥfūẓ, Najīb [= Mahfouz, Naguib], 'Zaabalawi', (trans. Denys Johnson-Davies) in Johnson-Davies (ed.), *Modern Arabic Short Stories*, London, Heinemann, 1981, 135–45.

Maḥfūẓ, Najīb [= Mahfouz, Naguib], *The Thief and the Dogs* (trans. Trevor Le Gassick and M.M. Badawi, revised by John Rodenbeck), Cairo, The American University in Cairo Press, 1984.

Maḥfūẓ, Najīb [= Mahfouz, Naguib], *Autumn Quail* (trans. Roger Allen, revised by John Rodenbeck), Cairo, The American University in Cairo Press, 1985.

Maḥfūẓ, Najīb [= Mahfouz, Naguib], *The Beggar* (trans. Kristin Walker Henry and Nariman Khales Naili al-Warraki), Cairo, The American University in Cairo Press, 1986.

Maḥfūẓ, Najīb [= Mahfouz, Naguib], *The Search* (trans. Mohamid Islam; ed. Magdi Wahba), Cairo, The American University in Cairo Press, 1987.

Maḥfūẓ, Najīb [= Mahfouz, Naguib], *The Day the Leader Was Killed* (trans. Malak Hashem), Cairo, General Egyptian Book Organization, 1989.

Maḥfūẓ, Najīb [= Mahfouz, Naguib], *Palace Walk*, Volume One of *The Cairo Trilogy* (trans. William M. Hutchins and Olive E. Kenny), Cairo, The American University in Cairo Press, 1990.

Maḥfūẓ, Najīb [= Mahfouz, Naguib], *Palace of Desire* (trans. William M. Hutchins and Olive E. Kenny), New York, Doubleday, 1991.

Maḥfūẓ, Najīb [= Mahfouz, Naguib], *Sugar Street* (trans. William M. Hutchins and Botros Samaan), New York, Doubleday, 1992.

Maḥfūẓ, Najīb [= Mahfouz, Naguib], *Adrift on the Nile* (trans. Frances Liadet), Cairo, The American University in Cairo Press, 1993.

Maḥfūẓ, Najīb, [= Mahfouz, Naguib], *The Harafish* (trans. Catherine Cobham), Cairo, The American University in Cairo Press, 1994.

Maḥfūẓ, Najīb, [= Mahfouz, Naguib], *Thebes at War* (trans. Humphrey Davies), Cairo, The American University in Cairo Press, 2003.

Mahjoub, Jamal, *Navigation of a Rainmaker*, Oxford, Heinemann, African Writers Series, 1989.

Mahjoub, Jamal, *Wings of Dust*, Oxford, Heinemann, African Writers Series, 1994.

Mahmoud, Mohamed, 'The Unchanging Hero in a Changing World: Najīb Mahfūz's *al-Liss wa'l-Kilāb*', *Journal of Arabic Literature*, XV (1984), 58–75.

Majaj, Lisa Suhair, 'Talking with Poet Naomi Shihab Nye', *al-Jadid* 13 (November-December 1996), 4–5, 22.

Makarius, Paul and Laura, *Anthologie de la littérature arabe contemporaine*, Paris, Editions du Seuil, 1964.

Makdisi, Saree S., 'The Empire Renarrated: *Season of Migration to the North and the Reinvention of the Present*', *Critical Inquiry*, 18, (Summer 1992), 804–20. [Published under the same title in Patrick Williams and Laura Chrisman (eds), *Colonial Discourse and Post-Colonial Theory: A Reader*, London, Harvester Wheatsheaf, 1994, 535–50].

Mann, Thomas, 'Tonio Kröger' in *Death in Venice, Tristam, Tonio Kröger* (trans. H.T. Lower-Porter), London, Penguin Books, 1995 (1st ed. 1928).

Matar, Nabil, 'Tayeb Salih's *Season of Migration to the North*: Circles of Deceit' in Takieddine Amyuni (ed.), *Tayeb Salih's Season of Migration to the North*, 113–22.

Al-Māzinī, Ibrāhīm 'Abd al-Qādir (Al-Mazini, Ibrahim), *Ibrahim the Writer* (trans. Magdi Wahba), Cairo, General Egyptian Book Organization, 1976.

McHugh, Neil, *Holymen of the Blue Nile: The Making of an Arab-Islamic Community in the Nilotic Sudan, 1500–1850*, Evanston, Northwestern University Press, 1994.

McKean Parmenter, Barbara, *Giving Voice to Stones: Place and Identity in Palestinian Literature*, Austin, University of Texas Press, 1994.

Mehrez, Samia, *Egyptian Writers Between History and Fiction: Essays on Naguib Mahfouz, Sonallah Ibrahim, and Gamal al-Ghitani*, Cairo, The American University in Cairo Press, 1994.

Meisami, Julie Scott and Paul Starkey (eds), *Encyclopedia of Arabic Literature*, London, Routledge, 1998.

Memmi, Albert (ed.), *Écrivains francophones du Maghreb: Anthologie*, Paris, Editions Seghers, 1985.

Memmi, Albert, *The Colonizer and the Colonized* (trans. Howard Greenfeld), Boston, Beacon Press, 1991.

Merriam-Webster's Encyclopedia of Literature, Massachusetts, Merriam-Webster, 1995.

Meyer, Stefan G., *The Experimental Arabic Novel, Postcolonial Literary Modernism in the Levant*, New York, State University of New York Press, 2001.

Mikhail, Mona N., *Studies in the Short Fiction of Mahfouz and Idris*, New York, New York University Press, 1992.

Milson, Menahem, 'Najīb Maḥfūẓ and the Quest for Meaning', *Arabica*, 17 (1970), 155–86.

Milson, Menahem, 'Medieval and Modern Intellectual Traditions in the Arab World', *Daedalus*, 101 (summer 1972), 17–37.

Milson, Menahem, 'Reality, Allegory and Myth in the Work of Najīb Maḥfūẓ', *Asian and African Studies*, 11:2 (1976), 157–79.

Milson, Menahem, 'Najīb Maḥfūẓ and Jamāl 'Abd al-Nāṣir: The Writer as a Political Critic' in Elad [-Bouskila] (ed.), *Writer, Culture, Text*, 9–25.

Milson, Menahem, *Najib Mahfuz: The Novelist-Philosopher of Cairo*, New York and Jerusalem, St. Martin's Press, The Magnes Press, 1998.

Milton, John, *Paradise Lost*, fourteenth impression, London, Longman, 1991 (1st published 1667).

Mīna, Ḥannā [= Mina, Hannah], *Fragments of Memory: A Story of a Syrian Family* (trans. Olive Kenny and Lorne Kenne), Austin, University of Texas, 1993.

Mishra, Pankaj, 'A Spirit of Their Own', *The New York Review of Books*, (May 20, 1999), 47–53.

Moosa, Matti, *The Origins of Modern Arabic Fiction*, 2nd ed., Boulding and London, A Three Continents Book, Lynne Rienner Publishers, 1997 (1st ed. 1983).

Morrison, Toni, *Beloved*, New York, New American Library, 1987.

Al-Mousa, Nedal, 'The Nature and Uses of the Fantastic in the Fictional World of Naguib Mahfouz', *Journal of Arabic Literature*, XXIII:1 (1992), 36–48.

Al-Mousa, Nedal, 'The Arabic *Bildungsroman*: A Generic Appraisal', *International Journal of Middle East Studies*, 25 (1993), 223–40.

Moussa-Mahmoud, Fatma, *The Arabic Novel in Egypt: 1914–1970*, Cairo, The Egyptian General Book Organization, 1973.

Moussa-Mahmoud, Fatma, 'A New Oriental Bird with Leaden Wings: On Saad El-Khadem's *Ajniha min Raṣāṣ*', *International Fiction Review*, 2 (1975), 67–70.

Munīf, 'Abd al-Raḥmān [= Munif, Abdelrahman], *Cities of Salt* (trans. Peter Theroux), London, Jonathan Cape, 1988 (1st ed. 1987).

Munīf, 'Abd al-Raḥmān [= Munif, Abdelrahman], *Endings* (trans. Roger Allen), London, Quartet Books, 1988.

Munīf, 'Abd al-Raḥmān [= Munif, Abdelrahman], *The Trench* (trans. Peter Theroux), New York, Pantheon Books, 1991.

Munīf, 'Abd al-Raḥmān [= Munif, Abdelrahman], *Variations on Night and Day* (trans. Peter Theroux), New York, Vintage Books, 1994 (1st ed. 1993).

Mūsā, Ṣabrī [= Moussa, Sabri], *Seeds of Corruption* (trans. Mona Mikhail), Boston, Houghton Mifflin, 1980.

Myers, Richard K., 'The Problem of Authority: Franz Kafka and Nagib Mahfuz', *Journal of Arabic Literature*, XVII (1986), 82–96.

Naddaff, Sandra, *Arabesque, Narrative Structure and the Aesthetics of Repetition in the 1001 Nights*, Evanston, Northwestern University Press, 1991.

El-Nagar, Kamal A. and Salah Hassan, 'Tayeb Salih: Patterns and Ambiguities', *Sudanow*, 77 (December 1977), 51.

Nash, Geoffrey P., *The Arab Writer in English, Arab Themes in a Metropolitan Language, 1908–1958*, Brighton and Portland, Sussex Academic Press, 1998.

Nasr, Ahmad, 'Popular Islam in al-Tayyib Sālih', *Journal of Arabic Literature*, XI (1980), 88–103.

Naṣrallāh, Ibrāhīm [= Nasrallah, Ibrahim], *Prairies of Fever* (trans. May Jayyusi and Jeremy Reed), New York, Interlink Books, 1993.

Nassar, Christopher S., 'Beckett's *Waiting for Godot* and Salih's *Season of Migration to the North*', *Explicator*, 56:2 (Winter 1998), 105–8.

Nazareth, Peter (ed.), 'African Writing Today', *Pacific Moana Quarterly*, VI, 3/4 (July-October 1981).

Nazareth, Peter, 'Out of Darkness: Conrad and Other Third World Writers', *Conradiana*, 14:3 (December 1982), 173–87.

Nazareth, Peter, 'The Narrator as Artist and the Reader as Critic in *Season of Migration to the North*', in Takieddine Amyuni (ed.), Tayeb Salih's Season of Migration to the North, 123–34.

Neilands, Robin, *The Dervish Wars: Gordon and Kitchener in the Sudan 1800–1898*, London, Murray, 1996.

Nicholson, Reynold A., *A Literary History of the Arabs*, Cambridge, Cambridge University Press, 1956.

Nuttall, Anthony David, *Openings: Narrative Beginnings from the Epic to the Novel*, Oxford, Oxford University Press, 1992.

O'Connor, Evangeline M. (eds), *Who's Who and What's What in Shakespeare*, New York, Gramercy Books, 1996.

O'Fahey, R.S. (ed.), *The Writing of Eastern Sudanic Africa TC. 1900 Arabic Literature of Africa*, vol. I, Leiden, New York, Koln, E.J. Brill, 1994.

Ostle, Robin C. (ed.), *Studies in Modern Arabic Literature*, Warminster, Aris and Phillips, 1975.

Ostle, Robin C., 'Maḥmūd al-Mas'adī and Tunisia's "Lost Generation"', *Journal of Arabic Literature*, XVIII (1977), 153–66.

Ostle, Robin C., 'The City in Modern Arabic Literature', *Bulletin of the School of Oriental and African Studies*, XLIX:1 (1986), 193–202.

Ostle, Robin C. (ed.), *Modern Literature in the Near and Middle East 1850–1970*, London, Routledge, 1991.

Ostle, Robin C. (ed.), *The Quest for Freedom in Modern Arabic Literature, Journal of Arabic Literature*, XXVI:1–2 (March-June 1995).

Ostle, Robin, Ed De Moor, and Stefan Wild, (eds), *Writing the Self: Autobiographical Writing in Modern Arabic Literature*, London, Saqi Books, 1998.

Parker, Michael and Roger Starkey (eds), *Postcolonial Literatures: Achebe, Ngugi, Desai, Walcott*, London, Macmillan Press, 1995.

Peled, Mattityahu, 'Portrait of an Intellectual', *Middle Eastern Studies*, XIII, 2 (1977), 218–28.

Philip, Vellacott, *Sophocles and Oedipus, A Study of Oedipus Tyrannus*, Ann Arbor, University of Michigan Press, 1971.

Piamenta, Moshe, *Islam in Everyday Arabic Speech*, Leiden, E.J. Brill, 1979.

Pinault, David, *Story-Telling Techniques in the Arabian Nights*, Leiden, E.J. Brill, 1992.

Al-Qadi, Wadad (ed.), *Studia Arabica and Islamica: Festchrift for Ihsan Abbas on his Sixtith Birthday*, Beirut, Imprimerie Catholique, 1981.

Al-Qa'īd, Muḥammad Yūsuf [= Al-Qaid, Mohammed Yusuf], *News from the Menesi Farm* (trans. Marie-Therese F. Abdel-Messih), Cairo, General Egyptian Book Organization, 1987.

Qāsim, 'Abd al-Ḥakīm [= Kassem, Abdel-Hakim], 'The Trial of the Small Black Woman', in Denys Johnson-Davies (ed. and trans.), *Arabic Short Stories*, 137–42.

Qāsim, 'Abd al-Ḥakīm [= Kassem, Abdel-Hakim], *The Seven Days of Man* (trans. Joseph N. Bell), Cairo, General Egyptian Book Organization, 1989.

Qāsim, 'Abd al-Ḥakīm [= Kassem, Abd al-Hakim], *Rites of Assent: Two Novellas* (trans. Peter Theroux), Philadelphia, Temple University Press, 1995.

Al-Raheb, Hani, 'Two Invasions and One Tragic End: The Dialectics of North and South in Conrad's *Heart of Darkness* and Salih's *Season of Migration to the North*', *New Comparison*, 17 (1994), 50–66.

Al-Rawi, Karim, 'The Village and the World: Tayeb Salih', *Afkār Inquiry*, 2:iii (1985), 72–3.

Rimmon-Kenan, Shlomith, *Narrative Fiction: Contemporary Poetics*, London, Routledge, 1996 (1st ed. 1983).

Richter, David H (ed.), *Falling into Theory: Conflicting Views on Reading Literature*, Boston, Bedford Books of St. Martin's Press, 1994.

Rooke, Tetz, *In My Childhood: A Study of Arabic Autobiography*, Stockholm, Almquist and Wiksell International, Stockholm University, Stockholm Oriental Studies, 15, 1992.

Rosenhouse, Judith and Ami Elad-Bouskila (eds), *Linguistic and Cultural Studies in Arabic and Hebrew*, Wiesbaden, Harrassowitz Verlag, 2001.

Rosenthal, Franz, *A History of Muslim Historiography*, 2nd ed., Leiden, E.J. Brill, 1968.

Roth-Laly, Arlette, *Lexique des parlers arabes Tchado-Sudanais (An Arabic-English-French Lexicon of the Dialects Spoken in the Chad-Sudan Area)*, Paris, Edition du Centre National de la Recherche Scientifique, 1969–72.

Rugh, William A., *The Arab Press, News Media and Political Process in the Arab World*, 2nd ed., Syracuse, New York, Syracuse University Press, 1987.

Said, Edward W., *Joseph Conrad and the Fiction of Autobiography*, Cambridge, Mass, Harvard University Press, 1966.

Said, Edward W., *Orientalism:* New York, Pantheon Books, 1978.

Said, Edward W., *The World, the Text and the Critic*, London, Boston, Faber and Faber, 1984.

Said, Edward W., *Beginnings, Intention and Method*, New York, Columbia University Press, 1985.

Said, Edward, 'Embargoed Literature', *The Nation* (17 September, 1990), 278–81.

Said, Edward W., 'The Politics of Knowledge', in Richter (ed.), *Falling into Theory*, 193–204.

Sakkut, Hamdi, *The Egyptian Novel and its Main Trends from 1913 to 1952*, Cairo, The American University in Cairo Press, 1971.

Sakkut, Hamdi, 'Naguib Mahfouz and the Sufi Way' (trans. Noha Radwan), in Ghazoul and Harlow (eds), *The View from Within*, 90–8.

Salih, Mahmud Husein and Naser Y. al-Hassan Athamneh, 'Silence in Arabic-English Translation: The Case of Salih's *Season of Migration to the North*', *Babel*, 41:4, (1995), 216–33.

Ṣāliḥ, al-Ṭayyib [= Salih, Tayeb], 'C'est ainsi Messieurs' (trans. and ed. Paul and Laura Makarius) in Makarius, *Anthologie*, 397–404.

Ṣāliḥ, al-Ṭayyib [= Salih, Tayeb], 'The Doum Tree of Wad Hamid' (ed.. and trans. Denys Johnson-Davies), in *Modern Arabic Short Stories*, 83–94.

Ṣāliḥ, al-Ṭayyib [= Salih, Tayeb], *The Wedding of Zein and Other Stories* (trans. Denys Johnson-Davies), London, Heinemann, 1968.

Ṣāliḥ, al-Ṭayyib [= Salih, Tayeb], *Season of Migration to the North* (trans. Denys Johnson-Davies), London, Heinemann, 1969.

Ṣāliḥ, al-Ṭayyib [= Salih, Tayeb], 'A Handful of Dates' (trans. Denys Johnson-Davies), in T. Salih, *The Wedding of Zein and Other Stories*, 1969, 1–20.

Ṣāliḥ, al-Ṭayyib [= Salih, Tayeb], *The Wedding of Zein and Other Stories* (trans. Denys Johnson-Davies), London, Heinemann, African Authors Series, 1970 (1st ed. 1969).

Ṣāliḥ, al-Ṭayyib [= Salih, Tayeb], *The Wedding of Zein and Other Stories* (trans. Denys Johnson-Davies), London, Heinemann, Arab Authors Series, 1970.

Ṣāliḥ, al-Ṭayyib [= Salih, Tayeb], *The Wedding of Zein and Other Stories* (trans. Denys Johnson-Davies), London, Heinemann, 1971

Ṣāliḥ, al-Ṭayyib [= Salih, Tayeb], *Le Migrateur* (trans. Fady Noum), Paris, Sindbad, La Bibliotéque Arabe, Litteratures, 1972.

Ṣāliḥ, al-Ṭayyib [= Salih, Tayeb], *The Wedding of Zein and Other Stories* (trans. Denys Johnson-Davies), London, Heinemann, 1975.

Ṣāliḥ, al-Ṭayyib [= Salih, Tayeb], *Season of Migration to the North* (trans. Denys Johnson-Davies), London, Heinemann, reprinted with corrections, 1976.

Ṣāliḥ, al-Ṭayyib [= Salih, Tayeb], 'A Handful of Dates' (trans. Denys Johnson-Davies), *Azure*, 1 (1977), 44–6.

Ṣāliḥ, al-Ṭayyib [= Salih, Tayeb], *The Wedding of Zein and Other Stories* (trans. Denys Johnson-Davies), London, Heinemann, Arab Authors Series, 1978, 29–120.

Ṣāliḥ, al-Ṭayyib [= Salih, Tayeb], *Season of Migration to the North* (trans. Denys Johnson-Davies), London, Heinemann, 1978.

Ṣāliḥ, al-Ṭayyib [= Salih, Tayeb], *Season of Migration to the North: The Wedding of Zein* (trans. Denys Johnson-Davies), London, Quartet Books, 1980.

Ṣāliḥ, al-Ṭayyib [= Salih, Tayeb], 'A Letter to Aileen, by al-Ṭayyib Ṣāliḥ' (trans. N.S. Doniach), *Journal of Arabic Literature*, XI (1980), 76–9.

Ṣāliḥ, al-Ṭayyib [= Salih, Tayeb], 'The Cypriot Man' (trans. Denys Johnson-Davies), *Azure*, 8, 1981, 25–7.

Ṣāliḥ, al-Ṭayyib [= Salih, Tayeb], 'The Cypriot Man' (trans. Denys Johnson Davies), in Johnson-Davies (ed. and trans.), *Arabic Short Stories*, 75–83.

Ṣāliḥ, al-Ṭayyib [= Salih, Tayeb], 'The Cypriot Man' (trans. Constance E. Berkley), in Osman Hassan Ahmed (ed.), *Sixteen Sudanese Short Stories*, 1981, 9–15.

Ṣāliḥ, al-Ṭayyib [= Salih, Tayeb], 'A Date Palm by the Stream' (trans. Denys Johnson-Davies), *Azure*, 8 (1981), 21–4.

Ṣāliḥ, al-Ṭayyib [= Salih, Tayeb], *Die Hochzeit des Zain* (trans. Stefan Reichmuth), Berlin, Edition Orient, 1983.

Ṣāliḥ, al-Ṭayyib [= Salih, Tayeb], *Saison de la migration vers le nord* (trans. Abdelwahab Meddeb and Fady Noum), Paris, Sindbad, La Bibliotheque Arabe, Literatures, 1983.

Ṣāliḥ, al-Ṭayyib [= Salih, Tayeb], *Bandarchāh* (trans. Anne Wade Minkowski), Paris, Sindbad, La Bibliotheque Arabe, 1985.

Ṣāliḥ, al-Ṭayyib [= Salih, Tayeb], *Dos Novellas Sudanesas* (trans. M. Nuim), Madrid: Cantarabia, 1987 (*La Boda de Zayn: Bandar Shah*)

Ṣāliḥ, al-Ṭayyib [= Salih, Tayeb], 'A Handful of Dates' (trans. Denys Johnson-Davies), in Achebe and Innes (eds), *African Short Stories*, 90–4.

Ṣāliḥ, al-Ṭayyib [= Salih, Tayeb], 'The Doum Tree of Wad Hamid' (trans. Denys Johnson-Davies) in D. Lee Bowen and E.A. Early (eds),*Everyday Life in the Muslim Middle East*, Bloomington, Indiana University Press, 1993, 136–45.

Ṣāliḥ, al-Ṭayyib [= Salih, Tayeb], 'The Doum Tree of Wad Hamid' (trans. Denys Johnson-Davies) in A.W. Biddle (ed.), *Global Voices: Contemporary Literature from the Non-Western World*, Englewood Cliffs, Prentice Hall, 1995, 512–22.

Ṣāliḥ, al-Ṭayyib [= Salih, Tayeb], *Bandarshah* (trans. Denys Johnson-Davies), London and New York, Kegan Paul International, Paris, UNESCO Publishing, 1996.

Ṣāliḥ, al-Ṭayyib [= Salih, Tayeb], *Les Noces de Zeyn et autres récits* (trans. A. Wade Minkowski), Arles, Sindbad, 1996.

Schimmel, Annemarie, *Mystical Dimensions of Islam*, Chapel Hill: The University of North Carolina Press, 1975.

Schipper, Mineke (ed.), *Unheard Words, Women and Literature in Africa, The Arab World, Asia, The Caribbean and Latin America*, London, Allison and Busby, 1985.

Seikaly, Samir, '*Season of Migration to the North*: History in the Novel', in Amyuni (ed.), Tayeb Salih's Season of Migration to the North, 135–41.

Shaheen, Mohammad, 'Tayeb Salih's Mustafa Sa'eed: The Southern Invader in an Icy Battlefield', *Arab Journal for the Humanities* (*al-Majalla al-'Arabīya li'l-'Ulūm al-Insāniyya*), 4:16 (Fall 1984), 281–92.

Shaheen, Mohammad, 'Tayeb Salih and Wad Hamid: An Alternation of Vision', *Arab Journal for Humanities* (*al-Majalla al-'Arabiyya li'l-'Ulūm al-Insāniyya*), 5:17 (Winter 1985), 276–86.

Shaheen, Mohammad, 'Tayeb Salih and Conrad', *Comparative Literature Studies*, 22; (1985), 156–71.

Shaheen, Mohammad, *The Modern Arabic Short Story: Shahrazad Returns*, London, Macmillan Press, 1989.

Al-Shahi, Ahmed and Francis Charles Timothy Moore, *Wisdom from the Nile: A Collection of Folk-Stories from Northern and Central Sudan*, Oxford, Oxford University Press, 1978.

Shakespeare, William, *Hamlet*, London, Longmans, 1968 (1st ed. 1601).

Shakespeare, William, *Othello* (edited by Norman Sanders), Cambridge, Cambridge University Press, 1995 (1st ed. 1604).

Shammās, Anṭōn (=Shammas Anton), *Arabesques* (trans. Vivian Eden), New York, Harper and Row, 1988.

Sharabi, Hisham, *Arab Intellectuals and the West: The Formative Years 1875–1914*, Baltimore, The Johns Hopkins Press, 1970.

Sharkey, Heather, 'The Sudan's Ex-Slaves: A Study of Tayeb Salih's *The Wedding of Zein*', *Sudan Studies*, 11 (1992), 18–23.

Sharkey, Heather J., 'A Century in Print: Arabic Journalism and Nationalism in Sudan, 1899–1999', *International Journal of Middle East Studies*, 31:4 (1999), 531–49.

Al-Sharqāwī, 'Abd al-Raḥmān [=Sharkawi, A.R], *Egyptian Earth* (trans. Desmond Stewart), Delhi, Hind Pocket Books, 1972 (1st ed. 1962).

Shawabkeh, Mohammed Ali, *Arabs and the West: A Study in Modern Arabic Novel 1935–1985*, Karak, Mu'tah University, 1992.

Al-Shaykh, Ḥanān [= Al-Shaykh, Hanan], *The Story of Zahra* (rendered into English by Peter Ford with the author's cooperation), London, Quartet Books, 1986.

Al-Shaykh, Ḥanān [= Al-Shaykh, Hanan], *Women of Sand and Myrrh* (trans. Catherine Cobham), London and New York, Quartet Books, 1989.

Al-Shaykh, Ḥanān [= Al-Shaykh, Hanan], *Beirut Blues* (trans. Catherine Cobham), London, Chatto and Windus, 1995.

Al-Shaykh, Ḥanān [= Al-Shaykh, Hanan], *Only in London* (trans. Catherine Cobham), London, Bloomsbury Publishing, 2001.

Shikova, E (ed.), *al-Ṭayyib Ṣāliḥ's Three Novels*, Moscow, Raduga, 1982.

Shipley, Joseph T. (ed.), *Dictionary of World Literature*, Totowa, New Jersey, Littlefield, Adams, 1972 (1st ed. 1953).

Shoush, M.I., 'Background Notes on Modern Sudanese Poetry', *Sudan Notes and Records*, 44 (1963), 21–42.

Shukry, Ghali, 'The Beginnings of the New Generation in the Arabic Novel', *Lotus* (July 1972), 43–59.

Siddiq, Muhammad, 'The Process of Individuation in al-Ṭayyib Ṣāliḥ's Novel *Season of Migration to the North*', *Journal of Arabic Literature*, IX (1978), 67–104.

Siddiq, Muhammad, 'Deconstructing the Saint's Lamp', *Journal of Arabic Literature*, XVII (1986), 126–45.

Sivan, Emannuel, 'The Beginnings of the *Faḍā'il al-Quds* Literature', *Israel Oriental Studies*, I (1971), 263–71.

Smart, Jack R. (ed.), *Tradition and Modernity in Arabic Language and Literature*, Richmond, Curzon, 1996.

Smith, Bayron Porter, *Islam in English Literature*, 2nd ed., Delmar, New York, Caravan Books, 1975 (1st ed. 1939).

Somekh, Sasson, 'Za'balāwī: Author, Theme and Technique', *Journal of Arabic Literature*, I (1970), 24–35.

Somekh, Sasson, *The Changing Rhythm: A Study of Najīb Maḥfūẓ's Novels*, Leiden, E.J. Brill, 1973.

Somekh, Sasson, *Genre and Language in Modern Arabic Literature*, Wiesbaden, Otto Harrassowitz, 1991.

Sophocles, *Oedipus Tyrannus* (Trans. Philip Vellacott), Ann Arbor, University of Michagen Press, 1971.

Soueif, Ahdaf, *In the Eye of the Sun*, London, Bloomsbury, 1992.

Soueif, Ahdaf, *The Map of Love*, London, Bloomsbury, 1999.

Soyinka, Wole, *Myth, Literature and the African World*, Cambridge, Cambridge University Press, 1976.

Stagh, Marina, *The Limits of Freedom of Speech: Prose Literature and Prose Writers in Egypt under Nasser and Sadat*, Stockholm, Almqvist Wiksell International, 1993.

Starkey, Paul, *From the Ivory Tower: A Critical Study of Tawfiq al-Hakīm*, London, Ithaca Press, 1987.

Starkey, Paul, 'From the City of the Dead to Liberation Square: The Novels of Yūsuf al-Qa'īd', *Journal of Arabic Literature*, 24 (1995), 62–74.

Starkey, Paul, 'Narrative Structure in al-Ṭayyib Ṣāliḥ's *Mawsim al-Hijra ilā al-Shamāl*', in Elad-Bouskila and al-Shahi (eds), *Al-Ṭayyib Ṣāliḥ*, *Edebiyât*, 33–42.

Steingass, Francis Joseph, *A Comprehensive Persian-English Dictionary*, second impression, London, Kegan Paul Trench Trubna, 1930 (1st ed. 1892).

Stendhal, (Henri Beyle), *The Red and the Black* (trans. Catherine Slater), Oxford, Oxford University Press, 1991 (1st ed. 1830).

Stepanov, L, 'Between the Past and the Future' (trans. from the Russian into English by Ella London), in Shikova (ed.), *al-Tayyib Salih's Three Novels*, 3–14.

Stiansen, Endre and Michael Kevane (eds), *Kordofan Invaded, Peripheral Incorporation and Social Transfomation in Islamic Africa*, Leiden, Boston and Köln, E.J. Brill, 1998.

Stringer, Jenny (ed.), *The Oxford Companion to Twentieth Century Literature in English*, Oxford, Oxford University Press, 1996.

Sturrock, John (ed.), *The Oxford Guide to Contemporary Writing*, Oxford, Oxford University Press, 1996.

Suleiman, Susan, 'Ideological Dissent from Works of Fiction: Toward a Rhetoric of the *Roman à Thèse*', *Neophilologus*, 60:2 (April 1976), 162–77.

Sviri, Sara, 'On Trees, Dreams, and Holy Men: Notes on al-Ṭayyib Ṣāliḥ's The Doum Tree of Wad Hāmid', in Elad-Bouskila and Al-Shahi (eds), *Al-Ṭayyib Ṣāliḥ, Edebiyât*, 103–22.

Tarawneh, Yosif and John, J., 'Tayeb Salih and Freud: The Impact of Freudian Ideas on *Season of Migration to the North*', *Arabica*, 35 (1988), 328–49.

Tejani, Bahadur, '*The Wedding of Zein*: Short Stories by Tayeb Salih', *Zuka*, 4 (December 1969), 55–6.

Thacher, Jean-Louise N., *An Annotated Partial Bibliography of Contemporary Middle Eastern and North African Poetry, Prose, Dreams and Folktales*,6th ed., Austin Texas, A Middle East Outreach Council Publication, 1998.

Thompson, Smith, *Motif: Index of Folk Literature*, Indiana, Indiana University Press, 1958.

Al-Toma, Salih J., *The Problem of Diglossia in Arabic: A Contemporary Study of Classical and Iraqi Arabic*, Harvard, The Center for Middle East Studies of Harvard University, Harvard University Press, 1969.

Al-Toma, Salih J., *Modern Arabic Literature: A Bibliography of Articles, Books, Dissertations and Translations in English*, Bloomington, Asian Studies Research Center, Indiana University, 1975.

Tomiche, Nada, *La Littérature arabe traduite; mythes et réalités*, Paris, Librairie Orientaliste Paul Geuthner, Supplément 9, 1978.

Tompkins, Jane (ed.), *Reader-Response Criticism: From Formalism to Post-Structuralism*, Baltimore and London, The Johns Hopkins University Press, 1992.

Trimingham, John Spencer, *Sudan Colloquial Arabic*, London, Oxford University Press, 1946 (1st ed. 1939).

Trimingham, John Spencer, *Islam in the Sudan*, London, Frank Cass, 1965 (1st ed. 1949).

Trimingham, John Spencer, *The Sufi Orders in Islam*, Oxford, Oxford University Press, 1971.

Tube, Henry, Vivication: (*Season of Migration to the North*), *Spectator* (20 September 1969), 374.

Al-Udhari, Abdullah (ed. and trans.), *Victims of a Map: A Bilingual Anthology of Arabic Poetry*, London, Saqi Books, 1984.

Voll, John Obert and Carolyn Fluer-Lobban, *Historical Dictionary of the Sudan*, 2nd ed., New Jersey: Scarecrow, Methuen, 1992.

Warburg, Gabriel R., *Historical Discord in the Nile Valley*, London, Hurst and Co., 1992.

Wehr, Hans, *A Dictionary of Modern Written Arabic*, 4th ed., Wiesbaden, Otto Harrassowitz, 1979.

Weidner, Stefan, 'The Logic of Fame: A Biography of Tayib Salih – or is it Autobiography?', *Banipal*, 2 (June 1998), 70.

Wellek, René and Austin Warren, *Theory of Literature*, Harmondsworth, Penguin Books, 1982 (1st ed. 1942).

Wielandt, Rotraud, 'The Problem of Cultural Identity in the Writings of al-Tayyib Sālih' in al-Qadi (ed.), *Studia Arabica and Islamica*, 487–515.

Williams, Patrick and Christmas Laura (eds), *Colonial Discourse and Post-Colonial Theory: A Reader*, London, Harvester Wheatsheaf, 1994.

Wilson, Richard, 'Tayeb Salih's *The Wedding of Zein*', Sheffield Papers on Literature and Society, Sheffield University, 1976.

Young, Barbara, *This Man From Lebanon*, New York, Knopf, 1959.

Young, M.J.L. et al. (eds), *The Cambridge History of Arabic Literature: Religion, Learning and Science in the 'Abbasid Period*, Cambridge, Cambridge University Press, 1990.

Zeidan, Joseph T., *Arab Women Novelists: The Formative Years and Beyond*, Albany, State University of New York Press, 1995.

INDEX

Abbasid Caliphs, The, 155
'Abd Allāh, 'Arafāt Muḥammad, 8
'Abd Allāh, Malikat al-Dār Muḥammad, 8
'Abd Allāh, Muḥammad 'Abd al-Ḥalīm, 186
'Abd al-Ḥayy, Muḥammad, 13
'Abd al-Ṣabūr, Ṣalāḥ, 157
Abū Bakr, 'Uthmān, 13
Abū Māḍī, Īlyā, 183
Abū Nuwās, 6, 11, 12, 39, 40, 169, 219, 237n.25, 253n.69, n.70
Abū Rayya, Yūsuf, 26, 249n.7
Abū Rīsh, Muḥammad 'Abbās, 8
Abū Tammām (Ḥabīb b. al-'Aws), 12
Achebe, Chinua, 10, 202, 240n.45, n.48, 241n.55, 259n.152, 282n.78
Adab (Journal), 193, 244n.75, 280n.43
al-Ādāb (Journal), 212, 233n.1, 236n.22, 237n.29, 238n.32,n.34, n.36, n.37, 239n.38, n.41, 240n.43, 246n.87, 251n.45, 257n.120, 258n.139, 270n.18, 281n.49, 284n.5, n.7, n.11
al-'Adawiyya, Rābi'a, 12, 241n.58
Addressee, 43-4, 52, 53, 59, 142, 143
Adūnīs ('Alī Aḥmad Sa'īd), 154, 157, 166, 184, 247n.92
al-Afghānī, Jamāl al-Dīn, 157
Africa, African, Africanism, 4, 10-11, 29, 33-4, 39, 58, 110, 117, 130, 149, 150-1, 160, 165-9, 171-2, 174, 185-6, 208, 226-7, 230, 238n.31, 240n.44, 281n.44, n.58, 282n.78
(Culture, Language, Literature), 7, 10, 11, 25, 158, 160, 185, 202, 203, 204, 205, 234n.3, 235n.16, 236n.20, 240n.44, n.45, 241n.55, 242n.64, 247n.91, 250n.20, 263n.31, 282n.78
Aḥmad, Jamāl Muḥammad, 13
'Ajūba, Ibrāhīm Mukhtār, 5, 184, 192, 207, 237n.28, 238n.37, 239n.38, n.40, 240n.50, 244n.75, 250n.20, 257n.120
Alexandria, 133, 147
Alf Layla wa-Layla, 12, 48, 86, 143, 162, 265n.61, 279n.33
Algeria, Algerian, 69, 149, 162, 173, 222, 235n.16, 278n.21
(Literature), 4, 64, 69, 157, 235n.16, 251n.36, 277n.10, 278n.21
Alienation, Alien, 3, 15, 35, 87, 89, 103-4, 116, 122, 137, 143, 144-5, 146, 147-8, 149, 150, 164-5, 167, 176, 177, 221, 234n.5
Amado, Jorge, 9, 13
America, American (United States), 5, 17, 67, 77, 158, 165, 184, 213, 229, 232, 270n.26
(Literature), 55, 64, 77, 117, 242n.64, n.68
Amīn, Aḥmad, 157, 177, 178-9, 180, 276n.8, 283n.84, n.90
'Āmmiyya (Colloquial/Spoken Arabic), 20, 77, 220, 222
Anagnorisis, 35, 43
'Antara b. Shaddād, 12, 241n.58
al-Aqlām (Journal), 195, 212, 213, 233n.1, 234n.9, 241n.59, n.61, n.62, 242n.65, 251n.47, 258n.126, 264n.45, 280n.35
Arabian Nights, The (see *Alf Layla wa-Layla*)
Arabic (Classical/Modern Literatures), 6, 7-10, 11-13, 16-18, 20, 25, 28-32, 38, 40-1, 47, 58, 64-5, 67, 68-9, 73, 77-8, 82, 84, 87, 92, 94, 133-4, 137, 155-6, 158, 160, 165-6, 177, 183, 185-7, 201, 222, 229, 234n.5, 236n.21, 240n.49, 242n.64, 243n.70, 245n.78, 247n.91, 248n.2, 249n.14, n.18, 252n.48, 254n.75, 255n.103, 257n.118, 265n.62, 270n.12, 272n.48, n.55
Arabic (see 'Āmmiyya/Fuṣḥā)
'Arāidī, Na'īm, 5
Aṣwāt (Journal), 192, 208, 244n.75
Auerbach, Erich, 75, 154, 260n.1
Authentic, Authenticity, 62-3, 65-6, 133, 243n.73
Author (see Real Author)
Autobiography, Autobiographical (Semi-autobiography), 1, 5, 19, 35, 49, 72, 75, 84-5, 90, 91, 123, 137, 140, 142, 144, 152, 157-8, 161, 188-9, 216, 236n.21, 248n.2, 252n.48, 269n.3, 273n.70
'Awaḍ, Luwīs, 277n.10
Aylīn (=Aileen) (Character), 28, 43, 51, 84, 143, 197, 267n.76
Ayyūb, Dhū al-Nūn, 26, 157, 249n.5, 277n.10
'Azzām, 'Abd al-Wahhāb, 157
'Azzām, Samīra, 183

Babylon, 68

el-Badawī, Aḥmad Muḥammad, 184, 234n.3, n.5, n.7, 237n.25, 240n.43, 241n.56, n.63, n.64, 243n.69, 245n.79, n.85, 247n.91, n.92, 253n.65, n.67, 255n.95, n.97, 257n.120, n.124, 259n.157, 261n.5, 265n.58, 266n.66, 268n.99, 283n.2, 284n.3, n.13, 285n.18, n.20, n.21, n.23, n.26, 286n.29, n.31, n.40, n.42
Ba'labakkī, Laylā, 9, 22, 64, 248n.102, 257n.118, 258n.134
Balzac, Honoré de, 25, 137, 248n.4, 270n.26
Bandar, 36, 125, 252n.53
Bandar Shāh (Character), 36-7, 38, 57, 62, 72, 123, 125-30, 135, 139, 140, 153, 200-201, 262n.19, 269n.8, 274n.74
Bandar Shāh: Ḍaw al-Bayt, 2, 11, 18, 23, 26, 36-7, 38-9, 49-50, 56, 62, 64-5, 67, 72, 79, 82, 92, 102, 123, 129-30, 135, 136, 139-41, 151, 152-3, 154, 188, 195, 199-200, 206, 219, 224, 233n.3, 248n.107, 252n.56, 255n.99, 256n.114, 257n.124, 258n.130, 260n.168, n.169, n.170, 261n.5, 262n.19, 268n.91, n.96, 269n.6, n.8, 270n.11, n.13, n.14, n.21, 271n.31, 272n.43, n.55, 273n.68
Bandar Shāh: Maryūd, 11, 18, 23, 26, 29, 38-9, 50, 57, 63, 64-5, 67, 72, 79, 82, 91, 92, 129, 135-6, 140-1, 142, 152-4, 186, 195, 200, 206, 224, 234n.6, 243n.69, 248n.108, n.110, 249n.5, 250n.22, 253n.66, n.70, 255n.101, 257n.124, 259n.149, 260n.165, n.168, n.169, n.170, n.174, 261n.5, 262n.19, 268n.96, n.97, n.98, 269n.8, 270n.22, 272n.44, 273n.71, 285n.20
Barakāt, Hudā, 184
Barakāt, Salīm, 64, 133, 184, 255n.93, 258n.132, 261n.10, 263n.33, 269n.3, 270n.12
Barrāda, Muḥammad, 11, 41, 64, 133, 254n.78, 258n.132, 269n.3, 274n.73
al-Bāyitāt, Sa'īd 'Ashā (Character), 23, 200, 269n.8
al-Bayyātī, 'Abd al-Wahhāb, 154, 184
BBC, 2, 217-18
B. Shaddād, 'Antara (see 'Antara b. Shaddād)
Beckett, Samuel, 13, 55, 256n.110, n.112, 265n.58
Bedouin, 34, 96, 149, 158
Beginning, 22, 30, 41, 43, 46, 51, 54, 56, 102, 114, 167
Beirut, 17, 21-2, 67, 91, 152, 201, 209, 220, 223, 225, 244n.75
Bennīs, Muḥammad, 157
Bergman, Ingmar, 92, 219
Berlin, 159
Bilāl (Character), 23, 38, 50, 129, 130-1, 135, 140, 141, 262n.19, 268n.99
Bildungsroman, 35, 43, 154, 252n.48, 274n.77, 276n.9
Binary Oppositions, 32, 37, 104, 153, 155, 183, 251n.38, 274n.76
Bint Majdhūb (Character), 15, 66, 101, 119, 120, 173
Biography, Biographical, 1, 78-9, 152, 233n.3, 248n.1, 279n.26
Black, Blackness, 10, 15, 104, 105, 130, 149, 166, 170-1, 230, 265n.61, 268n.99, 271n.26, 274n.76, 281n.44
'A Blessed Day on the Umm Bab Shore' (see also 'Yawm Mubārak 'alā Shāṭi' Umm Bāb'), 3, 5, 31, 196, 201, 204, 245n.84
Boccaccio, Giovanni, 143, 272n.49
Borges, Jorge Luis, 40
Britain/Great Britain, British, 4, 89, 110, 121, 147, 156, 169, 174, 177, 189, 197, 237n.25, 275n.4, 276n.9
Brontë, Emily, 13, 117, 255n.94
Brook, Peter, 55
Bullāṭa, 'Īsā, 159, 278n.18
Būlus, Sargūn, 184

Cairo, 17, 20, 26, 34-6, 67, 70, 111, 115-16, 146, 159, 199, 223, 247n.92
Calvino, Italo, 40, 133
Camus, Albert, 9, 11, 13-14, 102, 117, 145-50, 185, 266n.74, 273n.58, n.59, n.73, 282n.67
Catharsis, Cathartic, 54, 109, 151, 199
Cervantes, Miguel de, 25, 248n.4
Characters (see also Figures), 2-4, 6, 18, 22, 26, 28-33, 35-6, 38, 44-7, 50, 53, 54, 56-7, 60-6, 68, 71, 72, 73, 75-95, 97-101, 104-7, 109, 112, 114-21, 123, 125, 128-31, 133-5, 137-44, 150-4, 158-61, 163, 167, 169-71, 176, 181, 187-9, 199, 201, 221, 224, 234n.8, 252n.53, 255n.91, 256n.110, n.113, 258n.126, 260n.1, 261n.3, n.11, n.15, 262n.19, 263n.33, n.36, 264n.56, 267n.77, n.80, 268n.99, n.101, n.1, n.2, 269n.6, n.8, 270n.26, 272n.40, n.47,

274n.75, n.76, 278n.21, 279n.26, 281n.49, 282n.70
(Archetype, Archetypical), 15, 79, 98, 100, 109, 131, 139, 169, 188,
(Central, Leading, Main, Major, Principal), 22, 28-9, 31, 36, 45-6, 50, 58, 60, 63-4, 65, 68, 69, 75-80, 82-5, 88-93, 95, 100-101, 109, 117, 123, 125, 127, 129, 131, 135-6, 138, 139-40, 140, 150, 158, 168, 173, 187, 197-9, 264n.45, n.56, 269n.8, 278n.21
('Flat'), 75
(Iconographical), 137, 142
(Marginal, Minor, Peripheral), 60, 63, 69, 75-6, 77-80, 82, 84-5, 89-90, 93, 98, 100, 119, 123, 127-9, 131, 135, 138-9, 173, 187, 264n.45, 268n.99
('Round'), 75
(Secondary), 43, 50, 63, 75-8, 80, 84-5, 87, 88-90, 93, 98-100, 115, 119, 123, 127, 129, 131, 135, 138-9, 259n.149, 269n.8, 270n.26
(Stereotype, Stereotypical), 53, 170, 182, 188
Climax (Anti-climax), 31, 46, 50, 52, 83, 107, 146, 166, 171
Colonial, Colonialism (Anti-colonialism, Neo-colonialism) Colonizer, 10, 11, 15, 149, 156, 166, 174, 176, 222, 228, 229, 256n.111, 274n.76, 275n.4, 276n.7
Complementary Opposites, 24, 32, 37, 104, 153, 155, 183, 189, 274n.76
Conrad, Joseph, 13-14, 56, 102, 117, 145, 150, 185, 220-22, 256n.107, n.111, 273n.57
Credibility, 43, 61, 63, 65-6, 76-7, 82, 86, 133-4, 142, 150, 224
Christians, Christianity, 7, 10, 72, 118, 125, 151, 156, 160, 164, 166, 185, 226-7, 264n.46, 265n.61
City, 2, 8, 15, 26, 29, 33, 36-7, 39, 44, 46, 67, 71, 85-6, 102, 103, 111, 115-16, 122, 125, 133, 135, 137, 138, 139-40, 145, 151, 157, 160, 169, 174, 197, 199, 230, 234n.5, 250n.21, 252n.53, n.54, 269n.3
Crusader, Crusades, 118, 155-6, 176
Cypriot, Cyprus, 5, 31, 45-6, 91, 152, 225
'The Cypriot Man' (see also 'al-Rajul al-Qubruṣī'), 5, 22, 30, 196, 201, 204, 245n.84, 250n.28
Cypriot Man, The (Character) (see also al-Rajul al-Qubruṣī), 31, 46, 53, 90-2, 201
al-Dabba (al-Debba, al-Dubba), 1, 192, 233n.2
al-Ḍa'īf, Rashīd, 133, 269n.3
al-Dā'im, 29
Damascus, 45
Dār al-'Awda, 23, 191, 194, 195, 196, 233n.1, n.3, 234n.6, 240n.46, 244n.75, 245n.84, n.85, 248n.108, 249n.5, n.10, 250n.34, 251n.36, n.37, 262n.24, 277n.9, 278n.16, 280n.36, 284n.14, 285n.16
Dār al-Hilāl, 16, 194, 195, 209, 244n.75, n.80, 278n.18
Darwīsh, Zakī, 249n.14
Ḍaw al-Bayt (see *Bandar Shāh: Ḍaw al-Bayt)*
Ḍaw al-Bayt (Character), 36, 57, 72, 79, 92, 112, 117, 123-5, 127, 130, 139, 140-41, 153, 200, 201, 262n.19, 268n.86, 269n.8
Dawma (see also Doum Tree), 29
'Dawmat Wad Ḥāmid' (see also 'The Doum Tree of Wad Hamid'), 2, 11, 28, 29, 32, 42, 43, 44, 52, 56, 58, 64, 67, 72, 73, 85-8, 93, 128, 135, 143, 181, 186, 188, 192, 197, 202, 234n.6, 241n.57, 244n.75, 249n.15, 254n.80, 260n.168, 268n.99, 269n.8, 272n.46, 284n.7
Dawmat Wad Ḥāmid, 3, 16, 21, 27, 38, 45, 80, 90, 92, 135, 165, 191, 192, 193, 194, 234n.6, 244n.75, 245n.78, n.84, 249n.10, n.12, n.15, n.16, 250n.19, n.23, n.27, n.29, 251n.44, 254n.84, 257n.121, 258n.142, 259n.156, 260n.168, n.172, 264n.49, 267n.76, 268n.95, n.96, 270n.9, n.11, n.13, n.14, n.15, 271n.31, n.32, 272n.50, n.51, n.52, 280n.41, n.43, 281n.45, 283n.82, n.101
Ḍayf, Shawqī, 275n.5, 279n.26
Death, 15, 23, 35, 53-5, 57, 65, 71, 72, 75, 91-2, 100, 101, 104, 106-8, 110, 113-15, 121, 125-6, 129, 130, 131, 133, 135, 146-50, 152, 168, 170-2, 189, 199, 201, 219, 226, 230-1, 256n.106, 265n.60, 267n.80, 273n.67
Dedication, 25, 38-40, 253n.63
Desdemona, 15, 118
al-Dhubyānī, al-Nābigha, 12
Dialogue, 7, 10, 15, 17, 20, 25, 27, 43, 46, 47, 52, 53, 56, 57, 58-63, 65-6, 77, 86, 134, 140-1, 142, 149, 160, 187, 211, 256n.108, 257n.120, n.122, 258n.142, 261n.5, 264n.45, 266n.66, n.76, 267n.82
Dīb, Muḥammad, 183

Dickens, Charles, 13, 214
Diglossia (see also Multiglossia), 20, 222
al-Dōḥa (Journal), 22, 23, 50, 196, 204, 208, 236n.19, 240n.49, 248n.103, n.104, n.105, n.106, n.107, n.108, 255n.102, 257n.120, n.124, 282n.65, 285n.16
Doum Tree (see also *Dawma*), 59, 69, 72, 86, 88, 181, 197-8, 254n.84
'The Doum Tree of Wad Hamid' (see also 'Dawmat Wad Ḥāmid') 29, 69, 192, 197, 202, 245n.77, 257n.121
Doppelgänger (Double), 144, 153, 274n.76
al-Ḍuḥā, 71-2, 249n.7, 260n.167
Durrell, Lawrence, 133, 222

East, Eastern, 15, 21, 30, 32, 34-5, 48, 84, 112, 116, 121, 144, 148, 154-6, 158-9, 161-2, 164-5, 167-70, 172-81, 188-9, 198, 213, 243n.73, 276n.9, 279n.29, 282n.70
(Characters) 3, 28, 53, 84, 88, 89, 90, 101, 112, 119, 144, 158-62, 164-7, 170-1, 173, 176, 178, 180, 187-8, 197-8, 272n.51, 278n.21, 282n.70, n.73
(Cultures, Literatures), 12, 25, 39, 44, 48, 84, 109, 117, 121, 135, 138, 144, 154-8, 160, 162, 165-6, 176, 178-9, 181, 185, 265n.61, 276n.8, 272n.51, 277n.10, 278n.17, n.21
Eco, Umberto, 133
Egypt, Egyptian, 7, 9, 16, 18, 20, 21, 27, 29, 33, 39, 41, 51, 53, 66, 77, 80, 81, 90, 134, 156, 159, 166, 168, 170, 172, 174, 180, 184-5, 191, 192, 194, 195, 197, 215, 223, 227, 229, 244n.75, n.76, 251n.44, 271n.36, 273n.73, 274n.78, 275n.5, 277n.10, 278n.21, 281n.58, 284n.9, 285n.16
(Literature), 2, 4, 7-9, 13, 16, 20, 25-6, 41, 67, 69, 77-8, 100, 137, 157, 159, 164, 177, 185, 222, 234n.5, 236n.21, 237n.29, 261n.10, 270n.12, 271n.36, 272n.40, 273n.73, 274n.78, 277n.12
Elad-Bouskila, Ami, 6, 210, 213, 234n.3, n.8, 235n.16, 236n.18, 237n.27, 241n.57, 242n.65, 246n.85, 250n.20, 253n.72, 254n.75, n.80, 265n.59, 274n.77, 275n.3, 283n.1, 285n.19, n.20
Eliot, T(homas) S(tearns), 13
Emigration, Émigré, 33-5, 159, 165, 183, 277n.14
Ending, 25, 30, 31, 42, 48, 50-8, 96, 187, 196, 255n.103, 256n.108, n.112
England, English, 2-6, 10, 16-17, 19, 21-2, 27, 28, 30, 34-6, 43, 45, 48, 61-3, 69-70, 88-90, 100-1, 103-4, 106-7, 109-10, 112, 114, 115, 117-18, 136, 144-5, 147, 149, 158-9, 163-81, 183-6, 188, 198, 199, 203, 206, 210, 212, 213, 218-21, 231, 233n.1, 234n.7, 235n.14, 236n.23, n.24, 240n.52, 242n.68, 243n.69, n.71, n.72, n.73, 268n.1, 269n.3, 270n.24, 271n.27, n.30, 272n,40, n.48, 273n.73, 274n.74, 278n.20, n.21, n.22, 279n.26, n.33, 282n.60, n.78, 283n.80, n.83, 285n.20, n.28, 286n.45, n.46, n.47, n.48, n.51
(Characters), 34, 53, 69-70, 88-9, 101, 111, 115, 164-73, 174-6, 188-9, 198, 267n.80
(Literature), 6, 8, 13, 25, 58, 185, 242n.64, 256n.111, 271n.30
Europe, European (see also West, Western), 4-5, 9, 10, 11, 33, 34, 47-9, 64, 67-70, 84, 89, 101-2, 111, 116, 117-18, 143, 144, 150, 153-4, 156-63, 164, 165, 168, 170, 172, 173, 174, 176, 179, 182, 199, 240n.49, 264n.45, 273n.57, 274n.76, n.78, 278n.21, 281n.44, n.58, 282n.60, n.64, n.78
Exile, 5, 158, 165, 183, 184
Existentialism, 11, 14, 58, 145, 240n.50, 273n.73
Exposition (Opening) (see also Beginning), 21, 25, 27, 30, 40-51, 53-4, 56, 83, 96, 102, 135, 187, 196, 198, 254n.75, 255n.91, n.94, n.95, 256n.108

Fabula, 68
Fahmī, Manṣūr, 157, 276n.8
al-Fajr (Journal), 8, 209, 264n.53, n.55, 266n.69
Fanon, Franz, 222, 280n.44
Faqīh, 103
Fallāḥ, 49, 135, 159, 197
al-Faraj ba'd al-Shidda, 11, 42, 73, 187, 241n.57, 254n.80
Faṣl, 32
Fāṭima (Character), 90, 92, 110, 124, 125, 141, 172, 200, 269n.8
Faulkner, William, 13, 40, 64, 67, 77, 108, 117, 137, 151, 185, 261n.4, 263n.33, 264n.52, 270n.26

Faust, Faustian, 55, 115
al-Faytūrī, Muḥammad Miftāḥ, 9-10, 11, 13, 23, 39, 240n.46, 253n.68
Fayyāḍ, Sulaymān, 159, 278n.20
Fiction, Fictional, 1, 3, 4, 6, 7-9, 16, 24, 25, 35, 41, 42, 43, 49, 50, 53, 54-5, 59, 67, 72, 73, 75, 76, 78, 84, 91, 130-1, 133, 134, 141-2, 154, 157, 158, 181, 182, 187, 188, 189, 214-7, 221, 231, 232, 243n.70, 245n.78, 251n.44, 267n.76, 271n.27, n.30, 274n.76, 279n.31
Figures (see also Characters), 11-12, 14, 36, 72, 78-9, 89-90, 94, 99-100, 101, 106, 110, 115, 120, 129, 131, 137-40, 142-4, 150-4, 168, 187, 188, 227
al-Fikr al-'Arabī al-Mu'āṣir (Journal), 212, 238n.1
Flashback, 43, 72, 255n.91
Ford, Ford Madox, 13
French Invasion, 156
Foreign, Foreigner, Foreigness, 3, 15, 16, 27, 35-6, 45, 49, 52, 59, 66, 85, 89, 104, 116-17, 122, 137, 140, 148-9, 152, 164-5, 167, 174, 176, 178, 189, 220, 228, 273n.55, 277n.14
Forster, E(dward) M(organ), 13, 75, 213, 260n.2
Freud, Sigmund, 19, 104, 109, 145, 222, 247n.90, 260n.158, 266n.66, 267n.82
Fuṣḥā (Classical/Literary Arabic), 7, 20, 58, 60-3, 65-6, 77, 222-4, 257n.120, 258n.126, n.142

García Márquez, Gabriel, 9, 11, 40, 67, 133, 137-8, 240n.52, n.54, 271n.29, n.30, n.31, n.32
Germany, German, 16, 158-60, 164, 184, 186, 203, 204, 205, 232, 243n.69, 285n.20
Ghānim, Fatḥī, 11, 77, 134, 154, 157-8, 222, 250n.30, 257n.118, 261n.7, 271n.34, 274n.73, n.78, 277n.10
Goethe, Johann Wolfgang von, 13
Government, 8, 23, 52, 69, 85-7, 100, 115, 135-6, 138-40, 197, 240n.54, 268n.99, 271n.29
Grandfather, The (Character), 15, 28, 37, 38, 39, 43, 44, 51, 57-8, 62-3, 71, 82-3, 86, 101, 116, 120-1, 126-8, 129-30, 139, 140, 143, 151-3, 154, 187, 197, 200, 259n.149, 262n.19, 269n.8, 274n.74
Greece, Greek, 5, 73, 140, 155, 195, 243n.69 (Literature), 16, 133, 274n.77
Greenwood, Sheila (Character), 119, 149, 170-1
Gypsy, 34

Ḥabībī, Emīl, 40, 157, 235n.17, 253n.64, n.72, 263n.33, 264n.56, 272n.40, 274n.73
Ḥadīth, 40
'Ḥafnat Tamr', 2, 28, 29, 32, 37, 43-4, 51, 56, 58, 64, 67, 82-4, 93, 102, 126, 128, 142-3, 151-2, 191, 197, 202, 234n.6, 244n.75, 249n.15, 269n.6, n.8
Ḥājj Aḥmad (see The Grandfather)
al-Ḥājj, Unsī, 154
Ḥajjār, Walīd, 158, 277n.10
'Hākadhā Yā Sādatī', 29-30, 32, 45, 53, 58, 64, 67, 88-9, 143-4, 166-8, 176-88, 193, 198, 203-4, 217, 244n.75, 250n.29, 269n.8
al-Ḥakawātī, 47
al-Ḥakīm, Tawfīq, 4, 13, 67, 157, 161, 178, 235n.14, 259n.147, 277n.10, 279n.26, 283n.89
Ḥammād, Jum'a, 158, 275n.78, 277n.10
Hammond, Ann (Character), 119, 149, 169-71
al-Ḥanīn (Character), 32, 54, 79, 95-6, 98-100, 135, 139, 269n.8
Happy End, Happy Ending, 54, 56
Ḥaqqī, Maḥmūd Ṭāhir, 177, 283n.83
Ḥaqqī, Yaḥyā, 4, 13, 67, 69, 158, 180, 185, 235n.14, 259n.147, n.154, 262n.23, 264n.46, 274n.78, 276n.9, 277n.10, 281n.48, 282n.60
Hardy, Thomas, 25, 213, 248n.4, 271n.30
Ḥāwī, Khalīl, 157, 277n.12
Ḥawwā' (Character), 38, 92, 141
al-Ḥayāt (Journal), 9, 210-11
Ḥaydar, Ḥaydar, 22
Haykal, Muḥammad Ḥusayn, 26, 248-9n.5, 272n.40, 275n.4
Headmaster, The (Character), 46-7, 61-2, 66, 267n.81
Hebrew, 5, 16, 18, 191, 192, 193, 194, 195, 202, 203, 204, 205, 206, 208, 209, 219, 237n.29, 243n.69, 247n.94, 256n.110, 261n.3, 269n.4, 272n.40, 274n.75, 275n.3, 276n.7, n.8
Hero (Anti-hero), 25-8, 31-2, 35, 42-3, 63, 76, 101-2, 109-10, 115, 118-19, 145, 147-50, 157-67, 170-1, 180, 197, 198, 201, 250n.21, 258n.134, 259n.152, 265n.56, n.62, 281n.58
Hijra, 32-4, 251n.43, n.45

al-Hilāl (Journal), 21, 23, 50, 90, 191, 192, 194, 195, 210, 244n.75, 285n.16
al-Ḥilū,' Īsā, 9, 210, 238n.32, n.34, n.36, 239n.38, n.40, 257n.120, 267n.77, 284n.7, 285n.17
Ḥiwār (Journal), 17-18, 21, 90, 191, 193-4, 220, 244n.75, 245n.79, 270n.16, n.18, 272n.51, 284n.8, n.9
Holy Man, 85, 87, 100, 110, 230, 241n.57, 250n.20, 254n.80, 265n.59, 268n.99
Homer, 73, 79, 140
Ḥusayn (Character), 66, 80-2, 84, 197, 269n.8
Ḥusayn, Ṭāhā, 4, 9, 20, 100, 157, 231, 235n.14, 249n.14, 252n.58, 262n.24, 263n.43, 271n.35, 274n.78, 277n.10
Ḥusna (Character), 15, 33, 69, 71, 79, 92, 98, 105, 107, 112, 113-14, 119, 121-2, 126, 138, 141, 151, 168, 169, 172-3, 228, 264n.45, 267n.80, n.81, n.82, 282n.70

Ibn al-Fāriḍ, 12
Ibn Jallūn, 'Abd al-Majīd, 159
Ibn Jallūn, al-Ṭāhir, 4, 9, 183-4
Ibn Ziyād, Ṭāriq, 171, 282n.59
Ibrāhīm, Ibrāhīm Isḥāq, 2, 7, 9, 184, 234n.5, 237n.28, 238-9n.37, 239n.38, n.41, 250n.20, 255n.92, 257n.124, 261n.5
Ibrāhīm, Muḥammad al-Makkī, 13, 241n.60
Ibrāhīm, Sa'dī, 4, 69, 158, 162, 173, 235n.14, 259n.155, 277n.10, 282n.72
Ibrāhīm, Ṣalāḥ Aḥmad, 10, 13, 184, 209, 239n.42, 286n.38
Ibsen, Henrik, 219
Identity, 75, 122, 144, 149-50, 179, 185, 200, 280n.42
'Idhā Jā'at', 29, 32, 45, 52, 58, 64, 88, 166, 193, 198, 203, 217, 250n.29, 254n.84, 280n.43
Idrīs, Suhayl, 4, 9, 11, 13, 67, 147, 157, 161, 235n.14, 259n.147, 274-5n.78, 277n.10, 279n.27, 282n.60
Idrīs, Yūsuf, 9, 13, 158, 186, 250n.20, 277n.10, 278n.16
Ifrīqiyā (see Africa)
'al-Ikhtibār', 10, 89-90, 144, 167, 193
Image, 65, 104, 115, 119, 127, 162-4, 168, 182, 199, 279n.31
al-Imām (Character), 21, 66, 72, 93, 95, 100, 128, 139, 142
Imperialism, 10, 15, 33, 110, 116, 118, 157, 160, 162, 166, 169, 174-5, 176, 179, 189
Implied
(Author) 64, 134, 141-2, 144, 150
(Listener) 44
(Reader) 30, 53, 142
Ionesco, Eugéne, 13
Iran, Iranian (Persia, Persian), 16, 36, 125, 155-6, 180
Irony, Ironic, 41, 45, 47-9, 80, 86-7, 109, 171, 173, 198, 262n.22, n.23, 264n.56
'Īsā (see Bandar Shāh)
Islam, 130, 151, 155, 160, 180, 185, 208, 227, 265n.61, 271n.35
Israel, 5, 18, 165, 171, 209, 229
Italy, Italian, 40, 186, 202, 203, 205, 207, 243n.69, 285n.20, n.25

al-Jābirī, Shakīb, 4, 158-61, 275n.78, 277n.10, 278n.18, n.19
Jabrā, Jabrā Ibrāhīm, 4-5, 18, 26, 67, 134, 157, 159, 183, 235n.17, 244n.74, 246n.88, 249n.5, n.6, 259n.146, 278n.18
al-Jāḥiẓ (Abū 'Uthmān), 12, 262n.23
Jakobson, Roman, 155
James, Henry, 143, 272n.49
Jerusalem, 156, 159
Jesus, 125, 265n.61
Jewish, Judaism, 151, 155, 264n.46, 265n.61
Jibrīl, Ṭalḥat, 79, 102, 210-11, 233n.1, n.3, 234n.4, 235n.10, n.11, n.12, 236n.22, 241n.54, n.55, n.59, n.60, 243n.69, 245n.80, n.82, 246n.89, 247n.92, n.101, 249n.13, 250n.26, n.33, 251n.45, 252n.53, 253n.65, n.66, n.70, 255n.89, n.98, 260n.175, 261n.14, 262n.15, n.20, n.27, 263n.36, 268n.85, n.100, 270n.18, 271n.29, n.37, n.38, 273n.70, n.72, 280n.40, n.43, 281n.58, 283n.88, n.91, n.93, 284n.7, n.9
Johnson-Davies, Denys, 19, 21, 186, 202, 204, 205, 206, 233n.1, 234n.3, 240n.45, 242n.64, 243n.72, 245n.77, n.78, n.83, 247n.91, 249n.5, 250n.28, n.34, 251n.37, 254n.74, 257n.120, 262n.16, 269n.5, 285n.20, n.22, n.24, 286n.30
Jordan, Jordanian, 2, 64, 157-8, 229, 259n.148, 275n.78, 277n.10, 288n.33

Journey, 34-5, 43, 69, 100, 110-11, 147, 149, 152, 154, 157-8, 163, 251n.43, 252n.48
Joyce, James, 25, 40, 64, 248n.4, 252n.48, 255n.94, 274n.75
Jubrān, Jubrān Khalīl, 5, 154, 183, 265n.56

Kafka, Franz, 9, 11, 273n.73
al-Kafrāwī, Sa'īd, 26, 249n.6, n.7
Kalīla wa-Dimna, 11, 12, 40, 253n.70, n.71, n.73
Kanafānī, Ghassān, 64, 183, 257n.118, 265n.56, 272n.48
Karāmāt, 110, 265n.59
Kātib, Yāsīn, 183-4
al-Kātiba (Journal), 5
al-Khādim, Sa'd, 78, 261n.10
Khālid, Abū Bakr, 9, 239n.40, n.41
al-Kharrāt, Edwār, 26, 246n.89, 248n.5
al-Kharṭūm (Journal), 9, 21, 194, 196, 210, 237n.30, 239n.41, 240n.47, 244n.74, n.75, n.76, 247n.100, 250n.20, 254n.73, 263n.31, 265n.61, 266n.71, 268n.94, n.99, 270n.16, 277n.12, 281n.47
Khartoum, 1, 21, 33, 35, 45, 49, 67, 68, 70, 81, 85, 90, 103, 106-7, 110-11, 115, 116, 120, 123-4, 149, 199, 219, 236n.22
Al-Khayyām, 'Umar, 162, 279n.33
Khuḍayyir, Muḥammad, 157
Khulayyif, 'Abd al-Sattār, 137, 270n.23
Khūrī, Ilyās, 133, 269n.3
'Khuṭwa li'l-Amām', 10, 53, 89-90, 144, 167, 193, 198
Kitchener, H.H., 110, 169-70, 175
Koran, 11, 20, 40, 71, 241n.56, 252n.57, 259n.151, 260n.167
Kurdufān (Journal), 8
Kurtz (Character), 15, 56, 117, 150-1, 256n.111
Kuwait, Kuwaiti, 20, 209

'Laka ḥattā al-Mamāt', 45, 58, 89-90, 135, 144, 167, 193
Lāshīn, Maḥmūd Ṭāhir, 26, 249n.6
Latin America, Latin American (Literature) (see also South American), 9, 11, 40, 133, 240n.54, 271n.29
Lawrence, D(avid) H(erbert), 13
Legend, Legendary, 29, 36-7, 40, 46, 57, 67, 71-3, 79, 88, 96, 104, 110, 112, 114-15, 123-8, 130-1, 135, 140, 153, 176, 187, 189, 200-1, 224, 226-7, 250n.20, 255n.93, 259n.151, 262n.19, 265n.61
Leitmotif, 44, 50, 117
Levi-Strauss, Claude, 155
Liminal, Liminality, 139, 145
Liqā' (Journal), 202-3, 233n.3, 238n.35
Listener, 30, 44, 53, 58, , 73, 143, 187
Listener, The (Character), 44, 52, 58-9, 69, 86-7, 197-8, 254n.84
London, 2, 3, 4, 10, 17, 22, 35-6, 49, 67, 70, 71, 85, 91, 104, 111, 115-16, 147, 159, 160, 169, 191, 192, 194, 197, 199, 210, 213, 219, 234n.7, 236n.22, 237n.25, n.26, 244n.75, 270n.18, 273n.57, 278n.21

al-Ma'arrī, Abū 'Alā', 232, 250n.18
Macondo, 67, 138, 271n.30
Maghrib, Maghribi, 156-7, 162, 174, 177, 277n.14
(Literature), 4, 11, 78, 157, 162, 165, 183-4, 189, 235n.16, 279n.30
al-Mahdī, Muḥammad Aḥmad, 72
Maḥfūẓ, Najīb, 9, 11, 13, 22, 26-7, 42, 64, 67, 78, 81, 134, 137, 154, 157, 186, 234n.5, 240n.51, n.52, 243n.71, 245n.78, 249n.6, n.7, 254n.81, 255n.103, 257n.118, n.122, 259n.144, n.146, 261n.8, n.9, 262n.16, n.21, 265n.56, n.62, 269n.5, 271n.27, n.36, 273n.73
Mahjar/post-*Mahjar* (Literature), 5, 24, 165, 183-4, 236n.19, n.24
Maḥjūb (Character), 15, 28, 42-3, 49, 50, 51, 54, 56-8, 65, 69, 72, 79, 80-3, 93, 95-6, 101, 103, 105, 107, 113, 119-21, 128, 130, 136, 139-40, 153, 172, 181, 197, 200, 201, 251n.44, 261n.15, 264n.45, 282n.70
Maḥjūb, Muḥammad Aḥmad, 8
al-Majalla (Journal), 6, 209, 233n.1, 237n.26, 264n.54, 286n.29
al-Majdhūb, Muḥammad al-Mahdī, 10, 239n.42
al-Makhzanjī, Muḥammad, 78
al-Makk, 'Alī, 9, 13, 191, 192, 237n.28, 238n.34, n.36, 239n.40, 244n.75
Makkī, Buthayna Khaḍir, 9
Makkī, al-Ṭāhir Aḥmad, 53, 196, 234n.6, 248n.103, 250n.28, 254n.87
Malḥama, 18, 225, 246n.87
al-Ma'lūf, Amīn, 9

al-Manfalūṭī, Muṣṭafā Luṭfī, 8
Mann, Thomas, 13, 252n.57, 274n.75
Manṣūr, 'Atāllāh, 5
Marawī (Merwi, Merowi), 100, 123, 135, 233n.2
Marlow (Character), 15, 150-1
Maryam (Character), 38, 57-8, 72, 90, 92, 129-30, 141, 152, 160, 201, 229, 269n.8
Maryūd (see *Bandar Shāh: Maryūd*)
Maryūd (Character), 23, 37, 38, 57, 62, 72, 79, 125-31, 140, 153, 188, 200-1, 253n.60, 268n.92, 274n.74
Mas'adī, Maḥmūd, 13
Mashriq, Mashriqi (Literature), 2, 4, 11, 27, 78, 157, 161-2, 184, 189, 245n.78, 246n.89
Mas'ūd (Character), 28, 44, 51, 82-4, 197, 269n.8
Mawāqif (Journal), 5, 236n.21, 242n.66, 255n.100
Mawsim, 32-3, 251n.39
Mawsim al-Hijra ilā al-Shamāl (see also *Season of Migration to the North*), 2-3, 9-10, 13-15, 16-20, 21-2, 30, 32, 37, 43, 47, 49-50, 52, 54, 58, 60, 61, 64-5, 66, 67, 68-71, 79, 82, 83-4, 88, 89, 90, 91, 92, 93, 95, 98, 100-22, 123-4, 126, 127, 128, 131, 135, 136, 137, 138, 139, 140, 141, 143-52, 153, 158, 160, 162-8, 174-6, 178-9, 181, 186, 188-9, 194, 198, 199, 200, 205, 207, 209, 211, 212, 213, 217, 233n.1, 234n.6, n.7, 240n.49, 241n.56, n.59, 242n.65, n.67, 243n.69, 244n.74, n.75, n.76, 245n.78, n.80, n.82, n.84, 246n.86, n.87, 247n.91, 250n.20, n.26, 251n.46, 252n.49, 255n.94, n.96, 256n.106, n.107, n.108, n.112, 257n.118, n.123, 258n.135, n.139, n.140, n.141, n.142, 259n.156, n.157, 260n.158, n.159, n.160, n.161, n.162, n.163, n.164, n.165, n.170, n.171, 262n.19, 263n.39, 264n.45, n.48, 265n.58, n.59, n.60, n.62, 266n.66, n.67, n.70, n.71, n.75, 267n.76, 268n.91, n.99, 269n.6, n8, 270n.10, n.13, n.14, n.18, n.19, 271n.26, n.31, n.34, 272n.42, n.54, 273n.60, n.61, n.62, n.63, n.64, n.65, n.66, 274n.76, 277n.9, n.10, 279n.26, 280n.36, n.41, n.44, 281n.52, n.53, n.56, n.57, n.58, 282n.61, n.62, n.63, n.66, n.68, n.69, n.70, n.71, n.74, n.75, n.77, n.79, 283n.80, n.81, n.86, n.87, n.91, n.92, n.98, n.99, 285n.16, n.28
al-Māzinī, Ibrāhīm 'Abd al-Qādir, 13, 262n.23
MBC, 211, 237n.26
Mecca, 33, 128
Meddeb, 'Abd al-Wahhāb, 184, 205
Medina, 33, 226
Mediterranean, 155-6, 159
Melville, Herman, 55
Meursault (Character), 15, 145-9
Middle East, Middle Eastern, 4, 29, 170, 205, 275n.4, 281n.49
Migration, 33-6, 48, 108, 155, 251n.44, n.45, n.47
Mimesis, 75, 154, 260n.1
Mīna, Ḥannā, 26, 157, 159, 245n.78, 249n.5, 274n.73, 278n.17
al-Misnāwī, Muṣṭafā, 11, 27, 41, 249n.9, 253n.64, 254n.78
Modern, Post-modern, Modernity, Modernism, Modernization, 4, 6-11, 13, 16-18, 20, 25-6, 28-34, 37-41, 47-8, 52, 54, 56, 58, 64-5, 67-9, 71, 73, 77-8, 80, 82, 84, 86-8, 94, 98, 106, 122, 133, 136-7, 139, 155-6, 158-60, 162, 165-6, 168-9, 174, 176-7, 179-81, 183, 185-7, 189, 193, 197-8, 202, 205, 207, 210, 212, 222, 231, 234n.5, 236n.18, n.21, 237n.28, 240n.49, n.50, 242n.64, n.68, 243n.70, n.71, 245n.78, 247n.91, 248n.2, 249n.14, 250n.18, 252n.48, n.53, n.54, 255n.103, 256n.112, 257n.118, 259n.152, 262n.22, n.23, 265n.62, 270n.12, 271n.36, 272n.40, n.48, n.55, 273n.73, 274n.75, n.77, 275n.4, 279n.31, n.32, 282n.70
Monologue, 15, 25, 43, 58, 63-5, 187, 258n.134
Morocco, Moroccan, 177, 178, 222-3, 229, 235n.16
  (Literature), 4, 9, 27, 41, 64, 157, 159, 184, 235n.16, 247n.92, 253n.64, 274n.73, 275n.78, 277n.10
Morris, Jean (Character), 70, 101, 111-13, 115, 118-19, 122, 148-9, 160, 169, 171-2, 174, 212, 267n.82, 282n.64
Muḥammad, The Prophet, 33, 109, 131, 155, 265n.56, n.61
Muḥaymīd (Character), 23, 37, 50, 90, 126, 129-31, 151-3, 188, 200-1, 259n.149, 269n.8
Mu'jizāt, 110, 265n.59

Multiglossia (see also Diglossia), 20, 222
Munīf, 'Abd al-Raḥmān, 5, 13, 64, 67, 157, 159, 235n.17, 249n.14, 258n.132, 259n.144, 260n.165, 270n.12, 274n.73, 278n.18
'Muqaddimāt', 21, 30, 32, 45, 53, 88, 89, 90, 123, 166, 167, 178, 188, 193-4, 219, 220, 236n.23, n.24, 247n.95, n.96, 262n.26, 269n.8, 272n.51, 280n.43
Mūsā, Ṣabrī, 78, 261n.10
Muslim, 7, 10, 12, 19, 22, 33, 92, 110, 122, 130, 149, 156, 160-1, 163, 165, 166, 167, 169, 171, 177, 180, 188, 226, 227-8, 230, 247n.91, 259n.151, 264n.46
Mustajāb, Muḥammad, 41, 254n.78
al-Mutanabbī, Abū al-Ṭayyib, 6, 12, 219, 231-2, 237n.25
Muw'adhdhin (Muezzin), 130, 131
Mystic, Mystical, Mysticism (see also Sufism), 50, 54, 71, 72, 92, 95, 98, 139, 188, 201, 213, 254n.79, 271n.36
Myth, Mythical, Mythology, Mythological, 46, 67, 72, 79, 87, 94, 110, 131, 138, 140, 145, 168, 178, 210, 241n.54, 250n.21, 253n.70, 259n.151, 263n.31, 271n.29, n.36

al-Nabiyy al-Khaḍir, 110, 265n.58
al-Nahḍa (Journal), 8
Najd, 231
Nakhla (Date Palm, Palm Tree), 27-8, 29, 42, 49, 51, 63, 72, 80, 83, 85, 104, 135, 197, 249n.14
'Nakhla 'alā al-Jadwal', 2, 3, 5, 11, 27-9, 32, 38, 42-3, 44, 49, 51, 56, 58, 64, 66, 67, 72, 80-2, 83-4, 87, 88, 93, 123, 128, 191, 197, 202, 234n.6, 244n.75, 249n.15, 251n.44, 269n.8
al-Nāqid (Journal), 5, 283n.96
al-Naqqāsh, Rajā', 16-17, 243n.74, 244n.76, 245n.79, n.80, 246n.87, 253n.70, 257n.122, 258n.139, 261n.13, 266n.65, 268n.98, 280n.39, n.44, 281n.54
Narrator (External, Internal), 52, 59, 64, 85-7, 88, 90, 143, 150, 152
Narrator, The (Character) (see also *al-Rāwī*), 3, 14, 15, 28, 30, 31, 34-5, 37, 42-6, 47-50, 51-60, 62-4, 68-72, 81-6, 88-93, 98, 100-9, 111, 113-17, 120-3, 126-31, 134, 136, 138-45, 148-54, 160, 163, 166-7, 171-3, 174-5, 179, 181, 187, 188, 197-201, 216, 226, 243n.72, 251n.43, 256n.106, n.108, n.110, 262n.19, 264n.45, n.48, 266n.71, 267n.76, n.80, n.81, n.82, 269n.8, 273n.57, 282n.70
Narrator's Father, The (Character), 31, 37, 90, 116, 152, 201
Naṣrallāh, Emily, 26, 249n.7
Naṣrallāh, Ibrāhīm, 64, 133, 157, 258n.132, 269n.3
Nicosia, 45, 67, 201
Nile, The, 28, 34-6, 92, 103, 112, 115, 135, 148, 172, 245n.78, 259n.149, 266n.64
Ni'ma (Character), 47, 69, 79, 92, 93, 95-9, 141, 198, 259n.150, 267n.81
Nobel Prize, 9
North (see also West), 32-6, 108, 110, 112, 148, 155, 157, 165, 181, 199
Nouveau Roman, 11, 240n.53
Nu'ayma, Mīkhā'īl, 183, 276n.8
al-Nu'aymī, Khalīl, 78, 134, 261n.10, 269n.7
Nubia, Nubians, 227
Nūr, Mu'āwiya Muḥammad, 8
Nūr, 'Uthmān 'Alī, 8

Omdurman, 1, 8
Oppressor, 156, 166, 276n.7
Orthodox Caliphs, The, 155
Othello (Character), 15, 54, 117-19, 172, 281n.58
Outsider, 3, 110, 140, 162, 228, 262n.19
Other, Otherness, 48, 84, 144, 162, 181-2, 207, 219, 266n.75, 276n.7, 277n.12
Ottoman Empire, The, 155
Oxford, 70, 209, 236n.23, 237n.26, 243n.70

Pagan, Pagans, 185, 227
Palestinian (Literature), 4-5, 13, 17-18, 26, 40, 64, 157, 159, 165, 183, 185, 235n.17, 236n.18, 246n.87, 249n.14, 250n.18, n.25, 253n.64, n.72, 257n.118, 272n.40, 274n.73, 275n.3
Paris, 2, 4, 10, 25, 35, 67, 158, 160, 275n.5, 278n.21
Place, 2, 15, 25, 26, 34, 40, 45-6, 66-8, 71, 73, 90-1, 108, 112, 117, 131, 141, 142, 154, 187, 188, 255n.91, 256n.113
Plato, 35, 188

Plot, 21, 26, 29, 31, 45, 51, 53, 61, 65-8, 70, 72, 78, 82, 84, 88, 90, 91, 92, 93, 96, 101, 109, 112, 123, 127, 128, 130, 131, 137, 144, 150, 158-9, 161, 174, 187, 198, 199-200, 255n.91, n.92, 278n.21
Poetic, Poetical, 1, 9, 19-21, 25, 39, 40, 42, 51, 58, 73, 109, 137, 181-2, 187, 214, 224, 238n.34, 248n.2, 251n.38, 261n.3, 275n.1, 279n.26
Politic, Political, 1, 2, 5, 7-9, 16, 17-18, 20, 33, 70, 72, 80, 110, 115, 119, 120, 138, 156, 158, 165, 166, 174-5, 177-8, 181, 183-5, 187, 189, 219, 259n.158
Preacher, The (Character), 85, 87, 128, 138, 272n.46
Prix Goncourt, 9
Protagonist, 45, 46, 76-8, 80, 90, 95, 112, 117, 137, 138, 150, 172, 199, 264n.46
Proust, Marcel, 64

Qabbāl, al-Mu'ṭī, 184
al-Qa'īd, Muḥammad Yūsuf, 2, 11, 26, 41, 69, 157, 240n.53, 249n.6, 253n.64, 254n.76, n.77, 259n.153, 273n.55
al-Qāsim, 'Abd al-Ḥakīm, 2, 26, 69, 137, 154, 159, 249n.6, n.7, 252n.48, 257n.118, 259n.153, 270n.24, n.25, 272n.48, 275n.78, 277n.10, 278n.20
al-Qāsim, Afnān, 5, 246n.85, n.87, 256n.106, n.113
Qatar, 2-6, 22, 30-1, 50, 196, 257n.124, 285n.16
al-Qays, Imru', 12
al-Qiṣṣa (Journal), 9, 191, 244n.75

Rabāb (Character), 3, 46, 68, 92, 188, 201-2, 227, 228, 259n.150
Rajab, 'Abd Allāh, 8
'al-Rajul al-Qubruṣī' (see also 'The Cypriot Man'), 2, 5, 22, 30, 45, 53, 58, 67, 90, 152, 196, 201, 204, 219, 225, 234n.6, 245n.84, 248n.103, n.106, 250n.28, 254n.87, 269n.8
al-Rajul al-Qubruṣī (Character) (see The Cypriot Man)
al-Rasā'il, 29, 249n.18
al-Rasūl, Ḥasab (Character), 57, 124, 228, 270n.8
al-Rāwī (Character) (see also The Narrator), 30
al-Ray' al-'Āmm (Journal), 8, 191, 194, 244n.75
Real Author, The, 4, 29-30, 35, 37, 41, 44, 47, 67, 75, 81, 89, 114-15, 118, 123, 133-4, 142, 149, 152, 154, 188, 241n.56, 253n.73, 255n.91, 262n.23, 266n.69, 268n.86, 269n.6, 281n.47
Reader, Readers, 1, 3, 7, 8, 11, 16-19, 22, 24, 25 27, 29, 30, 36, 41, 42, 43, 44, 46, 47-8, 50, 52, 53, 54, 55-6, 57, 59, 60, 64, 65, 70-1, 72, 76-7, 81, 83, 84, 85, 87, 94, 96, 100, 102, 105, 109, 115, 133-4, 138, 142, 144, 149, 168, 172, 183, 186-7, 197, 216, 223-4, 225, 228, 229-30, 243n.72, n.73, 256n.104, n.108, 264n.56, 269n.6, n.8
Realism, Realistic, Reality, 1, 3, 5, 8-9, 11, 18, 25, 27, 37, 39, 40, 43, 51, 55, 57, 65, 66-8, 72-3, 75-6, 78, 79, 87, 98, 104, 105, 115, 119, 123, 125, 126, 131, 136, 140, 141, 142, 148, 154, 168, 169, 187, 188-9, 201, 215, 216, 217, 226, 227-8, 234n.7, 241n.57, 249n.11, 250n.20, 254n.80, 258n.134, 259n.158, 260n.1, 261n.15, 265n.59, 267n.76, 271n.36, 274n.76, 283n.100
Refugee (Literature), 165
Religion, Religious, 7, 11, 15, 22, 31, 32-3, 42, 50, 54, 67, 68-9, 72, 73, 81, 84, 87, 92, 93, 95, 96, 100, 120, 122, 138, 139, 151, 156, 157, 160, 164, 168, 171, 175, 177, 180, 181, 183-4, 185, 187, 227-8
Rifqa, Fūād, 154
'Risāla ilā Aylīn', 2, 10, 28-9, 32, 45, 51, 58, 64, 84, 88, 102-3, 123, 143, 166, 167, 176, 188, 192, 197, 202, 234n.6, 244n.75, 267n.76, 269n.8, 280n.43
Rithā', 225
River, 35, 54-6, 57, 82, 85, 108, 112-13, 115-16, 119, 123-4, 133, 135, 140, 148-51, 199, 200, 220, 227, 231, 256n.106, 266n.65
Riwāya, 18
Robinson, Mr (Character), 101, 111, 119, 160, 189
Robinson, Mrs (Character), 101, 111, 119, 147, 189
Rushdie, Salman, 22
Russia, Russian, 8, 16, 159, 165, 205, 206, 243n.69, 274n.74, 279n.26, 285n.20, n.28

Sa'īd, Muṣṭafā (Character), 3, 14-15, 34-6, 48, 54-6, 60, 64-5, 68, 70-1, 79, 83-4, 88, 92, 95,

98, 100-19, 120-2, 123-5, 127, 131, 135, 138-41, 143, 144-51, 153, 160, 165, 167-73, 174-5, 178, 180-1, 188, 199, 216-17, 221, 228, 251n.43, 256n.106, 262n.19, 264n.45, n.56, 265n.58, n.61, 266n.64, n.66, n.69, n.71, 267n.76, n.80, n.82, 268n.99, 271n.26, 273n.57, 281n.50, n.58, 282n.64, n.70
Saint, 87, 100, 110, 135, 139
al-Ṣalaḥī, Ibrāhīm, 164, 218-19, 280n.37, 283n.80
al-Sālimī, al-Ḥabīb, 158, 277n.10
Sammān, Ghāda, 13, 246n.87
Sartre, Jean-Paul, 11, 273n.73
Satanic, 55, 105, 119, 161
Saudi Arabia, Saudi Arabian, 5, 157, 184, 237n.25, 249n.14, 274n.73, 277n.10
Sayf al-Dīn (Character), 65, 269n.8
Ṣāyigh, Tawfīq, 17, 185, 220, 245n.79
al-Sayyāb, Badr Shākir, 154, 157
Scotland, Scottish, 2, 16, 28, 84, 165, 188, 197
Season of Migration to the North (see also *Mawsim al-Hijra ilā al-Shamāl*), 9, 32, 194, 198, 199, 204, 205, 207, 208, 211, 216, 217, 221, 224-5, 229, 234n.3, 236n.20, 242n.64, 243n.72, 245n.85, 246n.85, n.90, 247n.92, 250n.20, 251n.37, 255n.91, n.95, 256n.107, n.108, n.110, n.112, 257n.123, 258n.136, 259n.156, 263n.39, 264n.45, n.51, 265n.58, 266n.75, 270n.20, 273n.56, n.60, n.61, n.62, n.63, n.64, n.65, n.66, 274n.76, 277n.11, 280n.36, 282n.68, n.79, 283n.81, 284n.7, n.11, 285n.16, 286n.34, n.35, n.36, n.37, n.39, n.42, n.44
Sennar (Kingdom), 72
Seventh Seal, The, 92, 219, 262n.28
Seymour, Isabella (Character), 117, 119, 135, 149, 170-1
Sex, Sexual, Sexuality, 15, 19, 21-2, 88-9, 110, 115, 138, 166-72, 189, 247n.91, 267n.82, 275n.4, 276n.9
Shāh, 36, 125, 252n.53
al-Shahrazūrī, 12, 241n.58
Shakespeare, William, 13-14, 54, 73, 117-19, 145, 185, 219, 242n.64, 263n.33, 266n.74, 267n.76
Shalabī, Khayrī, 159, 278n.18
Shamāl, 32, 34
al-Shāmī, Rafīq, 184
Shammās, Anṭōn, 5, 272n.40
al-Sharqāwī, 'Abd al-Raḥmān, 2, 9, 82, 254n.83, 262n.17, 263n.33, 271n.34, n.35, 272n.40, n.48, n.55, 273n.55
al-Shawādhdh (Characters), 95-6, 100
'al-Shay' al-Ākhar', 21, 45, 58, 90, 166, 174, 193, 198, 244n.75, 247n.97, 254n.86, 262n.26, 272n.51, 280n.43, 282n.76
al-Shaykh, Ḥanān, 5, 157, 159, 166, 184, 278n.22
Sindbad, 69
Six-Day War, 18
Sjuzet, 68
Slave, Slavery, 39, 110, 130, 170, 171, 265n.61, 268n.99, 274n.76
Soueif, Ahdaf
South (see also East), 32-5, 108, 110, 148, 155, 165, 181, 199, 270n.26
South American (see also Latin America), 11
Space, 25, 66-8, 71, 187-8, 256n.113
Spain, Spanish, 25, 137, 171, 184, 204, 206, 243n.69
Stendhal (Marie Henri Beyle), 13, 77, 117, 145, 261n.6
Storyteller, Storytelling, 20, 30, 41, 137, 254n.84
Stranger, Strangeness, 36, 45, 49, 82, 84-85, 87, 88, 91, 96, 99, 112, 116-17, 124, 127, 139, 141, 146, 262n.19, n.21, 271n.26, 272n.55
Stream of Consciousness, 9, 15, 58, 64, 187, 207
Sudan, 1-2, 4-10, 29, 31, 33-5, 38, 44, 54-6, 60-1, 63, 65-72, 78, 79-80, 84, 86, 93-4, 99, 107, 109-10, 112, 121, 123, 125, 135-6, 139-41, 152, 153, 154, 164, 165-6, 167-8, 170, 172-3, 175-6, 179, 180-1, 183, 184-5, 187-9, 192, 197, 199, 209, 222, 224, 226-7, 229-30, 234n.7, 244n.76, 247n.101, 251n.45
Sudanese, (Colloquial, Dialect, Spoken, Vernacular), 7, 9, 17, 23, 58, 60-3, 65-6, 77, 222-4, 237n.30, 248n.110, 251n.35, 257n.120, 258n.125, n.126, n.129, n.142, 261n.5, 268n.92
(Literature), 2, 5, 7-11, 13, 26, 39, 68-9, 184-5, 207, 237n.28, 238n.33, 240n.50, 244n. 76, 261n.5, 277n.12

Ṣūfī, Sufism, 1, 11-12, 31, 36, 38, 42, 53-4, 96, 99-100, 185, 225, 259n.151, 262n.29, 263n.31, 265n.59, 271n.35
'Suzān wa-'Alī', 45, 144, 167, 193
Swift, Jonathan, 13
Swiss, 159
Syria, Syrian, 5, 158, 184, 223
(Literature) 4, 5, 13, 22, 26, 64, 78, 157, 158, 160, 184, 245n.78, 251n.36, 255n.93, 274n.73, 275n.78, 277n.10, n.12

Ṭāhir, Bahā', 159, 277n.10, n.12, 278n.18
al-Ta'īshī, 'Abd Allāh, 72
Tāmir, Zakariyyā, 5, 13, 184
al-Ṭarīfī (Character), 61, 98, 128, 136, 269n.8
Tawakkul, 42, 254n.79
Taymūr, Maḥmūd, 9, 20, 247n.94
Taymūr, Muḥammad, 67, 249n.6, 259n.146
al-Ṭayyib, Aḥmad, 13
al-Ṭayyib, Ṭāriq, 5, 209, 250n.32, 262n.23, 286n.53
Technology, 36, 156-7, 166, 179-81, 189, 273n.73
al-Thaqāfa al-'Arabiyya (Journal), 22, 195, 196
Theme, Thematic, 15, 20, 21, 117, 135, 137, 138, 166, 182, 207, 214, 216, 224, 249n.8, 270n.26, 273n.73, 276n.9, 279n.26
Time, 2, 15, 18, 25-6, 32, 34, 38, 40, 45-6, 52, 66, 68-73, 79, 91, 105, 112, 117, 123, 131, 140-2, 154, 187-8, 218, 256n.113
Title, 10, 25-39, 41, 45-6, 50, 53, 69, 126, 135, 187, 192, 193, 194, 203, 204, 206, 218, 226, 246n.87, 248n.2, 249n.14, 250n.25, 251n.36, 252n.53, 253n.60, 279n.26
Tunis, Tunisia, Tunisian, 18, 23, 34, 195, 196, 222, 246n.85, 248n.108, n.110, 253n.70, 285n.20
(Literature), 13, 158, 184, 243n.69, 249n.14, 255n.96, 257n.124, 262n.23, 277n.10, 281n.49
al-Tūnisī, Bayram, 158, 278n.15
Turābī, Ḥasan, 180, 247n.92
Turkey, Turkish, 180, 205, 243n.69

'Ughniyat Ḥubb', 45, 58, 64, 90, 144, 193
Uḥdūtha, 37
'Ujaylī, 'Abd al-Salām, 13, 157-8, 277n.10
Umayyad Caliphs, The, 155
al-'Umda (Character), 93, 96
Umm Durmān (see Omdurman)
UNESCO, 2, 6, 206, 234n.3, 245n.83, 249n.5
'Urs al-Zayn (see also The Wedding of Zein), 2, 16, 31, 33, 38, 46, 49-50, 54, 56, 58, 61, 64-5, 67, 69, 79, 87, 90, 92-3, 142, 186, 188, 192-4, 198, 204-5, 209, 217, 234n.6, 244n.75, 245n.78, n.84, 247n.98, 258n.137, 259n.150, n.156, 262n.24, 263n.31, n.36, n.38, n.40, 265n.58, 267n.81, 268n.99, 269n.6, n.8, 270n.13, n.16, n.17, n.18, 271n.31, 280n.43

Village, Villagers, 1-3, 5-6, 8, 15, 20, 21, 26, 27-8, 29, 30, 31, 32, 34-7, 43, 44, 46-7, 49-50, 51-2, 54, 55, 57, 59-60, 61-2, 63, 65-6, 67-73, 78-80, 82-3, 84-8, 90-1, 93-100, 101-7, 109-17, 119-22, 123-8, 129-31, 133, 135-45, 151-4, 157-9, 163, 165, 172-4, 180-1, 187-9, 197-201, 227, 230, 235n.11, 237n.29, 240n.53, 250n.21, n.29, 251n.44, 252n.53, 254n.76, n.83, 255n.92, 257n.120, 259n.145, n.148, n.152, 262n.15, n.18, n.19, n.24, 263n.33, n.36, 265n.58, 267n.81, n.82, 268n.99, 269n.8, 270n.12, n.18, 271n.30, n.35, 272n.40, n.55, 273n.55, 274n.76, 277n.13, 282n.70, 284n.7
Violence, Violent, 15, 55, 119, 122, 138, 149, 166-7, 171-2, 189, 229, 267n.81, 271n.26, 282n.65, n.70

Wad Dulayib (Character), 87
Wad Ḥabīb, Naṣrallāh, 130-1, 140
Wad Ḥāmid (Village), 29-31, 49-50, 59, 67, 73, 91-2, 123, 129-30, 135-6, 138, 142, 151-2, 153, 154, 187, 197, 201, 250n.29, 252n.53, 259n.148, 262n.19, 269n.8, 282n.70
Wad Ḥāmid (Character), 29, 69, 85, 87, 135, 197, 268n.99
Wad al-Rawwās (Wad al-Rawwāsī), al-Ṭāhir (Character), 22-3, 58, 63, 72, 79, 90-1, 130, 140, 152, 200, 201, 269n.8
Wad al-Rayyis (Character), 69, 71, 98, 101, 107, 119, 120, 121, 122, 126, 138, 141, 168, 172-3, 229, 264n.45, 267n.81, n.82, 269n.8
Wad Ṭāhā, Ibrāhīm (Character), 130, 269n.8
al-Wā'iẓ (see Preacher)
al-Wasaṭ (Journal), 210, 213
Waṭṭār, al-Ṭāhir, 64, 157, 251n.36, 258n.132

Wedding of Zein, The (see also *'Urs al-Zayn*), 21, 31, 194, 198, 202, 204-5, 217, 224, 230, 243n.72, 244n.77, 250n.34, 255n.91, 257n.121, 258n.127, 259n.156, 265n.61, 285n.22, n.24
West, Western, 3-5, 11, 15-16, 18, 21, 28, 30, 32, 34-7, 39, 47-8, 53, 84, 88-90, 93-4, 101-3, 105, 110, 112, 115-19, 121, 138-9, 143-5, 149-51, 154, 155-81, 183-5, 187-9, 197, 198, 213, 234n.5, 242n.64, 245n.82, 271n.26, 272n.51, 273n.73, 275n.4, 276n.5, n.8, n.9, 277n.10, n.11, 278n.17, n.21, 279n.25, n.29, n.31, 281n.44, 282n.60, n.70, n.73, 283n.95, 285n.22
(Cultures, Literatures), 6, 8, 11, 13-14, 16, 18, 25, 28, 32, 36, 38, 40-1, 44, 47, 58, 63-4, 67, 71, 73, 77-8, 102, 106, 109-11, 117, 133, 135, 138, 143, 150-1, 154, 155-7, 162, 166, 175-81, 185, 187, 189, 199, 252n.48, 260n.1, 271n.30, 273n.73, 276n.8
Woman, Women, 2, 8, 19, 25, 28, 29, 30, 33, 35, 45, 53, 63, 81, 84, 88-90, 91, 92, 96, 97, 99, 101, 102, 110-11, 115, 121-2, 130, 137, 138, 141, 143-4, 147, 149, 150, 157, 159-62, 165, 166-74, 178-9, 187, 189, 197, 198, 264n.45, 267n.80, n.82, 272n.39, n.40, n.51, 278n.21, 281n.49, 282n.60, n.64, n.73
Woolf, Virginia, 40, 64, 207, 266n.75

Yāsīn, Kātib (see Kātib, Yāsīn)
'Yawm Mubārak 'alā Shāṭi' Umm Bāb' (see also 'A Blessed Day on the Umm Bab Shore'), 3, 5, 11, 31, 38, 46, 53, 58, 67, 68, 90, 92, 131, 186, 187, 196, 201, 204, 219, 225, 227, 231, 235n.13, 245n.84, 254n.88, 259n.150
Yeats, William Butler, 13, 185, 219

'Za'balāwī', 27, 42, 78, 81, 134, 240n.51, 249n.8, 254n.81, 261n.8, 265n.62, 271n.36
Za'balāwī (Character), 42, 134
Zarrūq, al-Ṭayyib, 9, 239n.40
al-Zayn (Character), 31-2, 46-7, 54, 61, 65, 69, 79, 93-100, 109-10, 139-41, 198-9, 258n.126, 263n.31, n.35, 265n.58
Zifzāf, Muḥammad, 4, 11, 157, 158, 235n.14, 275n.78, 277n.10